W9-DAA-776

MASTER ROGER WILLIAMS

By Ola Elizabeth Winslow

JONATHAN EDWARDS, 1703–1758
MEETINGHOUSE HILL, 1630–1783
MASTER ROGER WILLIAMS

Master Roger Williams

A BIOGRAPHY

by

OLA ELIZABETH WINSLOW

THE MACMILLAN COMPANY · NEW YORK

1957

Published simultaneously in Canada

First Printing

Printed in the United States of America

Library of Congress catalog card number: 57-10016

This Book is for

MARILYN AND KENNETH

"It is a great work and too heavy for one
man's shoulders, but somebody must begin."

JEREMY TAYLOR

PREFACE

IN searching out the materials for this book, I chanced upon George Herbert's *Jacula Prudentum,* in the edition of 1640. His preface seemed a model in such sort, and with (I trust) due respect, I borrow it entire. It consists of a single sentence—this one.

"The best of the sport is to do the deed and say nothing."

Why indeed say more, except to thank those without whose help no book about times long past could be written at all. The materials for this one have been collected and studied in many places, but mainly in the Boston Athenaeum Library, the Massachusetts and Rhode Island Historical Society Libraries and in the British Museum. In the richness and friendliness of human association these centers provide, one finds unfailingly materials for other and perhaps better books that will never be written, nor perhaps can be, but the experiences themselves have made many days memorable. In this fresh discovery, time after time, there is a renewed sense of gratitude, which it is a pleasure to acknowledge.

I wish to mention also the helpfulness of Mr. Evan James of the Merchant Taylors' Company of London, Mr. N. Long-Brown of Charterhouse, Mr. S. C. Roberts of Pembroke College, Cambridge, Mr. F. G. Emmison of the Essex County Record Office in Chelmsford, and Mrs. C. P. Hall of the University Registry, Cambridge. In fairness the list should be far longer, including always gratefully the interest of my colleagues of Wellesley College which has been a continuing incentive and encouragement.

OLA ELIZABETH WINSLOW

London, November 11, 1955.

CONTENTS

PREFACE vii
PROLOGUE 1

LONDON, 1603–1623

I. "THE WONDERFULL YEARE, 1603" 3
II. MERCHANT TAYLOR'S SON 9
III. BOY IN SMITHFIELD 19
IV. "FITTE SCHOLAR" 35
V. PROTÉGÉ 43

CAMBRIDGE, 1623–1628

VI. PENSIONER 56

OTES, 1628–1630

VII. CHAPLAIN 74

PLYMOUTH, 1630–1633

VIII. "GODLY MINISTER" 95

SALEM, 1633–1635

IX. TROUBLER OF THE PEACE 107

THE NARRAGANSETT COUNTRY, 1635–1643

X. "FIRST BEGINNER" OF A COLONY 125
XI. ROVING AMBASSADOR 144
XII. LINGUIST 161
A Key into the Language of America

LONDON, 1643–1644

XIII. Diplomat 176

XIV. Controversialist 189

Mr. Cotton's Letter . . . Answered

Queries of Highest Consideration

The Bloudy Tenent of Persecution

PROVIDENCE PLANTATIONS, 1644–1651

XV. "Chiefe Officer" 208

Christenings Make Not Christians

XVI. Trader 221

Experiments of Spiritual Life and Health

LONDON, 1651–1653

XVII. Colony Agent 235

Major Butler's Fourth Paper

The Hireling Ministry None of Christs

The Bloody Tenent Yet More Bloody

The Examiner Defended

PROVIDENCE PLANTATIONS, 1653–1663

XVIII. Mediator 249

RHODE ISLAND COLONY, 1663–1683

XIX. Elder Statesman 267

George Fox Digg'd Out of His Burrowes

Epilogue. "The Root of the Matter in Him" 289

Notes 293

Bibliographical Statement 313

Index 317

ILLUSTRATIONS

MEMORANDUM ON THE BACK OF ANNE SADLEIR'S COPY OF A LETTER TO ROGER WILLIAMS, 1652 — *page* 47
Trinity College Library, Cambridge, England

SIR EDWARD COKE, BY PAUL VON SOMER — *facing* 114
Niblett Hall, The Inner Temple, London

A CORNER IN WASH HOUSE COURT, CHARTERHOUSE, LONDON — 115

THE CHURCH AT HIGH LAVER, ESSEX COUNTY, ENGLAND — 146

THE PEQUOT FORT ON THE MYSTIC RIVER, CONNECTICUT — 147
From an engraving of 1637

SIR HARRY VANE THE YOUNGER, BY SIR PETER LELY — 242
From a photograph in the Boston Athenaeum Library

TITLE PAGE OF *The Bloudy Tenent of Persecution,* LONDON, 1644 — 243
From a copy in Yale University Library

INTERNATIONAL MONUMENT OF THE REFORMATION AT GENEVA — 274

STATUE OF ROGER WILLIAMS, BY H. BOUCHARD — 275
From the International Monument of the Reformation at Geneva

ROGER WILLIAMS' PROTEST TO PROVIDENCE, DECEMBER 8, 1680 — *page* 287
Rhode Island Historical Society

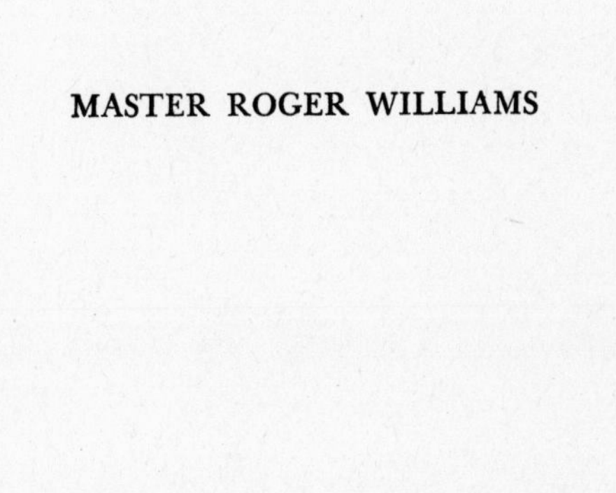

MASTER ROGER WILLIAMS

PROLOGUE

THROUGHOUT his generous eighty years, Roger Williams was no darling of the gods. Man of peace though he was, the lion rampant on his crest was fitting symbol, for his was a life of battle and his sword (which was argument) seldom rested in its scabbard. Man of gentleness that he also was, abuse, calumny, even hatred, were often his portion. Nevertheless, for him the cause was all and his heaped-up sorrows light in the balance. In a letter written late enough in his life to be called his valedictory, one finds this sentence,

> "And as to myself, in endeavouring after your temporal and spiritual peace, I humbly desire to say, If I perish, I perish— It is but a shadow vanished, a bubble broke, a dream finished. Eternity will pay for all."

Nearly three centuries toward that eternity have now passed, and payment has begun, but in an earthly coin for which Roger Williams would have cared little. His life story has been told many times and will be told many more. He would scarcely have known why. Statues exist to him; imaginary portraits have been painted; schoolboys know his name. He is enrolled among the great ones of America's earliest struggles to survive in peace and righteousness and to build toward a future they would never see. He lived in stormy times and was himself part of the storm. The idea now all but inseparable from his name was anathema to his contemporaries and he himself something of a conundrum because of it. Nevertheless he dared to put it to the test in the small corner of America in which he was permitted to live, when declared unwelcome elsewhere.

Now that the passing of many generations has reversed the earlier harsh judgments, his personal story has sometimes invited to myth and romantic legend. He requires neither. His story is better as he lived it. Also his contribution to things American has sometimes been oversimplified and sometimes overstated. His ideas have been fitted to later theories impossible to him. We do him greater honor to let him remain the pioneer he was.

But that is not quite enough. Like other men whose thought has at some point been built into a nation's way of life, he has laid on his posterity an obligation to try to understand him, first, in the context of his own time, and then to test the validity and continuing relevance of his thought for later times. After nearly three hundred years we still know less about him as a man among men than about almost any other man of comparable importance in the America of his own time. As to understanding him, now that the romantic cobwebs are being brushed aside, we have made only the merest beginning. For these reasons and many others which come readily to mind, the passing years are not likely to let Roger Williams alone. He belongs in the sparse category of those for whom no generation speaks the last word.

CHAPTER ONE

"The Wonderfull Yeare, 1603"

THE curtain rises for Roger Williams in Long Lane, London, probably in "the wonderfull yeare, 1603." "Wonderfull" in the awesome sense it was, for this was the year in which, as Thomas Dekker of London put it, the "great Land-Lady" of England was summoned "to appeare in the Star-chamber of heaven." For more than a fortnight there had been persistent rumors that her end was near, yet in spite of these warnings, the impact of the early morning announcement on March 24th was staggering in proportion as finality had been daily expected. At last it had come. Queen Elizabeth had "obayed Death's messenger, . . . resigning her Scepter to posteritie, and her Soule to immortalitie." The report was like a thunder clap, Thomas Dekker continued; "it took away hearts from millions," as "a nation that was almost begotten and borne under her," stood stunned, unable to comprehend what "that strange out-landish word *Change* signified." [1]

But they were not stunned long. At the sound of the trumpet, first before the palace gate at Whitehall and then at Cheapside, the "just feare of 40 yeres" as to the succession was dissolved in a bare moment of time, and at this new certainty, the citizens "did so rejoyce, as few wished the gracious Quene alive againe." [2] Once more it was true that "in England is no interregnum, because the King never dieth." Londoners listened to the proclamation of James I as King of England, Scotland, France and Ireland, "with greate expectacion and silent joye," though "noe great shouting." Bells stopped tolling and began to ring, continuing throughout the day. At sundown bonfires were lighted, but still there was "noe tumult, noe contradicion, noe disorder in the city; every man went about his busines, as readylie, as peaceably, as securely, as though there had bin noe change." [3] At least, so it seemed on this longest of London days. Life was lived by the hour and every hour was memorable.

Likewise in the days immediately following. The solemn magnificence of a royal funeral had no counterpart in the memory of an adult generation that had never looked on "the face of any Prince but herselfe." Every day brought strange new sights to be reported from house to house with mingled awe, sorrow, and also relief, until finally the day came on which in Thomas Fuller's word, "Her Corps was solemnly interred under a fair Tomb in Westminster." [4] As the funeral cortege proceeded thither, the London thousands poured forth from every street and crooked lane in the city. These men and women were well used to the pageantry of royal progresses, but this procession was like no other in their experience. They knelt in the street as the open chariot bearing the body of the dead queen passed. On top of the leaden casket lay her "image in her parliament robes, a crown on her head and a sceptre in her hand, all very exquisitely fashioned to resemble the life." At the sight many "fell a weeping," others exchanged dire portents presaging this very hour.[5] Still others, as always on great occasions, spoke of ordinary things, but to all it was a day of awe in its very strangeness.

Six weeks later, these same London crowds, now in gay holiday mood, streamed rejoicingly toward Stamford Hill to greet James I on his triumphal progress from Scotland. To the "unspeakable nomber of citizens" who "covered the beauty of the fields" on that May morning, seeming in their haste "rather to flie than to runne," the line between Tudor and Stuart seemed already invisible. What no one in that welcoming throng could yet know was that between the March 24th tolling of the bells and these May 7th shouts of rejoicing, an era had ended as well as a reign. England had turned a corner. Henceforth, perhaps far sooner than anyone might have thought possible, Englishmen on all levels of society would live with *Change* in ways hitherto undreamed. Their disillusionment would be profound. Their peace of mind would vanish along with the comfortable, measurably safe world that was now gone. Change would seem sudden, but really it was not so. Rather currents of change, long in the making, could no longer be ignored.

In consequence, very shortly the air was charged with manifold uncertainties. Violently opposed forces, hitherto held in check by Queen Elizabeth's strong arm, were unleashed, making England once more a divided kingdom. Ominous mutterings of unrest, long suppressed, were plainly audible, "manie having discontentment in their private opinions" and being newly "inclined to alteracion in government." [6] Only a short time before, Westminster schoolboys, practicing their skill in impromptu Latin verse, had reflected the confidence of their elders when they wrote in their copybooks what may be freely translated,

"Everybody is scared of Queen Elizabeth, and so we have peace." [7]

How long would "everybody" remain "scared" now? Prosperity, would it continue? Popery, would it again threaten? So numerous and so increasingly loud were these persistent questionings, that had a London soothsayer dared to voice the uneasy dread in men's minds during this same "wonderfull yeare, 1603," he might well have predicted that any English child born in this perilous in-between period, would by that fact alone be headed toward a stormy springtime and summer of life. Roger Williams was one of these children.

Looking backward, however, with his peculiar gifts in mind, one is impelled to reverse the prediction and to say that stormy times were perhaps his greatest good fortune. Disorder and turbulence need be no occasion of pity for one of his temperament. Parlous times became him, framed as he was always to stand at one passionate extreme or another and to risk all on a single throw. "Moderate men" are out of fashion at such a moment; mere "Owles in the Desart" to be hooted at, Thomas Fuller observed ruefully, being himself a man of the middle course. Roger Williams was of another sort. Moderation by any label was not for him, and one of "God's Doves" he could never be. In any or all climates of opinion, the golden mean would never be for him to discover, much less to advocate. Give him rather a single bastion of truth, fiercely held under equally fierce attack; no compromise, no surrender, no quarter. It was the only way he knew how to fight. It was also a way his seventeenth century brethren in both the Old and the New World would well understand. Better still for an uncompromising crusader, he could be at peace with himself and at home in the very swirl of the storm, and at its direst peak of peril his best visions would be born. Moreover, in a world of violent upheaval, when great principles were in conflict and all lines of difference were sharply drawn, his own "dangerous opinions" would have a good chance to catch the ear.

He was also fortunate in being born a Londoner, and thereby at this particular moment of English history not only to stand at a focal point of cataclysmic change, but also to be the direct heir of such ferment in men's souls as inspires fresh, bold vision in those capable of it. His boyhood peace would be disturbed by thronging incentives to immediate and sometimes unwise action, but in his first passionate responses to these incentives he would find his own life purpose and direction. Civil and religious, where is the line between? In the general mind, at this date, a knife-blade could not have separated them. Religion and politics, church and state were one and indivisible. Freedom for the individual, what are its limits under law? Conscience, dare it oppose established authority? Seldom have differences on these great questions bred more bitter antagonisms than at this particular moment, and out of such tempests, ideas, if not newly born, at least become newly articulate. For this and other reasons, London at this turning point in English history was perhaps the most fortunate schoolroom in the entire world for one who would do lifetime battle on these particular fronts.

Nor was this all. Born a Londoner at this particular moment, he would grow up in a larger world than Queen Elizabeth had ever known. By a poetic inspiration, Sir Walter Raleigh had christened his ship *Destiny* and the name was prophetic. Thanks to him and to the whole fraternity of intrepid Elizabethan voyagers, England's westward windows were opening and possibilities yet unspoken and undreamed were just beginning to emerge from the first romantic haze. Presently these windows would be flung wide and a whole generation of English children would realize hopes of the hitherto impossible. Roger Williams was one who would do more than gaze dreamily toward these new horizons. He too was an Elizabethan.

At the turn of the century London was the natural gateway to this larger world. Although with her approximately 300,000 inhabitants, she was still a city somewhere in the present Omaha, Fort Worth, Toledo, or Jersey City bracket, population totals tell little of her importance. By virtue of her amazing merchant activity, she was already at the very forefront of European centers of trade. "London is a large, excellent, and mighty city of business," [8] had been Duke Frederick's verdict on his official visit in 1592, and other visitors had echoed him. Another decade had now brought her close to being the most important city in all of Europe. Success in trade was nourishing still bolder ambitions in her merchants, men who were holding the whole earth in the compass of their thought, and dreaming of ways to make England the "common emporium and staple" not only of Europe but of the entire world.

Prosperity in trade was also declaring dividends not only in still greater prosperity, but also in power and the sense of power. English merchants were not yet "princes, greater, and richer, and more powerful than some sovereign princes," [9] but there were some in the merchant ranks who were beginning to sense such a possibility and some outside the ranks who were beginning to fear it. This zestful, outward-looking spirit was shared alike by merchants who kept small shops, possibly supporting only one or two apprentices, and those greater ones who went daily to the magnificent new Royal Exchange to display their wares, to buy, to sell, and to carry on their merchant adventures in their more than two thousand ships daily upon the seas.

As the son of middle-class parents, Roger Williams was the heir of this energetic, forward-looking spirit, and in view of what was ahead of him, his middle-class heritage was distinctly favorable. English society at this date was still firmly stratified, but in the early years of the new century there was greater mobility at the middle level than ever before. Particularly, lines between upper and lower middle-class were breaking down, and a man not only had a better chance to move up a few steps but he was beginning to make his individual will effective within his own stratum. Whether a middle-class boy's father was or was not of any special importance in his own group was of no great consequence; what mattered far more was that in a middle-class home, a wide-awake boy would have sensed the social restlessness belonging to his father's world, and that such a home would be a natural seedbed of confident aspiration. Without knowing how he had learned it, an alert boy in such a home would grow up knowing that age-old traditions might be challenged and that boldness in quite new directions might be justified in its fruits. His young thought would take shape amid the loud mutterings of middle-class discontent and a growing disrespect for kingly authority as vested in so inglorious a monarch as James I presently turned out to be.

For one who in his manhood was to be concerned with the things of government, particularly one destined always to speak for the protesting minority, a discontented middle-class England afforded far better tutelage toward spirited, non-conforming action than the outwardly tractable but inwardly restless England during the proverbially spacious days of the great queen. From every corner of England men of great gifts and great distinction in the use of them would come from the resolute, high-reaching middle-class stratum of English society at this date. Moreover, not so far distant from it, as history is written, there would be a reckoning, and the middle-class man would be a chief actor. He would shake a throne and topple a king. He would change England and build America. In such terms and with his own rich gifts in mind, who shall say that in the deeply troubled time of his birth Roger Williams was not a lucky man? But back to Long Lane, London, where his story begins.

CHAPTER TWO

Merchant Taylor's Son

SOMEWHERE along this Lane "truly called Long," an undistinguished passageway in Farringdon Ward without the city wall, lived James Williams, "Citizen and Merchant Taylor of London." He had rented the Long Lane house, or "messuage" as the record has it, in 1594 and was presumably occupying it early enough for his four known children to have been born there. The stamp of trade was upon them all: upon Sydrach, the oldest, who followed in his father's steps and became a merchant taylor, then climbed a few rungs higher, broadened his horizons and became a "Merchant to Turkey and Italy." It was upon Catherine, the only daughter, who married a merchant taylor; upon Robert, the youngest, who first apprenticed himself to his brother Sydrach, later broke away, came to America and settled in Rhode Island. It was also upon Roger, whom the world knows otherwise, but who among his many interests, remained something of a trader all his life. His trading post at Wickford Point, Rhode Island, was better known to his contemporary Rhode Islanders than his *Bloudy Tenent of Persecution,* and had a list of the colony residents, classified as to occupation, been issued at any time during his life, he would have been set down as a trader; quite fairly so.

Of his merchant taylor father, James Williams, little is known. He had been admitted to the freedom of the Merchant Taylors' Company "by servitude" on April 7, 1587, having previously been apprenticed to Nicholas Tresswell. The fact of this apprenticeship would indicate that his father before him had not been a merchant taylor, else he would have been admitted "by patrimony," as was later recorded for his own son Sydrach. Presumably when this seven year apprenticeship began, James Williams, according to the usual custom, would have been no more than fifteen or sixteen years old. Ironically, the Apprentice Book of the Company, which would have given his precise age and his father's name, begins in 1583, three years too late to include him. Other records also fail us, most lamentably those of St. Sepulchre's church, over against Newgate. Had he been born in this parish, where he lived until his death, his parentage and family station would have been matters of record, but ironically again, the records of this church were destroyed in the Great London Fire of 1666, nearly a century before anyone cared to know the antecedents of Roger Williams of America. As a result, the ancestral story on his father's side remains (to date) almost a blank back of the 1587 admission record of James Williams to the Merchant Taylors' Company.[1]

He would not have been a tailor in the more modern sense of one who cuts and fits men's outer clothes. In his day the word *taylor* more usually signified either a manufacturer of ceremonial robes of state, of canopies and pavilions to be carried over exalted personages in processions, or more frequently a shopkeeper who dealt in various kinds of imported cloth. By this date the older monopoly of the tailor's trade was gone and commercial enterprises had taken over. Many members of the Merchant Taylors' Company had nothing whatever to do with clothworking; they were merchants and wished to be known as such. Thomas Dekker, speaking satirically, wrote that their shops "all lead foorth in leases to be turned into ships," and that "with their shears (instead of a Rudder) they would have cut the Seas (like Levant Taffaty) and sayld to the West Indies for no worse stuffe to make hose and doublets of, than beaten gold." [2] The Long Lane neighborhood was crowded with their shops of the smaller sort, each one displaying wares from far away. Most of these shops formed the front part of a dwelling house, with quarters for apprentices and a warehouse behind. Very probably James Williams' relation to the trade was of this sort, with the Long Lane house serving both as home and place of business.

By his will, discovered some years ago in the records of the Commissary Court of London,[3] he seems to have been moderately prosperous, but probably no more so than thrift and industry would have made him. He presently owned a new home in Cow Lane, several other "tenements" in the Smithfield neighborhood, and small properties elsewhere. He provided a modest dowry for his daughter Catherine, and at his death left small legacies to his children and friends, together with the customary largess to the poor of the parish. He died in 1621, nine years before his son Roger left England for America.

During his thirty-four years as Merchant Taylor he appears to have held no office or performed no special service calling for record in the books of the Company. It is just possible that he may have been the "Mr. Williams" who, on occasion of the great banquet given to King James on July 7, 1607, received five shillings for two days' work in the kitchen, plus the apron such service demanded. This quite inconsequential item catches the eye in the Company's records only because in the same expense account, Thomas Morse, a fellow member and friend to whom James Williams left a small legacy, is named as one of the "Sheriff's Officers" who "waited at the dinner." [4] The fact that Ben Jonson on this same occasion received twenty pounds for writing the eighteen verses to be spoken by the "very proper child" and also the songs sung by the "three rare men" suspended from the ceiling in a boat, not only pays tribute to Jonson's current reputation for topical hits, but also honors poetic gifts as compared with apron service. As for James Williams, even though he were the "Mr. Williams" of the five shilling item, we are none the wiser for it. What his life was made of, aside from the day's work and particularly in what directions he may have helped to shape his son's thought, is not to be found in such details, even though they existed by the score. Except for his name, his occupation, his mark on various legal papers, his small holdings at the time of his death, his request to be buried in St. Sepulchre's parish, he remains throughout his life story, a virtual unknown, "James Williams, Citizen and Merchant Taylor of London."

Long-continued search also fails to extend his lineage further backward. The name *Williams* is a poor one for searching in any time or place, and in his particular London generation, its bearers were already legion. Almost every London parish had its Richard, John, Robert, or Thomas Williams, among many others, and even the names James and Roger appear with some frequency. The persistent tradition of Welsh ancestry for the American Roger is of no help, since it would hold equally for all bearers of the Williams name. Through the years one more or less plausible clue has been singled out for hopeful attention, but as yet no reliable sustaining proof has been established for any one of them.

The most teasing and one of the most persistent of these vague possibilities would derive James Williams from the picturesque Morgan Williams of Glamorganshire, Wales, later ale-brewer, beer-seller, and innkeeper of Putney. This Morgan Williams by his marriage to Catherine Cromwell, daughter of Walter Cromwell and sister of Thomas Cromwell, Earl of Essex,[5] became a paternal ancestor of Oliver Cromwell. The name Cromwell was assumed by Richard Williams, son of Morgan, from Sir Thomas his patron, and as a result, the Williams name was lost subsequently in the Cromwell line. This Richard Williams, born in Wales in 1529, was the father of Sir Henry Cromwell, the Golden Knight, grandfather of Robert, and great-grandfather of Oliver, the Protector. Such derivation, however oblique, for James Williams, Citizen and Merchant Taylor of London, makes a pleasant enough assumption for his son's sake, since faced by the mystery of genius, one gropes to find some path by which it may be connected with other greatness. However, it would take more than Roger Williams' apparently easy access to Oliver Cromwell and to other members of the Cromwell and Whalley families to make this assumption other than the merest conjecture. These associations can be quite satisfactorily explained on other, though less picturesque grounds. At the same time the tradition remains plausible enough to tease speculation and invite further research.

Somewhat more plausible, but also lacking in proof, is the suggestion of possible kinship between James Williams and the Rev. Roger Williams, vicar of St. Peter's Church in St. Albans, Hertfordshire. Search lingers here because St. Albans was the childhood parish of Alice Pemberton, who became the wife of James Williams. Search, however, is unrewarded. The career of the Rev. Roger is out in the open and well-documented from the time of his ordination at Payneswick in the diocese of Gloucester, Monmouthshire, through his various labors and honors, to his death in St. Albans in 1626,[6] but no extant record connects him unmistakably with

James Williams. The name Roger did not come from him or from any other member of the Williams family, but from Roger Pemberton, brother of Alice Pemberton, uncle and godfather to her son, Roger Williams of America.

For Alice Pemberton the immediate family connections are clear. She was the daughter of Robert Pemberton and Catherine Stokes, both of St. Albans. Both families belonged to the trades and were of distinctly better fortunes than James Williams was ever to be. There was also the occasional distinction of title and office in the family story. Alice Pemberton's father, according to tradition and probably also according to fact, belonged to a branch of the Pembertons of Pemberton who from very early times had flourished in Lancaster County. Quite probably he was the son of Geoffrey Pemberton, and if so, he was the first of the line to settle in St. Albans. He lived until 1578, when his daughter Alice was fourteen years old. Her brother, Roger Pemberton, godfather to Roger Williams, was a wealthy landowner of Walton Shelton, county Bedford, and a man of some local consequence. At one time he had been High Sheriff for Herts. He lived until 1627, only three years before his godson and namesake left for America, and he may very well have been an important influence in the boy's life during his early years. At his death, aged seventy-two, he left a legacy of ten pounds "unto my cosen [nephew] and Godsonne Roger Williams." With James Williams whom he called "brother-in-law," he had engaged jointly in various land transactions through the years.[7]

Another uncle, Sir James Pemberton, a goldsmith of London, was a man of large benefactions and some local prominence. He was High Sheriff from 1602 to 1603 and Lord Mayor of London from 1611 to 1612. At this time Roger Williams, then a boy of eight or nine, was old enough to feel the prestige of such a family connection, particularly on the occasion of the inauguration of Sir James as Lord Mayor on October 29, 1611. On this day, as Mayor-elect, he was honored by an elaborate pageant, *Chruso-thriambos: The Triumphes of Golde,* written by Anthony Munday, and performed by the Goldsmiths' Company. "Sparing no cost," says the title page, "that they might expresse their love to so Honorable a Brother." Seen through a boy's eyes, the spectacle of Sir James as the Golden King, taking barge toward Westminster with his Queen, or later riding in the triumphal chariot driven by the Indian King and Queen mounted on golden leopards, would have made a memorable day in a young nephew's life. The still more illustrious Sir Francis Pemberton, who rose to be Lord Chief Justice of the King's Bench, and later Chief Justice of the Common Pleas, was only a boy of six when Roger Williams left England, and it is not likely that this cousin relationship was of any special significance in his later life.

The marriage record of James Williams and Alice Pemberton is missing. It may have been destroyed with the burning of the Registers of St. Sepulchre's parish, their home throughout the remainder of their lives. If this were a first marriage for either or both of them,[8] the traditional date, 1597, seems late, for by this time James Williams had been an independent tradesman for ten years and Alice Pemberton was thirty-three years old. No license or other record of an earlier marriage having come to light, however, for either of them, there is only the fact of the Long Lane house in the tenure of James Williams by 1594[9] (and possibly earlier) to suggest that their home in St. Sepulchre's parish may have been set up near to this date. The birth records of their children, which most certainly would have been included in the church registers, are also missing. In fact, the first dated mention of these four children occurs in the will of James Williams in 1620. Their names are repeated in the same order, possibly of age, in the will of Alice Williams in 1634, long after all four had attained their majority. There may have been deaths in the family circle also, for in a plague-ridden city few families survived entire for so long a time. But of all that a blank page.

In consequence of these lost records, the precise birth date of Roger Williams has been a matter of much speculation and eager research, but so far it has not been authoritatively established. Roger Williams himself is of little help. In extant letters and in various Providence papers he mentions his age, but always vaguely, even riddlingly. How old is a man who says (in 1632) that he is "now in the days of my vanity nearer upwards of 30 than 25"; (in 1662) "about 56"; (in 1672/73) "now about three-score years"; (in 1677) "aged about seventie-five years"; (in 1679) "now neare Foure score years."[10] These vague statements do not square even with themselves. Taken literally, the 1632 statement would mean a 1603 or 1604 birth date; the 1662 one would push it ahead, possibly to 1605; the 1677 one would confirm 1603 or 1604; the "now neare Foure score years" might mean a year or so earlier. Until a more reliable statement comes to light, we shall probably not go far wrong to assume that he was born in "the wonderfull yeare, 1603."

If this be indeed true, his preservation throughout early infancy was something of a miracle, for in this memorable year the "arrow of God" was once again flying through London. Life was reckoned by the hour and to be safe at dawn was no guarantee of safety at sunset. The plague was afoot and more devastatingly than at any earlier time within the memory of parents young enough to have a child in the cradle. It was a year of terror, so much so that the passing of a great queen and consequent uncertainties as to England's future peace and prosperity became dim, or at least dimmer, as the "greatest pestilence that ever was heard or known by any man living" stalked through London streets. Even had this crucial year been recognized as a turning point in England's history, the fact would have seemed less momentous to Londoners than the crimson-circled words

Lord have
Mercy upon
Us

appearing on door after door as day followed day.[11]

Once again men and women of all classes ate garlic root spread with butter and salt, drank sack mixed with salad oil and gunpowder, and smoked tobacco before breakfast. When they ventured forth they chewed angelica root or lemon peel, held cloves in their mouths, wore bags of arsenic next to their skin, and carried orange cups containing sponges saturated with all manner of liquids which gave off pungent odors. Within their own houses by day and night they endured the smell of hot bricks sizzling in vinegar, or the smoke of smouldering leather, as well as the more pleasant frankincense, rosemary, bay leaves or juniper. They sprinkled their floors with rose water and scattered peeled white onions in their dooryards. Those able to pay for it thought to fortify themselves with a draught made from what passed as the dust of a unicorn's horn, albeit a talisman too costly for its alleged magic often to be put to the test. Infected ones wore poultices of garlic and white onions with tail feathers of cock, pigeon or pullet laid on their sores, and suffered nostrums almost as loathsome as the disease itself. But in spite of all known skills and these abounding quackeries, sextons and winding sheet weavers profiteered and prospered. As the weeks passed, plague orders posted on church doors became sterner, and examiners carrying red wands grew more diligent, yet day by day the crimson-circled placards were nailed on more doors, and night by night the dead carts rattling to the plague pits told the story, "husbands, wives and children being led as ordinarily to one grave, as if they had gone to one bed." Bodies were thrown in the pits at the cost of one penny apiece. One out of six died in London in the year 1603. Meanwhile though dogs, cats and rabbits were ordered killed, the black rats multiplied by thousands and ran unsuspected through London's crooked lanes and unpaved streets.

St. Sepulchre's parish, home of James and Alice Williams, and one of the "more sinfully-polluted Suburbs" where "Death hath pitcht his tents," fared among the worst. No wonder, for as London had sprawled rapidly outside the wall in this "farthest west ward of the city," it had become something of a Mecca for the poorer sort as well as a residence and business area for lesser merchants. In the preceding year (1602) an alarmed City Council had given order to pull down dwellings "over stables, in gardens and in other od corners," and to forbid the building of any new houses either "at London or three miles around." In 1603 they had forbidden the "filling and pestering of houses with Inmates not of the family." [12] But they were too late; besides the orders were ignored and more residents poured in.

The sequel in Farringdon and other outlying wards was disastrous. In St. Sepulchre's parish alone after early summer, 1603, the most musical bell in London tolled night and day without ceasing,

"And every stroake the bell doth toll,
Up to heaven it windes a soule."

From July to September of this same year it wound one thousand eight hundred and sixty-one souls to heaven from this one parish and all of them by the plague path. Even before Queen Elizabeth's death on March 24th, the pestilence was already within the city wall; by the end of the month it had appeared in nearly every ward and by midsummer it was raging. Before July 25th, the day appointed for the coronation of James I, the situation had grown desperate. Rather than risk infection in the streets, the king proceeded to Whitehall by water. A proclamation was issued forbidding any Londoner to presume to approach to the court, "the City having buried that week above a thousand of the plague." Nevertheless, throngs attended. Four days later, on July 29th, another order went forth, urging all those able to leave the city to do so immediately. Over night fear took on the proportions of panic.

Those able to find conveyance fled to the country, until presently watermen and hackneys, and even many of the official custodians of the city's safety had vanished also. The unfortunates left behind had no means of transportation save on foot. "There was not a good horse in Smith-field, nor a Coach to be set eye on," [13] wrote Thomas Dekker. London became a ghost city. The grass grew in Cheapside, as after more than three centuries, moss and flowers grow again in London cellar holes and over broken walls. The Globe theatre was closed for eleven months and Shakespeare had leisure, possibly to revise *Hamlet,* perhaps also to think of *Othello.* The trophies set up in honor of the coronation, wrote John Speed, stood "rather like the ruines of some old decay, than the Princely Pageants of a new Triumph." [14] Trade was at a standstill. No one dared to come in and all goods shipped out were under suspicion. The Merchant Taylors' Company gave up their annual dinner and distributed one third of the money it would have cost among the families of those "whose houses it shall please Almighty God so to visit." Other livery companies did likewise.

So far as is known, the Long Lane home of James and Alice Williams escaped the stroke which had fallen so heavily on their neighborhood. Very probably they were among the fleeing ones, for Alice Williams had numerous family connections in St. Albans, twenty miles away. Here they would have found a relatively safe harbor for their small family during the early months of the peril. As to a means of livelihood, James Williams would have nothing to lose by even a long absence from his taylor shop while only winding sheets were in demand. Very soon, however, they were in demand in these outlying districts also, for with the large-scale egress from the city, infection spread in new directions, so that by the beginning of 1604 London was safer than the country. The fleeing ones came home and gradually life became normal again, or nearly so. The terror would return, as all Londoners knew, but in the intervals between one onslaught and another, they could almost forget it, except in their public prayers.

> "Good Lord, keepe this noble citty of London, and defend it from grievous plauges and contagious sickines, that wee may often in brotherly and trewe love assemble and meete together, to thy glory and our mutuall comforte in Christ Jesus." [15]

So prayed the members of the Merchant Taylors' Company, at the sessions of their Quarterly Court, every man "kneeling upon his knees," James Williams probably among them. In this grievous visitation of his infancy, his son Roger had been spared, and he would be spared again; in his boyhood, in his early youth, and most mercifully of all perhaps, in the Great Plague Year, 1625, when he was a pensioner at Cambridge.

CHAPTER THREE

Boy in Smithfield

At some time, probably in his early boyhood, the Long Lane home, held by lease, was exchanged for the one in Cow Lane, purchased by James Williams. The date is not recorded, but whenever the change came, it would have made little difference in the outer look of life to a West Smithfield boy. Cow Lane, now King Street, is only a step from Long Lane, and in the early seventeenth century both were at the busy heart of old London. This dense center of life, interlaced with narrow lanes and overcrowded with "small Inns, Brew-houses, tenements for brokers, tiplers, and such like," dwelling houses with shops in front and warehouses behind,[1] hardly looked like the heart of a nation's prosperity, but such it was. The foreground was drab enough. Only a few imposing houses, such as High Hall, the city residence of the prior of Sempringham, an ancient structure of wood and stone, and St. Sepulchre's Church in the Bayley, towered high above the level of small houses and shops.

Out of the windows of either the Long Lane or Cow Lane house, the scene was of hurrying men and women carrying burdens in the "narrow, crooked, and incommodious Streets, fitter for a wheelbarrow than any nobler Carriage." Roger Williams' earliest impressions, possibly also many of his earliest memories, would have been connected in some way with displays of merchandise, with buying and selling, competitive industry, and with ships bound for far places. Young John Milton, over in Bread Street, only a little way toward St. Paul's, would have looked out on similar scenes: more crowds of heavily burdened men and women, more displays of merchandise. For both of these boys, destined in maturity for the battle of ideas, the earliest invitation was to action, not reflection; to insistent haste and the fever of striving rather than to inward quiet.

Long before the birth of either of them, historic Smithfield had greatly changed character. Gone were the one-time open spaces for seven-day jousts, military exercises, exhibitions, lavish processions, entertainments for royal guests. Through the centuries the "most part of the chivalry of England, and of France, and of other nations" had shared in these gorgeous pageants either as guests or participants. Here in the reign of Edward III rode "Dame Alice Perrers (the king's Concubine) as Lady of the Sunne . . . from the Tower of London, through Cheape, accompanied of many lords and ladies, every Lady leading a Lord by his horse-bridle, till they came into West Smithfield, and then began a great just, which endured seven days after." [2] Here in the reign of Richard II rode sixty lords and sixty ladies, each lord led by a chain of gold, trumpets announcing their advance. No hint remained that this spot was once a theatre of such grandeur. Gone also was the famous grove of elms which had given its name to the spaces between Turne-mill Brooke and the once "Great Water" known as "Horse-poole." The scaffold which anciently stood in Cow Lane had long since been moved to Tyburn. Pressure for building space had so increased that in John Stow's word, "now remaineth not one tree growing." After the suppression of the religious houses, their gardens and enclosures, which had made up nearly two thirds of the city area, had been crowded with dwelling houses of all sorts. In any direction one now walked between rows of small structures whose overhanging second stories cut off all view save of themselves. Even a portion of the "fayre Churchyard of St. Sepulchre's" was now "letten out for buildings, and a garden-plot." [3] Within the city wall London was changing from wood to brick, but here in Farringdon Ward Without, it was still a wooden city and one of little beauty.

Fortunately for those disposed to quietness, the open fields were not far away. A few steps down Chicken-Lane toward Turne-mill Brooke, over the brook by a bridge of timber or down Oldbourne Hill to Gold Lane, and there were the fields, stretching out into that "Garden without Wall" which was still part of Ward No. 25, or Farringdon Ward Without. Perhaps better still for teasing a boy's imagination and inviting his thought to the unknown parts of the enlarging seventeenth century world, were the docks with their forest of tall masts, their sailor talk of ships and shipping, their cargoes from far places. All this was almost within shouting distance of the Williams home, to add a dimension to a boy's thinking and to engage his dreams. Roger Williams' most famous sentence begins, "There goes many a ship to sea." [4] The sea figures in everything he wrote, and whenever his thought left the ground and sought imagery to suit, the sea answered his need. It is his most persistent metaphor. Why not? In later life he crossed the Atlantic five times in voyages of many weeks and long before one could be quite casual about such a crossing. The persistence of the image probably owed more, however, to the fact that his boyhood years in Smithfield were lived close to "the River," white with its hundreds of swans, and the docks to which it led. For him as for other London boys who grew up on the fringe of the Elizabethan era, the New World began at London docks, and as he watched ship after ship disappear over the far horizon, the Smithfield area henceforth claimed only part of him.

In the neighborhood of his own streets, as everywhere else in London at this date, everything was small scale, as compared with London after the Great Fire, but even so, urban problems were already pressing insistently. Traffic congestion in these narrow, winding streets, lanes and alleys, with consequent danger to pedestrians, was the first impression recorded by various foreign visitors. "Unwieldy engines [carts] which have begun to choke the streets so that a stranger, instead of finding time for observation, is happy if he escapes being crushed to pieces," wrote one. "It is a very populous city, so that one can scarcely pass along the streets on account of the throng," wrote another.[5] Truly, this "great Bee-hive of Christendome" held a bustling life, and it grew more so by the month, as tradesmen increased and prospered.

City authorities were paying intelligent heed to these traffic problems. There were already forty-seven laws on the London books about what not to do in the streets by day or night. Regulations as to speed limits, night-parking, lighting-up times, all were there. No man might "ride, or drive his car or Cart atrot, in the Street, but patiently, under paine of two shillings." No man might "Gallop his horse in the Street," also "under paine of two shillings." At no time might he "set any Carts in the Street by Night time, under paine of twelve pence," and if anyone were hurt by disobedience to this rule, the guilty one must "Recompence to such Persons as shall be hurt thereby." No one might go forth "by nightertaile without a lantern." Every householder must also "hang one out" at his door.[6]

Noise made another problem. From four in the morning until nine at night the air was rent with a bedlam of sound belonging to this dense center of activity. At mid-day in every street "Carts and Coaches make such a thundring as if the world ranne upon wheeles." Besides, "hammers are beating in one place, Tubs hooping in another, Pots clincking in a third, Water-tankards running at tilt in a fourth." Everywhere a drama of hurrying life: "heere are porters sweating under burdens, there Marchants-men bearing bags of money, Chapmen (as if they were at Leape-frog) skippe out of one shop into another; Tradesmen (as if they were dancing Galliards) are lusty at legges and never stand still; all are as busie as Countrie-Atturneyes at an Assises. How then can Idlenes thinke to inhabit heere?" [7] So wrote Thomas Dekker, who would not have exchanged this noisy, bustling, untidy London for any other spot on the globe.

Ordinances intended to control this bedlam out of hours were numerous on the City Books. Promptly at nine P.M. when the curfew rang from St. Sepulchre's tower, all sounds both of labor and merriment must cease, under pain of various shillings, or possibly of imprisonment. "No Hammer-man, as a Smith, a Pewterer, a Founder, or any Artificer making great sound" might work after "the Houre of nine in the Night, nor afore the Houre of four in the Morning, under paine of three shilling foure pence." No one might "blow any Horne" or whistle in the street "after the houre of nine of the clocke" under pain of imprisonment. Even in his own house "in the still of the night" no man might make any "sudden Outcry, cause any Affray," as by beating his wife or his servant, by "Singing or Revelling" which might disturb his neighbor.[8] Only the bleating of sheep in the Smithfield "Pennes and Folds" awaiting market day and the footsteps of those going up and down carrying *lanthorns* might lawfully interrupt the quietude of Long Lane and Cow Lane until the ban was lifted at dawn. The safety of one's own hearthside as compared with the perils of night life in London streets no doubt made such laws palatable enough to be observed by all except "the Banckrupt, the Fellon" and those who for any reason feared arrest by day. Such now crept out of their shells and "like so many Snayles stalked up and down" with a proud gait while "birds sit silent in bushes and beasts lie sleeping under hedges."

Once every month "at the Sessions holden for prisoners in Newgate," the "quiet of the Night" in the Cow Lane neighborhood was broken by the solemn tolling of St. Sepulchre's famous Hand-bell for the stirring to repentance of those condemned to die on the morrow.[9] "About the Hour of Ten of the Clock" the crier appointed to the task gave "Twelve solemn Towles, with double Strokes" under the window of the dungeon where the condemned ones lay, and then "after a good Pause," faced the window and "with a loud and audible Voice" recited a set speech of warning intended to arouse the victims to their last watchfulness and prayer. They were enjoined to "Pray all this night for the Salvation of your own Soules, while there is yet Time and Place and Mercie."

> "And when St. Sepulchre's Bell in the morning tolls,
> The Lord have mercy on your souls."

At six in the morning and continuing until ten, it tolled. Then precisely on the stroke of ten, the dead cart which would bear the victims to the gallows, was halted by the church wall, while the crier again tolled the "Twelve solemn Towles with the Hand-bell." After the dead cart had rumbled off, there was again tolling of the Great Bell until the execution was over, when it rang out "for the Space of one Half-hour or thereabouts." After many repetitions this grim reminder of mortality for lawbreakers might become mere routine to those who lived near enough to count the strokes while they tried to sleep. Perhaps not, but at any rate it was part of life in the Long Lane and Cow Lane neighborhood, and might well have given a sombre connotation to the ringing of bells anywhere for a lifetime.

The Smithfield neighborhood had also quite opposite moods. Once a year it was the gayest spot in all London, if not in all England. The occasion was Bartholomew Fair, for centuries one of the great fairs of the world. Originally born of religious zeal and for a long time a means of enriching the ancient priory of St. Bartholomew, by the seventeenth century it had long since lost its religious significance, overflowed the priory precincts and become a great Cloth Fair. In Roger Williams' boyhood it had lost even this importance and was little more than a riotous carnival, an object of concern to London authorities, the haunt of small dealers and holiday makers of all sorts,

> "A Variety of fancies where you may find
> A faire of wares, and all to please your mind." [10]

Truly so, and whether one regarded it as the Mecca of boisterous pleasure, or the "very shop of Satan himself, a wicked and foul Fair," everybody came, and for the fortnight of its duration put themselves at the mercy of the pig women, the gingerbread vendors, ballad singers, wrestlers, gamesters, applemongers, purveyors of all manner of gadgets, rattles, toys, dolls, hobby horses, trinkets and other small joys. They patronized the puppet shows, motions, side shows of many sorts, and if possible dodged the light-fingered rogues and pickpockets who were as much a part of the fair as the roast pig sizzling piping hot on the stalls. Strange sights and distracted noises, and "You who are wise, Preserve your purses, whilst you please your eyes."

All this went on every August almost at the Williams front door, and whether it presented invitations to enjoyment, or Puritan reproaches strong enough to compel three small boys to look in the opposite direction, it was an inescapable fact in the Smithfield section and in some form or other must have left its deposit in a boy's memory. Roger Williams and his brothers would have been strangely unnatural children, if among all these excitements they had not engaged with the other Smithfield youngsters in chasing the "parcel of live rabbits" turned loose for their delight, when the Lord Mayor rode away in great dignity at the opening hour.

As to which of all the Smithfield associations may have cut deeply significant grooves in his boy thought, the field of conjecture is large, as well as completely uncertain. It may or may not have been significant, for example, for one whose mature life was to be spent "beyond the seas" that during these same boyhood years, this very phrase was a household word, having immediate, almost intimate associations with St. Sepulchre's parish, and for no other reason than Captain John Smith himself. The Captain was a worshipper in St. Sepulchre's church, was well known there for his previous escapes and other adventures, and on the eve of his first setting forth to Virginia, he had knelt at this altar to receive "that most comfortable sacrament" as part of his last preparation. Roger Williams was too young at this time to share in the impressiveness of the occasion, or to be aware of the controversy it touched off, but possibly he was not too young to have some wisp of child memory of Smith's triumphant return in 1609 and again in 1612. In a sense the Captain's triumphs were neighborhood triumphs, and he could hardly have escaped being the particular hero of every boy in the parish.[11]

Even before his *Generall Historie of Virginia* stimulated a wide interest in Virginia colonization, the livery companies of London were well aware of the urgency of colonization plans. As early as 1609 the Merchant Taylors' Company had been requested by the Lord Mayor to contribute generously to the project. This was a request without benefit of choice or the privilege of refusal. The time had come (so reads the official *Precept*) when it was no less than imperative

> "to ease the City and Suburbs of a swarme of unnecessary inmates, as a contynual cause of dearth and famyne, and the very originall cause of all the plagues that happen in this Kingdome." [12]

The Merchant Taylors' Company, along with the other livery companies was promised in return for this voluntary contribution a hundred acres to every man with a trade. The contributors would also have "ratably according to their adventure, theire full parte of all such lands, tenements, and hereditaments, as shall from tyme to tyme be recovered, planted, and inhabited." The motive back of this proposal and the others which followed was well sharpened to the self-interest of merchants. In addition to the glory of God and the easing of an overcrowded city, they were lured on by "the visible hope of a greate and rich trade, and many secrett blessings not yett discovered." The Merchant Taylors, both as a company and as individuals, made generous response to this 1609 plea, as was expected of them, and they continued to do so as other appeals followed.

It would seem that henceforth colonization projects would have been matter of familiar knowledge and frequent conversation in a merchant taylor's home. In fact, much more widely, for the subsequent announcements of ships ready to sail, of places of rendezvous for those willing to go, in addition to the bizarre romance of Captain John Smith's adventures or the exhibit of live Indians brought back for Londoners to gaze upon, made Virginia a very real place, almost a place within reach. For years popular broadsides had made it also a place of fabulous plenty in comparison with the pinch of life in overcrowded London. As early as 1605 the Chapman-Marston-Jonson play *Eastward Hoe* had given it a romantic extravagance no "truth" accounts thereafter could quite effectively deny. Through Captain Seagull's eyes it was a land where gold is more plentiful than copper in England, where dripping pans and chains across the streets are of gold, where prisoners are fettered in gold, where rubies and diamonds are picked up on the seashore, "to hang on their children's Coates, and hang on their childrens Caps," where wild boar is as common as mutton, "where any man may be an alderman, never a Scavener, . . . and never a slave . . . a land where there is no more Law then conscience, and not too much of either." [13]

"How far is it there?"

asked Spendall in the play, and thereafter everyone in London asked the same question. Forthwith Captain Seagull stepped out of *Eastward Hoe* and his words assumed the authority of fact.

In 1616 when the much-heralded Pocahontas arrived with her husband, her son and her Indian retinue to receive London's acclaim, the long hero tale of Captain John Smith took on the solidity of flesh and blood history. The Virginia Company announced a lottery, and once again the talk of Virginia was as wide as London. In this same year Smith's *Description of New England* ("the Paradise of these parts") was published, bringing a fresh flurry of interest. As a boy in Captain John Smith's parish, Roger Williams could hardly have missed the dreams all this invited. Years later, when it came his turn to sail in "the good ship *Lyon,*" however individual or even grim the reason, and however sudden or compulsive his decision to embark, it must have seemed to him as inevitable to be going as though he had never intended to do anything else, for as a boy in West Smithfield, he had already been "beyond the seas" many times in his dreams.

His boy's thought would also have been expanded by the great doings of his father's fraternity, standing as they did at the opposite pole from the endeavor to ease London of its indigents and undesirables, or to invite the adventurous to seek a new home and a new chance. In 1609 the banquet to King James was one such occasion. As the date drew near, plans straightway became a subject of much controversy and debate among the members of the company, since they had not yet paid the deficit remaining from the like festivity of 1607. No wonder, in terms of the astounding list of what had been provided and no doubt eaten at that lavish feast. The itemized toll begins with five and a half calves and seven lambs, and then proceeds (to select at random) on through seventeen swans, ten old pheasants, sixteen pheasant pouts, two cocks, eighteen geese, sixty-two capons, a hundred and fifty-eight pullets, thirty-six turkey chickens, three hundred and thirty-four more chickens (variously classified), a hundred and seventy-two quail, eighty-one partridges, eighty-seven rabbits, fifty-seven house pigeons, ten owls, cuckoos, ring doves, peacocks, mallards, teals (variously numbered), thirteen hundred eggs, three hundred and sixty pounds of butter, enough beer to drown in, and in case they ran short, a buck and a hogshead of wine supplied by the king himself. Now in 1609 it was all to do over again, but "Forasmuch as all victualls are grown to a very high rate," they were loath to proceed with a feast to match this 1607 lavishness.[14] Hence, discussion waxed spirited.

Whether any echoes from such affairs ever reached the Cow Lane home no one can know. In Roger Williams' own writings there is only one item of boyhood reminiscence, and that concerns neither the Virginia excitements nor the magnificent displays which were almost commonplaces of London life in his boyhood. This one item of recall concerns religion. "From my Childhood," he wrote, "the Father of *Lights* and *Mercies* toucht my Soul with a Love to himself, to his only begotten, the true Lord Jesus, to his *holy Scriptures*." That his experience was not altogether happy is apparent in a second reference, made in a letter to John Winthrop in 1632, two years after Roger Williams had come to America. This second recall has been quoted many times, "Myself a child in everything, though in Christ called, and persecuted in and out of my father's house these 20 years." [15] The application of these brief statements is nowhere made specific, but there they are, not a boy's recollection, but a man's, and the second made in all candor by one not inclined to feel sorry for himself. They may not be important in proportion to their singleness, except that they put the accent where, in the sweep of his whole life, one might expect to find it—namely, on the things of religion. In the light of what became the ruling purpose of his life, it belongs nowhere else. Making allowance for the probability that he was speaking in round numbers, as he often did, twenty years would take him back to his eighth or ninth year, by no means too early for a memorable religious experience or a sense of persecution because of it. Certainly at that time, West Smithfield, London, would have been one of the best places in all England for a child to get an impression of persecution for religion's sake. No one with ears to hear or eyes to see could have missed knowing quite literally what it meant.

In March, 1611/12, when Roger Williams was presumably eight, "the very unblameable Bartholomew Legate," a lay preacher and dealer in cloth, was burned in full sight of the Williams home as a notorious heretic. Among his heresies was the view that Christ was "begotten and made," not "God of God begotten, and not made," that he had not "existed from everlasting," that he had not made the world and was not to be prayed to. For these and other "monstrous views" Legate had been apprehended, imprisoned in Newgate, tried by the Consistory Court and found guilty on thirteen counts. Given an audience before King James, his Majesty "had spurned at him with his foot" and said, "Away, base fellow." Pronounced an "obdurate, contumacious and incorrigible Heretic" by a *significavit,* he had been turned over to the secular power. After the civil writ for his execution had been issued, he was given a chance to recant, had refused, and forthwith been "burned to ashes" before "a vast Conflux of people." "Never did a scare-fire at night summon more hands to quench it, than this at noonday did eyes to behold it," Thomas Fuller wrote, being almost afraid to expose Legate's damnable opinions in print, lest he who wrote them down and those who read them on the printed page be polluted. His own final comment on Legate is eloquent of the unshakable certainty of justice with which Legate's judges, both civil and ecclesiastical, had condemned him. He wrote,

> "And so we leave him, the first that for a long time suffered death in that manner; And, Oh that he might be the last to deserve it!" [16]

This case made a great noise all over England, partly because the victim was young, comely, of a bold spirit, confident carriage, fluent tongue, excellently skilled in the Scriptures: "Well would it have been for him if he had known them less or understood them better," was another comment of Thomas Fuller, to which he added that the poison of heretical doctrine is "never more dangerous than when served up in clean cups and washed dishes." He was right, but for another reason than the one he had in mind. It was so dangerous in England at this time that its punishment at the stake raised such a cry that the Smithfield burnings were ended. In the same year the burning of Edward Wightman in Litchfield raised a similar cry. The Wightman martyrdom may have been remembered in the Williams household because of the marriage of Roger's sister Catherine to a man of the same name, though apparently no blood relation.

The Legate burning may very probably have recalled the earlier Smithfield martyrdoms, and made them subjects of pious conversation. There was, for example, John Badby, a tailor, who had been burned there in 1409/10. Encased in an empty barrel, and tied to the stake with chains, he had been given a last minute chance to make the *right* answer concerning the sacrament which was offered him. "What is the nature of it?" was the question. "It is hallowed bread, not God's body," he had replied, and the torch was forthwith applied to the circle of wood around the barrel. And lest later times forget, there was the picture of the horrid scene in Foxe's *Book of Martyrs* for children to gaze upon.[17] Here in Smithfield also, opposite the west gate of St. Bartholomew's, Anne Askew, too weak to stand, had been tied to the stake with a chain around her waist in 1546, the only mercy accorded her being gunpowder laid to her body to end the torture sooner. Her heresy also had concerned the nature of the sacrament, but though suffering the rack, to her honor it was written that she "would not convert for all the pain." Nine years later, the most famous Smithfield martyr of them all, John Rogers, vicar of St. Sepulchre's church, had gone to his burning "as though he had been led to a wedding." He also had refused to recant as the torch was applied, and instead had "washed his hands in the flames." Roger Williams himself mentions John Lambert, burned at Smithfield in 1538.[18] The edition of Foxe's *Martyrs* which he would have grown up with pictured Lambert's dying words, "None but Christ, none but Christ," issuing from his mouth as the flames ascended. The story of these Smithfield burnings had been so deeply built into neighborhood tradition through the generations that a boy who was feeling persecuted for religion's sake might naturally enough have thought of himself as one of their later number, as he walked over the ground hallowed by their physical anguish.

More realistically, Roger Williams may have been made aware of persecution through the experiences of his Dutch neighbors and boy playmates in the church of Austin Friars. This church, known as the "Mother of all Reformed Dutch Churches," stood next to Drapers' Hall, and close enough to his own home so that down any street or lane the members of this community were his near neighbors. In his boyhood it numbered some four hundred and fifty families of non-conforming Dutch and French refugees who by royal permission, confirmed by a charter, maintained their own preaching, administered their own sacraments and church discipline, elected their own officers, with this church as their worshipping center.[19] A child to whom religion was important, or even if it were not so, could hardly have escaped being acutely aware that here were people worshipping very differently from his own family at St. Sepulchre's, and that these differences mattered intensely on both sides. He might have sensed the uncertainties with which these non-conforming neighbors maintained not only an unorthodox church life but also their own personal lives because of these differences of faith and practice. The members of this community, adults and children as well, were ridiculed, hooted at and abused in the streets as strangers, although the Austin Friars neighborhood had been home to their fathers and grandfathers before them. As late as Roger Williams' boyhood occasional threats and warnings were written on the walls of the Dutch churchyard by night.

> "You, strangers, that inhabit in this land,
> Note this same writing, do it understand.
> Conceive it well, for safeguard of your lives,
> Your goods, your children, and your dearest wives." [20]

It is difficult to evaluate the effect of such a neighborhood association in the thought of one who stood outside of it and yet was intimately involved. These were his playmates who lived with fear because of their religious beliefs. These were their parents, called "beastly brutes, drunken drones," who had made a "cowardly flight from your own natural countries" by a "counterfeit show of religion." To sympathize with their sorrows would have meant to share in the persecution they suffered and to be on the unpopular side in a thorny neighborhood issue. Much of the abuse heaped upon them was motivated by the jealousy of craftsmen who were outdone by the skills of these "foreigners." The apprentices who staged some of the local riots against them were boys in their teens and they would also have been Roger Williams' companions. A conflict of loyalties would have been inevitable for any boy who lived on terms with both groups.

Undoubtedly, Roger Williams' later familiarity, even facility with Dutch and French as spoken languages, had its beginning in his daily intercourse with these neighborhood children. He had a Dutch Testament which he later gave to a boy who was his household servant in Providence. Very probably he had learned to read it himself in the church school kept for the children of the community. The teaching of languages was one of the acknowledged purposes of this school and Roger Williams' own flair for language may have received something of a spur from instruction there. If so, he would have learned a great deal more than language from his attendance.

Another possible clue to the persecution reminiscence, as well as another source of religious views other than the orthodox, leads one to the secret meeting-places in Smithfield of non-conforming groups representing various shades of Dissent and various degrees of Separatism. Unlike the Austin Friars community, these groups were without royal permission to carry on a different worship or to think for themselves as to doctrine and church polity. They met at private houses, came separately, left separately, and kept a guard stationed at the door during their half hour of prayer and hour of sermon. One such group had met in Cow Lane at the home of Nicholas Lee, who in 1616 became the minister of the group. He was strongly Separatist, and the leader of the London Barrowists. When others of the group emigrated to Holland, he remained behind and escaped capture. Another earlier group had met at "Mr. Bilson's house near Christchurch"; still another by St. Bartholomew's Hospital, one at the home of John Barnes, a tailor in Duck Lane, others at "Mr. Boyse's house in Fleet Street," and at Daniel Bucke's in Aldgate within the Wall. In St. Nicholas Lane there were two such places, one at a schoolhouse, probably George Johnson's, and the other at the house of John Nicholas of St. Sepulchre's, late of Cow Lane. He was presently imprisoned.[21] The fact that dissenting groups were meeting so close to the Williams home suggests that from his childhood up, Roger Williams had been a neighbor to unorthodox opinion and the persecution it invited, not only from ecclesiastical authority but from orthodox St. Sepulchre's worshippers as well.

He does not specifically mention these groups at any time in his later life, and at his boyhood stage he may have been quite as appalled by their boldness as his orthodox neighbors professed to be. He could hardly have failed, however, to know of the secret meetings and there is a strong probability that he had attended some of them. Certainly somewhere in his early years he had been "infected" with the notion that nothing less than complete separation from the established church would do for those who aspired to be "a pure communion of saints on earth," and some upper room in West Smithfield would have provided the place. Some of the men and women who dared to jeopardize their week to week safety in order to give some reality to their convictions were his neighbors and the parents of his boy companions, and he had reason to respect them.

During these same years *Separatism* was beginning to be a word not to be indifferent about, and since its justification was to be one of the goals of his own later thinking, it may or may not be significant that he would first have heard the label applied in derogation to men and women he knew. In his thirteenth year Henry Jacob's London church was gathered from one of these groups. Later still a small number seceded under John Spilsbury, the issue being that the Jacob group was not truly "separated." Henceforth the spotlight was on them, and what felt like *persecution* was only a step away. A reminiscence of Richard Baxter suggests that the line between safe orthodoxy and accusation of heresy may be thin indeed, and that *persecution* may have many definitions. In the Baxter reminiscence, some neighborhood revellers had called his father *Puritan,* not for scruples against the Book of Common Prayer or ceremonies, not for speaking against Bishops, or denouncing set prayers, but only for reading his Bible when the rest were dancing on the Lord's Day and for praying in his own house. As a boy Baxter had been so hurt by the reproachful stigma hurled at his father that he himself was "cured" of revelling and also alienated from his companions henceforth.[22] To a sensitive boy, *persecution* may need no broader base than this. The "in and out of my father's house" of Roger Williams' recall raises the question of disharmony within his own family group. Possibly, but his phrase is too dark for certainty.

In any or all of these conjectures about a boyhood of which he is all but completely silent, of course one treads on dangerous ground. As a place to grow up in during these important years, West Smithfield may not have been important for any of the details which in his boyhood caught the eye of strangers or have provided material for social history in the centuries since that time. It may be significant, however, that during his pre-University years Roger Williams was a city boy, and that the sights, the sounds, the local interests, large and small, the pleasures and excitements, the personalities, the sins of the greatest city in the world in his day were the background of his first thoughts and questionings. He was born to trade, and at the very center of the center of its London life. He knew the busyness, the clamor, the jealousy, the insistent haste, the fierce competition, the far-stretching ambitions of those who did business on the sea, and he knew it all so intimately that he could take it for granted along with the jostling in the street, the ringing of the prisoner's death bell, or the identity of the thirty-four heads on the thirty-four spikes of London bridge. For one who was to spend his mature life in wilderness places, the London background of his boyhood would seem to provide something of balance requisite for what lay ahead. Perhaps not, but at any rate, it was the fact.

CHAPTER FOUR

"Fitte Scholar"

FROM his sixth or seventh year forward some now forgotten Smithfield schoolroom was probably his larger world. In the absence of precise record or personal reminiscence prior to his Charterhouse years, one can construct the previous chapters of his schoolroom story only within the standard framework for a middle-class boy's early education. From one school to another there would have been only slight variation in the learning sequence, perhaps also in the degree of strictness, even rigor, with which these first steps would have been guided, for until Comenius made his plea for delight in learning as the schoolroom ideal, an English boy's education was conceived and planned in distinctly sober terms. "No slavery in the world like to that of a Grammar Scholar," Robert Burton wrote, remembering his own boyhood anguish in his suffering school days.[1] His verdict had many contemporary parallels.

Unless he were taught privately, as would seem unlikely for a boy in his station, Roger Williams would have set forth, aged six, to some neighborhood school for "Pettyes and Punies." Here he would have been "initiated into his Rudiments," as the saying was, by a teacher of the lowest pedagogical rank, namely an *abecedarian,* whose realm was the Hornbook. "Good scholars," John Evelyn lamented, will not "abase themselves to the *Elementarie,*" unless ill fortune should make them "stoop so low." This, he continued, is a great pity, for the first grounding should be handled by the best." Granted, but it was not always so, and the helpless "Pettyes and Punies" must take what guidance was offered, be it mediocre or otherwise.

Some schoolmasters urged an earlier start than the sixth year, both for the boy's sake and their own. "The sooner a child is put to school, the better it is," wrote Schoolmaster Hoole, "both to prevent ill habits, which are got by play and idleness, and to enure him betimes to affect learning and well doing." Hoole would have put this seasonable age for beginning between three and four years, "when a childe hath great propensity to peek into a book," but he preferred that such *peeking* be superintended at home. Merely to keep children "from troubling the house at home" was not the schoolmaster's business.[2] He would have approved of John Evelyn who wrote, as though apologetically, "I was not initiated into any rudiments until neere four years of age." [3] Thomas Hobbes who had also begun at four, was commended by John Aubrey for his skill in reading and numbers, aged eight. How to go further, faster and younger, was the issue in all such discussions. Evelyn, Aubrey and Hobbes had all gone to the *elementarie* in the church porch and Roger Williams may have done likewise, for there is a record of a school kept over the gate of St. Sepulchre's early in the century. Aubrey's own reminiscence supplies a smug note of privilege for his own primary school days. "I had then a fine little horse and commonly rode," he wrote. "I was not a vulgar boy and carried not a satchell at my back." [4] By this implication of social status, Roger Williams probably was a "vulgar boy," satchel and all.

There were only two R's in the *Elementarie* for a beginner in those days, Reading and Religion. Reading meant running backwards and forwards over the Christ-Cross-Row, sounding the vowels "like so many bells upon his fingers ends," putting vowels before consonants and consonants before vowels, until presently, when a boy had grown "pretty nimble in the most," he might go on to greater things.[5] Religion meant Bible history, the Catechism in both English and Latin, prayers four times a day "on his knees" and on Monday morning questions as to what he had "borne away" from the Sunday sermon. Long before he had learned how to write it down, he must be prepared to give an account of what he had heard.

When he was seven, he would "stay in his Bible" and in addition "go into his Accidence," or rudiments of grammar, both English and Latin. Queried the Catechism in such sort:

Ques. What booke do you learn?
Ans. Myne Accidence.
Ques. What booke is that?
Ans. It is the first booke which we use to learne to teach us the groundes and principall rules of Grammar.
Ques. What is Grammar?
Ans. It is an art which teacheth the right and due order of speech as well in writing as in speaking.[6]

Another current *simplification* "for young Punies" as to the nature of Grammatical Construction calls it "the concord and agreeing of words together: and the governing or ruling of one word of another." [7] So enlightened the little Punies were off to the first *Concord,* each step of their future progress to be clarified by further mouth-filling definitions in kind. When a boy reached the Genitive Gerund and the Supines of compound verbs, he would eschew English and return all grammar rules in Latin. He would live his school life in grammar; it would be almost the beginning, middle and end of his pre-University training. Hence "to say without book all the usual and necessary rules," to recognize their application, and to "give a right reason of every word why it must be so and not otherwise" became one of the foundation laws of the *Elementarie.*

In due course writing and numbers were added to a boy's program, with some three hours' practice in each daily. With the importance attached to being a "good penman" who "could make flourishes nimbly" and "never a bad letter," it seems strange to find writing in many schools slipped into the week's program on Saturday afternoons, playing days, in vacations, and (for boarders) "after supper." A Bury St. Edmunds statute, having specified Saturday afternoons after three o'clock as the time "for the mending of their hands," adds, "And when they have to write, let them use their knees for a table." [8] Inconvenience notwithstanding, however, good penmen were made, Roger Williams among them.

Rigidity in discipline and repetition in method were the twin laws of the *Elementarie,* and it would seem they were pressed to the limits of endurance for master and boys alike.

"I have so disposed the placing of my first booke,"

wrote Schoolmaster Coote,

> "that if the child should teare out every leafe as fast as he learneth it, yet it shall not be greatly hurtfull, for every new following chapter repeateth and teacheth againe all that went before." [9]

This discouraging practice was true in the book and out of it. "Rehearse" and then "Rehearse" again was the watchword of every schoolroom. From six A.M. in the summer, when a boy must be in his seat, "his satchell unknyt" and his mind adjusted to the day's rigors, until four or five in the afternoon, nothing else was to be expected. In addition, for most schools Friday was Repetition Day in all Forms, both of the *Elementarie* and the Grammar School to follow. The entire week's recitations were rehearsed according to a set schedule for each hour of the day. Competition after the Quiz Program pattern added zest and no doubt made Friday the best day of the week for the participants. Lined up in two ranks, the boys, each in turn, asked a question of the boy opposite and then counted to ten. If the correct answer were not forthcoming in time, "let the boy who missed be coptus" and on to the next boy went the question. A monitor was on hand to keep the score. In the Grammar School, this whole exercise would be in Latin, and the questions asked would concern only the points of greatest difficulty in the week's lessons.

Aged nine, his "Rudiments" behind him, his handwriting presumably decipherable and the Catechism imprinted on his memory for life, a boy was ready for the next stage. At this important gateway, Roger Williams' record is still blank. His name appears on no extant Grammar School record so far discovered. The Free School of the Merchant Taylors' Company, already one of their darling projects for more than fifty years, would seem to have been a natural choice for a Merchant Taylor's son, but his name is not on the extant list. Nor is it likely that he was either one of "Paul's Pigeons" of the St. Paul's famous Grammar School, or one of "Anthony's Pigs" at St. Anthony's School in Threadneedle Street. One thinks first, perhaps wrongly, of such well known schools. There were many other possibilities, less well known, whose records have perished, and in whichever of them he may have been enrolled, the training received would have been standard both in materials and method.

It would have been training mainly in Latin, Logick and Rhetorick and the greatest of these was Latin.

> "All men covet to have their children speake Latin, and so do I very earnestly too," [10]

said Roger Ascham of *Scholemaster* fame and also of fame in St. Sepulchre's parish where he is honored in burial. In so speaking he voiced the ambition of generations of fathers, James Williams no doubt among them. Latin being currently esteemed the international language, fluency in reading and speaking it was the *sine qua non* of the educated man. Accordingly every boy "born to be educated" faced seven years of declining, conjugating, parsing, rendering Latin into English, and then back into Latin (his own), turning prose into verse and verse into prose, reading the "best" Latin authors, memorizing "gems" from their works, struggling to Latinize his own best thoughts with strict grammatical correctness, "using no barbarous phrase," and imitating such "elegance" in his exemplar as he could comprehend. The process was unhurried. Thoroughness was more important than speed and a good grounding worth all it might cost in the "bitterness of learning." A "fitte scholar" must not only "know his declensions orderly," he must know them "every way, forward, backward, by cases, by persons; that neither Case of Noun, nor Person of Verb can be required, that he cannot without stop or study tell." [11]

The reward for such diligence may have been out of sight to a boy's eyes, except as success in competition made it desirable, but at any rate he had no choice. Mastery was expected of him, and interest must lie in mastery alone. As to any connection between the world schoolboys live in, outside of school hours, and the requirements of the Grammar School between six A.M. and five P.M., there was little enough. A boy lived in a past world. Within the school precincts he spoke no English word. Latin and Latin only was his medium of communication, and this under penalty for the merest lapse. Later in their lives both Milton and Williams were to be sharp critics of this Latinized training, but in their own school days they succumbed to it, of necessity.

Of concessions to boyhood restlessness, there were next to none.

The fifteen minute interval for breakfast or recreation at nine o'clock, after the first three hours of study and recitation, must be "countervailed" by fifteen minutes added to the morning session at eleven. Likewise the brief intermission at three-thirty in the afternoon. Some masters looked sourly on even these brief respites from steady application, holding that time out for "bever" (any kind of drink, but usually beer) was time wasted. Schoolmaster Brinsley took the opposite side, but only because in his opinion, these intermissions, plus the "bever," might "prevent many inconveniences," and make it easier to keep boys in their places and "hard to their labours." [12] In spirit this last phrase was written large over every schoolroom of the century, and if a boy survived as a learner, his will bent to the demand.

Even when the master "slept his hour" at his desk during a study period, his sleep was too light for safe dalliance. The famous Mulcaster, recalled by Thomas Fuller as one of the *sleepers,* was remembered as possessed of a sixth sense which could detect even a momentary blink on the part of some helpless boy entrapped before him. When he awoke, the boys must be ready "on the instant" to construe and parse according to his pre-napping instructions. In spite of all these rigidities, however (and they were very numerous) schoolmasters counselled each other to "punish unwillingly," control their anger, and to use "mildness of speech," that so they might "inflame the dull-headed dullard (if any such there be) to study and learning." If such an unrealistic hope savors of schoolroom inexperience, it also suggests that the master's sights were high, and that ideally he admitted that his patience should be equal to the strain.

What came of it all? For one who had acquitted himself as a "fitte scholar," it would seem that in addition to measurable familiarity with the materials over which his mind had been "incessantly worked" during his Grammar School years, a boy who survived would be likely to emerge with some zeal (partly unconscious) for mastery as the goal of his own striving; with composure enough to deliver "on the sodayn" what knowledge he could command in a given subject, some ability to express himself in acceptable English, and possibly some acquaintance, if in samples only, of what certain ancients had thought and written. Perhaps more determining than any other of these fruits of study, would be the unconscious following an approved sequence of steps for arriving at his own conclusions on any subject.

1st, learn the precepts;
2nd, note the best examples of the precepts;
3rd, imitate these examples;
4th, make somewhat alone without the examples.

These same four steps [13] had been accommodated to simple materials at the Hornbook stage, and they would still be a basic pattern in the entire university training. Roger Williams' writings, along with those of his contemporaries in the same field, show on almost every page that his mind worked according to these steps. They had been cut to lifetime depth and permanence. Likewise the continual stress on confuting another boy's position and ferreting out the weak places in his argument had shaped his own processes of thought and fitted him for the controversial battles of his manhood. No doubt this intensely competitive spirit encouraged from the Petty School days forward sharpened the wits, as was intended; such unceasing emphasis also made it more natural for a generation of thinkers to say a thing in refutation of some one else's statement than to say it directly. The pamphlet warfare of the 1640's reflects this training so unmistakably that from a few thousand pages of these controversial treatises, a schoolman could construct a textbook of educational principles and methods fundamental to this training.

Presumably when the Charterhouse doors opened to him in 1621, Roger Williams had behind him the fundamentals of such a training, wherever he had acquired it, and at whatever point it may have been interrupted. Otherwise, he would not have been admitted as a Foundation Scholar. Private instruction being probably unlikely, there is also the chance that after the *Elementarie* and possibly the earlier Forms of the Grammar School, he had been apprenticed to some member of the Stationers' or Scriveners' Company, and that impelled by what he himself called his "natural inclination to study and activity," he was serving this apprenticeship when the Charterhouse opportunity came. Such an opening as also the employment which preceded it, and in which he established his fitness for further study, would hardly have come to a schoolboy with a satchel, safely immured day after day within schoolroom walls. Neither would it have come to a boy without the fundamentals of early Grammar School training behind him. In any case this fortunate opportunity put Roger Williams on his lifetime track.

CHAPTER FIVE

Protégé

THIS determining event was of course the meeting with a great man, Sir Edward Coke, Chief Justice of the King's Bench, and in the opinion of many unto the present day, England's greatest man of law. Speculation as to the circumstances of the first meeting between this "Oracle" of the English law and the Merchant Taylor's son, has naturally enough led to picturesque exaggeration. A great man taking notice of an obscure and ungrown boy, who in his turn becomes another great man, is itself the chart for romantic legend. Posterity likes such tales. Roger Williams' life at various other points also invites to legend, although not seldom truth itself, according to human lives, has been known to follow a picturesque pattern. Certainly in this significant Man-Boy meeting there is no reason to doubt the pleasant tradition that on a certain Sunday morning in St. Sepulchre's church, the attention of the great Sir Edward was attracted to a studious looking boy diligently taking sermon notes in shorthand, and that forthwith he engaged this boy to take notes for him at the hearing of certain cases in the Star Chamber.

Conceivably enough, it may have been even so. Sir Edward was an occasional worshipper at St. Sepulchre's church, where the Williams family also worshipped. Young Roger, like any other English schoolboy of the period, had been obliged on Monday morning to stand before the schoolmaster's desk, present in writing an outline of the Sunday sermon, and then suffer more or less minute questioning on the text, the doctrine, its reasons and the applications thereof. Shorthand, or "secret writing," as it was often called, was a subject in which he might have received formal instruction at any Grammar or

Free School. Simonds D'Ewes tells of inventing his own "strange handwriting consisting of an alphabet and strange letters." He did it for "secrecy." [1] Whether invented or standard, such a shorthand system would have served a boy well for the Monday sermon ordeal and various other schoolroom necessities. Roger Williams himself continued to use a shorthand system throughout his life and the St. Sepulchre sermons of his boyhood may well have afforded him early practice. At any rate the employment by Sir Edward for the taking of shorthand notes is a fact of manifold importance in the life the boy was to lead. Attested years later by Anne Sadleir, daughter of Sir Edward, this employment is the first established fact of his life, although undated.

At this time Sir Edward was a man somewhere in his sixties. Behind him were great honors, great victories, great defeats. More and greater were to come in all three directions. Always they would come with attendant drama, for Chief Justice Coke was the kind of public servant whose every move made copy. Extravagantly admired, passionately hated, he could never be ignored and he knew it. Moreover, as King Charles is reported to have said on one desperate occasion, "he ever fell upon his legs." So it was, and so it would be, whatever disaster was still ahead. Already he had held high office under two monarchs. He had been Speaker of the House and Attorney General under Queen Elizabeth; Chief Justice of the Common Pleas and Chief Justice of the King's Bench, or as he dared to amend his own title, Chief Justice of England, under King James. He had conducted the trials of the Earls of Essex and of Southampton, of Sir Walter Raleigh and of the Gunpowder Plotters. The impeachment of his arch-enemy, Sir Francis Bacon, was still to come. Eleven volumes of his famous *Reports* had already appeared.[2]

For all this and much more in kind, no doubt his was a name and a presence to awe his fellow-worshippers at St. Sepulchre's Church when he walked to his pew on Sunday, although his far-flung honors may have been less impressive in this London section than around the law courts. According to John Stow, Coke had for some years before this date, owned and operated a dilapidated manse or "messauge" in Lime-Street Ward, "lately new-builded into a number of small tenements, letten out to strangers, and other meane people." [3] Not an improvement to the neighborhood apparently or an enterprise calculated to make him popular. Neither could anyone, high or low, anywhere in England, forget certain sensational details of his conduct during the state trials. In his most irascible moods he never uttered a more unfortunate word than when, raising his voice, he had shouted to Sir Walter Raleigh, "Thou art the most vile and execrable traitor that ever lived. . . . Thou art a monster. . . . Thou hast an English face and a Spanish heart and thy self art a spider of hell. . . . There never lived a viler viper, upon the face of the earth. I want words sufficient to express thy viperous treason." [4] Such words "lost him many friends," to put it gently.

In 1615, shortly before he probably came into the Roger Williams story, the famous Commendams case had once again put him in the bright spotlight, this time largely to his own praise. Even Francis Bacon had spoken favorably of his great courage. He had stood alone against the eleven other judges, declaring that he could do only what an honest and just judge must do, no matter what the odds. "When the case happens, I shall do that which shall be fit for a judge to do," he had said, and he had proceeded to challenge the king's own power. The boldness of his action and his high-principled explanation of it in such words provoked much comment in a restless time. In the following year, 1616, when conducting the sensational Overbury trial, his hint of foul play in the death of beloved Prince Henry aroused all England. He had even dared to say,

> "God knows what became of that sweet babe, Prince Henry, but I know somewhat."

This remark had so inflamed suspicion and so angered the king that Coke was sequestered on the charge of "perpetual turbulent carriage," deposed from his high office and sent to the Tower. But not to stay. His greatest achievement of all, his part in the Petition of Right, was still to come.

His employment of Roger Williams would seem to follow quite directly upon his release from imprisonment in 1617, and his recall to the Council table, "the king being loth to lose his abilities." In addition to sitting in the Privy Council, he also often appeared in the Star Chamber. During this period he was living in his chambers in the Inns of Court, where he was readily accessible to Londoners. By the fact of the immediately previous incarceration with its reasons therefor, the situation was abundantly favorable to hero worship on the part of a boy in his teens, and perhaps also favorable to some awareness of the moral issues involved in the imprisonment. No personal details of the Man-Boy association have come to light. There is only Anne Sadleir's manuscript note written on the back of her copy of a letter to Roger Williams on the occasion of his 1651/52 return to England. Thanks to this brief note, two facts in Roger Williams' young life are attested: first, his employment by Sir Edward, and second, his attendance at Charterhouse School. The portion of the note establishing both facts reads,

> "This Roger Williams when he was a youth would in a short hand take sermons, and speeches in the Starchamber and present them to my dear father, he seing him soe hopefull a youth, tooke such likeing to him that he put him into Suttons hospitall and he was the second that was placed there." [5]

Anne Sadleir's phrase "sermons, and speeches in the Starchamber" tells all that we know as to the nature of his service. Some part of it may have concerned Sir Edward's conviction in 1618 of a number of Dutch merchants who had illegally transported gold and silver, money, plate and bullion "beyond the seas." [6] If so, stenographic record of these hearings would have called for someone able to handle Dutch as a spoken language, a capacity in which young Roger could have qualified. Inquiry in the St. Sepulchre's neighborhood as to one so fitted would naturally have led to the Austin Friars' community, where Roger Williams would possibly have been known to the schoolmaster, the minister of the Dutch church, or possibly to John May, scrivener and friend of the Williams family who lived close by. But whatever may have been the circumstances, he was found and employed. As to the duration of the employment, there is the fact of Sir Edward's recall from imprisonment in 1617, as one limit, and his second incarceration in 1621 as another. Any period in this three year span would have fallen in an impressionable time in Roger Williams' adolescence, when employment, however humble, by such a man in the high concerns of his office would naturally enough have cut a deep groove in his young thinking. Coke's imprisonment in

For my much honoured kind
friend Mistress Sadler
at Stondon
near Puckridge
these

this Roger Williams when he
was a youth would in a short
hand take sermons, and speeches
in the starchamber and present
them to my dear father, he seeing
him (see how hopefull a youth) tooke such likeing to him
that he put him in to suttons
hospetall and he was the second
that was placed there full little
did he think that he would have
proved such a reble to god the king
and his cuntry, I leave his letters
that, if ever he has the face to return
into his native cuntry Tyborn may
give him welcome

Memorandum on the back of Anne Sadleir's copy of a letter to Roger Williams, 1652. Trinity College Library, Cambridge, England.

1621 followed upon his vindication of the privileges of Commons, and again in 1623, upon his motion advocating free speech as the "ancient and undoubted birthright of the subjects of England." Good seed this to be sown in the mind of the future founder of a colony.

In the light of what he was to be and to do, the significance of so unusual a chapter in the life of a middle-class boy during these turbulent years stirs one's imagination. Roger Williams, the merchant taylor's son, sitting under the glittering ceiling of the Star Chamber and knowing that he had a right to be there, might in the fact alone have been important. What he saw and heard there was as remote from life in a Smithfield schoolroom as though it belonged on another planet, and all at once he was part of it. Did the experience lessen any awe he might have felt for the tangible dignities and splendors of high office and those who performed them? Probably. Did it feed any resentment he may have shared with thousands of his class toward the Star Chamber as a symbol of arbitrary power, tyranny over human rights and the conscience of men? Probably, once more. Did it define *persecution* in ways not yet experienced directly? Possibly. Verdicts of slit noses, cropt ears, branded faces, whipped backs, gagged mouths, victims thrown in prison suited ill with the "glorious sight upon a Star-day, when the Knights of the Garter, with the Stars on their Garments, and the Judges in their Scarlet" took their places in the court. Many cases concerned religious beliefs. During these years there was, for example, the case of John Thraske, whose offence had been "venting his opinions in an unforgettably loud voice." He had recanted and lived. Shortly before, had come a typical case in the aged Edmond Peacham, who for one sentence in an unpreached sermon, found in his study when it had been broken into and searched, had been tortured, condemned, and had died in prison. No less a person than Francis Bacon had drawn up the questions to be put to him under the torture.[6] To a boy who had already thought about persecution and had even felt himself the victim of it, such cases would have raised fundamental questions as to the protection of the individual within the sanctions of law. Scant acquaintance with only the fringes of all this might have been deeply confusing.

To what extent this association with Sir Edward was personal is not a matter of record. In addition to Anne Sadleir's letters, there is only Roger Williams' own tribute, written in reply to one of them. He wrote,

> "My much honored friend, that man of honor, and wisdom, and piety, your dear father, was often pleased to call me his son." [7]

The word *son* deepens the significance of the relationship on both sides and makes it something more than a busy man's employment of a gifted boy, who at the moment could be of convenient service to him. Something about this boy called forth tenderness, perhaps affection, from one who was an uncanny judge of human worth. Many years later, Roger Williams, grown man, would be called *son* by another man of great power and dignity, and also a leader of men. This would be Canonicus, Chieftain of the Narragansett Indians, a savage, who for this young man's sake would make peace instead of war with the struggling English settlements in a far wilderness, and in testimony to an Indian's trust in this white man, would keep the peace as long as he lived. As a last request on earth, this Narragansett chieftain would ask this same man to close his eyes in death. Roger Williams walked many miles to fulfil this dying wish of Canonicus, whom he had loved and trusted in return. "He was buried," Roger Williams wrote, "in cloth of my own gift."

Unfortunately, the relationship between Sir Edward and his promising young protégé was not lifelong, and the hints of tenderness and affection on both sides merely make the eventual break between them more unfortunate. Whatever the full reason for the estrangement, in the fact alone it would seem a great pity, and for both of them. It was also an exception to Roger Williams' usual record. He kept his friends, and even those who opposed him as to religious or civil practice remained on friendly terms personally. The best example of this continuing friendship was with Governor John Winthrop, who sanctioned his exile and opposed many of his Rhode Island policies, chiefly that of granting freedom of conscience to heretics, but who to the end of his own life loved him as a man and as a friend. Governor Edward Winslow, another leader, who was glad to be rid of Roger Williams' troubling magnetism in Plymouth, called him "the sweetest soul I ever knew."

In the light of what we know of Sir Edward's personal feuds and estrangements, the rift with his young protégé is not surprising. He had his blind spots, many of them and amazing. He was often arrogant in his opinions, inconsistent in his actions, mixed in his motives. He was also a man of ineradicable, unalterable conviction as to justice between man and man, governor and governed, and a living example of the principles he championed. In an affair touching his principles, his courage was superb. Under attack he was often harsh, matching the scurrility of his opponent with invective and abuse still more reckless. Doubtless he deserved the royal rebukes which again and again put him unfavorably in the spotlight, but few even of his enemies, would have felt that the indignities thrust upon him in any way touched his honesty, his uprightness, his sense of justice as a judge and as a man. History knows him best in his great public moments when he forgot his personal advantage, said and did what made English history. It knows him less as a neighbor at his Stoke Poges estate, host to his friends, landlord to his tenants, scrupulous in his attentions to their just claims, as a man of books in his own library, advocating for younger students, "conference with others, (which is the life of study) and meditation upon what they have read (which is the life of reading)." [8] In the word of a contemporary who knew him in his private life, he was "the most religious and orderlye man in his house that ever lived in our state." [9] He followed his own code, and what some acquaintance with both code and example might have meant to a young boy of Roger Williams' sensitive awareness goes well beyond detailed specifications. He had known a man who dared oppose a king for a principle in which he believed, and a man to whom imprisonment in the Tower for such courage was merely incidental. He had heard much of human rights and the obligation of government to respect them. He had seen the law in action and had learned that its sanctions did not always protect the individual. He had learned something of the power of a strong minority voice. As to what the association may have meant personally, there is his own word for it, written in maturity,

"But how many thousand times since I had the honorable and precious remembrance of his person, and the life, the writings, the speeches, and the example of that glorious light. And I may truly say, that besides my natural inclination to study and activity, his example, instruction, and encouragement, have spurred me on to a more than ordinary, industrious, and patient course in my whole course hitherto." [10]

Late in 1621, upon the breaking up of a Parliament session in which he had been a "chief speaker," Sir Edward was again in the Tower, this time for a nine month period. At this last session he had been a leader on the popular side, and according to Sir Simonds D'Ewes, his speeches had won him "much love and credit." Upon the fall of Bacon, who was "outed his office for bribery," he had just missed being made Lord Chancellor, an honor he had long coveted. He had been one of those to draw up the charges against Bacon, and at last had seen his great enemy go down in final disgrace and defeat. Bacon's sun had set, and Sir Edward faced a long period of solitude, but solitude with honor. Not before he had seen his young protégé, however, a Gownboy at Charterhouse School. Apart from whatever richness the association had brought young Roger on the personal side (and that was probably a great deal) the Charterhouse opportunity was Sir Edward's best gift.

At this date, Sutton's Hospital, as Charterhouse was popularly called, was only six years old. The buildings had been completed in 1615, and the first twenty-five scholars admitted in that same year. By 1621, forty Foundation Scholars were accommodated, each boy being one of the personal nominees of one of the Governors and each one voted on by the whole body. Coke had been one of the sixteen original Governors, named by Thomas Sutton himself at the time of the founding, and by Anne Sadleir's statement, Roger Williams was the second boy his nomination had placed there. The signed nomination is not extant, but on the records of the school, the admission entry reads,

"25 June, 1621
Roger Williams (in place of Francis Wittie)." [11]

This date, in its probable relation to Roger Williams' age has been the subject of much discussion, since the rules of Charterhouse (until 1666) permitted boys only between the ages of ten and fourteen to enter. If the admission of Roger Williams conformed to this regulation, he would not have been born earlier than 1607, and if so late a date be correct, all of his own allusions to his age would be distinctly out of line with it. Moreover, had he been fourteen in 1621, he would have been a boy no older than ten at the time of his services in the Star Chamber, and obviously too young to perform them. The usual explanation has been that the great Sir Edward had only to demand an exception to the rule and it would forthwith be set aside. Possibly true in this instance, but doubtful reasoning, since first and last, Sir Edward's reverence for law and precedent was basic, so much so as to be one of his very real limitations. Had he been strictly literal in his reliance on precedent in this instance, the doors of Charterhouse would have closed on Roger Williams irrevocably. Had he wished this rule set aside, however, for a protégé of his own choice, the other governors might have been willing to make the exception, remembering that without Coke's legal aid, the school would never have come into existence.

It was one of Sir Edward's minor victories over his great rival Francis Bacon. Thomas Sutton, the richest commoner in England, had barely completed plans for this very lavish philanthropic project and made a will to insure its continuance, when he suddenly died. Immediately his nephew and heir, one Baxter, had sought to break the will and gain for himself the vast revenues settled upon the school *in perpetuum*. He enlisted the services of Francis Bacon who, hoping for royal preferment, devised a smooth scheme by which the will might be broken and the king gain much credit thereby. Justice Coke took the side against him and in favor of Thomas Sutton's own plan. Bacon's letter to the king urged him to seize Charterhouse and use its revenues for installing numerous charities, training servants and apprentices instead of scholars, of whom there were already far too many. His letter was a shrewd, even masterly political manoeuvre. Its flattery of the king was veiled, its suggested substitute for the institution Thomas Sutton had envisaged plausible and seemingly more far-reaching in its ultimate value to England. Francis Bacon never wrote a smoother letter or one more oily in its self-interest, but he had reckoned without the blunt, high-thoughted tactics of his arch-enemy. Coke won the case and saved the school according to its founder's intent. The stakes had been fabulous, the legal battle worthy the powers of these two great rivals.

No chance that Sir Edward's contemporary fellow-Governors would ever forget the debt they owed him, and in comparison with such signal service, a vote to admit one of his nominees, who happened to be over age, would have been a trivial exception to make, with or without Sir Edward's own request. Furthermore, the nomination may even have been made at the proper age, and the admission delayed until a vacancy occurred. The phrase, "in place of Francis Wittie," suggests that Roger Williams' acceptance came by the withdrawal of another boy's name, whatever may have been the reason. His fitness was probably established by examination, certified by an examiner appointed by the Archbishop of Canterbury. No exceptions to this rule were ever permitted, and the fact of Roger Williams' acceptance indicates a previous training within the standard framework.

In the London of the 1620's Charterhouse stood at the very edge of the city's open spaces, with the village of Islington still one mile further on. Its history prior to Sutton's purchase stretched back to Norman times and included many diverse chapters of honor and tragedy. More recently Queen Elizabeth had been entertained here and King James, en route to London on his first coming, had held court in its stately hall. Many generations earlier, when a Carthusian monastery had been built on this site, it was a No Man's Land. Later still Pardon Churchyard had been added to its spaces, an area for the burial of those who had taken their own lives or been executed for felony. Some 50,000 victims of the Black Death had also been buried here. Now that by Thomas Sutton's purchase, it had become a boys' school, its grimmer associations were being forgotten, and the forty Gownboys lived their lives in work or play, unaware of the story of human loss written under their feet.[12] Something survives, however, even today, from these past layers of magnificence and tragedy, and this in spite of the 1940 firebombs which reduced most of the venerable buildings to ashes and made of the whole area a relief map of broken walls. It will still survive in the new beauty of its restoration.

No personal record exists to make individual the story of Roger

Williams' life here. As for John Milton, we know only the beginning and end of his school life. Within these official limits all is by inference only, and through the pattern by which we know his course to have been charted. It was a rigid pattern, as in any Grammar School of the period. There were no extras and no surprises. All was as sober as the black robe of the Gownboy he had come to be. His studies were strictly classical. He read none but "approved Authors, Greek and Latin." At daily chapel, he used his Greek Testament, the only book furnished by the school. His boy associates were for the most part, sons of "poor Gentlemen," some of whom could write Esq. after their names, as James Williams could not. The Master at this date was Francis Beaumont, and the Schoolmaster Nicholas Gray, a young man only twelve years older than Roger Williams.

The world these Gownboys lived in was a world still remote from the clatter of London streets, a world of enforced quietness and obedience to rigid discipline. The tone of life was religious, as in all Grammar Schools of the time. The attitude of the scholar was one of receptivity. In the words of the *Prayer for a Young Scholar of the House,*

> "I am now soft and tender, apt to receive the first Impressions that are laid upon me, suffer me therefore not to be led aside by the whispers of sin, . . . Frame in me an humble and submissive mind, that I may be willing to be taught and obey, to entertain all godly and profitable Instructions." [13]

Roger Williams was too old on his admittance to be required to repeat this prayer, but the spirit underneath it had been instilled in him since his *Hornbook* days. It was the attitude of the conformist entering a world of unquestioned authority and certainty. Over against it somewhere in his developing years, prior to this time, there was whatever lay back of the single reminiscence "persecuted" to indicate that even in his "soft and tender" years, he had not always been a conformist. Possibly he was not completely tractable at Charterhouse; possibly his studies did not always engage him solely; apparently, however, during his two and a half years in residence, he met the requirements and acquitted himself acceptably.

On July 4, 1624, at the regular meeting of the Governors "to dispose of the Scholars to the University and to the trades," he was "elected out" as one "fytte for learninge," and on July 9th he was voted an "Exhibition" to the University,[14] to continue annually during his stay if he maintained himself creditably. This sum of sixteen pounds was not a scholarship earned by any special distinction in his studies but a stipend which belonged to all those who by examination were adjudged capable of further study. Those not "fytte for learninge" were sent out by another door, either to the trades or to some handicraft. For some reason, not explained in the record, the first allowance granted to Roger Williams was given to him as "John," but in the subsequent entries of renewal and in the final withdrawal of the stipend, it appears under his name correctly. The simplest explanation and probably the correct one, is that the *John* is a scribal error, as there was no one in the school at the time to whom it would apply, nor does it have any known connection with the son of James Williams.

The die was now cast. During these pre-University years he had been prepared for a particular kind of English life, and a life that was beginning to be challenged both within and without the University precincts. It was a life walled off from the common life of the multitudes. By virtue of the training he would receive, he would henceforth belong to the determining minority. By birth he also belonged to the common life. Within the quadrangles this dual heritage might not make for happiness, but in the life that was waiting for him beyond the gates, it would prove fortunate indeed.

CHAPTER SIX

Pensioner

THE lot fell upon Pembroke Hall, Cambridge. No known reason explains his choice, but it would have required no special justification. Pembroke, as one of the oldest of Cambridge colleges, had an honored tradition as "studious, well-learned, and a good setter-forth of Christ's Gospel and of God's true Word," and that would have been quite enough for Sir Edward, for Roger Williams' Charterhouse counselors, possibly enough to satisfy himself. No doubt also, Smithfield's prideful remembrance of certain great Pembroke names had created something of a neighborhood legend in its favor. John Rogers, first of the Marian martyrs, and briefly vicar of St. Sepulchre's church, had honored both his college and his pulpit when he had been led to his burning a few paces from the gateway to St. Bartholomew's. That was a long lifetime ago, but Smithfield still remembered. John Bradford, martyred in the same year, had also been a Pembroke man. Edmund Spenser had been a Merchant Taylors' Schoolboy before he was a Pembroke student. So had Lancelot Andrewes, who had later been Pembroke's great Master. Andrewes was still alive in 1623, and in spite of the rich honors of his later life, it was this Mastership that had spread his fame farthest. Along with other Smithfield boys, Roger Williams would have grown up sharing the neighborhood pride in these men. Also like any other potential college student, he would have had his own notions about where he wanted to go to college. He did not disclose them.

His choice is surprising only in that ever since Lancelot Andrewes' day, Pembroke had maintained a reputation for being strongly Anglican, strictly orthodox and anti-Puritan. If prior to this time, Roger Williams had acknowledged any sympathy with Dissenting opinion, why not Emmanuel instead of Pembroke, for at this date Emmanuel was openly recognized as a stronghold of Dissent. The easier answer and probably the correct one is that the staunch Anglicanism of Sir Edward Coke would have been outraged by such a choice, and at this stage of their relationship, his young protégé might not have dared or even wished to displease him. Coke himself was a Trinity man, and since 1614 he had been High Steward of the University, a post he continued to hold throughout Roger Williams' college residence. But whatever the reasons, Pembroke Hall it was to be. Perhaps better so, since here Roger Williams' unorthodox views would develop against the current rather than with it, and his convictions possibly grow more muscular in consequence.

At this date Pembroke Hall stood ninth in the list of Cambridge colleges for numbers, housing about one hundred and fifty persons, including tutors and lecturers as well as students. Its buildings enclosed a single court, ninety-two by ninety-five feet, with a single gateway from Trumpington Street on the west. The inner court had not yet been built. Although students were free during their hours of "Liberty" to go into the precincts of the other colleges, for the most part their lives were lived within the narrow limits of this small enclosure. To a London boy, even after the Charterhouse experience, such a life must have had its limitations. The entire University population was only about three thousand and that of the town of Cambridge some three times as large.[1] Within his own college limits a small world perhaps, yet large enough for kindred spirits to be present among the number, and intimate enough for them to find each other.

London, in terms of the muddy, uneven, and at times impassable roads, was further away than its miles. Once a week the boys had a chance to go by Thomas Hobson's horse and wain as far as the Bull Inn in Bishopsgate, or on any other day by "Hobson's choice," that is, by the horse that stood nearest the stable door, "this or nothing." In his young days, Lancelot Andrewes had preferred to go on foot and he may have had imitators in these later generations, though only hardy souls could qualify. For most students the Cambridge precincts were the limits of life, and this in spite of minor relaxation of older rules concerning absence in term time.

Roger Williams' entering date is recorded in the Admissions Book of Pembroke Hall under date of June 29, 1623.[2] This was almost at the end of the third or midsummer term, and in 1623 only two days from the commencement occasion on the first Tuesday of July. The entry consists of the single word *Williams*. Space is left for the usual details of birth, parentage, previous school and schoolmaster, as are entered for other names on these pages, but for Roger Williams the space remains blank. Presumably the scribe did not have these details at hand when he made the entry, and having turned the page, he forgot to fill them in later. At any rate the blank space remains, thereby disappointing one more hope for precise knowledge of these important facts in Roger Williams' earlier story.

For some reason his formal matriculation was delayed until June 7, 1624, nearly a year after his admission. This disparity in dates is puzzling, but not irreconcilable. The fact that his first Exhibition from Charterhouse was voted by the Governors on June 9, 1624, only two days after his formal matriculation, suggests that the entry may have waited on the fulfilment of some requirement during this intervening year. A deficiency would have been likely enough since he had been in residence at Charterhouse only about half of the usual time, and whatever Grammar School training may have preceded would probably have been interrupted by the service for Sir Edward. He may even have been in residence at Pembroke Hall during a portion of the year 1623–1624 while he demonstrated his abilities to pursue more advanced work. Whatever the reason, however, the disparity in dates, which remains unclarified on the official record, is not unique. The gap between admission and matriculation is merely longer than usual.

Thanks to the Charterhouse Exhibition, he was enrolled as a pensioner, that is, one able to pay for his living in Commons. So small a sum as sixteen pounds, while adequate, would permit of no extravagance, and though possible, it is hardly likely that Sir Edward augmented it with an allowance. As a pensioner, he belonged to the middle and largest group of the student numbers, both numerically and socially. At the top socially were the Fellows, the M.A.'s, the earls and sons of earls, barons, other noblemen and gentlemen commoners. At the other extreme were the numerous sizars and sub-sizars, who supported themselves by performing various personal services for tutors, other students, or by assisting in Commons. During mealtime the walls between these social groups were strictly observed. The Fellows, nobles and gentlemen sat at the high table on a raised dais. The pensioners sat at small tables around the wall. The sizars and sub-sizars usually ate in the kitchen after they had performed their share of mealtime duties. At all other times in the daily routine, social lines were being less sharply drawn, as the student population shifted from upper- to middle-class.

By Roger Williams' time the influx of sons of merchants, of husbandmen, of tradesmen, had already changed the once markedly aristocratic character of the quadrangles, and with some University authorities this increase was causing distinct concern. It was too late, however, in the first quarter of the new century to attempt once more to limit by statute the number of pensioners, as had formerly been tried at Trinity College. The statute had given as a reason,

> "in order that their rawness (imperitia) and predominance may not obstruct the general progress of the students." [3]

Rawness or not, however, the middle-class boy was now present in large numbers; he had come to stay, and from his rapidly increasing group would come some of England's great leaders of church and state in the cataclysmic mid-century. Over at Christ's, John Milton, son of a scrivener, at Gonville and Caius, Jeremy Taylor, son of a barber, William Laud, son of a clothier, John Preston, son of a farmer. Preston, though still under forty, had been made Master of Emmanuel in the preceding year, and was at the moment enjoying a popularity among students which was distinctly disturbing the orthodox. They would hear more of him.

Unfortunately, Roger Williams left no record of his college days as a personal individual experience. Once more we know only the official beginning and end, as for Milton, Thomas Fuller, Jeremy Taylor, among other of his contemporaries of whose youth one would like to know all possible details. The perhaps life-determining middle of their college experience is a blank for them all. Simonds

D'Ewes, who was something of an exception, confided some of his college thoughts to his *Autobiography,* one of the few such records of this college generation. He had come to the University, he says, "supposing there was no earthly happiness like unto that which might be enjoyed in it." [4] No merchant taylor's son, with a Smithfield boyhood behind him, would have been capable of such naïvete; hence Roger Williams was probably spared the disillusionment which D'Ewes, pampered son of privilege that he was, had to suffer. Even he, however, had begun realistically, endured the indignities of the "salting" and "tucking" initiation, spoken the demanded nonsense as he stood on the high table, "kissed an old shoe and was one of them." Roger Williams, Milton, Taylor, Fuller, and all the other notables of their generation probably did likewise and with sufficient good nature to make them acceptable. Stripped of their gowns and made to look like scoundrels, they had the skin scraped off their chins by a Senior thumbnail, drank the caudle of warm, salted beer, paid the bill and felt themselves initiates of merit. At Pembroke Hall, D'Ewes wrote, "a great deal of beer was drunk."

The externals of their subsequent lives within the walls would seem to bear out the verdicts of various foreign visitors, to whom the University scene presented an aspect of medieval remoteness and cloistered quietude. "The students live a life almost monastic," one after another remarked. Externally viewed, yes. According to a pattern that had changed little over many lifetimes they rose before dawn, attended chapel between five and six o'clock, breakfasted, and then divided their morning into private sessions with their tutors, attendance on lectures, "public school exercises," the disputations and sophisms in which they were first listeners and then participants in their turn. "Liberty" came briefly after the 11:00 o'clock dinner, to be followed by more lectures, more "public school exercises" and declamations. Then came private study, either in one's room, or in the library, if one were "a student of standing," and trusted with a key. During the later afternoon they might leave the University grounds by permission, albeit rarely alone. The required two by two custom was breaking down at this date, but it was still honored in the statutes. Supper in the Great Hall was a silent, solemn meal, as the student appointed for the day read the Bible aloud from a raised platform in the center of the hall. After the final grace came "liberty" to walk in the garden or to go to one's room, and the day was over. By 9:00 every boy was supposedly in his own corner. No wonder the word *monastic* came easily to the visitors who looked only on the stately buildings, the courts, the gardens, the black-gowned boys walking up and down. Some of these black-gowned boys, grown to manhood, would echo their verdict, among these Roger Williams, who twenty-five years later called the University regimen of life "Monkish and idle." [5] He probably did not think so during his own Pembroke days.

His studies concerned the culture of a bygone age, not the stirring cataclysms of the new century. The medieval trivium—grammar, logic, and rhetoric—was still the basis of all that was taught and learned, although there was some relaxation as to the amount of time a student must devote to these standard disciplines. As preaching had grown more important and become open sesame to high place, theology (especially Calvin's) had gained greater importance. The logic of Ramus, honoring human reason, had already modified somewhat the Aristotelian logic of the schoolmen. The *Dialectia* of Ramus had become a chief study. Nevertheless, the differences between what had been and what now was were as yet minor, and as to the shattering realization that

> "The new philosophy calls all in doubt,"

there were only muffled voices and these soon stilled. The philosophy of the lecture halls was not "new" and it called nothing in doubt. Moreover, erudition, not scholarship was the ideal. Classical learning was not pursued for its own sake but for its prefiguring of Christianity. The church fathers were read for the ammunition they could furnish against Papists and Arminians. If tradition may be trusted, there was one notable exception to this sturdy adherence to authority. Within the privacy of his own chambers, Joseph Mede, tutor of Christ's, was said to preface his evening tutorial sessions unfailingly with the query, "Quid dubitas?" Unfortunately for Roger Williams, who was likely to have been a questioner and doubter in his early as in his later years, there is no tradition of a similar invitation ever being issued from Master Jerome Beale's quarters in Pembroke Hall.

Instead Master Beale was continuing worthily the reputation of great learning established by his predecessors. With Lancelot Andrewes it had been learning nothing less than vast, although it was as a linguist that his fame as a scholar had gone farthest. He might have served, said Thomas Fuller "as interpreter general at the confusion of tongues." The learning of Samuel Harsnett, who followed him, was that of a high-churchman and "zealous asserter of ceremonies." Jerome Beale was now turning the emphasis toward controversy. Himself the target of sharp criticism because of his suspected Arminianism, he kept the arena of current dispute in sharp focus with his students as well as with his peers. This emphasis is clearly apparent in the training of Roger Williams' generation, and obviously it left its mark on his own ways of thought.

As to the student life of the University in his day, too much attention has been paid to the sweeping accusations of Simonds D'Ewes of St. John's concerning laxness of discipline and disregard of University authority during these same years. That there was laxness of discipline is clear enough and from several sources, but the accusations of Simonds D'Ewes as to "swearing, drinking, rioting, hatred of all piety and virtue under false and adulterate nicknames which did so much abound in his own college and in all the University," [6] require some discounting. So also William Laud's report written in 1630, when he had become Chancellor, that Oxford students were "Sunk from all discipline and fallen into licentiousness." [7] It is the "all" of both reports that needs discounting, as anyone familiar with University life in any age would quickly recognize. Simonds D'Ewes was an aristocratic young man of great sensitivity, fineness of nature and also a large measure of fastidiousness. His previous life had been singularly protected from acquaintance with the *Vices* he now wrote in large capitals. Hence he gave one frightened look around, decided to live almost a recluse's life "conversing in our college with some of the honester fellows thereof for the avoiding of the unnecessary society of all debauched and atheistical companions (which then swarmed there)." Presently even this righteous seclusion was not enough; he became "weary of the college" and largely because of these "vices of the times," consented to a "willing departure." Without question these are the sincere words of a very shocked young aristocrat who presently outgrew his priggishness and became one of the most trustworthy reporters of the contemporary scene in Parliament. When he fled the college wickedness, he still had much to learn about the world he lived in. The *Diary* of Samuel Ward of Sidney Sussex College, covering these same years, lists as "Sinnes of the University," "Excess in apparel, Excess in drinking and Disobedience and contempt of authority in the younger sort." [8]

That disregard for discipline was periodically flagrant is attested by periodic attempts of the authorities to bring student conduct more nearly in line with the statutes on the books. The fact that some of these statutes were long obsolete in terms of the ongoing life of the university lessens somewhat the implied blackness of guilt in transgressing them. To speak English in private instead of Latin, to keep a dog or a "fierce bird," to go boating or play "hot football," to bathe in the river, attend dances, play cards, go to cock-fights, are hardly sins of such dark depths as the remarks of Simonds D'Ewes would suggest, except possibly in the "disobedience" involved. The ban would not hold against any of them and it was useless to renew it. Nor would English boys much longer endure the public whippings on Friday afternoons for even more grievous offences. Among these, as one might imagine, tavern-haunting was the arch iniquity, against which all rules and threats were futile.

One of the periodic reforms aimed at restoring that "long-banished Pilgrim, Discipline," was in progress during Roger Williams' undergraduate days.[9] The fact that one of the changes instituted was the shifting of the dinner hour from 11:00 to 12:00 o'clock, with the purpose of discouraging the practice of lying in bed until the bell sounded, and thus perhaps improving the attendance at morning lectures, perhaps provides a fair sample of one sort of "Vice" and the reform needed to curtail it. Previously the dinner hour had been moved from 10:00 to 11:00 for the same reason, and presently it might need to be moved yet again. These student infringements owed something, no doubt, to the changing character of the university group, but they owed far more to the confusions of a disturbed time. Not war as yet, or quite the threat of war, but a tumult of questioning in men's minds, tenseness in their behavior, restlessness, fear, uncertainty in their every outlook. The quadrangles offered no escape from current unrest; rather, as always, the students were sensitive to every movement of restlessness beyond the gates, and the apparent triviality of some student transgression is misleading in terms of its underlying causes.

Roger Williams' entire period of residence was set against a background of events which kept all England in a state of fevered agitation for weeks on end. Cambridge was remote from theatres of action, and yet in spite of Thomas Hobson's slow-paced transportation, news of current happenings came to the colleges with amazing regularity and promptness. The letters of Joseph Mede, tutor of Christ's, to Sir Martin Stuteville of Daltham in Suffolk are veritable news broadcasts, "up to the chinne" in their fulness.[10] Every week there was a new crisis somewhere, and thanks to the correspondents Tutor Mede had subsidized all over Europe, Cambridge knew about it before Suffolk. Mede had no official reporting responsibility. He was merely interested enough to be willing to pay his correspondents to find out "how the world goes." In differing degrees the whole University shared this eagerness of interest. Masters, Tutors, Fellows, and most undergraduates lived one life in their all but endless Confutations, Philosophy Acts, Commonplaces, Declamations, their Latin, Greek, Hebrew exercises, and quite another in their intense concern with the current European and Parliamentary ferment.

At the very beginning of Roger Williams' first term of residence in the fall of 1623, London was launched into a fever of excitement and rejoicing thus far unmatched in the outwardly placid reign of King James. The occasion was the arrival at Southampton of Prince Charles, without the Spanish Infanta as his bride. For more than seven months previously England had been stirred to the depths by the proposed match with Donna Maria. To the Protestants this marriage would be "the funeralls of their Religion." "Popery" would again be enthroned. The excesses of Queen Mary's reign would be reenacted. Queen Elizabeth's work would be undone. All men's mouths were filled with discourse and dread of it. So inflamed was the feeling that Catholic and anti-Catholic response led to many excesses. Nothing happening in Parliament during these months could touch the "Spanish match" for importance.

Tension regarding the whole affair had first come to Cambridge in the spring of 1623, when James I, on the occasion of his much-heralded visit to the University, had announced that he would bring with him the Ambassadors of Spain and Brussels. In honor of the King, the students of Trinity College had prepared a play, *Ignatius Loyola,* which concerned a Jesuit and a Puritan, to be presented on Ash Wednesday. "Either the Ambassadors must not come or the play must not be acted," Joseph Mede wrote, but his warning passed unheeded. The Ambassadors came; the play was acted before the royal party, and when James "laught once or twise toward the end," Cambridge breathed again. In retrospect the excitements attendant upon the kingly visit were distinctly minor, in fact forgotten with the outbursts of joy which greeted the anti-climactic end of the whole Prince-Infanta affair. Not only the quadrangles, but all England now breathed again.

The release was in proportion to the tenseness of the preceding months of anxiety. Week by week ever since the Prince and Buckingham had set sail for Madrid, on February 17, 1622/23, contradictory reports had come back. He had married her; no, he had not married her. The dispensation permitting the marriage had come from Rome; no, it had been denied. The King commands that bonfires be lighted and bells rung when the Prince lands with his bride; no, he has not even sailed; he may not come until spring. "This whole Spanish business is so carried in the Cloudes that what effect it is like to take it is not possible to be yet discerned," Joseph Mede had written on July 5, 1623. Uncertainty had continued for three more months, and when the public was at last assured that the Prince had actually landed "without the Infanta," had been seen in London without her, excitement went out of bounds. "The greatest expression of joy by all sorts of people that ever I saw," William Laud wrote in his *Autobiography.*[11] On all sides there were veritable explosions of rejoicings.

In Cambridge the University bells rang for three days. Bonfires were lighted every night. On the second day a special dish was served at supper in every college and in place of the solemn Bible reading during the meal, there was a speech. On the third day the entire University assembled at Great St. Mary's for a sermon and public thanksgiving in the morning and an oration in the afternoon. Throughout the three day period student demonstrations continued. For students mature enough to ponder the issues underneath this seven month hysteria, the affair was not over when the last rocket was fired. Out of it came the word *toleration* which soon began to be heard on all sides. "All the talk is of toleration," wrote Joseph Mede. But this was not toleration as the 1640's would use the word; it was toleration as a political necessity in the Catholic–anti-Catholic battle, rather than a principle of human respect. Moreover, as popular opinion was quite against even this political policy, the word acquired unfortunate connotations which would linger long. Toleration, said many of the elder clergy, would mean the overthrow of England's religion, and might again mean bloodshed. "Sermons were turned into satires against Papists and non-conformists," wrote Thomas Fuller. Less than a fortnight after the Prince's return, anti-Catholic feeling was again inflamed by the tragic accident in London known as the "fatal Vespers." Two floors of an upper room in Blackfriars had collapsed while Father Drury, an ardent Romish priest, was preaching a denunciatory sermon against Luther and Calvin. Nearly a hundred persons were killed and many injured. A beam had broken, but in Protestant interpretation, God had done it. At this supposed sign from heaven the pulpit grew louder against the *Toleration* reported to be in the King's intent.

King James had already taken measures to silence his critics on this account. In August, 1623, two months before the Prince's return, he had issued *Directions* to regulate preaching. These were sent to every "parson, vicar, curate, lecturer & minister in the realm. . . . letting them know that we have a special eye unto their proceedings, and expect a strict account thereof." All preaching was henceforth to keep within the Articles of Religion as of 1562. All afternoon preaching was to be cut off (funeral sermons alone excepted). Approved preachers would spend Sunday afternoon "in the examination of children in the Catechism." No preacher under the degree of bishop or dean was to presume to preach on the "deep points of Predestination, Election, or Reprobation," but must leave these themes to be handled by the learned men. No preacher of any rank was in any case to meddle with affairs of state, or to rail against Papists or Puritans "without invitation from the text." Most fearsome of all to young men resolved upon the pulpit as a life calling, bishops and archbishops were solemnly counselled to "be more wary" in licensing such. Even lecturers were henceforth to be licensed only upon recommendation of their bishop, "with a fiat from the lord archbishop of Canterbury, a Confirmation under the Great Seal of England." [12]

The publication of these *Directions* was almost precisely coincident with Roger Williams' enrolment at Pembroke Hall, and as one already presumably committed to the pulpit as his life purpose, he must have felt almost as though the door before him were closing even as it was first opened. That the *Directions* meant what they said would have been particularly clear to Pembroke boys, as three men of the college were almost immediate victims of the clause forbidding meddling in affairs of state. One William Knight, M.A., had preached a sermon at Oxford in which he had quoted the learned Pareus, a Silesian scholar in the chair of Divinity at Heidelberg, as saying that in a case of life or chastity, a private subject might offer resistance to the civil ruler. The sermon was immediately branded as seditious, Knight and two other Pembroke men who defended him were jailed after examination by William Laud, then Bishop of London. Two years later Knight died as a result of this imprisonment. Roger Williams had just missed the public burning of the works of Pareus in Regent Walk, Cambridge,[13] although he may have been present at their burning at Paul's Cross, London, during the preceding summer. Certainly he could hardly have been unaware of this and later affronts to freedom of thought and speech which each subsequent year of his college course would accent in some new instance.

One of the most dramatic of these later incidents in kind was the silencing of Isaac Dorislaus, a Hollander, Doctor of Civil Law, appointed in 1627 to the chair of History founded by Lord Brooke, Fulke Greville. The misstep of Dorislaus had come in his very first lecture on this distinguished foundation, when with Tacitus as his subject, he had praised the shift in Rome from a government by kings to one by consuls. To "high monarchial ears" suspicious in advance because the speaker was a *foreigner,* he was "overpraising a State in disgrace of a Kingdome" and such advanced political ideas were not acceptable.[14] In fact, *History,* as popularly conceived, had as its legitimate province rather the fulfilment of biblical prophecy, a concept which Dorislaus had ignored. On the occasion of this first lecture, Matthew Wren, an auditor, wrote William Laud, and in ten days, the appointment was ended and Dorislaus was silenced by royal injunction. "Who can in this Confusion discerne truth from falsehood?" Joseph Mede wrote.

Whether Roger Williams, along with other spirited young protesters against such hostility to whatever lay outside the white lines of conformity, became openly troublesome at such times, is not known. Non-conformity, both civil and religious, smouldered in every college, sometimes under cover and sometimes not. In matters religious it flourished openly around John Preston, Master of Emmanuel. Young, magnetic, fearless, he had adherents in every college. His lectures and sermons were crowded by students and townsfolk alike. His election to the mastership of Emmanuel had been a triumph. He had won by his own popularity, bolstered with an alliance that could not fail; namely, with the Duke of Buckingham. His appointment as preacher at St. Mary's had been another victory, since no office was more coveted by those qualified to fill it. Under his preaching, the church became so crowded that townspeople had to be forbidden welcome.

The next year, 1625, was the most disturbed year of Roger Williams' university residence. Known in English annals as The Great Plague Year, it also brought the death of King James and the most heated period in the long public furor over the Duke of Buckingham, ending with his assassination three years later. Quadrangle life was affected by all three events, but most seriously by the plague. Infection came early, for Cambridge was on the way of those fleeing from London. "We are wonderfully troubled [Joseph Mede wrote] to keep out Londoners, who come sometimes 50 horse in company." Fifty were not required; one was enough, and he came in the person of a journeyman tailor to visit his mother, Joseph Mede's sempstress. Straightway, the infection was with them. Her scholars were sent from her, and she was commanded "to keep private." Pitiful precautions of other sorts were taken. When "the Plague broke out in the Pantry" and the cook's son died, Joseph Mede reported, "The bread was all given away." Nothing daunted by the warning, Mede himself set forth to London to see the new Queen, and reported in detail the impressive scene he had witnessed. Her magnificent escort had numbered "Thousands of boats" passing in procession under London Bridge, en route to Whitehall, bonfires in all the streets, thirty in Fenchurch Street alone, and all of London out to see the display. The sequel came in the Bills of Mortality for the following weeks, and before respite came, some 35,000 Londoners had died. Mede wrote hopefully that a royal proclamation against Popery had caused some abatement. Back in Cambridge he found the life of the University totally disrupted. Food was scarce; nothing but "eggs, applepye & custard," he wrote, and "We cannot have leave scarce to take the air." As for the University work, it was in paralysis and the students dispersed, not to reassemble until late November.

In 1626, Roger Williams' last undergraduate year, the election of Buckingham as Chancellor of the University upon the death of Thomas Howard, caused one of the greatest stirs of a generation in all ranks. This time it was the college Heads as well as students, who were all but in open rebellion at this forced election in compliance with the King's wish. The Bishop of London came in person to see that the royal will was obeyed. Some of the Heads departed, thinking to dodge a direct facing of the issue, with the result that by their absence Buckingham "carried it by three votes." Parliament was exasperated; the University in tumult. The Heads had their hands full, trying to quiet the students, particularly those Heads by whose absence the victory had come about. Jerome Beale of Pembroke had previously canvassed for the Duke, but on the election day had abstained from voting. So had nine other Heads. Buckingham was installed as Chancellor in March, 1626/27. The bells rang, posts wound their horns in every street, the University assembled, but few were pleased. Opposition to kingly authority, already openly apparent, gained measurably by this coercive success. No student could very well have dwelt above the tempest, nor have missed the issue underneath.

Roger Williams took his A.B. degree at the July Commencement, 1627. By this date, he would have completed the required four years in residence, assuming that he had begun his work at the opening of the fall term, October 10, 1623. The *supplicat* indicating its completion was filed in the University Registry prior to March 25, 1626. It was signed by Harrington Boteler, Praelector. Roger Williams had signed his name in the *Subscription Book,* also prior to March 25th. His is the twelfth in a list of fourteen names from Pembroke Hall. This signature, intended as a test of sound religious faith, had been required of all graduates only since 1623, and that by express command of King James. Prior to this date only graduates in divinity were required to sign, and the tightened regulation had provoked much discussion. The formality of the occasion was impressive. All graduates were assembled, and in the presence of the University Registrar, each signed in turn under the words,

> "We whose names are here und'rwritten doe willingly & *ex animo* subscribe to the three articles before mentioned and to all thinges in them contayned."

These Articles, popularly called James' *"three darling Articles,"* read as follows:

> "1. That the King's Majesty under God is the only supreme Governour of this Realm, & of all other his Highnesse's Dominions & Countries, as well in Spiritual or Ecclesiastical things or causes as temporal, & that no Forreign Prince, Person, Prelate of State or Potentate hath or ought to have any Jurisdiction, Power, Superiority, Preheminence, or Authority, Ecclesiastical or Spiritual, within his Majesty's said Realmes, Dominions and Countries.
>
> "2. That the Book of Common Prayer, & of Ordering of Bishops, Priests, and Deacons containeth in it nothing contrary to the Word of God, & that it may lawfully be used & that he himself will use the form in the sd. Book prescribed in Publick prayer and Administration of the Sacraments, & no other.
>
> "3. That he alloweth the booke of Articles of Religion agreed upon by the Archbishops & Bishops of both Provinces, and the whole Clergy in the Convocation holden at London in the Year of our Lord God One thousand five hundred Sixty and two; and that he acknowledgeth all and every the Articles therein contained, being in Number nine & thirty, besides the Ratification to be agreeable to the Word of God." [15]

The Long Parliament abolished this Subscription requirement in 1640, declaring it to be "against the Law and Liberty of the Subject, and ought not to be pressed upon any Student or Graduates whatsoever." In 1627, however, it was still being "pressed," and not to sign was not to be awarded any degree whatever. The result was a deep sense of injustice and resentment. Some students, having come to the end of their course, refused to sign. One name in the Pembroke list for 1626 is scratched out; had this student thought better of his first willingness and lost his degree? Probably. The surprise some have expressed that Roger Williams should have been willing thus to pledge himself would hardly seem to be justified. His quarrel was not with doctrine, nor ever to be. Neither would he have staged a major battle over forms and ceremonies and set prayers, although he declared himself against them later. His protests would go deeper and attack the very nature of the church on earth, as currently defined. Even so, he may have signed with "misgivings," as some of his fellow students were doing. More probably, however, aged only twenty-three, he may not yet have stepped out of orthodox ranks consciously enough to have had serious scruples as to the pledge asked of him. All that we really know is the fact of his name in the list. The peculiar storms of his college career had provided enough examples of affront to individual thinking so that, given perspective, he was not likely to forget the issues they underscored.

He remained at the University for about a year and a half after taking his degree in July, 1627. These eighteen months were to be a turbulent time in English public life, and to presage still greater upheavals to come. Sir Edward Coke would again be at the vortex of the storm. Returned to Commons by Buckinghamshire and Suffolk, he was to make several of the greatest speeches of his life during this period and to carry Commons with him. Greatest among them were the speeches against imprisonment of the subject without showing cause, against taxation without consent of the subject, and against the implications of the phrase "Sovereign Power." He also brought in the Bill of Liberties out of which grew the Petition of Right. His words, "Sovereign Power is no Parliamentary word; In my opinion, it weakens Magna Charta. Magna Charta is such a fellow that he will have no sovereign," were echoed all over England. He also spoke out against the Duke of Buckingham, the author of all England's miseries. On August 23rd, the Duke was assassinated. "After Thirteen years triumphing in Grace and Gallantry one stab dispatched him," [16] wrote John Hacket, and he might have added that temporarily this stab almost made a hero of his assassin.

Restlessness in the Cambridge quadrangles was greatly increased by these disturbing events, but whether they had anything to do with Roger Williams' decision to leave the University is matter for conjecture only. The fact is that he left, probably at some time near the end of the Michaelmas term, December 16, 1628, and the opening of the Lenten term, January 13, 1628/29. This assumption is sustained by a letter from Sir Robert Barrington to his mother, Lady Francis Barrington, on February 20, 1628/29, indicating that at this date Roger Williams was in residence as chaplain at the manor of Sir William Masham at Otes in Essex County.

On the records of Charterhouse for the Governors' meeting, July 2, 1629, this entry appears, indicating his departure from Cambridge.

> "Wee being informed that Roger Williams who hath his yerely exhibition and allowance from the Hospitall to keepe and mayntayne him at the University and so hath for about fyve yeres hath forsaken the Universitye and is become a discontinuer of his studyes there contrary to the orders of the Hospitall in that behalfe and therefore ought not to have his said yerely exhibition from the Hospitall any longer: We doe therefore henceforth suspend his allowance and reliefe from the said Hospitall untill wee shall at an Assembly give order to the contrary."

By the time of this action he had already been at Otes for five or six months, but since no Governors' meeting had been held during that time, formal notice of his withdrawal from Pembroke Hall would not have been entered on the books prior to this meeting. Hence the usual assumption that he had neglected to notify them does not hold. All we have is the record of the suspension of the exhibition at the July meeting, action entirely regular in such a case.

He probably had personal reasons for leaving the University at this time, aside from his intense interest in parliamentary affairs. If his birth is correctly assumed as of the year 1603, he would have been eligible in 1627 or 1628 for the legacy of twenty-five pounds from the estate of his father, James Williams, who had died in 1621, and also for the ten pounds left him by his uncle and godfather, Roger Pemberton, who died in December, 1627. These combined sums, as compared with the sixteen pounds annually awarded by Charterhouse, may have looked like a considerable amount to a young man thirsting for independence. Besides, even without the M.A., he was now ready to take orders and thereafter eligible for appointment. If the offer of the Otes chaplaincy had come without solicitation, it may have been an element in his decision. Silence in this eighteen month period, however, does not necessarily mean suddenness of departure, as has been supposed.

In view of what was ahead of him, his decision was probably wise. The M.A. would have meant at least two more years of the cloistered life. He would have continued to live his days in ancient and medieval thought instead of in the upheavals of his contemporary world which were so deeply engaging him. His own phrase, "My natural inclination to study and activity," comes to mind. His nature demanded both, with activity gradually winning. All that he was to say later in criticism of the "monkish and idle" life of the English Universities involved no disaparagement of learning for its own sake. "Knowledge of Languages" and what he called "the good Arts" headed his list among what he considered "outward gifts of God," excelling all other such gifts "as far as light excels darknesse." [17] His later quarrel had rather to do with the throttle hold the Universities had upon the "Trade of Preaching," but he was not ready to bear such crabbed witness against them until after twenty-five years of schooling in the harsher ways of the wilderness. Such astringent reflections as to campus life belong to middle age rather than to youth, and in his own Pembroke days possibly he thought differently of this cloistered, leisurely life. Possibly not, but surely there is little in his mature life to suggest that the lure of scholarship with its patient, lonely discoveries was the world toward which his heart inclined. His treasure lay elsewhere than in Minerva's tower.

CHAPTER SEVEN

Chaplain

THE move to Otes would determine many things in the life of the young minister. By going into Essex County he was putting himself in the main stream of migration to New England in the great migrating decade of the 1630's. In this quarter he would come to know certain leaders and promoters of this great enterprise, among them John Winthrop, a Suffolk neighbor only twenty miles away who would be one of those to determine his American career. As a chaplain in the Masham household he would have direct association with the more restless non-conformist ministers of the Essex neighborhood: Thomas Hooker, John Eliot, Hugh Peter, and more notably, John Cotton, who would later bring confusion into his life. Still later, in their long-continued paper warfare, John Cotton would call forth the best thought of which Roger Williams was capable, and the sequel would be a great book, and his greatest.

By becoming a member of Sir William Masham's household he would also meet a group of the most powerful Puritan leaders in Parliament, some of whom were interested in American colonization, and others who were to shape the future of England in the years immediately ahead. Among them was young Oliver Cromwell, four years his senior, a nephew to Lady Francis Barrington and a frequent visitor at both the Barrington and Masham households. At the hands of several of these leaders, as Roger Williams later recalled more than once, he might have had preferment at home. He chose otherwise, but they did not forget him, and presently, when he needed a charter for the colony he had founded, they saw that he got it. Determining decisions were ahead for him in these years 1629 and 1630, and this stop-gap appointment in a noble household would both clarify and shape them. Far more than a ship passage to the New World would come out of it.

The circumstances back of the appointment are not known, but there need have been nothing special about them. Until Laud, then Bishop of London, very shortly issued orders forbidding such appointments, a chaplaincy in a nobleman's country estate was one of the natural openings for a young cleric while he waited a vacancy toward a settled living. There were always more posts than candidates and this was a good way to try a man out. As a young man Laud himself had held such an appointment in the household of the Earl of Devonshire, at Wanstead in Essex. Now, however, in his intent to eliminate all likely seedbeds of Puritan Dissent, he saw fit to restrict the employment of private chaplains.[1] Roger Williams was just in time to escape this restriction. His qualifications were standard; he had an A.B. degree behind him and had made a beginning toward further study. In addition, he would have needed an influential word from a person of rank. Once again, such a word may have come from Sir Edward Coke, whose championship of the group of Puritan leaders around Sir Francis Barrington in their resistance to the King, particularly his part in the Petition of Right and his great speech against Tonnage and Poundage, had made him the staunch ally of these men, and the recommendation of a young chaplain to fill a vacancy in one of their houses would have been a small favor to grant. Whoever was responsible, however, in the shift to Otes Roger Williams was fortunate.

He had come to a hotbed of Puritan sentiment of the more militant sort, both ecclesiastical and political. Essex County at this date was a shire "well-planted with gentlemen," among whom none had been more effective thus far than the group surrounding the Barringtons of Hatfield Broad Oak. These men had made up the inner circle concerned in the Petition of Right and they continued to represent the King's most formidable opposition in Parliament as champions of the people's rights against kingly sovereignty. Sir Francis had represented Essex for seven Parliaments and twenty-seven years. Both he and his son-in-law, Sir William Masham, were men of stout courage and both had proved it lately in the matter of the Essex levy. Sir Francis had refused to sit on the Commission in

Essex for the forced loan to the King and Sir William had supported him in this refusal. In consequence both men had gone to prison, Sir Francis to the Marshalsea and Sir William to the Tower. Both had been released in the preceding year,[2] Sir Francis upon direct appeal to the King because of illness contracted in prison. Release had come too late, however, and he had died in the midsummer of 1628.

His death left Lady Joan Barrington mistress of Hatfield Broad Oak. She was the daughter of Sir Henry Cromwell, alias Williams, the Golden Knight of Hinchinbrook in Huntingdonshire, a woman strong-willed, high-principled, and of tenacious religious convictions. She was made of stern stuff, and when her husband, Sir Francis, had been condemned and sent to the Marshalsea, she had accepted imprisonment with him and had remained for the duration of his sentence. At home in Essex, she was quite the central figure in the Masham household as well as in her own. Her will was law and her wish a command. She expected deference and received it, and as is apparent from the many extant letters written to her by her sons and her daughter, Elizabeth Masham,[3] it was a deference willingly given. "I will do nothing without your advice," wrote Lady Masham again and again. Her sons and son-in-law, Sir William, did likewise. Perhaps they only knew, as Roger Williams was soon to learn, that from her authority there was no appeal, nor would anyone dare oppose her save to his own hurt. In the young chaplain's career, she was to be the most important member of the two households.

As Sir William's chaplain, he would to some extent share the life of Hatfield Broad Oak as well as of Otes, for only a short distance separated the two estates and the families were on terms of close intimacy. By virtue of his University degree, Roger Williams was now a *gentleman* in his own right, and therefore freely admitted to the life of both manors.

His duties as chaplain were both formal and informal, the informal doubtless being the more exacting. Otes was in reality a small parish, in which he was charged with the soul welfare of the entire household from master and mistress to servants, and they kept him at it seven days in the week. This was no Sunday assignment alone. In the social structure of the time, such manor houses as Otes and Hatfield Broad Oak were recognized units of life; intellectual, religious and economic centers of varied activity. Within their own borders they were almost completely self-sufficient, and therefore required for their maintenance scores of workers representing an array of skills as various as the needs of life. Almost everything a twelve-month living required was homemade and homegrown. Bread, their staple of diet, meant crops planted, tended, harvested, and the harvest milled before it was kneaded and baked. Clothing meant sheep cared for, flax planted, tended, gathered, spun, both the thread and the fabric, before it was woven, dyed, cut, and fashioned into garments, all by hand labor. Candles were peeled rushes, dipped in tallow. For all this and very much more, many hands were required, as the seasons passed.

An inventory of the household goods of Sir Francis Barrington,[4] when at his death Hatfield Broad Oak passed to his son Thomas, suggests the scale on which life was lived in the new world to which Roger Williams had come. The manor house had fifty-three rooms, every room completely furnished, and every room the particular charge of some member of the servant staff. Even to list these rooms is to call to mind the small army required to keep life functioning smoothly from day to day and season to season. There was a scouring house, a wash-house, a folding chamber, a brewhouse, a malt house, a dairy, a milkhouse, a cheese loft, a buttery, a dry larder, a pastry house, a bolting house, a dying chamber, and every other sort needful, as well as ample barns, granaries, orchards, fields, animals and men to care for them all. The Masham seat was smaller, but it too had its host of those whose "souls" Roger Williams had taken under his hourly care.

The *Diary* of Lady Hoby, wife of Thomas Hoby of Hackness, for the early years of the century (1599–1605) supplies detail for the seven-day program of her chaplain, a certain "Mr. Rhodes," whose duties would in general parallel those of Roger Williams at Otes. Lady Hoby, like Lady Barrington and her daughter, Elizabeth Masham, had been brought up in the womanly ideal of her time and station to fear God, love the Gospel, and hate Popery, and she worked hard in all three directions. Her *Diary* reports the day to day and sometimes almost hour to hour process,[5] suggesting in its details that had "Mr. Rhodes" known in advance what was to be expected of him, he might have thought twice before engaging himself, except that he too probably took his own religious life and his ministerial functions with the same desperate seriousness.

Many score of daily entries in Lady Hoby's *Diary* make it clear that private prayers, meditations, "mournings to God" for pardon, Bible readings, writing in her "sermon-book," self-examinings, with "praiers" before and after each of these, had first place in her daily scheme of things at Hackness. In addition, twice a day she attended public prayer and a "lecture" in the family chapel, and at intervals throughout the day, in the midst of her busy supervision of the distaff side of the manor, she required the personal attention of "Mr. Rhodes." He read to her, she talked with him, he prayed with her, she wrote out "spiritual exercises," notes, "positions," under his direction. He read aloud from the Bible, the *Book of Martyrs,* Latimer's sermons, while she "wrought with her maids" at needlework, or performed "other things wch was to be done in the House." Presumably while she supervised the preserving, distilling aqua vitae, dyeing wool, making candles, attending to bees, buying and selling sheep, or measuring corn, she required no devotional accompaniments to her task. Typically, after the evening "lecture" in the chapel, each day closed with the item, "talked with Mr. Rhodes, and so went to bed."

Such entries day by day suggest not only that the life of the titled lady at this date was after all not so different from that of her middle-class, country neighbors, but also that the life of the country chaplain was exacting to discouragement. Lady Masham was less demanding, it would appear, than Lady Hoby had been with her chaplain. Her letters abound with pious phrases in standard idiom, together with cravings for the prayers of her correspondents, but there is scant evidence of any such habits of exaggerated self-inspection and religiosity as seem to have been the groundwork of Lady Hoby's musings. By contrast Elizabeth Masham seems a quite agreeable young matron, genuinely considerate of her chaplain. Certainly while a member of her household, Roger Williams had enough freedom to take numerous horseback journeys to London and to remain several days together during the great parliamentary commotions of early spring, 1628/29, almost immediately after his appointment. Accessibility to London was one of the special advantages of the Otes location. The distance was considerably shorter than from Cambridge and apparently even the road conditions of springtime were no deterrent to the Barrington family. Back and forth they went, week by week, women as well as men, making so light of the long horseback journey as hardly to mention the inconvenience and weariness of it. Roger Williams did likewise.

From the letter of Sir Robert Barrington to his mother, Lady Joan, February 20, 1628/29, it would seem likely that between the opening of Parliament on January 20, 1628/29, when it reassembled, and March 10th, when it was dissolved, not to meet again for eleven years, he had made several such journeys. Of the February 20th session, Sir Robert wrote Lady Joan,

> "Mr. Williams who walkes the citty will be able to say more than I can who have not ye least tyme to be from the busines of ye hous, . . . he can partly tell you what late rubbs we have mett with, to our greate Distraction."

Of the March 2nd Parliamentary crisis, his brother Sir Thomas wrote,

> "What the perticulars were, you have an eye wittness to report at yor leisure." [6]

Both men of course referred to the final chapters in the long-drawn-out battle between King Charles and his third Parliament. From March 17th of the preceding spring to this March 2, 1628/29 date, much water had flowed under several very important bridges. The Petition of Right had been brought in May 28, 1628, and on June 7th Charles had given his reluctant consent, making it henceforth a law of the land. This Petition had ended the forced loans, taxes, compulsory billeting of soldiers without Parliamentary grant, imprisonment without showing just cause. Next had come Parliament's refusal to grant the customs duties known as Tonnage and Poundage for more than one year. Charles was indignant but his opponents had resisted all pressures, and in the midst of the ensuing debate he had prorogued Parliament until October 20th, and then changed the date to January 20, 1628/29. Everything had pointed to a storm and it had come. There were two main issues:

first, the right of the Crown to raise money without the consent of Parliament, or the Tonnage and Poundage question, and second, the royal attitude supposedly favorable to the spread of Arminianism and Popery. The fact that Queen Henrietta Maria was a Catholic naturally intensified the fear of Popery and made the situation almost too delicate to be handled peaceably. On the occasion of February 11th, while Commons constituted itself a Committee of Religion, citing those who had offended, Cromwell then thirty years old, and member from Huntingdon, had made his maiden speech, accusing his former schoolmaster, Dr. Beard of Huntingdon, of "flat Popery at Paul's Cross." Whether Roger Williams was present on this occasion is not clear; it was of the March 2nd session that he could give Lady Joan an eyewitness account.

The March 2nd crisis provided one of the most dramatic scenes ever enacted in the House of Commons.[7] The details have passed into tradition familiar to every English schoolboy. The occasion was the attempt to put to a vote the *Remonstrance,* branding as an enemy to the State and Kingdom anyone who should encourage either Popery or Arminianism, should advise the levy of Tonnage and Poundage without the consent of Parliament or should himself pay such a levy. The Petition of Right fortified Commons in such an attitude, and Charles had given his consent. Now, however, he denied the right of Commons to act, and had put Speaker Finch under orders not to permit a vote to be taken. Upon Finch's refusal to do so, Denzil Holles and Benjamin Valentine seized him, held him forcibly in his chair, the doors were locked, and while Sir John Eliot, framer of the *Remonstrance,* shouted the reasons therefor, and the King's messengers pounded on the door, the measure passed. The doors were broken open, but it was too late. The vote had been taken. Eight days later Parliament was dissolved. Meanwhile the leading spirits of the opposition had been conveyed to the Gatehouse and the Tower. These were the "perticulars" which Sir Thomas Barrington had written would be brought Lady Barrington by an "eye wittness." Roger Williams was the man. To have been present on this stirring occasion, to sense the London response to it, and then later to hear it discussed in the Barrington and Masham circles in Essex might well have opened new doors in the thinking of a young man fresh from his Cambridge disputations and his own commonplacing in the college chapel. It was also important that this experience came at the very outset of Roger Williams' new independence.

The dissolution of Parliament so soon after his arrival may have made the horseback journeys to London less frequent, but within the moat that surrounded the manor of Otes, life was anything but cloistered. Not many days passed between visits of Essex M.P.'s and other Puritan leaders who took the side of the people against the autocratic authority of the king, and mapped out their campaigns to that end. To have listened to some of these discussions was itself a tutelage in the ways of government and may have fostered a concern for human rights in the young cleric, who one day would found a colony for the oppressed. These men of experience to whom he was privileged to listen were concerned with the practical applications of much that he may already have learned from Sir Edward Coke as to the nature of law, and the respect for precedent, as to English rights and the basis for them in English experience. The Essex chapter may have supplied no more valuable contribution to his own education.

During his early months as chaplain he lost his heart to a young woman of the Barrington household, and had his skies temporarily darkened by the failure of his suit. In the small Essex world of these two neighboring establishments, it was written in the stars that soon or late the comely young chaplain would be thus ensnared. In fact, precisely this had happened so many times in the story of private chaplains at country manor houses as to have passed into tradition and become matter for jest.

> "If they come single, its a thousand to one but they will either bee in Love or Married before they goe away," [8]

Donald Lupton wrote in safe enough prophecy. This had been the fate of Lady Hoby's "Mr. Rhodes," who had fallen a prey to the charms of Mercy Hunter and had married her. Roger Williams' mistake on his first venture, had been to aim too high, for the young lady of his choice was no other than Jane Whalley, daughter of Richard Whalley of Kirkton Hall in Nottinghamshire, and niece of Lady Barrington herself. Apparently he had quickly won the love of the young lady, but as he would soon know, he had reckoned without the blessing of her haughty aunt, the mistress of the manor. Nor could he ever hope (in her eyes) to deserve it.

An attachment from which both lovers recovered so quickly and found consolation elsewhere would hardly merit space in Roger Williams' annals except for the fortunate preservation of two letters which he wrote to Lady Barrington relative to the affair: the first, in the full ardor of his devotion to Jane Whalley, and the second, out of the depths of his disappointment at losing her, and with his consequent ministerial reproaches incident to Lady Joan's fiat against him. The fact that these two letters [9] are the earliest extant words from his mind and heart and pen would make them invaluable whatever their occasion, but since in addition they establish certain conditions and facts of his early life, and also reveal something of his inner spirit under stress, they become doubly so. The first letter is undated, but was presumably written in late April, 1629. It is frankly confident, although recognizing that he solicits favor from one who is his social superior, and who holds all the keys to his happiness. He is ardent in his declaration of love for Jane, and suitably deferential toward her aunt. He respects the formalities of the situation, is appropriately humble, though not obsequious, and fully expects to win his case with his "honorable good ladie, ye Lady Barrington." In every sentence he is also the young cleric, full of the Bible and plainly concerned with the soul's health of her Ladyship.

Between the lines it is also apparent that he has had advance hints that his suit may not be welcome and that he has been staying away from Broad Oak for a time in consequence. Meanwhile "Flying Report" has been busy between the two houses. The names of Lady Barrington's "neare kinswoman" and his "unworthy selfe" have "fluttered or flowne abroad" until the time has now come for him to know her mind in the business. He admits his unworthiness in terms of social status, and also his "poore estate" in comparison with Jane Whalley's, but since her portion cannot be available to her in the present state of English affairs, he is not counting on it. His own prospects are bright. In addition to his "many former offers" and the "late New England call" [10] which he did not accept, he has since had "two severall livings" proffered him. At present he prefers to stay at Otes rather than to accept either of them. He also expects in time a small legacy from his mother. His personal possessions are few, "7 score pieces & a little (yet costlie) studie of books." To have so little is to be poor indeed. Another offer of marriage is pending, but at present there is "none in the world I more affect" than your "worthy niece."

He ends this straightforward declaration by expressing ministerial concern for Lady Barrington's soul welfare, though making the fatal mistake of referring to her "gray hairs," the near approach of her "last days" and praying that the Lord will make these "last days (like ye close of some sweet harmonie . . .") and her "rest fruitful (like Sarah) in old age." If his case had not been lost with the previous recital of his unworthiness, this monstrously untactful finale would have lost it for him irreparably.

His second letter, dated May 2nd, shows that a rebuff had come in no uncertain terms and doubtless promptly. His suit to Jane Whalley was not in order and he had lost her forever. Nevertheless he consoled himself by saying,

> "We hope to live together in the heavens though ye Lord have denied that union on earth."

Instead, they would live in adjacent settlements in the New World, for young Jane was quickly pledged to another minister, William Hooke of Upper Clatford, Hants. He presently came to Taunton, Massachusetts, where he labored for some twenty years and then returned to England to be domestic chaplain in Oliver Cromwell's household.

William Hooke's various letters to Lady Barrington after his marriage give little enough hint as to why he should have been preferred as a husband for her niece over Roger Williams. His social status was slightly better; he was the son of a gentleman. Financially, he would seem to have been even less favored; at least he gave thanks more than once for Lady Barrington's generous purse, her servants, as well as her prayers sent to them in need. Also more than once he wrote about his wife's portion, pleading that he had no money to proceed with the business and was loath to acquaint any of his own kindred or friends with his predicament, lest he become "an object either of derision or pittie" among them. For Lady Barrington's assistance he will requite her by his tender regard of her niece's welfare both of body and soul. Jane's sister, Mary Whalley, also solicited help in "my sister Hooke's behalf." On one occasion she was importunate and besought Lady Joan to send someone "with all speed." In one letter William Hooke admitted that he had "well tasted of yor munificence" and that he is endeavoring in his best recompense by "tendrest care of yor beloved niece" to approve himself to "ye greate Match-maker of heaven." In such blunt appeals and demands, he seems a man of little grace.[11]

Nor do the letters of Jane Whalley after her marriage suggest that Roger Williams had lost a jewel. She wrote as one of a pious turn, with no hint of the "spirit . . . hastie, rash and unconstant," which had been his only qualification of her merit. Six months after she had transferred the "loving and strong affection" she had entertained for the young chaplain to William Hooke, she begs Lady Joan to forgive her for her "carelessness and untowardness" while in her service, being conscious that she had also offended God by such behavior. Her eyes are now open to her sin and she craves pardon against the time the devil and her conscience together will accuse her. Was this "carelessness and untowardness" in whole or in part the love she had acknowledged for Roger Williams? If so, she had forgotten it in the solicitous attentions of his successor, for whom she desires to "blesse God," hoping with all her heart that her dear cousin might find "no worse yoke fellow." In spite of what would appear to be weakness of body, to judge from her many symptoms, she survived the rigors of Taunton, Massachusetts, for some twenty years, returned to England and outlived both her husband and Roger Williams. In her late years she was a correspondent of Increase Mather, sent donations of old clothes to New England ministers, regretting that she could not mend them first, and was piously saddened at the reports of New England's growing wickedness.[12]

The disfavor in Lady Barrington's eyes which his presumption had brought upon him made a painful chapter in Roger Williams' early days at Otes. Her rebuke was tantamount to excommunication and in the first blast of her anger, added to the failure of his suit, he may well have felt that his sun had set twice. With a bevy of maidens at both houses still unpledged, he could sooner be comforted over the loss of Jane Whalley, than over the loss of favor and the consequent denial of hospitality at Hatfield Broad Oak. Almost immediately he was reported "sick of a burning fever," which seems nearly to have cost him his life and may have owed something to Lady Barrington's unknown response to his second letter. In this letter he had shown no resentment for her denial of her niece's hand. He assumed this was born of "good wisdom and love," but having so spoken, as courtesy required, he then proceeded to preach Lady Joan a sermon after the fashion of Jeremiah, issuing from a veritable fire in his bones which could not be stayed. In so doing he was quite within his ministerial privilege, as it was currently understood, but in so delicate a situation as this one, he was untactful to blindness.

How could he be other than upright with her, he asked. In fact, she herself had encouraged him to be naked and plain. Well, here it is. Madame, certainly the Lord hath a quarrel against you. Professing Christians, both ministers and laymen, have suspicions and doubts of you. You are not in spiritual fellowship with God's people. You are worldly. You are less fruitful in holiness than those far younger than yourself. You are greatly favored in your high birth, your ample means, your long life. For all this God expects much in return. He owes you no mercy. Remember, your candle is twinkling. Your glass is nearly run. You have ample warning.

This was a good deal to take, even from one charged, as God's emissary, with keeping her soul in health, and even the remembrance that other ministers had likewise made her sins their target and her gray hairs their argument for speed in reform, softened the blow not at all. Ezekiel Rogers, once her chaplain, had said it in almost the same words.

"Forgett not yt yor time cannot be long,"

and so husband what time is left to you that "when death cometh it may be welcome." He had singled out her "olde disease of melancholy" and warned her it was high time she had banished it away by faith. He had also told her that

> "ye opinion yt others have of you, doth sometime sway you more than yor own knowledge." [13]

To judge from such frank accusations ministerial reproach was no novelty in her experience, but she was not minded to suffer another from the young chaplain of Otes, and she sulked in her tent.

The situation naturally put a strain on the Masham household and both Sir William and Lady Elizabeth were deeply concerned. They may also have been embarrassed by the persistence of Lady Joan in her anger. Throughout the whole affair they were on Roger Williams' side and there would seem to have been affection as well as a sense of justice back of their successive pleas for a return of Lady Joan's favor toward him. They nursed him through the "burning fever" and Sir William reported to Lady Joan, during her absence at her town house, that "in the depths of his sickness (when he and we all tooke him for a man of another world) he desired me to remember his humble and affectionate service to yo, and to let you know as from a dying man, that what he wrote to your [Ladyship] was out of the depth of Conscience, and desire of yr spirituall good, wch is most pretious to him; These might have been his last wordes." Now that he had begun to recover, a kind word from her would refresh the chaplain in his weak state. The news made little impression on Lady Joan. The kind word did not come and she kept her face turned away through the summer and until into harvest time when Sir William wrote again,

> "I am right glad to heare of yr inclinations to Mr. Williams, . . . a good man and a good friend." [14]

The clouds had dispersed; the thunders were past.

Once again in health, Roger Williams performed his chaplain's duties as before, and presently bestowed his glances toward another young woman, this time one within his reach. She was Mary Barnard, maid to Jug (Johanna) Altham, Lady Masham's daughter by a former marriage. For many months the attentions of both houses, even their worried concern, had been focussed on finding a suitable husband for Jug before it was too late, for as Sir William wrote to Lady Barrington,

"Fit matches in these partes are rare. We had best take the first that come (having your approval) fearing the longer she staies the harder itt will be to bestow her." [15]

It was hard enough as it was, for in her station, choice must be highly selective. Qualifications were many and difficult to fill, not the least difficult being Lady Barrington's approval. There is a touch of desperation about various of the letters in "this watye [weighty] business." Young Oliver St. John was finally voted acceptable, although he was not perfect. His father was a bastard, his own competence was scanty, but he had prospects. The contrast between the many Masham letters written to Lady Joan during the summer and autumn of 1629, mentioning this candidate and that, his social rating, his prospects as a man in high place, his inheritance, his willingness to negotiate the alliance, and the last minute postscript to one of Lady Masham's letters late in autumn, 1629,

"Mr Willyams is to marrye Mary barnard, Jug Altham's made," [16]

is an eloquent commentary on the current social structure. The poor parson and the maid settled it between themselves without benefit of protocol. It was all very simple.

The marriage took place December 15, 1629, at the parish church of High Laver, about a mile and a half south from the Masham estate. The record reads,

"Roger Williams clarke and Mary Barnard were married thee 15th day of December anno domini 1629." [17]

The church still stands, a lonely reminder of other days when this corner of Essex was the home of men of power and influence whose counsels many came to seek. Over these roads, now bordered by pasture lands and fields noisy with rooks, men of power and influence went back and forth to London, musing on far-reaching constitutional changes and vast projects, commercial, religious, colonial. Travellers from afar still come by, not often for Roger Williams' and Mary Barnard's sake, but to honor the memory of John Locke, who is buried in this quiet churchyard. A black marble stone enclosed within iron rails marks the spot, and on the church wall just inside is the epitaph, now barely decipherable, which he wrote for himself. For the last ten years of his life, he spent much time in the manor house of Otes, and doubtless worshipped in this church, which still serves its greatly changed countryside.

In Roger Williams' story and out of it, Mary Barnard, whom he married here, is a somewhat dim figure. Despite long search, her lineage is not yet unmistakably clear. The most thoroughgoing inquiry to date [18] makes her quite plausibly, though not certainly, the daughter of Richard Bernard, minister of Worksop in Nottinghamshire. The parish record shows Mary Bernard (or Barnard) to have been christened in Worksop, September 24, 1609. She was the third child and only daughter of Richard Bernard, who remained here until 1613, when he moved to Batcombe, where he lived until his death in 1641. She had five brothers whose names are fortunately individual enough to make identification easy. They were Besekiel, Hoseel, Masakiell, who later came to America, Beniamine, who died in early childhood, and Cannanuel, who became a minister in England.

Mary Barnard's position as maid to Jug Altham was no mark of humble origin or low social standing. She was maid in the sense of companion rather than servant, a position highly desirable in current rating and urgently sought after, particularly for daughters of the upper gentry or of clergymen. Such a connection with the household of a nobleman conferred a certain social dignity and also gave opportunity for training in manners, household arts and management. Sir Hugh Cholmley, in paying tribute to his wife, Lady Cholmley, speaks of the "perpetual obligation" owed her by all the people round about, "for as divers (and the best in the country) desired to have their daughters in service with her," her influence did thereby "much improve" the neighborhood.[19] Others of her class were similarly thanked and well deserved to be. One Mary Long, who in her youth had been in Lady Barrington's household, later requested the same privilege for her own daughter and thanked Lady Barrington "for the best part of my education." In Lady Hoby's household, her own cousin, Jane Sutton, was a maid; so was Jane Gates, granddaughter of Sir Henry Gates. There were of course maids of lower class also, and Mary Barnard may have been one of these, but it would seem otherwise. The fact that Richard Bernard's living at Worksop had come to him through Richard Whalley, brother-in-law of Lady Joan Barrington and father of Jane Whalley, whom Roger Williams had failed to win in marriage, suggests an obligation and an acquaintanceship which might have made it natural for his daughter to be a member of the Barrington household.

The Rev. Richard Bernard himself was a clergyman of some importance in his own day and neighborhood. He was the author of many books, one of them an allegory, *The Isle of Man,* which became something of a best-seller.[20] Described as "a conformable Puritan" he was at one time in trouble with Laud, but he managed to escape heavy censure, probably because he continued to use some ceremonies, though decrying others. Roger Williams said of him, "A man though upright in the mayne, yet of very great weaknesses." When he died in 1641, Roger Williams and his Mary had been in Providence for some ten years. The most desirable piece of evidence toward establishing her identity as his daughter would be his will, which as yet, despite extended research, has not come to light.

Mary Barnard's brother Massachiel (variously spelled) sailed from Weymouth, England, to Weymouth, New England, with the Rev. Joseph Hull, arriving in March, 1635. Land was assigned to him and his name appears at various later times in the records of the town. Once he was fined for giving "strong water" to Clement Weaver, a man at work on his house. He had a daughter whom he named Mary.[21] At one time William Harris, of Providence, mentions "Mr. Barnard the brother of Mr. Williams his wife," but the omission of the given name makes identification with Massachiel only probable. There were other Barnards in New England, as also in Essex County, England. Roger Williams himself had a cousin, William Barnard of Margaretting, but there appears to have been no Mary in this family.[22]

For some months after his marriage, he apparently remained at Otes, performing his chaplain's duties as before. It was a time of maturing decisions, leading to a break with all he had known. When he had written to Lady Barrington in the spring of 1629, he had had no intention of leaving England. The "late New England call" had been refused.

"Nor doe I seek nor shall I be draune on any tearmes to part (even to my last parting) from Oates so long as any competence can be raised or Libertie afforded."

Presumably to this later date neither had been denied. The strength of his protestation is a little surprising, for such a chaplaincy was far from an ultimate post for a young clergyman of parts, unless it opened the way to further preferment. After these months he now saw his future differently. It is possible, even likely, that the painful rift with Lady Barrington had altered his perspective considerably, for as soon as he had recovered from his illness, he either attended the Lincolnshire meeting of the Massachusetts Bay Company at Sempringham, country seat of the Earl of Lincoln, together with John Winthrop, Thomas Hooker, John Cotton and other clergymen of Essex, or met them en route. This was an important meeting for Dissenting clergy interested in emigration.

As they rode along together, the talk of the three clergymen fell upon forms and ceremonies, one of the most natural subjects of the hour for such a group to discuss. Years later when Roger Williams recalled this conversation, he remembered that he had given *"Arguments* from *Scripture,* why he durst not joyn with them in their use of Common prayer." [23] Two years earlier, he had signed the Cambridge Subscription book, agreeing to do so. In the interim something had led him to change his mind. One would expect him to have been uncompromising in his rejection of forms and ceremonies, and yet at no time in his life, early or late, were these his major quarrel. The fiery protests of his Dissenting brethren against the sign of the cross in baptism, the ring in marriage, kneeling at the sacrament, and the wearing of vestments, seem puny indeed when placed beside his insistence that church and state be completely separated and that biblically "pure saints" within the fellowship withdraw themselves completely from the established church. It would seem that these non-conformist views had become matured convictions with him at some time within this year, 1629, but without the knowledge of John Winthrop, who was surprised and shocked by them immediately upon Roger Williams' arrival in America.

His unorthodox views seem also to have been back of his break with Sir Edward Coke, which came within this same year. The reasons are nowhere stated, but the accusation, "rebel to God, the king and his country," written by Anne Sadleir,[24] Sir Edward's daughter, implies at least anti-royalist sympathies in some application. The fact that Sir Edward himself was anti-royalist wherever the rights of the people were concerned, suggests that his former protégé's fault in her eyes was otherwise. Religiously, Sir Edward was staunchly Anglican and his daughter blindly so. The whole tone of her condemnatory letter suggests a mind unalterably closed to the slightest deviation from the beliefs and practices of the established church. To her father as well as to herself separatism, with its opposition to the king as head of the church would be equivalent to treason, and therefore unforgivable. Roger Williams' only word as to this estrangement, was purely personal, and gives no hint of the cause. "I say it was as bitter as death to me, when I rode Windsor way, to take ship at Bristow, and saw Stoke House where the blessed man was, and I then durst not acquaint him with my conscience, and my flight." [25] He owed Sir Edward much, and the breach between them was a great pity. Coke had only six more years to live and there was to be no reconciliation.

During the late months of 1629, while Roger Williams still remained at Otes, he would have heard much of American colonization plans. The Barrington connections were particularly interested in the venture of the Providence Company for settlements in the West Indies. This project had been launched slightly earlier than that of the Massachusetts Bay Company, and several of the same leaders and backers were involved in both enterprises. In the Providence venture the moving spirits were close friends, some of them connections by marriage with the Barrington household. Among these were Oliver St. John, finally chosen as husband for Jug Altham, Sir Gerard Gilbert, who married Mary, daughter of Lady Joan Barrington, and Richard Knightley, who married another daughter. The Earl of Warwick himself, Nathaniel Rich, John Dike, and John Pym were also members of this intimate group. Pym had had more to do with the initial plans of the Providence Company than anyone else. He was one of the heaviest financial backers, had provisioned the *Seaflower* and made detailed plans for her first voyage. The leading motive back of this pioneer colonization plan was commercial, not religious, although like any other group of devout Puritans of their day, these leaders acknowledged a religious obligation and made plans for a settled ministry in their island colony. Their main purpose, however, was otherwise. They envisioned vast plantations, cheap Negro labor, and great financial profits.

For this reason alone the Providence Island venture was not for Roger Williams. He had been born to trade and later he would serve trade in humble ways, but from necessity, not choice. As a boy he had heard merchant talk, years of it. He knew the feverish drive toward economic success; he knew also the far goals of trade, for which the Royal Exchange had been a magnificent symbol on his West Smithfield skyline. But trade had not been his choice and it was not his choice now. His sympathies would be more naturally enlisted with the acknowledged purpose of the Massachusetts Bay enterprise, as expressed in their original charter, "the propagation of the Gospel is the thing we do profess above all to be our aim in settling this Plantation." To this purpose his deepest desires responded, or in his own words,

> "That which I long after, the natives' soules." [26]

During this year of decision he would have heard much of the Company's plans. He probably attended other meetings at Sempringham or at the home of Robert, Earl of Warwick, "the common Randesvouz of all Schysmatical Preachers."

Events were moving fast in the direction of the Company's first settlement. In July, 1629, ever since Laud had been transferred from the see of Bath and Wells to London, pulpit oppression had taken on new and frightening proportions. Thereafter also, colonization plans slipped into sharper focus. As early as March 4th, two days after the stormy Parliament session, a royal charter had been granted to the New England Company. A fortnight later they were given a grant of land known as Warwick's patent. Five months later, on August 26th, the government was transferred to America and John Winthrop was deep in plans for assembling his fleet. On March 29, 1630, he was on his flagship, the *Arbella,* headed westward. In between each week and the next during this entire period, determining events came to pass. Essex County, which was one supplying the largest number of immigrants, was astir with eager interest. Opposition also became more vocal. A letter of Robert Ryece, renowned antiquary of Suffolk, in his attempt to dissuade John Winthrop from embarking, lists various of the arguments being currently voiced in popular debate. Church and state need you here more than any "remote plantation," he had written. "How harde wyll it bee for one broughte up amonge bookes & learned men, to lyve in a barbarous place, where is no learnynge & less cyvillytie." [27] The dangers, hardships, sacrifices were in turn offset by their opposites, of which "the natives' soules" were ever the argument most heavily stressed.

Roger Williams could not possibly have missed the pros and cons of current exchange, but whether his decision to embark was a reasoned conclusion or one made in haste is not known. To judge from the later friendly concern and help from the Mashams, he had not fallen into disfavor at Otes. Nor so far as ecclesiastical records go, was there any official censure against him, although he may have had a warning. That at some time in his Essex career he had talked unwisely is apparent from a letter of Sir William Martin, a neighbor, to John Winthrop, but nothing stands against him on the records of the Consistory Court of London and Essex. There is only his own word, "When Bishop Laud pursued me out of the land." [28]

Possibly he had heard of the vacancy in New England resulting from the return of Francis Bright, a young non-conformist minister, sent out the year before under contract to remain for three years. Bright had served restlessly in Salem, Plymouth and Charlestown, but finding himself out of sympathy with New England church practices, had returned with Captain Pierce in the ship *Lyon* in May, 1630. There had been increasing prosecution for non-conformity in Essex. Thomas Hooker, at his school in Little Baddow, had been cited and had fled to Holland. The Alexander Leighton case had noisily warned all Dissenters to beware. Leighton had been caught, imprisoned, tried, fined ten thousand pounds, had his ears cut off, his nose slit and his cheeks branded. The plague had again broken out. At Cambridge Joseph Mede wrote that the University was "in a manner dissolved." No exercises or meetings were permitted, the gates were strictly kept and the few who remained inside were virtual prisoners.

But why search for a reason satisfying to logic? A ship was sailing and Roger Williams came. Why not? Throughout his life there was to be no settled plan working itself out by carefully ordered steps. So far as what might be called events in his life go, and surely changing continents is one of these, he was something of an opportunist as to the where and what of his life. Looked back upon, his life shows no central unity of place or profession, but of an idea alone.

As winter came on, Captain Pierce of the *Lyon* was eager to be off. He had spent busy weeks assembling a cargo to meet the urgent entreaty of Governor Winthrop that supplies be rushed to New England with all speed. Captain Pierce's letter to John Winthrop, Jr., on November 18th reports that he had first been in great perplexity to obtain what was needed but that now his ship was so full it could hold no more. A relief ship departing from Barnstable would carry the residue, and since his part was done, "I do now with all my strength endeavor to be gon to sea," he added. He weighed anchor at Bristol, on December 10, 1630, Roger Williams and his wife being among the twenty passengers aboard. They faced a winter voyage of which we know only that it was "a very tempestuous passage." Ahead of them were nearly two months of rough weather, cold, discomfort, danger, possibly illness, monotony; "Salt Beefe, Salt Porke, Salt Fish, Butter, Cheese, Pease, Pottage, Water-grewell, good Biskets and sixe-shilling Beere"; [29] prayers, sermons, determination, hope, a new world and a new life. "Plantations are for yonge men, that can enduer all paynes & hunger," Governor Winthrop's dissuaders had said by way of settling the matter. In this as in other ways, Roger Williams could qualify. He was twenty-seven and his wife was twenty-one.

CHAPTER EIGHT

"Godly Minister"

THE Nantasket welcome on February 5th, fifty-seven days later, was not for the twenty passengers so much as for Captain William Pierce and his blessed cargo. He had kept his word to John Winthrop and saved the settlement. Two hundred tons of food would see the colony through until spring. The good news of his safe arrival spread and there was grateful rejoicing, followed three days later by an official welcome. With Governor Winthrop on board and probably the whole settlement assembled at the shore line, the "good ship *Lyon*" came to anchor in Boston harbor, "where she rode very well, notwithstanding the great drift of ice." Five days later the frost broke up in the harbor and provisions were distributed to the people, "proportionable to their necessities." Meanwhile the previous proclamation for February 6th as a day of fasting and humiliation before God was exchanged for one of thanksgiving instead. God had heard their prayers twenty-four hours before they were uttered. Therefore it was meet that they thank him, as they did, "by order from the governor and council of the colony, directed to all the plantations." [1] It had been a notable deliverance.

When John Winthrop recorded this timely arrival in his *Journal* under date of February 5th, he mentioned by name only four of the twenty passengers, who had sailed aboard the *Lyon*. The first of these and the only one to be adorned with an epithet was "Mr. Williams (a godly minister,) with his wife." [2] This epithet on the Governor's lips amounted to a recommendation and not only assured Roger Williams of a warm welcome but made him immediately employable. It also indicated that any "dangerous opinions" he might have uttered in Essex during the months since Winthrop's fleet sailed, had not as yet reached New England, which at the moment was urgently in need of another "godly minister." Sermons were as necessary to Boston life in those winter days as the thirty-four hogsheads of wheat meal, the peas, the oatmeal, the five kinderkins of butter, the cheese, the seed rye, the barley, the oakum, the suet, the three hundred trees; in fact, the whole cargo, not even excepting the doubly precious lemons.

Besides the pulpit shortage occasioned by the return to England of Francis Bright, another vacancy was now waiting, and quite the most enviable one in the whole settlement. This was none other than the post of Teacher in the Boston church, to be made temporarily vacant by the Rev. John Wilson's projected visit to the homeland. He was going with Captain Pierce on the return voyage of the *Lyon,* and his place must be filled at once for the interval of his stay. No young minister ripe for appointment could have hoped for a greater compliment or a better chance both in present honor and future promise. If the substitute could sustain himself acceptably in the bright light which shone on this front rank pulpit position, he might reasonably hope some day to be in line for the mantle of John Wilson himself. Meanwhile he would work with leaders both civil and religious at the controlling center of the colony. Such a chance did not often come to a young man under thirty.

Furthermore, he might begin almost at once. On March 29th, John Wilson gave formal notice to the magistrates of his intention to be absent for several months. They granted his request, received his suggestions as to an interim arrangement in the Boston church, and on his sailing day accompanied him to the boat with honor. Promptly thereafter Roger Williams was "unanimously chosen teacher at Boston" in his place. The magistrates informed him of the choice and made formal offer of the vacant post. They did so with a due sense of the honor they were conferring. Would he accept? No, Roger Williams replied with blunt finality. His reason? He "durst not officiate to an unseparated people." [3] Boston had not cut loose from the Established Church of England with all her corruptions upon her. Herein they had sinned before God. Let them repent and be a pure church.

Magistrates and congregation were alike astounded. What could such words mean? They were neither worthy an approved minister, nor did they make sense. For one in Roger Williams' situation, they were queer indeed. Here he was in a strange land with a wife to support and a home to establish. He had cut all connections with the first twenty-seven years of his life. He had come with no committals, no plans for self-support. Harvest was still many weeks distant. Here was an immediate way of independence, a position which would take care of his physical needs, give him a work to do, an honored place in the community and perhaps a future. It was a position for which he was professionally trained and in which he had already made a successful start. He was equipped for no other. The offer had come without seeking. But no, he "durst not officiate to an unseparated people," and accordingly he shut the door in his own face. He did so not only against his own interest but against all common sense.

His refusal was also an affront to the magistrates, to the much-beloved John Wilson and to God Himself. He even refused to join in communion with the Boston church membership on the same grounds. They were an "unseparated people," as he had found upon examination and conference with them, and he "durst not officiate" to them. This was enough and to spare, but there was more. Magistrates, said he, may not lawfully punish swearing, Sabbath-breaking, and all other offences against the first four Commandments. Had they even heard him correctly? To rob officialdom of the plentiful offence of Sabbath-breaking alone would be to deprive the magistrates of half their week's business and in addition of a goodly share of their dignities as deputies of the Almighty. It was unthinkable. Pray, what kind of a "godly minister" is this who has come among us?

After many generations the puzzle disappears. This was Roger Williams to the life and his brusque refusal of this first offer becomes a clue to his whole career, to his successes as well as his losses. In this initial act his personal history was casting its long shadow before. At the very entrance to the new life he was acknowledging conviction to be regnant, whatever the odds might be to him personally. Henceforth neither argument nor entreaty would avail a hair. The matter was settled and his decision sealed. In this answer to the Boston magistrates he had said no to the best pulpit offer he would ever have and he had said it with his eyes wide open. The door was now closed. This same tenacity to conviction would close other doors to him as long as he lived. For months and years it would cut him off from his own race and generation and reduce life to a staff and compass in the wilderness. Also, on some far distant day, when he had been long asleep, it would put him in the Hall of Fame. At this date he had not yet learned to honor other men's convictions equally with his own, but in this early acknowledgment of conviction as a compelling guide to action, though to his own ruin, he was already on his lifelong track and following his own star.

Moreover, by this initial episode, he was already a marked man in Massachusetts colony. The Boston leaders whom he had affronted were also men of conviction, and they had acted on it to the investment of life, property, what hope they had of happiness in this life and of salvation in the next. This young man was barely older than their own eldest sons. He knew nothing of the situation which had challenged them and their people for more than a year, yet here he was, not only spurning the best honor in their gift, but branding their church as corrupt and calling on them to repent. John Winthrop had been one of the four men, who after solemn prayer and fasting, had stood under the giant Charlestown oak and taken covenant together to "unite ourselves into one Congregation, or Church, . . . in such sort as becometh all those whom He hath redeemed, . . . & to Promise, & bind ourselves to walke in all our wayes according to the Rule of the Gospell . . . so near as God shall give us grace." [4] Governor Winthrop knew the earnestness, even anguish of spirit, with which every step of this same founding had been undertaken by leaders and covenanting members alike. Hence the verdict "corrupt" on the lips of this bold young man seemed a word carelessly spoken. His behavior was bumptious; his opinions half-baked. Worse still, the very word *separatist* was synonymous with the word *anabaptist,* and whoever came under that label was by the same token a subversive, dangerous alike to church and state. Was this personable young man likely to be a troublemaker of that stamp in their midst? Apparently John Winthrop had been sadly mistaken in his recommendation.

Aside from disappointment in him and a suggestion that he had probably better be watched, there is no indication that this first brush with the magistrates caused more than the merest temporary ripple in their councils. Unsavory opinions and the rebuke they invited had already become routine cause for court action along with "scandalous conduct" of more tightly classified sorts. Every ship brought undesirables fitting all these classifications and if their indiscretions and offences were extreme enough, the next ship took them back again. So far Roger Williams' overbold criticisms were no cause for action, only regret and possibly caution. Time would dictate the next step. Therefore on to more pressing matters.

The issue of *separation,* however, which his refusal had underscored, was very much alive in New England at this date, as at home, and at times was proving highly inflammable. The question as to what is a true church and by what marks do we know it to be true, was duly belabored month after month in the pulpit until even children knew the approved answers, with Scripture to support them. Such vigilance, however, did not prevent a new skeptic from arising in nearly every flock, as the months passed. Shortly after Roger Williams had landed in Boston, John Wilson and Elder Nowell of the Boston church went to Watertown to confer with George Phillips, the pastor there, about one Richard Brown, an elder in the Watertown church, who was reported to have said that even Roman churches are true according to Scripture. His opinion was debated "before a large assembly, a vote taken, and by the majority present Roman churches were declared to be not true but false churches." [5] That settled the matter officially. Watertown also had a group at this time who frankly labelled themselves Separatist, and by that label were making a great stir in the community. Under threat of excommunication if they did not comply, the orthodox congregation gave them a day to "come in," with the result that all submitted except one who was promptly excommunicated. He stayed out for a fortnight and then "came in" [6] also. The courage to talk loudly on this inflammable issue was one thing; the courage to take the official consequences was quite another. There had been nothing noisy or sensational about Roger Williams' refusal to serve an "unseparated people." He had merely stated his position and thereafter remained unemployed.

Not for long, however. Whether because of the Boston incident, in spite of it, or merely because a preacher was sorely needed, Salem almost immediately called him to be Teacher in the place of John

Higginson who had died in the preceding summer. If "the late New England call," which Roger Williams had mentioned in his letter to Lady Barrington in 1629, had indeed been that of Salem, as is possible, even likely, then Governor John Endecott would already have been familiar with his qualifications, and turning to him again in their need would have been thoroughly natural. In any case, the post was offered; Roger Williams accepted it and moved to Salem. Promptly alert orthodox townsmen reported the fact to Governor Winthrop, who on April 12th called the General Court in session to consider the matter. The Court at once dispatched a letter to Governor Endecott, recalling Roger Williams' refusal either to join with the Boston congregation or to serve them, and detailing his "dangerous opinions." Why had Salem chosen him without first advising with the Council? Boston's magistrates "marvelled" at such precipitate action and warned Salem "to forbear to proceed until they had conferred about it." But it was too late; Roger Williams had already been elected to the post. Shortly thereafter, on May 18, 1631, he signed the Freeman's Oath and was admitted a freeman of the Massachusetts Bay Colony. Henceforth they would deal with him not as a stranger, but as one of themselves.

What happened in the next few months is not clear, except that he appears to have proved his gifts in the pulpit and to have made warm friends in the town. He would need them. Remembering his recklessness at this early stage, one may imagine that he continued to voice his convictions as to the corruptness of unseparated churches, and to repeat his second Boston heresy concerning the rights of magistrates to punish Sabbath-breaking and all other offences of the First Table. Even though he had kept complete silence in Salem on these delicate issues, as is not likely, the fact that he had already challenged orthodox procedures in both directions would have prevented colony leaders from feeling at ease about his presence in the colony, especially now that he had a pulpit from which to disseminate error. Whether Massachusetts fears of him expressed themselves in pressures public or private during his Salem ministry, or whether he was officially spied upon is not clear. No official action is recorded against him, but after a short time he left Salem and went to Plymouth. Had this move been from personal choice, there would have been no reason for official silence, nor need silence necessarily imply something withheld. The fact is that once again, as so often in his life, no surviving record clarifies the deciding step. There is only the statement of his departure.

As a refuge from Boston control, Plymouth was a natural choice; in fact, the inevitable one. Being admittedly Separatist, the Plymouth people could receive him on their own terms as one of themselves without qualification or suspicion. They may even have invited him to join them upon hearing of the "discontent" of Boston leaders over his acceptance of the Salem post. At any rate, he came, and according to William Bradford's record, was "friendly entertained, according to their poore abilitie." This apologetic phrase meant nothing grudging in their hospitality; only that life in Plymouth was straitened in some ways that Boston escaped. In further proof of their acceptance, and presumably upon their invitation, he "exercised his gifts amongst them, & after some time was admitted a member of ye church." [7] Later still, he was made assistant to the Rev. Ralph Smith, their pastor, and thereafter had a free chance to preach and teach among them.

Although Plymouth was out of their jurisdiction, Boston leaders could hardly have been pleased and they appear to have kept a wary eye upon him. In October, 1632, shortly after his appointment as assistant pastor, Governor Winthrop, John Wilson, and a delegation went to Plymouth on an official visit. Captain Pierce, who was again in port, carried them as far as Weymouth in his shallop, and from that point they went on foot. Some distance outside of the town they were met by Governor Bradford, Elder Brewster and a company who officially welcomed them. In Plymouth they were entertained at the Governor's house for several days. There was much feasting and exchange of counsel. On Sunday afternoon they had their chance to see Roger Williams in action, quite probably one of the main objectives of their visit. John Winthrop's account, which is fullest at this point, reported that according to custom, Roger Williams propounded a question to which the pastor, Ralph Smith, spoke briefly. Then Roger Williams "prophesied" and after his sermon, both Governor Bradford and Elder Brewster spoke to the question. Elder Brewster then invited Governor Winthrop and John Wilson to speak, as they did. Apparently since no suspicion or derogation is voiced in this *Journal* account,[8] Roger Williams had met the test favorably. He had of course been duly warned by the presence of the formidable delegation in this little town of "some three hundred souls" for several days, and he may have screened his own remarks accordingly.

So far as surviving Plymouth records go, church surfaces appear to have continued unruffled for a long time under Roger Williams' ministrations, and his own personal life during these months to have been measurably serene, though straitened. In his own words he got his bread "by as hard *digging* as most *diggers* in Old or New England have been put to." [9] He was learning a great deal about life on the fringe of the wilderness and no doubt finding it far different from the pictures. At the same time, the shift from the near-magnificence of Otes and Hatfield Broad Oak to a village dwelling house in Boston, Salem, and now Plymouth, furnished with only such comforts as some ten years of building and living experience yet afforded, although at first blush suggesting an astonishing contrast, was not after all so startling a change. A huddled village, plenty of wood to burn, small houses, simple fare, probably made a dawn to dusk day, even in winter, rather more comfortable than the great manor house with its stone floors, spacious rooms, tapestried walls, servants and formality.

As to remoteness from other settlements with attendant difficulties and dangers, it was merely an exchange of hazards. Essex County, England, reached today by electric trains, seems an easy suburb of London, as indeed it is, but on horseback or by weekly coach over muddy roads, at times impassable, with markets widely scattered, and footpads, vagrants, beggars always lying in wait, woods to get lost in, swamps to be mired or drowned in if one lost the way, it was after all not so different. His Essex neighbors had been country men and women, skilled in husbandry and whatever else pertained to country living. In the New World they merely had to work at it harder. In Roger Williams' own day to day life possibly the most insistent difference was the fact that responsibility for food and shelter was now directly on his own shoulders. Up to the day he sailed from Bristol, two years earlier now, he had known the protection of an institution, of Charterhouse School, of Pembroke Hall, of the manor house at Otes. Here in New England it was a different story. He must himself plant, tend, and reap, or there would be no bread. Accordingly "wrought hard at the hoe for my bread" became the formula for survival in the "beyond the seas" life he had chosen, and he accepted it without complaint, along with his brother clergymen of University training.

In view of the Narragansett chapter which was so quickly coming for him, perhaps the most valuable and important opportunity which these Plymouth months afforded was the chance to learn a great deal about the "natives" whose souls he so earnestly desired to save. What he had known about Indians prior to his embarkation had perforce been drawn mainly from the spate of descriptive accounts, beginning with Thomas Hariot's official report of the Raleigh expedition of 1588. Later books had continued to ring the changes on Hariot's observations as to Indian customs, mode of life, dress, food, hunting skills, religious rites and strange beliefs, with an increase of emphasis on the need to convert these "savages." Roger Williams' own longing after Indian souls probably owed much to these books and may very well have dated from an early lustrum of his life. The Plymouth residence now gave him opportunity to turn bookish knowledge into personal experience and to look at his own missionary hopes somewhat more realistically. He proceeded to do so.

In between Sabbaths he eked out his meager pulpit support by trading with the Indians of the Cape, and as their willingness permitted, trying to preach to them. The time would come when his expectation of their eventual Christianization would be at low ebb indeed, but that time was not yet. His youthful hopes were now high, and as would appear from later statements, already the plans for a missionary settlement among them began to take shape in his mind. His first overtures toward purchase of Narragansett lands had reference to such a purpose. During these same months he first came to know the Indians as individuals. A few of them won his respect and he in turn won theirs. He came to know a few of them as friends, almost to be trusted. Here for the first time he also knew the occasional hospitality of their "filthy smoke holes," which had at first repelled him. Little by little, thanks to his natural flair for languages, he began to talk with them in their strange tongue, and as opportunity offered, to preach to them with all the fervor of his first zeal toward their conversion. He also began to assemble notes and perhaps to entertain the idea of putting a *Key* to their language in print. In the beginning a practical necessity both for his trading operations and his preaching, this project presently became the interest of a scholar for whom the "Tongues" had been something of a talent since boyhood.

For a time the combination of Sunday and weekday labors, preaching and trading, went smoothly, but it could not last. The time came when Roger Williams' presence in the Plymouth pulpit again caused "discontent" among some of the brethren, as previously at Salem. How long this dissatisfaction rumbled along underground is not recorded, but probably from the beginning, since his first coming had been under something of a cloud of uncertainty or perhaps even suspicion. He may also have given fresh cause for discontent. William Bradford's verdict, written years afterward, was based on long range observation rather than memory of a sudden explosion or crisis in the relationship. In his mature view Roger Williams was "a man godly & zealous, having many precious parts, but very unsettled in judgmente." His teaching had been "well approoved," and Bradford was generous enough to add that he himself could bless God and be thankful to Roger Williams "even for his sharpest admonitions and reproufs, so farr as they agreed with truth." [10] Had they sometimes gone past truth?

What finally, in Governor Bradford's view, made an end to the pastoral relation desirable was not his "sharpness" in such sort, extravagant or not, but his "strange opinions" which from opinion proceeded to practice, and "caused some controversie betweene the church & him, and in ye end some discontente on his parte, by occasion whereof he left them some thing abruptly." The nature of these strange opinions is not stated, but they could hardly have concerned separateness, unless to a degree beyond what Plymouth already professed. According to John Cotton, at least one of them concerned the King's Patent, which was very shortly to plunge Roger Williams into deep trouble with the Massachusetts Bay Colony, and also with John Cotton, who would oppose him "with much vehemency" and in the end be victorious. Unfortunately for his continuance in Plymouth or his peace anywhere on this side of the ocean, Roger Williams had already put his views on the Patent in writing and the resulting *Treatise* would presently prove his undoing. Prudence and forethought in such matters were non-existent with him, and caution was not in his books where conviction was involved. He would probably have called it cowardice to withhold expression of a conviction even at the moment of greatest tension on any such inflammable subject. Governor Bradford's final word, as he recalls the end of Roger Williams' Plymouth ministry is that "he is to be pitied, and prayed for, and so I shall leave ye matter, and desire ye Lord to shew him his errors, and reduce him into ye way of truth, and give him a setled judgment and constancie in ye same; for I hope he belongs to ye Lord, and yt he will shew him mercie." [11]

Roger Williams' conviction that the King's Patent was invalid probably owed something to the Indian land grievances with which he had become familiar in his trading operations on the Cape. In his contention the assumption that these lands belonged to the English crown by virtue of discovery and that therefore they were within the king's gift for purposes of colonization was false. He held with the disgruntled Indians, that by virtue of possession, they belonged to the Indians alone, and that they could be taken over for colonization only by direct purchase from their Indian owners. There was logic on both sides, so that an ordered conclusion favorable to both white and red interests would be long deferred, and while battle waged on this issue, Roger Williams would be both right and wrong. Chiefly he would be indiscreet and his indiscretion would change the direction of his whole life. Very probably this Patent issue was only one item in the Plymouth unrest, but since the unity of the church body was threatened, the membership was doubtless wise to take the counsel of Elder Brewster, the peacemaker, and consent to his "dismission." The meagerness of the record leaves some doubt as to whether Roger Williams had taken the initiative and requested the dismission, or whether he had been given no choice. In either case, the situation had become so serious that the church felt obliged to send along some caution regarding him, as he returned to Salem, followed by some of his adherents. In this situation, as in all the other crises of his life, the line between friends and foes was sharply drawn. His personal magnetism was strong and it provoked a hostility equally strong, so that the peace of the Plymouth church was more likely to be durable without the presence of these ardent supporters, as well as of their leader.

One of these ardent and affectionate supporters, who did not accompany him, was beloved Samuel Fuller, deacon and physician, who died in this year, 1633. Nevertheless, his affection was registered in his will, by which he left to Roger Williams a plot of land on Strawberry Hill, but "if Mr. Roger Williams refuse to accept of them as formerly he hath done," these lands were to be assigned otherwise. There is also this note, that "whatsoever Mr. Roger Williams is indebted to me upon my books for physick I freely give him." [12] One would like to know more of the association to which these friendly provisions testify.

Roger Williams himself left no direct comment on this Plymouth chapter of his life except as such is written into the account of Indian life which he first observed there. His *Key* to the Indian language owes not only much of its content but also its freshness of a first observation and its youthfulness of spirit to the fact that these first-hand experiences were those of a young man new to the ways of the wilderness and its strange people.[13]

CHAPTER NINE

Troubler of the Peace

To return to Salem was to invite further trouble, as he must certainly have known, but where else could be go? He had warm friends there, and now with a group of adherents coming with him, he already had an audience, if not an office, and at the 1633 temperature of his zeal, an audience was imperative. He bought a house, as though intending permanent residence and once more took up his daily life in this frontier settlement. Very soon after he arrived, and presumably on invitation, he began to "exercise his gifts" publicly on the Sabbath, with the result that his audience grew, to the deep distress and worry of Massachusetts colony officials. For one reason and then another, Salem had been a trouble spot ever since the Brown brothers had attempted to read the Church of England service privately, immediately upon the gathering of the Salem congregation. They had been promptly deported for so doing. Now with this magnetic young rebel from Plymouth back in the town, further flare-ups were inevitable. Massachusetts scouts were at once put on the alert for the first signs of unorthodoxy or worse. They would not have to wait long.

Governor Winthrop's first concern was to get hold of the "dangerous" *Treatise* condemning the Patent. He requested a copy from Roger Williams and received it promptly. According to the entry of December 27th in his *Journal,*[1] Winthrop then called the members of the Council together to consider it. He also solicited advice from "some of the most judicious ministers of the colony, who much condemned Mr. Williams' error and presumption." To have "faulted King James" for granting land to Massachusetts and to have made "other reflections on him and his successor Charles I" was a very serious matter. Unfortunately the text of the original *Treatise* is lost but from John Winthrop's brief record of the Council's deliberations, it appears that Roger Williams' contention that the colonists had no right to New England lands except as they "compounded with the natives" was not all of this matter. His more serious offence in the Council's eyes lay in his "reflections," more properly labelled blunt accusations, of both King James and King Charles. King James, he had asserted, was guilty "of telling a solemn public lie" in claiming to be the "first Christian prince" who had discovered these lands. He was also guilty of blasphemy "in calling Europe Christendom or the Christian world." The accusation against King Charles was expressed in three uncomplimentary passages from the Book of Revelation: interpreted to mean that Charles had received the spirit of devils; that he was on the side of anti-Christ; and that he had drunk of the whore's cup.[2] At these charges the Governor and Council were "deeply offended." John Winthrop forthwith wrote to Governor Endecott who had not been present at the Council meeting, reporting their deep concern and laying upon him the responsibility of dealing with Roger Williams and gaining retraction of these errors. In further sequel to his bold revilings against "the Lord's annointed," Roger Williams was summoned to appear at the next session of the General Court to receive censure.

He did even better. Prior to the court session, he wrote to Governor Winthrop, stating "very submissively" that his offensive *Treatise* had been written for the private satisfaction of the Plymouth Governor "without any purpose to have stirred any further in it." Burn it or any part of it if you like, he added. He also obeyed the court order on the required date; appeared "penitently" and gave satisfaction of his intention and loyalty. Meanwhile the Governor and Council had reconsidered the *Treatise* and again weighed its "offensive passages," with the verdict that these were not "so evil as at first they had appeared." Let Roger Williams retract them or take the oath of allegiance and go free.[3] Since he had already done both, the episode was apparently ended and for the moment all was quiet. But for the moment only.

In challenging the Crown's right of patent as he had done in this *Treatise* and as he would soon do again, he was taking a strange view for a seventeenth century Englishman. For nearly a century and a half now the figure of John Cabot standing at the shore line of the New World, and taking possession in the name of his king, Henry VII, had been a vivid picture in the imagination of Englishmen everywhere. Their prideful knowledge of this dramatic moment in their history had been passed down the generations, until English schoolboys hardly remembered learning of John Cabot from a schoolmaster. They had grown up knowing that his discovery and the priority of claim which it had established for England was an event of vast significance to England and to the world. In Roger Williams' own school days, thanks to Captain John Smith and the London stir over Virginia colonization, these earlier discoveries had gained a contemporary significance. Post-Elizabethan England regarded New World colonization as their own special enterprise, and the right "to sit down" on these far-off lands as a right not open to challenge. For his own day Roger Williams' view was distinctly un-English.

It was also out of line with a current pulpit assumption familiar to all New England pioneers. In sermon interpretation the text, "The earth is the Lord's and the fullness thereof," meant New England earth in a very particular sense. In this far wilderness God had made room for a selected company of His own people, and in this spacious New World they would dwell as "Freeholders in a place of their owne," from which they need move no more. With their coming in mind, God had even sent a plague to kill off the natives in those parts especially designed for His New England Zion. Who shall put compulsions on God if He wants His own people to possess this land? Permission of men or payment to them is not necessary. God Himself is Landlord and where He has made "so convenient a vacancy," the sons of Adam and Noah may come freely and inhabit. So had John Cotton preached in farewell to the vanguard of John Winthrop's company in 1630, and in so saying he had voiced an assumption basic to the theocratic state.[4] It was an assumption long past any need for argument. To brand taking possession by royal grant as a "sinne" and to call upon English colonists to "repent," as Roger Williams was doing, was strangely twisted logic, particularly from one who was a sharer in these privileges. Such talk did not make sense. Besides, at the moment it was exceedingly out of order. The relation with the crown was delicate to the danger point. Had Roger Williams forgotten the triumph of the Massachusetts Bay Company when the precious Patent was permitted to be taken aboard the *Arbella* and brought to New England? To denounce it at this particular moment when the Crown was demanding it back again was madness. In the eyes of Massachusetts Bay Colony, this document was almost the Magna Carta in token. Why would this young minister "have provoked our Kinge against us, & putt a sword into his hande to destroy us?" [5] Why indeed?

As to the rights of Indians, neither the king, the Massachusetts Bay Colony or the original proprietors of settlements had been disregardful. Towns had paid for their territory and received Indian deeds in return. There had been frequent disputings about bounds, pasturage, depredations upon settlers' cattle and upon Indian corn fields; resentment both ways, but for the most part, at least officially, the rights of the natives to the lands they roamed over had been respected. Violations had been individual, not corporate. Governor Winthrop had expressed the official view when he wrote that since the natives inclosed no land, had no settled habitation, and no tame cattle to improve the land by, they "have noe other than a Naturall Right" to this territory. "Soe," he continued, "if we leave them sufficient for their use, wee may lawfully take the rest, there being more than enough for them & us." [6] Justice by this comfortable assumption would depend on the integrity of the individual colony. At the same time it was true that land transactions in the thought of the early colonists had been secondary to their desire to convert these "heathen," whom they regarded not as a nation or nations, but as individual candidates for salvation. To Christianize them was not just one purpose of the migration. With the first comers, it had been all but foremost. In the language of the royal Patent, their Christianization, "in our royal intention, and the adventurers' free profession, is the principal end of this plantation." These were not mere words. They represented a deep sense of obligation as well as a zealous desire. Roger Williams shared both, but in his 1632 *Treatise* he had shifted the emphasis to the legal rights of the Indian.

In this emphasis he was not voicing a new or novel point of view. The question had been debated in print and out of it ever since he was born. In 1609 Robert Gray lists as the first objection to be met,

"By what right or warrant we can enter into the lands of these Savages, take away their rightfull inheritance from them, and plant ourselves in their places, being unwronged or unprovoked by them." [7]

Although not yet quite sure of the answer, he ventured it as "likely to be true" that since these savages have only a "general residencie there, as wild beasts have in the forest," and since they are willing to yield up these lands "on reasonable conditions," and since there is "more lande than we shall bee able this long time to plant and manure," there is no reason to delay taking possession. Other pleaders for emigrants reason likewise, more or less confidently. Captain John Smith had dealt with the question twice, most recently in his 1631 *Advertisements for the Unexperienced Planters of New-England, or any where.*

"Many good religious devout men have made it a great question as a matter in conscience,"

he wrote,

"by what warrant they might goe to possesse those Countries, which are none of theirs, but the poore Salvages."

He found the question to answer itself. There was land enough for all the people in Christendom, and

"if this be not a reason sufficient for tender consciences; for a copper kettle and a few toyes, as beads and hatchets, they will sell you a whole Countrey." [8]

Later on the answer would not be quite so simple. In raising the legal issue at this early date, Roger Williams was anticipating a controversy which would go on for generations. The basis of argument as to natural rights would shift, but a century later men would still be arguing the questions involved. Is natural right the only basis for a true title? What constitutes native improvement, or are these lands still as free as the ocean itself? John Locke's phrase "state of nature" would give new life and also new vagueness to the apparently endless discussion. "For my own part," remarked a 1724 protagonist, "I have ever thought this a matter more talked of than understood." [9] In Roger Williams' day there were fewer hairs to split; he was merely opposing the comfortable official view that God had granted the land and the king had granted the power of governance over it. He was doing so on religious as well as on legal grounds. As he said himself many years later, "these thoughts so deeply afflicted [his] Soule and Conscience" that he came to the conclusion "that such Sinnes could not be *Expiated* without either returning to England or making public acknowledgment and confession." [10] The much beloved John Eliot was later of the same opinion as to Indian rights, but being shown his error by the magistrates, he repented and was still beloved. In Roger Williams' thought, repentance was due from his accusers.

Strangely enough for one who was later to prove practical in such matters, he was not pleading for the restitution of lands unfairly taken, or for constructive legislation by way of making such unfairness an offence under the law. He was merely denouncing the Patent and saying *Repent,* thereby depriving some three thousand English settlers of the protection of the crown and putting nothing in its place. In his own land dealings with the Indians, he would always be scrupulously fair in accord with the principles of fairness he was now espousing. As he himself wrote on one later occasion, "When ever ye Natives have desir'd Satisfaction (as knowing yt we have exceeded ye Bounds set us by yr Sachems) we have satisfied them."

Reconstructed in the bare outline possible from John Winthrop's scant record, this early *Treatise* from his Plymouth days throws some light on Roger Williams' characteristic ways of thought as a young man and to some extent throughout his life. It shows his emotional response to a situation to be so strong as to blot out all thought of expediency in remedy, of tact, even of courtesy, of danger to himself or to the cause he thought to serve. Without looking to the right or the left, he struck with all the force of his argument at his main objective, ignoring all logically contingent arguments. Characteristically also, his court of last appeal was the Bible, interpreted to the letter. In this early *Treatise,* the three passages from the Book of Revelation are an example. There is not a shred of logical correspondence between King Charles and the ten kings of the earth who receive the spirit of devils, make war with the Lamb, or partake of the cup of abomination, but to Roger Williams, the likeness was incontrovertible, as though God Himself had made the identification. Before such analogies he was helpless. William Bradford and John Winthrop also read their Bibles, and sometimes accepted Old or New Testament analogies as powerful arguments, but both these men also had a hard sense of present fact which saved them from such flimsy vagaries as these Revelation passages invited.

Roger Williams' attack on the Patent could hardly have been more ill-timed than in 1633. The order to revoke the royal charter of Massachusetts Bay Company and to empower a royal governor to assume complete management of the colony was pending. Archbishop Laud headed the Commission to carry out the new policy in detail. A ship was under construction to bring the new governor and his assistants from the twelve English provinces.[11] As announced on paper, Archbishop Laud's policy would cut the very taproot of New England independence in church polity as well as civil government and put worship once more strictly in line with English practice and under English supervision. Yet at this peak of danger Roger Williams not only dared to denounce the Patent, but to write a letter of protest to King Charles himself

> "humbly acknowledging the *Evill* of that part of the *Patent* which respects the Donation of Land, &c." [12]

At this point, in the eyes of the magistrates, he stepped past the nuisance stage, and became a positive danger to the commonwealth. It was a danger increased fourfold because he was a minister, had friends, was persuasive in convincing others, and even under reproof would not stop talking.

Routine punishments hardly fitted his offence. Clearly it was no case for the stocks, for public whipping, branding, or lopping off of ears. There was only one way to deal with such a man, and that was to put him on a ship and send him over the borders of the colony, or better still, back to England. So had Massachusetts dealt with Thomas Morton, a far different sort of troubler, and with others who had offended with their minds. Who even remembered them a fortnight later? To get them out of hearing and being heard was the remedy. From the day this unfortunate *Treatise* was first perused by the "most judicious ministers," the shadow of exile was on Roger Williams and he knew it. He made plans. Meanwhile the magistrates increased their watchfulness. Murmurs of agreement with his "dangerous opinions" began to be heard, making it doubly necessary that they have a clear case before taking action against him.

The situation quickly became tense, when in the early fall of 1634, upon the death of John Skelton, the Salem church invited Roger Williams to become Teacher in his stead. He accepted. By choosing him the church had offered contempt to the magistrates, since Roger Williams stood "under question of authority." By accepting their offer, he had done likewise. What was assumed to be punishment of the Salem church by the Boston magistrates took the illogical form of ignoring a petition previously filed by some men of Salem for a piece of land on Marblehead Neck, until such time as the church cleared itself of the contempt charge.[13] Angered, the church retaliated by writing a letter to other churches of the Bay, urging that the magistrates be admonished for this "heinous sin." The magistrates in their turn struck back by refusing at the next General Court to receive the Salem deputies until the church "gave satisfaction" about this letter. Meanwhile the petition for the land on Marblehead Neck continued to be ignored as though it did not exist. As Teacher of the Salem church, Roger Williams of course shared responsibility for this offensive letter, and when the elders of the Boston church refused to allow it to be read to their congregation, he and Samuel Sharpe offended a second time by writing a second letter of protest.[14]

Several weeks later, in October, trouble sprang up on a new front, this time in the spectacular action of Governor Endecott of Salem who defaced the royal ensign by cutting out the red cross of St. George. An idolatrous symbol, he declared, and struck it out with his sword. By this rash act, he put himself under charge of treason. King James had placed the red cross there in 1606, thinking by joining the red cross of St. George with the white cross of St. Andrew to denote the union of England and Scotland. Endecott's boldness made local turmoil for many months and greatly worried the Bay authorities, not only because of the already strained relations with

Sir Edward Coke, by Paul von Somer
Niblett Hall, The Inner Temple, London

A Corner in Wash House Court, Charterhouse, London

the Crown, but because many people, including some of the magistrates, thought Endecott had been right. The fact that this disturbance was another Salem affair, threw suspicion in Roger Williams' direction, although there is nothing to show that he was back of it in any way. Governor Endecott may naturally enough have consulted with him either before or after taking such action, and Roger Williams may have concurred, but this was not his kind of quarrel. Nothing in his whole career matches Endecott's action. A sword was not his weapon, nor a painted symbol his enemy. Governor Endecott was of an entirely different cast of mind and temper. He was quick to anger, fiery, and given to blows in the direction of his sudden rages. A short time before he had become so inflamed against Goodman Dexter, who stood before him "daring of me with his arms akimbo," that he struck him down, although himself justice of the peace. His sudden changes of front time after time, when faced with rebuke for his opinions or actions, showed him quite as unsteady in conviction as uncontrolled with his sword or his fists.

Records of the red cross incident show that, shocking as the defacement action may have been, and serious with respect to current attitudes of the Crown toward New England, the chief concern of the magistrates had been the threat to their own authority from such free thinking and acting. According to the official verdict in the case, Endecott's offence had been "very great, rash and without discretion." He had not asked the advice of the court beforehand, had exceeded "the lymitts of his calling" and taken upon himself more authority than he had. As to the use of the cross in the ensign, the magistrates sidestepped this issue, but they saw to it that Endecott was "disabled for one year from bearing any public office." [15] In an effort to allay the local excitement and also to remain safe with the Crown, they forbade any displaying of the ensign until advisement should come from England as to the whole affair. This incident, said Captain Israel Stoughton, "hath bred some evill blood in our body." In official Massachusetts Bay memory, Roger Williams suffered from this "evill blood" as well as Endecott, although there is no evidence that he was to blame in any way.

Official reports of this red cross incident, together with the various personal records which gave it space during the uproar, proclaim eloquently to a later day that no age dare call the issues of another age trivial. In the decade of the 1630's protest and counter protest were seething underneath the surfaces of life and almost any unconventional action, particularly in high place, might cause an explosion. It was still too early for the principles which would emerge from this ferment to be articulate, but great principles were underneath it. Roger Williams, along with various others whom later times have less reason to remember, was conducting a somewhat vague opposition and conducting it prematurely. The time would come when his protest would become affirmation, but that time was not yet.

While the verdict against Endecott was still pending, Roger Williams was summoned to appear before the General Court on April 30, 1635. His offence this time was to have taught publicly that "a magistrate ought not to tender an oath to an unregenerate man." An oath, he contended, is an act of worship and should not be used to establish communion with the wicked. In other words, sacred and secular, in this example, should be kept apart. "All the ministers," wrote Governor Winthrop, heard him state and substantiate his opinions, but they did not agree and he was "clearly confuted." [16] Even Governor Endecott, who had come to the meeting on Roger Williams' side, upon hearing the ministers, "gave place to the truth." Not so Roger Williams. He went away unconvinced. The matter of the oath would be on his agenda again. The magistrates, sensitive to any new challenge to their prerogatives, went away newly suspicious of this exceedingly troublesome young man. There would be no peace while he still continued to raise his voice against the existing order, now at this point and now at that. The shadow of grim future action now lay clearly across his path and both sides knew it.

The affair of the oath, like that of the Patent, was at the moment a topic of current concern to every freeman and to the magistrates, and a ticklish one. In May, 1634, the General Court had revoked the former oath, which one had been free to take or not to take, and on March 4, 1634/35, they had replaced it by the Residents' Oath, which they had made obligatory on every man over sixteen years of age. It was against this new oath that Roger Williams had preached in Salem, thereby giving some standing ground to those who were objecting to take it. The magistrates had been disturbed by a rather sudden and a large influx of strangers with no intent to settle in the colony, and they had devised the Residents' Oath in order to meet what seemed to them a threat to future peace. Roger Williams had spoken out with apparently no recognition of the problem the magistrates were attempting to meet.

His second challenge to the authority of the magistrates was a repetition of the charge he had made upon his first arrival in Boston. They should not punish offences of the First Table, meaning those against the first four Commandments, one's duty to God not being enforceable by civil power. Had this limitation been approved, the bulk of town books and sessions records would have shrunk appreciably during the lifetime of the first and second generations, for it was the profane swearers and Sabbath breakers who took the time of the magistrates and filled the pages of the official records. The power to enforce this portion of the Decalogue had also given them a hold on the common life which it would be hard to measure. No wonder they were unwilling to relinquish it. Had Roger Williams' view prevailed, the magisterial figure of colonial times would have lost much of its terror, and the Monday morning victims for the whipping post, the stocks and the cage would have dwindled to a minority. His challenge ran counter to one of the foundation principles of New England's Zion. The civil magistrates were God's own deputies and to have this upstart cutting the very ground from under their feet was monstrous. Those of Boston became thoroughly aroused.

Accordingly, after this April hearing, the pace of the threatened condemnation quickened. At the General Court session of July 5, 1635, four of his "dangerous opinions" were brought together under a single charge. No one of these was new, as of that date; the list merely reiterated those already considered; namely, the magistrate's right to punish offences of the First Table, his right to administer an oath to an unregenerate man, the prohibition against a man's praying with an unregenerate person, or giving thanks after a meal. These last two "errors" were less inflammable than the first two, but the fountain was flowing too freely, and the time had come to administer a public rebuke. Roger Williams heard the charges, and was given time "to consider of these things," until the next meeting of the Court, eight weeks hence. The alternatives were named: either to "give satisfaction to the court, or else to expect the sentence." [17]

Meanwhile, John Cotton, presumably at the suggestion of the magistrates, attempted to convince him of his errors. Letters were exchanged, but Roger Williams remained obdurate.

Not so the Salem church. They began to see the error of their way. Whether or not the tabling of the Marblehead Neck petition was a "heinous sin," as they had declared, the price of condemning magistrates was too high, and their protest softened. Apprised of this shift of front, Roger Williams wrote to his church that he could no longer have communion with them unless they refused communion with the churches of the Bay. They replied that they were "much grieved" at this ultimatum but Roger Williams had meant what he said. Sunday came and he did not appear in the pulpit, nor so far as is known, did he ever do so thereafter.

Salem's "grief" was Boston's chance, and on the second day of the court session on September 2nd, a letter was dispatched to Salem to "fetch satisfaction" for the letters wherein they have "exceedingly reproached and vilified the magistrates and deputies of the General Court," and if the major part of the freemen of Salem shall disclaim these letters, "it shall be lawfull for them to send deputyes to the General Court." [18] This action, looking toward finality on the whole affair, meant that the petitioners for the Marblehead Neck land would get the land they had asked for, as they presently did. Perhaps it is well to be reminded that during the entire year that the Williams case had been on their agenda, the Assistants had been harassed with the threat of the royal Commission to take over the government. At the September session, 1634, the ship *Griffin* had been in port, having brought word of its establishment, with power to call in all patents, and henceforth to order all colony affairs. At this session the court ignored the establishment of this commission entirely, took measures to fortify themselves, drill troops, and then went on to deal with the one hundred offences on the docket for their attention. The same mixture of major and minor affairs and issues, the same calm detachment was true of the session a year later.

After two days, the September court adjourned until October 8th, when in addition to the assistants, all the ministers of the Bay had been summoned. Governor Haynes presided. Roger Williams was charged with the two letters he had written, one to the churches of the Bay and one to his own church in Salem. He justified both and "maintained all his opinions." The Court offered further consultation, a month's respite and an opportunity to debate these opinions. He refused the consultation and also the month's respite, offering to debate at once. Thomas Hooker, his friend of the Essex days and companion on the rides to Sempringham, was chosen to debate with him. If anyone could convince him, Thomas Hooker was the man, but he "could not reduce him from any of his errors."

From this point on, the official record of the whole affair takes little space; similarly the private record of John Winthrop. It would have taken even less space, if like most other culprits in kind, Roger Williams had bowed to authority, repented his errors and "given satisfaction" to the magistrates. Nothing else was expected. The thorniness of this case and that of John Wheelwright and Anne Hutchinson so quickly to follow, was that these three individualists held to their "erroneous opinions," justified their grounds, and talked back to their accusers. Such was not standard behavior. Accordingly, their cases settled nothing; they merely created new problems.

On the following morning, October 9th, amid a welter of miscellaneous business: to do all that is necessary to the prison at Boston, to lay upon a committee the forwarding of the fishing trade, to press men and carts toward the finishing of the fort at Castle Island, to buy lead for the covering of said fort, to swear William Westwood constable *pro tem.* of the plantations at Connecticut, to license several ordinaries, to license John Holland to keep a ferry, to deport John Smith for divers dangerous opinions, to repeal various price ceilings, to mend various highways, Roger Williams was called to the lower end of the table, where a culprit stood, and heard the verdict addressed to him.

"Whereas Mr. Roger Williams, one of the elders of the church of Salem, hath broached & dyvulged dyvers newe & dangerous opinions, against the aucthoritie of magistrates, as also writt l[ett]res of defamacon, both of the magistrates & churches here, & that before any conviccon, & yet mainetaineth the same without retraccon, it is therefore ordered, that the said Mr. Williams shall dep[ar]te out of this jurisdiccon within sixe weekes nowe nexte

> ensueing, wch if he neglect to p[er]forme, it shalbe lawfull for the Govn^{r} & two of the magistrates to send him to some place out of this jurisdiction, not to returne any more without licence from the Court." [19]

His was the twentieth banishment from the colony since John Winthrop's company came and the first in three years. It was entirely legal for the causes named, and wholly in line with the charter of Massachusetts.

Three days before the verdict was given, young Harry Vane, aged twenty-two, had arrived in Boston. Behind this young man also were various displays of stiff individualism that had put him in a troublesome category somewhat analogous to that of Roger Williams. Upon entering the University, he had balked at the required taking of the Oath of Supremacy, "quitted his Athenae gown, put on a cloak and studied notwithstanding in the same hall." He had declared himself against bishops and against the formal service of the Church of England. His father, deeply disappointed in him, had tried one way and then another to bring him in line with his family traditions and prospects. Now in Thomas Wentworth's word, he had "gone into New England for conscience sake." Reckless, charming, unstable, he had as yet given hardly a hint of the statesmanlike sagacity which would later distinguish his services to England during the Revolution.[20]

Temperamentally, Roger Williams and Harry Vane were framed to understand each other, and apparently during the three days between Vane's arrival and Roger Williams' edict of banishment, the two young rebels discovered their capacities for mutual understanding and sympathy. For Roger Williams this was to be the closest friendship of his life. Seven months later Harry Vane was Governor of Massachusetts Bay Colony and Roger Williams was dealing with him in Narragansett affairs. Their relation personally and officially would continue for thirty years before Vane went to his execution, and more than once he would be the "sheet anchor" of Rhode Island's hope for existence as a civil body. Had the life of either one of these promising young men ended near to the time of their first meeting in 1635, he would have been written down as a troubler of the peace and nothing more. But life was to be kinder to them than that. Each of them needed time; time to learn, to grow, to discover his own powers, and then to forget them in a selfless devotion to great principles of human action.

To assume, as later generations have sometimes done, that Roger Williams as a headstrong, impulsive young rebel in 1635 was already the man to whom these same later generations call themselves deeply indebted, or that his Massachusetts rashness in 1634–1635 concerned the principle of "soul-liberty," which has come to be almost synonymous with his name, is to read history backward. There are hints here and there, as in his reply to the Boston church, that he already saw *civil* ways and *church* ways as clearly distinct. There are also hints as in the July, 1635, list of charges against him, that already a man's conscience was to him a realm sacred to the individual man alone and therefore not to be invaded by magisterial authority, but these are hints only. He was on his way to the far-reaching principle he was to enunciate, but it did not as yet possess him. He was approaching it negatively, as was entirely natural in a restless time. His apparent blindness to the unwisdom, if not the positive peril of his opposition to the existing order at such a time of crisis as Massachusetts Bay Colony faced in 1635, is the most amazing part of his story at this stage. When his insubordination is placed in its contemporary local setting of 1634, with Matthew Craddock all but on his way to New England to demand the return of the patent, the patience and forbearance of the magistrates does them great credit, as it also shows that they recognized him as a man "of precious parts," in spite of the problem he was proving to be at the moment.

After the verdict against him, he returned to Salem to find that his church had "openly disclaimed his errors," and written "an humble submission to the magistrates, acknowledging their fault in joining with him in the offensive letters criticising the magistrates." The church had been forgiven; Salem was back in the fold, and Roger Williams was left alone. Perhaps one may read a very private comment of Roger and Mary Williams on the exile they now faced in the fact that their second child, born in this same month of October, 1635, was christened *Freeborn.*

Before a month had passed, the Boston authorities heard that in spite of the order of silence laid upon him, and presumably agreed to by him, he was again going about "to draw others to his opinion." Once again he received an immediate summons to appear at the next session of the General Court. He could have expected nothing else. What was in his mind? Surely he had nothing to gain for the Indians or for the cause of religion by such beating of the air. He was apparently unable, or at least unwilling, to keep his convictions to himself, or in his own word, written later in a quite different connection,

> "I have not hid in my breast my soul's belief."

Clearly he had not. Speaking out would seem to have been an obligation, if not a virtue. As for the broken promise, he says nothing. Was this a lesser obligation or had he merely forgotten? It would not matter which. The patience of the magistrates was at an end, no matter how severe the winter. They accordingly decided

> "to send him into England by a ship then ready to depart."

Once outside of Boston harbor, he might talk as much as he wished. He replied in answer to their summons that he was grievously sick, and could come to Boston only on hazard of his life. Very well; they would go to him. Forthwith Captain Underhill was dispatched to Salem with a pinnace to convey him back to Boston, but "when they came at his house, they found he had been gone three days before; but whither they could not learn." His Salem friends would have seen to that. No pursuit was undertaken.

In Boston the waters closed over this whole affair very quickly. There were a few regrets. Sir William Martin of Essex wrote to John Winthrop, "I am sorry to heare of Mr. Williams separation from you," but he was hardly surprised. He gave no instances, but continued,

> "He is passionate and precipitate, which may transporte him into error, but I hope his integrity and good intentiones will bring him at last into the waye of truth, and confirme him therein. . . . I praye shew him what lawfull favore you can, which may stand with the common good." [21]

There is probably an Essex story back of this fair judgment, which if it could be known, might illuminate Roger Williams' own word that Archbishop Laud pursued him out of England. Some months later John Winthrop received another letter from another English correspondent commending him for "disclayming Mr Williams' opinions," and dealing with him as Massachusetts had done. This action, "tooke off much prejudice from you with us, and hath stopt the mouths of some," this correspondent reported, thanking God that some letters coming from New England reporting "dangerous passages" which if known, "would attempt your undoing," had not as yet come to the wrong eyes.[22]

John Winthrop's problem in this affair, painful to him in its ending, had been to separate the personal from the official and to remember that he was guardian of magisterial authority, which at all cost must not be endangered. He was also entirely convinced that the magistrates, under God, were charged with the rooting out of error. He would keep his public trust inviolate. At the moment he was also somewhat under a cloud himself because of an accusation of too much lenity with previous offenders and he felt obliged to redeem himself from the scathing attack of Thomas Dudley. Privately, he was kindly disposed to Roger Williams, who once out of Massachusetts jurisdiction, would be deserving of assistance toward his immediate safety. The project of a trading post in the Narragansett country was no secret. Roger Williams had confided his plans to Winthrop and the two men had discussed them together. In the light of future developments, it is also altogether likely that John Winthrop was thinking in the direction of Massachusetts expansion to the southward, and he was glad enough for this daring young man to break the ice in that wild territory ahead of the time when more space would be needed. Let him begin a settlement there, and thus make it easier for those who would follow later.

So far as Massachusetts officially was concerned, the affair was over, at least for three hundred years, when the sentence of banishment was revoked in honor of the place Roger Williams has won in a nation's thought. In midwinter 1635/36, when as an exile he took the path toward Narragansett, the possibility of such a reversal would have seemed even further off than three hundred years. His ideas were not then conceivable as being merely too advanced for his time. They were poison in the church body and treason in the state, and for that reason must be torn out root and branch. What the magistrates had yet to learn was that by the method of excision, they would but grow the faster.

The vexed question as to whether he was banished for civil or religious reasons will probably continue to be debated, although it would seem that long ago enough has been said on that matter.[23] The text of the banishment itself has too often been forgotten in these discussions, and also the fact that in 1635 civil and religious were one and inseparable. Religion was a part of everything in a theocratic state, and the rooting out of error was an obligation to which the magistrates were pledged. As to how far his "soul-freedom" conviction was a cause of his expulsion, he himself would not have been able to say. The leaven was at work in his own thought, and he was exercising a privilege which presently he would justify as a human right. One might expect the abstract principle to precede the action, but in Roger Williams' life, and not in this instance only, the practical application preceded and clarified the principle in his own thought.

In the lengthening perspective of the generations, the decree of banishment against him was, in Justice Holmes' phrase concerning another sort of crisis, "the stroke of lightning which changed the whole course of [his] life." Roger Williams' change was fortunately toward giving the high endeavor that was in him a chance to become articulate in action more worthy of itself. Perhaps it is sometimes fair to think of the story of human lives in terms of the might-have-beens. If so, for Roger Williams to have remained in Salem, or wherever else he might have found a brief hospitality, might predictably have meant that with his individual thought throttled at every new birth, he might presently have become no more than a perennial rebel, increasingly aggressive, and futilely spending his force in embattled opposition. He had already been one man against everything too long for his own good. One might conjecture also that had Captain Underhill and his pinnace caught up with him before the three day head-start through the snow, and carried him off to England in his 1635 frame of thinking, he might one day have shared a scaffold on Tower Hill with impetuous, high-thinking Sir Harry Vane. Instead, he was given a chance, first to learn, and then to throw his weight for nearly a half century against controlled thinking, and to do so on the affirmative side of rebellion.

CHAPTER TEN

"First Beginner" of a Colony

In John Cotton's self-exonerating phrase for his share in the business, Roger Williams' banishment was not to be counted so much a limitation as an *enlargement*. He was right; enlargement it was, though in ways Cotton would not live to know, possibly also in ways he might not have cared to grant. The same suggestion, made in a different spirit, was also in Edward Winslow's letter written soon after Roger Williams' escape from his pursuers at Salem, advising him to move across the Seekonk River, where, as Roger Williams later quoted Edward Winslow's phrase, "I had the country free before me." Free; yes, in retrospect, but in the bitter winter season of mid-January, 1635/36, enlargement and freedom of this sort appeared to be exactly what it was; namely, exile in a vast, unsettled, and dangerous country; "a sorrowful winter's flight" into a world made of nothing but air and snow and such sharpness of cold as when an old man in his late seventies, he could "feele yet." [1] Aged thirty-three, he had gone forth as a lonely, discredited man. But he would have been lonelier had he stayed.

If like William Bradford, or John Winthrop, or Samuel Sewall, he had been minded to keep a personal record of the forty-seven years of life still left to him, America would have had one more priceless early record, this time of man against the wilderness in an almost strictly literal sense. It is easy to understand why he kept no such record. Those who live an epic seldom have time to write it down, even if they recognize its probable epic quality to later times. They have other things to think about. In the beginning Roger Williams fought for bare survival, and against great odds.

Yet he made himself a new home, accepted the new pattern of life in untamed places, met the day's urgencies as they came, and although he never forgot that "unkindly and unchristianly," as he believed, he had been "driven from my house, and land, and wife and children," to the day of his death he did not know the magnitude of what he had done. It is better so.

Failing a current record, we must piece out the stark beginnings of his exile's story largely from his own phrases of fragmentary recall years later, usually under oath, and from his few extant letters to John Winthrop belonging to these earliest experiences. From the several details these sparse fragments supply, only the barest framework of his first movements emerges, and often with such vagueness as to be subject to differing interpretations or even flat contradictions. The fact is we do not know of a certainty how he "steered [his] Course" during these first "fourteen weekes," when he was so "sorely tossed" as hardly to know what "bread or bed did meane." [2] Neither do we know much more about the ensuing weeks and months, first on one side of the Seekonk River and then on the other. Fact and tradition are too much tangled to be separated conclusively.

From such light as is available at present, however, it appears that he left Salem on foot about January 15th, accompanied only by Thomas Angell, a young domestic servant of the family whom he had brought over from England with him five years earlier. The two men made their way to an Indian settlement somewhere over the border of Massachusetts into Plymouth patent. Here they probably remained for some time with the Indians, for on account of Roger Williams' illness shortly before leaving Salem, he may still have required the ministrations which tradition has assigned to his Indian friends on this first leg of his flight.[3] It is also likely that this Indian settlement was the point at which, by pre-arrangement, his four Salem companions joined him before the little company set out across country to the Seekonk River on the far boundary of Plymouth territory.

Although Roger Williams expected these companions, from his own testimony as to the beginnings of the colony, they had joined him at their own solicitation, not at his invitation. Even so, he should have denied them, as four less suitable associates in the venture before them could hardly have been assembled. He should have known their unsuitableness and probably did; nevertheless, "out of Pity," as he said later, he gave leave to William Harris, an attorney's clerk, "then poor and destitute," also to John Smith, miller of Dorchester, banished also, of whom he later admitted a "dislike & especially of his wife," and at John Smith's desire, to "a poor young fellow, Francis Wicks, as also to a lad of Richard Watermans. These are all I remember." [4] The descendants of other early Rhode Islanders are ready to assist his memory at this point, but available evidence to increase the number in this pioneer company remains too hazy to be credited. From the subsequent actions of these four, particularly of William Harris, one may strongly suggest that except as six against such winter hazards as they faced were better than two, he might far better have continued his journey with Thomas Angell alone. It was a thousand pities he did not.

According to various private accounts in addition to John Winthrop's, the 1635/36 winter was a "very bad season" indeed; in fact, something of a "foul weather" record. The foulness had not abated since the great hurricane of the preceding August, "a mighty wind" which had blown down many hundreds of trees, overthrown houses, driven ships from their anchors, created great waves which overtook fleeing ones to their deaths. The toll of lives lost had been high. As winter came on, destruction and tragedy continued. Ships were driven out of their course, shallops broke loose from their moorings, snow was knee deep, many cattle were lost, many people in great straits for food. Those of Dorchester were reduced, John Winthrop reported, "to acorns, malt and grains." [5] Later in this same year, and wiser for waiting, Thomas Hooker led his caravan out on the Old Bay Trail to find a new life and to found a new colony. He was going voluntarily and had choice of season for his historic exodus; Roger Williams did not.

After what would seem to have been a considerable sojourn with the Indians, he and his companions made their way to a cove on the eastern shore of the Seekonk River, presumably near the present site of Rehoboth. Here they built themselves a shelter and waited for spring to break. As soon as the ground could be worked, they began to plant from their store of corn and beans and grain which each man had carried, along with the hoes, spades, axes, hammers, and all other implements and tools required for the beginnings of a new life. There was nothing haphazard about this expedition, nor about the site chosen as a base of operations. "Many years before I, came in person to the Nahiganset," Roger Williams later testified, he had purchased this piece of land from Ousamakin (Massasoit), chieftain of the Plymouth Indians, "and therefore when I came I was Welcome to Osamaquin and that old prince Canonicus, who was most shy of all English, to his last breath." [6] He was now claiming this site for residence. If the purchase had been made during the Plymouth years, as is likely, his "many years" could have been no more than five, possibly less.

What had been in his mind at the time of the original purchase is hardly matter of surmise, for in his own words, oft-quoted,

> "My souls desire was to do the natives good, and to that end to have their language (which I afterwards printed) and therefore desired not to be troubled with English company." [7]

Now, pressed by necessity, he had come to this same corner of Plymouth patent as to a haven. Doubtless he had been here many times and knew the landmarks, even in winter snows. Both Governor Winthrop and Governor Winslow knew the place and also his plan in banishment to steer his course "unto these parts, wherein I may say, as Jacob, Peniel, that is, I have seene the face of God." The biblical analogy which he felt himself to be living at this moment may have mitigated somewhat his sense of uncertainty and desolation. Whether at his 1635 coming, the missionary purpose was still a compelling motive in his thought he does not state, but there is no reason to think that he had abandoned it. The phrase, "desired not to be troubled with English company," certainly belongs to this later time, not to the Plymouth residence.

While the building of the shelter and the planting were still in progress, a messenger came from Governor Winslow, bringing word that Seekonk was within the jurisdiction of Plymouth, and therefore advising Roger Williams "in the name of their government to remove but over the river unto this side, (where now, by God's merciful providence, we are,) and then I should be out of their claim, and be as free [as] themselves, and loving neighbors together." [8]

Accordingly, leaving their newly planted crops behind them, the six men abandoned Seekonk and moved across the river.

The traditional story of their historic landing on the opposite shore is well known, particularly as imagined in a painter's thought. Who would want to change it in a single detail? Besides, it is probably literal fact as well. A slender canoe coming down the river, carrying white men, not red, and few enough in number to be counted from a distance; the huddle of Indians at the shore line watching; would it be in friendliness or hostility? Then, as the canoe came nearer, the Elizabethan greeting, "What cheare, Netop?" called out by the leader of the white men, indicating that these strangers meant no harm. Next, his gestures signifying that he intended to land on the neck of land around the bend of the river; Indians and canoe moving slowly by land and by water to the spot indicated; then Slate Rock and the historic meeting of white and red.[9] So should a great enterprise begin. Simply, and yet with enough risk for it to have ended at the outset, except it be saved by some unpredictable fraction of judgment, of tact, or something more intangible than either. So it was on this early spring day in 1636, and in this pregnant moment something more than colonial enterprise had its beginning. The imagined picture of the first step in so notable an achievement belongs where Rhode Island has put it for all time; namely, on the seal of the colony and state which thus began.

From time to time through the years the number of men in the canoe, as represented in various official statements, and even on the seal itself, has been changed: from two to five, from six to three. The Ordinance of 1845 made it four; the City Manual of 1861 increased the number to six; the latest official count would seem to be three. The matter is best left with those whose responsibility it is to reconcile conflicting traditions. Slate Rock is no longer visible except in a painter's imagination. The site, long buried under made land, is marked with a monument northwest from the corner of Williams and Gano streets. Better still, this traditional landing place in its original promise and beauty still teases the imagination of those to whom a monument must always be too unpoetical a reminder of great moments. The date remains a matter of some uncertainty and dispute. It was probably mid-April. The statement of Benedict

Arnold, "We came to Providence to Dwell the 20th of April, 1636," [10] would seem to mean on the territory across the river to which the name Providence was first applied. Roger Williams' first extant letter to John Winthrop from this point, undated, is headed New Providence, probably in distinction from the Old Providence settlement off the coast of Central America.

Having crossed the river, they were now out of Plymouth patent and in the territory of the Narragansetts, near unto the Indian village of Mashasuck. Strictly, the Narragansett country at this date was a small area of about twenty square miles; in John Winthrop's description, "all champain for many miles, but very stony and full of Indians." Not all stony, however, and as Roger Williams' quick eye had no doubt noted on his first coming, it was exceedingly fertile in a narrow strip on both sides of the river. In terms of such prosperity as these rich fields could promise, the location was hopeful, and once again they planted from the store of seed they had left. Until their own first crops could take care of their needs, they could purchase from the winter supplies of the Indians, after their own were exhausted. Besides, each new recruit carried additional store with him, so that at least for the spring and summer season, some of the initial hardships were behind them.

In terms of permanent settlement two things were immediately needful, land enough for all and a form of government. Unfortunately, neither was provided and planned on a safe basis for continuing peace. The perennial harvest, particularly of land troubles, which Roger Williams was to reap throughout the remainder of his life, and then leave behind to plague the colony for years thereafter, was implicit in these first land transactions and the first arrangements for group control of community affairs. Both were personal and proprietary instead of corporate. Both mistakes are understandable and reflect no discredit on Roger Williams. Founding a colony had not been his prime objective, and all at once he found himself in a situation for which he was not prepared. Moreover, quick action was imperative, and in these first decisions a stormy future was shaped. As for long range planning, there was almost none. The beginnings of Providence Plantations were almost fortuitous. One man, deeply harassed, had come to a remote spot for refuge. Others followed him, and a colony resulted. It was almost as simple as that. Nevertheless, as the natural leader of this little band of wayfarers, quickly augmented by others, Roger Williams assumed responsibility with complete selflessness. Mistakenly he took it for granted that his fellow settlers shared his high motives, as some of them did not. He seemed to have had no understanding of the selfishness of men without a country, when they saw fertile lands spread out, as it were endlessly before them. He also lacked as yet, a political philosophy requisite for the founding of a state. However, not knowing that he lacked either, he assumed charge, and faced the immediate problems of survival and group peace.

The purchase of land came first. As one might expect, in view of his attitude toward the royal patent, these land transactions from the beginning show him respecting what he believed to be Indian rights of ownership to the letter. He had come to the Narragansett country as a private person, fleeing pursuit. He had no patent, no deed, no boundary lines, no financial or legal backing, no authorized claim of any sort, no capital except the small sum for which he had mortgaged his house in Salem, and a bundle of such toys and necessities as served for exchange with the Indians. His only basis for negotiating a bargain with them was the claim of mutual friendship with the sachems Canonicus, chieftain of the tribe, and Miantunomi, his nephew and co-ruler. In their eyes as well as in his own, this friendly relation was sufficient. In the official English view, such a transaction conferred squatters' rights only. The land of America, which belonged to England by right of discovery, became the possession of English colonists only by royal patent. All the Indians could do was to give permission for co-inhabitation merely by way of neighborly courtesy. Ignoring this view, Roger Williams immediately and with the full willingness of the sachems, purchased of them the territory enclosing the Indian village of Mashasuck, thereafter to be called Providence. In his own word, "And having in a Sence of Gods mercefull providence unto me in my destresse, called the place providence," [11] he took possession in full confidence that henceforth it was his, as he was later to say, "as much as the coat upon my back." The name, at first given to the whole section he had acquired, was presently used for what became the town of Providence only.

There is a tradition that his "out land," which included the landing site, was later given to him by Canonicus, and though in default of record, the assumption is likely enough. In the 1657 deed Roger Williams used the greeting *What Cheare* as a place name referring to this landing site, and wrote,

> "Reserved to my selfe the two Indian fields called *whotcheare* and *Saxifrax Hill* . . . and also planted both those fields at my first coming as my owne pecular: with mine owne hand." [12]

The original purchase, which would seem to have been by verbal agreement only, was confirmed two years later (March 24, 1637/38) in an impressive ceremony at Pettaquamscutt Rock. On this occasion Roger Williams, William Coddington, Randall Holden and John Clarke met with the chieftains; the deed was drawn up and signed in the presence of a large number of Narragansett Indians. With this confirmatory deed, later to be known as *The Towne Evidence,*[13] now badly mutilated, the documented history of Providence begins.

An ingenious story, obviously invented later to explain the mutilation, is a fair example of the kind of subterfuge and rationalization which punctuates the record of Providence land transactions throughout the lifetime of Roger Williams and his first companions. This important paper, so runs the story, had been on one occasion used as wrapping for garden seeds, and being left out in the rain after the seeds were planted, had required cutting, pasting, re-tracing around the mutilated area, which happened to concern the original boundaries agreed upon. One's speculations may or may not be teased by the record of many years of lawsuits and counter lawsuits which dealt with this torn area, for which the custodian of the document at the time of the mutilation became an unremitting claimant throughout these legal procedures. However that may be, the significant fact about this precious scrap of paper is that it documents a private purchase, made in a private necessity by one white man from two Indian chieftains, who already possessed satisfying evidence of the white man's good faith and friendly intent. By Roger Williams' own sworn statement, prior to this purchase, there had existed "several treaties with Canonicus and Miantunomi" and this deed of March 24, 1637/38, "thereof established and confirmed the boundes of these landes." In his eyes this procedure was legal and final. The land was his. So far as Indian rights were concerned, his preachment and practice were one. If at this date Massachusetts or Plymouth had chosen to move in, with an additional royal grant behind them, he would have been helpless. Had he taken time to go to England to petition for a royal grant, he would have been refused, because of his standing as an exile from Massachusetts colony. Besides, in view of the time required for even a hearing, to say nothing of delay in arrangements, he would probably have returned to find this purchased territory in other hands. He was wiser to remain a squatter for the seven years just ahead, and to apply for a charter at that later time, as he did.

Subsequently he made other land purchases, all of them likewise personal. On this same March 24, 1637/38 date, he received deeds for Aquidneck Island and for Prudence Island, purchased jointly for himself and John Winthrop in the preceding November. "I have bought and paid for the island," [14] he wrote, inserting Winthrop's name in the Prudence Island deed with his own. In his own word the term applicable to these various purchase prices was *gratuities*. "The truth is," he wrote, "not a penny was demanded by either [Canonicus or Miantunomi], and what was paid was only *gratuity,* though I choose, for better assurance, and form, to call it sale." He repeats the word at various times in his later sworn statements, making a pointed distinction between such gratuities and *monies*. Of his first purchase he wrote,

> "not by monies nor payment, the Natives being so shy And jeloues, that monies could not doe it; but by that Language, Acquaintance and favour with the Natives. . . . And also bore the charges and venture of all the Gratuetyes which I gave to the great Sachems." [15]

Of the Aquidneck and Prudence purchases he wrote, "For a thousand fathom would not have bought either, by strangers." Fortunately, he had come with these gratuities in his wallet and pack, having "mortgaged my house and Land at Salem (with some hundredths) for supplies to go through." Those harried last days in Salem had been spent in more than talk.

It was not until 1658, when amid the "noise of purchase and purchasers," Roger Williams saw fit to declare anew "the rise and bottom of the planting of Rhode Island in the fountain of it," that he wrote the memorable sentence,

> "It was not price nor money that could have purchased Rhode Island. Rhode Island was purchased by love." [16]

Something of the spirit of his own thought of both his Indian and white associates; in fact, the spirit of his whole life is caught in that declaration. At another time he phrased it thus,

> " 'Tis true he recd presents and gratuities many of me, but it was not Thousand not Ten Thousands of money that could have bought of him an English Entrance into the Bay. Thousands could not have bought of him Providence or Pawtuxet or Aquideneck or any other land I had of him." [17]

The phrase "land I had of him" gives a clue to the question of tenure as Roger Williams regarded it. He and his companions were not buying it as a group, of whom he was merely leader and spokesman. He was buying it individually, and then assigning portions to them equally to use, not to own. In the beginning no deeds were transferred to them, for he thought of these co-inhabitants as cosharers, or feoffees in the earlier English sense, not as absolute owners in their own right. William Harris, most obstreperous of these first associates, represented the newer English view of individual ownership and acted in accordance with it through all of his subsequent tempestuous dealings with Roger Williams. This view Williams not only did not accept; he did not understand it. It was of Pawtuxet, the tract around which dispute raged most fiercely and for many years, that he said, "It was my own as much as the coat on my back." From this view he never retreated. The tenacity of William Harris on the opposite side was not entirely malicious, although at times it appeared to be so. Both men grew so bitter and so blind to the other's point of view as to obscure the legal implications and deadlock the case irremediably. To both of them the feud became deeply personal. Both were right, but according to views of land tenure generations apart. In a later day William Harris could not have been effectually opposed in his claim of absolute ownership, nor would Roger Williams have had any legal ground to stand upon.

Precisely what was in his mind as to the intended use of the land he had purchased before it was divided among his twelve associates is not entirely clear, but his word *yielded* in his 1677 testimony as to the colony beginnings, suggested that it was something other than what came to pass. He wrote,

> "The Truth in the Holy Presence of the Lord is this.— Wm H[arris] Pretending Religion, wearied me with desires that I should admit him and others into fellowship of my purchase. I yielded and agreed that the place should be for such as were destitute (especially for Conscience Sake) and that each person so admitted should pay 30/ country pay, towards a town stock, and myself have £30 toward my charges, which I have had £28. in broken parcels in 5 years." [18]

The phrase "town stock" is never made entirely clear as to its intended use. It appears not to have been used for schools, bridges, roads or other community improvements, although sparseness of record may account for such omission. He continued,

> "This sum I Received, And in love to my Freindes, And with Respect to a Towne, And place of Succor for the destressed as afore said, I doe Acknowledge the Said Sum, And payment, as full Sattisfaction." [19]

Both the plan of payment and the amount had been agreed upon in consultation with the settlers. No one seems to have objected. Such an arrangement was natural enough and fair enough for a small group of something less than a score, who called themselves friends, but its workability would lessen as the number mounted.

Formal record of this land allotment appears in the document known as the Initial Deed, so called because only the initials of the co-owners appear. Herein Roger Williams stated that he

"Doe freely and fully pass grant and make over Equall Right and power of Injoying and dispossing the Same grounds and lands, unto my loveing Friends and Neighbours [their initials appear here] and Such others as the Major part of us shall admitt unto the same fellowship of Vote with us." [20]

These twelve proprietors were a joint company, but they held their titles to their assigned lots under Roger Williams, not individually. It was a voluntary association and without power except of mutual agreement. This important document is undated, but it would seem to belong early in the arrangements for group living. Until lots were assigned, houses could not be built nor families sent for. There was not a day to lose. As to Roger Williams' own share, he wrote,

"Reserving only unto myselfe, one single share, equall unto any of the rest of that number, . . . and agreeing—never to lay claime nor cause any claime to be laid to any of the landes aforementioned . . . more than unto my owne single share." [21]

This deed bears also the mark of Mary Williams, wife of Roger. It was re-executed in 1661, with the names in place of the initials in the original document.

Unfortunately, for future peace the plan of governance was less definite. Roger Williams had come without a well-worked-out plan; in fact, without a conscious plan of governance at all. Why expect it of him in the light of his later assertion,

"It is not true that I was employed by any, made covenant with any, or desired any to come with me into these parts." [22]

As a result he met emergencies as they came, and then as later circumstances demanded, modified the earlier arrangements, added to them, feeling his way as he went. It was a piecemeal adventure at first, always with a high regard for individual human rights and an assumption (often false) of a comradely solicitude for the good of the whole on the part of his companions. Much was adopted from the practices of Plymouth and Massachusetts Bay. There are also suggestions that something of the fraternal spirit of the English guild administration, which he had known as a merchant taylor's son, was carried over into the organization of town and colony. The permissive element as to newcomers is one such detail. The social order in which the guild was the unit was not strongly centralized, although there was a firm loyalty within the individual group and a sense of obligation to the commonwealth of which all guilds were a part. Stronger than any other principle underneath the structure of early Providence government was the hatred of oppression and the militant resentment at meddling with personal freedom in any form.

Formal record of the incorporation of Providence as a town exists in a copy only. It bears the date of August 20, 1637, nearly a year and a half after Roger Williams and his companions had taken possession. Prior to this date, what Thomas Lechford called "a kind of government" had existed, "of their own erection." In both idea and practice, to judge from references to it in Roger Williams' letters to John Winthrop, this "kind of government" was scarcely more specific than the majority vote of the "masters of families," who "ordinarily met once a fortnight and consulted about our common peace, watch, and planting, and mutual consent have finished all matters with speed and peace." Such a loose arrangement was natural enough so long as the group was small in number and comprised of friends and adherents of the leader, with whom they were in essential agreement as to their mutual purpose, but neither speed nor peace would be possible long. For the first year the number of residents hardly exceeded thirty, with the voting "masters of families" possibly no more than eight. The organization which presently evolved out of the "mutual consent" of this small group was a continuing response to successive urgencies, not a well articulated system conceived as a whole. No wonder the going was at times rough.

The earliest extant covenant after this 1637 incorporation is a simple statement of mutual obligation.

"We whose names are hereunder, desirous to inhabit in the town of Providence, do promise to subject ourselves in active or passive

> obedience to all such orders or agreements as shall be made for public good of the body in an orderly way, by the major consent of the present inhabitants, masters of families, incorporated together into a Towne fellowship, and others whom they shall admit unto them, only in civil things." [23]

Thirteen names are signed to this instrument. What was probably the prior version of this signed covenant is preserved in a letter to John Winthrop, together with another version intended for the "young men" who were not yet admitted to the vote. In reporting the two versions of this covenant to Winthrop, Roger Williams adds, "until we heare further of the King's royal pleasure concerning ourselves," [24] suggesting that he intended to regularize his claim with the mother country as well as with the natives. This letter concerns the inevitable unrest over the admission of newcomers, some of whom were not in sympathy with the essential purposes of the controlling masters, and who were now demanding the vote.

This letter makes it quite clear that in the beginning Providence was not the democracy it has sometimes been asserted to have been, nor was such a way of government intended. The burden of Roger Williams' inquiry of John Winthrop is whether he may not properly have power of veto over the admission of those undesirable to him. The logic of his position is that since he has subjected himself to the common consent in that he will not bring into the town anyone who did not meet the approval of the group, why should anyone against his consent be "violently brought in and received." Clearly he regarded himself as proprietor in the current sense, and he was seeking to extend his permissiveness as far as personal approval of applicants. The urgency of his inquiry at this point suggests that the discontented young men were making a difficult situation.

John Winthrop's reply is not extant, but in view of the trouble he had brought on himself by a similar proposal in Massachusetts Bay Colony, he would probably, at this date, have advised against the exercise of such a veto, although agreeing in principle with the logic under it. Keeping out undesirables, or ejecting those who had smuggled themselves in unaware, had been one of the thorniest problems Massachusetts Bay Colony had undertaken to solve and they had not been successful. In spite of having been a victim of their efforts in this direction, Roger Williams' query shows that he had taken the principle along with him to Providence. Had he persisted in it, the history of Rhode Island would have been very different indeed. At this stage he seems not to have realized that a colony must grow in numbers if it would survive, and that growth by permission defeats itself, particularly when it is the younger generation that must be suppliant. Apparently he dropped the matter upon receipt of John Winthrop's reply, for nothing in his own future leadership of Providence shows him putting up barriers to those unwelcome elsewhere, no matter how undesirable their reputations announced them to be. The doors were open to troublesome Samuel Gorton whom nobody wanted, and who with his riotous company, "madded poor Providence" almost past endurance for forty years. They were open to Anne Hutchinson and her following, to William Coddington, who became a traitor to the colony, to the Quakers, who in Massachusetts thought, were most undesirable of all comers. In some way this early crisis, while the disgruntled young men raged, may have been a determining incident as to this change of view.

Although not expressly stated in their first extant covenant, liberty of conscience as to religious practice was permitted from the beginning. John Winthrop's word in an entry concerning this freedom, reads,

> "For whereas, at their first coming thither, Mr. Williams and the rest did make an order, that no man should be molested for his conscience, . . ." [25]

No *order* to this effect is extant, but apparently none was needed. Also, the word *formerly* in the phrasing of the covenant of 1640 testifies to the earlier practice.

> "Wee agree, as formerly hath bin the liberties of the towne so still, to hould forth liberty of Conscience." [26]

Subsequent covenants repeated this provision, which seems never to have been so much as challenged. When the towns of Portsmouth and Newport united in 1641, they included in their joint agreement,

"It was further ordered, by the authority of this present Courte, that none bee accounted a Delinquent for *Doctrine,* Provided, it be not directly repugnant to ye Government or Lawes established." [27]

Breach of covenant in this respect was duly punished. Some hair-splitting was indulged when defendants of Jacob Verin, who had forcibly, even brutally, restrained his wife from attending religious meetings at Roger Williams' house, contended that a wife's obedience to her husband was scriptural and should be maintained; therefore Verin, who had beaten her for this disobedience, which was a matter of conscience with him, was not guilty. Nevertheless, he was censured by the court, debarred from the freedom of Providence, and disfranchised. William Arnold, his defender, and a stolid opponent of Roger Williams, saw to it that the Williams credit suffered in this affair, which according to Arnold, was an affront to civil liberty.

"I presume," Roger Williams wrote to Governor Winthrop on this occasion, "the end is to make me odious both to the King's majesty, as also to yourselves." [28] Certainly, and the Verin affair continued to reverberate in hostile corners.

In spite of all such unfavorable reports, however, the "none bee accounted a Delinquent for *Doctrine*" provision became an invitation, and as the word spread, Providence gained new recruits, "so as those parts began to be well peopled." As John Winthrop saw it, such a provision was an invitation to the devil, who very soon "was not idle at Providence." The other side of the coin was that gain for Providence was good riddance for Boston, although the distance was too short for safety against heresy. Hence the many ruffles in their subsequent relationship. Aquidneck, the island portion of the colony, got its start in 1637 with the expulsion of the Hutchinson party. Unwelcome in Plymouth as well as barred from Massachusetts, says John Clarke in his *Ill Newes,* years afterward,

"So to a town called *Providence* we came, which was begun by one M. *Roger Williams* (who for matter of conscience had not long before been exiled from the former jurisdiction) by whom we were courteously and lovingly received." [29]

On Roger Williams' advice, William Hutchinson, John Clarke, and other leaders of the party went to Plymouth with him to learn the bounds of Plymouth jurisdiction, and being assured that Aquidneck was outside these bounds, they were content to search no further, their resolution being, as John Clarke expressed it, "to go out of them all." Roger Williams immediately arranged to buy the island from Canonicus and Miantunomi, and the little town of Pocasset (later Portsmouth) was settled. In Roger Williams' own record,

> "And because Mr. Coddington and the rest of my loving countrymen were to inherit the place, I drew up a writing in Mr. Coddington's name;"

a kindness Coddington would later forget.

In the midst of the Hutchinson-Wheelwright uproar, Samuel Gorton arrived in Boston and thence went to Plymouth, where he was speedily in trouble. Forced to "depart the colony" in fourteen days, he went next to Aquidneck, where his presence was so disrupting that Coddington together with nine others, in fact, the entire government, left and founded Newport at the other end of the island. Gorton, soon in trouble again and denied the freedom of the island, next tried Providence, and when, after some stormy weeks there, he was again denied settlement, he moved to Pawtuxet, subsequently the trouble zone, par excellence, of the whole colony. Undoubtedly, the all but unending troubles he caused, both within and without his own party, have resulted in harsher judgments for him than he deserved, but the exasperation John Winthrop, William Coddington, Edward Winslow, and Roger Williams suffered for his sake at least makes such verdicts understandable. There would be no peace even among his own followers while he lived. In the welcome accorded groups in trouble elsewhere lay the basis for such eventual unity of purpose as was to be achieved in Rhode Island colony, but it was a stormy process and also a long time coming.

To what extent, amid all the first labors of building houses, planting crops, arranging for the coming of wives and children, and ordering a government, Roger Williams' own skies had been darkened by conscious awareness of the battles ahead, is not clear, but certainly his answers to a questionnaire sent him by Governor Winthrop after some six months of exile, are the answers of a man who has no intention of retracing his steps or of coming to terms on the issues which brought about his banishment. Six months were of course too short a time for any answer to get below the surface with any of these queries; the perspective of all the years remaining to him would still have been too short, but Roger Williams complied, and returned a six month answer, professing "double diligence" in the heart-searching required.[30]

"What have you gained by your new-found practices?" was the first question. "Loss of friends, esteem, maintenance," was the reply, if gains were to be "cast up in man's exchange," but such was not his standard of measurement. Such gains he counted loss, as in the scriptural balance. Tribulation had indeed brought some consolation and a "weak victory" within himself.

To the second question, "Is your spirit as even as it was seven years since?" he replied, "I will not follow the fashion either in commending or condemning of myself." He then interpreted *evenness* as meaning a spirit of esteem and respect toward those from whom he differed and a willingness "to spend and be spent in any service (according to my conscience) for your welfares." That opportunity was already at the door. To the third question, "Are you not grieved that you have grieved so many?" the answer was yes, but that he grieved more for the "soul defilements" of God's people. "Do you think the Lord hath utterly forsaken us?" No, but I beseech you to "remove the stumbling blocks."

Words could hardly suffice for a man to answer the next query, "From what spirit, and to what end do you drive?" Using scriptural language, Roger Williams acknowledged religion to be the goal of his life's quest, as his forty-seven more years of living would abundantly bear out. "I ask the way to lost Zion," he said. Lastly, the enigmatical question, "Would not your former condition have stood with a gracious heart?" In other words, couldn't you have stayed with us and been at peace with yourself? The answer was that as between judgment and conscience, conscience must win, for the soul that "feels a guilt hath broken bones." Practical, high-minded John Winthrop would have understood all these answers, even where he did not agree. The friendship between this exile and the head of the state which had exiled him was based on a sympathy which remained untouched by the externals of their respective positions.

A letter of the following year belongs with this six month retrospect. Hearing of a rumor that had come to him that "I am weary of my station," Roger Williams replied, "If I was to choose, I would be where I am." Everything in his subsequent life would indicate that he meant exactly what he said. This shaggy world of primeval forests, red men and freedom, was henceforth his country, and given chance after chance of preferment, position, honor elsewhere, it remained his country from choice. There would have been a far easier way, even in the wilderness, than the life of incessant battle that lay ahead of him. Only a few miles from the Slate Rock landing, was Study Hill, the retreat of William Blakston, the first white settler on Boston Neck. A scholar, Cambridge trained, a Church of England man who had taken orders, this other prickly individualist, who also had chafed under what he considered Boston's meddling ways, had settled his own peace by merely walking away to this remote spot. Here he was enjoying his freedom from the "Lord Brethren" both on Sundays and weekdays, indulging his scholar's tastes in his library, planting his orchards of "yellow sweetings" and living a friendly life with his neighbor Indians. Occasionally he preached, and the figure of this stately man riding his bull to meeting was well known to those who came by. He too lived nearly a half century in this corner of the wilderness. Such a life would have been no life at all to Roger Williams. From whatever angle his wilderness years are viewed, the life he lived here was in no way that of a recluse. His chance for action was coming in the public concern and in a way he could not have guessed.

CHAPTER ELEVEN

Roving Ambassador

DURING those same months of spring and summer, 1636, when as the "first beginner" of a colony he had been assailed day after day by problems which had no counterpart in his previous experience, another new rôle was thrust upon him quite without warning. This one was ironic in the extreme. When Massachusetts had pushed him over her borders as one dangerous to her peace, she had thought to act purely in her own interest. She acted better than she knew, also purely in her own interest. Many scores, perhaps many hundreds of men, women and children would owe their lives to the unsuspected skill of this young rebel, as he was called time after time to the "smoke-hole" councils of Indians in deadly war mood. The magistrates and ministers who had sent him away were first amazed, then humbly grateful, when in place of the recklessness, the blunt speaking, the intractable behaviors which had made him unwelcome in the Commonwealth, he displayed quite other qualities, proving himself a skillful negotiator with the canny natives, matching his foresight, his mental agility, his fearless honesty against their devious wiles, and again and again coming off victor at the councils. Massachusetts did not know the man she had exiled. Perhaps in this new rôle he did not know himself.

His preparation for this service had been incidental, not deliberate, and stretched back to his Plymouth days. Thanks to his brief residence there, he had not come to the Narragansett country as a stranger to Indians and their ways. Nor was he strange to them. "That old prince Canonicus," chief sachem of the tribe, and his nephew Miantunomi, who would soon succeed him, were already his friends. Fortunately also, he knew Massasoit, chieftain of the Wampanoags, and also understood something of the background of suspicion and enmity between his people and the Narragansetts. He knew the Narragansett distrust of Uncas, chief sachem of the Mohegans, and something of the long story of family feuds, inter-tribal jealousies, and lusty revenges which slumbered among the Pequots, fiercest and most unscrupulous of all the Indians in the region. An Indian to him was not just an Indian; he was a Pequot, a Cowesett, a Mohawk, a Nyantic, a Wampanoag, a Nipmuc, a Shawomet. In his trading operations along the Cape and inland thus far, he had dealt with members of the rank and file of all these tribes, but fortunately for what was yet to come, he had seen to it that he knew them also at the top level through their chieftains. By all this previous knowledge and direct acquaintance, he had laid foundations which would serve him well as ambassador of peace between red and red, as well as between white and red.

Among his acquired qualifications for such a rôle, his ease with the Indian language was by all odds the most important. Long before 1636 he was familiar enough with the several dialects of the region to carry him well beyond the daily exchange of courtesies, of hospitality, and of trade. He had often preached to the Indians of the Plymouth and Mount Hope regions in their own tongue. Both in Plymouth and later in Salem he had already made a substantial beginning toward assembling data for his *Key* to the Indian languages of these related tribal units. In addition to his own readiness in acquiring vocabulary, he was also enough of a linguist to recognize some of the basic laws of Indian speech and to handle its variants between one tribe and another. He had not conversed in Latin as a schoolboy, debated and declaimed in Greek and Hebrew as a university student for naught, and he knew how to use this training in practical ways. Language behavior interested him and he could catch the nuances of tribal difference as he went to and fro from one Indian settlement to another. The resulting ease and accuracy in his intercourse with them won him respect from Indian messengers, emissaries, and interpreters, with whom he was now obliged to treat. The sachems soon discovered that they could not deceive this man, and would not be deceived by him through misinterpretation. At this date no Englishman in New England was so well equipped as Roger Williams to handle their strange speech; consequently as soon as he was known to be in their territory, he was in demand at one council after another.

Need for negotiations arose almost immediately. When he arrived on the Narragansett side of the Seekonk River in the spring of 1635/36, a four year off and on war between the Narragansetts and the Pequots was just ending and the situation was still strained. Minor skirmishes and surprise attacks still went on. In midsummer an "incident" having more serious implications took place. Captain John Oldham, a white trader on Block Island, who had aroused the enmity of the Narragansetts by trading with their enemies the Pequots, was murdered in his boat by four minor chieftains of the Narragansetts. Canonicus, recognizing the seriousness of the situation, came immediately to Roger Williams to disclaim responsibility for instigating the crime, and to secure assistance in explaining the circumstances to Governor Winthrop. At this very moment a delegation of inquiry was on its way from Boston to the court of Canonicus. This delegation was received in state, and while formal assurances of continuing friendship with the English were in progress, the Pequots, always suspicious of any alliance between their enemies and the English, dispatched another delegation to Canonicus, intending to prevent just such assurances of friendship. This intent became doubly urgent when they learned that the Massachusetts Court had sent ninety men under Endecott to Block Island, had taken the Island and already advanced some distance into the Pequot country. Forthwith alliance with their Narragansett enemies became a clear necessity. At this point Governor Winthrop sent a messenger to Roger Williams, urging him to hasten with all speed to the court of Canonicus. This summons marked the beginning of his career as Ambassador of Peace without portfolio, and from this time forward his offices toward a "peaceful coexistence" between English and natives became far more than a part time responsibility.

Of this first summons, with no diplomatic victories yet behind him, he wrote, years later,

> "The Lord helped me immediately to put my life in to my hand, and scarce acquainting my wife; to ship myself, all alone in a poor canoe, and to cut through a stormy wind, with great seas, every

THE CHURCH AT HIGH LAVER WHERE ROGER WILLIAMS AND MARY BARNARD WERE MARRIED

THE PEQUOT FORT ON THE MYSTIC RIVER, CONNECTICUT From an engraving of 1637

minute in hazard of life to the Sachem's house. Three days and nights my business forced me to lodge and mix with the bloody Pequod ambassadors, whose hands and arms, me thought wreaked with the blood of my countrymen, murdered and massacred by them on Connecticut river, and from whom I could but nightly look for their bloody knives at my own throat also." [1]

His fears proved to be naught. He not only escaped personal harm, but the Pequot intent failed and his own succeeded. The Narragansetts withstood all Pequot threats and enticements, and though for three breathless days the issue hung perilously in the balance, they finally refused to join with them in any way, agreeing instead to an alliance with the English. Not all the credit for this shift belonged to Roger Williams, but unmistakably he could claim a share. The Narragansetts feared Pequot treachery and had been only half willing to risk an alliance with them. Roger Williams increased this fear in their minds. They also feared English powder, and he gave them added reasons to fear it. They decided that it was safer to be on the English side. Throughout the discussions Canonicus had been hardest to convince, for he preferred any such arrangement to be pure Narragansett. The odds, however, were against him and he yielded. As early as 1636 the shadow of eventual surrender to the whites, if not extinction, was on the Indian race and the older sachems knew it. Moreover, Canonicus had learned well before this date that he could trust Roger Williams, but he did not trust the English as a race. It is not too much to say that in return Roger Williams loved Canonicus, but that he neither loved nor trusted the Indians as a race. When he knew them better, as he was to say later, he would trust them less.

The geographical position of the three powerful Indian nations which separated Providence from Massachusetts increased the hazards from Pequot treachery. Nearest to Providence was the territory of the Narragansetts, who occupied a strip extending as far as the Pawtuxet River. Then came the Pequots, most formidable of the three to the English, and most inclined to hostility toward their Indian neighbors. Their land extended as far as the Pequot River, beyond which the Mohegans occupied the area stretching as far as the Connecticut River. Because of their middle position, the Pequots felt obliged either to subjugate one or both of their rival Indian nations or else to form an alliance with one or both of them against the English. They preferred, in spite of long-standing jealousies and antagonisms, that because of their great strength, this alliance should be with the Narragansetts. It was just this alliance that Roger Williams had succeeded in preventing.

The treaty was duly concluded, but it did not bring an end to "incidents" of violence, each one to threaten war afresh. The murder of Oldham was soon followed by the murder of six other English, this time by Pequots, and in the spring of 1637 by two more and the capture of two women. In addition, the Pequots made continual forays into Massachusetts and Connecticut, burning houses and barns, shooting cattle, trapping horses, always secretly and always with no harm to themselves. We need not come to battle with them, they said; only lie in wait and shoot them as they go about their business, and they will soon be forced to leave the country and Indians not exposed to much hazard. Their plan was long-term total destruction of the English, either through tormenting them past endurance, so that they would withdraw voluntarily, or if the Pequots could eventually win the Narragansetts as allies, to exterminate them in war. To this end they kept on, first with one design and then another, each time hoping afresh to break the Narragansett alliance with the English.

By early fall, 1636, they were again active toward accomplishing this design. Word also came that the Mohawks had killed several English at Saybrook. "I hope it is not true," [2] Roger Williams wrote Governor Winthrop, but it was true. Meanwhile Connecticut authorities were much aroused, and each succeeding report from the outposts confirmed their fear that war was coming. By spring, 1637, plans were in the making on both sides, Pequots against English and Narragansetts together. In March Miantunomi sent a Pequot's hand to Winthrop to signify that the Narragansetts would do their part in their alliance with the English. These dead hands were never a "pleasing sight" to Roger Williams, as he remarked more than once.

Tension increased on all fronts until May 1st, when the Hartford Court declared an offensive war on the Pequots. Straightway Captain John Mason with his ninety men began his march toward the Pequot Fort on the Mystic River, collecting Indian reinforcements as he went. Uncas, sachem of the Mohegans in revolt against Sassacus, a Pequot, contributed a hundred men and went along. Roger Williams hastened to the court of Canonicus and found him in sour humor. He thought to blame the English for sending a plague which had killed some Narragansetts, and even accused them of plotting against his own life. Quite probably Pequot propaganda was to blame for both accusations. After a considerable time, Roger Williams succeeded in sweetening him somewhat and the two men talked of plans. In an immediate report sent to Harry Vane, still in the Governor's chair, and to John Winthrop, Deputy Governor, he stressed the necessity of acting "with speede" and listed nine observations "which you may please (as cause may be) to consider and take notice of." [3]

He ended this detailed report characteristically with the suggestion that Canonicus "would gladly accept of a box of eight or ten pounds of sugar, and indeed he told me he would thank Mr. Governor for a boxfull." Give it to him. He reported in another letter that he had given the sachem his own sugar supply "in the depth of winter and his sickness." [4] The alliance between the Narragansetts and the English was not won by sugar, but as for Roger Williams' share in it, it was won and maintained in part by such an understanding of the workings of this sachem's mind as the small favor of a gift of sugar might suggest. A few days later he repeated the suggestion, adding that Miantunomi likes powder. Give it to him. His suggestions were also practical down to small details. When some Narragansetts were hurt in the Mystic River battle because they were not easily recognized as allies, "You may please therefore to provide some yellow or red for their heads," he wrote. Such care with details has frequent example in these letters.

During the first two weeks of May, 1637, one council followed hard on another. Miantunomi "with a great train" came to Roger Williams' house in Providence and there "kept his barbarous court." "He takes some pleasure to visit me," Roger Williams reported, "and sent me word of his coming over again eight days hence." [5] The suggested picture of this occasion and various others like it invites the imagination. No house was large enough to entertain such a company, even if they had deigned to come inside. Very probably they were accommodated close by, in a space temporarily enclosed with poles, covered with mats and furnished with a hole in the center to let out the smoke. In this enclosure the sachem lay on a mat in the place of honor, his nobility hunched up around him in a double or triple circle, knees touching chins and the Indians sitting so close together that two of them occupied less than the space of one white man. "Every man hath his pipe of their *Tobacco,* and a deepe silence they make, and attention give to him that speaketh." [6] These speeches were sometimes an hour or more in length, and punctuated with "very emphaticall speech" and "great action." Not once but many times this tiny outpost of Providence witnessed such a scene around "Master Williams' " house.

On the May, 1637, occasion Miantunomi was easier to convince than Canonicus had been. He accepted Roger Williams' explanations of delay in English preparations, and together the two men mapped out a plan of action which was immediately forwarded to Governor Vane and John Winthrop. A diagram of the Pequot positions had been sent previously. The details of this memorandum have the crispness of a military directive, with reasons assigned for each movement of the soldiers. Roger Williams' strategy was psychological as well as military. Of a certain movement of Miantunomi's troops he wrote,

> "It will at present wedge them in from any starting aside until your forces shall follow; if they speed, it will weaken the enemy and distress them, being put by their hopes: as also much enrage the Pequots for ever against them, a thing much desirable." [7]

The decisive battle of the war was fought ten days later. This was the second engagement of the campaign, the first having been a successful attack on Block Island by Miantunomi. Captain Mason with his ninety men, Uncas with his hundred Mohegans, Captain Underhill from Massachusetts and Miantunomi returning from Block Island arrived at the Pequot Fort on the Mystic River on May 25th at nightfall, made a surprise attack by night, set the fort on fire and slew some seven hundred Pequots. Butchered them, in fact, for this was a battle after the Indian fashion. In its ghastly and inhuman details, it well deserved Captain Mason's own remark of the Indian slaughter of Indians in the minor engagement several days later.

"Indeed it did hardly deserve the Name of Fighting," he wrote. Neither did this one.

When Mason's troops had arrived, after marching all day, they made camp in a swamp between two hills, "keeping great Silence, supposing we were very near the Fort. . . . The Rocks were our Pillows; yet Rest was pleasant: The Night proved Comfortable, being clear and Moon Light." [8] In the stillness their sentinels could hear the Pequots singing until midnight. Before day they marched the remaining two miles to the Fort, where "commending ourselves to God [we] divided our Men," one group at each of the two entrances. A dog barked; an Indian called out, "Owanx!! Owanx!!" (Englishmen! Englishmen!) and the fight was on. The Indians were taken completely by surprise. The English leaders forced their way in and "fell on with courage, . . . but being straitened for room, because of the wigwams," Captain Mason gave order, "We must Burn them." The fort was surrounded, the mats covering the wigwams were kindled, the wind carried the flames and those inside had no chance. Those who dared to come forth were killed with the sword. Those who crept under their beds fared worse. Those trying to escape "ran as men most dreadfully amazed," some of them into the "very Flames." "Thus were the Stout Hearted spoiled, having slept their last Sleep." [9] Only seven were taken captive; seven escaped; some seven hundred were burned alive, women and children along with warriors. The victors were horrified at their own success by such means. No wonder Captain Underhill wrote, "Great and doleful was the bloody sight to the view of young soldiers that never had been in war." And not to young soldiers only. Yet the victors searched their Bibles and referred their critics to the wars of David. "We had sufficient light from the Word of God for our proceedings," they said and believed it. The Pequot war was over.

But as Leift Gardener, one of the reporters of this grim battle, remarked, "Policy is needful in wars as well as strength," and had this Mystic River slaughter not been followed by immediate and successful negotiations leading to a treaty, even this major victory would have lost its decisiveness. In these negotiations Roger Williams was the key figure, as Captain Mason had been in the military engagement. The parley was long and stormy and the details wearisome.

How many captives to this sachem, and how many to that one? Who will have this squaw and who this one? Where are the squaws who were too lame to travel, and who has made off with the promised wampum? It was a tedious business and at times another war seemed imminent, but Roger Williams stayed on duty, mediated the charges and counter charges, until November 1, when Miantunomi made an official visit to Governor Winthrop in Boston and the two men parted "upon fair terms." Except for minor uprisings, secret forays and numerous incidents yet to come, the Pequot menace was ended. Their power as a nation was broken and their plan to annihilate the English thwarted in time and for all time. Another such threat to the survival of the New England colonists would not come until King Philip put on war paint in 1675, nearly forty years later, and tragic as that war would prove to be, by that time New England would be strong enough to endure in spite of it. In the earlier decade of the mid-century, however, it is doubtful whether any event was more vital to New England's survival than this hideous success of the Mystic River battle.

Another major test of Roger Williams' skill in conciliation came late in September, 1638, when he was summoned by Connecticut to a council at Hartford between Connecticut leaders, Mohegans and Narragansetts. Connecticut colony did not feel sufficiently protected by the Narragansett treaty with Massachusetts and wished one of her own. The situation had grown suddenly tense, preparations for peace talks had been slow, and once again, Narragansett enemies sought to prevent a treaty. Connecticut insisted, against Roger Williams' advice, that the council be held at Hartford, although every mile thither was beset with dangers to the caravan making the long journey.

Roger Williams' account of this trek through the autumn woods with Miantunomi and his retinue [10] deserves to stand beside the story of Thomas Hooker's spring journey en route to the founding of Hartford in 1636, although this time no white woman was riding in a "horse-litter," no cows were being driven before them to provide milk by the way. Instead, this was a company under armed guard and vigilance by the minute. Roger Williams with his two English companions, Richard Scott and Thomas Cope, Miantunomi, his wife and children, were at the head of the line, protected by an escort of forty or fifty armed warriors on either side to "prevent sudden surprisals." Three nights they encamped in the woods, twenty or thirty fires lighted around them and armed warriors on guard. Sunday came, and in deference to Roger Williams' way of life, progress was halted; "staying for me," he wrote, "until the Lord's day was over." These were not "praying Indians," but "heathen." They were not honoring the white man's God or the Sabbath day. Their action was a tribute to one white man whom they trusted. They could pay him none higher.

Arrived in Hartford, the party met with Connecticut leaders in council, and a tripartite treaty was signed on September 21, 1638, looking toward a perpetual peace. By the terms of this agreement, no Indian tribe was to make war on another tribe without appealing to the English, who were by this treaty bound to help the side they thought was right. There were holes in such an agreement and the Indians found them, with the result that council after council would still be necessary. The subsequent trouble stemmed not so much from anti-English feeling as from anti-Narragansett, anti-Pequot, anti-Mohawk feeling, all of which kept the need for conciliation constantly in focus.

One of the most vexatious and delicate of these many minor occasions came when Janemo, sachem of the Niantics and subject to Miantunomi, plundered some Long Island Indians, who were English subjects, and while Roger Williams, at the behest of Massachusetts, was attempting to negotiate between Miantunomi and Janemo, four Plymouth white men murdered a Narragansett messenger. No incident of all his ambassadorship called for more patience and tact than these two episodes which had occurred almost simultaneously. One might have thought from the ensuing uproar that a whole tribe had been slaughtered. "The Indeans sent for Mr. Williams & made a greeveous complainte . . . fearing that the English would fall upon them," wrote William Bradford. Massachusetts and Plymouth also both appealed to him to prevent another tribal war. "But Mr. Williams pacified them," William Bradford continued, "and tould them they should see justice done upon the offenders;"[11] thus one more crisis was passed.

This sentence in William Bradford's account of one affair could be written over many similar proceedings of these years. It should be written in capitals. Was this man who could bring such an uproar to a peaceful conclusion the troublemaker who only a short time before had been thought so dangerous to colony peace that he had deserved banishment, or was it someone else by the same name? What had happened? Who had been wrong? It is easy, too easy, to oversimplify the answer, and perhaps one should not be tempted to reply. If a hint toward an answer may be ventured, however, it might be that the change in him had something to do with the life and death necessity for concrete action in a situation which depended on him alone: possibly something also with an almost untrammeled initiative in devising such action, and with the confidence and respect shown him by both sides, while plans were in the making. Instead of being silenced, he was listened to, and somewhere in these desperate procedures, he had learned to listen likewise, and when he spoke, not to speak out of turn. He who knew no fear, had learned caution, quietness, respect for those from whom he differed. When he saw that "the Busines is ravelld and needs a patient and gentle hand to rectifie Misunderstanding of each other and Misprisions," he became patient and gentle and the ravelling ceased. He handled delicate situations delicately.

Did freedom from outside authority make part of the difference? Did the magnitude of the responsibility thrust upon him awaken powers he did not know he possessed? Back in Essex William Laud had "pursued him out of the land." In Boston he had been suspect almost from the day he arrived; in Salem, in Plymouth, and then back in Salem again, he had been unwelcome. There had been no room for Roger Williams in New England. Even in his own house he might not speak freely to his friends. There had been no audience for his opinions, except as these might condemn him. But here in the Narragansett country "The Indeans sent for Mr. Williams," and he sat with their chieftains in council. In the short space of a year the wilderness had released something in him and liberated him from something stubborn in himself. He was beginning to be a free man.

In minor episodes as in greater matters his success as a negotiator would seem to have been due first of all to his recognition that every grievance has two sides, and that the Indians as well as English were entitled to unqualified justice. He weighted no decision, no verdict, no plan for future action in favor of his own race, and the Indians knew that he would not. Basically, of course this meant that he considered them as equals, though barbarians. His remark,

> "From Adam and Noah that they spring is granted on all sides,"

and again,

> "Another miserable drone of Adam's degenerate seede, and our brethren by nature," [12]

suggests the antithesis in his own thought. In his own dealing he lost sight of neither half of the verdict. He treated them without either sentimentality or a breath of condescension. He knew their cupidity and they knew that he knew it. Again and again they tried to fool him, but he read their hearts and the truth came out. The situation was favorable to a mutual exchange. They also knew that he was not afraid of them and his stature increased in proportion as they gloried in their own strength and skill. He kept his promises to them to the letter, even making good the promises of his countrymen when on occasion they forgot. "Sir, for the young man that accompanies my man," he wrote, "the country may please to recompense him or I shall." "Wequash wants a Coate, Wascote and shirt." Of the two Pequot squaws, half starved, and one of them badly burned "with fire sticks," he reported, "I promised them, if they would stay at my house, and not run away, that they might be used kindly." Such details are everywhere in his letters.

In their personal need his friendliness knew no limits. Indians as well as English found their way to his door in confidence at all times, a fact more important than the list of services he rendered. His house was a council chamber, a hospital, an inn, whatever was needed at the moment. "5 or 6 Indians at my house;" "One of Uncas' men, having hurt his foot, and disabled from travel, turns unto me;" a Narragansett man, "turned in to me for lodging;" some one else "took sick" on the way, and would stay until he was well. If they needed a canoe, shelter in "foul weather," food, whatever it was, "Mr. Williams, his house" was the answer. To read the casual allusions to such services in his letters makes one wonder whether there was ever a time when his household, in addition to an Indian servant or two, did not include several more who had "turned in" for some service or other. To read between the lines in such an entry as of a Boston soldier, "neere death," but "my wife hath got him upon his legs, though very weak," is to get a true picture of more than hospitality. His heart went out to Indian children. "I have fixed mine eye on this little one with the red about his neck," he wrote about a captive in war. He would bring the child up in his own home. Of one such child it was written later, "Mr. Roger Williams hath an Indian boy who chose his master's house rather than his mother's."

There is another side to the story, and a necessary one, for the rôle he played. In all these dangerous dealings time after time, he learned many things about Indians and grew realistic and canny in his negotiations with them. "Their treacheries exceed Machievelli's," he reported. He learned that messengers could not always be trusted. They kept letters a long time, and if they suspected a letter concerned themselves, they suppressed it. He learned how to get information from them indirectly. When Wequash, a Pequot, who had gone over to the Narragansetts, was lodged at his house together with the messengers who had abused him, Roger Williams wrote to John Winthrop that he had caused them "solemnly to parley of what I knew was grievance betwixt them," took notes on all they said and whatever else "I could any way pick out from either of them, concerning ourselves the English, or the Pequots, or themselves," and here it all is. Another time when awaiting a reply from the sachems, he held four Indians hostages at his house until the answer came.

> "I am not yet turned Indian, to believe all barbarians tell me . . .
> I commonly guess shrewdly at what a native utters,"

he wrote, and much came of these guesses. He learned to deal with them "wisely as with wolves endowed with men's brains." [13]

He knew their passions and the cruelties of which they were capable, their fierce pride, their inability to endure defeat or subjugation. When some Pequot chieftains arrived at Mystic too late for the battle and saw their fort in flames, they stamped and tore their hair in their rage. To parley with such men one must know how far they could be pushed and what restraints they could endure.

"Poor wretches," he called some of the Pequot victims, but they must be dealt with justly as human beings. "If they have deserved death, 'tis sin to spare," but if not, why not train them up to labor, and after a due time set them free, "for perpetual slavery they cannot endure."

He took no credit to himself for any of these services. "God preserved me," he wrote at the time of the Narragansett-English treaty of 1636, "and enabled me to break in pieces their design." Late in life, as he looked back over his own story, he still took no credit. In a letter to the Massachusetts General Court, he wrote,

> "It hath pleased the Lord so to order it, that I have been more or less interested and used in all your great transactions of war or peace, between the English and the natives, and have not spared purse, nor pains, nor hazards, (very many times), that the whole land, English and natives, might sleep in peace securely." [14]

There it was, and he meant it. God had done the rest. He would not have disagreed with the verdict of Massachusetts leaders that the great victory over the Pequots at Mystic River owed less to the skill of one captain in war and one missionary-trader in council than to the fact that the day before had been kept as a fast day. "It happened the day after our general fast," was in reality the official record of this great victory.

The prolonged absences, the many negotiations these first years required had all but disrupted the trading operations upon which he was now mainly dependent for a livelihood. They also sometimes delayed the planting and harvesting of crops and the care of many other interests vital to pioneer living. As to leisure for study and thought, there was none. Indeed, if such leisure were requisite to life as he wished it, the wilderness was the last place on earth where it might be found. The tenseness in inter-tribal relations, and between white men and red, also made labors for the "natives' souls," for which he had longed, all but impossible. The Narragansett country had been turned into a battlefield.

Providence settlement also suffered from these prolonged and frequent absences. A strong hand and a clear brain had been critically needed during these months, but that hand and brain had been busy elsewhere. As a result, almost before the little settlement had even begun to feel itself a unit, it had begun to fall apart. There were reasons for disunity in the very geography itself. Mainland and island were two settlements, not one, and their separateness could not be easily combatted by canoe and rowboat. The two separate halves had been settled at different times and by diverse groups, living too near each other to develop very far separately, and too distant to make one unit. The loose governmental structure had not welded the separate units into one body in the beginning, and once having pioneered in their own way, they were reluctant to change. All who came had previously suffered oppression in some form, and were therefore sensitive to the first breath of authority over them. The leading spirits were stout individualists, inclined to force their wills on the more yielding. All these causes for disunity were deeply and loudly personal in consequence.

During the relatively peaceful years after the signing of the tripartite treaty of 1638, the Providence situation grew worse instead of better. Semi-security from Indian disorders brought new settlers who demanded space. Some of these comers, in their desire for land and more land, presently forgot why they had come or the welcome they had received. Moreover, Massachusetts Bay Colony, Plymouth and Connecticut began to look southward toward these unchartered, fertile lands and wide boundaries. Trouble lay ahead, deep trouble, from pressures both within and without. The story of Rhode Island fighting for her lands against these pressures is a story by itself, intricately tangled in its details, clear in its motivations; a story of years of incessant strife which at every turn begot more strife. Not a pretty story in such terms, but one that takes high ground again and again in the selfless determination of men who could forget their own interests in a great human cause.

This great land battle determined many things for Roger Williams, not only in his leadership of the colony, but in his personal life as well. One of the first consequences and also the most important was his return to England in 1643. The occasion recalled in large outline, goes back to the coming of Samuel Gorton in 1638. He had been in trouble at Plymouth and came to Aquidneck for protection and a haven. In trouble thereafter at Portsmouth, Newport, and Providence, by 1643 he had moved to Pawtuxet, where William Arnold and his party had settled. Trouble came quickly here also.

Meanwhile Arnold, by connivance with the local sachems, Saconomoco, a Narragansett in rebellion against Canonicus, and Pomham, also in rebellion, had secured what he called a confirmatory deed to a large tract of land which he claimed had been included in the mutilated portion of the "Towne Evidence." This tract included the land originally bought by Roger Williams from Canonicus and Miantunomi and divided by him among his twelve associates, of whom William Arnold was one. Saconomoco had re-sold it illegally. Annoyed by the behavior of Samuel Gorton, Arnold twice appealed to Massachusetts for protection against him, and was twice told that there could be no such protection given without voluntary submission to her jurisdiction. William Arnold took the hint, and on September 8, 1642, together with his son, his son-in-law and Robert Cole submitted himself and his lands to Massachusetts colony. Six months later, Saconomoco and Pomham did likewise. Samuel Gorton, once banished from Massachusetts, and fearing a second such verdict, bought the tract known as Shawomet and moved thereon with his company.

The submission of Arnold and the Indian sachems of their now very large tract, was of course precisely what Massachusetts colony wanted, and as John Winthrop reported, her acquiescence was designed "to draw in the rest of those parts, either under ourselves or Plimouth, who now lived under no government, but grew offensive, and the place was likely to be of use to us, . . . and seeing it came without our seeking, and would be no charge to us, we thought it not wisdom to let it slip." [15] Massachusetts then sent a letter to Providence, informing her of Arnold's action and warning her to exercise no more jurisdiction in those parts.

It was now clear to both the Island and the mainland settlements, that if they were to survive as an independent colony, they must have royal warrant for their existence. The alternative was to become no more than an outpost on the fringe of Massachusetts and Plymouth. The Island towns had twice appealed to Sir Harry Vane in their own behalf, but no answer had yet come. It was time to act. Accordingly, only eleven days after Massachusetts had accepted the submission of the Arnold party, the Assembly at Newport voted to look into the possibility of an English patent for Rhode Island and the lands adjacent. As to the agent to be sent, there was no question. Roger Williams was the man.

He set forth probably in late February or early March, 1642/43, taking ship from New Netherlands, as on account of his banishment, he might not set foot in Massachusetts territory. He arrived at Long Island either shortly before or immediately after the outbreak of a serious Indian war on February 22, and while he waited for a ship, was in council with Governor William Kieft in this connection. John Winthrop's record indicating that Roger Williams had a determining part in the peace negotiations, however, is an error. There was a brief truce declared in early March, but the records show no mention of Roger Williams' offices. By his own statement when he finally sailed away,

> "Mine eyes did see that first breaking forth of that Indian war, which the Dutch began, and they questioned not to finish it in a few days, But before we weighed anchor, their bowries were in flames. Dutch and English were slaine. Mine eyes saw their flames at their towns, and the flights and hurries of men, women and children." [16]

This was the war in which Anne Hutchinson met her death, with her family, all save one, near to the Parkway which bears her name, thoroughfare of the daily thousands, of whom few now remember her stout battle for the truth as she saw it.

Roger Williams was now off to another kind of battle which would test his powers in new ways.

CHAPTER TWELVE

Linguist

On board ship he found the leisure which the wilderness had thus far denied him. He used it to write his first book, *A Key into the Language of America.* Had this been his only publication, his posterity would have been harder put to it than they now are to make him come together as an understandable human being. Once again, is this the disseminator of "newe and dangerous opinions," or someone else by the same name? Surely the man who wrote this quiet book is no incendiary, to be quickly hustled over the border lest he wreck the state. Instead, at least in these pages, he is a soft-spoken linguist, with something of the scholar's interest in language behavior, a lively enthusiasm for his subject, and a large endowment of the scholar's patience in assembling data over a long period of time and under the most untoward conditions. Also as a shipboard adventure, the mere putting into an orderly structure of these 2500 separate items, doubtless without an inch of privacy adequate to such a task, calls for the persistence and concentration of a man of the cloister, trained to quietness.

His purpose was essentially practical and is clearly so stated. First, he wished, as he says, "a private *helpe* to my owne memory, that I might not by my present absence *lightly lose* what I had so *dearely bought* in some few yeares *hardship* and *charges* among the *Barbarians.*" Second, some of his *"worthy friends,* of all sorts" needed to know the Indian language as he had needed to know it. They had frequently "importun'd" him to "afford them some helps this way." His own experience had given him the opportunity to come by these materials, and being reminded by his friends "what pitie it were to bury those *Materialls* in my *Grave* at land or Sea," he had "resolved (by the assistance of *the most High*) to cast them into this *Key, pleasant* and *profitable* for *All,*" but especially "for my *friends* residing in those parts." [1] The book is a "rude lumpe" drawn into this form at sea, but here it is, and may it be useful. These are hardly the words of a scholar, dedicated to pushing out the boundaries of knowledge for its own sake, but of a practical man, who has put his own discoveries into a convenient handbook for the everyday use of himself and his friends.

He meant exactly what he said. There is not a shadow of ambitious authorship, of literary consciousness, or more than a hint of the importance such a book might have for later times or for a wider audience. "I have not heard of the like," he says, in addressing his "Deare and Well-beloved Friends and Countrymen, since it pleased God to bring that mighty *Continent* of *America* to light," [2] and so far as a book in English on the language of the American Indian is concerned, neither had anyone else heard of the like at this date. This *Key* is the first comprehensive book-length attempt in English to put the Indian language into print. It preceded John Eliot's Indian Bible by twenty years—fortunately early enough so that the various tribal dialects he was to deal with had not yet been sufficiently modified by interchange between English and Indians to have a pidgin character.

The title page of the first edition in the Thomason collection bears the date September 7, 1653, suggesting that the manuscript found its way into Gregory Dexter's printing office very soon after Roger Williams had reached London. It gave the censor no pause. On the last page he wrote,

> "*I Have read over these thirty Chapters of the* American Language, *to me wholly unknowne, and the* Observations, *these I conceive inoffensive; and that the Worke may conduce to the happy end intended by the* Author.
>
> "Io. Langley"

The fact that Roger Williams was an unknown writer at this date was no impediment to bookstall demands, for the widespread interest in the American Indians made any new array of facts concerning them immediately welcome to English readers. For those concerned with their Christianization, this *Key* answered a need already acknowledged to be critical. President Dunster of Harvard College, Thomas Lechford, lawyer, and other far-seeing ones had already realized, and said so, that preaching to Indians in English was all but futile. Missionaries must know the native tongue or they did but beat the air. Accordingly, this little handbook was commended as meeting an urgent need. Roger Williams' name on the title page would also conduce to his success in the charter business, although he did not know that when he sat down on shipboard to frame this "lump."

His equipment for the undertaking was no more than the standard university training in the ancient languages, particularly Greek, Latin and Hebrew, a speaking knowledge of at least French and Dutch among the modern ones, the blessing of an exceedingly good ear, and best of all some twelve years of fairly continuous association with Indians who knew little or no English. In his own word, "(out of desire to attaine their Language) I have run through varieties of *Intercourses* with them Day and Night, Summer and Winter, by Land and Sea." [3] The result was a compendium considerably richer than any irreducible minimum of day to day exchange could have been. Of his own title he wrote, "A little *Key* may open a *Box*, where lies a *bunch* of *Keys*." [4] Truly spoken, and every key in this bunch unlocks the door to something more than an aboriginal language.

His practical purpose led him to present his material in the form of a phrase book rather than a dictionary or formal grammar and in this choice he was wise. Neither a dictionary nor a grammar would have been "so accommodate to the Benefit of all," as these thirty-two chapters made up of blocks of words, phrases and more often whole sentences, classified as to subject and occasion, and often cast in simple dialogue form after the fashion of a travellers' guide. The structure of such a book almost makes itself. Once one has started with Salutations, he proceeds to Food, Shelter, Weather, Land and Sea, Sun, Moon and Stars, Money and how to count it, the Days of the Week, the Directions of the compass, Birds and Beasts, Human Relationships, Buying and Selling, and so on down the list. Such a handbook naturally puts the accent on strangeness, with implied comparison to that which is familiar in each of the several classifications. This is precisely the effect of this *Key*. One lays it down, having in imagination looked in on the Narragansetts, and seen them in action "from their *Birth* to their *Burialls*." It is a story, told with spirit and warmth, and quite untouched by controversy. There is a lightness and youthfulness of touch, an element of surprise and eager interest, as though the writer himself were new come to these strange people.

Models for such books are plentiful in all ages. For the phrase lists of this one, Roger Williams probably owed something, consciously or not, to the Latin-English conversation manuals written by Renaissance schoolmasters for the agonized use of boys compelled by school regulations to use only Latin throughout their ten-hour school day. A certain *Phraseologia Puerilis,* compiled by Master Clarke of the Free School of Lincoln may speak for the type. Made up of a hodgepodge of everyday details, it served for purposes of talk on an A B C level for twelve-year-olds, albeit talk conceived by an unimaginative schoolmaster. The adult speaks in it oftener than the boy. "Read on where you left off last. Stand bare, Put off your hat. Shut the door. Go to bed. Make haste. To be a laughing stock. Who heard the clock? I am as hungry as a horse. I am angry with you. I fished faire and caught a frogge." [5] These books typically abounded in clichés: as white as snow, as soft as silk, as black as night; also in familiar proverbs, such as pride goeth before a fall, with an occasional surprise, "Fair words butter no parsnips." No English schoolboy was innocent of the help such a book supplied, and if Roger Williams had not worn out his own copy in his school days, he may still have had such a book in his library. In any case he would not have forgotten it.

His own exhibit of the Narragansett tongue consists in some 2500 separate items or speech units, most of them elaborately compounded of many syllables after the fashion of all primitive languages. As presented, this body of material is sufficiently explicit to enable a modern linguist in many cases to distinguish roots from prefixes and suffixes, and to catch hints of a certain typical agglutinative structure in the compounding process. However, even though Roger Williams had been interested in studying such aspects of language behavior, it was still two centuries too early for such analysis to have been expected of him. Seventeenth century English linguistic scholars had not yet grasped the possibility of what is now called the science of language. In their thought the origin of all language difference was Babel. The parentage of all language was Hebrew, which would of course be the language of Paradise. This assumption put them on the alert to discover similarities between each new language they came to know and the Hebrew. Roger Williams notes such occasional resemblances to Hebrew and also to Greek, but with him such interest was incidental only.

He also pays scant attention to one of the historical dilemmas of the hour concerning the Indians; namely, how to derive them from the sons of Noah, for in the opinion of various writers of his day, unless this derivation could be established, the Indians as a race could hardly exist on the drowned earth. He speaks of discussing the matter of their origins with the Dutch governor of New Netherlands, who "drew their *Line* from *Iceland,*" and also of talking with other "Wise and Judicious men," but this was not a main interest with him. Nor were the nature of language, its remote origins, its interrelations areas to which his thought inclined. His emphasis was neither analytical nor philosophical. He was thinking of language as communication, and in one specific example, the "Barbarous and Rockie speech" of the Narragansetts. He is saying in effect no more than here is a storehouse of words and phrases which I have used. It may help you also to carry on life in the Narragansett country. As he wrote it down, he heard it, and hoping that his readers might hear it also, he was "at the paines and charges to Cause the Accents, Tones, or sounds to be affixed;" his reason, "because the Life of Language is in the Pronuntiation." [6]

For the *Observations* on Indians and their ways which make up about half of each of the thirty-two chapters, he also had numerous models, ready to hand. Thomas Hariot had begun it in 1588, with the section on the "Nature and Manners of the People" in his official report of the Raleigh expedition, and others had followed him in their accounts of America ever since.[7] Roger Williams had been familiar with these books since his London boyhood and his indebtedness to them is apparent on page after page of the *Key*. At the same time his informality and easy reminiscence make his *Observations* something very different from these earlier categorical arrays. Every page of his book is full of life, motion, color, and there is little of the encyclopedia about it. Read without the word lists, it becomes a sequence of personal experiences to which the lists supply an implicit dialogue, dealing with the same detail of Narragansett life. In addition, it has more to offer as to the day to day life of Roger Williams himself as pioneer, trader, and sometimes preacher, through the first twelve years of his wilderness life than anything else that has survived from his pen. Much of it is frankly autobiographical, although clearly without any such intention. He is merely attempting to clarify his observations by recounting his experiences in the first person, as was completely natural. The result of this direct personal recital, in addition to the fresh vividness it provides as to the Indians and their ways, is that it reveals the narrator's inner springs of thought and action far more simply and clearly than his later controversial writings, complicated as these are by devious argument and counter-argument, and often emotionally overcharged, as he aimed his thrusts at a straw antagonist or at his perennial real one, John Cotton. By comparison in spirit and purpose with these justly more famous books, the *Key into the Language of America* is a quiet book, spoken in a conversational tone to a small group of "worthy friends" eager to hear and to know.

Each page is a drama and as its particular scene is reenacted before us in the wilderness setting, we feel the presence of the actors as they go about their daily lives.

Customer and trader bargain together. Have you any cloth? Thick cloth, thin cloth, black, red, or inclining to white? They like sad colors best. What of the quality? "woolie on both sides" or "bare of wool?" Open it up, shake it, feel it, fold it up. How much shall I give you? You ask too much. It is dear. You are very hard. No, it is cheap. It is worth it. Let us agree. Do not make adoe about a penny.

A hunter tells of his skill. How many have you killed? I have killed two, three, four, ten, twenty. I must go to my traps: old traps, new traps. I have found a deer. It is lean. It is fat. It is sweet. It smells ill.

War comes. Are you afraid? I fear none. Let us pursue. They fly from us. The Pequots are slaine. We are confererates. Save me. I am shot. I am dying. Quarter! Quarter! Mercy! Mercy!

We look in on a peace conference. Who drew the first bow or fired the first shot? He shot first at me. I scorne or take it indignation. Let us cease arms. Let us parley. Let us make friends. Remember your wives and children. I love you. My heart is true.

In the wigwam. I am very sick. Bind my head. I have a feaver. I cannot eat. I am all on fire. I shake for cold. I shake as a leafe. Cover me. Reach me the drink.

The missionary-trader speaks. Why do you paint yourself? Wipe off. You spoile your Face. The God that made you will not know you.

In each of these word groups we hear "the propriety of language in common things." No mere sojourner between one boat and another could have looked in on so rich a panorama of Narragansett living as these brief sentences and phrases suggest. Back of them are miles of journeys, not of an observer seeking copy, but of one who has lived in these woods, journeyed along these paths with these people, eaten with them, slept by their fires, had abundant conversings with them, shared wilderness dangers, ministered to them and been ministered unto. The word brings back the experience. After the word for "Parch'd meale, which is a readie very wholesome food, which they eate with a little water, hot or cold," he writes,

> "I have travelled with neere 200 of them at once, neere 100 miles through the woods, every man carrying a *little Basket* of this at his *back,* and sometimes in a hollow Leather Girdle about his middle sufficient for a man three or foure daies."

Content with this one detail of the suggested picture, he stamps it with his own signature, as it were, by adding,

> "With a *spoonfull* of this *meale* and a *spoonfull* of water from the *Brooke,* have I made many a good dinner and supper." [8]

Again, at the end of the chapter on *Eating and Entertainment,*

> "Many a time, and at all times of the night (as I have fallen in travell upon their houses) when nothing hath been ready, have themselves and their wives, risen to prepare me some refreshing." [9]

After the phrase *under a tree,* he recalls a custom and an experience to illustrate it.

"I once in travell lodged at a house, at which in my return I hoped to have lodged againe there the next night, but the house was gone in that interim, and I was glad to lodge under a tree." [10]

Of Travelling brings back another reminiscence.

"I have heard of many *English* lost, and have oft been lost my-selfe, and my selfe and others have often been found, and succoured by the *Indians.*"

"I have often been guided twentie, thirtie, sometimes fortie miles through the woods, a straight course, out of any path." [11]

"It is admirable to see, what paths their naked hardned feet have made in the wildernesse in most stony and rockie places." [12]

The verses which conclude each chapter exhibit nothing more commendable than obedient practice in Grammar School Objective, No. 22, in Brinsley's *Ludus Literarius,* which reads, "To write verses extempore of any ordinary Theames." Roger Williams was no poet and his efforts in kind have no merit beyond the necessary four lines, and because thus limited, a little less of the clutter so characteristic of many of his over-busy prose sentences. The quatrain form also tempted him to a neat didactic observation in which the red man comes off better than the white.

"God gives them sleep on Ground, on Straw,
on Sedgie Mats or Boord:
When English softest Beds of Downe,
sometimes no sleep afoord." [13]

As one might expect, the longest chapter concerns their religion. It contains some surprises, in comparison with the current view. Shocked as he naturally was at the plurality of their gods (he had once counted thirty-seven by name) and at the grossness of many of their religious rites, he did not pronounce their religion the work of devils and witches. Other ministers did so without qualification. "I believe they are *lost,*" he said, and yet he hoped that somehow "(in the Lord's holy season) some of the wildest" of them might know salvation according to the Christian way. "With how little *Knowledge* and *Grace* of Christ the Lord may save," he did not assume to know; "therefore will neither *despaire,* nor *report* much." [14] Surprisingly for one so literal in biblical interpretation, he recognized certain fundamentals of religious belief in their body of tradition and honored them. "He that questions whether God made the World, the *Indians* will teach him," [15] he said, and he built on such basic essentials in his own preaching to them.

Unfortunately, no sermon of his to them has survived among his papers, but the chapter on Religion provides some suggestions as to approach and method which may have been typical. The telling of the creation story may stand as one such example. "Many hundreths of times," he wrote, "great numbers of them have heard with great delight, and great convictions," while he taught them, catechism wise, thus:

Friend, I will aske you a Question.
Speake on.
Who made the Heavens?
The Earth, the Sea?
The World.
Some will answer Tatta' I cannot tell, some will answer Manittowock the Gods.

How many gods bee there?
Many, great many.
Friend, not so.
There is onely one God.
You are mistaken.
You are out of the way.
A phrase which much pleaseth them, being proper for their wandring in the woods, and similitudes greatly please them.

Friend, I will tell you newes.
One onely God made the Heavens, &c.
Five thousand yeers agoe.

And upwards.
He alone made all things.
Out of nothing.

In six dayes he made all things.
The first day Hee made the Light.
The second day Hee made the Firmament.
The third day hee made the Earth and Sea.
The fourth day he made the Sun and the Moon.
Two great Lights.
And all the Starres.
The fifth day hee made all the Fowle.
In the Ayre, or Heavens.
And all the Fish in the Sea.
The sixth day hee made all the Beasts of the Field.

Last of all he made one
Man
Of red Earth,
And call'd him Adam,
or red Earth.

Then afterward, while Adam,
or red Earth slept,
God tooke a rib from Adam,
or red Earth,
And of that rib he made One
Woman,

And brought her to Adam.
When Adam saw her, he said,
This is my bone.
The seventh day hee rested,
And therefore Englishmen
Worke six dayes.
On the seventh day they
praise God.[16]

The *Genesis* story won the Indians, as one might expect, and Roger Williams did not spoil the beautiful simplicity and dignity of it in the telling. They could also understand it, for they had one to match, which someone would always volunteer to add. One of their gods had made man out of a stone and also woman, but disliking them both, he had broken the stone in pieces and made another man and woman out of a tree. These two were "the Fountaines of all mankind." If a stone or a tree, why not "red Earth" for Adam and a rib for Eve? It was the preacher's chance. They could also understand the miracles of Jesus. One of their gods, "having a broken resemblance to the Son of God," had also walked on the water. "We have heard this before," they would say, and then some-one would tell the Indian tradition.

It is a revealing picture, and on both sides. If a single mural were to be painted of Roger Williams' wilderness life, this would be one to choose. A clearing in the forest, with wigwams in the near distance and dark trees behind. The huddled, attentive Narragansetts, sitting "in a round" very close together, the firelight on their faces, an expression of solemn wonder on every face, as they listened to this white man who did not lie to them. At this moment they seemed like satisfied children, rather than warriors, as they followed his every word. The discourse ended, they did not hold back their doubts as to the white man's God. He tells of one time when after he had "discoursed of many points of God, of the creation, of the soule, of the danger of it, and the saving of it," an Indian listener assented; "but when I spake of the rising againe of the body, he cryed out, I shall never believe this." At another time, when he, being over-wearied with travel, lay down to sleep in the wigwam after his "discourse," a skeptic among his listeners said, when did he see a soule goe to heaven or Hell? [17] In Indian tradition, souls went to the Southwest instead, and the direction was not subject to change.

Roger Williams kept no list of such questions as John Eliot often did, but no doubt he had to meet the same stolid literalness whenever his teaching left the concrete level. Their Narragansett language had no words for spiritual truth. Following the example of Canonicus, he could take a stick and break it into ten pieces to show them that they had broken their promises to the English ten times, but when such demonstration would not serve, he was helpless. Some of their questions as reported by John Eliot underscore the missionary's difficulty in illuminating examples.

> Do they dwell in severall houses in heaven, or altogether, or what do they?
> How do you know what is done in heaven?
> Doth the Devill dwell in us as we dwell in a house?
> Shall we see God in heaven?
> When a Soule goes to heaven, what doth it say when it comes there, and what doth a wicked soule say when it commeth into Hell?
> I see why I must fear Hell, and do so every day. But why must I feare God?
> Why is God so angry with Murtherers?
> If God made Hell in one of the six dayes, why did God make Hell before Adam had sinned?
> I finde I want wisdom, what shall I do to be wise?
> Why must we love our enemies, and how shall we doe it?
> If a man be almost a good man, and dyeth; whither goeth his soule?
> If all the world be burnt up, where will Hell be?
> Why did not God kill the Devill that made all men so bad, God having all power?
> Whither their little children goe when they dye, seeing they have not sinned?
> Whether the devill or man were made first?
> Where is Christ now?
> Does God understand Indian prayers? [18]

From such questions, and John Eliot lists them generously, one can infer something as to his preaching, although such inferences are dangerous. The safer inference concerns the concreteness which the Indian understanding demanded.

Their localizing of all goodness in the heart gave the missionary at least one chance and he took it. Various of the questions John Eliot lists concern hard hearts and soft hearts, as does also the story of Wequash, Roger Williams' Pequot guide, whose alleged conversion got into print and was widely repeated. The story bears another repeating for the sake of Wequash's own phrasing of his inner state.

He had first learned Christian teaching during a long illness at Roger Williams' home in Providence, but had not accepted what he heard. Nevertheless, what orthodox evangelists would call *conviction* for sin followed him after he went forth cured of his illness. When Roger Williams saw him again, many months afterward, he was greeted by the Othello-like confession,

"Me so big naughty Heart, me heart all one stone." [19]

No wonder the story got into print, and when Roger Williams was in London again, he found that his countrymen had been encouraged by it in their hope for the Christianization of the red man. Roger Williams was sent for by Wequash on his deathbed, and walked two miles to comfort him. "My old friend Wequash," he called him, saying that he hoped he had been saved, but "I dare not be so confident as others."

He felt that change of heart was rare indeed among these wilderness children, and he was not content to accept mere appearances or lip service. More than once Miantunomi had discoursed with his people "of keeping the Englishmans day of worship, which I could easily have brought the Countrey to," [20] Roger Williams wrote, but he would not permit this wholesale gesture of conversion. It would have been too easy, and was not God's way. A soul must turn "from its Idolls, both of heart, worship, and conversation, before it is capable of worship, to the true and living God." It was in part his refusal to permit this outward sign of "conversion" that led English observers to speak disparagingly of Roger Williams' small results as a missionary, as compared with those of John Eliot and others who gave estimates in numbers. We know little of his preaching, but from what he was willing to say about it, apparently he made no attempt to frighten his hearers into belief by pictures of eternal damnation. Instead, he seems to have been the quiet teacher, answering their questions about God, the sun, moon, stars and the Great Water, as he might have explained these marvels to his own children.

It is also clear from this *Key* and also from his many references to Indian life throughout his letters, that to him these "savages" were not a lower order of creation, nor were they curiosities to be exhibited with mild interest or with abhorrence. To him they were his equals among God's creatures, "(their spirits in naked bodies being as high and proud as men more gallant)." Some of their practices were abhorrent in his eyes also and he knew their treachery, but he could respect their culture in its totality. Again and again he found something in it to rebuke his own. This attitude not only sets him off from most of his contemporary observers of the Indian and his ways, it also uncovers something in Roger Williams which went deeper than his training or experience. In this application as elsewhere in his thinking and acting, "the root of the matter in him" was something no one had taught him. Herein lies one clue to his greatness. As to the goals of his missionary labors with them, he would have agreed with Gandhi that religious faith does not admit of mere telling; but that it has to be lived, and once lived, it becomes "self-propagating." From what can be known of Roger Williams' own Narragansett years, one may dare assert that his best sermon to those he called "my Indian friends" was the life and example he lived among them.

From such hints of his own personal life as appear perhaps unintentionally in these pages, one may gather here and there that the wilderness life was not all Indian forays, stolen cattle, war paint, treacherous messengers, sometimes bloodshed. These made up only the warp of life, to be accepted as such, dealt with promptly, as one danger succeeded another. "Halfe inche from death;" certainly, many times, but there were long stretches in between when one might almost forget the hazards, except as these translated themselves into an attitude of unceasing vigilance. To first generation pioneers this was a lifelong attitude of which presently they were only half conscious. To their children such an attitude would be almost, as it were, congenital. They too would accept the warp of their generation and busy themselves with the woof. Could the history of the little knot of families that made up Providence during these earliest years be written in line with their own focus of thought and activity, their story, like that of most other early New England settlements, would have been only incidentally a tale of dangers, or rumors of dangers. Whatever it is that makes men venture the unknown (or be forced to accept it unasked) presently dwarfs the importance of much that those who live more safely and comfortably are likely to underscore too heavily.

As Roger Williams met the "barbarous distractions" of his near half century on the fringe of the Narragansett country, he also lived another life of study, of thought, of religious satisfactions, of inward growth, to which the outer background of his life gives little clue. His mind roamed far places; his very large correspondence with men in England, as well as in the other colonies, brought him in touch with the ongoing life of those who spoke his language; he read; he learned. The wilderness extended his view, not only by making the universe more vast to his eyes, but also by resolving its contrasts and strengthening the sense of unity in its vastness and diversity. In this unity he found a sustaining comfort. His life with the Indians also enlarged his view, and made him hospitable to ideas sharply different from his own. This should not be a hard lesson for an individualist to learn, but it was hard for Roger Williams. In the wilderness he also learned quietness, inner quietness. One of his unpoetic quatrains says it.

How busie are the sonnes of men?
How full their heads and hands?
What noyse and tumults in our owne,
And eke in Pagan lands?

Yet I have found less noyse, more peace
In wilde America,
Where women quickly build the house,
And quickly move away.[21]

In ministerial fashion he ends the book with a benediction. May the God who has mercifully preserved him through all his distresses with the Barbarians and has assisted him to "frame this poor Key," in His owne good season use it to "open a Doore." A prayer well prayed and answered in ways he did not yet know. It opened an immediate door for him as soon as his ship docked in London. It also opens a door for those who wish to understand some things in him centuries later. His leading ideas are nearly all here, to be slowly clarified and made more articulate. Present also are the determining lines of his own self-portrait. In nothing else that he wrote, except in some of his letters, would he paint it more clearly.

CHAPTER THIRTEEN

Diplomat

WITH the "dreadful Atlantick Ocean" now safely behind him, he was once again a free man among his peers. For the space of a little above a year, he would speak English instead of Narragansett, have no need of a compass, the little emergency bag of "parch'd meale," deerskin boots and an Indian chimney to dry them in at nightfall. He would parley with Puritan leaders instead of with Indian sachems, match wits on occasion with Presbyterians and Independents instead of with jealous land-grabbers at stormy town meetings. He would be at home again in his native country, and would sometimes wonder whether he had ever gone away. Inducements to stay would besiege him, and possibly he would be tempted; but unlike the two Massachusetts colony agents,[1] who were in London at this same time, he would say no to these offers, one and all. His mission was a charter for Providence Plantations, and when he took ship back to the wilderness again, he would have the charter safely in his pocket. Nor would this be all. In these months of 1643 and 1644, his life purpose and direction would be sharpened to a new goal. He would return as a recognized leader in the bitter current battle of ideas. Full days were ahead; fuller than he could yet know in midsummer, 1643, and he was ready for them.

He had arrived at a moment of crisis within a crisis, always his best time for clear thought and bold action. The Civil War had been in progress since the preceding August. The battle of Edgehill had been fought, but without victory for either side. The battle of Marston Moor was a full year away. The King was at Oxford, whence he would return to London only to die. Cromwell was at Cambridge, training his Ironsides and himself learning the ruthlessness by which battles and wars are won. On June 6th, when Roger Williams was probably still on the sea, a majority of Commons had taken covenant to support Parliament against the king. Three days later a majority of the Lords present had done likewise. Henceforth there would be no effective peace party in Parliament. On June 15th this same covenant of loyalty to Parliament against the king was taken freely in London, although possibly not one man in fifty could have stated the issues clearly.

"Both sides promises are so fair that I cannot see what it is they should fight for,"

Lady Sussex is reported to have said. She spoke for hundreds who also could not see, although they died on the battlefield for one side or the other. They only knew that England was in convulsion and that the end might be fatal.

"God put an end unto these wofull times, before they put an end to us," [2]

Thomas Fuller prayed. It was a prayer all men could pray.

Speaking for the bewildered man in the street, John Taylor, the Water Poet, had for months been reflecting the current confusion in men's minds by his serio-comic verses and broadsides which were hawked about the streets for a penny. One of these, bearing the title "Mad Fashions, Od Fashions, All out of Fashions; or, the Emblems of these distracted times," [3] suggested the upside-down-world of the moment with ridiculous literalness. It showed a church balanced on its steeple, a candle burning upside down, the wheelbarrow pushing the man, the horse driving the cart, the rat chasing the cat, and man, the central figure in this absurd array, wearing shoes and spurs on his hands, gloves on his feet, and his trousers and waistcoat reversed.

"And this is England's case this very day,
All things are turned the clean contrary way."

Obviously, popular entertainment of this absurd stamp (and such efforts were legion during these years) expressed something recognizably true in the comprehension of the level at which they were aimed, else no printer would have touched them, nor would the non-reading public have parted with the penny price. The populace merely knew that in some way they did not understand their English world was out of joint and that somehow religion was both the cause and the issue of the confusion.

On a higher reading level, printing presses were busy with tracts bewailing the diseases of the times, particularly such as the "Immedicable Tumor of Faction," the "stupendous innundation of Heresie," the "strange diffusion of Brownism." The times groan with these diseases, said the alarmed clergy; "our streets swarm with the tumultous division of Schisme." They looked to Parliament to find some speedy cure, ere the church itself sink into a "deep Consumption." Religion itself was in grave danger, they said, and they expressed their fear with frightening imagery of destruction. Parliament had long been aware both of the threat to religion, and also of their own responsibility to take suitable action in safeguard. "If we can secure our Religion," said Sir Benjamin Rudyard, addressing Commons in 1640, "we shall cut off and defeate many Plots, that are now on foot." [4] He spoke to those who needed not to be told that religion was politics and that politics was religion. Other sermons echoed the warning, until by 1643, clergy and Parliamentarians alike agreed that the danger they had envisaged was upon them. "Confusion lies at the door," they said, and no one was surprised.

On June 12th, six days after they had declared themselves against the king, Parliament authorized the calling of the Westminster Assembly for the large purpose of "securing" religion in England by reforming it, particularly in the matter of church government. On July 1, shortly after Roger Williams had arrived in London, this body held its first meeting and from this day forward until February 22, 1648/49, (five years, six months and twenty-two days later) the one hundred and twenty-one "Divines" elected by the House of Commons, together with the Deputies from Scotland and the twenty members from the Lower House, sat through one thousand, one hundred and sixty-three sessions to effect this reform. Every session was a storm center.

"Our toyle is exceeding great; every day from eight in the morning till near one, and it is oft in the afternoon, from three to half six, we are in exercise; . . . All of us longs much to be at home; but we are all commanded to stay, and attend this great service." [5]

So spoke Robert Baillie, minister of Glasgow, and as England's leaders, civil as well as religious, saw it, his phrase "great service" was amply justified. In these councils as well as on the battlefield, the future of England was at stake.

Obviously such a moment of great stress and danger was not an auspicious time for an obscure emissary from a struggling plantation an ocean away to solicit favors. Whatever Roger Williams wanted, it would seem that he had come at the wrong time and with the wrong plea. Besides, to members of Parliament not immediately concerned with American colonization, the word *Providence* either meant a half-forgotten enterprise of the Bahamas which had failed, or a small group of south of Boston heretics with whom Massachusetts colony had had trouble. Whichever it might be and whatever they wanted, Parliament had other things to consider. Roger Williams either sensed the inopportuneness of his plea or took advice as to procedure and made plans accordingly. In treating with the Indians he had learned something of the importance of timing in such affairs, and though news by every boat from America would make prompt action in the charter negotiations increasingly urgent, he knew that undue speed at such a critical time in England might well mean failure. He also knew that he could get a favorable hearing in only one way; namely, through the patronage of influential members of Parliament. Fortunately he had powerful friends in Commons and they had not forgotten him. He sought their help at once.

The key figure in all matters of American colonization at this time was Sir Robert Rich, an Essex man, the close friend and associate of Sir William Masham, Roger Williams' former patron at Otes, and also Sir Thomas Barrington of Broad Oak. During the years he had been away, these two men had increased in stature as leading Puritans. Of the two Sir Thomas was closer to the Earl of Warwick in knowledge of colonizing activities, and in the single year he had yet to live, he would prove as valuable a sponsor as Roger

Williams could well have expected to find. Both men were more hopeful of the American colonization venture than they had been in his chaplain days. Another key figure and at the moment, far more powerful, was Sir Harry Vane, Roger Williams' personal friend since the day of his banishment. During his Governorship of Massachusetts in the period of the Pequot war, their association had been official as well as personal. Since Vane's return to England they had kept in close touch and Sir Harry was conversant with Rhode Island affairs, as well as in sympathy with Roger Williams' hospitality to settlers of differing religious faith.

In their own personal religious beliefs, they shared much common ground and in their intensity of religious concernment, they spoke the same language, as also in the lengths to which loyalty to principle could take them. One might search a long time in the churchly annals of William Laud's day for an example of the thin edge between truth and error, peace of mind and torture for sin, to match the youthful figure of Sir Harry depriving himself for two years of the blessing of the sacrament of communion so necessary to his peace, because he could find no Church of England clergyman to administer it to him standing. Kneel he would not though the thunders descended. Even though forms and ceremonies had never been Roger Williams' particular battleground, he had understood Sir Harry's strictures on such points and respected him for them. As for liberty of conscience as all men's right, both saw eye to eye unswervingly.

Shortly after Roger Williams had arrived in 1643, he heard Vane's "heavenly speech," as he called it, and quoted him in print soon after. The adjective "heavenly" was no doubt called forth by Vane's echo of his own thought when he had said,

> "Why should the Labours of any be supprest, if sober, though never so different? We now professe to seek God. We desire to see light!" [6]

Vane had already proved himself completely fearless in speech as well as action. Two years earlier, when the bill against Episcopal Government had been before Commons, he had made an unforgettable accusation,

"For the whole Fabrick of this building is so rotten and corrupt from the very foundation of it to the top, that if we pull it not down now, it will fall about the eares of all those that endeavour it, within a very few yeares."

This was the speech in which he had also accused Episcopal Government of "displacing of the most godly and Conscientious Ministers" in the kingdom, and "banishing out of the Kingdome, the most religious of all sorts and conditions." [7]

During the years since 1638 when he had all but fled New England in defeat, Sir Harry had learned many things. He had grown up and had already gone far toward redeeming the hopes of his father and other leading Parliamentarians as to his possibilities for distinguished service. In this year, 1643, he was nearing the peak of his fullest success in Parliament and he would soon be second only to Cromwell. His peculiar gift of discerning the purposes of other men with, as Clarendon said, "wonderful sagacity, although no man could make a guess of what he himself intended," fitted him for situations of extreme delicacy and Parliament was making use of his powers.[8] His word carried authority, and when the time came to weigh Roger Williams' plea for a charter, no voice at the council table would be more likely to be heard and heeded. He alone of all the Commissioners could say, I was there; I saw with my own eyes; I know this man who makes plea. No wonder then, that in Roger Williams' own word, Sir Harry became the "sheet anchor" of his hopes.

In July, almost immediately after Roger Williams had arrived, Vane was assigned the delicate mission of accepting for England the ancient Scottish covenant known as the Solemn League and Covenant. While he and his two companions, Philip Nye and Stephen Marshall, were absent, there was suspense in Parliament. The *Commons Journals* followed his movements on almost every page. The English wanted a civil league. The Scots demanded a religious covenant. The English wished a door left open for the Independents, who could no longer be ignored, but the Scots were wary of any such provision. Vane diplomatically met this situation by inserting in the clause pertaining to government the words "according to the word of God," to allow for debate. Likewise he added in the clause pertaining to reformation of the Church of England, the phrases "according to the same Holy Word and the example of the best reformed churches." These phrases might possibly preserve the peace.[9]

Only the urgency of their need for military aid could have reconciled Puritan leaders to the framing of such a covenant in any form. They were as hostile to presbytery as to the king, but their case was all but desperate. On their side the Scottish leaders saw their advantage and pressed it. Every step of the negotiations leading to the alliance was of the utmost delicacy, but Sir Harry proved himself an able diplomat, and the Covenant, which was to be a sword in English political and ecclesiastical life for many months, passed the Council of Estates in Scotland on August 17th, was forwarded to the Council of Divines on August 26th, and amended by them on August 28th. Commons amended it still further, and sent it to the Lords, September 7th, and on September 25th it was sworn to by both Commons and the Assembly of Divines in a solemn service at St. Margaret's. Vane and Cromwell were among the signers. In immediate sequel the Scots, 20,000 strong, poured over the northern borders and the Parliament cause took on a more confident hope. For his share in preventing a stalemate and framing a covenant that had won at least the acceptance of both sides, Sir Harry Vane was accorded a triumphant welcome. No man in England had done more at this crucial time to put Parliament in control of the kingdom than he.

Bolstered by this new confidence, Parliament took over various royal prerogatives, among them the control of all English colonial enterprise. Eighteen Commissioners, six Lords and twelve Commons, were forthwith named on November 2nd, and entrusted under Sir Robert, second Earl of Warwick, with all matters relating to the islands and other plantations of the English crown. Warwick himself bore the mouth-filling title of *Governor-in-Chief and Lord High Admiral of the English Fleet Governor in Chief of all the Islands and other Plantations of the English Crown.* Under his leadership, these Commissioners were the group by whom Roger Williams' petition for a charter would either be granted or rejected, and there would be no appeal. Only ten signatures would be required. Of the eighteen men, in addition to Vane and Cromwell, Roger Williams' friends were the Earl of Warwick himself, Lord Saye and Sele, John Pym (King Pym), who died December 8th, too early to cast his favoring vote, Sir Arthur Haselrig, and Cornelius Holland.

Even with these men on his side, the issue was by no means certain. Opposition was formidable. His two American countrymen who were representing Massachusetts claims to Rhode Island territory, Thomas Welde and Hugh Peter (his successor and not always his friend in Salem), also had powerful supporters among the Commissioners. Both Welde and Peter were able men for the business, and they also had the supreme advantage of being on the side of orthodoxy. This fact alone possibly more than equalled the influence of at least half of Roger Williams' supporters. Thomas Welde had been in London for two years and he had laid his plans carefully. Furthermore, the Massachusetts arguments made sense. As a growing colony she needed more territory and expansion southward was the natural direction in which to grow. Providence territory would meet her needs precisely. The Arnolds on Pawtuxet, by their own desire, were already under her jurisdiction. Given a patent to the whole area of Providence colony, she could suppress heresy not only among local obstreperous groups, but prevent its further spread. The influx of heretics throughout the colony was already alarming; it was high time that an authoritative hand prevent a still more serious threat to orthodoxy. To devout Puritans this argument was all but unanswerable in 1643, and besides, Providence was riven by parties and in constant turmoil of dissension. Discipline is the answer, and now is the time to impose it; so spoke the agents of Massachusetts.

All this was of course no secret to Roger Williams. These were the arguments and the pressures which had made it necessary for him to come to England at this time. Nothing but a charter would determine who had a right to rule the colony he had planted. It was a race, and he too had certain equipment toward victory. Doubtless under the advice of his friends, he set about the preliminary spade work which might lead to a favorable hearing. Such involved winning over by personal solicitation more than the ten required signers of his petition, a task that would take time and deliberate preparation more than ten times over. In these personal interviews nothing helped him so much or pled so eloquently for the cause he represented as his little *Key into the Language of America.* Surprising as it seems, this tiny volume, flanked as it had been on the bookstalls by Parliamentary appeals for money, for loyalty, by orders concerning the assembling, training and equipping of troops, by announcements of engagements fought here and there, had somehow found its way to interested readers, even in so stormy a time. It fed their concern for the Christianization of the American "natives" in new ways and in fuller detail than any of its predecessors. Of all the books Roger Williams was ever to write, this one alone had been printed at precisely the right time and had concerned the right subject to enlist immediate sympathetic interest. In the charter race on which he was now engaged, it was by all odds the best card he had to play. The fact also that he had been the first "to break the ice" with these natives by purchasing from them the territory now called Providence, not only added to his personal distinction, as he stated his case, but also weakened somewhat in their eyes the justice of Massachusetts claims for the same territory.

While he made haste slowly in his personal solicitation of the Commissioners, there was much else to engage his abundant energies, quickened as they were by the swirl of great events around him. He was at home again, but it was a very different London to which he had returned after this long absence. The West Smithfield neighborhood of his boyhood was hardly recognizable. The city had pushed its boundaries in this direction until the once open fields were now far away. His mother had died nine years before. His home had passed into other hands. His older brother, Sydrach, now a successful Turkey merchant, was at home again from one of his voyages to the Levant, and the two men had much to say to each other. They also had joint legal business to get under way. This involved instituting suit against their younger brother Robert, in the hope of recovering the legacies left them by their mother, in total amounting to one hundred pounds for Sydrach and two hundred for Roger. Robert, the only one of the sons in England at the time of their mother's death, had been made executor, but he had not been faithful to his trust. According to the record of the proceedings in the Court of Chancery, he had "failed in creditt and became unexpectedly much impoverished by reason of some accidental misfortunes." The suit against him would take time, but the two older brothers set the legal process in motion on August 15th.[10]

Meanwhile there was a practical emergency to be met. This was the coal shortage of 1643/44 which soon took on alarming proportions. Roger Williams had arrived shortly after it began and already the situation was grave. It would grow more so week by week as winter came on. The reason for this "stop of Coale" was that Newcastle, London's main source of supply, was possessed by forces hostile to the King and Parliament, and that by Parliament order, all importation was under strict ban until such time as "that Towne be reduced into such hands, as shall declare themselves for King and Parliament." Royalists and Parliamentarians alike were shaken with foreboding, but the prohibition held, as London shivered. Coal vendors, having any supply on hand at all, immediately raised the price beyond the power of the poor to buy. Parliament acted, also immediately, to prevent such profiteering by fixing the price at "23 shillings the chaldren at the most." Even at this rate, which was high, the scant supply dwindled, until presently in spite of black markets and evasion of the whole sequence of Parliament orders, there was no coal left. The winter of 1643 was unusually cold and there was much suffering. The Assembly of Divines moved into the Jerusalem Chamber, made somewhat warmer by the tapestried walls, but even so they shivered and many were ill.

The makers of "Artificial Fire" used their wits and devised substitutes for coal which were noisily advertised in broadsides and news sheets, and probably did not live up to the predictions made for them. One of the most entertaining of these extant broadsides to later well-warmed generations is labelled *Artificial Fire, or, Coale for Rich and Poore,* and adorned with three pictures of three grades of wares announced. It begins,

> "Fire and Water be two of the most excellent Creatures that ever God created."

Now for want of one of these those who never stole before, now

> "stele *Posts, Seats, Benches* from *doores, Railes,* nay the very *Stockes* that should punish them, and all to keep the cold Winter away." [11]

The practical author of this penny sheet then details his invention whereby the rich may keep warm with "half a Chaldren of Sea-

Coales" mixed with sawdust, chopped straw, and coal dust. The poor may use either "Cowdung mingled with Sawdust and Smalcoale" made up into Balls or squares and dried, "a very good Fewell, but something noisome," or "Horse-dung in balls plus charcoale dust, but the smell is offensive." He closes with the warning, "Above all things, let me persuade all men to sweep their chimneys clean against winter."

As the blockade continued through the winter, the suffering became acute. A Parliament proclamation as late as the following summer permitted the cutting of turf for burning and promised satisfaction to landowners whose property was damaged thereby. Even after the Scottish army was on English soil and the ban was lifted, coal shipments continued to be inadequate for many months and help was urgently solicited toward easing the suffering of the poor. In June, 1644, the Lord Mayor of London issued proclamation, promising free leave and liberty at their pleasure to all such good-affectioned ones as shall "undertake to bring Seacoales, Pitcoales, or any other manner of Fewell from any part of this kingdome, into the Port of London, . . . especially for the poor and needy. All such doings shall be taken as a very acceptable service to this City, and not to bee forgotten." [12] It was this "very acceptable service" by which Roger Williams' time, as he himself said, was "eaten up in attendance upon the Service of the *Parliament* and *City,* for the supply of the poor of the *City* with *Wood* (during the stop of coale from *Newcastle,* and the Mutinies of the poor for firing.)" [13] A Merchant Taylor's son with nearly thirteen years of pioneering experience behind him would need no instructions as to how to arrange for finding, cutting, and transporting the needed cords of wood from outlying districts, and no doubt making scores of friends the while.

In addition to these services, his own personal matters, and the Rhode Island business for which he had come, the sessions of the Assembly of Divines claimed a large share of his time and thought. He attended many of the debates, became known to various leaders, both Presbyterian and Independent, and used his powers of persuasion in lobbying with clergy and laymen, whenever he had the chance. Robert Baillie's word, "My good acquaintance, Mr. Roger

Williams, has drawn a great number after him to a singular Independencie," [14] suggests some success from these interchanges.

During the early months of their discussion, doctrine was not on the Assembly's agenda except tangentially. Church government was their concern, or more specifically, how to find a middle way between Presbyterianism, which was too rigid, and Brownism, which was too loose. This must be a way which would square with Scripture at all points, and also a way that would not bind future generations. Such a necessity was of course asking too much for anything approaching agreement from men so wide apart in their views and so vehement in their loyalties. It was a political battle for power that was being waged, and with such spirit that John Selden was well understood when in jocular comment, he said that he went to "enjoy the Persian pastime of seeing wild asses fight." Had a majority decision been all that was required, debate would have ended very quickly, but the Independents, led by Messers Goodwin, Nye, Bridge, Burroughs, and Simpson, were obdurate and they were also able fighters.

A church government battle in its multitude of specifications may not have seemed vital to Roger Williams, as he listened to these fiercely contended items, one after another. Such specifications were not his theatre of conquest, and yet as he listened, his thought reached out to the wider areas involved. His own convictions deepened, as he pondered the relation of sacred and secular, church and state, civil and religious. The brethren in wider audience than in this shivering assembly would soon hear from him.

Meanwhile he did not forget why he had come. In spite of all the comings and goings his varied activities required, and particularly in spite of the disturbed state of English officialdom at this time, in something less than ten months' time after he had landed, a virtual stranger, he had secured his charter for Providence Plantations. The date was March 14, 1644. To have accomplished such a mission at such a time speaks well for his diplomacy and his persuasiveness. He had won by only two votes among the Commissioners, but he had won. His opponents, Thomas Welde and Hugh Peter, had lost by one vote, but they had lost. The margin of victory was even narrower, for by an error, which has never been satisfactorily explained, three months earlier, on December 10, 1643, these two agents for Massachusetts colony had secured what has since been referred to as the Narragansett Patent, or a charter for the same territory as was granted to Roger Williams on March 14, 1644, as Providence Plantations. Some of the same commissioners had signed both charters. As appeared later, the Narragansett Patent [15] not only lacked one necessary vote, but the nine names signed to it had apparently been secured at different times, not in official session, and the document also lacked seals. The charter for Providence Plantations had eleven signatures, in proper order, and affixed in regular session, with seals added. Satisfying himself that the Narragansett Patent had "never past the table" and was therefore spurious, Roger Williams rested his case.

The March 14th charter he had secured was not a land grant or a trading charter only. It gave full power and authority to Providence Plantations to rule themselves by such a form of civil government, as by the voluntary consent of all, or a greater part of them, they should find most suitable to their estate and condition, provided only that such government be "conformable to the laws of England, so far as the nature and constitution of the place will admit." It was a "Free Charter of Civil Incorporation and Government for the Providence Plantations in the Narragansett Bay in New England." [16] On the preceding day, at the Court of Elections in Newport, the name of the island colony had been changed to Rhode Island,[17] although Roger Williams would not know that until he reached home. The charter he had secured was not for mainland or island alone, but for both; wisely so.

His mission was now accomplished. He had been far more successful than he might have dared to hope at the outset. The prospects for the colony were now brighter than ever before. Then why not down to the docks and home again with all speed? Because, as happens now and again in the fortunes of men who cast a wide net, out of one battle had come the call to another. By following his main track through to a successful end, another path now opened to him. He would take it.

CHAPTER FOURTEEN

Controversialist

HE shot his first bolt in the current battle of ideas on February 5, 1644, about nine months after he had arrived in England and one month before he had secured the charter for Providence Plantations. During the very active weeks immediately preceding, his pen also had not been idle. Four days later a second publication appeared. These two brief pieces, which were the first fruits of his thinking during this exceedingly busy time, served in different ways to introduce a bold new spokesman who was not likely henceforth to be ignored. Soon or late what he had to say would have to be answered, even though he himself were disposed of by authority, as from the outset seemed likely; in fact, all but certain.

The first of these pieces gained an immediate hearing by the use of John Cotton's name in the title. It was called *Mr. Cotton's Letter Lately Printed, Examined and Answered,* and bore Roger Williams' name as author. Since Cotton's letter, published shortly before, had been openly addressed to Roger Williams [1] and had concerned his banishment, both the letter and the answer to it were connected in the reader's mind with the *Key into the Language of America,* which had been so favorably received only five months before. In this second publication the banished author was in quite different mood. He was now telling a story which seemed to put the great John Cotton in an unfavorable or at least an equivocal light. For this reason alone, Roger Williams' answering letter would have found readers, particularly among churchmen to whom Cotton's name had news value and would continue to have it to the day of his death.

In February, 1644, however, there was an even better reason for the alert interest this publication aroused among the brethren. The

Independents of the Assembly of Divines, in their eager desire to strengthen their position against the Presbyterian majority, were tacitly inviting the support of the numerous sectarian groups in the current religious body. This meant a softened criticism of Dissenters, particularly those who had migrated to New England, and an increased hospitality to the ways of the New England churches. The name of John Cotton and this New England Way were all but identical in the mind of churchmen at this day, and at the moment he was almost on a pedestal of Independent approval. In this answering letter of Roger Williams he took a heavy fall, and with him the carefully planned strategy of the Independents to win a political advantage over their Presbyterian opponents. Read in the light of this 1643 situation, the staleness of the charges and counter charges of these two letters is displaced by a current liveliness of import not easily exaggerated. Both letters should be read in the context of fierce debate in the Assembly sessions, not in that of a Boston court of 1635, when a troublesome man was banished the Commonwealth.

Otherwise the rehearsing of a personal grievance now eight years old might be rightly dismissed as unworthy the writer and also quite inconsequential among his extant writings. This letter deserves both verdicts, except as it supplies several details not elsewhere recorded as to his trial and banishment, and for that reason has some biographical value. On the personal side it also shows that Roger Williams' sense of the wrong done him was sufficiently alive after eight years to put a sting in every sentence which concerned John Cotton's part in his sorrows. He had brought Cotton's letter along with him, together with his own long-delayed answer to it, presumably to show to his Essex friends, but when through some circumstance of which he professes ignorance,[2] John Cotton's letter appeared on the book stalls, the urge to print his own answer, with timely additions, was irresistible. He even rejoiced, as he admits, at the "present opportunity of answer," and forgivably or not, took satisfaction in what he thought would be the last word in this chapter of personal resentment.

He might have known that Cotton would answer his charges, and that on and on the feud would go. Even when he himself had almost reached his three score and ten, and John Cotton had been long dead, he wrote words to Cotton's son which still sent off sparks.

> "Sir, I pray forget not that your father was not God, but man,—sinful, and failing in many things, as we all do, saith the Holy Scriptures," [3]

he wrote, although adding that he had "tenderly loved and honored his person." Theirs had been a battle of argument, yet the tenacity with which he all but hugged his sense of unjust treatment in this affair is manifest also in some of his other human relationships. "The unlamblike frame of his Spirit," Cotton called it, not without justice.

What is significant in this 1644 skirmish is that once he had voiced his grievance, and in so doing effectively removed the halo from John Cotton's head, he freed the main issues underneath this eight year grudge and struck a blow in the current battle of ideologies. As a result, he turned the spotlight of the Assembly debates squarely on himself. This letter announced his arrival as a controversialist.

The gist of John Cotton's argument in the banishment decree had been that by announcing himself to be a Separatist and demanding that other New England worshippers break all ties with the Church of England he had become a menace to the church of God in the New World. To Cotton also there was evil in the parish system of the Mother Country, but to cut one's self off completely was neither necessary nor expedient. Instead, he had advocated a middle position between rigid Separatism and whole-hearted adherence to the Established Church. Let us make less of the evils of Old England, he had said, and unite in the greater battle against prelacy. To him Roger Williams' uncompromising Separatism was poison in the church body.

In his reply, Roger Williams bluntly asserted that Cotton's arguments had been used to "take off the edge of censure from himself," that he had taken a safe middle way, endeavouring "to walke with an even foote between two extremes." While "swimming with the stream of outward credit and profit," he had been "smiting with the fist and the sword of persecution such as dare not joyn in worship with him." Roger Williams had dared, and in consequence had been "denied the common aire to breath in, and a civill cohabitation upon the same common earth." [4] By following this safe middle way for himself and advocating the way of persecution for those who differed from him, Cotton had missed the vision of the communion of saints on earth as Jesus himself had revealed it. If Cotton had the power of empire in his hand, he would persecute likewise "all other consciences and wayes of worship but his own, in the civill state and consequently in the whole world." [5]

The brethren of the Assembly were astounded. The most explosive issue of the moment was persecution for religion, and if John Cotton and the New England churches were advocating such a policy, then the Independents were off on the wrong path entirely in sanctioning their procedures, to gain the support of the sectaries. As for Roger Williams' arguments in favor of Separatism, they were hardly interested. In these he was back in the climate of the 1630's, when the core of anxiety among pious churchmen had been how to get a pure church and how to keep it pure. Those who had separated from the Establishment had done so mainly in order to approach more nearly to the scriptural ideal of a communion of saints on earth. In 1644 the sights were lower. Although there were still those to whom such high motivation had vitality, for the majority now flocking into the many sectarian groups, the chief reason, acknowledged openly by many, was to free themselves from the tightness of the established system. They wanted to handle their own affairs and to that end the elaborate hierarchy of the Presbyterians was as intolerable as the control of bishops had been. The "gathered churches" of New England had looked like a way out, and now by this revelation of New England's persecuting ways, Roger Williams had spoiled the hope of the Independents for a political alliance with these sectarian groups.

Still back in the climate of 1630 Separatist thinking, he ended his treatise with an appeal for the scriptural ideal of a church society, and in so doing, made it seem almost within reach in Old England as well as New. He ends very simply by saying,

> "I desire Mr. *Cotton* and every soule to whom these lines may come, seriously to consider, in this Contraversie, if the Lord Jesus were himselfe in person in Old or New England, what Church, what Ministry, what Worship, what Government he would set up, and what persecution he would practice toward them that would not receive Him?" [6]

Wisely he did not attempt to answer his own question, but left it to work as leaven in the minds of such of his readers as cared to follow him to his own conclusions. They would hear from him again. These eighty-one pages in answer to Cotton's fourteen were only the preamble to what was seething within him, as he listened to the Assembly members wage a political battle in which this treatise had made him an unwelcome participant.

Four days after this answer to Cotton's letter had appeared on the stalls, his second blast was published, this time anonymously, but his authorship was not a secret long. The style of this impassioned piece, to which he gave the title *Queries of Highest Consideration,*[7] as well as its repetition of the arguments for separation, almost immediately identified the author as the antagonist of John Cotton. He now appeared as the antagonist also of the five Independents in the Assembly, whom he named on his title page. It was their publication, *The Apologeticall Narration,* published on January 3rd, to which his *Queries* purported to be a direct answer. He had written it at headlong speed, and gotten it into print less than five weeks afterward. It was the first answer to be published. Their pamphlet, in reality a manifesto of their position, and intended to make a bid for sectarian support, had given a new turn to the pamphlet warfare. Roger Williams' answer now gave it another.

Messers Goodwin, Bridge, Burroughs, Simpson, and Nye, together with their followers, advocated what in their own words amounted to

> "a *middle way* betwixt that which is falsely charged upon us, *Brownisme;* and that which is the contention of these times, the *authoritative Presbyteriall Government* in all the subordination and proceedings of it." [8]

They supplied abundant scriptural warrant for their plan for preserving orthodoxy. Give us a chance, they said, and we will rid English Christendom of heresy. We shall not separate from the national church but we will purify it. They had put their position strongly, and both sides were reading it, both being also conscious that this was a plain call for support from the sectarians, and for the political advantage such an alliance would bring against the Presbyterian majority.

Ignoring all political considerations entirely, Roger Williams struck out against both sides. Herein lies the only hint that this anonymous protest was not the work of an English pen. Not only did he not take the side of one party or the other in the Assembly, but he rebuked Parliament for having called it. Even so, strangely enough, he hardly spoke as an outsider. Perhaps the most arresting thing about this brief piece, as the work of a New England exile "among the barbarians," is that although he had been nearly thirteen years absent, what he had to say seems to issue directly out of an intimate and precise awareness of English ecclesiastical and political turmoil during these same years, as well as of the immediately preceding Assembly discussions. Roger Williams was not essentially a man of books, even though in his wilderness situation he had been free to import them, and certainly after 1636 his chance to see any current printed matter at all had been a scant privilege. He had a few English correspondents, Sir Harry Vane among them, but even a generous correspondent could hardly have told him all he needed to know in order to handle his weapons so adroitly at this crucial time. In controversy the temperature of feeling is as important as fact; perhaps more so, and in this outburst what he had to say was tuned to the temper of the moment, as well as born of a deeper understanding of the intellectual and emotional context than five months of observation as an assembly lobbyist could very well have supplied.

Boldness is written all over this piece, albeit boldness with appropriate deference, even humility. "Humbly bold" is his own phrase and it is apt. He states his position without hesitation or apology and admits from the first sentence that his music will not please. In his Address to both houses of Parliament, he says, "It is fitted not to your Eares, but to your Hearts, and the bleeding Heart of this afflicted Nation." The theme of this unpleasing music is that no model of a church yet in existence is worthy imitation.

> "It shall never be your Honour to this or future Ages, to be confined to the Patterns of either French, Dutch, Scotch or New-English churches. We humbly conceive some higher Act concerning Religion, attends and becomes your Consultations," [9]

he declared, showing himself to be a Seeker as to a church Pattern as well as in religion itself. He was dedicated to a search which could not end in this life, but was supported by a confidence that, according to Scripture, the Kingdom of Heaven was near at hand, so near that he might almost hope to experience this ideality.

No doubt you are men of conscience, he continued, addressing both parties at once, but while you fight each other, you are fighting Christ Jesus, in whose cause you gather here. Not even the professed reformation of religion which has brought them together is worthy their counsels. Addressing Members of Parliament,

> "Most Renowned Patriots, You sit at Helme in as great a Storm, as ere poor Englands Common-waelth was lost in: Yet be pleased to remember that religion is not your care. The Bodies and Goods of the Subject is your charge. Leave their Souls to the Messengers and Embassadors sent from Heaven to them." [10]

Strange words these, ignoring the specifications and limitations and minutiae which were being so hotly debated in the Assembly, and saying in effect, who are you who thus debate them, and by what right are you here? Look to the Scriptures for your answer. What warrant have you from Christ Jesus himself? How dare you call yourself the Assembly of Divines? If Parliament have its power only by the Commonweal, of which it is the representative, who then is the true head of the Church? In attempting the present reform, are you not once again repeating past mistakes? "Your wisdomes know the Fatall Miscarriages of England's Parliaments in this point." Our history is full of them. What one Parliament sets up another casts down. Where in the doctrine of Jesus himself do you find warrant for a "Nationall holy Covenant and a Nationall Church" whereby a whole nation must "walk in one way of Religion"? Can a Nationall Church be fitted to every conscience?

> "Sooner shall one suit of Apparell fit every Body, one Law president every case, or one Size or Last every Foot." [11]

Why may not the Papists themselves and their Consciences be permitted in the world?

There were those in the Assembly to whom such words made sense, until he reached this last query, but at that point his logic failed. Queen Mary was still too recent an historical fact to Englishmen of the 1640's for such a suggestion to be even worthy of respect, and to be among the first to utter it was not courage; it was madness.

The churchmen of the Assembly were even more likely to have been shocked by the heresy of his final paragraph, in which he asserted without argument, annotation, or proof that the things of Moses were done away. His "Pattern" for Israel, which the Assembly was trying to imitate in their plan for the "true church" in England, was one of the "Shadows" which had vanished at the coming of Christ Jesus and was therefore not to be taken as a model. It was directly opposite to the very nature of a Christian church, of Civil Magistracy, and a Civil Common Weal. It was a "type" only. There could be no long-lived Peace or Righteousness from such a root.

In John Cotton's disparaging label, such notions were merely Roger Williams' "high thoughts," worthy only to be dismissed. Seen in longer perspective, they amount to a preliminary, incomplete and undeveloped expression of his lifelong convictions. Some of it has had little pertinence beyond the convulsions of 1644. Some of it has for so long now been adopted into the experience of men and nations that the signature of no one man is any longer very important. Some of it is still a far-off ideal. Reduced to its lowest terms what he was saying was

The "Precept and Pattern" of Jesus is the foundation of all religious concerns.
The Old Testament is a type and a type only.
The civil magistrate is to rule in civil things only.
A national church does violence to the individual conscience.
Persecution for religion has no sanction in the teachings of Jesus.

To the passionate championship of these convictions he would apply himself in argument and in practice for the remainder of his years.

For the moment the response of his fellow controversialists was silence, at least in print. Had he aligned himself with one side or the other, there might have been an "Answer to Queries of Highest Consideration," but since he had attacked both sides, the usual missiles missed fire. Therefore, let him alone. For Roger Williams, however, with or without answer, these two skirmishes in print had been of immense value. In the first, he had learned how to add to the zest of battle by making the attack personal. In the second, his own thought had found a center and focus. He had discovered and isolated what for him was the main issue underneath the current conflict. In differing ways each of these hastily written pamphlets had clarified his own thought and sharpened his sense of direction. He had learned the feel of his weapons, gotten the scent of battle, and discovered that he liked it. He was now ready for more dangerous warfare. In fact, his pen was already engaged upon it.

Four months later, on July 15th, the book which posterity calls his best was selling on the bookstalls. Somehow amid all the energetic busyness of the immediately preceding weeks, he had managed, as he said, "to gather and scatter his loose *thoughts* and *papers*" into a book which in its first edition ran to two hundred and forty-seven pages. He had done it piecemeal, "in change of *roomes* and *corners* . . . in variety of strange *houses,* sometimes in the *fields,* in the midst of *travel.*" [12] One wonders how, but there it was, printed and for sale, a book whose every page was a lash for his own times and in which some pages still remain a beacon well ahead of our own. In form disorderly, lacking any firm organization, unpruned of needless repetition and excessive verbiage, it is at one and the same time unforgivably ragged for the talent that produced it, and also magnificent. At its best quotations do it far less than justice. These ringing pages can be fairly sampled only by being heard in their Elizabethan exuberance and King James rhythms.

His sensational title, *The Bloudy Tenent of Persecution,* put him with the wrong crowd and marked his book for destruction, but it was also a stroke of genius for catching attention on the bookstalls. Had the licenser seen no more than these five words, the book would have been banned at birth, and had he turned the page and read any one of the twelve statements of purpose, he would have seen more than enough, for Roger Williams had concealed nothing.

> "God requireth not an *uniformity* of *Religion* to be *inacted* and *inforced* in any *civill state,*"

he wrote, as Purpose No. 8, and any one of the other eleven purposes would have condemned him roundly likewise. Besides, they were all written plainly enough for the wayfaring man to understand.

How a book with such prefatory dynamite slipped by the censor's desk is no enigma. It was probably never submitted, or else in the blockade of printed matter it escaped examination. Apparently the censor was duly reproved for his carelessness, for in defending his licence policy two years later against repeated censures, he mentioned the *Bloudy Tenent* together with Milton's *Divorce Treatise,* "and others that have affinity with these," as among "those I have been so farre from licensing, that I have not so much seene or heard of them, till after they have been commonly sold abroad; and how many such like I have refused to license, some scores can witness." The possibility that Gregory Dexter may have been the printer of the *Bloudy Tenent,* as he was also of the *Key,* is likely enough, but there is no convincing proof of his official guilt in the matter. At the time of the Parliament order, January 17, 1644/45, he was safely enrolled as a freeman in Providence.[13] On this date the House of Commons had instructed their Committee of Examinations to "send for the Company of Stationers; and to know of them, by whose Default it happens, that such scurrilous, libellous, and seditious Pamphlets are every Day printed and published; and to enjoin them to be more diligent in suppressing such Licentiousness; and to acquaint them That the House doth expect a better Account of them and their Proceedings herein hereafter."

But it was too late. It had also been too late less than a month after the *Bloudy Tenent* came off the press (twenty-five days to be precise) when the House had ordered it publicly burned. At this date and in the current fury of protest against such boldness, nothing else was to be expected. On August 7th Roger Williams had been mentioned for censure, and on August 9th, it was

> "Ordered, That Mr. *White* do give Order for the publick Burning of one *Williams* his Booke, intitled, &c. the Tolerating of all Sorts of Religion." [14]

On that date Roger Williams was well out on the Atlantic, homeward bound, his charter for Providence Plantations safely with him. The burning order would have been carried out by the public hangman, probably at Paul's Cross, or at the plane tree in the court between Stationers' Hall and St. Martin's Church, and in the presence of a noisy crowd. In spite of having witnessed many such spectacles, those who came could always summon the appropriate marks of enjoyment. In the fast-moving story of printed matter, one more printer had lost his paper and his labor, and certain booksellers their small profit, but incredulity would have gone out of bounds could either of these groups have been informed of the value to their successors of this particular bonfire in pounds and shillings.

On the same day this burning was authorized, Commons had acted on a petition from "many ministers in the several Counties," who had previously requested action against the spreading doctrines of Anabaptism and Antinomianism together with the "turbulency" these doctrines encouraged. The previous answer of Commons had been to forbear for a time, but now the members recognized that they had made a mistake. It was high time to "suppress" purveyors of such doctrine and accordingly they took action against various individuals. One of them, a Mr. Knoller, had preached openly in Cornhill against the baptizing of children; another, a Mr. Penrose, "attended with many People, in a tumultous Manner" had entered a church in Southwark and prevented "with a kind of violence" others from coming there; still another, a Mr. Simpson, formerly forbidden by Commons to preach, had asserted that "the Lord Jesus Christ is in Hogs, Doggs and Sheep;" a certain Mr. Randall had held that if a wicked woman married a godly man, she was thereby sanctified. The conclusion had been that "These things will admit of no longer sufferance." Surely, so far as his companions in guilt were concerned, Roger Williams was in bad company indeed. Ironically, three days later, Sir Arthur Haselrig made report concerning the "Reprisal of such foreign Ships as trade in Parts in Hostility with the Parliament," that

> "Without Breach of the Treaties, Strangers cannot be hindered in the Trade of free Goods with this Kingdom." [15]

Free trade; yes; Free Ideas, no; not yet.

Six weeks later, Lazarus Seaman, preaching before both Houses on a Fast day, mentioned Roger Williams' *Bloudy Tenent* as one of four dangerous books on Toleration, adding this prophetic comment,

> "The shell is sometimes throwne into the fire, when the kernell is eaten as a sweet morsell." [16]

The toleration morsel was not very sweet as yet, except to a feeble minority, but even so, it had been eaten. So had the kernel of the other three books the preacher mentioned: *John the Baptist, The Compassionate Samaritan* and *Liberty of Conscience*. He might have added also Milton's *Divorce Treatise* and the *Areopagitica*. All were now beyond the power of any hangman and his fire to destroy. All over England men's minds had begun to move in the direction of greater freedom to speak and to believe, particularly in the matter of religious concernments, and with a momentum no power on earth could stop. Roger Williams' bold plea at this early stage gave the movement an energetic push at a determining time, for in this particular battle of ideas, midsummer, 1644, was a strategic moment.

Early in the year the spate of pamphlets protesting against the Solemn League and Covenant had changed its direction. In part this change resulted from a new order of Parliament on February 2nd, requiring all persons above eighteen years of age to swear to this Covenant with "their hands lifted up to the Most High God." The names of those who refused were reported. For thousands this was an odious demand and "against their Consciences," with the result that the word *Conscience* acquired a new connotation and with this, also new dignity. Slightly earlier, the *Apologeticall Narration* had put the question,

> "What amount of Non-Conformity is to be allowed in the new Presbyterian Church which is to be the National Church of England?"

Every sect in England waited for the answer, and in the discussion which promptly followed, the word *toleration* began to be heard, although the Independents themselves had carefully avoided it. From midsummer forward, 1644, these two words *conscience* and *toleration* were on the public tongue, in pamphlets, sermons, and official censures of protesting sectarians.

Very soon, as nearly always happens in ideological warfare, these two words had many meanings. To those of long historical memory, toleration meant either the danger of Papist control and the possible shedding of blood, or the excesses of the peasant revolt from which the word *Antinomian* could never free itself. To others it meant such indiscriminate licence as would be the end of law and order in both church and state, and the painting of disaster to England along such a road soon waxed fantastic to the point of absurdity. Yet the writers were serious men, expressing sober convictions. It would take years of time and many thousands of thousands of words before either freedom of conscience or toleration would acquire a good name. In the long story of popular comprehension, and still longer in popular acceptance, toleration had to come first. From conformity to freedom of conscience was too long a span for even one generation to achieve. Toleration would be a necessary intermediate step.

Roger Williams was not concerned with intermediate steps. He thought in ultimates. To him, as to Justice Holmes in a far later day, toleration is an insult to the human spirit. It is a permissive act, implying superiority in those who confer it. He admitted no such superiority. Both his conviction and his plea in this treatise were for complete liberty in religious concernments. "Soul liberty" was his best word for it, and this was a human right, which could be conferred by no power on earth, nor could any power on earth take it away. It belonged to man by virtue of his human nature alone. That such a plea would have no chance in 1644 he knew as well as his opponents, but he did not make his decisions by expediency, nor did he hide within his breast his soul's belief, no matter what contrary winds of doctrine were blowing.

The plan of this *Bloudy Tenent* treatise can be simply stated. It has three main parts: first, the letter of a prisoner in Newgate (presumably John Murton) protesting the persecution he is enduring, together with John Cotton's reply to this letter, justifying the persecution; second, a dialogue between Truth and Peace, dealing with John Cotton's answer to the prisoner's letter; and third, a Model of

Church and Civil Power, composed by several ministers of New England and sent to Roger Williams during his pastorate in Salem. This Model is also discussed by Truth and Peace. The dialogue form frequently used in pamphlets of the period and with the same speakers, Truth and Peace, halts the argument at times and invites to repetitions and windings harmful to the continuity of the thought. It was a form Roger Williams should never have chosen, since his greatest fault as a writer (and he had many) was "prolixitie," as he himself admitted, and in this piece he indulges in it sometimes unforgivably.

Both the persecuted prisoner's letter and the Model of Church and Civil Power belong to a date preceding Roger Williams' banishment. He had turned them over in his own thought many times during these intervening ten years, and very probably long before 1644 had committed his ideas to some of the "loose thoughts and papers" which he now gathered into this pamphlet. The disjointed and repetitious character of the published whole would seem to owe something to this method of composition. These two units, however, merely stand as examples of what he is now opposing with all the vigor and fire of his matured convictions. Cotton's *Reply* to the prisoner's letter represents the arrogance of authority in matters of conscience and the Model the "meddling" of the state in what concerns religion. The principles which Roger Williams isolates from these two ten-year-old occasions were as contemporary in their up-to-the-minute connotations and significance as news of the battle of Marston Moor fought on July 2nd, only a fortnight earlier.

The two ideas which emerge from these many pages of dialogue are those which in later generations have come to be all but identified with the name of Roger Williams. Freedom of conscience in matters of religion is an individual human right, and civil and religious must be kept separate in the government of a state, the second being so deeply involved in the first as hardly to require being stated separately. It is perhaps impossible three centuries later to imagine the passion with which each of these ideas would be opposed in 1644 by men as deeply religious as Roger Williams, as earnestly concerned that Truth should prevail on the earth, and that the government of the state should be built on a fair and a safe foundation. Truth to many of these men was as priceless as it was to him, and they did not want nor intend to sell it cheap. They merely differed as to the way of keeping it inviolate.

The distinction of the *Bloudy Tenent,* as a tract for this particular time in the history of things English, does not consist in its being a pioneer plea for freedom of conscience or for the separation of church and state. It was by no means the first, or even a very early proclamation of "soul freedom" as a human right. The ideas that have transformed human society have seldom gotten a hearing through their first spokesmen. Nor is this strange. Behind the best remembered books in all great battles of ideas are forgotten men; so here. The freedom of conscience idea had been simmering in various minds for over two generations and from time to time had had an able spokesman in print. The special distinction of this 1644 proclamation and plea is that it is an idea plus the kind of man who by his impulsiveness, his intensity of conviction, his courage to the point of recklessness, dared to make passionate espousal of a dangerous idea, at what would seem to have been precisely the wrong time. In sequel, July 15, 1644, proved to have been precisely the right time, as has happened more than once when dangerous ideas make headline news. In this detail, as in others, the history of ideas, in their birth, their long battle for acceptance, and their final triumph, seldom follows a logical, a predictable, and almost never a safe course. Had Roger Williams been a sensible man, who took thought for the morrow, solicited advice from wiser men than himself in the conduct of affairs, and watched the favoring signs, he would have kept silence in the London crisis of 1644. Instead, he waited only to get his charter for Providence Plantations safely in his possession; then walked out in the arena and spoke his mind without fear or caution. The prophet Amos might well have been his model.

Seen in the long perspective of many generations (from the air as it were) and held firmly in its chronological niche among the pros and cons of 1644 debate, the appearance of this book at this particular time, the explosions it set off, the hundreds of pages it provoked, and the eventual contribution it made to the victory of a great principle, have many parallels in the history of thought. The test of validity for ideas at first unwelcome and inflammable, is of course their ability to get themselves accepted in the market place, and for ideas which reshape society significantly, such acceptance has usually been long delayed. It would be so with this 1644 plea. Roger Williams' part was only to proclaim the truth as he saw it, and then to go about his Rhode Island business as before. Fortunately both for him and for his idea, a ship took him away at once, so that his answer to his answerers could at least wait until this first thrust had struck home with all its force. Had he remained in London longer at this time, he would have spoken out again and yet again, and in so doing he might have blurred the issue. In this cause he need never have said another word. His book had been printed and ordered burned. That was enough.

As to the sum of his indebtedness for what he had said, speculation is idle. He was probably familiar with most of what had been written on the subject, at least during his lifetime. His own conviction had been long in the making and to it his whole experience of living had contributed. Among London imprints he might have known, there was Leonard Busher's *Religion's Peace,*[17] presented to King James when Roger Williams was a boy of ten or eleven. Identified only on his title page as "Citizen of London," Leonard Busher according to one surviving tradition, was a member of John Smythe's congregation in Amsterdam, and according to another, was linked with Austin Friars' parish in London. Both are plausible enough, but lack proof. One would like to think that as a boy in Smithfield, Roger Williams might have read this gentle book, or that possibly Leonard Busher was one of his Cow Lane neighbors, but there is not a shred of evidence for either conjecture. Leonard Busher was a man of quiet speech, given to no denunciations or harsh words for kings or bishops; he said only that "as they cannot command the wind, so they cannot command faith." Men may be forced against their consciences, but they will believe as they did before. "Error and heresy cannot be killed by the fire and sword, but by the word and Spirit of God." Therefore is "persecution" for difference in religion "a monstrous and cruel beast," which hindereth the gospel of Christ and scattereth his disciples that witness and profess his name. But permission of conscience saveth both prince and people, "for it is a meek and gentle lamb." [18]

Obviously a plea for its quite different day, neither this book nor its author would have been fitted for the furious warfare of the 1640's. *Religion's Peace* would not have been banned nor would

Leonard Busher have been sent to prison. The battle issues had changed several times since 1614. One era had ended when Archbishop Laud went to the Tower where he was now languishing. In a few more weeks he would lay his head on the block and the event would be news only briefly. Not forms and ceremonies, not even doctrine was of first importance now. Instead, the battle between the Presbyterians and the Independents was a party war for power and power of two distinctly opposed patterns. Unknowingly both parties were searching for an anchor which would replace the authority of king and the aura of the bishop. Neither could any longer be endured, but both were missed. As to the union of church and state, that was not even open to question.

The other books pleading for liberty of conscience before Roger Williams spoke out, were also out of line with the current temper. Had he given his book so mild a title as *The Compassionate Samaritan,* published four months before his own, it might have escaped the flames unread by the censor, or if he had addressed Commons "without boldness and without fear," as the author of this tract announced, he might have escaped censure. At this date a little of both was requisite. Another of the four books labelled dangerous by the Parliament preacher was nimble-pated Henry Robinson's, quite frankly entitled *Liberty of Conscience.* No man, he argued, has a monopoly of truth. Give each man all the rope he wants and we shall have more truth discovered. The Westminster Catechism is for Englishmen, not for the whole world. Why can't we tolerate other faiths as well? It will make for good business. Henry Robinson was a mercer's son, and he had his feet flatly on the earth. Yet he was not an irreligious man. He talked sense, business sense. His book would be discussed in a natural tone of voice, even in 1644. The best thing about it is that he is speaking outside of party lines, as churchmen could not yet do.

Through the months immediately ahead, repressive measures as to printed matter reform at the censor's office continued to be met with such a flood of pamphlets as laid sheet to sheet, said John Taylor, the Water poet, wasted enough paper to "goe neere . . . to cover the whole Kingdome." Religion itself became a controversy, and week by week an additional grist of pamphlets was issued to prove it. Propaganda was discovered for the power it is. Bookselling became so profitable as to be followed by those who had never read a book. Why, one may ask, did not this whole structure of controversy topple by its own weight? Why did not some sharp-tongued satirist reduce this much speaking to absurdity and end it all? The obvious answer is of course that the questions being so repetitiously debated were too fundamental, the issues too vital. Both sides believed that the stability, in fact, the very life of England depended on a workable settlement as to church government, and they were right. Both parties in the Assembly debates were concerned with the minutiae by which such a settlement could be accomplished. Roger Williams started with a principle and was content to let the minutiae follow. Any reform of course needs both approaches.

His opponents did him the honor of a prompt reply. These men were the brains of the Church of England. His colleagues, in so far as any rallied to his side, were in Robert Baillie's phrase, "men of that stamp," meaning something decidedly inferior. As for Roger Williams himself, Baillie called him "my good acquaintance, Mr. Williams," adding "I have often pitied that poor man's spirit." He meant it kindly, but he could not follow. To him as to the stoutest of those who answered in print, to make conscience umpire was to open the door to all error and to exchange what to them looked like scriptural certainty for "the reelings of windmills, fair forms and dreams, beliefs bottomed on fallible opinions." They were afraid of liberty. Belief by authority and government machinery to keep it unchanged was a wall to preserve the doctrine. If liberty of conscience were permitted, religion itself would soon be lost in a "crowd of sects." The more timid among the warriors tried to find middle ground, substituting the word *accommodation* for the word *toleration* and sloping their arguments toward a peaceful coexistence of opposing camps. Like its modern counterpart, *appeasement,* however, their substitute soon acquired a bad name and was heard no more.

Roger Williams missed all this; fortunately so. Had he stayed he would have been too much tempted to answer Robert Baillie to whom toleration was "so prodigious an impiety" that Parliament could not but "abhor the very naming of it;" or Richard Baxter, to whom it was "soul-murder;" and most of all, the extremist Thomas Edwards, to whom it was the "grand design of the devil, his masterpiece, and chief engine he works by at this time to uphold his tottering kingdom." Back in New England, Nathaniel Ward, outdoing them all in native wit, laid a wager that if a "worse Assertion than that men ought to have liberty of Conscience" could be devised, he would "Petition to be chosen the universal Ideot of the World." [19] Personal abuse knew no limits in this warfare and logic could prove anything. What was needed was a new vision, and it had come. Roger Williams had spoken at a strategic moment, and when he came back to the battlefield again eight years later, many things would be different.

CHAPTER FIFTEEN

"Chiefe Officer"

In a life almost bare of splendor, Roger Williams could name one day of brief homage and glory. Perhaps that day would be brighter in his memory because of its dark preamble.

He landed at Boston on September 17, 1644, and presented the letter from "divers lords and others of the parliament" to the Governor and Assistants of Massachusetts Bay. It bore twelve signatures, among them those of William Masham, Thomas Barrington, and Oliver St. John, among his Essex friends, and of Miles Corbet, Cornelius Holland, and Philip Wharton, among those who had signed the charter. In it these men testified to their notice of Roger Williams' "good affections and conscience, . . . his sufferings by our common enemies, . . . the prelates, as also of his great industry and travail in his printed Indian labours." They sorrowfully resented that "amongst good men (our friends) driven to the end of the world, there should be such a distance," and expressed their "great desires" that this breach might be more nearly closed, and that Roger Williams might be shown "all friendly offices." [1]

But it was not to be so. Instead, the magistrates returned a stiff answer, reporting that they saw no reason to condemn themselves for their previous action against him, and that unless he would recant his previous opinions as to separation, the colony could not grant him "free liberty of ingress and egress" through their territory. So long as he held these opinions, he might infect others. For this one time he had their permission to pass through Massachusetts on his way back to Providence, but that was all. John Winthrop records his arrival,[2] but gives no hint as to whether any personal cordiality was shown him. At least officially, no one rejoiced in his safe return, or spoke a "Well done" for what he had accomplished in the common cause. He could hardly have expected felicitations in that direction, however, since his success in securing the charter had been failure for Massachusetts in the same endeavor. The cool reception over, he set out at once on foot, probably accompanied by the two or three English families who had come with him as co-settlers.

After eight years, the one-time trail through the woods was now a broad path. Many passed this way, white as well as red. There was no longer any danger of being lost, although the landmarks he had known were no longer recognizable. He was now a stranger on this once familiar way. Flanked on either side at this season with the beginnings of autumn glory, he travelled through a goodly world, as compared with that last time, in the bitterness of winter snow and cold. There is a passage in his book of the following year which might recall emotions belonging to this homeward journey of 1644. He wrote as one newly returned.

> "New English Voyages have taught most of our *Old English spirits,* how to put due prices upon the most *common* and ordinary *undervalued mercies;* how precious with some hath been a little *water?* how dainty with others a piece of *bread?* How welcome to some the poorest *howsing?* Yea the very *Land* and *Earth,* after long and tedious passages." [3]

As he drew nearer to Rhode Island borders, the consciousness that he had accomplished his mission, and that because of it better days might be ahead for the colony, and also personal anticipations of home and family, probably pushed the coolness of the Boston reception into the background of his thought. At least one hopes so. There would be a son he had never seen, Joseph, born the preceding December. But bright as these prospects might be, he was probably unprepared for the cordiality of the welcome just ahead.

When he came to the Seekonk River on the Plymouth side, probably very near to the spot where he and his four companions had built their first rude shelter and planted their first crop in the spring of 1635/36, the triumph awaited him. No more suitable spot could have been chosen. There it was: a fleet of fourteen canoes filled to capacity with his Providence friends and neighbors who had come out to meet him, and as he and the little company of foot-travellers with him came into sight, they sent up a ringing shout of welcome. It was a high moment. This greeting was personal and affectionate as well as official. These men had come as friends and neighbors, glad to see him, as well as official representatives of the town, grateful for what he had accomplished. He was given a seat of honor in the center of the little flotilla and proudly escorted down the river to Providence, where more friends and neighbors waited to do him honor. As a boy in Smithfield, a university student at Cambridge, and a grown man in London, he had witnessed many royal pageants and seen many proud triumphs, but this simple village honor was his own, and the only such event in his whole life story. His heart must have been warmed by this welcome.[4]

Unfortunately, the original record of whatever first steps were taken by Providence toward organization in line with the charter provisions is lost. One might suppose that the town assembled at once to hear the charter read, and after due discussion to make formal acceptance of it, although as in the other three towns of the colony, acceptance may have been delayed. Presumably also, the election of Roger Williams as "chiefe officer" was also immediate, but no record of this action is extant. The first reference to him in the office is of August, 1645,[5] nearly a year later. He held this position for three years, or until all four towns had accepted the charter and organized themselves into a united body. This was on May 18, 1647, nearly three years later.

In between these two points of time lay three stormy years, years in which more than once Roger Williams must have felt that he was doing his first works over again, and almost from the starting line. So far as continuing peace and harmony were the fruits, the eight years of community living sometimes seemed to have passed almost for naught. Why indeed so little peace? Such limited growth and prosperity? There were many reasons for it to be otherwise. Here were four towns in a tract of almost fabulous fertility. The coastline provided numberless small harbors inviting to shipping enterprise. The forests were all but untouched; fish and game abounded. Space for expansion and development was lifetimes long and wide. There were already enough settlers in each of the four towns with sufficient diversity of gifts to lay foundations for a state, but not so many as to make group agreement other than a neighborhood affair. Perhaps that was a main barrier to community peace. By the terms of the charter now presented for adoption, freedom in self-government was almost absolute. It was a moment and an opportunity which called for vision, for leadership, most of all for some invulnerable basis for unity and the will to achieve it.

Fundamental unity had always been lacking, except as these remote spaces had offered hospitality to those unwelcome elsewhere. Too many difficult and disgruntled individuals had come and they had come too fast. Already they had lived too long according to their own untrammeled desires to be greatly interested in an organized community life other than that of the loose give and take of town meeting agreement. They preferred to continue to do as they individually pleased. The more aggressive leaders among them had learned how to get enough votes to carry out their individual purposes, some of which were monstrously selfish. As to union with the other three towns, the reasons did not look compelling. Up to this time the chief reason for union had been for common defense against Indian danger, and for some six years now, since the Pequot power had been crushed, neighboring Indians had been friendly. Why unite now? Portsmouth, Newport, and Warwick were not disposed to do so.

As "chiefe officer" Roger Williams faced the necessity of overcoming this reluctance or else losing nearly all the territory of the newly chartered colony to Plymouth and Massachusetts, both of whom now pressed their claims afresh. He also faced, and immediately, new Indian dangers of serious proportions. These were in direct sequel to what had happened to English-Narragansett relations during his year and a half of absence. When he had sailed in the spring of 1643, the Narragansetts, under the able leadership of Miantunomi, were the acknowledged friends of the English, not only of Providence Plantations, but of Massachusetts and Connecticut as well. The tripartite treaty had held. Whenever the Narragansetts were in trouble with another tribe, they had laid their grievance before the Boston Commissioners, as they were pledged to do. Before Roger Williams was out of sight of land in 1643, a grievance had arisen. It had come about through the rebellion of the two minor chieftains, Pomham and Saconomoco, who had illegally re-sold lands to William Arnold and then with him had submitted to the jurisdiction of Massachusetts.[6] Against hostile Indian testimony Miantunomi had been unable to convince the Commissioners of his claim to sovereignty over the two rebel chieftains, and by the refusal of the minor sachems to acknowledge this claim, the Narragansetts had lost another large tract of their lands.

Nor was this all. Uncas, sachem of the Mohegans and unalterably hostile to the Narragansetts, saw his chance of involving the English against them and proceeded to do so. Roger Williams had never trusted Uncas and had warned Massachusetts again and again of his perfidy. He had always maintained that the Narragansetts were friendly to the English, but this time, in his absence, Miantunomi had no friend at the council. Uncas was believed instead, and the murder of Miantunomi was the grim sequel. The treachery of Uncas in this whole affair affords a sample of what the wisdom of the serpent needed to be in Indian-English negotiations of the mid-seventeenth century in America.

Uncas first sent a messenger to Boston with the word that Miantunomi had made an attempt on his life. He then cut his own arm with a piece of flint to prove his lie. Massachusetts summoned Miantunomi to Boston, but refused to believe the innocence he protested. Shortly thereafter, Sequassen, one of Miantunomi's kinsmen, attacked one of Uncas' warriors. Uncas appealed to the Commissioners for justice and was told to take his own revenge; he did so by making a raid on Sequassen and burning a village. Miantunomi retaliated by asking permission of both Massachusetts and Connecticut to avenge this injury. He too was told to go ahead. The two armies, totalling some fifteen hundred Indians, met on Sachem's Plain. Miantunomi, clad in medieval armor, unwisely lent him by Samuel Gorton, was called out in the open for a personal interview with Uncas. In the sight of both armies, Uncas, having the smaller force, challenged Miantunomi to single combat, but Miantunomi refused, giving the expected answer,

"My men came to fight, and they shall fight."

At this point, by pre-arrangement with his chieftains, Uncas threw himself on the ground, and the Mohegans fell upon the Narragansetts, who though twice their number, were so taken by surprise that they fled in confusion. Miantunomi, hampered by the armor, never meant for an Indian, was captured, his own brother was killed, two of Canonicus' sons were wounded, thirty of his best warriors killed, with the remainder of his army put to confused flight.[7]

Uncas had been victorious, but while Miantunomi lived, Uncas could have no security, and he was wily enough to seek English warrant for the murder of his great rival. John Winthrop's report of the Commissioners' decision and their secret instructions to Uncas makes sad reading from the side of Providence and Roger Williams. The Commissioners feared Miantunomi's power and prowess in war, and were all of the opinion that "it would not be safe to set him at liberty, neither had we sufficient grounds for us to put him to death." In this dilemma, they called in the "most judicious elders" and "they all agreed that he ought to be put to death." [8] Secretly the Commissioners authorized Uncas to do so, sending along two English to see the execution, and promising Uncas that if he were invaded for the murder, "we would send men to defend him." One blow of the hatchet did the rest, as Miantunomi was being led through the woods, a captive. In this murder more was ended than the life of the ablest chieftain of the Narragansetts, whose friendship, skill in war, and scrupulous keeping of the treaty with the English had been a guarantee of survival to all English settlements on the Atlantic seaboard. He had taken his grievance with Uncas to the Commissioners, as the treaty required, and they had betrayed him. Had Canonicus remembered the incident Roger Williams tells in the *Key*, of the stick broken in pieces to indicate the breaking of English promises, he would have felt doubly justified in his interpretation of this simple object lesson. For a year and a half, according to tribal custom, the Narragansetts made lamentation, morning and evening, the women with blackened faces. Nor was the story ended, when these months had passed. The tribe thus wronged would never rest until they had executed vengeance in return. As to where justice had lain, or whether it had merely been a choice between treacheries for the Commissioners, it is perhaps too late to say. The story varies, according to the sympathy of the teller.

One of Roger Williams' first responsibilities as "chiefe officer" was to deal with one sequel to this breach of the long peace with the Narragansetts. The situation was deeply complicated by the fact that both Indian and English loyalties were involved on both sides. While he was still in London, Samuel Gorton had arrived, bringing with him the *Act and Deed of voluntary submission to King Charles* of Pessicus, successor to Miantunomi. Canonicus had also signed this agreement. This meant that another large section of territory over which the charter, just granted, had given complete jurisdiction to Providence Plantations, was now directly under the Crown. Guerrilla warfare between the rebel Narragansetts and the Mohegans had been going on for some time, and by September threatened any day to be full scale war. The Narragansetts were demanding return of the ransom they had given for Miantunomi's life, else they would settle the score on the battlefield. Their threat became fact in the early spring of 1645, when Pessicus fought the Mohegans disastrously, refused to obey the summons of the Boston Commissioners, and as a result brought upon his tribe a declaration of war from the United Colonies of which Providence Plantations was not allowed to be a member. It was a critical situation.

Having tried to dissuade the Commissioners from what he thought was a rash step, Roger Williams then attempted to protect his own colony by negotiating a treaty of neutrality with the Narragansetts. Naturally neither Massachusetts nor Plymouth was pleased, but thanks in part to his presence at the council, in fact, by offering himself as a hostage, further open war was averted, and a treaty effected in August, 1645. There is a suggestion of grim humor in the fact that when Benedict Arnold was appointed by the Commissioners to attend this conference as interpreter, he could not be found, and something too grim for humor in the wrath of some of the Boston Commissioners when Roger Williams was a successful substitute. A good many things about the subsequent doubtful loyalty of the Narragansetts to the Boston Commissioners can be explained by such an incident as was later reported—Captain Atherton's dragging of Pessicus by his hair into the presence of the white soldiers at the door of his wigwam, and demanding the immediate payment of the tribute due. Such methods were as costly as they were stupid, nor would such a scene ever be forgotten by a chieftain whose idea of a present to his allies was thirty fingers and thumbs of the enemy.

In their subsequent relations with the English of Rhode Island, the Narragansetts remained friendly, in spite of their resentment toward the United Colonies, and in spite also of the *Act and Deed of voluntary submission to King Charles,* which Samuel Gorton had carried with him to England in April, 1644, when Roger Williams was still absent. The shift in loyalty this surrender involved was long in coming, chiefly because of intra-mural jealousies and tribal strifes which sorely ruffled the surfaces of Narragansett life. Moreover, disturbing as their submission was at this time to the hope of a united colony, in the end, and entirely without Gorton's intention, this foothold of the Crown would be a help when it came time to secure a new charter at the Restoration.[9]

But the unity of the Narragansetts as a tribe had been broken with the death of Miantunomi and when two years later Canonicus died, a long chapter in neighborly English-Indian relations ended. Canonicus had been an old man when Roger Williams first came to the Narragansett country, and found him the venerated sachem of a powerful Indian nation. During the space of these eleven years he had seen his one-time vast kingdom slip away to the white man and at no time had he been blind to what was happening. He knew what this partitioning of his lands, these deeds and confirmations of deeds meant for the future of his race. He knew that the 1644 treaty demanded of him by the Boston Commissioners was a virtual mortgage on what remained of his diminished lands. It spelled ruin for his tribe. He had lost his own son, he had lost his brilliant nephew and co-ruler, Miantunomi, and he had lost the submission of one minor chieftain after another. There had been breaches of faith in his subject tribes, and breaches of faith in the white man who had won their allegiance. It had not always been easy for Roger Williams to win Canonicus to the defence of English lives in war, but the old sachem had never questioned the integrity of this younger leader, and during the eleven years of their continuing association, Roger Williams had not had a better friend (English or Indian) on this continent. As he had written in the *Key,* quoting the old chieftain's

> "—solemne Oration to my self, in a solemne assembly," " 'I have never suffered any wrong to be offered to the *English* since they landed; nor never will: . . . if the *Englishman* speake true, if hee meane truly, then shall I goe to my grave in peace, and hope that the *English* and my posteritie shall live in love and peace together.' " [10]

He meant it, and to the end of his life he kept the pledge without qualification. Long before this June 7, 1647 day when he died, he had asked Roger Williams to attend him in death, and he had received the assurance it would be so, as it was. In the last sworn testimony of his life, Roger Williams paid his tribute to the long friendship with this veteran chief. It belongs on the same page with the great chieftain's. In recalling God's goodness, he wrote,

> "When the hearts of my countrymen and friends failed me, His infinite wisdom and merits stirred up the barbarous heart of Canonicus to love me as his son to his last gasp." [11]

Both men honored themselves as well as each other in these testimonies of unswerving friendship.

The Indian disorders of the first months after his 1644 return and the strained relations with the Boston Commissioners in consequence, disturbed the surfaces of Rhode Island life for a long time, and postponed the urgent business of accepting the charter and effecting a union of the four towns under it. Meanwhile Rhode Island remained a pariah in the thought of the northern colonies, who continued to press their claims for her lands. Plymouth claimed Aquidneck, of which she had given assurance in 1638 that it lay outside her claim. Connecticut claimed Shawomet where the Gortonists now lived, and Massachusetts, with Pawtuxet now under her jurisdiction, pressed for still more land. Any discontented Rhode Islander, wherever he dwelt, could have a friend and a promise of orderly government, if he would submit to one or another of these rival claimants. On August 27, 1645, Massachusetts sent a letter to Roger Williams, forbidding him to exercise any jurisdiction whatever over Aquidneck, Pawtuxet or Mishamet, and this on authority of the Narragansett Patent.[12] Officially, he appears to have ignored the demand completely, but privately, he wrote to John Winthrop, stating clearly his assurance that on the word of the Lord High Admiral himself, no charter existed for these parts except the one he himself had obtained; the other one "had never past the Table." No answering letter from John Winthrop is extant, and apparently this Massachusetts order of August 27, 1645, was not repeated.

During this three year period of office Roger Williams divided his time and effort between the two goals, union under the charter and constructive legislation toward greater harmony in each individual town. The balance which resulted between powers belonging to the whole and those belonging to the individual towns looks far ahead to a union of separate states he would never see. There is not the slightest hint that he envisaged such a far future. He was acting in a present crisis, and acting with what proved to be great wisdom. The extent to which the laws and other governmental provisions which belong to his period of "chiefe officership" can be attributed to his initiative is of course a question mark. The fact merely is that they are on the books as of his term of office. His peculiar genius in the matter of government was of the sort which grasps a principle in the abstract, paints its working on a large canvas, and then leads by evoking a response in others, not by holding the reins himself. There were those in Providence at this date who were immune to such evokings, but there were others, who could, as we say in this later day, *implement* these principles for everyday use, and no doubt, at this critical juncture, they helped him significantly.

In a single instance, such measures toward greater contentment in Providence during these years, have illustration in the granting of small plots of land to a number of newcomers, young men, and too poor yet to purchase a full right in the town lands. They were granted "a quarter right," or twenty-five acre plot, in advance of admission as freemen. In exchange they signed an agreement not to

> "claim any right to purchase of the said Plantations, nor any privilege of vote in the town affairs" [13]

until they were admitted as freemen. For some of them this meant a waiting period as short as one year; for others longer. These grants to the "25 acre men," as they were later called, eased much tension among the hitherto unprivileged as to ownership of land, rebuked the monopolists, who wanted to own it all, and also encouraged new settlers to come. It was a far-seeing change, and is only one of several such constructive measures.

The full story of the long delay in the acceptance of the charter is one of intricate cross-weavings, plots and counter plots, disloyalty within and persistent encroachment from without, of English-Indian disaffection, most of it manipulated by personal, selfish interests. It is a revealing chapter in one colony's struggle to come to terms with itself. As such it is the story of a state rather than of a man and belongs to Roger Williams' life only because he sat in the leader's seat during these difficult months. He labored incessantly, journeyed from town to town, rowed his boat from island to mainland, patiently, persistently, week after week. Warwick took longest to persuade, largely because it had had no part in the initial move to request a charter, since it had been last of the four towns to exist as an incorporated unit.

At last the union was accomplished. A majority from each town had agreed to accept the charter with its grant of self rule to Providence Plantations as an independent colony. Ten men from each of the towns, Providence, Portsmouth, Newport and Warwick, met at Portsmouth on May 18, 1647, officially acknowledged acceptance of the charter and made final arrangements toward union, which guaranteed to each town equal rights in the management of its affairs. These ten men had been duly appointed in their respective town meetings, given instructions and full power to act toward this May 18th settlement. Roger Williams had presided at the Providence town meeting and led the delegation for the town. These ten men of Providence, together with their friends and neighbors, embarked in canoes, carrying with them the good wishes of their fellow townsmen, who had assembled to bid them a "comfortable voyage, a happy success and a safe return." It was even so. The result was the "Incorporation of Providence Plantations in Narragansett Bay in New England." This was the long-delayed conclusion to Roger Williams' fifteen months in London. He had waited nearly three years for the official stamp of approval, and before as many more months passed, much of his work would need to be done over again. Out of the tumult of English affairs, another charter need was already in the making.

At this same May meeting a code of laws was adopted and a Bill of Rights. The preamble to this document declared the government of Providence Plantations to be "Democratical, that is to say, a government held by the free and voluntary consent of all, or the greater part of the free inhabitants." The code of laws ends,

> "These are the lawes that concerne all men, and these are the Penalties for the transgression thereof . . . and otherwise than this, what is herein forbidden, all men may walk as their consciences persuade them, every man in the name of his God. And lett the Saints of the Most High walk in this Colonie without Molestation in the name of Jehovah, their God for ever and ever." [14]

At this Portsmouth meeting the delegates made public recognition of Roger Williams' labors in securing the charter, and levied a tax of one hundred pounds to him as a free gift. Unfortunately, it would never be paid in full, but at least the debt had been acknowledged by representatives of the whole colony. During these three years as "chiefe officer" he had been severely straitened financially, and in order to re-establish some substantial means of livelihood for his growing family, he had gone frequently to his trading post for brief periods. Now that the union of the colony had been effected, and his three year term of office had expired, he gave more time to trading, remaining for long periods at the post, sometimes alone, sometimes with one of his two older daughters, Mary or Freeborn, and sometimes with Mary Williams, his wife. Although hardly a week passed without Providence business or Indian affairs calling him away, the four year period before a second trip to England became imperative, was the longest stretch of outward quietness, or semi-quietness, in his life. He needed it, and it came at a good time for one who by choice and by compulsion, lived the very active life. He was now in the full maturity of his powers, and when these four years were over, he would not yet be fifty years old. This four year period would not correspond to Paul's years in Arabia. Roger Williams' Arabia, in so far as he had one at all, had come during the far briefer solitudes of his earliest months in the wilderness, and the experience had shaped his thought in significant ways. This later quietness was a privilege not given to many mature men; a mid-campaign chance, as it were, to step out of the battle ranks and take sights afresh. He was fortunate to have it.

The only publication which had appeared during the preceding busy three years, was a brief pamphlet, *Christenings Make Not Christians,* which came out January 16, 1645. He had probably left the manuscript behind him when he took ship home in mid-summer 1644. It belongs with the interchange of opinion, which had been enlivened by the publication of his *Key* to the Indian language in 1643, and in content is mainly an elaboration of his own view of conversion, expressed therein. This view consists in a sharp distinction between conversion as an inner change, and mere outward observance of the forms of Christian worship. As he saw it, the compulsion to worship must be inner. "It is like a free Vote." He had said all this to his friends in London, and one of them, Robert Baillie, gives it back again in his *Dissuasive,* published only one day before this little pamphlet appeared. Baillie may have seen the manuscript of the piece before publication.

There is one idea which Roger Williams would develop more fully later, the need for what he calls "a Commission" from God Himself before carrying on his labors among the Indians. Lacking this, he had refused "proffers of assistance" from friends in the Bay, among whom he mentions Colonel Humphries. The argument for this later treatise which he called *The Hireling Ministry None of Christs,* was already clear in his mind. Had he not returned to England, he might never have written it at all. It was not only the incessant busyness of the Providence life, it was also that he seemed to need the stimulus of opposition to bring his own ideas to expression. As a University student, he had been trained to confute another man's thinking, and to the end of his days, this training determined his most natural patterns of expression. The one significant departure from it would belong to the solitary trading house life to which he now turned.

CHAPTER SIXTEEN

Trader

It is quite likely that Canonicus had laid out the site for the trading house at Cocumscussoc "with his own hand" as early as the Plymouth chapter of Roger Williams' life, and that one of the "treatyes" he mentions as belonging to this period concerned this purchase. It is also quite likely that he had occasionally used this site for trading operations before he came to Providence as a fugitive, and that it was one of the reasons for his choice of refuge in these parts. The exact location, in recent years a matter of dispute, was probably very near to that of the present structure at Wickford Point. This location, with its quiet coves suitable for the loading and unloading of cargo, the many trails leading inward to neighboring Indian villages (as many as twenty to the mile, Roger Williams once said) made it admirably suited to trading purposes, as the Dutch had discovered long before Roger Williams came. Richard Smith had also previously used this site and he would use it again. Providence was only six miles away and conveniently accessible at most seasons by either land or water. Newport, where most of the supplies were landed, was even more convenient.[1] Roger Williams had a "great Canow," a pinnace, and several small craft, and he seems usually to have made the trip from Providence by water. The trading house was probably not built until some time shortly before his more settled residence here between his term of office and the second trip to England.

As to the trading operations themselves, they were probably considerable in volume and diverse enough to call for ingenuity in supply. The Indians were willing customers and they needed everything: pans, kettles, knives, cooking utensils of all sorts, spades, hoes, and other garden implements, cloth, pins, needles, thread, beads, trinkets, toys, and in largest demand of all, tobacco, and pipes to smoke it in. Even more they wanted whiskey, but Roger Williams refused all pressures and temptations. He might have made "thousands," he said, as those less scrupulous ones of Rhode Island, Massachusetts and New Netherlands were doing, but where a principle of right action, as he saw it, was concerned, money was less than no temptation to him. Presumably at his instigation, Rhode Island had made an order prohibiting such sale, but there were frequent violations. Convinced that the Indians sometimes needed a little "strong water" in sickness, he later petitioned the colony for permission to supply them and was granted "leave to sell a little wine or stronge water to some natives in theare sickness." At the same session, May 25, 1649, he was also "granted leave to suffer a native, his hyered household servant, to kill fowle for him in his piece at Narragansett above his house." [2] Individualist that he was, it was his lifetime practice to use lawful channels only for privileges not his to assume.

In addition to the commodities in steady demand, any trader could create a new demand by merely displaying new wares. The difficulty was how to get them and to get them promptly. Shut off from Boston, as Roger Williams was, such problems were major. Remoteness meant many letters to far places, and then long delays while he waited for messengers going thither and boats returning with the commodities he had ordered. Shipping of all sorts was attended by peril and frequent mishap. Small boats foundered and were lost; cargoes of tobacco "took wet" and were ruined, those commissioned to make purchase and payment proved irresponsible. Roger Williams' surviving correspondence shows items on all these counts and the resulting losses were sometimes heavy. His surest and perhaps his largest profit was in furs, skins, and baskets, in which his Indian customers paid him or which he bought from them. As a merchant taylor's son, he knew how to find an English market for greater demands than he could meet. Details as to his profits are lacking, except in his own single statement that his profit amounted to £100 annually, a sum which for his day and situation suggests no small degree of success. The Indian population of the section he served was roughly about three thousand, sufficient to make the flow of commodities considerable.

Was his heart in it? Probably not, except that it was his livelihood, and except for his farm in Providence, he had no other. Six children were growing up in the Providence home, and it would be several years yet before his three boys would be able to take over the farm responsibilities. By leaving his partner, Richard Wilcox, in charge of the trading post, and making the six mile journey to Providence frequently at seed time and harvest, and various times in between, he somehow managed both farm and shop. He also raised swine and goats on the nearby island. It was a busy life, and except for the trading a life very little different from that of his fellow townsmen. They were all farmers, the more prosperous among them raising sheep, cattle, goats, and especially horses, their best export to the West Indies.

Roger Williams was farmer and trader by necessity, but he was still preacher by choice. Preaching was the best of all callings, he said, but a poor trade. Some of his brother ministers spoke slightingly of him because he was not preacher and preacher only. "Mr. Williams spending his life trucking with the Indians," [3] was John Eliot's disparaging verdict. Not quite, although perhaps it looked so from a well-approved orthodox position. Roger Williams' little trading post in the heart of the Narragansett country was also his pulpit, where he continued to satisfy his longing after "the natives' soules." His Indian customers were his parish and he seems to have preached to them with some regularity during these years. Very informal sermons these no doubt were, such as he had illustrated in his *Key*, and in addition to them, almost any chance for conversation presently got around to religion, so that he was as much missionary as trader, and that not on Sundays only. One hint of his preaching to them comes in his own word that

> "When we deal with *Indians* about *Religion,* our work is to prove unto them by Reason, that the *Bible* is *Gods Word,* for by Nature they are much affected with a kind of Deity to be in Writing." [4]

Their sense of awe and reverence for this strange Book which he used to find out their secrets had something to do with their thought of him as a sachem, for as he observed, "this Scripture agrees with their own Consciences, reproving them for those sins their Souls say they are guilty of." This observation also suggests a conversational exchange rather than a formal sermon. One may imagine many such, as his customers lingered after the bartering.

Late in this period of residence at the trading house, possibly in 1650, he wrote a little book, which from what we know of his preaching, would seem to correspond with it in its spirit of helpfulness, its dependence on Scripture at every turn, as well as in its sermon form. He entitled it *Experiments of Spiritual Life and Health*. He wrote it, as he states in his introductory letter, to comfort Mary Williams, his wife, who was at the time recovering from a serious illness, and was apparently depressed about her religious life. It is a very revealing book. According to the dedication, it was written "this last year" when during a time of disturbed Indian relations, "it pleased the Lord . . . more than ordinarily to dispose of [his] abode and travel amongst them." In any case it was a wilderness book, written "in the thickest of the naked Indians of America, in their very wild houses, and by their barbarous fires." He called it "an handful of flowers made up in a little posy for thy dear self and our dear children to look and smell on, when I, as the grass of the field, shall be gone and withered." He had intended to let it remain the "private and sudden discourse" it had been, but later upon his return to England, being persuaded by friends to print it,[5] he had consented, hoping thereby to sow "a little handful of spiritual seed" while the short minute of his own seed time (the opportunity of life) lasteth." There is not a word of controversy in it.

To have written so quiet a book at a time of outer confusion, danger and turmoil was for him quite in character. Not only are the outer circumstances utterly unimportant to the content, but the fact of tumult around him drove his thought inward to those hidden values which were his springs of action. This had happened before in his life. The peculiar significance of this little book in his life story is that it reveals the place which religion had in his own thought more clearly and more completely than anything else he ever wrote, and also the nature of religion as he conceived it. The *Experiments* of his title are "experiences" of personal communion with God "in the spirit of holiness." He writes not of sickness, but of health; not of strife, but of peace and joy. "Cheerfulness" is one of the most frequent words in these pages.

> "For the Lord loveth a cheerful giver, so loves he also a cheerful preacher, a cheerful hearer, a cheerful pray-er, and a cheerful sufferer for his name's sake." [6]

Under three main heads, the Marks of Spiritual Life, of Spiritual Health, and the Helps to Preserve Spiritual Health and Cheerfulness, he details the tests by which a living, growing, joyous Christian life may be known to the individual Christian himself. He pays Mary Williams the tribute of saying that he and others have discerned these marks in her, and he prays that she herself may rejoice in the reality of them, "and not in another's good opinion of thee." His own tenderness and sweetness of concern for her, his recall of their life together, his regret at the long enforced absences, slight as all this is through these pages, it suggests an area of his life about which literal record is almost wholly lacking. Once later, in a letter to Providence about the probable date of his return after his prolonged stay in England, he wrote this sentence,

> "Remember I am a father and a husband." [7]

Not only during these long periods abroad, but for weeks out of any year of his wilderness life, he had been denied the comforts and sweet refreshings of his own home life; he had been a traveller and sojourner for a night, so that when he says, as he does several times in this book, "to be content with a traveler's and stranger's portion of such as may serve our journey," he knew whereof he spoke.

The spirit as well as the text of this little manual for Christian living is far removed from that of other current books of its kind with which it might suitably be compared. Roger Williams draws up no schedule of virtues, or corresponding lapses from godliness, such as abounded among pious helps for the pew. There is nothing about never allowing one's self to go to sleep at night without remembering that the last thought must be of God, or rising in the morning likewise, nothing about never allowing one's thought to wander during sermon time or having bythoughts during prayer, forgetting to list one's sins for the day at the day's end, supping too liberally, or rejoicing in things earthly. There is nothing whatever in this book about conduct. The tests to be applied are principles, not rules. The difference between all such tables of behavior and this glowing vision of passionate religious attainment in one's personal life is a difference too wide to bridge. Roger Williams approached the experience of Christian living with criteria of measurement having nothing whatever to do with things outer. The "marks of spiritual life" which he considers valid come by soul-searching, not by consulting the daily tally of outward observances or lapses from them. Does one's soul long for more knowledge of God? Then consider that a "mark." Does one have no peace in sin? Consider that another. Does one long after the "grace" one sees in others, but has not yet attained for himself? Then consider yourself in the way and press on joyfully. Even the desire for spiritual life is a "mark" that it exists. Had Roger Williams not known the peace and joy which these experiences of which he speaks bring to the individual Christian, he could not have written this book.

Not that the yearning after spiritual satisfactions puts him with those who are content to meditate on perfection, and in the intensity of their meditations sometimes feel themselves caught up into the Ineffable and made, though momentarily, one with the divine. Not at all. There was next to nothing in Roger Williams which allies him in any way with those whom we call by the loose term *mystics,* the seers of visions and dreamers of dreams. He would have had nothing whatever to say either to Madame de Staël, St. John of the Cross or even John Bunyan of his own century. They spoke a quite different language. To him divine revelation came through the Word of God, and through the Word only. His guidebook was the Bible, and the Bible only. In his own words here as elsewhere in his thought of religion, "All my flowers" in this little nosegay, are "picked out from the garden of the Holy Scriptures for our spiritual refreshing and consolation." [8] Bible in hand, he searched out scriptural warrant for even the restless desires of his own heart after things of the spirit. The "particulars" which he presents in this wilderness volume are among the fruits of these personal searchings.

In addition to the *Experiments,* the semi-seclusion of these months saw the writing of his second plea for "soul liberty," *The Bloody*

Tenent Yet More Bloody, not to be published until he reached London on his second long visit, but written and sent over earlier.

> "It is a controversie wherein I am much engaged, of which you will (if God please) see more," [9]

he wrote John Winthrop. There is also correspondence about books bought, books borrowed, suggesting paths down which his own mature thought was travelling, and not all of them predictable. One of the books he requested was Carpenter's *Geography,*[10] or some other book treating of the earth's diurnal motion. In this 1625 volume, which he might have known as a university student, he would have read that there is more earth than water, that the terrestrial globe is round and its motion probably circular, that the earth is the center of the whole universe, and that by observing the moon shadows one might find out its measure precisely. Some hints are also given of the use of an artificial globe. Had solitary sunrises and sunsets fostered an interest in such queries? Probably.

In the second volume he would have read even stranger things. The entire globe is habitable. The sea is salt not by nature, but by accident. Navigation, first taught by God Almighty, was afterward "seconded by the industrie of famous men in all ages." The people of the eastern hemisphere are far superior to those of the west. Colonies translated from one region to another gradually decline and suffer alteration. In requesting these volumes, he ended the letter, "Spare it a little to your most unworthy Roger Williams." A chance sheet such as this, surviving by the merest accident, suggests the likelihood of a mental life rich in directions unknown and unguessed.

The semi-seclusion of these trading house months might have given him further chance to garner his own thoughts, but even here the necessity for active participation in colony affairs pressed hard. Before he had been away half a year, trouble multiplied in every corner of Rhode Island. Disorders in Pawtuxet could not be controlled, because it was under Massachusetts jurisdiction, but too far away for Massachusetts authority to be effective; disorders in Shawomet, subject to the Crown, likewise could not be controlled. Rhode Island was helpless in both areas, and disorder was perennial. On Aquidneck, though both towns had accepted the charter, William

Coddington saw to it that this acceptance made little difference in his domination. Disappointed in not having been made first president of the united colony, he made plans which might yet gratify his ambition, although to the ruin of colony unity. Providence was riven by factions more seriously than at any other time in its previous history, and plans were on foot to carry their grievances directly to the Crown.

As in preceding years of the colony's existence, the blame for most of these troubles is not to be laid on the body of settlers, men who tilled their small farms and lived an orderly, peaceable life, but rather on the same contentious spirits, who had frustrated all plans for a settled community peace since the beginning. William Coddington, William Harris, Samuel Gorton, William Arnold were not evil men. They were ambitious men, greedy of power, greedy of land and ever more land, and having attained wealth and prosperity, their ambitions rode them. As Roger Williams admitted, they had gotten the power out of his hands, and now they had also gotten it out of the hands of the colony, and though Roger Williams had neither power of land, nor authority, nor office, it was to him that all riven corners of the colony turned for help.

In August, 1648, he wrote an answering letter to the Providence plea for his intervention,[11] asking that the rival factions be at least willing to be "pacifiable . . . reconcilable . . . sociable," and to listen to his suggestion outlining a program of arbitration toward the ends of town peace and harmony. To try out matters by disputes and writings, he wrote, is "sometimes endless;" to do so by arms and swords is "cruel and merciless;" to trouble England with our disagreements is "most unreasonable;" to trouble our neighbors is "neither safe nor honorable." Let us try to do it ourselves. Let each party nominate three men, with authority to "examine every public difference, grievance, and obstruction of justice, peace and common safety." Let these men, by majority agreement, give judgment in the case, and by their sentence, "end all, and set the whole into an unanimous posture of order." He requested that the names of those chosen be sent to his house within twenty days, when he would appoint a time and place of meeting. This time he signed himself,

"Your mournful and unworthy Roger Williams."

"An unanimous posture of order" did not result, and five months later he wrote John Winthrop, "Our poore colonie is in civill dissension, their meetings fallen into factions." Opposing groups continued to seek his intervention, but for a time, he held off, being resolved, as he wrote, "not to ingage, unless with great hopes of peace-making." [12]

His letter written early in the year 1649/50 came near the end of the long friendship and mutual exchange of counsel between these two colonial leaders. Once again, it concerned Indian affairs: in particular, another perfidy of Uncas. Winthrop died two months later, in March, 1649/50. Through the years Roger Williams had borne no grudge toward the older man who had had a controlling voice in his banishment, and on his part, John Winthrop had respected the advice and been grateful for the many services of this younger colleague. There was also a mutual affection between them which had surmounted all obstacles. "We have often tried your patience, but could never conquer it," John Winthrop, Jr., had said. For both father and son it was a distinguished human relationship.[13]

Early in the preceding spring, news of the death of King Charles had reached America by slow sail. On May 26, 1649, Roger Williams had written,

> "Sir, tidings are high from England; many ships from many parts say, and a Bristol ship, come to the Isle of Shoals within a few days, confirms, that the King and many great Lords and Parliament men are beheaded." [14]

For Rhode Island the death of the king would mean renewed authentication of the charter by Parliament, or the colony's right to govern herself was gone.

But William Coddington had acted faster than the colony. At the second election, May 16, 1648, he had been made President of the colony, but this was not enough. He had other ambitions. Eight months later, January, 1648/49 he was off for England to have the charter abrogated and to secure for himself life tenure as Governor of the Island portion of the colony. This action had a long foreground and was no secret to Roger Williams. As early as 1644, immediately after Roger Williams' return from England, he had twice tried to secure recognition for Aquidneck as an independent colony unit, either under Massachusetts or Plymouth, or as a separate colony, in federation with the United Colonies. He had written John Winthrop of this desire, requesting him "to burye what I write in deepe silence." [15] The death of the king now opened a new path to him, and accordingly, he walked away from his obligations as president of the United Providence Plantations and was off to England, leaving the colony without an official head. Roger Williams was summoned to act as Deputy President in his stead, and at first refused. His refusal was ignored, and he presently yielded. This responsibility of course meant many visits to Providence, although the fact that his letters for the next two years continued to be written from Cocumscussoc, suggests that he continued to make the trading post his headquarters for a goodly portion of his time. In 1650 came the Indian troubles which he mentioned in his *Experiments,* as requiring continued absence both from home and from the trading post. He held the Deputy Presidency until the next election, May, 1650.

Meanwhile the petitions of both Edward Winslow and William Coddington, both claiming the territory of Aquidneck, were presented to the Council of State, and William Coddington was successful. He represented himself as discoverer and purchaser of both the island of Aquidneck and of Quunungate from the Indians. He had "quietly enjoyed" these territories ever since and he now wished to govern them by English laws and to be dependent on the Commonwealth. He therefore asked for a life commission so to do. This was on April 17, 1650.[16] After waiting nearly a year, his request was granted and he was given a commission by the Council of State to govern them for life. He returned to America and made a beginning. Plymouth having lost her claim to Aquidneck, attempted to take over Warwick on the mainland.

The time had come to act or Rhode Island colony was gone. Providence and Warwick promptly appointed Roger Williams to secure confirmation of the 1644 charter. A majority of the Aquidneck freemen appointed John Clarke, physician and Baptist minister, to secure revocation of Coddington's commission. Roger Williams sold his trading house, or rather gave it away, for fifty pounds to finance his own voyage.[17] He also sold his two big guns, his fields and the fencing around them; in fact, everything he had except his Providence home, "for the public peace sake." The personal price he was willing to pay that Rhode Island colony might endure, is all the evidence needed to prove how much this concrete example of the principle he had proclaimed meant to him. When William Arnold heard of this intended mission, he wrote to the Governor of Massachusetts that it would be "a great mischief" and at all cost must be prevented in time. Otherwise

> "under the pretence of liberty of conscience about these partes there comes to live all the scume the runne awayes of the country."

In time these undesirables will bring a heavy burden on the whole country.

> "We humblie desire God their purpose may be frusterated for the country's peace." [18]

It was not frustrated, however, nor was his name, as he requested, concealed for having advised it.

While preparations for the mission of Williams and Clarke were going forward in midsummer, 1651, John Clarke became the center of a sensational episode, which centuries later might appear entirely extraneous, and yet which strangely enough, contributed materially to the success of the mission; in fact, may have tipped the balance in its favor. It may indeed have been deliberately planned to that end, for John Clarke was a shrewd man. Fortunately also, he could use his pen, and he saw to it that the episode got into print at precisely the right moment after arrival in England. The tale itself though shabby, slightly ridiculous, and trivial to later eyes and ears, is a first rate example of the kind of incident which in its hour can assume such importance as to swing popular feeling in a great cause with far-reaching effect. It could not have been better timed.

In outline the tale runs like this.[19] Three Rhode Islanders, John Clarke, Obadiah Holmes, and John Crandall, went to Lynn, Massachusetts, ostensibly to pay a call on their Baptist friend, William Witte. Report of their presence went forth and various neighbors assembled at William Witte's house, hoping for a sermon from John Clarke. It came. He preached from Rev. iii, 10, and inevitably, the sermon swung around to infant baptism, the most explosive subject of the hour in Massachusetts church circles. John Clarke apparently left nothing unsaid as to the falseness of this doctrine. Only a visible believer, repentant for his sins before God, had any right to this holy sacrament. Obviously, no infant could qualify.

News that such heresy had been spoken in the town was quickly sped to the magistrates, but before the three intruders could be called to account, they had added to their guilt. They had gone to a church meeting and kept their hats firmly on their heads. As of course they had expected (and probably hoped), their three hats were knocked off and themselves borne off to the town jail. At their trial they were fined in different amounts according to the estimated enormity of their guilt: Holmes thirty pounds, Clarke twenty, and Crandall five, in default of which they were to be publicly whipped in similar proportion. Upon hearing their sentence, Obadiah Holmes made the proper reply of a self-considered martyr,

"I bless God I am counted worthy to suffer for the name of Jesus."

At this point, the Rev. John Wilson, long accounted one of the holiest among the Boston orthodox, stepped briskly forward, and slapping Holmes in the face, delivered himself of the unsaintlike words,

"The curse of God and Jesus go with thee."

As the thirty strokes descended on his bare back, Obadiah Holmes prayed aloud that the smiters be not charged with this sin and gave evidence of great religious exaltation. The whipping master struck harder with his three-corded whip, but the victim seemed to feel the lash not at all. At the thirtieth stroke of this ugly scene, the sympathizing crowd surged forward, blessing God. All of the town of Lynn had seen a 1651 supplement added to Foxe's *Book of Martyrs* before their very eyes. Obviously no one present would forget it, no matter on which side of the infant baptism fence he had staked out his hopes of eternal bliss.

When, in May of the following year, John Clarke's *Ill Newes from New England* detailed this story for English consumption, various doors in England opened to him and Roger Williams, and the words of his prefatory letter, "Rhode Island where my residence is, and a town called Providence, which was begun by one Mr. Roger Williams," became a topic of conversation to the dispraise of Massachusetts Bay leaders. Sir Richard Saltonstall wrote to John Cotton and John Wilson,

> "These rigid ways have laid you very low in the hearts of the saints."

Nothing daunted, however, John Cotton replied that as to the punishment, the culprits had fared better in prison than at home, and that Obadiah Holmes had not been so well clad in years. As to compelling men to conform to orthodox beliefs and ways, even though it made them hypocrites, "Better be a hypocrite than a profane person." When John Cotton entered glory later in 1652, he went stedfast in orthodoxy and undefeated in supporting argument. Thomas Cobbett also replied, supporting the magistrates in their action, and conversation thrived on the pros and cons of this episode.

Besides settling up his personal affairs before he sailed on what looked like another long absence, there was only one more thing for Roger Williams to do, and that was to secure some guarantee that he and John Clarke represented the desire of loyal English subjects. Therefore, with the help of Gregory Dexter, Town Clerk, he drew up an Oath of Allegiance which read,

> "I do declare and Promise that I will be true and ffaithful to the Comonwealth of England, as it is now Established without a King or house of Lords." [20]

No fuzzy specifications; just a clean-cut, unequivocal statement of purpose, which the wayfaring man would understand when he affixed his name or his mark, as about one third of the Providence freemen did immediately, and others throughout the colony later. Getting a new charter would require some such assurance, and it was a wise move to have fortified themselves with such an instrument in advance of presenting their petition. Roger Williams may not have meant to found a colony when he floundered through the

1635 snowdrifts, but like a score of other pulpit men of his generation, he had learned through his exile years to use his talents and his training toward a minor statesmanship which did him great credit.

CHAPTER SEVENTEEN

Colony Agent

HE sailed from Boston in November, 1651. John Clarke, just out of jail, and William Dyer went with him. Permission to pass through Massachusetts jurisdiction had come this time by his own personal application to the General Court then in session. Might he have leave to pass, as a stranger for a night, "to the ship, and so (if God so please) may land there again from the land of our nativity" on his return. His phrase "inoffensively behaving myself" seems strangely misapplied, but there it is. He made it clear also in his petition that he went "not only as a private passenger, but as a messenger and agent to the high court of the Parliament of England," and that the occasion was the late grant obtained by William Coddington. He knew of course that Massachusetts would not be pleased with this mission, but he made no attempt to obscure it. They would also not be pleased with the recall of his banishment, which he stated he had desired "to endure with a quiet and patient mind," but something in Roger Williams made it impossible for him not to mention his sufferings. He also recalled once again his services to maintain peace with the Indians through these sixteen years of banishment. "Scarce a week hath passed," he wrote, but in some way he had been instrumental "to the peace and spreading of the English plantings in this country." [1] All true, of course, however much one might wish the recall might come from the other side. In the face of all this, the Deputies could hardly refuse his plea and it was granted, "provided he carry himself inoffensively according to his promise." They did not yet trust him, nor was his passage through the colony "without molestation," probably thanks to the Clarke episode.

The voyage was rough, but "blessed be God, we live, and through the jaws of death are landed safe," he reported.[2] He appears to have gone immediately to Sir Harry Vane's residence in Whitehall, whence he looked forth on a greatly changed England, politically and religiously. The eight years since his last visit had ended the monarchy, brought victory to Cromwell and also nourished his ambitions. The House of Commons was now reduced to only a fragment of its former self and a House of Lords did not exist. Young Charles II was safe in France, but already eyes were beginning to turn in his direction. During this interregnum the Council of State constituted the ruling majority in Commons and whatever passed its table was sure of Parliamentary approval. It was virtually the power in the land. Cromwell was its chairman, Sir Harry Vane, Cornelius Holland and William Masham were among its members. The position of these influential friends in high place gave Roger Williams' plea a better chance to be heard favorably than would be likely after Commons was once again an elected body in full numbers. He saw his opportunity, and took it, probably on the advice of Vane.

This first action took the form of a petition, asking that the commission of Coddington be revoked and that the former royal charter of 1644 be confirmed. This confirmation was of course only an intermediate step, but since at the moment no power existed to grant a new charter, Rhode Islanders had best keep what they had for what protection it might afford against successful encroachment from the northern colonies. Massachusetts and Connecticut also had royal charters and were in precisely the same uncertain situation. At first Roger Williams' petition met with vigorous opposition, led by Sir Arthur Haselrig, previously a friend of Rhode Island, and one of the signers of the 1644 charter. William Coddington had pressed his claims personally and had made a good impression. Before Roger Williams and John Clarke had a chance to challenge the truth of these claims, English events forced postponement, and then a long delay. Sir Harry Vane was sent to Scotland to secure voluntary assent to union with England; the Dutch war was at hand; in fact, almost at the shore line; the bill for dissolving Parliament had already been brought in. The Council of State obviously had no time to consider Rhode Island affairs. The petition was shelved.

Delay was not altogether unfortunate, however, for it gave Roger Williams a chance to become better known to those members of the Council who were already inclined to be friendly, and to confront his opposers personally. During this same interval of waiting he also went to a London printing house five times and the five titles which issued forth were the best of introductions to Cromwell's circle whose help he solicited. Two of these publications had been written earlier: *Experiments of Spiritual Life and Health* and *The Bloody Tenent Yet More Bloody*. The first, written for Mary Williams alone, but now printed at the earnest desire of friends, bore a dedication to Lady Vane, his hostess at various times during his stay. The second *Bloody Tenent* treatise, sent over prior to his own coming, had prefatory addresses added only. Two sides of Roger Williams speak in these two books, the preacher and the controversialist, and the London of 1652 provided an audience for both. The other three pamphlets, two of them appearing in this same month of April, concern issues of the immediate moment.

As on his previous visit, his thought was fired by the controversy going on around him, and the urge to engage in it was irresistible. Had his residences in England been for decades not months, his shelf of contributions would have been several shelves, for his thought seemed to require outside stimulus, particularly the stimulus of opposition. Heated difference set him off; also sympathetic understanding kindled his own fires. In the Narragansett country he had few associates whose intellectual interests belonged to his own world. He crossed swords with his fellow townsmen over practical everyday matters of governance and was obliged to give the largest share of his thought and energy to keeping the peace. Here in London his associates were men of stature comparable to his own. They too were grappling with problems of governance, but problems set in a larger context. Both their differences of view and their agreements fructified his own thought and immediately he had things to say. The circle in which he moved was a circle of English leaders, among whom he took his place with as much ease as in a Providence town meeting. In addition to Cromwell, Sir Harry Vane, Sir William Masham, Cornelius Holland, and others who had helped him to secure the charter in 1644, the circle now included Major General Harrison, Sir Henry Lawrence, John Owen, Colonel Danvers, Major Butler, Charles Vane, to mention only a few. In terms of the interest and stimulus such associations provided, these months of waiting must have been some of the most deeply satisfying of all Roger Williams' life, and this in spite of the weight of anxiety he was carrying for the colony, and the personal deprivation of absence from his home and family.

His friendship with John Milton belongs to this period also. Whether the two men had met on the 1644 visit is not known, but the likelihood is strong. Sir Harry Vane and Milton had been close friends at that time, and it would have been natural for Vane to bring about an introduction. All three men had been much in attendance upon the sessions of the Assembly of Divines, where during these earlier months Milton's Divorce treatise had made him a storm center of Assembly criticism. Roger Williams' answer to Cotton's letter and his *Queries* had brought him into prominence with Assembly members also, and it is difficult to see how the two men could have missed each other. As to the 1652 association, there is Roger Williams' oft-quoted statement as to the language exchanges.

> "It pleased the Lord to call me for some time, and with some persons, to practice the Hebrew, the Greek, Latin, French and Dutch. The Secretary of the Council, (Mr. Milton) for my Dutch I read him, read me many more languages." [3]

A glance at the Council of State orders, issued to Milton as Latin Secretary, suggests that the burden of work upon him was such as to require a large corps of helpers, even though he were in full possession of his own eyes, and at this time he was threatened with total blindness. Any help Roger Williams might have given was probably informal, not official, and besides, Milton had a Dutch assistant, but even so, he might have been very useful. The Dutch war made a particular necessity for the speedy translation of Dutch communications into the official Latin. How to interpret the "read me many more languages" is puzzling, but surely it testifies to an association of some duration and a chance for mutual exchange of more than linguistic matter.

The two men would have had much common ground in the cause of freedom to which each had made such significant contribution. Milton's plea for liberty of conscience had a more practical basis than Roger Williams'; it was a "high intellectual persuasion" for a course of action of proved expediency. Roger Williams based his plea on the authority of Scripture and the inherent rights of man as man, but fundamentally the two men were in agreement basic enough to make differences arguable. As Roger Williams grew more experienced in the problems of government, he too grew more realistic and tested his own high notions in terms of their workability in everyday affairs. His most significant growth as a political thinker is in this direction, and since 1644, it would have brought him closer to Milton's tests of "utility." Milton's distrust of universal suffrage would have been a significant point of difference in their views, but

> "That all men are born free, that kings and magistrates are but agents of the people acting with delegated power and that the form of government is unimportant, provided only that popular sovereignty is its method of being"

—in all this they were agreed.[4]

At some time before April, 1652, the month in which four separate units of his thought issued from London printing houses, he composed the introductory addresses prefaced to his *Bloody Tenent Yet More Bloody*. These addresses to Parliament, to the General Courts of New England and to the Reader are the freshest part of this long, slow-paced second dialogue of Truth and Peace. This book would not be ordered burned by Parliamentary vote. Not that Roger Williams now spoke too mildly, or that the battle he fought had already been won; far from it. But the climate had changed. In the eight years since his first "soul-freedom" treatise had shocked his friends and angered his enemies, the word *toleration* had grown a little more than respectable. The Declaration of Parliament in 1648 that "religion is a thing intrincicall between God and the soul" and that there is "no humane power of coertion thereunto" had not only brought ease to the non-conformist, but had encouraged rigorists for conformity to become liberal over night and to call themselves "well-wishers to the Kingdomes Good" or some other such flattering title.

It is true that "God's Diamonds" still found vulnerable places at which to "cut each other," but the "Great Stirre" of the mid-forties was no longer in full fling. It was a cold war now and the resulting treatises make dull reading in comparison with the fiery vehemence of combatants when the battle was young and swords were newly sharpened. Whether, as one writer had put it, the fiery trial of contention or persecution itself had been the greater evil, it was hard to say. Now in placating terms tired antagonists on both sides were saying, "Let us no more devour each other." Why cannot "Variety of opinions and unity of those who hold them stand together?" But official toleration and "soul-freedom," as Roger Williams had conceived it, were a long way apart, and if anything, the oppressed were in a worse case than before. There was still room for another plea, but it must be differently shaped.

The second *Bloody Tenent* treatise hardly met the need of these changed times. In the semi-solitude of his trading house clearing, Roger Williams had gone right on fighting the battle from the point where Cotton's answer to his first blast [5] had left it in 1647. Cotton had waited three years to answer, and since then Roger Williams had waited five. No battle of ideas stays at the same point more than a fraction of either span, and the line by line refutation of that which was already long cold in print, as Truth and Peace talk it out page after page, is pale by comparison with the 1644 treatise. In this first piece, Roger Williams had occasionally forgotten John Cotton and his fallacies in logic, and had found words to express a flaming personal conviction and an uplifting vision. He would not do it again, nor was a second such flight needful. The battle front had shifted.

At the same time the later skirmishes in a great struggle between opposed principles of human action have their place. Men hack away at rough places, chipping here and mending there, concerning themselves with minutiae. Had Roger Williams built this second discourse on his introductory plea that Parliament would distinguish between freedom of conscience as a state necessity and "the Equity and Piety of such Freedom" he would have done well. Instead, it is his intent "to unwash Cotton's washings" and to prove

Persecution more "notoriously guilty" than on his earlier arraignment, and to that end he defines persecution afresh as to its nature and then goes on to the power of the civil sword in spirituals and the Parliamentary permission of Dissenting Consciences. A good many of his readers no doubt availed themselves of the concluding summary to which he invites them if their reading time be brief. Read, however, in its entirety, as a thinker's second thoughts on the subject to which his life was all but dedicated, every page of this repetitious dialogue reveals the depth of his conviction, the strength of its buttresses, and the affirmative cast of his thought. There is much of Roger Williams in these pages: his learning, his logic, his utter literalness, his ruthlessness of pursuit, his detective awareness of misty corners where error might lurk, his meticulous care of detail. In its intensity of earnestness, this book is also, if one may use one of his own figures, a window into a man's heart. What one sees there above all is unswerving selflessness in a great cause.

In the other three publications of 1652, he addressed himself to immediate issues of the hour. His part in *Major Butler's Fourth Paper* was slight. The whole pamphlet runs to only twenty-three pages. The occasion was the drawing up by John Owen of *Fifteen Proposals* submitted to the Committee on the Propagation of the Gospel with the intent to set certain limits as to freedom of worship and belief. This Committee had been appointed in answer to the action of a company of ministers who had appeared at the doors of Parliament in personal protest against the printing of a Racovian catechism in February, 1652. The book had been ordered burned by Parliament and the newly appointed Committee, with Sir William Masham as chairman, had gone to work, meeting daily for many weeks.[6] On March 2nd, Major Butler had printed his protest against the Fifteen Proposals of John Owen, and on March 30th, Roger Williams reprinted Butler's protest with what he called "Humble explications" of his own. It is easy to see why he supported Major Butler so earnestly, for the proposals of Owen had put the brunt of the responsibility for limiting freedom of worship and belief in the hands of the civil magistrate, and "the state's power in spirituals" was a subject on which Roger Williams could not by any possibility keep silence. The first three of Butler's counter proposals repeat familiar arguments, but the fourth proposal was itself relatively new in 1652. It concerned permitting the Jews, "whose conversion we look for, to live freely and peaceably amongst us." As one might expect, this proposal and Roger Williams' endorsement of it would presently become fact in Rhode Island, as it did. Neither Major Butler nor Roger Williams had much weight with the Committee which adopted Owen's first three proposals, giving the magistrate the power against which both men had protested. The dissolution of Parliament in the following April put a quick end to the Parliamentary discussion of the Committee's report, which was submitted only in February, 1653.

His fourth publication, *The Hireling Ministry None of Christs*, concerned the current discussion of forced tithes for support of established ministers, an issue being debated in the Commons and arousing intense feeling all over England among sectarian groups. Since the larger issue of the civil authority in matters of religion was again involved, once again Roger Williams "being desired by eminent friends to cast in my mite," struck a hard blow against compulsory support of the clergy in a church not of one's own faith. The word *hireling* in his title put him on the wrong side at once with ecclesiastical leaders, for this was George Fox's word, as also was the plea for voluntary support of the ministry. No matter, he meant *hireling* with all its unfortunate connotations.

More than any other of his printed statements, this treatise clarifies Roger Williams' own personal position as to a church affiliation. His Epistle Dedicatory is in effect an autobiographical declaration. He recalls the whole panorama of his life in a single sentence. He has trod

> "the hopefullest paths to Worldly preferments, (which for Christ's sake I have forsaken) since I know what it is to Study, to Preach, to be an Elder, to be applauded, and yet what it is to tug at the Oar, to dig with the Spade, and Plow, and to labour and travel day and night amongst English, amongst Barbarians! why should I not be humbly bold to give my witness faithfully, to give my counsel effectually, and to persuade with some truly pious and conscientious spirits rather to turn to Law, to Physick, to Souldiery, to Educating of Children, to Digging (and yet not cease from Prophecying) rather than to live under the slavery, yea and the

SIR HARRY VANE THE YOUNGER, BY SIR PETER LELY
From a photograph in the Boston Athenaeum Library

THE

BLOVDY TENENT,

of PERSECUTION, for cause of CONSCIENCE, discussed, in

A Conference *betweene*

TRVTH and PEACE.

VVHO,

In all tender Affection, present to the High Court of *Parliament*, (as the *Result* of their *Discourse*) these, (amongst other *Passages*) of *highest consideration*.

Printed in the Year. 1644.

TITLE PAGE OF *The Bloudy Tenent of Persecution,* LONDON, 1644
Yale University Library

censure from Christ Jesus and his Saints and others also of a mercenary Hireling Minister?" [7]

In the "poor small span" of his life, he has desired to be a "diligent and Constant *Observer,*" seeking in many ways "in *City,* in *Country,* in *Court,* in *Schools,* in *Universities,* in *Churches,* in *Old* and *New-*England," and yet he could not discover that "the ministry of the Apostles according to first *Institution* of the Lord Jesus Christ are yet restored and extant." Twenty years later in the debate with the Quakers he repeats this testimony of his unending quest. To the end of his life he did not find what he sought and he would accept no lesser substitute.

The ministry of Christ as he conceived it called for something different from a University degree. Look at Samuel How,[8] "that despised and yet beloved . . . Cobbler," who without humane learning, merely by searching the Scriptures, "grew so excellent a textuary, or Scripture-learned man, that few of those high Rabbies, that scorn to make or mend a shoe, could aptly and readily, from the Holy Scripture out-go him." Such knowledge of the Scriptures was the equipment of a minister, and a "Commission" from God Himself, not a University degree, was the warrant.

"Christ never appointed nor needed the divinity degrees of universities and colleges,"

he wrote. Churches themselves were the only "Schools of the prophets," and need have no alliance with secular institutions. No disparagement of university training is intended; this verdict is only one more application of his mature view that whatever concerns religion must be separate unto itself alone.

The fifth of these 1652 publications, *The Examiner Defended,*[9] was an answer to twenty-two questions asked in an immediately preceding pamphlet, *The Examiner Examined,* itself an answer to one still earlier, entitled *Zeal Examined.* These three pamphlets appeared in quick succession, were the work of three friends, all of them on the same side of the 1652 issues being discussed. The third, only recently identified as the work of Roger Williams, bears his signature unmistakably both in matter and style, even phraseology.

It is again "humbly bold" and begins with his favorite figure, the Ship of State, with its "commanding orders," its "obeying stations," its "sheet-anchor," and various other familiar details. In accepting the challenge of these twenty-two questions, Roger Williams says,

> "I confess, my Principle of Soul-freedom commands me to *applaud,* and *honour* this *searching* and *proposing* from the holy Scripture." [10]

His answers to these questions present nothing new, but merely emphasize afresh his insistence that the civil magistrate has no power in "spiritualls," and that the salaried minister makes his calling as "Mercenary and unChristian" as his who "stands at the Corners of the streets in dark Nights," saying "Will you have a light Sir!" Roger Williams is at home in this quieter exchange, as he had been in the two more temperate publications of this same year on the same subjects, but this last one adds little to the sum of his thought.

In April, the same month in which four of these publications had appeared, he had his delayed hearing before the Council of State. He was well prepared and well furnished with proofs as to the fraudulency of Coddington's claims. He himself had been a signer of the Aquidneck deed in 1638, and he had documentary evidence to prove it. He also had the authorization of the majority of freemen in Aquidneck, protesting against Coddington's usurpation and delegating John Clarke as their representative to petition that his commission be revoked. The hearing seemed favorable, and both agents were encouraged. Fortunately, during the following month of May, while the findings were being discussed, Sir Harry Vane was appointed to act as President of the Council of State. On October 2, 1652, six months later, Coddington's commission was revoked, and the 1644 charter of Providence Plantations confirmed.[11]

The usurpation was over. After this rebuke one might wonder how William Coddington could walk erect through the streets of his own town; however, he not only did so, but held offices thereafter by election. He was an able man, one of the ablest in the colony, and in the light of his whole career, is no enigma. His abilities fitted him for calm weather, not for storms, and when things went against his peace, he merely built a new utopia and walked out of the mess. He had large holdings on the island, had built himself a mansion, and he wanted peace in which to enjoy his prosperity. Tired of the petty bickerings around him, he had thought to end them by wearing the crown of his small kingdom, and as this solution tempted him, he conveniently forgot the warmth of Roger Williams' welcome when he had come to Providence as a refugee in 1638, and had been helped to this very home on Aquidneck. He had overreached himself; gaining the life commission had been easier than he might have thought possible, but he had reckoned without the astuteness and diplomatic skill of this same Roger Williams in an affair of clear truth and justice.

Now that the Coddington claim was foiled, the mission of the two agents was half over, but only half. Getting a new charter had already begun to look years distant. Had either Roger Williams or John Clarke realized that it was still eleven years distant, they might have been disheartened indeed although they were well aware that uncertainty as to the final issue increased with each succeeding month. The representatives of Connecticut, Edward Hopkins and George Fenwick, were also in London, together with Edward Winslow who was pleading Plymouth's claims. All three were men of moderation and fairness, and already they had gone a long way toward impressing the Council of State that their claims were valid. Massachusetts also had not relaxed her efforts. If the demands of any one of these three claimants were allowed, it would be difficult to deny the other two. Would Rhode Island ever be able to call herself her own? Even so, to challenge these counter claims too early or too hotly might be to lose all. It was wiser to risk the mounting unrest at home than to lose the very ground under their feet by too great urgency or too frank hostility.

Foreseeing the long delay still ahead of them before they could hope for any chance for success, Roger Williams had written Gregory Dexter in September, 1652, to report encouragement in the Coddington affair, and the likelihood of a long-deferred charter settlement. "The determination of it, I fear, will be a work of time," he wrote, adding that he could have no thought of returning until at least a year from the coming spring. Facing this longer absence, he was considering asking Mary Williams to come over to share these months with him.

"Joyful I should be of her being here with me,"

he wrote, but

"our many children, the danger of the seas, and enemies,"

made him unwilling to press his desires against her own judgment.

> "I *freely* leave her to wait upon the Lord for direction, and according as she finds her spirit free and cheerful, to come or stay." [12]

This sentence opens a window into the Providence home. She decided not to come, and though he doubtless thought her answer wise, the letter of the following April reflects his disappointment. There is a distinct note of homesickness in this official letter.

"I have longed earnestly to return with the last ship,"

he wrote; nevertheless, he was willing to stay, "except you are pleased to give me a discharge." [13] Besides, if he came now, the burden "might pinch others" and might fall heavy upon all. What was their wish in the matter?

The answer of Providence, written October 28, 1652, before they had heard of the cancelling of Coddington's commission, is one of the most appreciative statements of Roger Williams' abilities and endeavors he was ever to receive from his fellow townsmen. One hopes it rested in his memory in the same niche with the shout of welcome from the shore of the Seekonk in 1644. He needed such encouragement and it was rare enough. This town reply, penned by John Greene, General Recorder, may have more of John Greene in it than the tone the town action warranted, but at least Roger Williams had the comfort of such healing words as

> "Wee may not neglect any opportunity to salute you in your absence, and have not a little cause to bless God, who hath pleased to selecte you to such a purpose. . . . Wee perceive your prudent and comprehensive mind stirreth every stone to present it unto the builders, to make firme the fabricke under us. . . ." [14]

Obviously, the main intent of this letter was the suggestion that the Council of State appoint him as Governor of the colony for a year, that the government might be stabilized while a charter decision was awaited. This suggestion he did not accept, as it would seem wisely, but at least he had had advance warning that the headship of the colony would probably await him on his return. He remained in England for more than another full year.

It was a year that would change many things in England, and once again as in his chaplain days, he would be a walker of London streets to witness the impact of some of them. His intimate association with Sir Harry Vane, one of the chief actors, would mean a shared knowledge of some details shut otherwise to all but the participants. Vane's break with Cromwell was one such event. How would Sir Harry have reported the cataclysm of April 20, 1653, in an intimate conversation? Written with stark literalness on a page of history, prejudicial to neither side, it leaps into drama, and takes on color and sound. It can hardly be read dispassionately; one takes sides unwittingly. The fact that it was a long-anticipated crisis would only have made the tenseness more insupportable to those who were of it.

It was a swift drama: Cromwell's arrival at Parliament in black suit and gray worsted stockings, as though he had come suddenly, and on impulse instead of with due preparation; the soldiers left outside; Cromwell's accusation, made with rising anger as he strode back and forth; Sir Peter Wentworth's protest at his unbecoming language, and then Cromwell's outburst.

> "Come, come, I will put an end to your prating. You are no Parliament. I say you are no Parliament. I will put an end to your sitting. Call them in."

Then the tramp of musketeers, the speaker removed from his chair, the mace removed, and Vane's voice, above the clamor,

> "This is not honest; yea, it is against morality and common honesty."

How would Vane have reported Cromwell's rejoinder, as tradition has passed it down?

"O Sir Harry Vane! Sir Harry Vane! The Lord deliver me from Sir Harry Vane." [15]

To have known the two principals in this final sad exchange, also Sir Henry Lawrence, Major General Harrison, who gave the order to the soldiers, and others within the chamber; to have been an eyewitness to the consternation, the anger, the fears for the future, the conflict of loyalties these events awakened in the London populace, would have raised many questions in the mind of a man deeply concerned in government, and committed to the belief in man's right to govern himself. What now? For as once more the old order changed, Englishmen realized afresh that all that had been wrong had not ended when Charles I put his head on the block; nor had the consequent order brought about all that was right. The feeling for a return to monarchy was rising all over England.

With the dissolution of Parliament, the Council of State had also been dissolved, and as this body was re-constituted on May 3, 1653, Vane, whose sun had set, William Masham and Cornelius Holland, three of Roger Williams' best friends in their sympathy for Rhode Island's claims, were not included. What had already looked like a long postponement in the charter business, now stretched out even longer. Every boat brought news of dissension in the colony. Roger Williams decided to go home, leaving John Clarke in charge of Rhode Island's fight for a new charter. He would have ten more years to wait for success to reward his efforts.

CHAPTER EIGHTEEN

Mediator

In early summer 1654, he landed in Boston, this time furnished with an order from the Lord Protector's Council, requiring Massachusetts to grant him safe conduct through her territory. Accordingly, in his own word, "once again saluting the wilderness," he set out staff in hand through the woods to Rhode Island. This time there would be no flotilla of canoes waiting to greet him, no grateful welcome from his own townsmen.

He had come back to far worse than he had left behind more than two years before. "The chaos of Rhode Island" indeed, for the phrase was woefully apt. During his absence the insistent claims of Massachusetts, Connecticut and Plymouth colonies had kept the settlers of the parts claimed in a continual state of tension and consequent friction among themselves. If these rival claimants only half succeeded, Rhode Island would be left in mere ribbons and patches. Moreover, the inhabitants of the unclaimed territories were so riven by factions that the colony was all but dismembered, Roger Williams' own town of Providence most seriously of all.

Faced by what looked like an almost hopeless continuation of strife, he sat down and wrote the town the sharpest letter they were ever to receive from him. Its sharpness may have been tempered a little by the note of bewilderment and deep personal hurt which sounded through it.

> "Well-beloved friends and Neighbors," he began. "I am like a man in a great fog. I know not well how to steer. I fear to run upon the rocks at home, having had trials abroad. I fear to run

quite backward, as men in a mist do, and undo all that I have been a long time undoing myself to do, viz.: to keep up the name of a people, a free people, not enslaved to the bondages and iron yokes of the great (both soul and body) oppressions of the English and barbarians about us, nor to the divisions and disorders within ourselves."

In the light of the next sentence his co-townsmen would hardly seem to deserve the affectionate caption with which his letter had addressed them.

"I am as good as banished by yourselves, and that both sides wished that I might never have landed, that the fire of contention might have had no stop in burning." [1]

Perhaps in his distress and bewilderment he overstated the case, but certainly his outburst is understandable. For more than two years he had put the interest of the colony uppermost, sacrificing his own personal concerns at every point. Having disposed of his trading post to finance his voyage, he was now without a means of livelihood. During his stay in London he had been obliged to borrow and to work for his very bread. He now came home to censure, even abuse, heaped on him by those in whose cause he had spent these difficult months. Present disappointment recalled past grievances in kind and he repeated them bluntly.

"Since I set the first step of any English foot into these wild parts . . . and spent almost five years with the state of England, to keep off the rage of the English against us, what have I reaped, of the root . . . of being the stepping stone of so many families and towns about us, but grief, and sorrow, and bitterness?" [2]

It was all true and more, one party having even called him traitor "against the state of England."

On the town's side, this attitude of criticism and harshness is also understandable, at least in part. He had come back without the charter, which alone would give them a right to the very soil under their feet and the grass lands over which their cattle, sheep and goats ranged. The explanations of delay which he had so carefully written them months before, "the mighty war with the Dutch," their enemies in high place, the risk of losing all unless one moved cautiously, all these reasons seemed remote and insubstantial to a provincial town in the far wilderness. Providence was the smallest of the four towns which made up Rhode Island and the least prosperous. Its entire population at this date was probably less than two hundred and fifty. Up and down the one long street, life rubbed on life and small quarrels grew large in the mere struggle to survive. Among the principal men of the town were few men of vision. Blessedly they had Gregory Dexter, who had done his best to hold the town together, but he had not always been wise, and he was still regarded as something of a newcomer, not quite accepted by the pioneer settlers. The issues underneath most of this party strife were personal.

Almost any pioneer town in early New England shows a similar picture at some time or other. Life was hard, and on the flat, everyday level of existence, party strife found a good soil in which to grow and increase. Usually such divisions localized around the meetinghouse, and the town minister took the blows. Providence had no meetinghouse for nearly half a century yet, and not even a fort or town house, in spite of Roger Williams' repeated efforts to encourage the building of one. The tavern was the usual meeting place for the town business. Even such an outward symbol of group unity as a common refuge or place of meeting to suggest the good of the whole against the will of each individually, might have helped, but Providence had neither the symbol nor the reality.

These 1654 manifestations of discord were no surprise to Roger Williams. He had had news of them by every boat, had talked them over with Sir Harry Vane, and had asked Vane to write a letter to the town, pleading for a better spirit. The letter is dated February 8, 1654, nearly six months before. Roger Williams now made four copies of it and sent one to each town in the colony. He acted unwisely, and so had Vane. Both men were forgetting what they had had a chance to learn many times as to the delicacy of human relations when the fires of contention are blazing. In the tenseness of feeling at the moment, Rhode Island was in no mood to be scolded. Addressing them as Loving and Christian Friends, Vane had written,

> "How is it that there are such divisions among you? Such headiness, tumults, disorders, injustice? The noise echoes into the ears of all, as well friends as enemies, by every return of ships from those parts. . . . Are there no wise men amongst you? No public self-denying spirits, that at least, upon the grounds of public safety, equity and prudence, can find out some way or means of union and reconciliation for you amongst yourselves . . . ? [3]

True, and needing to be said, all of it, but hardly the letter of a man to his equals, nor written in the spirit of an ambassador of peace. Had Sir Harry been in Providence, facing the assembled townsmen at the tavern or in someone's ample kitchen, he would have won them to a man, for the magnetism of his presence, like that of Roger Williams, was compelling, but on paper his words had a scolding sound. Besides, he was meddling in their own very private affairs, and the reception given these stern words was not pretty, whether Sir Harry was the "sheet anchor" of their ship or not.

Halfway through his own long letter to the town, Roger Williams became himself again, or rather, his wiser self, and proceeded to show the Providence malcontents a way around one impasse, their latest one. This was their opposition to a gesture of unity sent by the island towns of Newport and Portsmouth. They had invited Providence and Warwick to send their deputies to a conference, looking toward a restored union of the two halves of the colony. Roger Williams made no criticism of their refusal to do so, but wrote disarmingly, "If I were in your soul's case, I would send unto your opposites such a line as this," and he even supplied the phraseology by which they might retract their former refusal, and still save their pride. Let the conference be held, he suggested, and then "if yet aught remain grievous," let Providence and Warwick choose two men out of any part of the colony and let the island towns choose other two, to judge the matter between us.[4] So stated, it sounded simple and logical, and was so ordered.

In this letter, first, for its straightforward, unsoftened statement of the case as he saw it, and second, for the practical suggestion of a way out, Roger Williams revealed certain fundamental qualities of his own nature, and also one of the secrets of his best success as a mediator for troubled times. In both the rebuke and the remedy, he spoke as a man to his equals, proud as he was proud. Once again he succeeded. The conference was held on August 31st; a special election was called for September 12th, and on that day he was re-elected President of the colony. Thereafter he was re-elected in the two succeeding years. It had taken his presence and his voice to accomplish what a month before would have seemed impossible. He had been away too long.

Meanwhile, before the month of August had passed, Providence had asked him to draft a reply to Sir Harry Vane's letter of accusation. He did so, and the letter was sent under the signature of Gregory Dexter, Town Clerk. Every sentence of it is alive with the spirit of Roger Williams, and though there were probably those in the town meeting whose temperatures rose when the letter was read to them, it had already been accepted and sent. It had expressed thanks to Vane for "awakening any of our sleepy spirits by your sweet alarm," with these thanks being wisely matched by naming William Coddington and William Dyer as the chief offenders back of the dissension, thereby saving the town pride. Roger Williams had also taken this opportunity of saying some things to Providence as well as to Sir Harry. These concerned the charter and its privileges. If these things were only said often enough, Providence would remember them and presently give them back as their own. For example,

> "We have long drunk of the cup of as great liberties as any people that we can hear of under the whole heaven." [5]

He followed this sentence by listing these liberties for better emphasis. This too is Roger Williams to the life. Most of the encomiums upon liberty surviving in early town papers are in his words. Over and over he repeated them, sometimes in crisp epigrams, such as his own school days had honored; sometimes bolstered by Scripture warrant, but always he repeated them. This letter is only one example, but a fair one.

As the elected President of the riven colony, he now faced three more difficult years. These years would test afresh his patience, his wisdom, and his ability to separate the transient from the enduring. They would also test the workability of the principles of individual freedom upon which he had spent so many hundreds of words in his *Bloody Tenent* treatises. Many an Amos has spoken his piece in the market place, but to relatively few prophets have the gavel and the seal been handed immediately afterward. Such was Roger Williams' opportunity in 1654.

Looked back upon for what would seem to be the larger objectives of his plan during this three year period, his record shows him to have been driving first of all toward a sound union of four separate town states, no one of which really wanted union with the other three. Neither did they want increase of governmental machinery within their own town limits. "Nor doth the face of Magistracy suit with our present condition," Roger Williams had written to John Winthrop when the settlement was barely a handful; neither did they greatly want it in their September mood when they elected him President. The dangers of 1636 "(in the midst of these dens of lions)" were not actively present in 1654. The incentive to union now must be inner, not outer, and obviously that would take a long time. A start was made, however, when four months later they were "persuaded," as Roger Williams wrote to John Winthrop, Jr., "by the good hand of the Lord," to choose six men in each town as Commissioners to work out a plan of union.[6] The fighting went right on, but at least the initial machinery had been set up, and with the presidential chapter of Samuel Gorton on the mainland and the usurpation of William Coddington on the island officially ended, both of the sundered halves of the colony began to see the advantage of holding the reins themselves. The leaven was working and Roger Williams let it alone for a while.

His second objective was more difficult; namely, how to draw the line clearly between liberty as an individual human right with obligations toward other men, and freedom to act without reference to anyone else. In the powder keg of Rhode Island he did not need to wait long for an issue upon which to build this distinction. It happened to be Providence which exploded first, and ironically enough, over the issue of military service as a civil defense measure.

Pacifism was as good a reason as any for those who wished to defy the town order, and they proceeded to do so in militant fashion. Thomas Olney, William Harris, and a substantial following, Bibles in hand, attempted to rally supporters and confute the order on scriptural grounds. The situation quickly became confused and turbulent.

No doubt a great deal was said on both sides in the heat of the moment, but whatever Roger Williams' part in this first give and take up and down the long street of Providence may have been, his official answer toward clarification of the issue was a letter to the town. In calm mood he resorted to parable and wrote what has since become the best known paragraph in all his writing. He had said the same thing before, more than once, but this time he said it more succinctly and therefore more memorably. It begins,

> "There goes many a ship to sea, with many hundred souls in one ship, whose weal and woe is common, and is a true picture of a commonwealth, or a human combination or society . . ." [7]

The ship carries passengers of many faiths, and no one of these passengers is obliged to come to the ship's prayers if his conscience forbid, but everyone, whatever his faith, must, for the good of the whole, obey the orders of the captain or be punished for disobedience. May this parable, he prayed, "let in some light to such as willingly shut not their eyes," signing himself, "I remain studious of your common peace and liberty, Roger Williams." Apparently it helped, at least at this moment of insubordination, but the line between *my good* and *the good of the whole* was a long time invisible to certain "heady spirits" in Providence.

In later times a single sentence in this famous parable has had a fair share of attention. It is "if any should preach or write that there ought to be no commanders or officers, . . . the commander or commanders may judge, resist, compel and punish such transgressors, according to their deserts and merits." Was Roger Williams, say his modern critics, denying free speech? Was he forbidding to others that of which he himself had been accounted guilty at the bar of Massachusetts justice? In its village context of 1654, clearly *No.* Authority steps in at the danger point only, and restricts the privilege of him who would destroy all. On the town records of Providence, so far as they detail the month by month reproofs and punishments administered, clearly *No* again. Authority stepped in not at the point of difference, but at the point where difference spelled danger to the community. Even in his own boldness of 1634 (which must have looked a little callow to him in 1654) he had not incited a mob, defied civil authority, or advocated violence. He had not even raised his voice. He had merely spoken his protest, in a pulpit tone, as to the end of his days he insisted any citizen had a right to do. In the Massachusetts edict against him, there had been a relation between *heresy* and *security,* but a security against error in religious belief. In Providence the danger point concerned security to the civil state only. Within such limits his parable can still clarify the issue.

In the detached view of many generations, this simple parable in response to a village crisis is worth more than many thousand words of line by line confutation of dusty objections to objections in the current controversial pamphlets of the hour, but so to say is to step out of the seventeenth century, when controversy was a natural medium of exchange to thinkers in the cloister or village merchants in the street. It was itself a language. This famous ship passage was a single spark struck off in a tense moment. Behind it and underneath it were long slow fires which were still a long way from their own cold ashes.

While Roger Williams was giving himself during these three years to these two main problems, journeying back and forth incessantly from mainland to island, laboring personally with those who opposed union or defied laws on the basis of individual conscience, the colony books show legislation which gave concreteness to these principles of governance. Measures were worked out which gave increasing solidarity to each of the four town sovereignties and also drew more firmly the line between these and the obligations each town owed to the other three. Certain controls which had formerly belonged to the town individually and had varied in details of administration were now transferred to the General Assembly of the colony and made uniform. The system of taxation was no longer left on a voluntary basis, with contributions from each town; the

Assembly levied the taxes. The penal code was also made more nearly uniform, liberalized in certain directions and extended considerably in others. One of the first of the reform measures attempted was what Roger Williams called "A Speedie Regulacion of our Lawes (now under the Examination of a Committee as allso of a more Speedie course of hearing the Complaints and Grievances of the Colonie." [8]

These constructive measures have sometimes been obscured by noisier matters which of necessity required attention. Studied from the colony and town books, this record shows a grasp of the more active causes of these noisier matters and an understanding of practical ways to meet them, in so far as the machinery of government affords a means to that end. Of course Roger Williams did not do it all. Wisely he seems to have entrusted the creation of such machinery to the freeholders themselves, however his own guidance may have initiated various measures or shaped their results. His leadership in matters of town and colony public affairs was of the sort which evokes the desire and the willingness in other men, never the leadership of the driver and dictator.

In 1656 came the Quakers, to test afresh the practical working out of the freedom of conscience principle in everyday life. Rhode Island's part in this deeply involved story can be simply told. They merely held the door open while the other colonies shut it. Promptly upon the arrival of the first ship bearing Quakers to Boston, action was taken "by the prudent care of that Government" not to receive them. The Commissioners of the United Colonies informed Rhode Island of this action, whereupon the General Assembly of the colony, met in Portsmouth, replied that since

> "freedom of different consciences, was the principal ground of our Charter . . . which freedom we still prize as the greatest happines that men can possess in this world," [9]

Quakers will be granted this freedom so long as they subject themselves to all the duties required of other members of the civil society. The northern colonies were of course not pleased, but Rhode Island persisted, reporting that

"They have their liberty amongst us, are entertayned into our howses, or into any of our assemblies."

The colony then wrote John Clarke in London, empowering him in the new charter negotiations to plead Rhode Island's case in such sort that "we may not be compelled to exercise any civill power over men's consciences, soe long as humane orders, in point of civility, are not corrupted and v[io]lated." [10] Expressions of conviction such as this, and the resolute determination that nothing should be allowed to violate it, should be remembered to Rhode Island's praise, and set over against the long story of petty animosities, inter-village strife in its many ugly outbursts through the years. The history of towns, nations, and the men who try to lead them, is to be read, of course, on the pages of official records; fairly enough so. There is, however, an undocumented story which is unfortunately mainly lost, and this loss can leave gaps which can vitiate the whole story.

To read Rhode Island's history in the Providence town papers or in the colony records, both incomplete, one might wonder sometimes whether there was ever a season or a session when fellow townsmen worked together in harmony or neighbors were not at war with neighbors. Unhappily this peaceful side of the story called for no record, but somehow underneath the recorded tale of small strifes and the censures they invited, a body of pioneers had united in such a fundamental conviction as to human rights, as no command or threat from the outside, or any roughness from within could even touch, and they had done so in the short space of twenty years. How this had come about in the step by step application is a tale that can never be told. A long web had been weaving ever since six men in a canoe had come down the river to this remote spot, and by the decade of the 1650's, it was a web not to be torn apart. The mediation of small differences had a part in this process, but these noisy differences themselves are not the history of early Rhode Island. Already the inhabitants had done a greater thing than they realized, and when they could themselves see this achievement in perspective enough to recognize it for what it was, they would have a basis for unity that nothing could shake.

In this 1656–1658 chapter of the Quakers in New England, as is usual in such matters, it was their extravagances and noisy misdemeanors which caught the headlines. These have now so long fallen out of memory as to have no meaning whatever in connotations of the word *Quaker* to later times. They seem unbelievable, but they were earlier facts, requiring no present recall except to explain the sense of shock which in part lay back of seventeenth century inhospitality and persecution, both in England and in America. It should be remembered, however, that Rhode Island's attitude of welcome was also of the seventeenth century, and that they too were afflicted with these same noisy demonstrations of impropriety. Even so, they said, Come; live here. You are welcome.

Their hospitality also made headlines. In a typical example, a ship bearing Quakers docked at New Amsterdam in 1657. It was captained by one of them, a man who spoke hardly a word but (said the Director-General of the port) stood still with his hat firm on his head, "as if a goat." The passengers behaved strangely, and presently finding themselves unwelcome, they sailed away. The record of the New Amsterdam ministers reads,

> "We suppose they went to Rhod Island, for that is the receptacle of all sorts of riff-raff people, and is nothing else than the sewer (latrina) of New England. All the cranks of New England retire thither. We suppose they will settle there, as they are not tolerated by the Independents in any other place." [11]

One young man who had succeeded in landing, was imprisoned, fined one hundred guilders, and being given his choice, elected to stay rather than to be shipped out, he knew not whither. He was set to work at the wheelbarrow with Negroes, this service to last for two years. Refusing to submit to this verdict, he was whipped, and told that if he refused a second time, he would be whipped again. After several more days, a letter was brought to the Lord-Director which read,

> "Think, my Lord-Director, whether it be not best to send him to Rhode Island, as his labor is hardly worth the cost."

Such a judgment as to the practical import of Rhode Island's principle of soul-liberty had been only twenty years in the making, but it was as settled in the general mind as though it had endured for a century. Roger Williams was wise enough to know that words are futile to change the unfortunate side of such a connotation, and he was content merely to hold the door open and let the passing generations do the rest.

As always, both before and after, there were Indian uprisings during these three years of office. In the first month after his election, Ninigret, a Narragansett, was again on the warpath. The Commissioners of the United Colonies collected an army and sent them against the Narragansetts, whom they again suspected, in spite of Roger Williams' assurance, again repeated, that they had never stained their hands with English blood. The Massachusetts and Connecticut attitude, favoring alliance with Uncas rather than with the Narragansetts, was a matter of policy. Uncas was their nearer neighbor, and it was safer to be on his side. Alliance with him meant hostility to the Narragansetts, for there was deadly enmity between them. It was in his letter to the Massachusetts General Court, protesting this new march upon the Narragansetts in 1654, that Roger Williams called war one of "those three great, sore plagues, with which it pleaseth God to affect the sons of men." He declares himself not to be against the use of the civil sword in a defensive war, but he suggests that since all men are prone to think of their own wars as defensive,

> "I humbly pray your consideration, whether it be not only possible, but very easy, to live and die in peace with all the natives of this country."

A naïve assumption, one might say, but not from one who had so many times tested his own policy of *talks* with them around their own fires, instead of declarations of war and men marching. As to the Narragansetts, he added,

> "How can it suit with Christian ingenuity to take hold of some seeming occasions for their destructions?" [12]

particularly since God's name is also concerned in this business. Once more bloodshed was avoided, but so long as Uncas lived and the Commissioners supported his side of inter-tribal outbreaks, just so long would such counsels be deterrents for the moment and for the moment only. In this long 1654 letter of protest, Roger Williams had foreseen the possibility that all the Indians in America might one day join against the whites, and that the issue would spell disaster, as it did, twenty years further on. His dealings with the Narragansetts had also been directed by a policy which concerned all English in America, as well as his own Rhode Island colony, and he spoke this warning with the preservation of all in mind.

During his second year as President he had what must have been satisfaction indeed, when at the General Court of Trials in Warwick, on March 11, 1655/56, William Coddington arose and publicly professed,

> "I, William Coddington, doe freely submitt to ye authoritie of his Highness in this Colonie as it is now united, and that with all my heart." [13]

Roger Williams would be out of the presidential chair in June, 1658, when William Arnold petitioned the Massachusetts General Court, asking to be discharged from Massachusetts jurisdiction and declaring his willingness to accept certain proposals by Mr. Roger Williams. Arnold's return to Rhode Island jurisdiction ended many disorders on Pawtuxet. Massachusetts had been too far away to control them, and Rhode Island had had no power to do so. It had been a situation fraught with unending confusion. Now the two prodigals had come home. There was still Samuel Gorton, and always there was William Harris.

The Harris story is darker in its colors than any other of these intra-mural ranklings during Roger Williams' three years of office, darker even than the perpetual Indian troubles, and it would continue to be so for more than twenty years thereafter.[14] Nothing in his whole record is harder to reconcile with the spirit of his dealing with his fellow men than the "forty years' vinegar" of this affair with William Harris. Three hundred years later it is the dullest of stories, but while it raged, it was fire and brimstone in Providence, for this was a Providence affair, not one involving the whole colony. Roger Williams' personal story is blotted by it in the vituperation he permitted himself to express, both in public utterance and in writing. As to the moral issues underneath, the greater right would seem unquestionably to have been on his side. In part it was a matter of personalities. These two men should never have "sat down" in the same pioneer village. Roger Williams knew this in the beginning, when they got into the canoe together toward the landing on Slate Rock, but "William Harris, wearying me with desires . . . I yielded." It was a bitter mistake.

As to the quarrel itself, basically and from this beginning, it concerned land. Roger Williams, without a grain of acquisitiveness in his make-up, regarded his land purchases from the Indians in the beginning and always as a trust, to be divided among all comers equally, and used, always reserving space for other distressed ones who might come. His inherited theory as to land tenure was feudal, and even when England abolished feudal tenure in 1660, he still did not grasp the significance of the change. William Harris, whose basic quality seems to have been acquisitiveness, and whose cast of mind was legalistic, demanded an absolute right in the lands allotted to him in the beginning and in the later Pawtuxet Purchase of which he had been granted an equal share with the other twelve Proprietors. When Roger Williams recalled in his August, 1654, letter to Providence, that his purchases from Canonicus

> "were mine own as truly as any man's coat upon his back,"

and that he had reserved to himself not

> "a foot of land, or an inch of voice in any matter, more than to my servants and strangers," [15]

he spoke the literal truth. In his freedom from any desire for personal possessions or for gain, or for personal power, his record is unsullied. Unwisdom in the beginning consisted in the absence of any strong, centralized control which might have blocked selfishness in others of the group early enough to prevent what happened.

As one voice against the twelve he was helpless, and through the years the principle of fairness and equality to all, which lay back of the original distribution, had been buried deep under the greed which ruled several others of the group, particularly William Harris. In his thought ownership was absolute. The land was his, once he possessed the deeds. The matter was closed. He owned no obligation to the Indians or to later comers among the settlers. By 1654, when the quarrel broke out afresh, he had collected deeds for some 300,000 acres of land in the Narragansett country, and was exulting in its possession. He had paid the asking price and it was his. So had Roger Williams paid the asking price in the beginning, but he could say and mean it,

> "It was not price nor money that could have purchased Rhode Island. Rhode Island was obtained by love."

These were words William Harris could not understand.

The main issue of the 1656 outbreak in this long struggle between these two determined men concerned three words added (in another handwriting) to the Pawtuxet Purchase deed of 1639. These words were "upstreams without limits." Roger Williams' explanation of these words, for which he was not responsible, was that they referred to a courtesy of the Indians at the time of the purchase, permitting cows of Providence men to pasture along the meadows bordering the purchased lands. A very small area was involved, and near enough to the town for the cows to be driven home at night. It was permission to use these grass lands, not to claim them within the purchase. William Harris contended that these same words added to the Pawtuxet purchase all lands as far as the head of the river, a vast tract, comprising many hundreds of acres. By his "confirmation deeds," as he called them, thus evading the town's prohibition against other lands to be purchased privately from the Indians, Harris contended that all these lands were his, legally and finally. This claim of course involved a flat negation of Roger Williams' basic purposes for Rhode Island colony, as a place where those distressed might share equally in the distribution of land.

The explosion during this three year period of his presidency was oblique to this long-standing contention over land rights. During William Harris' long withdrawal in the woods, where in Roger Williams' acerbic phrase he lived like Nebuchadnezzar, he had written a book, unfortunately lost, in which according to report, he had made arraignment of all government, asserting that freedom of conscience was absolute. "He that can say," he declared, "it is his conscience; ought not to yield subjection to any human order among men." This sweeping assumption was of course the clear opposite of all Roger Williams had tried to clarify in the general mind, and he took extreme measures in rebuke; too extreme to square with wisdom. He charged William Harris with treason, which he defined as "open Defiance against the charter, and all our Laws, and against Parliament, the Lord Protector, and all Government." He placed the case before the whole colony Assembly instead of before Providence alone, since Harris had circulated his declaration against all civil government to all four towns.[16] The Assembly heard the evidence, required Harris to read his book publicly, and declared his behavior to be "contemptuous and seditious." Not feeling competent to decide whether it amounted to treason against the state, the Assembly ordered that report of the case be sent to John Clarke in London for a verdict.

Perhaps fortunately, the ship on which this report was dispatched, foundered, the materials were lost, and no verdict was ever secured. John Clarke would probably have had wisdom enough not to press for a decision, and had he done so, it is doubtful whether at the bar of English justice the treason charge could have been sustained. The noise which this whole affair raised in Rhode Island was costly to Roger Williams. He did not stand for re-election in 1657, and had he done so, he probably would not have been elected, for William Harris had an influential following. As to the land dispute, there were still twenty years of litigation ahead. In the end Roger Williams would achieve a canny victory,[17] too canny perhaps, and at great cost to his personal peace. In the long record of this bitter animosity, which became deeply personal on both sides, one remembers Thomas Fuller's word, which is applicable,

> "When worthy men fall out, only one of them may be faulty at first, but, if such strifes continue long, commonly both become guilty."

Unfortunately, it had been so with Roger Williams and William Harris.

In 1663 word came that the charter had been granted on July 8, 1663. Presently it arrived. The General Court held at Newport on November 24, 1663, received it and then adjourned. The announcement went forth, and "at a very great meeting" and assembly of the freemen of the colony on that same day, in the presence of the people, Captain George Baxter, "the most happy bringer and presenter," stepped forth, opened the box in which the charter was enclosed, and "with much becoming gravity" held it high "to the perfect view of all the people," so that the great seal was plainly visible. He read the charter to them, with becoming gravity, and then returned it to the box, which was again locked up in their sight by the Governor, "in order to the safe keeping of it." It was a great occasion. Before it closed, the thanks of the Assembly were voted to John Clarke, for his "above twelve years of service to the colony" and a generous payment authorized to him.[18] He had brought this long tedious business to a successful conclusion and at great personal sacrifice. This November 24, 1663, was his day of triumph, as it rightly should have been. Roger Williams was not officially mentioned on this occasion, nor would he have expected to be. His reward was in the satisfaction that the greatest battle of his life lay behind John Clarke's graceful phrasing of Rhode Island's purpose. One hopes that Captain George Baxter had read these words slowly.

> "Whereas . . . they have freely declared that it is much on their hearts (if they may be permitted) to hold forth a lively experiment, that a most flourishing civil state may stand and be best maintained, and that among our English subjects, with a full liberty in religious concernments." [19]

If Roger Williams had been concerned to name the great days of his life, very probably he would not have named this one or any other whose date is recorded in the annals of the colony. His word, written of later English affairs,

> "Eternity (O eternity!) is our business,"

suggests his standard of value, and yet there must have been quiet satisfaction for him on this November day, as he looked over the crowded Assembly, recognized that once more a new era of safe continuance lay ahead for Rhode Island, and knew that he had had a share in bringing it to pass. It was now twenty-seven years since the landing on Slate Rock.

CHAPTER NINETEEN

Elder Statesman

THESE twenty-seven years had taken sharp toll of his one-time abounding energies and the infirmities of age had come early. "Old pains, lamenesses, so th't sometimes I have not bene able to rise, nor goe nor stand," he wrote as early as his sixty-third year. Physically, he was an old man long before his time, and the staff was now a necessity. A whole generation of Providence children would never see him without it. Nevertheless, in his continuing services to town and colony after 1663, he made scant concession to age or infirmity, and neither did those who continued to solicit his help. Until a few months before his death, his rôle was never to be that of the sage, who sits comfortably in the shadow of his tent, perchance to be visited by those who wish his advice. Not Roger Williams. Until disease and weakness finally shut him in, he was up before dawn in answer to a summons or the likelihood of any emergency presaging one, and dragging his "old bones" down to the shore line or the path to the Narragansett country, he was off by canoe or on foot, unattended as before.

When King Philip, twelve years later, turned his warpath toward Rhode Island, it was then as Captain Williams that Providence knew their veteran founder. Commissioned with military authority, he took a leader's part in planning the town's defenses, mustering volunteers, evacuating women and children, ordering the drum beat, as occasion required. After the war, when the desolated settlement attempted to rebuild and to go on once more, the record shows few men a generation younger who were more active in its restoration.

The panorama of these later services for the years he had left, of course show differences, as compared with earlier decades. The long sea-journeys, the protracted absences were over. His area of activity was perforce local. He belonged to the town and colony for whatever was within his declining strength. Many of the tasks now laid upon him were mere chores, but not for that reason would he have refused to accept them. He had taken in sail, but he was still theirs for whatever was to be done. Presently his energy outran his strength, but even extreme bodily weakness could not defeat his spirit. There was to be no emptiness in his closing years.

Until five years before his death, he was one of the Assistants of the colony. In 1677 he asked to be excused, although he continued to be moderator of meetings, to serve on committees, to draw up letters, petitions, agreements, protests, instructions, even "our thoughts." At the request of the colony he transcribed the charter, was one of those to review the laws to see whether they were agreeable to the charter, then to put them "in a better forme for finding of them when ther is occasion to looke for any law." In 1664 he was named as one of four men to run the long disputed boundary line with Plymouth, and in 1672 he was again named for a similar service, this time as one of seven Commissioners chosen by the Assembly to meet with the Commissioners from Connecticut, "to heare, debate, agitate, determine, and putt a fynall issue and end to all differences betweene this collony and the Collony of Connecticut, in reference to the premises, untill the King's pleasure bee further knowne." [1] After the many years of dissension over both of these boundary lines, the word *fynall* in their instructions must have been a rare satisfaction indeed. The Connecticut boundary as established by this Commission held for seventy-eight years.

Early in this period of his "retirement," he took it upon himself to collect the money voted by the colony to John Clarke in payment for his long period of service for them in securing the charter of 1663. During the winter of 1664 he made a house to house canvass in Providence for the cause. He called it visiting his neighbors. Many met his plea with reluctance, even flat refusal to contribute their share to the amount voted. In a letter to the town of Warwick, where had not his lameness prevented, he had hoped to make personal appeal also, he listed some of the excuses his Providence neighbors had given. Some objected to certain words in the charter; some will pay if *all* do, but not otherwise; some will see the charter first; some are against all charters; some say, let those who sent Clarke pay the bill. Not one of these excuses is "Common Honesty," he declared with vehemence. Even the Indians do better. When they send a messenger, they reward him. Mr. Clarke has worked for us; he deserves his pay. He even mortgaged his house and lands "to go through our Worke." One might wish, he went on, that two such "inestimable Jewells" as our charter has bestowed on us, could fall from Heaven like manna "gratis and free," but that is not God's way. Have we no gratitude? Rhode Island means Isle of Roses. "Shall we now turne our Roses into Hemlock?" As for himself, he will do his share "although I part with my Cloths from my back." [2]

This letter gave him an occasion to eulogize the charter and he did so.

> "Such peace, Such security, such liberties for Soule and Body as were never enjoyed by any English men, nor any in the World yt I have heard of." [3]

This is a strong plea and revealing as to his thought of freedom in the state. He names five freedoms and the breadth of his conception is apparent in each of them: "freedom of our spirits, our persons, our estates, our societe or corporation, and of the Laws of England respecting our Wilderness estate." Perhaps the letter was too long, the tone too critical, the business too cold in Warwick memory. At any rate, despite his labors the money was never all paid, nor did he ever receive his own full share, either for his 1643 expenses or those during his second English trip in 1651.

During this last period of his life he still continued to preach with a fair degree of regularity. Once a month he travelled the six miles to his old trading post at Wickford Point, where according to young Richard Smith, son of his successor in trade,

> "he precheth well and abell, and much pepell comes to here him to theyre good satisfacion." [4]

On most other Sundays he held a service in Providence, possibly at his own house. The groups who came to hear him there were probably small, mainly the friends of his own generation. The Quakers, now resident in considerable proportion, would not have come, nor the Baptists, who had their own meeting, and many of his pioneer associates had now passed on. With no one to attack or confute in these Sunday discourses, he may have been content to speak more simply as a religious teacher, as he had done once in his little book of devotion, the *Experiments of Spiritual Life and Health,* itself suitable for pulpit use.

No sermon of his is extant, but there is among his papers a manuscript list of twenty-two sermon subjects entitled "The Contents or Heads of ye Nahigonset discourses." These would seem to be the discourses referred to in a letter to Governor Bradstreet some eight months before Roger Williams' death. In the quietness of his last days, he was again the preacher. He wrote,

> "By my fire-side, I have recollected the discourses which (by many tedious journeys) I have had with the scattered English at Narragansett, before the war and since, I have reduced them unto those twenty-two heads (enclosed) which is near thirty sheets of my writing." [5]

He lacks money to publish them and is soliciting subscriptions. He died before the project was carried out, and the thirty pages of manuscript have not survived. In his handwriting, thirty pages would have made a substantial beginning toward the development of these subjects in which more than a year's preaching would have been involved. The list bears repeating. It is as follows:

1. of Atheisme
2. of ye holy Scriptures
3. of ye Sower & his 4 sorts of Ground
4. of ye wise Marchant
5. of ye goulden Chaine of Predestination Vocation Justification & Glorification
6. of Salvation what it is
7. of ye power of Nature in Spiritual Matters
8. of Pardon of Sin
9. of ye Emptiness of ye Creatures as to Soule Comfort

10. of Eternitie
11. Mistakes about Christian life
12. ye 8 last things Death Resurrection Judgment Heaven & Hell
13. ye drowning of ye old World
14. Abraham killing his Son to offer him to God
15. Jobs trialls and Patience
16. ye wise and foolish builders
17. of Christ Jesus & Peters discourses about Love
18. Sheepe for the slaughter wi wch I humbly offer my Thought as to ye Late blazing starr
19. Comforts against drout
20. ye burning up of ye whole World occasioned by ye bloudie Jesuits burning of Boston
21. Meditations on Harvest, especially of Indjan Harvest
22. Considerations on ye Lylly

One can learn more from this list than merely the subjects of his discourses. The speaker is not an evangelist; he is a teacher. He is opening his Bible before his hearers and bringing from it things new and old; concrete things; things easily understood: seed in the ground, a blazing star in the sky, lilies of the field, a dry season, fire and flood. His analogies came close home: harvest, not in Bible lands, but Indian harvest, here in the Narragansett country, the burning of Boston, the teaching of the Jesuits. These could hardly have been heavily doctrinal sermons, and in so far as doctrine was preached, it was apparently orthodox Calvinist. Was the language plain? He hoped so. Was the composure "rude"? If so, so much the better. He knew how to dress up sermon matter. "But the Father of Lights hath long since shown me the vanity and soule-deceit of such points and flourishes." [6] Once he had been guilty of them, but all that had been laid away long since.

Incapacitated for most farm work during these later years, and his trading house gone, his sources of income were seriously limited. His three boys were now old enough to take over many of the farm duties, and whether as he attempted out of hours to give them something of an education, other Providence boys still joined them at the lessons is not known, but it may well have been so. Such an occupation would have been to his taste. Along with John Milton, he had

had notions about teaching, particularly of language, ever since his own university days, and he doubtless put these in practice, as he had done in his teaching of gentlemen's sons during his second long stay in London and during his years as President of the colony. The thought of him as schoolmaster invites a pleasant picture for these quieter decades.

Record of another small source of income during several of these years strikes a note of pathos as the assignment for an intellectual of Roger Williams' stamp. In February, 1677/78, he petitioned the town for the right to keep a toll bridge across the clam-beds of the Mossasuck River, previously forded at low tide. His letter to the much respected Inhabitants of Providence has a sentence using his favorite sea figure, in these words,

> "I am, therefore, bold, after so many anchors come home, and so much trouble and long debates and deliberations, to offer, that if you please, I will, with God's help, take this bridge unto my care, by that moderate toll of strangers of all sorts, which hath been mentioned; will maintain it so long that it pleaseth God that I live in this town."

He follows this offer with a six-point schedule of working specifications as to how toll shall be pro-rated according to a man's use of the bridge, and how it shall be kept in repair. He kept this bridge for four years, when, as it would seem summarily, he was "by acte of the Towne,"

> "wholly fforbid so to do ffrom this day fforward." [7]

The sharpness of phrasing on the Town Book suggests displeasure, but no details are given.

In 1672 he was again for the space of four days the warrior, in characteristic individual pose. This was on occasion of his debate with the three Quakers who answered his challenge in place of George Fox, who had departed. During this affair Roger Williams stood in a very bright light indeed, so bright that there can be no mistaking what it revealed. No public occasion since his trial and banishment in 1635, when he could not be "reduced" from any of his opinions, reveals the "rocky flintiness of his selfe-confdence" more clearly. That had been in his thirty-second year; this was in his seventieth. Also, no event in his whole personal story has been the subject of more controversy, usually with conclusions disparaging to him. Disparaging or not, however, it is a significant chapter in his life story, and by no means either to be ignored or apologized for. It belongs to him unmistakably, every inch of it.

It fell about thus. John Burnyeat, a Quaker missionary, on his second visit to Rhode Island in 1671, held a large meeting in Newport. Roger Williams attended this meeting, and after the discourse, rose to speak to one of Burnyeat's points. Whether intentionally or not, but probably not, he was "cut off" as he said, in the midst, "by the sudden *Prayer* of one, and the *Singing* of another, and then by the *Prayer* of another, and the sudden dissolving of the Assembly." The abruptness had offended him, and he "resolved to try another way," but by a public debate, not in private conversation. The next summer when George Fox came to Providence, Roger Williams did not go to hear him, or even show him the courtesy of a call, although Fox stayed in the town for several days. Of course such an affront to a man of George Fox's importance by a man of Roger Williams' standing in the community was missed by no one in Providence, now the home of many Quakers.

After George Fox had left town, Roger Williams challenged him to a debate on *14 Propositions* [8] he had drawn up concerning Quakerism. He sent the challenge, together with this list by boat to Newport, in care of Captain Cranston, himself a Quaker. The letter was delayed in delivery, supposedly deliberately, by Cranston who knew the contents, until George Fox was well out to sea, en route for England. He declared later that he had not received it in time, but Roger Williams would have it no other way but that he had been afraid to debate the Propositions and that he had "run for it." Perhaps he had, but it was a breach of courtesy, to say the least, not to accept his own statement that he had not received the letter before he sailed. His three deputies, John Burnyeat, William Edmondson, and John Stubbs, agreed to meet the challenge for him. They came to Providence, called on Roger Williams, arrangements were made and the announcement went forth. The ensuing debate was one in name only. Every one of Roger Williams' 14 Propositions [9] was a direct attack. Such sweeping denunciations do not admit of debate, only of equally sweeping denial, and unfortunately also, in this instance, of mutual abuse, name-calling, and angry exchange. Roger Williams says in his printed account, that he "laboured to keep down heat," but he did not always succeed. What both men lacked, in addition to a sense of humor, was enough common ground to make disagreement debatable. As a matter of fact, in their respective bodies of belief, they possessed more than enough common ground, but on this occasion, they refused to admit it. The result was not so much theological argument, as personal attack and personal rejoinder.

Report of the bout itself is extant in two versions: Roger Williams', written immediately afterward from memory (as he had been unable to secure a shorthand writer) but not published until four years later, and George Fox's, appearing in very prompt reply.[10] After four years it might seem that these two detailed records would have been too stale to interest even the principals, and that their heated accusations would have been matter for regret only. Not at all. The two treatises had been awaited with interest; they were read and discussed by adherents and opponents of both sides. Roger Williams himself was so far from regretting his former derogation of George Fox, that when letters of protest for his conduct of the affair came to him, he lashed back in a nine page answering pamphlet,[11] justifying himself and attacking his critic, who happened to be William Coddington. The Quaker battle had shifted center since the mid-fifties; persecution was officially over on both continents and with it the end also of indecorous behaviors, but Quaker doctrine still kept controversy active and bitter. Roger Williams contributed to this bitterness by his attack. So would John Bunyan and other religious leaders, whose zeal for what they believed to be the truth sometimes outran their wisdom.

The spirit of the 1672 encounter was caught in the titles of both books. *George Fox Digg'd Out of His Burrowes* was of course a pun which no one missed, for Edward Burroughs was a prolific pamphleteer in the Quaker cause. *A New-England Firebrand Quenched* was almost as easily recognizable, as Roger Williams had previously been adorned with the same epithet. Both books lack dignity at times. Both display regrettable qualities in these two notable religious leaders, each of whom had something better to say than appears

International Monument of the Reformation at Geneva

STATUE OF ROGER WILLIAMS, BY H. BOUCHARD
International Monument of the Reformation at Geneva

on some of these pages. Regret aside, however, both books are significant in different ways. In Roger Williams' story this debate underscores a paradox which lies at the very center of his Rhode Island leadership. While he was President of the colony from 1654 to 1657, he had defied both Massachusetts and New Netherlands in their policy of inhospitality to Quakers. Come, live here; the doors are open, he had said and they had come. When he wrote this fierce attack against their religious tenets in 1672, they were present in such numbers as to be politically in control of the colony. He had fought for their right to come, to stay, to hold their opinions. That was one thing. Their doctrines were quite another, and he would neither give an inch nor remain quiet in his opposition. We admit Quakers, he said, but we do not abet them. This treatise is the proof of that distinction.

It was a distinction well understood in Rhode Island Colony. Through the years the difference between civil hospitality and the right to speak against what one considered religious heresy had become utterly clear to the citizenry. Angry as some resident Quakers were at his shattering denunciations on this occasion, they did not share the sense of impropriety later generations have felt as to his boldness to utter them. Rhode Island spoke out, and why not? That was the peculiar privilege of this Isle of Roses. The speech of Elizabeth Williams, wife of Roger's brother Robert, at the end of the debate, might have come quite as sincerely from any one of several hundred auditors, possibly even from one on the opposite side of the argument.

"This man hath discharged his conscience,"

she said simply. Such was a Rhode Islander's privilege.

On the day before the announced date, Roger Williams had untied his rowboat at Providence cove and rowed the thirty mile distance to Newport, arriving just before midnight. The next morning the Quaker meetinghouse was crowded. Expecting possible disorders, the governor had come also. Roger Williams had begun to speak at nine o'clock and at six P.M. he was still on the first of his fourteen Propositions; namely, That the People called Quakers are not true Quakers according to the Holy Scriptures. He had been interrupted, heckled, jeered at and sometimes confused by being, as he said, assailed by three or four at once, but he had kept steadily on. His method, that of reading Fox's book, page by page, and then commenting on the matter presented, would seem to have made for intolerable tediousness. It also invited him to indulge his greatest fault, prolixity, but such was the approved method of religious controversy. His three antagonists, who sat high at the other end of the hall, had their copies of George Fox (as did some of the audience) and all turned the pages together.

During the morning an eclipse of the sun occurred, but that was incidental only; the company listened in the darkness. Had anyone trembled in the Bible? Yes, the opposition declared. Moses, by his own statement, had trembled in Hebrews xii, 21. "And so terrible was the sight that Moses said, I exceedingly fear and quake." Were Quaker demonstrations in kind thereby authorized? Were the tremblings identical? To reduce such minutiae to absurdity as the exercise of intellectuals is easy enough, given centuries, but 1672 was still early enough for certainty in all such matters to be possible, and one dare not be wrong. Therefore listen to the scholars who understand the tongues in which God (as it were), wrote it all down.

At the end of this first day, it was apparent to the weary audience that Roger Williams would not be able to complete the remaining six Propositions to be debated at Newport in the two days allotted, and they objected to the prolixity. Roger Williams blamed the interruptions and promised to speed the process. He made concessions, consented to a timekeeper for each point discussed, and permitted himself to be held to the schedule of minutes. Somehow it was all accomplished and at the end of two more days, hoarse, half ill and utterly weary, he returned to Providence where one more day's similar performance awaited him. The mainland settlers came in large numbers and even some from Connecticut, crowding the "mighty barn" to the doors. At the end of this day the issue was indeterminate. Some thought that Roger Williams' arguments had the greater weight; others thought not. Personalities had been as important as arguments. At Newport, William Harris, now turned Quaker, had spoken his piece, and also William Coddington. If Roger Williams reported such speeches correctly in his printed account, he matched those who abused him by harsher language than in any other of his published works. Since he was trusting to memory, he may have embellished his account at heated points. One wonders, for example, whether on the Newport platform he actually said that George Fox is like an old cow with a kettle on her head, giving every one warning to stand clear. If so, he would have said it unsmilingly, and it would have been unsmilingly heard.

The doctrinal matter of his book has usually been dismissed as adding nothing to his stature as a religious thinker. Perhaps there is a quibble in the word stature. Say rather that it contributes more to an understanding of his own religious beliefs than anything else he wrote except the *Experiments of Spiritual Life and Health.* In his prefatory address to Charles II, he calls it

> "the Lantskip of a Battle fought this last Summer in your Majestyes *New-England,* touching the difference between some of the Eminentest of the *Quakers* and my self." [12]

The center of the center of this difference concerned God's way of enlightening men, and in 1672 this was an all-sundering difference. How may man know God? By the inner light in his own soul, said George Fox; by the Bible, said Roger Williams, and in no other way. The emphasis given to the answer to this one question in this debate quite obscures the fundamental agreements between these two men. As to complete religious toleration and equality before the law they were on the same side, as also in the insistence that the individual soul was answerable to God alone without any priestly intermediary. The debate did not concern these points.

To Roger Williams the idea of the listening soul, awaiting God's revelation to each individual alone through the Holy Spirit dwelling within, caused his own "spirit to rise" in indignation.

> "Lazie fool under the Fig Tree,"

he shouted, as he recalled an emblem suggesting the receptive attitude.

> "I Charge upon this *Foxian party* the horrible Crime of a *proud Laziness* for not studying the *Original Languages* themselves." [13]

What is it but *"pride* and Ingratitude" to disregard and slight the writings of those who have labored and left their labors behind for the benefit of all? Roger Williams was too much the man of energy to be fair to the idea of passive receptivity. He lacked the capacity to understand so easy a way of arriving at truth. Truth is dear beyond price and one must pay his utmost to possess so much as a glimpse.

> "And why do they worship a dumb Devil in their dumb meetings, and stand still and listen and lie upon their beds of laziness for Revelations and Notions, &c."

When he himself said that he maintained the "inward breathing of the Holy Spirit" in the Bible more than they did by their inner light, the margin of difference between them was the merest promontory, as has been true in the fiercest of religious battles many times before and after, but when the wall between them was low enough to be no longer a barrier, they merely built it higher. In seventeenth century religious controversy, there was still no place for charity toward men of different opinions.

What the Calvinist in Roger Williams regarded as even more "abominable" in this doctrine of the light within was the magnifying of our "cursed human nature" by making it part of God Himself. Such magnifying was born of pride and nothing else. "My spirit rose up against me," he wrote, at such blasphemy.

> "Alas poor lump of clay and dust and ashes: poor finite vapours we are, and not able to give a guess at what Infinity, and an infinite Majesty and Godhead is." [14]

Squeeze the juice out of these statements about the indwelling God, and "the Quakers say they are equal in power and glory with God the Father, Son, and Holy Spirit. Blasphemy! Blasphemy!" In one of the letters preliminary to the debate, he stated his opposing belief clearly in these very personal words,

> "I believe that every *Hair of mine head,* and every *Minute* of my Life is in the mercifull hand of the *Father of Spirits.* I doe not simply and blasphemously think that my Soul is a piece or part of God." [15]

As to the claim that Christ had already come again to Quakers,

"I know that a man may feel this Lye with a pair of mittins."

Recalled in the quiet of his own chimney corner days afterward, the Quaker arguments evoked a fierceness of response, even anger, which comes through on nearly every page. This is not the fire of youth such as glows on the pages of his far greater book, *The Bloody Tenent*; it is rather the never-let-go tenacity of a far older warrior, whose ideas are, as it were, cast in stone. He will not permit the merest chiselling at the edges; his certainty is final.

In the nine page pamphlet he wrote in 1678, replying to Coddington's attack on his conduct in the debate, he agreed that the tongue is a sharp arrow, a sword, a viper, a fire from hell—certainly, but we must be "sure," and it was the certainty of his conviction that had called forth such sharpness. As he saw it, to confute error was as much an obligation laid on him by the Almighty, as it had been to the Massachusetts magistrates who had exiled him. Unfortunately in this 1672 attack, he failed to separate the personal from the doctrinal at times, and as a result blurred the issue. So did George Fox, whose saddest mistake was to use the word *lie* too often in lieu of an answering argument.

In this his last publication Roger Williams is not showing the side of either his mind or character that later times like best to remember, but a side that is none the less a rock-bottom element in both. In these adamantine views so fiercely defended, he was firmly and honestly a man of his time, as of course he had a right to be. Naturally he has been most honored in later times for those utterances in which he seemed to look beyond his own century, but even in these he is best understood, perhaps only understood, when his loyalty to his own heritage of thought is recognized for what it was. The acceptance of ideas depends on when they are uttered, but it is the fact that his most revolutionary convictions were uttered by him, as the man of a heritage in which they had no place, that makes him so significant a thinker. Generations had to pass before a general acceptance of these principles, for which statues now exist in his honor, could allot this honor to him.

His last book is also revealing in quite another way. It provides the external backdrop for his life in Providence Plantations. In his first book, the *Key into the Language of America,* we looked in on the Narragansetts. A panorama of their tribal life unrolled before us through the spirited story of a young man's observation. Roger Williams was part of it, and much that he said and did throughout his life is explained by it. In this last book we see a panorama of the other half of his wilderness life similarly unrolling before us. Here is a provincial society in action. Here are Newport and Providence as he knew them. This was his theatre of action. These were the people with whom he had worked out a way of life. These interruptions, hecklings, these cries of "Old man! Old man!" the affronts to his age and dignity, they were all part of the provincial mores. So also was the willingness of a large proportion of the two towns to sit for an entire day in a crowded, uncomfortable room to hear this line by line proof and disproof as to how God chooses to reveal Himself to man. This was Roger Williams' world, the world for which, as he said more than once, he had given up honors and preferments in university, state and church abroad, and by choice had come back to Rhode Island. He was as much a part of it as those who heckled him, and one may well linger at this picture of a four day tournament, which belonged to this time and this place, for the light it can throw on the life and thought of a man who belonged to it implicitly, and who also belongs to the centuries.

Shortly before the book was printed in 1676 came another battle, for Roger Williams the last of its kind, and the only one he ever lost. This was his part in King Philip's war, one of the saddest chapters in the long story of English-Indian relations in the New World. Viewed from any angle, this war was a tragedy, and one which in the long perspective of many lifetimes, seems a tragedy that might have been avoided. Six hundred English killed, many more hundreds of Indians, a thousand buildings burned, confidences built up over two generations shattered, and resentments newly awakened for generations to come; it is a black page in New England history for both white men and red.

Posterity knows the story best as written by white men, who told it as the story of a righteous war of self-defense in which the God of the Old Testament came to their aid and helped them to cut the heathen in pieces.[16] Had King Philip, son of Massasoit, written it, his would have been a tale of revenge and the settlement of an old score against the Boston Commissioners, and a settlement which in the end was foiled by the powder of the white man. The Narragansetts would have told it as the tragedy of a proud tribe, falsely accused of complicity with the bloody Philip, and in consequence paying the price of almost total destruction. The history of the Narragansetts as a great people ended with the Great Swamp Fight in the snowdrifts. Had Roger Williams written it, his account likewise would have lacked the detachment denied to all contemporary actors. He believed the declaration of war against Philip by the United Colonies to have been a mistake, and to the end he trusted in the good faith of the large body of Narragansetts whose destruction was a personal sorrow to him. He continued to trust in those who survived.

His own life, so crowded with irony, shows no irony more bitter than the burning of the town he had founded, even his own house therein, and by the race for whose souls he had longed, and with whom he had striven for forty of his manhood years to bring about a stable coexistence in peace. Personally, they bore him no malice, not even King Philip. Without a weapon he was safe, but Indians in war mood were no respecters of towns or houses within them. He lost everything he owned, and was henceforth dependent on his sons for a home. By this destruction posterity lost, in the accumulated papers of his lifetime, that which would no doubt have filled out the many blanks and silences in his wilderness story. In the saving of the bulk of the Town Books, John Smith, miller, was the village hero. Seeing his own house in flames, he dashed recklessly inside, seized the Books which were in his keeping as Town Clerk, and threw them out the window into the mill brook. Then when the Indians had departed, and the fires smouldered, he fished them out again, with the resulting distinction to Providence of a more nearly complete set of early records than is extant for any other New England town of the period. "Saved by God's merciful providence from fire and water," was Roger Williams' comment, although he withheld any praise of John Smith (whom he did not like) as God's agent in their rescue.

Roger Williams' part in these sad events was again that of a negotiator, only this time his offices were sought only the day before the first shot was fired. That was too late; years too late. At Plymouth's entreaty, four years earlier he had brought about a meeting between Philip and the Governor at which promises had been exchanged, but these had done no more than prevent an earlier outbreak. In

June, 1675, messengers had come in haste to his Providence house, urgently soliciting assurances from the Narragansetts, whom the Boston Commissioners again suspected of hostility. "Within halfe an houres warning," he was off to the meeting with Cachonet, Miantunomi's youngest son, and another chieftain. The Governor's letter was opened and read in their presence and the plea for a larger meeting with "Ye Old Queen Ninnicraft" and other Narragansett leaders readily accepted.

> "We condescended to meete them all neare ye great pond, at least ten miles from M. Smith's house," [17]

Roger Williams reported. This would have been in the very heart of the Narragansett country.

The meeting was held. The Narragansetts professed to have made no agreements with Philip in his rising against the English, to have sent no messengers to him and to have ordered all those who had made marriages with his people to return or perish with them. This was an inter-tribal war, as well as an Indian uprising against the English, and the Narragansett concern was for the privilege of settling the score with the Mohegans without white interference. They confirmed their promise to the Boston Commissioners as to the existing treaty, but they flatly refused the order to surrender the old men, women and children of Philip's Wampanoags, whom Philip himself had sent to them for refuge. "Not so much as the paring of a Wampanoag's nail," said Cachonet in anger. This refusal did not mean complicity with Philip (as the Boston Commissioners had supposed), but rather loyalty to an ancient tradition, even a code, of the Narragansett tribe, granting hospitality to the helpless. Surrender of these refugees would have meant their sale into slavery in the West Indies, a fate far worse than death to an Indian. Roger Williams understood this code, believed that refusal to surrender the refugees had no other basis, and was also in sympathy with the Narragansett demand to be allowed to settle their own quarrel with the Mohegans. Boston thought otherwise, and their reply to this refusal was a Proclamation of final warning to the Narragansetts. The next step was the despatching of a thousand soldiers against them.

The sequel was the Great Swamp Fight, fought on Sunday, December 19, 1675, near Kingston, Rhode Island, in which the helpless ones and the Narragansetts together were slaughtered in a winter battle too hideous to recall. They had been caught between the English army on the one side and that of Uncas, ally to the English, on the other. Rhode Island had no part in this fight. During the intervening months between King Philip's first onslaughts on Plymouth and Massachusetts colonies, they had taken warning. Women and children had been sent to the island towns, and there had been some attempt to fortify Providence and Warwick. Roger Williams had urged making a garrison out of one Providence house (the Field house) set high on the hill. His letters to John Winthrop, Jr., and to Governor Leverett of Massachusetts detail his further counsels. On December 18, 1675, the day before the Great Swamp Fight, he wrote,

> "I presume you are satisfied in the necessity of these present hostilities, and that it is not possible at present to keep peace with these barbarous men of blood, . . . I fear the event of the justest war; . . . Dear Sir, if we cannot save our patients, nor relations, nor Indians, nor English, oh let us make sure to save the bird in our bosom, and to enter in at that straight door and narrow way, which the Lord Jesus himself tells us, few there be that find it." [18]

This was the letter and the faith of one who had written earlier, "Sir, my old bones and eyes are weary with travel and writing to the Governors of Massachusetts and Rhode Island and yourselves." He had done what he could do, but it was too late. Besides, he dealt with an Indian generation that knew him not.

Warwick was burned on March 17th and Providence on March 26th. The familiar tradition that when the Indians came, he walked over to them, leaning on his staff, hoping to pacify them as he had often done, would seem to require some modification,[19] although essentially the story remains authentic fact. Modification consists only in the fact that the Indians had asked, not for him, but for one Valentine Whitaker, an interpreter, to speak with them. Hearing of this request, Roger Williams called to them, saying that he would parley with them, and then did so for an hour, but without succeeding in saving the town from their burning. The count varies, but apparently the greater number of the houses was destroyed; by the usual estimate, only twenty-three out of a hundred and three remaining.

Four months later, King Philip was slain in a swamp near the Swansea line, and sixteen days later the war ended at Annawan Rock on the Rehoboth side of the Seekonk River. Cachonet, son of Miantunomi, had been captured and killed by Oneko, son of Uncas. He had proved himself a true son of his great father, and had died like a prince. After his capture, he had refused to speak with anyone not his equal in rank, and when given his choice of submission to the Mohegans or death, he had chosen death, answering,

> "I like it well. I shall die before my heart is soft, or I have said anything unworthy of myself."

Sir Harry Vane's death speech on the scaffold was not more noble.

Five days after the burning, Massachusetts colony, hearing that Roger Williams' house was destroyed and "himself in his old age reduced to an uncomfortable and disabled state . . . out of compassion," revoked the edict of banishment against him conditionally to the extent that "if the sayd Mr. Williams shall see cause and desire it, he shall have liberty to repayre into any of our Towns . . . during these Public Troubles, he behaving himself peaceably and inoffensively and *not disseminating and venting any of his different opinions in matters of religion* to the dissatisfaction of any." [20] He did not avail himself of this permission, but remained in Providence. Two years later Connecticut "in the name of the Court" voted him a gratuity of ten pounds for his "courtesy to our army," and made provision for the "conveyance" to him of corn, together with a letter of appreciation for his many services.

The Providence Town Records for the months immediately following the burning of the town tell in scattered items the story of the rebuilding and beginning over once more. This record begins with the list of the twenty-seven men who "stay'd & went not away." [21] Roger Williams' name heads the list. History would expect nothing else of him. From this date forward, his name is on many pages, as in his younger years. On June 5th, six weeks later, he was Moderator of a Town Meeting called "under a Tree by ye Water side." The words bring a picture. At this meeting he was elected Town Clerk for the ensuing year and one of the members of the Town Council. As Town Clerk he would have the responsibility of putting the salvaged Town Records into order, a service entrusted to capable hands. Another immediate responsibility was disposing of the captive Indians then in the town. He was named as one of the five men to do this and report the following morning, the town promising to acquiesce in this disposition.

There is a hint of the temper of the town during these critical days and of the tenseness the presence of an Indian could create, in the item reporting the coming of Chuff, a ringleader in the destruction of the town. The date was on August 25, 1676, a fortnight after King Philip had been killed. Chuff had been badly wounded by Providence men several days before and had been hiding in the woods. When his suffering was no longer bearable, he had appeared in the town, presumably in the hope of mercy. If so, he was mistaken. He would get only justice. The record reads,

> "Capt. Roger Wms. Caused ye Drum to be beat, ye Town Councell & Councell of War called, all cried for Justice & Execution, ye Councell of War gave sentence & he was shot to Death, to ye great satisfaction of ye Towne." [22]

Presently these tense days passed. Many meetings were held under the "Tree by ye Water side," houses were rebuilt, women and children brought back from the island towns. There is a record for August 30, 1676, that

> "By Gods Providence it seasonably came to passe yt Providence Williams brought up his mother from Newport in his sloop & cleared ye Towne by his vessel of all ye Indians to ye great peace & Content of all ye Inhabitants." [23]

This is the last recorded item concerning Mary Williams. Whether she survived her husband, and whether they again set up their household in Providence is not known. Tradition has it that Roger Williams spent his last days with his son Joseph, but no dates or other details are extant. There is also a letter written long afterward by his son Daniel which suggests that both parents were recipients of his help for at least a time.

> "I do not desire to say" (he wrote) "what I have done for both father and mother. I judge they wanted nothing that was convenient for ancient people." [24]

Otherwise the record is a blank as to their subsequent private lives. What "near destitute" meant to Roger Williams in a single detail comes in the postscript to a letter written to Governor Leverett of Massachusetts, January 14, 1675. He wrote,

> "Sir, since I am oft occasioned to write upon the public business, I shall be thankful for a little paper upon the public account, being now near destitute."

After the burning of Providence, he had a little more than six years to live, and from the Town Records it is apparent that at least five of these were still active years in community service. As late as October, 1681, he was still Moderator of meetings, being sometimes continued from fall to spring and spring to fall. In June, 1680, he was again a member of the Town Council and asked to perform various other services. Something of the vigor with which he still performed them is suggested by his protest, dated December 8, 1680, against the legality of a meeting which had not been called by the specified "three days warning." [25] His handwriting had grown coarser with advancing years and failing eyesight, but he still held a pen firmly. He also still insisted that everything concerning the town business should be legal to a hair's breadth. The distinction between individual free thinking, which he claimed as a right, and absolute obedience to law and statute in all civil procedures was a distinction that nothing could blur.

Many letters continued to come from his pen, through these last years, to friends both in New England and abroad, suggesting that somehow in the absence of a half century and the remoteness of Providence, he had remained a citizen of the larger world of his own day. In one of his last letters he mentions among his many friends in Boston, Captain Brattle, Seth Perry, Joseph Dudley, Mr. Eliot, Israel

Stoughton and Captain Gookins, all men of consequence in the colony. Death had stripped him, he says in this letter, of all his friends in Charlestown, and very soon "Time and Death" would call him away also. He had outlived his generation. John Clarke had died in 1676, Samuel Gorton in 1677, Benedict Arnold, William Coddington, William Harris in 1678.

The precise date of his own death is not established, but according to Providence land records, it occurred between January 16,

Roger Williams entred his Protest agnst ye Legalitie or Lawfullness of this abovesaid Meeting as not being Lawfully Called in our Kings Maties name by his officer a Magistrate at three dayes warning: & Consequently he protested agnst all Acts & Orders & Adjournments yt were or should be made, upon ye illegal, factious, & dangerous foundation:

Roger Williams

This protest is Entered on ye 48th page of ye Towne booke of ye Entry of Towne orders:

p Dan: Abbott Towne Clk

Roger Williams' Protest to Providence, December 8, 1680
Rhode Island Historical Society

1682/83, when he signed a deed, and April 25, 1683, the date of a deed drawn up by William Carpenter who called himself the last survivor of the original thirteen proprietors of Pawtuxet.[26] Roger Williams was also an original proprietor. A letter of William Adams to J. Richards, dated March 15, 1682/83, narrows the margin more precisely in the statement,

"Mr. Williams of Providence is lately deceased." [27]

Later land records repeat his name as former owner, but do not record the date of his death. Tradition, entirely without documentary authentication, names his burial place as a garden "near Patience Ashton's grave," and the reminiscence of a late contemporary recalls "a considerable parade" and "guns fired over his grave." [28] One hopes it is true. His captain's commission would explain the guns and his venerable figure on the streets of the fast changing town he had founded, might have inspired the parade as the tribute of townsmen to one of themselves. Roger Williams would not have wished nor understood any honor more wide-circling.

His death would hardly have been ignored in official circles throughout the colony, although at this date he would have been mourned, if at all, by a generation that knew him not. They were also too near his period of active local service even to guess why far later generations would wish to honor him by statues in congressional halls of America, let alone in far off Geneva. Less still might they have understood why three centuries later his would be a familiar name and story to American boys and girls from coast to coast of the country he had once heard men say was as big as all of Europe.

The years have brought him many honors, some appropriate to his services and some not. Has anything yet offered in tribute to him matched the quiet simplicity of the inscription marking the site of the spring in Providence, near to the spot where he and his companions landed in 1636? It would seem not. By a Proprietor's grant in 1721, this site was enshrined and marked with a legend which unconsciously one translates into its deeper meanings. It reads,

"Liberty is reserved for the inhabitants to fetch water at this spring forever."

EPILOGUE

"The Root of the Matter in Him"

In Roger Williams' day for a man to be judged as having "the root of the matter in him" meant that at least in other men's eyes, he gave evidence of being one of the "elect." Surprising though it be for one of his troublesome unorthodoxies, this was the verdict of "many judicious persons" who had known him while he lived. A generation later it was still remembered, and Cotton Mather wrote it down to his praise and the praise of early New England. Taken quite out of its current seventeenth century setting and pondered as a query instead of an assertion, the figure is apt, the phrase pregnant of suggestion. As one looks back over Roger Williams' eighty years, what was the *root of the matter* in this man? Whence and what was the source of that which made him what he was? What is the clue or approach to a clue that unthreads the maze? For it is a maze. His was a complex personality, plenteous in contradiction and human inconsistency, as is true for most men of great gifts. Yet there was in him also a great simplicity, and that would seem to be the trail to follow.

If the trail is allowed to begin when and where his life began, and is followed forward, not backward, one walks with him in the midst of great events; in fact, through a cataclysm in human society. His entire life was not only lived, year by year, against this sombre backdrop, but his fortunes were time and again bound up with these same great events, of which the sequel was as yet hardly guessed. Bold and reckless men were dying for the truth as they saw it in those dangerous days, and some of them were dying for half truths. The one thing not quite possible for Englishmen who thought for themselves and cared deeply about their English situation, was indifference to the issues underneath the struggle, and the radiant hope to which it was giving birth. Things had to change; they could not possibly stay the same; hence wherever Englishmen lived in those days, they were minded to build the world over, as men have yearned to do at such hopeful moments, since the world began. In London, they could build only by first tearing down; in Boston, Plymouth, Salem, Providence (and a hundred other places) they had one of the best chances Englishmen have ever had to build freely according to their own conviction and desire. Roger Williams' mature life was divided (unequally) between the Old and the New Worlds of the mid-seventeenth century, and he had a share both in the rebuilding and the building. It was also his great good fortune, as a man of thought whose battlefield was the printed page, and also as a man of bold practical action, to be given an almost completely free chance to work out his own "dangerous" ideas in a small unit of human society, remote enough from outside interference, and for a long enough time, so that such interference could not quite spoil what he had tried to do. In sequel, his thought endured in more than words on a page.

His matter was not new to his age. It was no other than the common thought and experience of his own part of the century. Both his protest and his vision of possibility came from the group consciousness of his own countrymen in these tempestuous decades; else it would have failed of response. The times were not yet ready to accept what he had to offer by way of remedy, but the time to voice the protest was at hand. In a very explicit sense, he was not ahead of his day, not an inch. The power underneath his own expression of his conviction was the utter contemporaneousness of the need for just such a protest and vision. As a result, his words evoked a response from the deepest feelings of other men around him. It is also because this protest and vision were so deeply rooted in the feelings of his own day that later times still respond to them. His thought reached deep enough to get below the contemporary and touch universal human chords, as transforming thought in any age must do. Herein lies the power of great literature, great art, great leadership in church and state, or anywhere else in human society.

His strongest drives were also of his very own time. Puritan drives, as we say, but they do not stop there. A passionate religious zeal, relentless energy, stern self-discipline, capacity for sheer endurance, faith and the will to achieve even the impossible and to that end to be stopped by nothing, as well as the lonely courage to dare it. Perhaps most pervasive and most compelling of all, a consciousness ever present, that (in his own words)

"This life is a brief minute, eternitie follows."

Yet there was nothing of other-worldliness about him, nothing of obliviousness to the bustling, suffering human scene around his feet, nothing of Puritan austerity in its typical manifestations. He was impulsive, lovable, warm-hearted, magnetic; "a man lovely in his carriage," as a great contemporary put it, and "the sweetest soul I ever knew."

In the thought of his fellows he was only incidentally and secondarily the "man of God," in the usual lineaments and set-apartness of his calling. His feet were very firmly on the Narragansett earth, and he was far more practical in weekday wisdom than his posterity has allowed him to be. He dealt in things, concrete, tangible, necessary things, and made no apology for so doing. His zest to know went down many earthly paths, as well as behind the meaning of Hebrew words; his talents were expended in everyday chores; often dull chores. Yet whatever he did, whether he moderated meetings, kept shop, stood in the pulpit or wrote books, he was essentially in his deepest self, a religious man. Not in William James' sense of the man to whom religion is the whole of life, consciously and with a single-minded absorption and devotion. Rather that his springs of action, his standards of value, his tests of his own actions, his moral earnestness, his plea for soul-freedom itself, have their source in a religious view of life and not elsewhere.

It does not matter what we call him. His versatility was multi-faceted, and yet as the panorama of his life unrolls before us in its entirety, its slope and direction are constant. He saw what he had to do as a very simple thing, and he did it simply, without a thought of the consequences to himself. Personal ambition in him was almost totally lacking. Honors were dust. Size was naught. Money, time, possessions, talents, position, influence, all belonged to a cause greater than anything personal. The landscape of his life shows no ordered plan, driving toward a goal of individual achievement, nor to the last day that he lived would he have thought of anything he had accomplished in terms personal to himself. That the colony should endure mattered, and mattered intensely. That men should "live in peace securely" mattered even more. To be "Chiefe officer" or President, or even the Peacemaker, for any personal honor thereof, was not important. If a master strain in his character is to be named, there is not a doubt as to what it should be. It was selflessness, but selflessness of such a sort as confers dignity on the human race. In his own words, he used the world and all the comforts of it "with a weaned eye and mind," as if he used it not.

> "If riches, if children, if friends, if cattle, if whatsoever increase, let us watch that the heart fly not loose upon them."

His heart did not, and if he had a secret of personal living, it lies somewhere just here.

Perhaps that is the reason that somehow his individual life seems to lie outside and beyond all that he did. There was something in him more massive than his record can catch, a sense of amplitude and of greatness in him, out of proportion to any listing of his services to a colony, to a cause, even to a great idea. Much that he had to say belonged to his own time and not ours; it drops away easily. Much also is still an arrow's flight above our own. Something of his greatness is owing also to the strategic moment at which he lived and spoke. His story suggests in a significant example that the timing of a man's life and words can be of vast importance in human history. A moment earlier, or a moment later, and the difference is a gulf. Born at a time when a vast revolutionary movement was in confused ferment, he helped to give it direction as well as impetus at a critical early stage.

His victory (qualified of course) was by no means final, nor even acknowledged as victory. The battle for freedom, by any definition, is never won. Nor will it ever be quite lost. The meaning of freedom changes with the generations, but the fight is perennial and must be. Roger Williams symbolizes, and also personifies, something in the human spirit that perpetually renews the battle.

NOTES

CHAPTER I

1. *The Wonderfull Yeare, 1603,* London, n.d. (unpaged). In *Non-Dramatic Works of Thomas Dekker,* ed. by Alexander B. Grosart, 5 vols., London, 1884, I, 86–87.
2. *The Journal of Sir Roger Wilbraham,* 1593–1616, ed. by Harold Spencer Scott, *The Camden Miscellany,* London, 1902, Vol. X, p. 54.
3. *Diary of Sir John Manningham,* 1602–1603, ed. by John Bruce, Westminster, 1868, pp. 146–147. Manningham's entry for March 24th, is in a different tone from Thomas Dekker's. He wrote, "This morning about three at clocke, hir majestie departed this lyfe, mildly like a lambe, easily like a ripe apple from the tree."
4. *The Church-History of Britain,* London, 1655, Bk. IX, pp. 4–5.
5. "John Clapham's Memoir," in "Elizabeth of England," ed. by Evelyn Plummer Read and Conyers Read, in *Translations and Reprints from the Original Sources of History,* Philadelphia, 1951, 3rd ser., Vol. VI, pp. 110–113. See also *The True Narration of the Entertainment of His Royal Majesty,* by T. M., London, 1603, in *Stuart Tracts,* ed. by C. H. Firth, Westminster, 1903, pp. 46–47. Various other contemporary accounts repeat these details in almost the same words.
6. Wilbraham, *op. cit.,* pp. 54–55.
7. B. M. Royal MS. 12 A, XLI, quoted by Thomas W. Baldwin, *William Shakspere's Small Latine and Lesse Greeke,* 2 vols., Urbana, Ill., 1944, I, 385.
8. William Brenchley Rye, *England as Seen by Foreigners in the Days of Elizabeth and James the First,* London, 1865, p. 7.
9. Quoted from Daniel Defoe, *A Plan of English Commerce,* London, 1728, by H. R. Fox Bourne, *English Merchants,* 2 vols., London, 1866, I, 313–314. Thomas Fuller, quoting Isa. xxiii, 8, had expressed such a hope for English merchants nearly a century earlier.

CHAPTER II

1. Alphabetical List of Freemen, Records of the Merchant Taylors' Company, London. Previously he would have served a seven year apprenticeship.
2. *The Wonderful Yeare, 1603, op. cit.,* pp. 99–100.

3. By Henry F. Waters. Printed in his *Genealogical Gleanings in England,* 2 vols., Boston, 1901, I, 327–329. Also in *The New England Historical and Genealogical Register,* 1889, Vol. 43, pp. 291–293. The will of James Williams is dated, Sept. 7, 1620; proved, Nov. 19, 1621: of Alice Williams, dated Aug. 1, 1634; proved, Jan. 26, 1634/35.
4. Charles Mathew Clode, *Memorials of the Guild of Merchant Taylors,* London, 1875, p. 172. This *Williams* may have been John Williams, whose name occurs elsewhere in this same record. Mention of Thomas Morse is on p. 178.
5. Thomas Cromwell, 1485–1540, was a man of high administrative gifts. First a London merchant, he became successively agent of Wolsey, chief agent of Henry VIII in the destruction of the monasteries, Master of the Rolls, Chancellor of Cambridge, Lord Privy Seal, Vicar General and Earl of Essex. Although caring nothing for religion, he was honored by inclusion in Foxe's *Book of Martyrs.* He had been beheaded in 1540.
6. He was ordained at Payneswick, Glamorgan, Monmouthshire, in 1575; instituted to the rectory of St. Alban's, Mar. 7, 1582/83, and to the vicarage of St. Peter's, Mar. 1, 1591/92. There are many references to him in the *Records of the Old Archdeaconry of St. Albans,* ed. by H. R. Wilton Hall, St. Albans, 1908. He died Nov. 11, 1626. See also *The Parish Register of St. Albans Abbey,* 1558–1689, transcribed by William Brigg, Harpenden, 1897.
7. In these records of land transactions he is mentioned as "James Williams, citizen and merchant taylor of London." *Herts Genealogist and Antiquary,* ed. by William Brigg, Harpenden, 1899, Vol. III, pp. 241–243. Roger Pemberton died Nov. 20, 1627; will proved, Dec. 5, 1627.
8. *Pemberton Pedigrees,* compiled by Major General Robert C. B. Pemberton, ed. by his son, the Rev. Robert Pemberton, Bedford, 1923. Chart 10 states that Alice Pemberton, daughter of Robert, baptized Feb. 18, 1564/65, married either Francis Kempe, Nicholas Cotchett, or Jeremy Odell. No St. Albans record appears to confirm this assertion, which (if true) could have meant a first marriage. All three names, Odell, Cotchett and Kempe, occur in the St. Albans records. G. Andrews Moriarty, *Rhode Island History,* 1944, III, 23–30, 67–71, 91–102, summarizes data concerning the Pembertons of St. Albans. This account includes many items relative to James Williams.
9. *Abstracts of Inquisitiones Post Mortem for the City of London,* British Record Society, Vol. XXXVI, 1908, pp. 233–234. Inquisition for Thomas Castell, Jr., taken at the Guildhall, Oct. 3, 1594. "Long before his death," he was seized in his demesne of "1 messauge now in the tenure of James Willyams; . . . and all said messauges and tenement lie in Longe Lane, aforesaid in the said parish of St. Sepulchre without Newgate." *Chancery Inq. p.m.,* ser. 2, vol. 245, no. 53.
10. *1632,* in an undated letter to John Winthrop, c. July, 1632. *Narragansett Club Publications,* 6 vols., Providence, 1874, VI, 2 (*nearer up-*

wards, usually above). *1662,* Nov. 15, Deposition in Town Clerk's office Portsmouth. *Town Book,* p. 412. *1672/3, George Fox Digg'd Out of His Burrowes, Narragansett Club Publications,* V, lxiv. 1677/78, Testimony given Feb. 7, 1677/78, *R.I. Hist. Soc. Pub.,* 1900, VIII, 157. *1679,* July 2, *Records of Rhode Island Colony,* III, 57. For a listing of these, with comment, see a brief article, "The Date of Roger Williams' Birth," *Rhode Island Historical Society Collections,* XXVIII, 1935, pp. 112–115. His contemporaries also spoke of birthdays and ages without precision.

11. For an account supplying many details, see F. P. Wilson, *The Plague in Shakespeare's London,* 1927. The diagram is reproduced in color on p. 63. Earlier the sign had been a cross.
12. Rymer's *Foedera,* London, 1715, XVI, 448–450; John Stow's *A Survey of London,* Kingsford ed., Oxford, 1908, II, 367–368.
13. *The Wonderfull Yeare, 1603,* p. 111.
14. John Speed, *The Historie of Great Britaine,* 2nd ed., London, 1623, p. 1242, col. 1.
15. Clode, *Memorials of the Guild of Merchant Taylors,* pp. 130–131.

CHAPTER III

1. John Stow, *A Survey of London,* II, 28–29.
2. *Ibid.,* II, 29–30.
3. *Ibid.,* II, 33.
4. In a letter to the Town of Providence, Jan. 1644/45, *N.C.P.,* VI, 278–279.
5. This last was Duke Frederick, as early as 1592. Rye, *op. cit.,* p. 7.
6. Stow's *London,* brought down to 1633, by John Strype, 2 vols., London, 1720, under *The Temporal Government,* II, 306–307.
7. *The Seven Deadly Sinnes of London,* 1606 ed., pp. 25–26.
8. Strype's ed. of Stow, *op. cit.,* II, 307.
9. This bell is still in the possession of St. Sepulchre's Church. There are many contemporary allusions to it, the most famous being Lady Macbeth's "the fatall Bell-man, which gives the stern'st goodnight."
10. Henry Morley, *Memoirs of Bartholomew Fair,* London, 1859, quotes these lines from the title page of a small quarto tract of 1641, p. 185.
11. Capt. John Smith is buried in the south aisle of the church. A brass plate at the entrance to the Royal Fusiliers' Chapel marks his grave and another on the baptistery wall honors his achievements,
    "Done in Virginia, that large Continent."
12. From the Mayor's order, dated Mar. 27, 1609. Clode, *Memorials of the Guild of Merchant Taylors,* 143–144, 146.
13. Act III, Scene 2.
14. Clode, *op. cit.,* pp. 164 ff.
15. *George Fox Digg'd Out of His Burrowes, N.C.P.,* V, prefatory state-

ment, unpaged; in a letter to John Winthrop, c. 1632, *N.C.P., Letters,* VI, 1–2.

16. Thomas Fuller, *The Church-History of Britain,* London, 1655, Bk. X, pp. 63–64.
17. *Acts and Monuments of John Foxe,* London, 1641, I, 681.
18. *Ibid.,* II, 427. Roger Williams' reference to him, *Bloody Tenent Yet More Bloody, N.C.P.,* IV, 464.
19. The history of this church has recently been written. Johannes Lindeboom, *Austin Friars: History of the Dutch Reformed Church in London, 1550–1950,* The Hague, 1950. The church building was completely destroyed, Oct. 16, 1940, when a landmine attached to a parachute exploded in the space enclosed by high offices around the church. The archives were destroyed. A few pages from the pulpit Bible were all that could be recovered from the rubble and dust.
20. John Strype, *Annals of the Reformation,* 4 vols., Oxford, 1824, IV, 235.
21. Champlin Burrage, *The Early English Dissenters,* 2 vols., Cambridge, 1912, I, 144–148, prints a list of 1592–1593 Barrowists, with their depositions. Most of those listed were young men.
22. *Reliquiae Baxterianae,* ed. by Matthew Sylvester, London, 1696, pp. 2–3.

CHAPTER IV

1. Robert Burton, *Anatomy of Melancholy,* 3 vols., London, 1893, I, 384.
2. Charles Hoole, *The Petty Schoole,* 1659, included in *A New Discovery of the old Art of Teaching Schoole,* in four small treatises, London, 1913, p. 2.
3. *Diary and Correspondence of John Evelyn,* 4 vols., London, 1850, I, 4.
4. *Aubrey's Brief Lives,* ed. by Andrew Clark, 2 vols., Oxford, 1898. He had gone to school in Leigh-de-la-mer, I, 332, marginal note.
5. Hoole, *op. cit.,* p. 5.
6. *Certaine Grammar questions for the exercise of young Schollers in the learning of the Accidence,* n.d. The book begins with this catechism.
7. John Stockwood's *A Plaine and Easie Laying open of the meaning and understanding of the Rules of Construction in the English Accidence,* London, 1590, p. 1.
8. Quoted by Foster Watson, *The English Grammar Schools to 1660,* Cambridge, 1908, pp. 190–191 note. One reason for the place of writing in the week's program may have been that writing masters were often itinerants, travelling through the country from school to school.
9. *The English Schoole-maister,* London, 1596, The Preface to the Reader. Coote was Master of the Free-Schoole in Bury St. Edmunds.
10. *The Whole Works of Roger Ascham,* ed. by the Rev. Dr. Giles, London, 1864, *The Schoolmaster,* Vol. III, Bk. I, p. 93.
11. William Haine, *Lily's Rules Construed, A Short Introduction to the Parts of Speech,* London, 1641 ed., Address to the Reader.

12. John Brinsley, *Ludus Literarius, or The Grammar Schoole,* London, 1627, pp. 298–299. This book is a gold mine for the subject.
13. William Kempe's summary of current practice, as quoted by Thomas W. Baldwin, *op. cit.,* I, 438 ff.

CHAPTER V

1. *The Autobiography and Correspondence of Sir Simonds D'Ewes,* 2 vols., London, 1845, I, 95–96. Various textbooks on shorthand were in print; for example, *The Art of Stenographie, wherein is annexed a very easie direction for Stenographie, or Secret Writing,* London, 1602. It was sometimes advertised as *Short-Writing,* or *Double Writing.* Roger Williams reports his own proficiency in short-hand, "Now I knowing what short-hand could doe as well as most in *England* from my *Childhood . . .*" *N.C.P.,* V, 131.
2. There are various lives of Coke: Cuthbert William Johnson, *The Life of Sir Edward Coke,* 2 vols., London, 1837; Charles Warburton James, *Chief Justice Coke, His Family and Descendants at Holkham,* London, 1929. A new life is announced as in preparation. It is badly needed.
3. Stow, Kingsford ed., I, 163.
4. Quoted wherever Coke's story is told. Cf. *D.N.B.;* Johnson, I, 157–163. For numerous quotations from Coke's speeches, *cf.* John Rushworth's *Collections,* 6 vols., London, 1703–1708, I, 497, *passim.*
5. A memorandum on the back of her copy of one of her letters to Roger Williams in 1652. MS. owned by Trinity College Library, Cambridge. These letters are reprinted in *N.C.P.,* VI, 241, 244, 249–253, and also by James, *Chief Justice Coke,* pp. 60–61.
6. For a brief account of Star Chamber, see John Rushworth, *A Discourse concerning the High Court of Star-Chamber,* in *Historical Collections of Private Passages of State, 1618–1629,* London, 1859, II, 471–480; Samuel Rawson Gardiner, *Reports of Cases in the Star-Chamber and High Commission,* London, 1886. John Lord Campbell, *Lives of the Chief Justices of England,* 2 vols., London, 1849–1858, mentions Coke's negotiations, 1617, against certain Dutch merchants, I, 304–305.
7. From his letter to Anne Sadleir, 1652, *N.C.P.,* VI, 239.
8. A recent catalogue of his library shows the range of his interest aside from the law: *A Catalogue of the Library of Sir Edward Coke,* edited by W. O. Hassall, New Haven, 1950.
9. Sir James Whitelocke, *Liber Famelicus,* 1609–1631, ed. by John Bruce, Camden Society, 1858, p. 50.
10. Letter to Anne Sadleir, 1652, *N.C.P.,* VI, 239–240.
11. Records of Charterhouse, fortunately preserved from the all but total destruction of this ancient foundation by fire in 1940. Rebuilding is now well advanced.
12. For the history of Charterhouse, see William Haig Browne, *Charterhouse Past and Present,* Godalming, 1879; G. S. Davies, *Charterhouse*

in London, 1921; David Knowles and W. F. Grimes, *Charterhouse: The Medieval Foundation in the Light of Recent Discoveries,* London, 1954. This account includes the finding of Walter Nanny's tomb during the present rebuilding. Records of the school are reprinted by Bower Marsh and Frederick Arthur Crisp, *Alumni Carthusiani,* London, 1913.

13. Quoted from the records of the school by Samuel Herne, *Domus Carthusiana,* London, 1677, pp. 282–283.
14. The July 9th record reads, "Wee doe also Order, Constitute and Ordeine, that Robert Capping, John Parlor, and John Williams, for that upon examynason, they are found to be good Schollers; shall between this and all Saynets next, be removed out of the said hospitall, and sent to the universitie, and to have such allowances, as is lately sett for the mayntenance of schollers."

CHAPTER VI

1. Fuller's estimate, *History of the University of Cambridge,* 1655 ed., I, 163. "An exact survey was taken of the number of Students in the University, whose totall summe amounted unto Two thousand nine hundred ninety and eight." John Scott, notary public of Cambridge, in his list, Add. MS. No. 11, 720, gives the Pembroke number as 140, although since he gives Peterhouse, King's, Sidney Sussex, and Corpus Christi as also 140, he may be speaking in round numbers.
2. P. 50.
3. Quoted, James Bass Mullinger, *The University of Cambridge,* 3 vols., Cambridge, 1884, II, 142.
4. *Autobiography,* I, 106–107.
5. In his *The Hireling Ministry None of Christs,* London, 1652.
6. *Autobiography,* I, 141–142, 147.
7. *William Laud,* ed. J. Bliss, 7 vols., Oxford, 1847–1860, V, 13.
8. *Two Elizabethan Puritan Diaries, by Richard Rogers and Samuel Ward,* ed. M. M. Knappen, London, 1933, p. 122.
9. Charles Henry Cooper, *The Annals of Cambridge,* 3 vols., 1866, III, 182.
10. These letters are invaluable, not only for their weekly catalogue of news, but also for judging the reflection of it in University Life. Harleian MSS. 389–390, British Museum.
11. *Autobiography,* p. 14.
12. Quoted, Fuller, *Church-History,* Bk. X, 108–110.
13. They had also been burned in St. Mary's churchyard, Oxford. The undoing of Pareus had been the *Quaestio* in his *Commentary on the Romans,* "Whether resistance to the civil ruler be lawful in any case, and, if so, to what extent?" *Cf.* Mullinger, II, 562–568.
14. Fuller remarked that because Dorislaus was a foreigner, not a theolo-

gian, "his lectures were listened to with the more critical attention of Cambridge auditors, *Church-History,* Bk. X, 163–164.

15. From a MS. copy in the University Registry.
16. *Scrinia Reserta, A Memorial Offer'd to the Great Deservings of John Williams,* London, 1693, Pt. 2, p. 81.
17. *The Hireling Ministry None of Christs,* 1652. This treatise concerns the current battle of the Independents against forced tithes for the support of the established church.

CHAPTER VII

1. This had been one of Laud's first moves to show his power. In addition to the instructions as to chaplains, he had said to his bishops, stay in your diocese, hang on to the lands belonging to it, keep control over lecturers, suppress afternoon sermons, and instead advocate catechisings.
2. 76 persons had been released at this time. For a history of the Barrington family, see Alan Lowndes, "The History of the Barrington Family," *Transactions of the Essex Archaeological Society,* New Series, Colchester, 1884, II, 3–24.
3. The Barrington Correspondence, Egerton MSS. 2643–2650, British Museum.
4. Lowndes, *op. cit.*
5. *Diary of Lady Margaret Hoby, 1599–1605,* ed. by Dorothy M. Meads, London, 1930.
6. Barrington Correspondence.
7. Samuel Rawson Gardiner, *History of England, 1603–1642,* 10 vols., London, 1883–1884, VII, 67–76. To Simonds D'Ewes, this dissolution of Parliament "in a tumultary manner" marked "the most gloomy, sad, and dismal day for England that happened in five hundred years last past."
8. D. Lupton, *London and the Countrey Carbonadoed,* London, 1632, pp. 123–127.
9. Barrington Correspondence. These letters are reprinted in the *New Eng. Hist. and Geneal. Register,* 1889, Vol. 43, pp. 316–320.
10. This "late New England call" is nowhere made specific. In order to come prior to this letter of Roger Williams, presumably written in late April, 1629, this call might logically have been to Salem at the time of the initial plan for a settled ministry in the new colony. If so, it probably would have been for the post accepted by Francis Bright, a non-conformist Essex minister, who in Feb. 1628/29, agreed to go and to remain for three years. It also might have been, but less probably, an early offer for Boston, but these plans were not yet far advanced until late summer, 1629.
11. Barrington Correspondence. A letter and two of Hooke's sermons are

preserved in *The Ministry of Taunton,* ed. by Samuel Emery, 2 vols., Boston, 1853, I, 63–129; Appendix, 130–154.

12. Barrington Correspondence. Her letters to Increase Mather are in *Coll. Mass. Hist. Soc.,* 4th ser., VIII, 261–267; to Rebecca Russell, 260–261; to John Wilson, 267–268.
13. Barrington Correspondence.
14. James Ernst has endeavored to put the six letters relative to this whole affair in chronological sequence. *Coll. R.I. Hist. Soc.,* 1929, XXII, 97–103. The time involved extends probably from April 1629 to late fall, 1629.
15. Many letters concern this family problem. Jug was finally married in the spring of 1630.
16. This is the only certain clue to her identity.
17. The records of the church are preserved in the Essex County Archives, Chelmsford, England.
18. The most thoroughgoing search has been made by Emily Easton. *Coll. R.I. Hist. Soc.,* 1936, XXIX, 65–80, "Mary Barnard."
19. Quoted from his *Memoirs,* pp. 49–51, by Dorothy Meads, *Diary of Lady Hoby,* pp. 267–268, note 361.
20. For a bibliography of his writings, see John Ingle Dredge, *The Writings of Richard Bernard of Epworth, Worksop, and Batcombe,* Horncastle, 1890, No. 1 of the Lincolnshire Bibliographies.
21. The record of his arrival reads, "Masachiell Barnard of Batcombe clothier of the County Somersett, 24 yeare." *Weymouth Vital Records,* I, lists a daughter, Mary, born Sept. 27, 1637. *Cf. History of Weymouth,* 3 vols., 1923, III, p. 77.
22. This William Barnard was nephew and heir of Ann Barnard Pemberton, wife of Sir James Pemberton, brother of Alice Pemberton, Roger Williams' mother.
23. "Possibly Master Cotton may call to mind," *Bloody Tenent Yet More Bloody, N.C.P.,* IV, 65–66.
24. *N.C.P.,* VI, 252–253.
25. *Ibid.,* VI, 239.
26. Repeated various times, early and late in life. In his 1677 testimony, "My soul's desire was to do the natives good."
27. *The Life and Letters of John Winthrop,* ed. by Robert C. Winthrop, 2 vols., Boston, 1869, II, 330–331.
28. In his 1652 letter to Anne Sadleir, *N.C.P.,* VI, 239.
29. William Wood, *New England's Prospect,* London, 1634, Chapter XII, p. 49.

CHAPTER VIII

1. *The History of New England,* 2 vols., Boston, 1853. Subsequently referred to as Winthrop's *Journal,* I, 51, 56.
2. *Ibid.,* 49–50.

3. March 25, 1671, *N.C.P.*, VI, 356. Letter to John Cotton, Jr. Neither John Winthrop nor the Boston Church Records mention this offer and refusal. There is only this statement of Roger Williams forty years later.
4. First Church Records, Boston (unpublished). Mass. Hist. Soc. custodian of MS copy.
5. Winthrop's *Journal,* I, 70.
6. *Ibid.,* I, 97. He reports that the minority numbered only three.
7. *The History of Plymouth Plantation,* Boston, 1898, Bk. II, p. 370.
8. *Journal,* I, 108–110, under date of Oct. 25, 1632.
9. *The Bloody Tenent Yet More Bloody, N.C.P.,* IV, 104–105.
10. *History of Plymouth Plantation,* Bk. II, pp. 369–370.
11. *Ibid.,* p. 370. The date of his departure is not recorded. Joseph B. Felt, *The Annals of Salem from its First Settlement,* 2 vols., Salem, 1827, I, 60–62, says that he returned in November. Felt's statement that Roger Williams' objection to the appellation "good man" except as applied to pious persons, was one of the reasons for the Plymouth uneasiness, appears to have no substantiation in the earlier records. Cotton Mather repeats the objection, but does not mention Roger Williams by name. *Magnalia,* 1820 ed., I, 117.
12. *The Mayflower Descendant* (1899), I, 25, 28. Will proved Oct. 28, 1633.
13. William Wood pays early tribute to his ability to use Indian language in preaching. *New England's Prospect,* London, 1634, Part II, "Of Their Language," pp. 91–92.

CHAPTER IX

1. *Journal,* I, 145.
2. *Ibid.,* I, 145. The passages from Revelation are identified in a marginal note in the MS. of John Winthrop's letter to John Endecott. They are Rev. xvi, 13, 14; xvii, 12; xviii, 9. This letter is printed in *Proc. Mass. Hist. Soc.* (1871–1873), pp. 343–345.
3. *Journal,* I, 147.
4. This sermon is entitled *God's Promise to his Plantation,* London, 1630.
5. In John Winthrop's MS. answer to the *Treatise* arguments. Owned by the Mass. Hist. Soc.
6. *Life and Letters of John Winthrop,* 2 vols., Boston, 1869, I, 311–312, under the title *Diverse objections wch have been made against this Plantation, wth their answears & Resolutions.* In Hutchinson's *Collection of Original Papers relative to the Colony of Massachusetts Bay,* it has the title *General Considerations for the Plantation of New England, with an Answer to several Objections.* Some doubt of Winthrop's authorship has been expressed.
7. *A Good Speed to Virginia,* London, 1609, unpaged.
8. Chapter 4, p. 10.
9. Rev. John Bulkley of Colchester in Connecticut, *An Inquiry into the*

Right of the Original Natives to the Lands in America, and the Titles Derived from them, Coll. Mass. Hist. Soc. (1794), Vol. III, pp. 159–181. He is in vehement opposition to the opinion that the natives had right of title to the lands they roamed over, quoting Locke's *Treatise of Government* in support.

10. *The Bloody Tenent Yet More Bloody, N.C.P.*, IV, 461–462. He asserts that the Letter to King Charles was one of the causes of his banishment. Whether in his use of the word, *Letter* is identical with *Treatise* is not clear.
11. It broke in two upon being launched. In John Winthrop's word, "God frustrated their design."
12. *The Bloody Tenent Yet More Bloody, N.C.P.*, IV, 462.
13. *Journal,* I, 195.
14. This letter is extant in Roger Williams' handwriting. It is printed in *N.C.P.*, VI, 71–77.
15. *Journal,* I, 188–189; *Massachusetts Bay Records,* I, 146.
16. *Journal,* I, 188.
17. *Ibid.*, I, 193–194.
18. *Massachusetts Bay Records,* I, 156, Sept. 3, 1635.
19. *Ibid.*, I, 160–161. Winthrop's *Journal,* I, 204.
20. Lives of Vane include J. K. Hosmer, *The Life of Young Sir Henry Vane,* Boston, 1888; W. W. Ireland, *The Life of Sir Henry Vane the Younger,* London, 1905.
21. *Winthrop Papers,* III, 240–241, Mar. 29, 1636.
22. *Coll. Mass. Hist. Soc.,* 4th ser., VI, 445.
23. Henry Martyn Dexter, *As to Roger Williams,* Boston, 1876, pp. 58–80.

CHAPTER X

1. Letter to Major Mason, June 22, 1670, *N.C.P.*, VI, 335.
2. *Ibid.*, VI, 336.
3. Elder James Brown of Providence, 1666–1732, left a memorandum naming Manton's Neck as the place where Roger Williams "abode the latter part of that winter." No source is given for the statement. Quoted, Howard M. Chapin, *The Documentary History of Rhode Island,* 2 vols., Providence, 1916, 1919, I, 14. The original is in the MSS. Papers of the R.I. Hist. Soc.
4. From Roger Williams' 1677 Testimony, Rider's *Historical Tracts,* No. 14, pp. 53–54. The portion naming his companions is quoted by Howard M. Chapin, *Documentary History of Rhode Island,* I, 5.
5. Winthrop's *Journal* records this storm, I, 195–198.
6. *Plymouth Colony Records,* II, 87, records ten fathom of beads given Assamequine at Mr. Williams' house "for his land at Seacunk." The deed is not extant.
7. Roger Williams' 1677 Testimony, Rider, *op. cit.*, p. 53.

8. His 1661 Testimony, taken at Providence Dec. 13, 1661, *N.C.P.*, VI, 316.
9. For various sources of the landing tradition, *cf.* Chapin, *Doc. Hist.*, I, 17–20.
10. *New Eng. Hist. and Geneal. Register,* 1879, Vol. 33, p. 428. From the family record of Benedict Arnold.
11. *Early Records of the Town of Providence,* V, 306–309. The 1662 acknowledgment is signed also by Mary Williams.
12. Chapin, I, 21.
13. Chapin, I, Chapter VIII, pp. 61–69; reproduced, pp. 64–65.
14. Letter to John Winthrop, Oct. 28, 1637, *N.C.P.*, VI, 70–71, and Nov. 10, 1637, *ibid.*, p. 78.
15. Quoted Chapin, *Doc. Hist.*, I, 27–28. *Early Records of the Town of Providence,* V, 306–309. The original is framed in the Office of the Recorder of Deeds, Providence.
16. Testimony relative to the deed of Rhode Island, Providence, August 25, 1658. *N.C.P.*, VI, 305.
17. Chapin, I, 25.
18. From his 1677 Testimony, Rider, *op. cit.*, No. 14, p. 55.
19. Chapin, I, 27–28.
20. Both the Initial Deed and the 1661 copy are printed in Chapin, I, 76–78. See also *Early Rec. of Prov.*, I, 22–25; *Providence Town Papers,* 0120. There are differences in spelling in these different versions.
21. *Rec. of R.I. Col.*, I, 23–24.
22. 1677 Testimony, Rider, *op. cit.*, p. 53.
23. *Rec. of R.I. Col.*, I, 14.
24. An undated letter to John Winthrop, *N.C.P.*, VI, 3–7. Two versions of a covenant are given.
25. *Journal,* I, 340. No *order* is extant.
26. From the Combination of 1640. Printed Chapin, *Doc. Hist.*, I, 110–115. Original document lost; copy made March 28, 1662. *Rec. of R.I. Col.*, I, 28. The first entry in the first extant town book is an undated covenant, agreeing essentially with the first one quoted in Roger Williams' letter to John Winthrop (Note 24 *supra*) except for the phrase "only in civil things." Thirteen names are signed to this instrument, among them only those of Thomas Angell and Francis Wickes of the original group of six men. Presumably all thirteen are the young men referred to in Roger Williams' letter.
27. *Rec. of R.I. Col.*, I, 113.
28. *N.C.P.*, VI, 124.
29. From the Address to Parliament and Council of State, unpaged, in a prefatory "discourse touching New England." The full title of this book is *Ill Newes from New England,* London, 1652.
30. Oct. 24, 1636, *N.C.P.*, VI, 7–13.

CHAPTER XI

1. Letter to Major Mason, June 22, 1670, *N.C.P.*, VI, 338.
2. To John Winthrop, Oct. 24, 1636, *N.C.P.*, VI, 13.
3. To Gov. Vane and Deputy Gov. Winthrop, c. May, 1637, *ibid.*, VI, 17–19.
4. *Ibid.*, VI, 87.
5. *Ibid.*, VI, 17.
6. *A Key into the Language of America, ibid.*, I, 82–83.
7. Letter of May 13, 1637, to Gov. Vane and Depty Gov. Winthrop, *N.C.P.*, VI, 25.
8. Four contemporary accounts of this battle were printed: Capt. John Mason, *A Brief History of the Pequot War;* Capt. John Underhill, *Newes from America, . . .* London, 1638; P. Vincent, *A True Relation of the Late Battell fought in New-England, . . .* London, 1638; Leift Lion Gardener, *Relation of the Pequot Warres,* written in 1660, first printed in 1901. All these narratives are reprinted in Charles Orr, *History of the Pequot War,* Cleveland, 1897. Mason, Underhill and Vincent had previously been reprinted in *Coll. Mass. Hist. Soc.,* 2nd ser., VIII, and 3rd ser., VI and VII.
9. The quoted phrases are from Mason's account, Orr, *op. cit.,* pp. 26, 30, 31–32.
10. *Key, N.C.P.,* I, 201.
11. Bradford's *History of Plimoth Plantation,* 1898 ed., under the year 1638, Bk. II, p. 434. Later Roger Williams gave testimony to all this in court.
12. *N.C.P.,* VI., 35.
13. *Ibid.,* VI, 22, 38, 101.
14. *Ibid.,* VI, 269–270.
15. Winthrop's *Journal,* II, 102.
16. Letter to the Mass. General Court, Oct. 5, 1654, *N.C.P.,* VI, 272–273.

CHAPTER XII

1. *N.C.P.,* I, 19.
2. *Ibid.,* p. 19. Johannes Megapolensis, Jr., in *A Short Sketch of the Mohawk Indians in New Netherlands,* 1644, Amsterdam, 1651 (*N.Y. Hist. Soc. Coll.,* 2nd ser., III, Pt. 1, 147–160) says he is making a vocabulary of the language, but finds it very puzzling.
3. *N.C.P.,* I, 25.
4. *Ibid.,* p. 20.
5. There were many such books. For example, Charles Hoole's *Pueriles Confabulantinculiae, or Childrens Talk English and Latine,* London, 1659; Maturinus Corderius's *Colloquia Scholastica,* London, 1657, each in many editions.

6. *N.C.P.*, I, 29.
7. Thomas Hariot, *A briefe and true report of the New found land of Virginia.* In addition to Capt. John Smith and various other Virginia and Maryland reporters, there were William Alexander, *An Encouragement to Colonies,* 1624; Francis Higginson, *New England's Plantation,* 1630; William Wood, *New England's Prospect,* 1634; Thomas Morton, *New English Canaan,* 1637, and various others, in each of which the Indians were discussed.
8. *N.C.P.*, I, 39–40.
9. *Ibid.*, p. 46.
10. *Ibid.*, p. 75.
11. *Ibid.*, pp. 97, 98.
12. *Ibid.*, p. 95.
13. *Ibid.*, p. 49.
14. *Ibid.*, p. 25.
15. *Ibid.*, p. 147.
16. *Ibid.*, pp. 155–158.
17. *Ibid.*, p. 160.
18. Included in one of Edward Winslow's letters to Parliament under the title, "The Glorious Progress of the Gospel amongst the Indians in New England," London, 1649, pp. 12–14, 20–21. More of these questions are included in Henry Whitfield's *The Light appearing more and more towards the perfect Day,* London, 1651.
19. It was printed in *New England's First Fruits,* early in 1643, by R. Overton and Gregory Dexter who also printed Roger Williams' *Key.*
20. *N.C.P.*, I, pp. 160–161.
21. *Ibid.*, p. 200.

CHAPTER XIII

1. Hugh Peter, who had succeeded Roger Williams as pastor of the Salem church, and Thomas Welde, who had participated in the trials of Anne Hutchinson and John Wheelwright.
2. *Truth Maintained,* 1643; in the Prefatory address to Master John Downam, he had said that the "only Good Token of such Times is, That they are so extreamely Bad they can never last long."
3. Thomason lists it as of March, 1642.
4. Nov. 7, 1640, printed, 1641, p. 4.
5. A public letter, June 7, 1644, *Letters and Journals,* transcribed by Robert Aiken, 2 vols., Edinburgh, 1775, II, 24.
6. Quoted in Address to the Reader, *Mr. Cotton's Letter Examined and Answered, N.C.P.*, I, 32.
7. In the House of Commons, June 11, 1641.
8. Quoted by William W. Ireland, *The Life of Sir Henry Vane the Younger,* London, 1905, p. 204. The Assembly of Divines was greatly

troubled by Vane's espousal of toleration. Baillie, *Letters and Journals,* II, 61, "The great shot of Cromwell and Vane is to have a liberty of all religions."

9. The first phrase was struck out; the second kept and also accepted by the House of Lords.
10. For a copy of this bill in Chancery and details of the procedure, see Sidney Rider, *Book Notes,* Vol. 29, 1912, pp. 89–93; Harley H. Bartlett, *New Eng. Hist. and Geneal. Register,* 1943, Vol. 97, pp. 176–181.
11. By Richard Gesling, 1644.
12. Dated at the Guildhall, London, the 27th day of June, 1644.
13. *The Bloody Tenent Yet More Bloody, N.C.P.,* IV, 103.
14. In a letter to Mr. David Dickson, July 23, 1644, II, 211–212.
15. For the text of the Narragansett patent, see *New Eng. Hist. and Geneal. Register,* 1857, Vol. XI, pp. 41–43. For a discussion of it, see Thomas Aspinwall, *Proc. Mass. Hist. Soc.,* 1862, pp. 41–47. His design is to prove this instrument spurious. See also Raymond Phineas Stearns, "The Weld-Peter Mission," *Col. Soc. of Mass. Pub.,* XXXII, 188–246.
16. The charter is extant in four copies. The original is lost. For the text see *Coll. Mass. Hist. Soc.,* 2nd ser., IX (1832), 185–188.
17. "It is ordered by this Court that the yland comonly called Aquetheneck shall be from henceforth calld the ile of Rhods, or Rhod-Island." Chapin, *Doc. Hist.,* II, 128.

CHAPTER XIV

1. Entitled, *A Letter of Mr. John Cottons, Teacher of the Church in Boston, in New-England, to Mr. Williams a Preacher there,* London, 1643. Reprinted, *N.C.P.,* I, 295–311.
2. Cotton himself, in his *Reply to Mr. Williams, his Examination,* 1647, p. 10, speaks of Sabine Staresmore as one who, "well affected" to Roger Williams, might have published it, but adds that he does not suspect him. Staresmore was a Separatist, several times the subject of criticism in print. Roger Williams does not mention him.
3. Dated Mar. 25, 1671, *N.C.P.,* VI, 354.
4. *N.C.P.,* II, 339.
5. *Ibid.,* 328.
6. *Ibid.,* 396.
7. John Cotton's *Reply,* 1647, also identifies it by title, p. 10, "above them all to address himself (according to his high thoughts) to propound Quaeries of high concernment (as he called them) to the High and Honourable Court of Parliament."
8. *Apologeticall Narration,* p. 24. A facsimile edition of this tract is included in William Haller's *Tracts on Liberty in the Puritan Revolution,* 3 vols., New York, 1933.

9. *Queries,* pp. 15–16.
10. *Ibid.,* p. 14.
11. *Ibid.,* p. 26.
12. *The Bloody Tenent Yet More Bloody, N.C.P.,* IV, 104.
13. Bradford Swan, who has looked into Dexter's activities more closely than anyone else, makes out a good case for his printing of this book. See his *Gregory Dexter of London and New England, 1610–1700,* Rochester, 1949.
14. *Commons Journals,* Vol. III, from Mar. 15, 1642, to Dec. 24, 1644, p. 585, col. 1, Die Veneris, Aug. 9, 1644.
15. Aug. 12, 1644.
16. Entitled *Solomon's Choice,* preached Sept. 25 at St. Margaret's, p. 41.
17. Reprinted, E. B. Underhill, *Tracts,* Hanserd Knollys Society, 1846.
18. *Ibid.,* 17–18, 22, 41.
19. *The Simple Cobler of Aggawam in America,* 1713 Boston ed., *Peter Force Tracts,* Washington, 1844, p. 11.

CHAPTER XV

1. Chapin, *Doc. Hist.,* I, 212–213.
2. Winthrop's *Journal,* II, 236–238, also copies this letter. Winthrop merely states, "here arrived also Mr. Roger Williams, and with him two or three families."
3. *Bloody Tenent Yet More Bloody, N.C.P.,* IV, 29–30.
4. There was one unfavorable report of this village reception, from his personal enemy, John Scott, who saw him "hemmed in in the middle of the Canoes . . . Elevated and Transported out of himself"; quoted, *Doc. Hist.,* I, 214.
5. In the subscription of the 25-Acre-Men, (Jan. 19, 1645/46) the phrase, "according to our charter" occurs. *Doc. Hist.,* I, 219.
6. The secret deed of Saconomoco to William Arnold belongs to Jan. 30, 1641/42, although it was not recorded until 1645, *Doc. Hist.,* I, 146–147. The subjection of Pomham and Saconomoco to Massachusetts occurred June 22, 1643, *Doc. Hist.,* I, 150–151; *Mass. Col. Records,* II, 40. They made their marks, expressing also their willingness "to be instructed in the knowledge and worship of God."
7. For a brief account of this affair, see Howard Chapin, *Sachems of the Narragansetts,* Providence, 1931, pp. 37–52.
8. Winthrop's *Journal,* II, 157–162.
9. As to the eventual consequence of this action, favorable to Rhode Island, although not so intended, see William Greene Roelker, *Rhode Island History,* II, 1–10, "Samuel Gorton's Master Stroke."
10. *N.C.P.,* I, 85.
11. In his 1682 Testimony, *N.C.P.,* VI, 407.

12. Plymouth Colony sent a similar letter. *Cf.* Winthrop's *Journal,* II, 270. For the text of both letters, *Doc. Hist.,* I, 227–229.
13. *Early Rec. of R.I.,* I, 156–190.
14. Reprinted, *R.I. Hist. Tracts,* No. 14, Providence, 1881.

CHAPTER XVI

1. Cocumscussoc was the name of a brook flowing into the harbor at this point. The best argument for the shore position rather than the rival site at Devil's Foot Rock, nearly two miles inland, is the greater convenience as a landing place for cargo brought by boat, and for Indian customers coming by canoe. Why the extra burden of transportation for either by foot trail? Howard B. Chapin, "The Trading Post of Roger Williams, and those of John Wilcox and Richard Smith," Society of Colonial Wars, Providence, 1934, brings together the available evidence on this matter.
2. May, 1649, *Prov. Town Papers,* I, 219.
3. "Description of New England in 1650," a letter, *Proc. Mass. Hist. Soc.,* 2nd ser., 1885, II, 46.
4. *George Fox Digg'd, N.C.P.,* V, 447.
5. In 1652, on the occasion of his second visit to England. Recently reprinted, with Introduction, by Winthrop S. Hudson, Philadelphia, 1951, pp. 40, 44.
6. *Ibid.,* p. 45.
7. Letter of Apr. 1, 1653, *N.C.P.,* VI, 255.
8. *Experiments,* p. 47.
9. Cotton's *Answer* had not yet come, he says. "If you heare, let me know."
10. Nathanael Carpenter, *Geography delineated foorth in two bookes,* Oxford, 1625. The second book concerned the inhabitants of the globe.
11. Aug. 31, 1648, *N.C.P.,* VI, 149–151.
12. Jan. 1648/49. *N.C.P.,* VI, 166–167.
13. There had been one slight rift toward the end, the occasion being the Massachusetts claims for Rhode Island lands and Roger Williams' refusal to admit their validity in any way.
14. *N.C.P.,* VI, 180–181.
15. *Winthrop Papers,* IV, 490, Aug. 5, 1644.
16. The record of this petition and the successive action of the Council of State upon it is to be found in the *Interregnum Entry Book,* Public Record Office, London, Vol. 92, under dates of Mar. 6 and Mar. 7, 1651; Vol. 146, under dates of Mar. 20, Mar. 27, Apr. 9, Apr. 17, 1651. The matter was referred to the Committee of the Admiralty, which reported back to the Council of State. His commission was revoked Oct. 2, 1652.

17. Action authorizing them to go was taken at the Assembly Oct. 26, 1650. *Early Records of R.I. Colony,* I, 231.
18. *Ibid.,* I, 234–235. Sept. 1, 1651.
19. Best told in Clarke's own *Ill Newes from New England,* London, 1652. Reprinted in *Coll. Mass. Hist. Soc.,* 4th ser., 1854, Vol. II, 1–113. Cobbett's answer, *The Civil Magistrates Power in Matters of religion modestly debated,* appeared in London, 1653. Henry Melville King rewrote the Clarke episode in *A Summer Visit of Three Rhode Islanders to the Massachusetts Bay in 1651,* Providence, 1896.
20. Mar. 7, 1651/52. See Richard LeBaron Bowen, *The Providence Oath of Allegiance and its Signers, 1651–52,* Providence, 1943, for a thorough investigation of this document and its importance.

CHAPTER XVII

1. *N.C.P.,* VI, 231–233.
2. To John Winthrop, Jr., *ibid.,* VI, 234.
3. Letter of July 12, 1654, *ibid.,* VI, 261–262.
4. The *Areopagitica* appeared Nov. 24, 1644.
5. Entitled *The Bloody Tenent, Washed, and Made White in the Bloud of the Lambe,* Thomason's date is May 15, 1647.
6. See Gardiner, *History of the Commonwealth and Protectorate, 1649–1660,* II, 208–210.
7. Reprinted, Cyrus Pitt Grosvenor, *A Review of the Correspondence of Messrs. Fuller and Wayland,* . . . Utica, 1847, pp. 155–183.
8. How had written a treatise, *The Sufficience of the Spirits Teaching without Humane-Learning,* London, 1640.
9. Identified as belonging to Roger Williams, by James Ernst. Fully entitled, *The Examiner Defended,* in a fair and sober Answer to the two and twenty questions which lately examined the author of Zeal Examined, 95 pages.
10. Pp. 6, 64–65.
11. By action of the Council of State.
12. Letter of Sept. 8, 1652, *N.C.P.,* VI, 236–237.
13. To Providence and Warwick, *N.C.P.,* VI, 255.
14. *Early Rec. of the Colony of R.I.,* Oct. 28, 1652, I, 248–249.
15. Gardiner, *History of the Commonwealth and Protectorate,* II, 207–210.

CHAPTER XVIII

1. Dated August, 1654, *N.C.P.,* VI, 262–263.
2. *Ibid.,* 263.
3. Dated Feb. 18, 1653/54, *ibid.,* VI, 257–258.
4. *Ibid.,* 266–268.

5. Dated Aug. 27, 1654, *ibid.*, 265–266.
6. Dated Feb. 15, 1654/55, *ibid.*, VI, 283.
7. Jan. 1654/55, *ibid.*, VI, 278–279.
8. Committee appointed, "ye last of August, 1654," *Records of R.I. Col.*, I, 278.
9. Dated Sept. 12, 1657, requesting that "you remove those Quakers that have been receaved, and for the future prohibite theire cominge amongst you." *Rec. of R.I. Col.*, I, 375. Rhode Island made reply, to the Commissioners, Oct. 13, 1657, *ibid.*, pp. 377–378; to Mass. Bay Colony, Mar. 13, 1657–58, *ibid.*, 378–80.
10. It was signed by the clerk of the Assembly, met in Warwick, *Coll. Mass. Hist. Soc.*, 2nd ser., Vol. VII, 1826, pp. 85–87.
11. From a letter of Johannes Megapolensis and Samuel Drissius, ministers in New Netherland, Aug. 14, 1657. *Ecclesiastical History of the State of New York*, Albany, 1901, I, 400, 410.
12. Oct. 5, 1654, *N.C.P.*, VI, 271.
13. Mar. 11, 1656, *Rec. of R.I. Col.*, I, 327.
14. This story is a volume by itself. *The Harris Papers, Coll. R.I. Hist. Soc.*, Vol. 10, supplies one side of it. *The Early Records of R.I. Colony, Records of Providence*, Roger Williams' correspondence, *N.C.P.*, all are full of it.
15. *N.C.P.*, VI, 263.
16. July 4, 1657. *Rec. of R.I. Col.*, I, 363–365.
17. This involved drawing of a thwart line, extending from the conjunction of the Pawtuxet and Wanasquatucket Rivers instead of all the way to the head of the Pawtuxet, thus reducing the territory claimed by Harris by the greater portion of that area which Roger Williams regarded as unfairly claimed by him.
18. *Rec. of R.I. Col.*, I, 508–511.
19. The text of the charter is printed in the Appendix, No. XXI, *Coll. R.I. Hist. Soc.*, 1838, IV, 241–261.

CHAPTER XIX

1. *Rec. of R.I. Col.*, 1664–1677, II, 74–75; 76. For boundary line with Conn., *ibid.*, 454–455.
2. Jan. 1, 1665/66, *Proc. R.I. Hist. Soc.*, 1872–73, pp. 58–62. The assessment to Warwick had been £80. They had objected and sent a protest.
3. *Ibid.*, p. 62.
4. Daniel Berkeley Updike, *Richard Smith, First English Settler of the Narragansett Country*, Boston, 1937, p. 97. Dated Wickford, June 25, 1673. See also, John Callender, *Historical Discourse*, Boston, 1838, *Coll. R.I. Hist. Soc.*, 1838, IV, 111.
5. *N.C.P.*, VI, 403–406. The MS. list of subjects is owned by the Mass. Hist. Soc.

6. Letter to Anne Sadleir, c. 1652, *N.C.P.*, VI, 239.
7. Feb. 10, 1667/68, *N.C.P.*, VI, 324–325; the Town order forbidding him to keep it longer is dated Mar. 1, 1671, *Early Rec. of Prov.*, III, 219. Plans for building this bridge go back five years in the town records.
8. *George Fox Digg'd Out of His Burrowes,* Boston, 1676, *N.C.P.*, V, 2–3.
9. Listed, *ibid.*, pp. 4–5. Also, *N.C.P.*, VI, 357–360.
10. Roger Williams' letter is dated July 15th. George Fox says that he received it, July 26th.
11. Entitled "Answer to a letter sent from Mr. Coddington of Rhode Island to Governour Leverett of Boston," printed by John Foster, Boston, *Proc. R.I. Hist. Soc.*, 1875–1879, 9 pages inserted between pp. 53–55.
12. George Fox says in his *Autobiography* that he and Burnyeat went to William Penn's Worminghurst seat, and in three weeks answered "a very envious and wicked book, which Roger Williams, a priest of New England (or some colony thereabouts) had written against Truth and Friends." This answer was published 1678 and bore both the names of Fox and Burnyeat. Fox adds, "of all the Books I ever read, I never saw so much *Foul Language* and *Contradictions.*" A letter from John Stubbs, one of the disputants in Rhode Island, written at the time to Margaret Fell, calls Roger Williams "this Roger," this "Old Man Roger Williams," "This Old doting Man."
13. *N.C.P.*, V, 388.
14. *Ibid.*, V, 225.
15. *Ibid.*, V, 34.
16. The best known is that of Benjamin Church, *The History of King Philip's War,* Boston, 1716; reprinted by Henry Martyn Dexter, 2 vols., Boston, 1865. A new account is currently announced. The earliest was that of Henry Oldenburg, written nine days after the battle, and published in London, Feb. 17, 1675/76. It is entitled, *A farther Brief and True Narration of the late Wars risen in New-England,* reprinted by the Society for Colonial Wars, 1912.
17. June 25, 1675, *N.C.P.*, VI, 367.
18. *Ibid.*, VI, 377–378.
19. This is a letter from Noah Newman of Rehoboth to John Cott, Jr., at Plymouth, Apr. 19, 1676, which reports that the Indians called for Valentine Whitman. Mr. Williams called to them and had an hour's discourse with them. He assured them he would be instrumental about a treaty. They said wait a month. Nothing came of it. Providence was burning while they talked. Richard LeBaron Bowen, *Early Rehoboth,* 1948, III, from chapter I, "New Source Material for King Philip's War," pp. 1–24. The Newman letter is printed, pp. 9–10, 15–19.
20. *Massachusetts Archives*, X, 233.

21. *Providence Town Papers,* June 5, 1676, XV, 151.
22. *Ibid.,* Aug. 15, 1676, p. 152.
23. *Ibid.,* Aug. 30, 1676, p. 152.
24. Included in Knowles, *Memoir of Roger Williams,* Boston, 1834, pp. 110–111.
25. *Early Records of Providence,* VIII, p. 89. "Voted, The meetting is Disolved."
26. Jan. 27, 1682/83, Town Meeting, *Early Records of Providence,* VIII, 122, 123. Apr. 25, 1683, William Carpenter's, "I the said William Carpenter only surviveing." *Deed Book,* I, 274.
27. In the unpublished *Winthrop Papers,* Mass. Hist. Soc. Reported in *Coll. R.I. Hist. Soc.,* XX, 59.
28. *Coll. R.I. Hist. Soc.,* XXVII, 54.

BIBLIOGRAPHICAL STATEMENT

Roger Williams' own writings are the principal source of material for the story of his life. Most of these writings, including a very large number of his surviving letters, are extant in print only. The manuscripts have perished. In addition to early editions of the separate works, now excessively rare, only the six volumes of the *Narragansett Club Publications,* Providence, 1866–1874, present these materials in anything approaching completeness. Each volume of this series has an introduction. The most recent offering from his work is a volume of selections, edited by Perry Miller in the *Makers of the American Tradition* series, *Roger Williams, His Contribution to the American Tradition,* Indianapolis, 1953.

In chronological sequence, his known works include:

A Key into the Language of America, London, 1643, *N.C.P.,* Vol. I.

Mr. Cottons Letter Lately Printed, Examined and Answered, 1644, *N.C.P.,* Vol. II.

Queries of Highest Consideration, London, 1644, *N.C.P.,* Vol. II.

The Bloudy Tenent, of Persecution, for cause of Conscience, discussed, in A Conference betweene Truth and Peace, London, 1644, *N.C.P.,* Vol. III.

Christenings Make Not Christians, London, 1645. Reprinted in *Rhode Island Historical Tracts,* 1st ser., No. 14, ed. by Henry Martyn Dexter, Providence, 1881.

Experiments of Spiritual Life and Health, written c. 1650, pub. London, 1652. Reprinted, with Introduction, by Winthrop S. Hudson, Philadelphia, 1951.

The Fourth Paper Presented by Major Butler, London, 1652. Reprinted by the Club for Colonial Reprints of Providence, R.I., ed. by Clarence S. Brigham, 1903.

The Bloody Tenent Yet More Bloody, written c. 1648–1650, pub. London, 1652, *N.C.P.,* Vol. IV.

The Hireling Ministry None of Christs, London, 1652.

The Examiner Defended, London, 1652.

George Fox Digg'd Out of His Burrowes, Boston, 1676. *N.C.P.,* Vol. V.

Letters of Roger Williams, 1632–1682, N.C.P., Vol. VI.

A few original letters are in the collections of the Rhode Island Historical Society, the Massachusetts Historical Society, the American Antiquarian Society, Yale University, Trinity College Library, Cambridge, England, and in single items elsewhere, but such are pitifully scarce. Aside from the letters, and his own sworn testimonies, original records of his private life have not survived, except for his name in school and college files, in the Barrington correspondence (Egerton MSS. 2643–2645, British Museum) and occasionally elsewhere.

Not so his public life, which is written on many pages of Providence town and Rhode Island colony records, as also on those of Massachusetts Bay Colony, Plymouth and Connecticut colonies. These records not only document specific details of his story, but also supply much material indispensable to an understanding of his public and private career. Until after his death in 1683, not a volume from any of these records can be spared.

The Early Records of the Town of Providence, 21 vols., 1892–1915. Vols. XV and XVII contain *The Providence Town Papers;* Vols. XIV and XX, *The Book of Deeds.*

Records of the Colony of Rhode Island and Providence Plantations, 10 vols., Providence, 1856–1865. Vols. I and II, particularly.

For convenient reference, though in excerpts only, Howard M. Chapin, *Documentary History of Rhode Island,* 2 vols., Providence, 1916, 1919, is useful.

Among secondary sources, for Rhode Island history, one may start with Irving B. Richman, *Rhode Island, Its Making and Meaning,* 2 vols., New York, 1902, and for New England history, Charles M. Andrews, *The Colonial Period of American History,* 3 vols., New Haven, 1934–1937.

Among personal accounts of his contemporaries, John Winthrop's *History of New England* (referred to as Winthrop's *Journal*), 2 vols., Boston, 1853 ed., is fullest in detail, but Roger Williams' story is illuminated similarly by the writings of William Bradford, Edward Winslow, Thomas Shepard, Edward Johnson, John Clarke, Samuel Gorton, Samuel Sewall, John Hull, Thomas Morton; in fact, by any New Englander who set pen to paper from the day of the first settlement throughout the whole span of Roger Williams' life.

Equally important are the many scores of extant sermons enforcing over and over the tenets of faith and practice which were the *sine qua non* of the Christian life, as currently interpreted by the pulpit. For evaluation of these sermon materials and the overhanging ideas they express, the work of Perry Miller may well head the list in *The New England Mind: The Seventeenth Century,* New York, 1939; *The New England Mind: From*

Colony to Province, Cambridge, 1954; and *Orthodoxy in Massachusetts,* Cambridge, Mass., 1933.

The English background of his childhood and youth is similarly illuminated and enriched by the personal accounts of his contemporaries, in letters, journals, autobiographies: Simonds D'Ewes, Richard Baxter, John Evelyn, William Laud, Samuel Ward, Walter Yonge, John Rous, and very many others. Among secondary accounts of these men and their times, Masson's *Life of Milton* is invaluable.

For an understanding of the relevance of his thought to his own time, the richest offering, not in scores, but in hundreds of items is the pamphlet literature of the 1640's and 50's. The most nearly complete source of this body of material is the Thomason Collection in the British Museum (*Catalogue of the Pamphlets, Books, Newspapers, and Manuscripts . . . collected by George Thomason, 1640–1661,* 2 vols., London, 1908). A few of these pamphlets are available in contemporary reprints, as in William Haller's *Tracts on Liberty in the Puritan Revolution,* 3 vols., New York, 1933–1934, but there is no substitute for a generous sampling of the whole collection, particularly in the decade of the 1640's. Cromwell's *Letters and Speeches,* ed. S. C. Lomax, 3 vols., London, 1904, are also illuminating.

Among secondary treatments of the liberty of conscience subject, Wilbur Kitchener Jordan's *The Development of Religious Toleration in England,* 4 vols., Cambridge, Mass., 1932–1941, lays sound foundations. One thinks also of Francesco Ruffini, *Religious Liberty,* New York, 1912; A. S. P. Woodhouse, *Puritanism and Liberty,* London, 1950; Sebastian Castellio, *Concerning Heretics,* translated by Roland H. Bainton, New York, 1935.

The principal full-length biographies of Roger Williams to date are:

James D. Knowles, *Memoir of Roger Williams,* Boston, 1834.

Romeo Elton, *Life of Roger Williams,* Providence, 1853.

Isaac Backus, *A History of New England, with Particular Reference to the Denomination of Christians called Baptists,* 2 vols., Newton, Mass., 1871. Not full length, but contains some letters no longer available elsewhere.

Oscar S. Straus, *Roger Williams: The Pioneer of Religious Liberty,* New York, 1894.

Edmund J. Carpenter, *Roger Williams: A Study of the Life, Times and Character of a Political Pioneer,* New York, 1909.

Emily Easton, *Roger Williams: Prophet and Pioneer,* Boston, 1930.

James E. Ernst, *Roger Williams: New England Firebrand,* New York, 1932.

Samuel Hugh Brockunier, *The Irrepressible Democrat: Roger Williams,* New York, 1940.

John R. Dos Passos, "Roger Williams and the Planting of the Commonwealth in America," in *The Ground We Stand On,* New York, 1941.

Limitations of space forbid even a selection of critical comment as to Roger Williams and his significance, as it has been evaluated over the years. The list is long, too long for justice to be possible in a brief selection of titles. One hopeful new direction is marked out by the researches of Mauro Calamandrei, in his "Neglected Aspects of Roger Williams' Thought," *Church History,* XXI (1952), 239–258. One hopes for more from this source.

INDEX

Act and Deed of voluntary submission to King Charles (Pessicus), 214
Adams, William, 288
Advertisements for the Unexperienced Planters of New-England (Captain John Smith), 111
Altham, Joanna (Jug), daughter of Lady Masham, 86-87, 88, 91
Anabaptist, 98
Andrewes, Lancelot, Master of Pembroke Hall, 56-57; fame as linguist, 62
Angell, Thomas, Roger Williams' companion in exile, 126, 127
Apologeticall Narration, The, 193, 200
Aquidneck Island, purchase of, 133; settlement of by Hutchinson party, 140-141; Coddington's ambition to govern, 229-230; life commission granted, 230; commission revoked, 244
Areopagitica, 200
Arnold, Benedict, records arrival at Providence, 129-130; fails as interpreter, 214; death, 287
Arnold, William, 228; defends Verin, 140; secures confirmatory deed and submits to Massachusetts, 159; tries to prevent Roger Williams' mission to England, 231; returns to Rhode Island jurisdiction, 261
Arnolds on Pawtucket, 183
Articles of Religion, 66
Artificial Fire (broadside), 185-186
Ascham, Roger, 39
Ashton, Patience, 288
Askew, Anne, 30
Assembly of Divines (Westminster Assembly), 185, 238; called, 178; sessions of, 178-179; swears to Solemn League and Covenant, 182
Atherton, Captain, 214
Aubrey, John, 36
Austin Friars (Reformed Dutch Church, London), 30-31, 32

Bacon, Sir Francis, praises Coke, 45; Peacham case, 48; his fall mentioned, 51; Charterhouse case, 52-53
Badby, John, Smithfield martyr, 29-30
Baillie, Robert, minister of Glasgow, quoted on Assembly sessions, 179; on Roger Williams, 186-187, 206
Banishment edict of Roger Williams, quoted, 119-120
Barnard, Mary (or Bernard), wife of Roger Williams, married to him, 87; position in Barrington household, 88-89; sails, 94; arrives in Boston, 95; signs Initial Deed, 136; *Experiments of Spiritual Life and Health* written for her, 224, 225; her joining Williams in London proposed, 245-246; brought back to Providence by her son after King Philip's war, 285
Barnard, "Mr. Barnard," of New England, 89
Barnard, William, of Margaretting, cousin to Roger Williams, 89
Barnes, John, non-conformist, 32
Barrington, Sir Francis, M.P., Puritan leader, 75; imprisonment and death, 75-76; inventory of his country seat, Hatfield Broad Oak, 77
Barrington, Lady Joan, widow of Sir Francis, aunt of Oliver Cromwell, 74, 77; mistress of Hatfield Broad Oak, 76; her sons' letters to her quoted, 79; Roger Williams' letters to her, 82, 83, 85; her favors to William Hooke, 83-84; criticized by her former chaplain, Ezekiel Rogers, 85-86; shows disfavor to Williams, 86; reconciled with him, 86

Barrington, Mary, daughter of Lady Joan, 91
Barrington, Sir Robert, son to Sir Francis, letter to his mother, quoted, 79
Barrington, Sir Thomas, son to Sir Francis, letter to his mother, quoted, 79; mentioned, 179, 208
Bartholomew Fair (in Smithfield), 23-24
Baxter, heir of Thomas Sutton, 52
Baxter, Captain George, brings Rhode Island charter, 265
Baxter, Richard, boyhood reminiscence, 33; on toleration, 206
Beale, Jerome, master of Pembroke Hall, 61; learning of, 62, on Buckingham election, 69
Beard, Dr., schoolmaster, accused by Cromwell of "flat Popery," 80
Beaumont, Francis, master of Charterhouse, 54
Bernard, Massachiel, Weymouth, England, to Weymouth, New England, 89
Bernard, Richard (or Barnard), father of Mary Barnard, minister of Worksop and Batcombe, 88; father of Beniamine, Besekiel, Cannanuel, Hoseel, Masakiell, 88; Roger Williams' opinion of him, 89; writes *The Isle of Man,* 89
Bill of Liberties, 71
Bilson, "Mr. Bilson's house" (in Smithfield), 32
Blakston, William, at Study Hill retreat, 143
Bloody Tenent Yet More Bloody, The, written at trading post, 237; published, 239; changed climate of toleration battle, 240-241
Bloudy Tenent of Persecution, The, 9, 197, 279; stated purposes of, 197-198; ordered burned by Commons, 198; labeled "dangerous" by Parliament preacher Lazarus Seaman, 199; plan and leading ideas of, 201-202; distinction of, 203-204
Book of Martyrs, 30, 78, 232
Boteler, Harrington, 69
Boyse, "Mr. Boyse's house" (in Smithfield), 32
Bradford, William, meets Boston delegation to Plymouth, 101; verdict on Roger Williams, quoted, 104, 105, 153; mentioned, 113, 125
Brattle, Captain, 286
Brewster, Elder, 101
Bridge, William, leading Independent, 187, 193
Bright, Francis, 93
Brinsley, Schoolmaster, 40, 168
Brooke, Lord (Fulke Greville), 67
Brown, Richard, 99
Brown brothers (Salem), deported, 107
Bucke, Daniel, 32
Buckingham, Duke of, 68; in Prince-Infanta affair, 65; elected to Cambridge Chancellorship, 69; assassinated, 71
Bunyan, John, 226, 274
Burnyeat, John, Quaker, meets Roger Williams' challenge to debate, 273
Burroughs, Edward, Quaker pamphleteer, 274
Burroughs, Jeremiah, leading Independent, 187, 193
Busher, Leonard, author of *Religion's Peace,* 204
Butler, Major, 238; writes *The Fourth Paper,* 241-242

Cabot, John, 109
Cachonet, son of Miantunomi, 282; capture and death, 284; his dying words, 284
Calvin, John, 61, 66
Cambridge, University of, population, 57; increase of middle-class student, 59; regimen of life, 60-61; alleged lawlessness and attempted reform, 62-63
Canonicus, chieftain of the Narragansetts, calls Roger Williams "son," 49; Williams fulfills his dying wish, 49; sale of lands to Williams, 128, 131-132, 133, 141; treaties with, 132; in council with Williams, 144; Williams calls him "that old prince Canonicus," 144; breaks a stick to indicate English broken promises, 171-172; lays out trading post, 221; speech of

loyalty to English, 215-216; death, 216
Carpenter, William, 288
Carpenter's *Geography,* Roger Williams wishes to borrow it, 227
Chapman, George, *Eastward Hoe* (with Marston and Jonson), 26
Charles I, King, 79-80, 236, 248, 277; and the *Revelation* passages, 108, 112-113; Roger Williams' alleged letter to, 113; his death reported, 229
Charterhouse (Sutton's Hospital), 51; Roger Williams admitted, 51; legal battle to maintain founder's intent, 52-53; Gownboy's life, 53-54; prayer for a young scholar, 54; Exhibition to him, 54-55, 58
Cholmley, Lady, 88
Cholmley, Sir Hugh, 88
Christenings Make not Christians, 220
Chruso-thriambos: The Triumphes of Golde, London pageant, 13
Chuff (Indian), ordered executed in Providence, 285
Clarke, John, physician and minister on Aquidneck, present at confirmatory deed ceremony, 132; quoted, 140, 141; appointed agent for Aquidneck, 230; in Lynn affair, 231-232; writes account of this incident as *Ill Newes from New England,* 232-233; left in England to complete securing of charter, 248; appealed to in Harris affair, 264; honored on his return to Newport, 265; secures charter, 265; Roger Williams attempts to collect money in payment to him, 268-269; death, 287
Clarke, Schoolmaster, 164
Cloth Fair, 23-24
Coal shortage in London, 184-186
Cocumscussoc, trading-post site, 221
Coddington, William, 132, 139, 141, 253, 274; ambition to rule Aquidneck, 227-228; applies for life tenure as Governor, 229-230; petition granted, 230; claims challenged by Roger Williams and John Clarke, authorized agents, 236; Coddington's commission revoked, 244-245; his motivation, 244-245; his submission to Rhode Island, 261; at Newport debate, 276; death, 287
Coke, Sir Edward, 57, 81; meeting with Roger Williams, 43; Coke's achievements, *Reports,* 44; employment of Williams as shorthand writer, 44; Commendams case, 45; imprisonments, 45-46, 48, 51; Williams' employment attested by Anne Sadleir, daughter of Sir Edward, 46, 47; significance to Williams, 48-49; rift between Williams and, 49-50, 90-91; in private life, 50; Williams' tribute to, 50-51; Charterhouse case, 52-53; great speeches, 71; Petition of Right, 75
Cole, Robert, submits to Massachusetts, 159
Comenius, 35
Compassionate Samaritan, The, 200, 205
Coote, Schoolmaster, 37-38
Cope, Thomas, 152
Corbet, Miles, 208
Cotton, John, 74, 90, 104, 166, 189, 196; sermon of, 109; tries to convince Roger Williams of his errors, 118; in banishment affair, 125; prestige in England, 189-190; charges against Williams, 191-192; death, 233; Williams' answer to Cotton's *The Bloody Tenent Washed,* 240-241
Cotton, John, Jr., Roger Williams' letter to, 190-191
Cow Lane, 11, 19-23
Cowesett (Indian tribe), 145
Craddock, Matthew, 121
Crandall, John, Lynn affair, 231-232
Cranston, Captain, 273
Cromwell, Catherine, 12
Cromwell, Sir Henry, 12, 76
Cromwell, Oliver, 12, 74, 177, 181; his maiden speech in Commons, 80; in Parliament crisis, 247-248
Cromwell, Robert, 12
Cromwell, Thomas, 12
Cromwell, Walter, 12

Danvers, Colonel, 238
Dekker, Thomas, quoted, on Queen Elizabeth's death, 3; on merchant

Dekker, Thomas (*continued*)
taylors, 10; on plague, 17; on London streets, 22
Description of New England, A (Captain John Smith), 26
Devonshire, Earl of, 75
D'Ewes, Simonds, quoted, on shorthand, 44; on Coke, 51; on university life, 59-60, 62-63
Dexter, Goodman (of Salem), 115
Dexter, Gregory, printer of London, prints Roger Williams' *Key into the Language of America,* 162; may have printed his *Bloudy Tenent,* 198; as Town Clerk in Providence, 233, 245, 251, 253
Dialectia, of Ramus, 61
Dike, John, 91
Directions of King James, as to preaching, 66-67
Divorce treatise (Milton), *Doctrine and Discipline of Divorce,* 238
Dorislaus, Isaac, 67-68
Drury, Father, 66
Dudley, Thomas, 133
Dunster, President Henry, 163
Dutch refugees in Smithfield, persecution of, 30-31
Dyer, William, accompanies Roger Williams to England, 235, 253

Eastward Hoe (Chapman-Marston-Jonson), 26
Edmondson, William, Quaker disputant, 273
Edward III, 20
Edwards, Thomas, quoted, 206-207
Elementarie, The (education), 35-38
Eliot, "Mr. Eliot," 286
Eliot, John, 74, 162, 173; his Indian questions quoted, 172
Eliot, Sir John, framer of the *Remonstrance,* 80
Elizabeth, Queen, 5, 6, 17, 53, 64; death of, 3; funeral, 4
Emmanuel College, stronghold of Dissent, mentioned, 57
Endecott, Governor John, in first case of charges against Roger Williams, 100, 108; Red Cross incident, 114-116; at Block Island, 146
Essex, Earl of, 44
Evelyn, John, 35, 36
Examiner Defended, The, 243
Examiner Examined, The, 243
Experiments of Spiritual Life and Health, 230, 237, 270, 277; occasion and plan of, 224; quoted, 224-226

"Fatal vespers," 66
Fenwick, George, agent of Connecticut, 245
Finch, Speaker, in Parliament crisis, 80
First Church, Boston, Covenant of, 98
Fox, George, 242; challenged to debate with Roger Williams, 273; his answer in print, 274
Foxe, John, *Book of Martyrs,* 30
Frederick, Duke, report of London, 7
Fuller, Samuel, his legacy to Roger Williams, 105-106
Fuller, Thomas, 40, 59, 60; quoted, on Queen Elizabeth, 4; on "moderate men," 5; on Legate, 29; on Lancelot Andrewes, 62; on the times, 177; on worthy men at odds, 264

Gandhi, Mohandas, 174
Gardener, Leift, 151
Gates, Sir Henry, 88
Generall Historie of Virginia, The (Captain John Smith), 25
George Fox Digg'd out of His Burrowes, 274; quoted, 277-278; differs from *Bloudy Tenent,* 279
Gilbert, Sir Gerard, 91
Golden Knight, The (Sir Henry Cromwell), 76
Goodwin, Thomas, leading Independent, 187, 193
Gookins, Captain, 287
Gorton, Samuel, a troubler, 139, 141, 158, 159, 228, 261; gives armor to Miantunomi, 212; brings *Act and Deed* of Pessicus, 214; death, 287
Grammar school education, 38-41
Gray, Nicholas, 54
Gray, Robert, 110-111
Great Plague Year, The (1625), 68-69

Great Swamp Fight (King Philip's War), 282-283
Greene, John, of Providence, 246
Greville, Fulke (Lord Brooke), 67
Griffin, ship constructed to bring royal governor, 118
Gunpowder Plot, Coke's prosecution of plotters, 44

Hacket, John, 71
Hamlet, 17
Hariot, Thomas, 103, 165
Harris, William, 89; one of Roger Williams' four companions in exile journey, 127; his theory of land tenure, 134-135; his ambition, 228; interpretation of liberty, 254-255; in contention with Williams, 261-265; at Newport debate, 276; death, 287
Harrison, Major General, 238, 248
Harsnett, Samuel, 62
Hartford Council, leading to Narragansett treaty, 152, 153
Haslerig, Sir Arthur, 183; quoted, 199, 236
Hatfield Broad Oak, country seat of the Barringtons, 77
Hayes, Governor, presides at court sentencing Roger Williams, 118
Henrietta Maria, Queen, 80
Herbert, George, Preface, vii
Higginson, John, minister of Salem, 99-100
High Hall, 19
Hireling Ministry None of Christs, The, 220; quoted, 242-243
History, in current meaning, 67
Hobbes, Thomas, 36
Hobson, Thomas, "Hobson's choice," 57, 64
Hoby, Lady (of Hackness), 81, 88; *Diary* of, 77-78
Hoby, Thomas, 77
Holden, Randall, 132
Holland, Cornelius, friend to Rhode Island, 183, 236, 237, 248
Holland, John, 119
Holles, Denzil, 80
Holmes, Obadiah, Lynn affair, 231, 232, 233
Holmes, Justice Oliver Wendell, 124, 201
Hooke, William, marries Jane Whalley, 83-84
Hooker, Thomas, dissenting minister, 74; meets Roger Williams at Sempringham, 90; cited and flees to Holland, 93; debates with Williams on "dangerous opinions," 119; migrates to Hartford, 127
Hoole, Schoolmaster, 36
Hopkins, Edward, agent of Connecticut in England, 245
Howe, Samuel, cobbler, 243
Hull, Joseph, 89
Hutchinson, Anne, 119, 139, 160
Hutchinson party, comes to Aquidneck, 140-141

Ignatius Loyola, play in honor of King James at Cambridge, 64-65
Ill Newes from New England (John Clarke), account of Lynn affair, quoted, 140
Independent leaders, 187, 193
Indian questions on religion, supplied by John Eliot, 172
Initial Deed of Providence Plantations, 135-136
Isle of Man, The (Richard Bernard), 89

Jacob, Henry, 33
Jacula Prudentum, Preface, vii
James I, 204; proclaimed king, 3; triumphal progress, 4; coronation, 17; entertainment by Merchant Taylors, 27; treatment of Legate, 28; at Charterhouse, 53; reign of, mentioned, 64; at Cambridge, 64-65; issues *Directions* concerning preaching, 66; death, 68; his "three darling Articles," 70-71; Roger Williams' "revilings," 107-108
James, William, 291
Janemo, sachem of Niantics, 153
John the Baptist, 200
Johnson, George, 32
Jonson, Ben, writes verses, 11; share in *Eastward Hoe,* 26

Key into the Language of America, A, 189, 198, 220; has inception in Plymouth experience, 103-104, 106; Roger Williams' qualifications for, 145; stated purpose in, 161-162; issued, 162; well received, 163; plan, and models for, 164; quoted, 166, 170, 175; Williams helped by, in charter plea, 183-184; panorama of wilderness life revealed, 279-280
Kieft, Governor William (New Netherlands), 160, 165
King Charles. *See* Charles I
King James. *See* James I
King Street, once Cow Lane, 19
King's Patent, Roger Williams' attack, 104-105
Knight, William, imprisoned for quoting Pareus, 67
Knightley, Richard, 91
Knoller, "Mr. Knoller," a culprit, 199

Lambert, John, martyr, 30
Langley, John, censor, passes *Key,* 162
Laud, William, 59, 89, 122, 154, 180, 205; on Oxford discipline, 62; on ending of Prince-Infanta affair, 65; case of William Knight, 67; order as to chaplains, 75; transferred to see of London, 92; Roger Williams "pursued . . . out of the land," 93; headed commission on royal governor of New England, 113
Lawrence, Sir Henry, 238, 248
Lechford, Thomas, quoted, 137; reported, 163
Legate, Bartholomew, Smithfield martyr, 28-29
Leighton, Alexander, case of, 93
Leverett, Governor, 283, 286
Liberty of Conscience, labeled "dangerous," 205
Lincoln, Earl of, 90
Locke, John, at Otes, 87-88; on "natural right," 111-112
London, merchant activity of, 7; street sights and sounds, 19-23
Long, Mary, 88
Long Lane, 19-23
Ludus Literarius, Brinsley's, 168
Lupton, Donald, quoted, 81
Luther, Martin, 66
Lynn episode, 231-232
Lyon, "the good ship," 27, 96

Machiavelli, 156
"Mad Fashions, Od Fashions, All out of Fashions" (broadside), 177-178
Marblehead Neck affair, 114, 118
Marshall, Stephen, 181
Marston, John (Chapman-Marston-Jonson play), 26
Martin, Sir William, 93; quoted, 122
Mary, Queen, 64, 196
Masham, Lady Elizabeth, daughter of Lady Joan Barrington, mistress of Otes, 77, 78
Masham, Sir William, Puritan leader, imprisoned, 75-76; on Roger Williams' side in rift with Lady Joan, 86; friend of Roger Williams in charter plea, 179; signs letter to Boston Commissioners, 208; on Council of State, 236; headed Committee for Propagation of the Gospel, 241; off Council of State, 248
Mason, Captain John, in war with Pequots, 148-149; account of Mystic River battle, 151
Massachusetts Bay Company, 90, 92
Massachusetts colony, claims to Rhode Island territory, 216; offers shelter to Roger Williams after burning of Providence, 284
Massasoit, chieftain of Plymouth Indians, 128, 145
Mather, Cotton, 289
Mather, Increase, 84
May, John, 46
Mede, Joseph, tutor of Christ's College, 61, 93; correspondence with Sir Martin Stuteville, 64; letters quoted, 65, 68, 69
Merchant Taylors' Company, 10; benefactions during plague, 17; their prayer quoted, 18; colonization projects, 25-26; dinner to King James, 27
Miantunomi, nephew of Canonicus and co-ruler of Narragansetts, 131, 132, 141, 144-145, 284; at Roger Williams'

home, 149-150; suspected by Massachusetts Commissioners, 212; captured and killed, 213
Milton, John, 19-20, 39, 54, 59, 60, 271-272; divorce treatise, 198, 200; associations with Roger Williams, 238; Latin Secretary, 238; idea of government, 239
Model of Church and Civil Power, 201-202
Mohawk (Indian tribe), 145
Mohegans, geographical position of, 147
Morse, Thomas, 11
Morton, Thomas, 113
Mulcaster, 40
Munday, Anthony, 13
Murton, John, 201
Mystic River battle, 150-151

Narragansett Patent, secured by agents of Massachusetts, 187-188; Patent invoked against Rhode Island, 216-217
Narragansetts, treaty with English, 146-148; geographical position, 147; treaty with Connecticut, 152-153; suspicions of Massachusetts, 212, 260, 282; tribal unity broken, 215
New England Company charter granted, 92
New England Firebrand Quenched, A (George Fox), 274
"New England Way, The," 190
New Netherlands, war with Indians, 160; Quaker incident, 259-260
New Providence, name first used, 130
Newgate sessions, 23
Nicholas, John, 32
Ninigret, a rebel Narragansett, 260
Ninnicraft, Ye Old Queen (Narragansett), consulted, 282
Nipmuc (Indian tribe), 145
Non-conforming groups in Smithfield, 32-33; in Essex, 75
Nowell, Elder, 99
Nyantic (Indian tribe), 145
Nye, Philip, Independent leader, 181, 187, 193

Oath, Resident's, 116-117
Oath of Allegiance (of Rhode Island), 233
Oath as an act of worship, one of Roger Williams' "dangerous opinions," 116-117
Oath of Supremacy (Vane refuses to take), 120
Oldham, Captain John, murder of, 146
Olney, Thomas, abuse of liberty, 254-255
Otes, Masham country seat in Essex, 72, 77, 88
Othello, 17
Ousamakin (Massasoit), 128
Owen, John, 238; proposals for limiting freedom of worship, 241
Oxford, William Laud on student excesses, 62

Pardon Churchyard, 53
Pareus, 67
Parliamentary crisis (1628–29), 79-81; (1653), 247-248
Pawtuxet, trouble zone of Rhode Island, 141
Peacham, Edmond, case of, 48
Pemberton, Alice, mother of Roger Williams, 12-13, 14
Pemberton, Sir Francis, cousin, 14
Pemberton, Geoffrey, first of the line in St. Albans, 13
Pemberton, Sir James, uncle, 13-14
Pemberton, Roger, uncle of Roger Williams, and his godfather, 13; legacy of, 72
Pembertons of Pemberton, 13
Pembroke Hall, great names, 56; size, 57; Roger Williams enrolled, 58; studies in, 61
Penrose, "Mr. Penrose," culprit, 199
Pequots, character, 145; geographical position, 147; enmity with Narragansetts, 147-148; war against, declared by Hartford, 148; Mystic River battle, 150-151
Perrers, Dame Alice, 20
Perry, Seth, 286
Persecution in Smithfield, 28-30
Pessicus, submission to King Charles, 214

Peter, Hugh, agent for Massachusetts, 183; with Thomas Welde, secures Narragansett Patent, 187-188
Petition of Right, 71, 75, 79
Petty School, 35-36
Philip, King, 267, 284
Phillips, George, of Watertown, 99
Phraseologia Puerilis, 164
Pierce, Captain, 93, 94, 95
Plague, 15-17, 68-69
Plymouth claims to Rhode Island lands, 216; boundary line, 268
Pocahontas, 26
Pomham and Saconomoco, surrender to Massachusetts, 159
Popery, fear of, 64; proclamation against, 69
Preston, John, 59, 68
Prince-Infanta affair, 64-65; celebration at Cambridge at end of, 65
Providence, original purchase of land, 131; name, 131; purchase confirmed, 132; government, 136-137; incorporation of as town, 137; covenant, 137-138; liberty of conscience in, 139-140; hospitality to undesirables elsewhere, 139; lack of unity, 158; dissension, 210-211, 228-229, 249; Vane's letter of criticism, 252; the town's reply, 253; town records preserved, 281; town burned, 283-284
Providence Company, 91-92
Providence Plantations, charter secured, 187; nature of charter, 188; charter accepted by all four towns, 218-219; charter confirmed, 244; need for new charter, 229-231. *See also* Rhode Island
Prudence Island, purchased, 133
Pym, John, 91, 182-183

Quakers, attitude of Massachusetts to, 257-258; coming of, 257-258; of Rhode Island, 257-259; of New Netherlands, 259
Queen Elizabeth. *See* Elizabeth, Queen
Queen Mary. *See* Mary, Queen
Queries of Highest Consideration, 193, 238; arguments listed, 196

Raleigh, Sir Walter, 44, 45
Ramus, logic of, 61
Randall, "Mr. Randall," culprit, 199
Religion's Peace (Leonard Busher), quoted, 204
Remonstrance (Sir John Eliot), 80
Resident's Oath, 116-117
Rhode Island, name adopted, 188; Roger Williams as Chiefe Officer, 210; dissension, 210-211, 228-229, 249; Williams' achievements in office, 211, 214, 217-218; Portsmouth meeting to accept charter, 218-219; code of laws and Bill of Rights accepted, 219; occasion for Williams' parable of the ship, 254-256; governmental machinery strengthened, 256-257; fundamental basis for unity recognized in hospitality to Quakers, 257-258; chartered as Rhode Island, 265. *See also* Providence Plantations
Rhodes, Mr., 77, 78, 81
Rich, Nathaniel, 91
Rich, Sir Robert, 179
Richard II, 20
Richards, J., 288
Robinson, Henry, 205
Rogers, Ezekiel, chaplain of Lady Barrington, his criticism of her, 85-86
Rogers, John, Smithfield martyr, 30, 56
Royal Exchange, 7
Rudyard, Sir Benjamin, quoted, 178
Ryece, Robert, attempts to dissuade John Winthrop from coming to New England, 93

Sachem's Plain, battle of Mohegans and Narragansetts, 212-213
Saconomoco, Narragansett in rebellion against Canonicus, 159; surrender to Massachusetts, 159
Sadleir, Anne, daughter of Sir Edward Coke, 44, 51; quoted, 46, 47; her accusation of Roger Williams, 91
St. Anthony's School, 38
St. John, Oliver, 91, 208; marries Joanna Altham, 87
St. John of the Cross, 226
St. Paul's School, 38
St. Sepulchre's Church, 19, 20; prison-

ers' hand-bell, 23; Captain John Smith a parishioner, 24-25, 26-27
Saltonstall, Sir Richard, quoted, 233
Saye and Sele, Lord, 182
Scott, Richard, companion of Roger Williams on trek to Hartford Council, 152
Seagull, Captain (in *Eastward Hoe*), 26
Seaman, Lazarus, labels *Bloudy Tenent* as "dangerous" in sermon before Parliament, 199-200
Seeker, 194-195
Selden, John, 187
Separatism, in England, 33; back of Roger Williams' refusal of Boston post, 96, 97; in New England, 98; in Watertown, 99; in Plymouth, 101; John Cotton's arguments against, 191
Sewall, Samuel, 125
Shakespeare, William, 17
Sharpe, Samuel, Salem elder, 114
Shawomet (Indian tribe), 145
Shorthand, 43-44
Simpson, "Mr. Simpson," culprit, 199
Skelton, John, Salem minister, 14
Slate Rock, 266; traditional landing spot, 129
Smith, "Mr. Smith's house," wilderness place for meeting of Indian council, 282
Smith, Captain John, 109; *Generall Historie of Virginia,* 25; in St. Sepulchre's parish, 25-27; *A Description of New England,* 26
Smith, John, deported from Massachusetts, 119
Smith, John, miller of Providence, 127; saves town records, 281
Smith, Ralph, pastor at Plymouth, 101
Smith, Richard, trader, 221
Smith, Richard, son of trader, 269
Smithfield, historical associations, 20; burnings, 28-30; as place to grow up in, 33-34
Smythe, John, 204
Solemn League and Covenant, 181; sworn to by Parliament and Assembly of Divines, 182
Southampton, Earl of, 44
"Spanish match," 64-66
Spendall, character in *Eastward Hoe,* 26
Spenser, Edmund, 56
Spilsbury, John, 33
de Staël, Madame, 226
Stamford Hill, 4
Star Chamber cases, 48
Stokes, Catherine, 13
Stoughton, Israel, quoted on Red Cross affair, 115; in Roger Williams' list of friends, 286-287
Stow, John, his *Survey of London* mentioned, 20, 44
Stubbs, John, Quaker disputant of Roger Williams, 273
Study Hill, wilderness retreat of William Blakston, 143
Stuteville, Sir Martin, correspondent of Joseph Mede, 64
Subscription Book (King James' three "darling Articles"), 70-71; Roger Williams signs, 69-70
Sussex, Lady, quoted, 177
Sutton, Jane, 88
Sutton, Thomas, founder of Charterhouse School, 51, 52-53
Sutton's Hospital (Charterhouse School), 51

Tacitus, Dorislaus on, 67
Tailor trade, 10
Taylor, Jeremy, 59, 60
Taylor, John, the Water Poet (broadside), 177-178; quoted, 205
Thraske, John, Star Chamber case, 48
Toleration, word becomes current, 65-66; new meanings, 200-201; official, 239-240
Tonnage and Poundage, Coke's speech on, 75, 78-79
Towne Evidence, document confirming original purchase, 132; mutilation of, 132; William Arnold takes advantage of, 159
Trading post, 9, 123; site of, 221; commodities, 221-222
Treatise (Roger Williams'), concerning King's Patent, 104-105; Council action on, 107-108; reveals characteristic

Treatise (continued)
ways of thought, 112-113; foreshadows coming banishment, 114
Tresswell, Nicholas, 9
Triumphes of Golde, Chruso-thriambos: The (pageant of Goldsmiths' Company), 13
"25 acre men," 217-218

Uncas, sachem of Mohegans, Narragansett distrust of, 145; his man mentioned, 155; relation with Massachusetts, 212, 260; perfidy of, 212-213, 229; forces of, 283; his son kills Cachonet, 284
Underhill, Captain John, dispatched to bring Roger Williams from Salem, 124; quoted on Mystic River battle, 151
"Upstreams without limits," key phrase in Harris land aggression, 263

Valentine, Benjamin, 80
Vane, Charles, 238
Vane, Sir Harry, 120, 124, 159; arrives in New England and meets Roger Williams, 120; Governor, 149; speech of, 180; his growth, 181; correspondent of Williams, 194; services to Parliament, 236, 237; President of Council of State, 244; in Parliament crisis, 247-248; his letter of criticism to Providence, 251-252; death, 284
Verin, Jacob, 140

Wampanoag (Indian tribe), 145
Ward, Nathaniel, quoted, 207
Ward, Samuel, of Sidney Sussex College, 63
Warwick, burned, 283
Warwick, Robert, Earl of, 91, 92, 179-180, 182
Waterman, Richard, "a lad of," joins Roger Williams in exile, 127
Weaver, Clement, 89
Welde, Thomas, agent for Massachusetts, 183; with Hugh Peter secures Narragansett Patent, 187-188
Wentworth, Sir Peter, in Parliament crisis, 247
Wentworth, Thomas, quoted on Harry Vane, 120
Wequash (Pequot guide), in parley at Roger Williams' house, 156; his alleged conversion, 172-173
Westminster Assembly, called, 178
Westwood, William, 119
Whalley family, 12
Whalley, Jane, niece of Lady Barrington, 85; and Roger Williams, 81-83, 84; marries William Hooke, 83-84
Whalley, Richard, 81, 89
Wharton, Philip, 208
Wheelwright, John, 119
Whitaker, Valentine, interpreter, at burning of Providence, 283
White, "Mr. White," ordered to burn Roger Williams' book, 198
Wickford Point, trading-house site, 221
Wicks, Francis, joins Roger Williams in exile, 127
Wightman, Edward, martyr, 29
Wilcox, Richard, partner of Roger Williams at trading post, 223
Williams, Catherine, sister of Roger Williams, 9, 11
Williams, Elizabeth, wife of Robert, brother of Roger Williams, at Newport debate, 275
Williams, Freeborn, second daughter of Roger and Mary Williams, 121, 219
Williams, James, father of Roger Williams, 54, 55, 72; admitted to Merchant Taylors' Company, 9; prosperity of, 10; death, will of, 10-11; conjectures as to possible antecedents, 12-13; marriage, 12, 14; land transactions, 13
Williams, Joseph, son of Roger Williams, born during his first visit to England, 209; quoted, on care of aged parents, 285-286
Williams, Mary, wife to Roger, marriage, 87; arrives in New England, 95; signs *Initial Deed,* 136; Roger Williams writes *Experiments of Spiritual Life and Health* for her, 237; wishes her to join him in London, 245-246; son, Providence, brings her

back to Providence after King Philip's war, 285
Williams, Mary, daughter of Roger Williams, 219
Williams, Morgan, of Glamorganshire, 12
Williams, Providence, son of Roger Williams, brings mother home, clears Providence of Indians, 285
Williams, Richard, father of the Golden Knight, 12
Williams, Robert, brother of Roger Williams, 9; suit against him, 184
Williams, Roger, known antecedents: father, James Williams, merchant taylor of London, 9-11; mother, Alice Pemberton of St. Albans, 12-13; conjectural earlier heritage, entirely unproved and probably entirely unlikely, even false, Morgan Williams of Glamorganshire, married to Catherine Cromwell, daughter of Walter Cromwell, a paternal ancestor of Oliver Cromwell, thus uniting the Williams and Cromwell lines, 12

Immediate family circle: brother Sydrach, merchant taylor and later Turkey merchant, 9; Robert, apprentice to Sydrach and later resident of Rhode Island, 9; sister Catherine married to a merchant taylor, 9

Birth, date uncertain, but probably 1603, 14-15; according to Charterhouse admission, 51-52; good fortune in the time of his birth, 5-6, 7-8

Childhood associations: in the Smithfield neighborhood (external), 19-24; Merchant Taylors' colonization projects, 25-26; voyages of Captain John Smith, 25, 26-27; his own boyhood reminiscences, 27-28; the Legate burning and the previous martyrdoms it recalled, 28-30; persecution of Dutch refugees, 30-32; other non-conforming groups, 32-33

Early education: petty school, 35-38; Grammar School, 38-40; employment by Sir Edward Coke, 43-44, 46-47; significance of this association, 48, 50-51; education at Charterhouse, 51-52, 53-54; Exhibition to the University, 54-55

Pensioner at Pembroke Hall, Cambridge, 58; University life, 60, 62-63; his studies, 61-62; repressive measures: political and religious tension throughout England, 64-66; King James' *Directions,* 67; silencing of Dorislaus, 67-68; signs Subscription Book and takes degree, 69-71; remains at University year and a half, 71-72

Chaplain at Otes, meets Puritan leaders, 74-76; duties as chaplain, 76-77, 78; present in London during Parliamentary crisis, 78-81; love affair with Jane Whalley, 81-82; ensuing rift with Lady Barrington, 82-86; marriage to Mary Barnard, 87; hears much of colonization ventures, 91-93; longs after "natives' soules," 92; sails, 94

Arrives in Boston, 95; refuses offer in Boston church, 96; criticizes magistrates, 97; under suspicion as Separatist, 99; made teacher at Salem, 99-100; moves to Plymouth, 100-101; trades with Indians and makes notes on their language, 103-104; leaves Plymouth and returns to Salem, 104-105

Treatise against King's Patent brings summons before magistrates, 107-108; again criticizes magistrates, 116-117; warned because of "dangerous opinions," 117; remains obdurate and is sentenced to exile, 118-120; Captain Underhill, sent to Salem to fetch him back to Boston, finds him "gone three days," 122

Leaves Salem on foot with Thomas Angell, 126; joined by four companions at Seekonk, 126-127; on advice of Governor Winslow, moves across river and lands at Slate Rock, 129-130; purchases land of Indians, founds Providence, 131-132

Negotiates treaty with Narragansetts, 146-147; strategy in Pequot war, 149-150; has share in Hartford

Williams, Roger (*continued*)
negotiations, 152-153; success as peacemaker, 154-155; understanding of Indian character, 154-157; made agent to secure charter, 159-160; goes to London, 160; publishes *A Key into the Language of America,* 161-162

Arrives in crisis, 176-179; helps sufferers in London coal shortage, 184-186; attends sessions of Westminster Assembly, 186-187; secures charter for Providence Plantations, 187-188; enters controversial battle, 189-190; published *Mr. Cotton's Letter Answered,* 189, 193; *Queries of Highest Consideration,* 193-196; *The Bloudy Tenent of Persecution,* 197; book ordered burned, 198-199; significance of his plea for "soul liberty," 203-204

Returns to Providence and is made "Chiefe officer," 209-210; achievements in office, 211, 214, 217-218; succeeds in getting charter accepted by all four towns, 218-219

Freed from office, goes to trading post and trades with Indians, 219-220; writes *Christenings Make not Christians,* 220; preaches to Indians, 221-224; writes *Experiments of Spiritual Life and Health,* 224-227; solicited by Providence in both town and Indian troubles, 227-229; made deputy president, 230; appointed agent with John Clarke to obtain new charter, 230-231; sells trading post and sails for England, 230-231, 233

Meets Puritan leaders, lays foundations for successful plea, faces long delay, 236-238; publishes *Experiments for Spiritual Life and Health, The Bloody Tenent Yet More Bloody, Major Butler's Fourth Paper, The Hireling Ministry None of Christs, The Examiner Defended,* 237, 239, 241, 243; acquaintance with Milton, 238-239; succeeds in getting original character confirmed and Coddington's commission canceled, 244-245

Leaves Clarke to continue struggle for charter and returns to Rhode Island, reported in serious dissension, 249; finds both town and colony hostile to him, 249-250; overcomes hostility and is elected President, 253; three years of constructive measures, 254-257; Quakers hospitably received, 257-258; long land quarrel with William Harris, 261-265; holds office until charter secured by Clarke and brought to Rhode Island, 265

Infirmities of last years, 267; continues services to town and colony, 268-269; continues preaching to Indians, 269; debates with Quakers, 269-271; reports debate in *George Fox Digg'd out of his Burrowes,* 284-286; death, 288

Williams, the Rev. Roger, of St. Albans, 12-13

Williams, Sydrach, brother of Roger, 9; Turkey merchant, 184

Wilson, John, of Boston, his post offered to Roger Williams during absence in England, 96; off to Plymouth with delegation, 101; his curse, 232

Winslow, Edward, 125, 141, 230; his tribute to Roger Williams quoted, 49; advice to him as to Plymouth bounds, 128; agent for Plymouth, 245

Winthrop, John, 74, 90, 92, 93, 95, 101, 103, 113, 160, 213; continuing friendship with Roger Williams, 49, 229; action on the *Treatise,* 107-108; on Indian lands, 110; in banishment of Roger Williams, 123-124; his questions to him in exile, 141-142; solicits help in Indian troubles, 146, 150, 156; in Rhode Island land struggle, 159, 216-217; death, 229

Winthrop, John, Jr., 94, 229, 254, 283

Wittie, Francis, 51, 52

Wittie, William, in Lynn affair, 231

Wren, Matthew, informant against Dorislaus, 67

Zeal Examined, 243

19. *Transforming Cape Town,* by Catherine Besteman
20. *Unimagined Community: Sex, Networks, and AIDS in Uganda and South Africa,* by Robert J. Thornton
21. *Righteous Dopefiend,* by Philippe Bourgois and Jeff Schonberg
22. *Democratic Insecurities: Violence, Trauma, and Intervention in Haiti,* by Erica Caple James
23. *Partner to the Poor: A Paul Farmer Reader,* by Paul Farmer, edited by Haun Saussy (with a foreword by Tracy Kidder)
24. *I Did It to Save My Life: Love and Survival in Sierra Leone,* by Catherine E. Bolten
25. *My Name Is Jody Williams: A Vermont Girl's Winding Path to the Nobel Peace Prize,* by Jody Williams
26. *Reimagining Global Health: An Introduction,* by Paul Farmer, Jim Yong Kim, Arthur Kleinman, and Matthew Basilico
27. *Fresh Fruit, Broken Bodies: Migrant Farmworkers in the United States,* by Seth M. Holmes, PhD, MD
28. *Illegality, Inc.: Clandestine Migration and the Business of Bordering Europe,* by Ruben Andersson
29. *To Repair the World: Paul Farmer Speaks to the Next Generation,* by Paul Farmer
30. *Blind Spot: How Neoliberalism Infiltrated Global Health,* by Salmaan Keshavjee (with a foreword by Paul Farmer)
31. *Driving after Class: Anxious Times in an American Suburb,* by Rachel Heiman
32. *The Spectacular Favela: Violence in Modern Brazil,* by Erika Robb Larkins
33. *When I Wear My Alligator Boots: Narco-Culture in the U.S. Mexico Borderlands,* by Shaylih Muehlmann
34. *Jornalero: Being a Day Laborer in the USA,* by Juan Thomas Ordóñez
35. *A Passion for Society: How We Think about Human Suffering,* by Iain Wilkinson and Arthur Kleinman
36. *The Land of Open Graves: Living and Dying on the Migrant Trail,* by Jason De León (with photographs by Michael Wells)
37. *Living with Difference: How to Build Community in a Divided World,* by Adam Seligman, Rahel Wasserfall, and David Montgomery
38. *Scratching Out a Living: Latinos, Race, and Work in the Deep South,* by Angela Stuesse
39. *Returned: Going and Coming in an Age of Deportation,* by Deborah A. Boehm
40. *They Leave Their Kidneys in the Fields: Illness, Injury, and Illegality among U.S. Farmworkers,* by Sarah Bronwen Horton

They Leave Their Kidneys in the Fields

Illness, Injury, and Illegality among U.S. Farmworkers

Sarah Bronwen Horton

UNIVERSITY OF CALIFORNIA PRESS

University of California Press, one of the most distinguished university presses in the United States, enriches lives around the world by advancing scholarship in the humanities, social sciences, and natural sciences. Its activities are supported by the UC Press Foundation and by philanthropic contributions from individuals and institutions. For more information, visit www.ucpress.edu.

University of California Press
Oakland, California

Library of Congress Cataloging-in-Publication Data

Names: Horton, Sarah Bronwen, author.
Title: They leave their kidneys in the fields : illness, injury and illegality among U.S. farmworkers / Sarah Bronwen Horton.
Other titles: California series in public anthropology ; 40.
Description: Oakland, California : University of California Press, [2016] | "2016 | Series: California series in public anthropology ; 40 | Includes bibliographical references and index.
Identifiers: LCCN 2015048171 (print) | LCCN 2015049983 (ebook) | ISBN 9780520283268 (cloth : alk. paper) | ISBN 9780520283275 (pbk. : alk. paper) | ISBN 9780520962545 ()
Subjects: LCSH: Migrant agricultural laborers—Health and hygiene—California—Central Valley. | Migrant agricultural laborers—California—Central Valley—Social conditions.
Classification: LCC HD1527.C2 H67 2016 (print) | LCC HD1527.C2 (ebook) | DDC 363.11/96309794—dc23

25 24 23 22 21 20 19 18 17
10 9 8 7 6 5 4 3 2

In keeping with a commitment to support environmentally responsible and sustainable printing practices, UC Press has printed this book on Natures Natural, a fiber that contains 30% post-consumer waste and meets the minimum requirements of ANSI/NISO Z39.48–1992 (R 1997) (*Permanence of Paper*).

They Leave Their Kidneys in the Fields

CALIFORNIA SERIES IN PUBLIC ANTHROPOLOGY

The California Series in Public Anthropology emphasizes the anthropologist's role as an engaged intellectual. It continues anthropology's commitment to being an ethnographic witness, to describing, in human terms, how life is lived beyond the borders of many readers' experiences. But it also adds a commitment, through ethnography, to reframing the terms of public debate—transforming received, accepted understandings of social issues with new insights, new framings.

Series Editor: Robert Borofsky (Hawaii Pacific University)

Contributing Editors: Philippe Bourgois (University of Pennsylvania), Paul Farmer (Partners In Health), Alex Hinton (Rutgers University), Carolyn Nordstrom (University of Notre Dame), and Nancy Scheper-Hughes (UC Berkeley)

University of California Press Editor: Naomi Schneider

1. *Twice Dead: Organ Transplants and the Reinvention of Death,* by Margaret Lock
2. *Birthing the Nation: Strategies of Palestinian Women in Israel,* by Rhoda Ann Kanaaneh (with a foreword by Hanan Ashrawi)
3. *Annihilating Difference: The Anthropology of Genocide,* edited by Alexander Laban Hinton (with a foreword by Kenneth Roth)
4. *Pathologies of Power: Health, Human Rights, and the New War on the Poor,* by Paul Farmer (with a foreword by Amartya Sen)
5. *Buddha Is Hiding: Refugees, Citizenship, the New America,* by Aihwa Ong
6. *Chechnya: Life in a War-Torn Society,* by Valery Tishkov (with a foreword by Mikhail S. Gorbachev)
7. *Total Confinement: Madness and Reason in the Maximum Security Prison,* by Lorna A. Rhodes
8. *Paradise in Ashes: A Guatemalan Journey of Courage, Terror, and Hope,* by Beatriz Manz (with a foreword by Aryeh Neier)
9. *Laughter Out of Place: Race, Class, Violence, and Sexuality in a Rio Shantytown,* by Donna M. Goldstein
10. *Shadows of War: Violence, Power, and International Profiteering in the Twenty-First Century,* by Carolyn Nordstrom
11. *Why Did They Kill? Cambodia in the Shadow of Genocide,* by Alexander Laban Hinton (with a foreword by Robert Jay Lifton)
12. *Yanomami: The Fierce Controversy and What We Can Learn from It,* by Robert Borofsky
13. *Why America's Top Pundits Are Wrong: Anthropologists Talk Back,* edited by Catherine Besteman and Hugh Gusterson
14. *Prisoners of Freedom: Human Rights and the African Poor,* by Harri Englund
15. *When Bodies Remember: Experiences and Politics of AIDS in South Africa,* by Didier Fassin
16. *Global Outlaws: Crime, Money, and Power in the Contemporary World,* by Carolyn Nordstrom
17. *Archaeology as Political Action,* by Randall H. McGuire
18. *Counting the Dead: The Culture and Politics of Human Rights Activism in Colombia,* by Winifred Tate

For my parents, Bronwen and Neil Horton
And for Don Abrán Villanueva

A portion of the proceeds from sales of this book will be donated to Mendota High School in California to fund an annual college scholarship for a child of farmworkers.

Contents

Acknowledgments *xi*

Introduction *1*
1. Burning Up: Heat Illness in California's Fields *17*
2. Entering Farm Work: Migration and Men's Work Identities *46*
3. Ghost Workers: The Labor Consequences of Identity Loan *72*
4. *Presión Alta:* The Physiological Toll of Farm Work *96*
5. Álvaro's Casket: Heat Illness and Chronic Disease at Work *124*
6. *Desabilitado:* Kidney Disease and the Disability-Assistance Hole *148*

Conclusion: Strategies for Change *173*

Appendix A. On Engaged Anthropology and Ethnographic Writing *185*
Appendix B. Methods *191*
Appendix C. Core Research Participants *195*

Notes *201*
References *221*
Index *241*

Acknowledgments

A number of people have helped to shape this book since its inception nearly a decade ago. Many colleagues were generous with their time and expertise, commenting on the manuscript and nudging it toward completion. Louise Lamphere has been a consistent mentor, and I am indebted to her for her advice and insight. Ruth Gomberg-Muñoz was a loyal writing buddy: the *coraje* (anger) she expressed at the circumstances described here provided me with moral support. Bill Alexander offered thoughtful comments on previous versions of the manuscript and helped me strengthen it. Catie Willging was a faithful sounding board, loyal friend, and insightful reader—even with only a day's notice. Angela Stuesse, Heide Castañeda, Cecilia Rivas, Whitney Duncan, and Emily Mendenhall kindly read and commented on drafts of chapters, and Joe Heyman, Carlos Vélez-Ibañez, Jonathan Xavier Inda, Jim Quesada, Luis Plascencia, and Alejandro Lugo offered helpful comments on versions of the conference papers that became this book. I am also indebted to Charles Briggs and Nancy Scheper-Hughes for their helpful suggestions and advice.

I am grateful to my colleagues at the University of Colorado, Denver (UCD), for providing me with the time and support necessary for finishing the book. John Brett, who said he didn't have the time to read the entire manuscript, somehow wound up reading nearly two-thirds of it. I am ever grateful for his generosity with his time and his consistent, unwavering mentorship. Steve Koester's passion for working with

vulnerable populations and keen appreciation of ethnographic writing served as an inspiration. Chris Beekman provided the humor, Tammy Stone the support and no-nonsense advice, and Jean Scandlyn the enthusiasm that helped lighten the load. And many wonderful UCD students helped me develop my thinking about various aspects of this project. Analisia Stewart, Alysa Haas, Casey Cole, and Tyler Lundy were all involved in projects that contributed to this book's publication, and Dalia Abdulrahman, Sarah Hall, and Gretty Stage provided invaluable editorial support.

This book has benefited from institutional support from the University of Colorado and University of California systems. Several internal grants from the University of Colorado, Denver, allowed me to conduct the research on farmworkers' work circumstances, and a leave from university teaching granted me the time to complete the project. A visiting scholarship at the Center for the Study of Law and Society at the University of California, Berkeley, provided me with the space and time to finish the manuscript. I am grateful to Cecilia Rivas, Pat Zavella, and Cat Ramírez for offering me a forum at the Department of Latin American and Latino Studies at the University of California, Santa Cruz, and for the thoughtful comments and questions of students and faculty at the colloquium. Finally, this book would not have been possible without the encouragement and forbearance of Naomi Schneider, Will Vincent, Erika Bűky, and Cindy Fulton at the University of California Press, who patiently waited as the book underwent multiple revisions.

Over the years, many friends, family, and fictive kin have put up with this project and supported it in multiple ways. My parents, Neil and Bronwen Horton, nurtured the interest in social justice that first led me to anthropology and then on to farmworker health. Together with my brother, David Horton, they loyally read chapters and provided the inspiration to make the book something they would want to read. Ben Gross was unfailing in his intellectual and technical support, Kim Todd kindly lent me her expertise in creative nonfiction, and Steph Cooper kept me on track with her humor and warmth. Meanwhile, my Denver "family"—especially Jo Panosky, Krystal Brown, Deborah Saint-Phard, and Wendy Flitter—loyally stood with me through the many ups and downs of writing. I am particularly grateful to Christine Nguyen for supplying the faith and unfailing support that allowed me to write from the heart, and to Kathleen Ashcraft for bringing me laughter, light, and sustenance in the long final stretch toward the book's completion.

Finally, I am grateful to the many individuals in Fresno County who helped me through the process of research and writing. Joe Riofrio is the kind of key informant anthropologists dream of; it was his masterful storytelling and deep knowledge of farmworkers' life circumstances that first piqued my interest in the themes discussed here and continued to provide inspiration throughout my fieldwork. Norma Ventura of California Rural Legal Assistance, Inc., helped with the workers' compensation intervention I describe in the conclusion, and Raúl Uribe, Robert Pérez, and Raquel García graciously donated their time to make it a success. Anne Katten of the California Rural Legal Assistance Foundation helped me understand the implications of the state's heat-illness prevention standard. And I am grateful to Judith Barker for first hiring me on the project on oral health that brought me to the Central Valley, and for her mentorship and thoughtful analysis.

Most important, I am grateful to the many farmworking men and women of Mendota who gave me their time, extended me their hospitality, and trusted me with their life experiences. This book owes its existence to their remarkable stories. To protect their privacy and confidentiality, I can only mention them by pseudonym. I am especially grateful to Elisabeta, the master storyteller, and Teo, her kind and thoughtful husband; to Sulema, who showed me how to suffer with dignity; to Don Tomás, who kindly withstood my many questions about the workings of the labor hierarchy; and to Yadira, whose passion for justice is inspirational. And I am grateful to René, Raquel, Alberto, Blanca, Gerardo, Leticia, Claudio, Don Santiago, Doña Rosa, Don Octavio, Doña Berta, Doña Linda, Don Miguel, José Angel, Ricardo, and Carlos for their insight and patience. Writing is an imperfect mirror of reality, and I regret that these pages can offer but a limited glimpse of their struggles and a hint of their dignity. If this book fails to move the reader, it is indeed my fault alone.

FIGURE 1. A picker's fingerprints slowly erode through contact with the tough skin of the melons, so farmworkers often wrap their fingers in athletic tape to protect them.

Introduction

Salud Zamudio Rodriguez, a forty-two-year-old undocumented farmworker from Michoacán, sparked a legislative firestorm when he met an untimely end one summer afternoon in California's Central Valley in 2005.[1] On a July day when the temperature soared to 105 degrees, Salud had been finishing a ten-hour shift picking bell peppers and running them over to a conveyor belt pulled by a tractor. As his coworker later stated in a brief filed by the United Farm Workers union (UFW), the labor contractor had allowed his workers only half the legally required thirty-minute lunch break. At the end of the break, Salud's foreman had asked the tractor driver to double his work pace so that the team could finish picking the field and be ready to start a new one the next morning. For more than two hours, the foreman set a pace that required the crew to pick six buckets of peppers every fifteen minutes. "In all my years of picking crops, I have never worked that fast," Soledad Reyes, one of Salud's coworkers, later told a journalist.[2]

Other workers skipped pepper plants to keep up with the tractor, but not Salud. Near the end of the day, Salud confided in Soledad that he felt ill and needed to quit. Instead, she later told the reporter, he began pacing back and forth as though delirious. Just minutes before the end of the day, he approached his foreman as if to say something but simply sank into his arms. The foreman took off Salud's hat and tried to revive him by fanning his face. The crew carried Salud to the shade provided by an adjacent orchard and tried to give him water. Yet

shortly after the ambulance arrived, the man they called "the machine" had expired.[3]

Salud's death was one of four in the Central Valley that summer that ultimately led to passage of California's Assembly Bill 805, the nation's first law establishing regulations to protect outdoor workers from heat illness. Three other farmworkers died at work during a three-week period that July in which the temperature exceeded 100 degrees every day. On July 14, the body of a melon picker was found next to a patch of ripe cantaloupes in Fresno County. A week later, the body of a deceased grape picker was found in Kern County, crouched beneath a grapevine; his brother later reported that he was attempting to take shelter from the sun.[4] Ten days later, also in Kern County, a twenty-four-year-old died in the hospital after suffering heat exhaustion while picking tomato for a farm labor contractor.[5]

It is well known that farm work places workers at a high risk of heat illness. Their work outdoors, sometimes without easy access to shade, exposes them to direct sunlight. The physical exertion of farm work contributes to their production of excess body heat, even as the clothing they wear to protect their skin from sun damage makes it more difficult for them to cool off by sweating.[6] It is perhaps unsurprising, then, that in the media frenzy that followed this string of deaths, journalists, government officials, and even farmworker advocates attributed them to the unusual heat wave striking the Valley that July. Observing that half as many farmworkers died from heat that summer alone as during the previous fifteen years, for example, the president of the UFW suggested that the "prolonged Central Valley heat wave . . . may have sparked the high death toll."[7] Meanwhile, the media cast the "blazing California sun" and "killer heat" as foes to be "battled" with the state's new protections.[8]

Heat waves, a phenomenon exacerbated by global climate change, disproportionately affect the most vulnerable members of society.[9] To combat rising and unpredictable summer temperatures, both California and Washington have implemented new laws protecting outdoor workers. California's was the first to mandate cool-down breaks when workers requested them and the provision of adequate water and shade.[10] But by focusing on the "relentless sun" of California's summers alone, journalists and policy makers naturalize the phenomenon of heat death, short-circuiting inquiry into the social and political factors that place farmworkers at greater risk. Indeed, nearly twice as many workers died in the three years after the implementation of California's heat illness law as in the three years prior to 2005.[11] Why, then, do farmworkers

continue to die of heat in California's fields, and what broader circumstances does an approach focusing on workplace protections alone obscure?

Heatstroke is the leading cause of work-related death for farmworkers. Members of this occupational group bear a higher risk of heatstroke than outdoor workers in any other industry, including construction.[12] According to the Centers for Disease Control and Prevention (CDC), all the heat deaths in farm work recorded between 1992 and 2006 were among men, and foreign-born Latinos accounted for 71 percent of such deaths.[13] Why do farmworkers suffer heat death at a rate higher than other outdoor workers, and why do foreign-born Latino men bear particular risk? Surveys suggest that farmworkers being paid by contract—that is, based on their productivity—may be more likely to forgo breaks than those being paid by the hour.[14] How does the organization of farm work itself play a role in heat death, and what broader labor and immigration policies shape work circumstances for farmworkers?

An emerging body of literature examines the social and political organization of "natural disasters" such as heat waves and—arguably—heat deaths.[15] Demonstrating that severe weather alone could not account for the mortality in Chicago during the 1995 heat wave (the Midwest's deadliest), for example, Eric Klinenberg argues that heat deaths call for dissection of the social and political structures that make them possible. He suggests that although heat deaths may initially appear to be isolated, chance, and extreme events, their very "excessiveness" lays bare the underlying social pathologies of which they are symptomatic.[16] Following Klinenberg's model of conducting a "social autopsy," this study subjects the public policies implicated in farmworkers' heat deaths to extended critical inquiry. I argue that for migrant men, heat simply catalyzes a chain reaction waiting to happen: for Salud, it set in motion a socially organized catastrophe that had been generated by myriad public policies.

MISPLACED AUTONOMY

Unlike heat waves, farmworkers' heat deaths raise the illusory issue of migrants' own agency and decision making. After all, deaths in the fields are partly the result of farmworkers' behaviors at work—such as not taking breaks when ill or not informing their supervisors of their illnesses. Indeed, work itself—which produces such heat deaths—is presumably a voluntary activity. It is therefore common for journalists to

wonder and the public to ask, why did Salud keep working? Did he not recognize that he was suffering from heat illness? Why didn't he say anything to his supervisor or request a break?

A growing literature in the occupational health sciences employs this focus on individual decision making in its attempts to reduce heat illness among farmworkers. Emphasizing the need for "health education and health promotion," the literature tends to portray heat illness as the result of poor knowledge and faulty choices.[17] It proposes training workers to recognize the symptoms of heat illness and to dispel farmworkers' erroneous, and presumably hazardous, beliefs.[18] It argues that farmworkers lack knowledge of how to appropriately cool themselves after heat exposure and underestimate the importance of adequate hydration and acclimatization.[19] Finally, it highlights "risky" behaviors among farmworkers that increase their chance of suffering heat illness, such as drinking sodas and caffeinated energy drinks to increase work efficiency and wearing heavy clothing to promote weight loss.[20] These studies thus individualize responsibility for heat illness prevention, portraying farmworkers' behaviors as though isolated from their work contexts and the labor and immigration policies that shape them.[21]

The theoretical model informing such studies emphasizes a rational individual actor who carefully weighs the pros and cons before engaging in any particular behavior. As the anthropologist and physician Seth Holmes points out, this approach ethnocentrically assumes actors who are able to exert "control over their destiny through 'choice.'"[22] This framing of individual acts as *choices*—whether describing migrants' crossing the border without papers or farmworkers' working through illness—in turn leads the public to blame migrants for their "irrational" or "impulsive" decisions. Our dominant framework for understanding illness and death chalks up the risks migrants face to their own personal failings, reassuringly implying that illness and accident lie within personal control.

As the critical medical anthropologist Paul Farmer has trenchantly observed, this framing uncritically assumes the unfettered agency of vulnerable populations, endowing their behaviors with a misplaced sense of autonomy. Farmer first developed this critique in his analysis of the *structural violence* that constrains the treatment options of poor residents living with infectious disease in countries such as Peru and Haiti.[23] Global public health officials tended to portray the populations of these countries as willfully noncompliant with treatment regimens and therefore as contributing to the global spread of epidemics. Yet

Farmer showed that a series of structural obstacles compromised their access to health care and to medications. Farmer's analysis of structural violence—that is, of the impersonal structures that systematically, yet invisibly, harm members of marginalized groups—drew attention to the constraints under which they must navigate. It has therefore led to many insightful analyses of the multiple social and political structures—"free trade" policies, immigration policies, and labor hierarchies—that place migrants in harm's way.

While the framework of structural violence has been instrumental in training anthropologists' gaze on the social production of bodily harm, many have pointed out that it lends itself to a dichotomous view of marginalized victims battling totalizing social structures.[24] Moreover, although it holds great relevance for understanding the health of vulnerable populations, its portrayal of social structures as violent may alienate otherwise sympathetic practitioners and limit its applications in the field of public health. In its place, critical medical anthropologists have recently proposed the concept of *structural vulnerability*. Rather than pinpoint the structural mechanisms that lead to the embodiment of ill health, the concept of structural vulnerability redirects our attention to the bodily, material, and subjective states that such structures produce. It refers to the kinds of risks with which an individual is saddled by virtue of his or her "location in a hierarchical social order and its diverse networks of power relationships."[25] As Quesada and colleagues argue, the concept of structural vulnerability points up the frequent exaggeration of the agency of vulnerable groups, redirecting our focus to the "forces that constrain decision-making, frame choices, and limit life options."[26] Because it suggests that migrants' illness is produced by their structural vulnerability—that is, by their positionality within overlapping social and political structures—this framework is particularly useful for the analysis of heat death. Indeed, this book aims to make visible the social and political contexts missing from the accounts of journalists, occupational health scholars, and policy makers. It describes the multiply constraining web of immigration and labor policies that ensnares migrant farmworkers and exposes them to the risk of illness and death in California's fields.

Even as undocumented migrants are often popularly understood as somehow existing beyond the reach of the government, public policies touch most aspects of farmworkers' lives, regardless of their legal status. Through labor policies, the state and federal governments shape farmworkers' work behaviors; they dictate how long they will work,

whether and when they can take breaks, whether they will be paid overtime, and when overtime pay kicks in. Government policies also shape the degree to which farmworkers must rely on their jobs for economic security. Farmworkers have the lowest incomes of any wage and salary workers.[27] As a result, state and federal programs must provide them with assistance. Food stamps, welfare, and Medicaid provide vital support for eligible farmworkers and their families, and federal disability payments offer those with legal status a form of "retirement" well in advance of retirement age. Thus any understanding of the behaviors implicated in farmworkers' premature illness and death must take into account how state and federal policies produce farmworkers' structural vulnerability—that is, how they shape farmworkers' opportunities and their need for work.

Moreover, the concept of structural vulnerability usefully directs attention to migrants' decisions as not only shaped by immediate social structures but also as emerging from their historically generated *habitus*. The sociologist Pierre Bourdieu developed the idea of habitus to draw attention to the fact that our largely unconscious bodily deportments and mental schema are forged within social environments. In this book, I examine what I call migrants' *work habitus* and *health care habitus*—that is, a set of attitudes regarding work and health care seeking that are shaped by their migration histories and precarious occupational and legal statuses. I use the term *habitus* in the sense of an "embodied feel for the game"—that is, to suggest that migrants' sense of what to expect in particular contexts is based on their past experience.[28] Thus I argue that the depth of the risk position that migrant farmworkers inhabit is difficult to fathom without understanding the weight of history. It is difficult to understand their work attitudes today without understanding the lingering influence of the guest-worker program their fathers and grandfathers experienced, just as it is impossible to understand men's learned avoidance of government-subsidized health care without understanding their historic exclusion. As I explain in chapter 2, the public policies that dictate the shape of farmworkers' lives leave memory traces that also influence the following generation's attitudes and behaviors.

ETHNOGRAPHY AND EPIDEMIOLOGY

This book is based on sixteen months of noncontiguous ethnographic research carried out over nearly a decade in Mendota, a small farmworking community just northwest of Fresno, in California's Central Valley. Ethnography's holistic perspective makes it a research method particularly well suited to situating phenomena such as heat illness within the

broader contexts that produce it. Thus ethnography can complement what is known about heat illness from the epidemiological studies described above: it can help explain known statistical patterns of illness by uncovering the invisible pathways through which a specific social positioning harms health.[29] Much as Klinenberg's inquiry used the statistical patterns of death illuminated by Chicago's heat wave as a means to conduct his social autopsy, this book undertakes a social-epidemiological analysis of the statistical patterns of heat death among farmworkers. It situates the individual-level factors associated with heat death—foreign-born status, "Latino" ethnicity, male sex, and contract work—within the social and political contexts that make them risk factors.

Such an analysis requires investigating the public policies and entrenched private interests that place particular farmworkers in harm's way. It demands an understanding of the way that immigration policies make Latino men particularly reliant on their jobs and the heightened work pressures entailed by the multiple layers of supervision created by subcontracting. It requires examining farmworkers' vulnerabilities at work—themselves created and sustained by labor and immigration policies—as well as the food-safety policies in the produce industry that compromise workers' safety. It demands attention to the social production of migrant men's chronic diseases that interact with their illnesses at work, as well as the health care and disability policies that allow such diseases to remain undiagnosed and untreated.

Ethnographic immersion not only allows us to contextualize the known risk factors as defined by epidemiologists, but it also provides an account of "risk categories" from farmworkers' own perspectives. Epidemiology typically concerns itself with identifying the causes of sickness and death, using broad data sets to statistically test hypotheses about the relationships between particular variables and health outcomes. Epidemiologists construct their hypotheses by relying on data sets of aggregated cases blanched of all but the most relevant preconstructed variables. They strive to eliminate the "noise" caused by local differences in order to develop universal theories of causation constructed from a bird's-eye view. In contrast, ethnographers build our accounts from the ground up, and we dwell in the particular. Because anthropologists recognize that the way we construct the categories we measure rests on a variety of assumptions, we are interested in the cases that fall through the cracks. We are interested in the chaff sloughed off in the process of creating the standardized categories used to yield epidemiological conclusions.

By paying close attention to research participants' narratives and points of view, ethnography can yield what we call *experience-near*

accounts that can illuminate unknown patterns of illness and new groups of people at risk. Thus this book uses ethnography to reveal the social and political logics behind a host of ethnographically grounded categories of farmworkers particularly vulnerable to heat illness and death: recently arrived migrants, "ghost workers" (see chapter 3), and those with undiagnosed chronic disease. In attending to these categories, this book provides an insider's perspective on heat illness, according as much value to farmworkers' own accounts as to the data abstracted from surveys. Indeed, one of the strengths of ethnography is its committed epistemological stance: in the words of Louise Lamphere, it positions farmworkers "not as objects of study but as subjects of their own experience and inquiry."[30] Thus this book is a form of "social epidemiology from the ground up"—it uses farmworkers' own experiences and analyses as the building blocks of its analysis. In short, listening to ethnographic "noise" —that is, examining the chaff that disappears from epidemiological accounts—can not only contextualize known statistical patterns but also provide valuable new information.

ETHNOGRAPHY IN AN "OTHER" CALIFORNIA

I did not come to Mendota with the goal of studying heat deaths. Yet farmwork fatalities were such an ever-present part of life there that it began to seem like an oversight, even irresponsible, not to study them. Every year, members of this town of 11,420 people died of heatstroke in the fields—most while harvesting corn and melon in the full summer heat, but a small number while harvesting spring crops. Moreover, heat deaths were just some of the work fatalities among town residents. I heard of other deaths, too, deaths caused by a tractor capsizing, tractors running over workers, crashes of certified farm labor vehicles on the way to work, and fatal anaphylactic reactions to insect stings.

When I first arrived in Mendota, I was struck by how far removed the Valley is from the prosperity of the California coast. The town's population is predominantly Latino and migrant; according to the 2010 U.S. Census, it is 97 percent Hispanic and 51 percent foreign-born.[31] Because of its high proportion of migrants and farmworkers, Mexican Americans in neighboring towns pejoratively refer to it as a "migrant labor camp." A sign at Mendota's entrance proclaims the town the "Cantaloupe Center of the World," but Mendota has also been dubbed the "Detroit of California" because of the high proportion of migrant farmworkers living in destitution.[32] The median household income in

Mendota is $25,845 for a median family size of 4.5, and 43 percent of households have incomes below the federal poverty line.[33]

I grew up just two hours away in the San Francisco Bay Area. Yet simply stepping into the town's 99 Cent stores, supermarkets, and convenience stores, I found myself in an "other" California. The ceilings were often hung with hats—baseball caps, straw sombreros, and Chinese paddy hats—sold to shield workers against the sun and protect them from heatstroke. Aisles were stocked with bandannas to tie across the mouth to screen out dust and pesticides. In the convenience stores' coolers, next to the soda and Gatorade, stood bottles of Pedialyte, called *suero* in Spanish. Designed for dehydrated children, *suero* is a lifesaver for farmworkers in the summer heat.

As a visible outsider in this farmworking community, I initially struggled to explain my objective to parents and establish trust. Migrant parents initially did not know what to make of me. I probably seemed like a peculiar variant of the many *gabachos* (white North Americans) who often intruded in their homes: social workers, school officials, health outreach workers. However, over time, the fact that I was a *gabacha* and that I was often indignant about their work conditions seemed to provide them with a sense of validation. Interviewees knew that I cared about their health and work safety; they knew that I was on their side. Soon, many wanted me to know as much about their lives as possible. They invited neighbors and friends to come and tell me their stories; they volunteered my services in contacting workers' compensation insurance carriers, doctors, and attorneys. In this highly segregated community, my English skills, legal status, and knowledge of the workings of state bureaucracies (however limited) were rare assets. I embraced my role as a researcher-cum-social worker, helping my research participants locate health care services, driving family members to appointments, translating letters from state and federal bureaucracies, and helping them navigate the eligibility rules for California and Social Security disability programs. Offering this assistance not only helped me establish trust with families but also gave me valuable insights into how state and federal policies themselves shape migrants' health, workplace vulnerabilities, and health care seeking behaviors.

Just as often as I was able to help, I found myself powerless in the face of tragedies: one participant's husband was deported, another failed to receive adequate compensation for a work injury, and—as I describe at the end of this book—several men faced kidney failure because of a lack of timely access to health care and social assistance.

Those who work with vulnerable populations often experience a kind of survivor's guilt: even as we record the difficulties of our research participants' lives, we have the luxury of being able to return to our own comfortable lives. When I needed to escape, a two-hour drive took me up the truck-choked Highway 5 to the metropolitan corridor of I-580, to a protected middle-class environment where 99 Cent stores gave way to malls, where furrowed fields became periurban sprawl, where no men I knew faced kidney failure.

My initial research on migrant farmworker children's health allowed me to establish rapport with a core group of migrant women, six of whom I was able to follow over the course of a decade. I also conducted interviews with these women's husbands. I added a seventh couple to the group in 2008 and an eighth in 2010. In sum, I conducted intensive ethnography and repeat interviews with a core set of fifteen research participants about the sociopolitical structuring of migrants' lives and their excess burden of death. Ten were migrants from Mexico, and five were from El Salvador. (See appendix B for the demographic backgrounds of the couples and greater detail on my methods). In addition, I conducted interviews with members of these core participants' families and with multiple other farmworkers to ensure that their experiences were not atypical.

To better understand the factors affecting migrants' work circumstances, I conducted interviews with an additional eighteen workers, six labor supervisors (three contractors and three *mayordomos,* or foremen), eight workers' compensation attorneys, and organizers in the UFW and California Rural Legal Assistance, Inc. (a legal advocacy agency for rural low-income Californians). To grasp how federal and global food safety regulations affect workers' health at work, I conducted interviews with officials in the Audits Services branch of the U.S. Department of Agriculture (USDA) and semiformal interviews with three food-safety supervisors in two different agricultural companies. To understand how social assistance programs affect migrant farmworkers' health and work histories, I conducted interviews with fifteen middle-aged, elderly, and retired workers as well as with workers in the state agency that administers disability insurance. To discern the long-term implications of work for migrants' health, I conducted interviews with five migrant farmworkers with kidney failure, as well as two nephrologists and one finance manager at the University of California, San Francisco Transplant Center. I complemented my interview data with observation of multiple types of farm work (weeding tomato and cotton, harvesting

corn, and harvesting melon); I also participated in packing watermelon, canary melon, and cantaloupe on three different farm crews.

Because of the duration of ethnographers' ties with their participants, longitudinal research with vulnerable populations enhances the validity of a study's findings. It increases rapport and thereby allows ethnographers to elicit narratives that participants may not divulge to researchers who remain strangers.[34] Moreover, it can shed light on the compounded effects of social inequality as they unfold over the life course.[35] Farmworkers' limited access to health care and high likelihood of undiagnosed disease impede synchronic studies of farmworker health, which examine their health status only at one point in time. Longitudinal analysis, by contrast, allows ethnographers to track the diagnosis, course, and progression of chronic diseases, illuminating the cumulative health toll of being a migrant farmworker.

Some suggest that because it places academic researchers outside their comfortable environs, ethnographic immersion in the lives of vulnerable populations has an inherently "transgressive" or even "transformative" potential.[36] Attending to research participants' own experiences, described in their own words, allows the ethnographer to serve as an "ethical witness"; by virtue of its methodology, ethnography demonstrates the researcher's "empathy and engagement" as a form of "solidarity with the afflicted."[37] Yet I suggest that ethnographers who work with vulnerable populations must go beyond the imperative of sympathetic representation: they must honor an unspoken ethical contract they establish with their research participants through the very conditions of their entry. My research participants allowed me into their lives on condition that I serve as an advocate. My knowledge of English, legal status, and therefore my relative ease in approaching U.S. bureaucracies facilitated my entrée and access to the information I present here. This book only partially satisfies the terms of our implicit contract. Intimate involvement in research participants' lives confers a particular burden of not only representation but also action, a subject I return to in the book's conclusion. (See also appendix A for a more detailed discussion of engaged anthropology.)

"THEY LEAVE THEIR KIDNEYS IN THE FIELDS"

In the course of my everyday life in the Valley and visits to my interviewees, I gained an oblique view onto the perplexing questions about blame and causality that heat deaths raise. Each story provided more

questions than answers, and following each string that I unraveled led me to new hypotheses. Below, I offer my first impressions of heat death in the fields to provide clues.

One Sunday in early May 2008, I emerged from Don Pablo's shack on the main drag of the town and stumbled on three men who were whiling away the afternoon in the shade of the street's olive trees.[38] They had set down their beer bottles, which were nestled inside brown paper bags, and leaned against the white fence that separates the sidewalk from Don Pablo's house. They were absorbed in their talk, and the tone of their conversation was angry, even strident. They were discussing a coworker who died while harvesting corn for a local company last summer. Their friend—a young man in his twenties—left behind a wife and two-year-old daughter in Mexico. The men were about to begin harvesting corn again, and they were pausing this afternoon to remember his death.

Picking corn in the summer is a particularly dangerous job. The corn stalks rise above workers' heads like trees in a forest. It is hot and humid in the thicket of corn, and the density of the stalks prevents the summer breeze—if there is one—from entering. Workers complain that they often overheat. The summer this man died, another local worker also died harvesting corn, despite the fact that growers had changed the time corn is harvested to make the job less risky. Workers now enter the cornfields in the dead of night: they harvest corn from 2 A.M. until 2 P.M.[39]

I had observed corn harvesting before, watching as a tractor outfitted with wings crushed the rows of picked corn, hauling the flatbed truck that workers call a *traila* (trailer) behind it. Men fanned in front of the tractor to pick the ears of corn from the stalks and throw them onto the trailer wings, where women gathered them and packed them into boxes. Atop the *traila,* men lifted the boxes of corn and stacked them on pallets into columns nearly eight feet high. The young man who died was a stacker. He had worked for several hours in the open sun without a break. He had informed his *mayordomo* of his exhaustion, the men say. Yet the foreman reportedly allowed him no rest; he relentlessly pushed his team on (*les daba carillas*) in order to clear the field.

One year after their friend's death, the men on the sidewalk were about to start work for this very same supervisor, whom they condemned. "The *mayordomo* was the one who screwed up—it was *his* responsibility to make sure his team was okay," one man said angrily. With a nod, his companion agreed. "In the corn, it's always hard to breathe. But it was his responsibility to let him rest or take him to the

hospital if he needed it," he said. A third man, reclining against the gate in sullen silence, suddenly came to life. Staggering into the circle, he weighed in, slightly inebriated and visibly enraged. "Us illegals, they treat us like burros," he spat (*los ilegales, nos tratan como burros*).[40]

This man's angry protestations lingered with me through the week. They suggested a pattern of unequal treatment of undocumented migrants in the fields, highlighting their particular structural vulnerability at work. Yet they also illustrated the way that the very circumstances of farm work could be invoked to obscure blame, the dense stalks of corn deflecting attention from the exacting demands of the man's supervisor.

Later that week, I was in a convenience store on the highway that runs through town when I heard about a local man in his fifties who died harvesting asparagus in March. As the cashier told the story, some of her patrons stopped browsing the aisles to contribute details. The woman said that the asparagus season had just begun, and it was an unusually hot spring day. The team had finished picking asparagus in one field and walked to another, a little more than a mile away, to begin picking there. Unprepared for such a hot day in early spring, the man had no hat to shield him from the hot sun. He fainted. Even though his supervisor called an ambulance to take him to the hospital, he later died.

Even as the patrons seemed relatively unperturbed, I was startled by the abruptness of this story's ending. Like so many stories of heat death I had heard before, it seemed to progress inexorably from a worker's fainting or heat exhaustion to the same final, unhappy outcome. So I prodded the cashier for more information. *Why* had he died? Why this man, on this team, on this day? Was his death due only to heat stroke, or were other factors at work? How had his work circumstances, his social circumstances, influenced his death?

"*Pues* [well], they say he was hung over, and his *mayordomo* was pressuring him," the woman replied.

A middle-aged patron in a baseball cap, browsing the snack aisle with a friend, assented with a grunt. "He drank too much cold water and they changed his field, so he had to walk the distance. His body probably went into shock because of the quantity of water," he added.

His friend nodded. "When you drink too much cold water at once, the pump of the gallbladder bursts," he said. "And the *mayordomo* was too demanding."

On the one hand, these explanations portray the man's death as something he could have avoided—by drinking less cold water, or perhaps by not getting drunk the night before. On the other hand, they indict the

man's supervisor for spurring on his workers in his desire for profit, echoing the criticism of growers and their intermediaries issued by Salud's coworkers above. But another man, who approached the counter with a gallon of milk, dismissed the chorus of explanations with a shake of his head. "Pressure is something that people bring on themselves," he said in a chiding tone (*la carilla se da a si mismo*). He elaborated: in some cases, workers' pay is tied to their performance, so they must push themselves hard to earn more. In other cases, they must work hard to impress the *mayordomo* to ensure job security. "You have to kill yourself so they'll take you to the fields every day," he muttered as he set the gallon of milk on the counter with a thump.

What allows *mayordomos* to push their migrant workforce to their limits, and how do state and federal policies fail to prevent heat-related deaths—or even contribute to them? If the man purchasing milk in the corner store is correct that "pressure is something that people bring on themselves," what are the unseen pressures that migrant men internalize to the extent that they achieve not a living but death in the fields?

At the end of the week, I asked a long-term research participant, Blanca, and her father, Don Santiago, about these stories. Don Santiago told me that he had been harvesting melon for the same company when the man died in the cornfield the previous summer. The man's coworkers had visited the melon-picking crew asking for donations to send the man's body back to Mexico. "We donated two, three dollars—what we could," he said. He could offer no more details than I had already heard from the men on the sidewalk, yet he dismissed my question about the cause of the man's death with a wave of his hand. "His kidneys dried up," he said. Despite my further questioning, he merely stated that the man must not have drunk enough water and consequently died of dehydration. Seeing that I was not fully satisfied, Blanca chimed in, as though attempting to translate between the local reality and mine. "They leave their kidneys in the fields," she said. "When they go back to Mexico, all used up [*agotado*], that's what they say. They say, 'I left my kidneys over there'—I left them in the fields from having done farm work."

Blanca's remark conjured up an image of tomato fields littered with arthritic knees and melon fields paved with the hunched backs that picked them. It was so darkly intriguing that I had to inquire further, asking whether this expression was but one of the many poetic aphorisms I had recorded that evoke the hardships of farmworkers' lives. When discussing immigration raids in town, I had heard Blanca reassure a neighbor with "God may shake us, but he does not strangle us" (*Dios*

nos aprieta pero no ahorca). And when discussing the hard work of her husband and father, I had heard her say: "The city lives off the countryside" (*la ciudad vive del campo*). When workers take leave of each other and plan a next meeting, a common response is "God willing" (*si Dios quiere)*. When discussing old age, some may say quite bluntly, "We'll see if I get there" (*a ver si llego)*—or, more obliquely, "When night falls, we don't know whether we'll see the dawn" (*si oscurece, mañana no sabemos si amanece)*. I asked Blanca whether this is a *dicho*, a common saying. Blanca gave me a level stare. "Well, sure, they're sayings. But they're sayings because they're true, no?"

This book places the high rate of heat deaths among farmworkers, and among Latino migrant men in particular, in the social and political contexts that saddle them with invisible pressures that make them particularly susceptible. It situates heat illness and death in the context of multiple levels of causation—from that of the individual to his *mayordomo* and all the way up to the labor policies that shape migrants' work environments and the immigration policies that influence their health. Chapters 1–3 examine the causes of farmworkers' vulnerability at work. I explore how U.S. trade and foreign policy first led Mexican and Salvadoran men to migrate to the Central Valley to fulfill their masculine responsibilities as breadwinners, and the ways that labor and immigration policies make them particularly dependent on the income derived from their jobs. I examine the limited types of agricultural employment open to undocumented migrants and the way that subcontracting abets labor abuses while intensifying the productivity demands placed on field hands. Chapter 3 examines the informal income-generating strategies farmworkers must use to survive and the ways that recent changes in immigration enforcement place all noncitizens engaged in these strategies at risk of arrest and deportation. Because of a trend toward rendering even legal permanent residents deportable, these policies jeopardize the working conditions of all migrants.

Chapters 4–6 explore the social production of chronic diseases among farmworkers that interact with unreported heat illness. Drawing on new theories of how minority status "gets under our skin," chapter 4 examines migrant farmworkers' high risk of cardiovascular disease. It places their high rates of hypertension in the context of the social stressors they face because of their precarious legal status. Chapter 5 examines why such chronic disease may go undiagnosed and how the current organization of farm work may cause untreated hypertension to interact with heat illness. Finally, chapter 6 examines the cumulative effect of farmworkers'

chronic heat illness, helping explain Blanca's matter-of-fact statement that farmworkers "leave their kidneys in the fields."

By producing an experience-near account of heat illness, ethnography can reveal the multiple factors that place migrant farmworkers' in harm's way. If we are to understand the many causes of heat illness, we must first examine migrant farmworkers' immediate work contexts and then the public policies that shape them. It is to the fields, then, that we will turn first.

CHAPTER 1

Burning Up

Heat Illness in California's Fields

Why do farmworkers die in the fields? On the highway in the Central Valley in the summer of 2013, the state's answer to this question is prominently displayed. As I drive, the wizened face and torso of a female farmworker loom into view on an oversized billboard. As she rests under a shade structure, a vast, cloudless blue sky and field stretching behind her, she stares down at drivers soberly. "If you want to last, don't forget to rest," she warns (*si quiere durar, no olvide descansar*). Down the road, another billboard features a young male farmworker shaded by a straw hat, his shovel slung over his shoulder as he raises a cup to his lips. "With water, you can deliver more," the billboard proclaims (*con agua, uno rinde más*). The captions reflect migrants' gendered work goals as imagined by the state: the women's goal is to endure, the men's to maximize productivity. These signs are part of a state campaign to reduce heat deaths in the fields by mandating that employers provide rest, shade, and water for farmworkers and by zeroing in on farmworkers' preventive behaviors themselves.

In 2005, after five farmworkers died from heatstroke, California became the first state in the nation to adopt emergency regulations to protect outdoor workers. With the motto of "Water, Rest, Shade: The Work Can't Get Done without Them," the heat-illness prevention standard established a series of protections for outdoor workers. It required that once the temperature exceeds 85°F, agricultural employers provide a shade structure that can accommodate at least a quarter of their crew

FIGURE 2. A Cal-OSHA billboard on a county road advising how to prevent heatstroke. This poster, showing a woman, advises the viewer that rest is necessary to endure (*durar*).

at any one time, and that the shade remain as close to the workers "as practicable."[1] It mandated that employers provide enough cold water for each member of a crew to drink at least a quart every hour. Finally, it permitted workers to request a minimum five-minute "cool-down rest in the shade" when they "feel they need to do so."[2]

California's regulations were hailed as the most far-reaching in the nation. Yet nearly twice as many workers died in the three years following their enactment as in the three preceding years.[3] Laying the blame for these deaths squarely at the feet of the state's worker safety regulatory agency, the American Civil Liberties Union (ACLU) and the United Farmworkers union (UFW) sued the state for inadequate enforcement—the ACLU in 2009 and the UFW in 2012.[4] The plaintiffs not only argued that the heat illness prevention law did not go far enough; they also claimed that the state's official tally of heat deaths undercounts the true extent of heat mortality. The state's numbers exclude those deaths in which heat was deemed by the county coroner a contributing factor but not the sole cause.[5]

FIGURE 3. A second heat-illness prevention billboard, this time depicting a man, claims that staying hydrated enables the worker to deliver more product (*rendir más*).

Based on participant-observation of melon harvesting during a heat wave in Fresno County in 2013, this chapter examines why heat deaths have continued among migrant farmworkers despite the state's protective regulations. It takes the reader on an ethnographic tour through the Valley's melon fields to explore the public policies and private interests that impinge upon farmworkers' immediate work environments. It suggests that the very organization of industrial agriculture contributes to heat deaths. Participant-observation in the fields illustrates how the farm labor hierarchy capitalizes on men's pride in their labor capacity, encouraging them to press on despite illness.

AN ETHNOGRAPHIC TOUR OF FARM WORK

An understanding of the broader contexts that contribute to farmworker deaths is notably absent from the state's campaign against heat mortality. The figures on the highway billboards labor as though in a vacuum: the images zoom in on the workers themselves, and the workers' supervisor and crew—let alone the federal and state policies that

shape their actions—are nowhere to be seen. The publicity campaign pictures workers as autonomous agents. With the refocusing of a wide-angled lens, heat deaths are reduced to an issue of poor individual decision making; the billboards imply that it is simply up to the worker to decide when to rest and rehydrate.

In June 2013, I decided to visit the fields to better understand the immediate work context in which heat-related illnesses unfold. Because farmworkers in California often work for large corporations and labor contractors, it can be difficult to gain access to the fields they harvest.[6] After weeks of leaving messages for local companies and contractors, I resorted to conducting unannounced visits to the fields. I interviewed workers and supervisors during breaks; I also worked packing cantaloupe, canary melons, and watermelon on three different labor crews.[7] Below, I use my field notes from trips to the cantaloupe fields during a historic heat wave in Fresno County to correct the myopic vision of farm work displayed on the state's billboards.

Friday, June 28, 2013

The air conditioning is on full blast as I drive down the highway, sunglasses shielding my eyes from the glare of the asphalt. It is only 11 A.M., but my car thermometer reads 110°F as I pass the cramped corner store that marks the dusty town of Tres Piedras (Three Rocks). Today's official forecast predicts a high of 105, but it is hotter out on the road, just as it will be hotter in the thick of the vegetation in the field.

The weather forecast has predicted highs between 105 and 111 all week. Warning of a "historic heat wave," the *Fresno Bee* ran an article stating: "The last time Fresno flirted with several days of 110 degree-plus weather, heat played a role in killing 14 people. Now at the doorstep of July, Fresno is flirting again."[8] Cal-OSHA, the state's department of occupational safety and health, has issued a press release warning employers of the heightened risks to outdoor workers. "Employers should know that workers who labor under excessive heat for extended periods are likely to exhibit fatigue more quickly than in shorter heat waves. The probability of serious heat illness for outdoor workers is much higher right now."[9]

The field I have come to visit today lies south of the city of Dos Palos (Two Sticks), near the small town of Tres Piedras. My long-term interviewee, Elisabeta, has told me where a local company named Fresco harvests its cantaloupe, and I have come to observe. "This way you will see it

with your own eyes: the field and the melon and the *casitas* [shade structures] and all," she had said with excitement. The worst that could happen, she had reassured me, was that a supervisor would ask me to leave.

I turn off the highway onto a gravel county road and cross an aqueduct. The valley gives way to fields of melon, lined with neat green furrows of vines. In the distance, I can see eight field-packing machines crawling up and down the rows like spiders.

Hauling a bag heavy with Gatorade, I begin the half-mile walk to the path where a machine has discharged a crew of workers to break for lunch. A crew of eighteen is eating lunch under a shade structure, and I approach. The men are wearing long-sleeved shirts to protect themselves from the sun, and some of the women wear white *pañoletas,* or coverings, over their faces. The men have been trailing the machine to pick melon for six hours, working without the benefit of the machine's protective awning. Their faces are flushed a deep red and appear swollen.

Usually, within minutes of my arrival at a field, the large white truck of a supervisor rolls up beside me to ask me my business. I brace myself for the familiar crunch of gravel under the truck's supersized wheels. Today I am in luck; there is no truck and no contractor.

I start the conversation by asking the men what they do to protect themselves from the heat. The table is quiet for some time, with only the soft sound of chewing and the occasional scraping of bowls. Finally, Samuel, a short man from Acapulco, speaks up as though irked by his coworkers' passivity. "*Pues,* drink water, take rest, find shade," he recites, with a shrug at the question's obviousness. He is parroting the state's recommendations, which he seems to think I want to hear. "Not a lot of water all at once—that isn't good for the body," he clarifies. "But water as often as you can."

Given his pat response, I suspect that Samuel has mistaken me for a visitor from Cal-OSHA. Despite the explanation of my purpose and research agenda, after all, I am a *gabacha,* like many well-meaning visitors from the state. This is but one of the limitations of conducting research on heat illness in the fields. While participant-observation reveals the immediate work contexts that cause heat illness, it only provides clues as to the invisible pressures that migrants themselves bring to work. Moreover, if supervisors are present, it is unlikely that migrants will discuss their work conditions freely.

I ask Samuel where his *mayordomo* is, and he gestures at the cars parked at the side of the road. So I ask Samuel whether taking such precautions is possible—whether he can in fact drink as much

water as he needs to when he's working. He scrunches his face into a frown of disbelief, as though insulted by the ludicrousness of the question. Drinking water, he explains, would interrupt the very process of production. "*Ni hombre* [no way]. They'd have to stop the machine for me to get at the water jugs. And they're not going to do that!"

A tall, ungainly man with a floppy straw hat—who I later learn is called Miguelito—chimes in excitedly, as though encouraged by the line of questioning. "A lot of people start to get sick, and they won't say anything. Better not to say anything," he repeats. I ask why not. "Because they're afraid the *mayordomo* won't believe them, that he'll just say, 'That one's lazy.'" There are mutters of agreement from around the table. Encouraged, the man continues. "That's the problem about preventing *la insolación* [heat illness]. It's better to wait until you are going to fall over. If you fall over, they'll believe you. If not, they'll just say, 'That lazy ass [*flojón*] just doesn't want to work.'" He screws up his mouth and dismisses the imaginary worker with his hand; the men laugh.

Samuel jumps in, warming to the discussion. "The law says that if we need to take a break, we should go to the side of the field and sit down if we need to," he says. There are knowing looks from around the table, preparing me for the caveat to come. "But it all depends on the *mayordomo*. There are some that will let you take a break, and you'll still have your job. In other cases, though, *ni modo* [no way]. You'll have to look for work elsewhere," he says.

A tall, pale man with broad shoulders—a man the crew later calls *El Güero* (the white guy)—seems unnerved by the dark drift of the conversation and its implication of powerlessness. He puffs himself up as he steps in to correct the tone. "I always take breaks if I need to; I can always find another job," he says.

There is an awkward silence. Then Samuel steps in to qualify Güero's statement. Whether taking breaks is safe, he clarifies, depends entirely on whether there is a surplus of workers. If workers are scarce, taking a break may not cost you a job. If they are plentiful, "Well, then you better start looking for work," he says with a morose chuckle.

These are abstract generalities, but I want to know how they play out on the ground. In his discussion of the formation of habitus, Bourdieu has called this embodied knowledge of social contexts a "feel for the game."[10] I want to know how workers decide whether it is safe to rest—whether the *mayordomo* is amenable, the company sufficiently short-handed, or one has displayed enough *ganas* [hustle] to earn oneself a five-minute respite in the shade. I am hoping to fill in the empty background on the state's

billboard—to understand the way that fieldworkers' work context shapes their everyday behaviors. So I turn to Samuel and ask, "Have you ever found yourself in a situation where you felt you had to choose between saying something to protect your health and possibly losing your job?"

The table is quiet, and Samuel gives me a level stare. "We've all been in that situation," he says, slowly circling his finger in the air to draw an imaginary lasso that will settle over all the men and women sitting at that bench. "*Todos*" (all of us).

THE CODE OF SILENCE

As Samuel's statement indicates, the organization of labor crews enforces a code of silence about workers' vulnerability. Migrant men eschew breaks out of fear that their *mayordomo* will fire them. Migrants' precarious status on labor crews can be traced in part to the Immigration Reform and Control Act (IRCA), an immigration reform bill passed in 1986. By imposing federal fines on employers who were found to have "knowingly" hired undocumented workers, IRCA created a subcontracting boom in California agriculture and deepened workers' precarity.[11]

Employers' degree of compliance with IRCA depends on the size and permanence of their workforce, which largely determines their risk of facing an immigration raid or audit. In the Valley, agricultural employers include small ranches, large packing and processing houses, and large commercial companies and growers. Small ranches, which face minimal risk, are known to hire undocumented migrants with impunity. However, there are few jobs on such ranches. Large packing and processing sheds with a semipermanent workforce face moderate risk and therefore check workers' documents more rigorously. Large agribusiness companies, and growers whose size and visibility might attract federal attention, often delegate their hiring to subcontractors in an attempt to insulate themselves from the risks of directly hiring a predominantly undocumented workforce. Because contractors often employ rotating rosters of workers for relatively short periods, they face less risk of attracting federal scrutiny than their larger and more visible employers. As a result, few contractors rigorously inspect employees' work authorization documents. Thus IRCA has made labor crews the primary source of work for undocumented migrants.

Subcontracting intensifies pressures on field hands by creating what farmworkers call a ladder (*escala*) of descending workplace pressures. Large commercial growers and agribusiness companies hire contractors to assume responsibility for the hiring and supervision of their workers;

contractors in turn hire *mayordomos* to command each crew and ensure their health and safety in the fields.[12] Because growers typically hire contractors to accomplish a particular task—such as weeding or picking a field—the work on labor crews is repetitive and narrowly specialized. Moreover, the gradated labor hierarchy on labor crews makes the labor process quite unlike that in packinghouses and small family farms. Subcontracting introduces an intermediate layer of supervisors who themselves must derive profit from field hands' labor. Growers pay contractors a fixed commission that covers overhead, the workers' wages, and the contractor's own pay. Therefore contractors squeeze a profit from their commission by maximizing workers' productivity; it is in contractors' best interest for field hands to work as quickly as possible.

The pace of work is very different on family farms because of the lack of a labor hierarchy and the varied tasks workers must perform. Elisabeta temporarily filled a position on a small ranch tending grape vines one summer when a permanent employee fell ill. After more than fifteen years of working on labor crews, she found the transition a shock. Rather than emphasize speed, her supervisors taught her to carefully tie and prune the vines. "I think God gave me this job *(me regaló este trabajo)*," Elisabeta tells me. At one point, Elisabeta says, the *mayordoma* even came over to tell her crew to proceed more cautiously. "And I said to my coworker, 'Ay, this is the first job in all my life where the supervisor said to not work so quickly!' And my *compañero* [coworker] just laughed and laughed."

Not only does the hierarchical supervision of labor crews intensify the pressures on field hands, but its competitive structure also undermines their job security. The job security of supervisors at each level of the hierarchy depends on the performance of workers at the level below. If a *mayordomo*'s crew fails to perform to the contractor's demands, both the *mayordomo* and the crew will lose their jobs the following season. If the contractor, in turn, fails to meet the grower's demands, that contractor and all his employees—all the *mayordomos* and all their crews—will lose their jobs. Thus workers on labor crews face heightened precarity. A field hand has the least job security; the downward pressure of the farm labor hierarchy reverberates most forcefully at the lowest level.

Saturday, June 29, 2013

It is 108 degrees at noon when I return to the fields near Tres Piedras. As I pull up to the field, I pass a white van with its windows rolled up. A man with tousled, damp hair is slumped in the passenger side as the air conditioner hums at full power.

Samuel's crew has already returned to work after their lunch, so I find another crew to talk to. I distribute the Gatorades and explain why I am there. The crew nods, eating their lunch silently.

I open the conversation by asking the group how they are coping with the heat. "Okay, but one of us is already sick," says a man to my side. He gestures at a crew member across the table with red crescent moons under his eyes. "Sick with what?" I ask. Another man pipes up. "He suffers from—well, they call it *la mano débil*" (weak hands), he says, letting his wrist go limp for effect. The men sitting beside him laugh uncomfortably and then become quiet. I turn to the man with the hollowed eyes, the butt of the joke, who is silent. On the table in front of him stand a salt shaker and a jar of salsa. As the others eat their lunch, he takes a lime out of his pocket, cuts and salts it, adds salsa, and then sucks it dry. *Sal y limón*— a poor man's oral rehydration salts.

I am concerned about the deep red circles below the man's eyes as well as the other crew members' seeming indifference to his condition. Why hasn't his *mayordomo* removed him from the heat and placed him with his coworker in the air-conditioned truck? "Are you going to go home?" I ask. His face is flushed red, like the others', but it is also covered by a visible film of sweat. The man pauses before he speaks, and the chatter of the table stops as the other crew members turn toward him, straining to hear his words. He speaks under his breath, as if fighting for air. "No, I'll be fine after the break," he says. I immediately realize I shouldn't have asked him anything at all. I have drawn further attention to him, and he is uncomfortable. A tall man seated in the middle—whom the men later identify as the crew's *mayordomo*—intervenes. He appears to wish to stop the line of questioning. "We won't be working the full day because of the heat," he informs me. "We'll be leaving at 2, 2:30." The men sitting next to him nod obligingly.

THE GENDERED DIVISION OF LABOR

Gendered constructions of male prowess and female frailty are inscribed in the division of labor in melon harvesting. Men take pride in working in the most physically taxing and dangerous jobs. Only men drive the tractors. On the field-packing machines, they work as pickers, shovers, and stackers. They trail the machine to pick melons in the open sun, and they shove boxes of melons down the conveyor belt leading from the field-packing device to the trailer. Men also work on top of the metal trailer, which has no protective canopy, lifting boxes of melons onto pallets stacked more than seven feet high.

FIGURE 4. In the gendered division of labor in the fields, women pack boxes of melon under a protective canopy, while men pick under the hot sun.

FIGURE 5. Men pick canary melons beside the field-packing machine, tossing them onto the machine for women to pack.

FIGURE 6. A stacker piling boxes of melons on the metal trailer in direct sun.

Women fill less strenuous jobs that involve less exposure to the sun. They round out melon-harvesting crews as packers, riding on the field-packing device, under the shade of the canopy. They stand on the machine's wings, folding sheets of cardboard into boxes. Packing and assembling boxes is seen as women's work, and men who engage in it face the stigma of debility. Only elderly men or men who have become sick from the heat deign to ride on the machine to pack or assemble boxes. Men view women's work as a temporary reprieve from the hard physical labor of picking and stacking.

The agricultural industry capitalizes on migrant men's pride in their work capacity. Supervisors use gendered barbs to encourage men's productivity, taunting men who become ill, like Miguelito, by saying they are merely "lazy" (*flojo*) or "weak." If middle-aged men are lagging in their work, supervisors may urge them on by saying that they can "no longer cut it" (*ya no la hace*), or worse, that "they have already hung up their gloves" (*ya colgó los guantes*). Meanwhile, they discipline women by implying that they cannot compete with men or by infantilizing them. For example, as Blanca told me, simply requesting that the tomato-harvesting

machine stop so that she could use the porta-potty would reduce her to the status of a *meona,* a bed-wetting child (see chapter 2).

Seventy-three percent of California's farmworkers are men.[13] Thus men establish a work ethic by which all workers are judged—one in which hard work is equated with masculinity. Even women feel compelled to uphold this ideal of manly prowess to be valued as members of the crew. Particularly adept female workers often assert their prowess by claiming quasi-male status. For example, one elderly farmworker recalls of her job in a packing shed, "I was a man driving that forklift." Thus even as women must conform to this norm of hard work, these gendered constructions of male worth place men at higher risk of heatstroke.

"Weak Hands"

Labor discipline is produced not only through the hierarchical organization of labor crews but also through the daily interactions of crew members. Farmworkers work in teams, and ensuring equivalent levels of effort and motivation is crucial to a team's success. Both workers' job security and their earnings depend on the efficacy of the crew as a whole. In contract work in particular, workers' pay is directly tied to the crew's performance, as the crew earns a set amount for every trailer or box it fills with melons. Thus coworkers as well as supervisors discipline underperforming workers by slighting their masculinity to spur productivity.

As seen above, supervisors and field hands portray labor power as intrinsically linked to masculinity. They blame field hands' illness on their constitutional weakness, in turn obscuring how the downward pressure of the labor hierarchy creates such illness. Thus these statements serve as a form of what Pierre Bourdieu calls *symbolic violence.* According to Bourdieu, symbolic violence is a process that masks the arbitrariness of the inequalities of the social order so that we come to perceive it as "natural." Because male dominance is imagined as rooted in innate biological superiority, Bourdieu uses the normalization of gender inequality as a case study in symbolic violence. Through symbolic messages and social interactions, dominant groups—such as men—assert the superiority of their position. Meanwhile, subordinate members—that is, women or "effeminate men"—internalize the dominant group's vision of the social order and come to view it as "just." As Bourdieu argues, subordinate members are made to feel sentiments such as "shame, humiliation, [and] anxiety" because of their difference from the male norm: such sentiments accept and uphold the justness of the social order itself.[14] The shame that

the ill fieldworker described above feels at being sick is the embodied imprint of symbolic domination.

Bourdieu points out that women are not the only victims of masculine domination. As he puts it, "Men are also prisoners, and insidiously victims, of the dominant representation." Men are the ultimate arbiters of "manliness;" they stand as sentries at the door of the exclusive club of "'real men' without weakness." Because they dread being demoted to the denigrated category of "'wimps,' 'girlies,' 'fairies,'" they overcompensate to prove their worth.[15] Symbolic violence not only legitimizes women's subordination but also justifies the violence men inflict on themselves and on each other. Manly honor, then, is an inaccessible and destructive ideal.

Symbolic violence serves to reproduce a social order in which manhood is linked to labor capacity; we will examine the social and political structures that generate this masculine ideal in the next chapter. This male ideal is not merely the reflection of gendered norms in Mexico and Central America; it has been intensified and transformed in the context of men's work in the United States. As men are forced to submit to rigid supervision that undermines their autonomy, many respond by emphasizing their labor capacity. Men's gender ideals must be understood within the context of their migration. Indeed, as we shall see in the next chapter, demotion to the category of "wimps" is particularly hurtful for migrant men because of the sacrifices they have made to fulfill their roles as providers.

These gendered barbs not only discipline lagging workers but also uphold a standard of tough masculinity by which all crew members are judged. By equating illness and breaks with weakness and effeminacy, migrant men set expectations for all crew members to work through illness, forgo breaks, and push themselves to the limit. As Bourdieu would argue, this ideal of masculinity is a trap. As men strive to prove their worthiness, they become prisoners of an elusive ideal of virility; when they fail—like the man above—they become its victims.

STACKERS: WORKERS WITH THE MOST "JUICE"

Saturday, June 29, 2013

Before evening falls, I decide to stop in to visit Sulema. After a fall from a tomato planting machine, she has been convalescing at home, while her nineteen-year-old son, Vicente, has been harvesting melon for a company called Maduro. His muddy shoes stand outside the door. Having changed out of his work clothes, he is slumped before the television on the couch in the living room with the blinds drawn.

Sulema, meanwhile, is vigorously washing out a large orange mini-cooler in the kitchen. She sets it to dry, and we sit at her kitchen table to chat. At the center of the table stands a shrine to preventing heat illness—a large salt shaker next to a wrought-iron bowl filled with limes.

Sulema sends Vicente to work each morning with the cooler filled with water, salt, and limes because he is working as a *cargador* (stacker), lifting and stacking boxes of melon on the trailer in direct sunlight. The job of *cargador,* which requires the heaviest physical exertion, is therefore typically reserved for the youngest and strongest men—men with the most *jugo* (juice). Each box weighs between twenty and forty pounds, and a *cargador* may fill seven to nine trailers each day. Each trailer carries a total of 736 boxes. Because the trailer has no protective awning, stackers are exposed to direct sunlight. In the noonday sun, farmworkers say, the metal floor of the trailer becomes a mirror; it reflects the sun's glare in a blur of blinding silver.

Sulema calls Vicente to join the conversation, and he stumbles over to the table with a yawn. His crew, he tells me, is working on contract. They arrive in the fields by 6 A.M. and try to meet their quota by 1 P.M., working swiftly to fill the trailers as quickly as possible. Because they are all young men, they have decided to forgo the state-mandated breaks. "We like to finish early. We try to beat the heat," he says, as Sulema shakes her head in concern.

Without breaks, and with new food-safety regulations limiting what workers can carry on the trailer, it is particularly hard for Vicente to drink. Stackers work farthest from the water jugs that are typically carried under the lip of the field-packing machine to which the trailer is attached. If Vicente were to request a cup of water, the machine would have to stop so that a coworker could fetch it for him. The only time he does drink, he says, is when the crew has filled an entire trailer; then work must stop in any case as the supervisor unhitches the trailer to take its precious cargo to the cooling shed.

In the past, Vicente used to tuck a water bottle into the back pocket of his jeans and take sips as he worked. But this year, Sulema says, the supervisors have become more strict (*corajudos*). They won't allow workers to bring their own water bottles onto the machine. They won't let them eat their lunches in the shade of its awning. All they talk about, Sulema says, is food safety inspections and salmonella.

Hence the orange cooler Sulema is cleaning: its bright orange serves as camouflage. "The coolers the supervisors bring for the crew are all orange," Vicente explains. He simply sets it on the trailer, and the

supervisors are none the wiser. "If they ask me what the cooler is doing there, I just say it belongs to a supervisor."

Sulema picks up a lime as though it were a talisman. "The supervisors all tell men to drink Gatorade. But salt and lime—it's the best protection against burning up," she says.

WHEN A BODY BURNS UP

In its campaign to prevent heat illness among outdoor workers, the state refers to heat illness as *insolación,* literally excessive exposure to sunlight.[16] Farmworkers sometimes use a related word, *soleado,* when referring to sun exposure. But for heatstroke, they most commonly use the colloquial term *quemarse,* "to burn up." The term is apt because heatstroke is both an acute and a chronic condition: once it strikes, the body is more susceptible to suffering it again. Burning up moves a healthy, productive body into the ranks of *los quemados*—those whose bodies bear an invisible susceptibility to heat. Once a body burns up, its *jugo* cannot be replenished. For this reason, heatstroke may spell not only the end of a farmworker's job but also the end of his career: it marks a worker as permanently depleted and may bar him from future employment.

As a strong nineteen-year-old, Vicente shrugs off the danger posed by working as a stacker in the summer heat. He is confident that he can "cut it" (*hacerla*), and that his body will not betray him. Yet Vicente's show of indifference masks a darker reality. Heatstroke, burning up, would permanently mark his body as spent. Thus working in high heat places migrant men in a double bind. They are unwilling to take breaks for fear of appearing weak, yet they risk being marked as "finished" if they succumb to heat illness.

Once heatstroke has hit, it may be just a matter of time before it will strike again. Thus a burned-up farmworker is a financial liability and a safety risk for his crewmembers and supervisor. As Elisabeta puts it: "They say of people who get heatstroke, '*Ya se quemó*' [he already burned up]. If a *mayordomo* tells a worker, 'Yes, and Fulano [So-and-So] will round out our crew,' that worker will say: 'Fulano? But don't you remember, he's the one who burned up last year! [*¡ese es el que se quemó el año pasado!*]' They won't ask him to work again."

Sunday, June 30, 2013

The thermometer in my car reads 112 when I pull up to the fields where Fresco is harvesting. It has been the third straight day of record heat in the

Valley, with the mercury consistently topping 105 degrees. As I step out of the air-conditioned car onto the gravel and am enveloped by warmth, I notice that at least today a faint breeze offers a reprieve from the heat. I can see it blowing gently through the trees in the adjacent apricot orchard.

As I walk to the field, Samuel's crew is climbing onto the machine, which is slowly drifting out into the field. They have just finished their lunch break. Miguelito jumps off the machine and runs over, excited. "You missed the ambulance! A guy from the other crew burned up yesterday," he says, pointing to the next crew over. I thank him for the tip and walk over to find out what happened.

The *mayordomo* stays to chat with me as the rest of his crew boards the machine to finish the afternoon's work. He is a squat Salvadoran man with silver grills around his front teeth. He is wearing jeans, a long-sleeved polo shirt, and a sombrero to protect himself from the sun.

The *mayordomo* keeps glancing down at my notebook, as though worried about what I am writing down. He speaks quickly and with concern and occasionally shakes his head. "The boy [*muchacho*] was only twenty-two," the *mayordomo* says, and he didn't see it coming.

Usually you can tell when workers are burning up, he says: they develop deep red crescents under their eyes. When he sees the warning signs, he sends workers to the van to sit in the air conditioning. But Jairo was young and strong; he had worked on his crew before, cutting broccoli and weeding cotton. He had never before showed signs of *insolación*.

It happened at 3 P.M., during the afternoon break. The crew had sat down under the *casitas* by the side of the field, as usual. The *mayordomo* had asked them how they felt, and they had responded—almost in unison—"*Bien.*" Jairo was drinking Gatorade, he says, and then he began to sway. "It looked like he wanted to faint," he remembers. "When someone gets heat illness [*se insola*], you have to clear room for them so they can breathe. So I pushed everyone away, and then I fanned him with my hat to give him air. I grabbed hold of his arms. But his arms were already tensing up; he was already starting to convulse [*acalambrear*]." The young man's body, he says, was on the brink of shock.

I ask whether there were any clues that could have alerted the company to Jairo's risk for burning up. Could anything have been done to prevent this? The *mayordomo* is sullenly quiet for a while; it is clear that he has mulled this question over himself. Then he shakes his head. "*Ni hombre,*" he says. "When people come from the coasts, you have to watch them. When they come from Salinas, when they come from Santa María, you have to be careful because they're from the cool coasts. But this boy, no—

this boy was from here, he had worked in the broccoli before, he had worked in the *azadón* [weeding]. But it was his first day as *cargador*. And up there on the *traila*, where they stack the boxes, it's an inferno. If it's 100 degrees here, on the ground, it's 112 up there. Because the metal of the *traila* floor reflects the sun. There's no awning like on the machine. And you're lifting and stacking boxes—that's the heaviest job there is."[17]

I consider what the *mayordomo* says. I know that the state's heat-illness regulations include measures that kick in to protect workers when the temperature exceeds 95 degrees. Supervisors are required to give new workers time to "'acclimatize' to the heat;"—supervisors must "lessen the intensity" of their work or reduce the "shift length." The regulations recommend that supervisors "provide close supervision" of workers in their first two weeks on the job and be "extra-vigilant" with those who may have not yet acclimatized to the high temperatures.[18] "Were you watching him closely because it was his first day stacking?" I ask. "Were you monitoring him because it's the heaviest job there is?"

He looks at the ground and does not answer the question. "The boy seemed fine," he says.

He shifts in his shoes and then launches into a complaint. What makes his job particularly hard, he says, is that workers rarely speak up when they're not feeling well. "They don't say anything," he says plaintively. "And if they don't say anything, how can you know? Especially if they're not showing symptoms. They *must* know they're not feeling well. When you get heatstroke, you get nausea. You start to vomit. You *know*. But no one wants to speak up."

Later that afternoon, I spot a white truck driving slowly towards us on the dirt track at the edge of the field, spewing a trail of dust. The *mayordomo*'s supervisor, Steve, has heard about the visitor poking around in the fields and is coming to investigate.

Steve's height and attire—jeans, a short-sleeved polo shirt, and a pair of sunglasses—immediately distinguish him from the workers in the fields. He has worked as a food safety supervisor for Fresco for eight years. "The food inspections are the worst," he says. This year Fresco has already had eight state food-safety inspections and passed them all. Last year, though, it failed its first two inspections, before the company owner hired more staff to work on the issue. He says that Cal-OSHA has visited Fresco's pepper harvesters once this season to ensure supervisors' adherence to the heat-illness standard. "And they passed the inspection like nothing," Steve says.

According to Steve, food safety inspections have increased dramatically over the past two years. Last year, to counteract the bad press from a severe multistate listeriosis outbreak linked to fresh cantaloupe in Colorado in 2011, the largest cantaloupe producers and distributors in the state—through their trade association, the California Cantaloupe Advisory Board (CCAB)—produced their own checklists specifying how cantaloupe should be grown, harvested, packed, and cooled. The checklists, based on the federal Food and Drug Administration's own guidelines to minimize the contamination of fresh produce, were in turn approved by the state and federal departments of agriculture.[19] Now Fresco, along with all the state's major cantaloupe producers, must undergo at least one unannounced and one announced audit by state inspectors each year. "It's all about maintaining public confidence," Steve says. If Fresco fails an audit, it must show that it has corrected the problem in a repeat audit if it is to continue to brand its produce as CCAB-certified and thereby gain access to a large market.

Steve says that in melon harvesting, state food safety inspectors check that the workers are not eating or drinking on the machines; that no one is driving the tractor but the tractor driver or the foreman; that no one is smoking; and that the workers don't have any exposed skin and are wearing gloves.[20] "Melon is high risk for *E. coli* or salmonella," he says. Last year, Fresco began prohibiting workers from drinking and eating on the trailer, tractor, and field-packing machine to comply with the CCAB's food safety guidelines.[21]

We talk about the heat and Jairo's hospitalization yesterday. Steve politely answers my questions and expresses his concern. In his view, what felled the young man was an unfortunate confluence of events. "It's hard with the heat," he says, shaking his head. "Yesterday we had four guys that wanted to faint, one that did. It's rough for the *mayordomos;* it's a lot for them to have to worry about," he says.

I ask what the *mayordomos* do for the men who wanted to faint. "They set 'em in the vans with the air conditioning on and monitor them. They give 'em something to drink. If it gets worse, they call the ambulance. No point in trying to play around and be heroes," Steve says.

Steve emphasizes that the supervisors did what they could given the circumstances. "The season just started, and at the same time we got a heat wave. That's a bad turn of events." He tells me that Fresco is a good company. "Other companies—they don't worry as much. But we get training in first aid. We learn how to perform CPR. We watch a whole video on it," he says.

So what happened with Jairo? I ask. Why did he faint? "It was too hot," Steve replies. "It was his first day working, and it was 106. His body wasn't accustomed to the heat." Skirting the issue of whether his *mayordomo* should have been monitoring the youth more closely, Steve asserts that the youth's hospitalization was a victory. The *mayordomo* was proactive, spotting the young man's heatstroke and removing him from the fields in time. He called an ambulance, preventing a worse outcome. Last week, he says, the company also sent home a man picking bell peppers, also for heat illness.

I think about Elisabeta's point that heatstroke fells a worker for life, that a worker who has "burned up" will never return to work at the same pace. Will Jairo get his job back, I ask? Now that his body has burned up, will it be difficult for him to get work in the melon fields again? Steve nods. "Well, he needs his *papelito* [little paper] from the doctor to say he's ready to work again," he says. "But this is a good company—they care about their workers. So he'll get his job back. He'll work again—but not as a stacker. He can work picking, maybe even packing melons. But he won't go back to work on the metal trailer in the open sun."

STATE ENFORCEMENT: ENABLING THE CODE OF SILENCE

The complaint of the *mayordomo* above, that workers do not speak up when feeling ill, draws attention to the code of silence that shrouds heat illness. It illuminates the pressures of a farm labor hierarchy that eliminates underperforming members—whether ill or slow— for the sake of expedience. Yet, as both supervisors' narratives show, state policies and industry profits also increase migrant farmworkers' risk of heatstroke. Cal-OSHA's anemic enforcement of the state's heat-illness regulations has done little to break this code of silence. Meanwhile, the cantaloupe industry's heightened concern for implementing food safety rules to ensure consumer confidence works at cross purposes with the state's regulations to protect against dehydration and heat illness.

Cal-OSHA itself has acknowledged that farm work presents challenges to state regulation and inspection, which are exacerbated by inadequate agency funding.[22] As of 2009, Cal-OSHA had only 187 inspectors to monitor more than a million workplaces in California, including an estimated thirty-five thousand farms. The agency can rarely investigate a complaint on the day it is lodged, and when inspectors do finally show up, employers may be in compliance. In 2007, state safety inspectors

found that more than half the farms they audited were in violation of the state's protective legislation.[23] In 2012, employer compliance had slightly improved; Cal-OSHA audited four thousand farms and found that a quarter were in violation of the heat illness standard.[24]

In 2009, the American Civil Liberties Union (ACLU) sued Cal-OSHA, charging that the agency was inadequately equipped to protect its outdoor workers. It argued that Cal-OSHA must go beyond merely requiring that employers provide workers with water and shade, the only protections initially offered by the state in 2005. The plaintiff recommended that employers be required to provide an additional five-minute break in "high-heat" conditions. The day after the organization filed suit, Cal-OSHA announced it would adopt a modified version of the recommended change. This modification created the heat illness prevention standard currently in force, stating that a shade structure large enough to shelter a quarter of a team should be erected once the temperature exceeds 85°F and that employees should be "allowed and encouraged" to take a break in the shade "to protect themselves from overheating."[25]

In the summer of 2012—during which there were four confirmed heat deaths among farmworkers—the question of the state's competence in enforcing its regulations arose once again. The UFW sued Cal-OSHA for "systematic failure" to enforce the law, blaming the deaths on agency negligence. The suit alleged that the agency did not follow up complaints of violations to its hotline, failed to initiate inspections on time, and did not cite or adequately fine violators.[26] It claimed that in the summer of 2011, the UFW had helped farmworkers report seventy-eight violations of the standard, yet only three were investigated.

The UFW suit contained a long list of such violations, including an example involving twenty-five workers at Valpredo Farms who were observed working in 90-degree heat with only a beach umbrella for shade. Another crew was working without any shade structure at all. Although a UFW organizer filed a complaint through the Cal-OSHA hotline, it took two weeks for the agency to investigate. When Cal-OSHA inspectors finally arrived on the scene, there were no workers at the site, and the agency subsequently closed the case.[27]

Cal-OSHA's lax enforcement of state law helps explain why migrant farmworkers continue to put their work before their health despite state assurances that they are entitled to breaks. Bourdieu's theory of habituated action illustrates this. Bourdieu suggests that individuals develop a sense of what they can expect in particular situations based on past experience, resulting in a "hysteresis effect": a lag between deliberate changes to social

structures and their effect on individuals' behavior.[28] Because habituated behavior occurs largely at a level below consciousness, the state's billboards and campaign to encourage preventive behaviors make little sense. In order to change farmworkers' behaviors, the state must normalize the practice of taking breaks by transforming the multiple policies that impinge on their work environments—and, as a first step, by enforcing its protective laws.

In addition, the state's approval of industry food-safety guidelines directly contradicts its stated concern for workers' health. The section of the CCAB guidelines devoted to "worker hygiene" prohibits workers from taking "personal items" into the harvest area and from eating or drinking on the farm machinery.[29] When I ask the vice president of a local cantaloupe company—who is also a member of the CCAB—whether the guidelines are indeed meant to prevent all cantaloupe harvesters from rehydrating on top of the machinery, he confirms the fact. "Well, let me tell ya. One of the common concerns in California is heat stress. When you get into consumables, like beers, sodas, Red Bulls, it's not only bad for their health, but it violates the heat stress/illness protocols," he says. This grower thus paternalistically draws on the heat illness law to justify the food safety guidelines, representing measures intended to safeguard industry profits as necessary to protect workers from themselves.

When supervisors prohibit workers from carrying their own water supplies onto the farm equipment, they make workers entirely dependent on the company-provided water stored underneath the field-packing device. Because production must halt in order for workers to access the water source, men typically follow the code of silence and refrain from drinking. Women often grumble inwardly as they outwardly comply with this norm. To avoid asking for the machine to stop, for example, Elisabeta hides a water bottle under a cardboard box so she can steal small sips. Yet drinking water inevitably means having to use the porta-potties, which also requires halting the field-packing machine so that workers can descend safely. To avoid this, *mayordomos* often encourage workers to urinate into the fields. Because women like Elisabeta consider this practice *cochino,* or "gross," they often forgo drinking large amounts of water. In sum, it is disingenuous to create a state law to protect farmworker safety without examining how food safety policies, combined with the pressure of the farm labor hierarchy, shape farmworkers' behaviors and undermine the state's new protections.

The state sends the workers a mixed message: its approval of rules to protect consumers from contaminated fruit directly contradicts its stated concern to protect workers from heat illness. To cope with the

regulations, workers smuggle water sources onto the machines and urinate in the field. Because the industry rules fail to take into account the pressures of labor crews, then, they backfire: they not only place workers at risk but also threaten consumer safety.

Sunday, June 30, 2013

As I drive back to Mendota that afternoon, an official from Cal-OSHA is speaking as the invited guest on a call-in program on how to prevent heat illness that is airing on the region's bilingual radio station.

The guest, Hector, is informing the audience of risk factors for heat illness as well as how to prevent it. He urges workers to drink Gatorade (unless they are diabetic) and other electrolyte-rich drinks, and to avoid caffeinated energy drinks like Red Bull. Workers should cover their bodies to protect themselves from the sun, but they should make sure that their protective clothing is lightweight and reflective of the sun. And it's important, he urges, for workers to remember the exact coordinates of the location of the field where they're working so they can inform the paramedics in case an emergency occurs.

And then there are their rights. He tells the audience that once the temperature passes 85 degrees, workers are allowed a minimum five-minute break. If a worker needs a break, he should inform the contractor that he knows he has the right to rest. And if the temperature rises above 95 degrees, a set of enhanced protections kicks in. The supervisor needs to accompany each crew and actively monitor its members for signs of heat illness.

What happens, the host of the show asks Hector, if a contractor or *mayordomo* refuses to honor a worker's request for shade? If the supervisor is negligent, Hector answers, Cal-OSHA will fine the company. He concludes his presentation by giving the workers a number they can call to complain and by directing them to the state's website.

The radio crackles as Hector fields calls. A woman wants to know what can be done when the contractors rush people more (*acarrea más a la gente*). What protection does the state offer workers from demanding supervisors? Can workers report contractors for attempting to accelerate the pace of work when it is particularly hot? Hector repeats that workers have the right to request a break when the thermometer hits 85 degrees, and that they can report their contractor to Cal-OSHA if they refuse. "Oh," the woman says flatly, and then hangs up.

A man calls in and asks what his crew can do when the *mayordomos* bring water that "tastes like chlorine" (*cloro*). Hector replies that by law, the water needs to be cool, but the regulations state only that it needs to be potable.

A woman calls in and speaks in a taut voice. On her crew, she says, four people suffered heatstroke last week and were sent to the doctor. The doctor said they had nothing wrong with them and should return to work. All four were fired. They reported the incident to Cal-OSHA, but so far, she says, the company has not even been fined.

Hector attempts to address her complaint, his voice growing tight. He says that the workers are entitled to a second opinion. He says that the state investigators are still working through the complaints left on the complaint line. The state only has so many inspectors, he says.

The next caller has no question, only an observation. "I just wanted to say, a farmworker has the rights of a dog in the street [*un perro en la calle*]," he says. He spits the aspirated *p* of the word, *perro* into the phone, and before Hectors can reply, a dial tone punctuates the caller's remark.

I am cooling down from the afternoon's visit in my air-conditioned motel room when I get a call from Yadira. Her friend's boyfriend fainted because of heatstroke yesterday, and she asks whether I would like to go visit him in the hospital in Fresno. She knows I am interested in such things, she says. Because both of them are undocumented and have no drivers' license, they would appreciate the safety of a ride. The sun is setting when I pick up Yadira and her friend, a forty-year-old woman called Martita, for the drive to Fresno.

Martita is dressed for the occasion with rhinestone-studded sandals, jeans, and a pink polo shirt. She fills me in about the young man as we drive. She says she tried to visit him last night, but he was still in the emergency room when she arrived at 8:30; he was only stabilized and admitted to the hospital at 1:30 A.M. She says he is a young boy [*mozo*] who arrived in the Valley from Guatemala just last year; he is still learning the ropes of farm work and working hard to repay his debts from his undocumented passage. Martita hopes she can take care of him when he is released from the hospital. "He lives in a house with five other men, but they don't take good care of themselves. They don't eat well, and he doesn't have any family here," she says. "I try to cook for him, and he tells me, 'Martita, you are my little angel, my precious *mamacita*.'"

As we drive, it becomes clear that she is speaking of Jairo, the young man who fainted at Fresco. "He called me from the ambulance yesterday," she says. "He said, 'Martita, you know where I am? I'm in an ambulance going to Fresno.' I thought he was joking."

She tells me that the pair met when they were planting tomato for Álvarez Contracting. They worked as a team. She rode on a planting wheel and placed tomato seedlings into its slots; his job was to walk behind and ensure they were planted. "And he was different. He was such a gentleman [*muy caballero*], very caring. He wanted to take care of me, you know?"

When we arrive at the hospital and obtain our visitors' passes, we find Jairo's older brother standing in the hallway outside his room, making a phone call. He has driven two and a half hours from the Salinas Valley. Martita greets him, and they discuss the young man in quiet tones. The brother reassures her that he seems to be doing fine, and the hospital will release him tomorrow. Martita asks whether the company is paying for his care. "So far," the brother says. She asks how the brother is planning to proceed. "If they behave well, we're all good. But if something comes up on the medical exams, then we'll get a lawyer," he tells her. He is referring to the fact that companies test injured workers for preexisting conditions—such as high blood alcohol levels—that relieve the company from liability and thereby from paying for a worker's medical care.

Inside the room, Jairo is lying in a hospital bed with a heart monitor attached to his chest. He has a full, round face and dark hair. We enter very slowly, and Martita approaches his bed and places her hand on his damp forehead.

Jairo opens his eyes and greets her. After a day and a half in the hospital, he is lucid but still seems weak. Without sitting up or moving his head, he tells the story of what happened.

It was his first season in the melon fields. The *mayordomo* had asked him to round out his crew, and he had asked to work as a *cargador*. Because he was young and strong, he thought he could handle it. *Cargadores* are compensated for the risk of the work by earning a dollar more per hour than the other melon harvesters. By working as a *cargador,* Jairo says, he could reimburse his brothers sooner for his debts. He told the *mayordomo* he had never worked as a stacker before. "And he said he would show me how," Jairo says. But when he was out in the fields on the trailer, the *mayordomo* never came over once to check on him. "And it was hot that day," he says. "And with the heat of the *traila*, it was even worse."

He describes how it happened. "It was on the third break, at three. I was sitting under the shade. And I couldn't see well, and I started to feel cold, and things that were very close suddenly seemed very far away. And then there were people running towards me," he remembers. "They caught me so I wouldn't fall." His brother mutters something under his breath.

Jairo says that if he hadn't fainted, it would have been someone else. "Everyone was getting sick that day, but no one said anything," he says. "I talked to a guy on my crew today. He said it's a good thing that I got sick, because then they took everyone out."

Jairo's brother's mutter explodes into an audible curse. "*Hijo de puta* [assholes]. That's what they do. Even if it's too hot. If no one faints, they just don't stop" (*si no cae alguién, no paran*).

As we drive home that evening, I think about what Jairo's story reveals about the causes of workers' silence. His story highlights the kinds of structural vulnerabilities that cause young, recently arrived men to assume the risk of jobs as *cargadores,* as they face hefty migration debts that make the additional pay attractive. It also points to a counternarrative that unsettles supervisors' complaints that workers don't speak up when they are ill. The state's billboards and supervisors' own statements place the onus on workers for their own safety. Yet as Jairo suggests, supervisors collude with workers by turning a blind eye to the visible signs of heat illness. Jairo's fainting broke the code of silence and forced supervisors to acknowledge the reality that was unfolding before their eyes. It takes a coworker's heatstroke to relieve other crew members from maintaining the code of silence.

Wednesday, July 3, 2013

Several days after Jairo has been discharged from the hospital, Yadira tells me what happened to him. The day after he was released, she took him to the Fresco company offices, where he gave a report of his illness. Fresco sent someone to accompany him to a doctor under contract with the company's insurance provider. She says she doesn't know what the doctor said, but he performed a series of tests and cleared the young man to work again. Fresco did not claim that he had any preexisting conditions that had led to his heat illness, so workers' compensation covered his hospitalization. The company hired him back.

But Jairo told his *mayordomo* that he didn't want to work picking melon any longer, and he switched to picking corn. That is a tough

job as well, Yadira says: the corn stalks grow tall and thick, blocking the circulation of air. The stalks are covered by a sticky substance called *guate* that makes your hands and arms itch. The more you sweat, the more you itch, so workers protect their skin with long-sleeved shirts.

Yadira says that Jairo likely made a calculated career decision to protect his body from the sun. To prevent heat deaths, corn harvesting now occurs at night. "He probably moved to the corn because he knows that now he could burn up," she says.

I ask, "If corn is now harvested at night, why can't melon harvesting be changed to the nighttime as well?" Yadira pauses. "Because nobody wants a green melon. Men have to be able to see the color of the melons so that they can pick them when they're ripe," she says with a wan smile.

Thursday, July 4, 2013

A few days later, I return to talk with Samuel and his crew. As we sit underneath a shade structure by the side of the road, their faces are red and swollen. They have been working since 6 A.M., and they are ready to go home. It is their last break of the day; they will stop shortly before 3 P.M.

Jairo's hospitalization is on everyone's minds. "Has anyone visited him?" Samuel asks. Had Jairo been discharged from the hospital, and when did the other crew's *mayordomo* say he would return? I tell them about visiting him on Sunday night, and we trade updates and news. Why had Jairo gotten heatstroke, I ask—why *him?* I want to know how the men understand the causes of heat illness and where they place the blame. Was the young man's illness the result of the individual-level behaviors that the state and supervisors are wont to emphasize: not drinking enough water or not asking for a break? Was it due to his *mayordomo*'s negligence and his company's turning a blind eye despite its workers' visible signs of fatigue? Was he the casualty of heightened food-safety regulations that compromise workers' rehydration, or of the state and its inadequate inspections? Or should we fault the invisible pressures this recently arrived man carried into the fields, where he deliberately chose the most dangerous job to earn more money? How, I wonder, is it even possible to separate individual behaviors from the social and political structures that shaped them, and which align so seamlessly to produce heat illness in the fields?

The men first hazard explanations they have heard in safety trainings that emphasize the need for shade, rehydration, and the importance of acclimatization. "*Pues,* it was his first day working on the *traila,*"

retorts a short man with a baseball cap abruptly as he takes a swig from a small plastic bottle. "His body wasn't used to the heat," offers another with a shrug. Then Samuel interrupts, fielding a more elaborate theory—imaginative and complex. It fuses an understanding of sweat as essential to cooling the body with a popular idea of the innate fitness of particular bodies for certain kinds of work. The men grow quiet and lean in closer around the table as they discuss the question of why some bodies burn up while others don't.

Some people, Samuel proposes, are simply better able to cope with heat than others. Different bodies are created with different capacities. Some bodies can labor better and harder, and others, he says surprisingly, lack the sweat glands that protect laborers. "Some bodies can withstand more. But other bodies don't even sweat. If they don't sweat, when it actually cools down, they won't be refreshed. So they have limited ability to work. Those bodies that don't sweat can only work seven hours or less. They burn up more rapidly," he says.

A man at the end of the table chimes in eagerly to elaborate on Samuel's argument. "Because not all bodies work or tire at the same pace [*al mismo ritmo*]," he agrees. "So you have to check how you're doing. Some of us are weaker than others; we are not all made the same."

The crew seems mollified by a theory that conveniently boils heat deaths down to an unfortunate physical defect. As Bourdieu would put it, they appear to have absorbed the ideal of masculine hardiness expressed in supervisors' gendered barbs and reinforced by labor crews. Bourdieu argues that symbolic violence produces a misrecognition of social inequality as "just" by portraying it as rooted in innate biological differences. Thus portraying ill workers as constitutionally deficient obscures how the farm labor hierarchy, combined with U.S. immigration and labor policies, combine to create heatstroke.

Then a short man with a very red face lets out a sigh, shaking his head skeptically. "*Ni hombre,*" he says with a growing smirk. "It's not that some bodies are simply weaker, it's that some companies just push them more. Before, companies used to just push, push, push to squeeze out every last drop of sweat they could [*sacarles la última gota de sudor*]."

Miguelito, who is wearing his straw hat with a tear in the front, pipes up, as though emboldened by the short man's skepticism. He grins, revealing front teeth framed by silver grills. "Before, I used to pick melon with a sack," he says. His eyes are distant as he recalls an earlier era of farm work, before the invention of the field-packing machine in the 1990s allowed the consolidation of picking and packing. Back then, demand for

labor in the fields and in the packing sheds was high. Work was plentiful and well reimbursed. He migrated from Mexico to work for Fresco each harvest season between 1985 and 1992. That was when companies always paid workers a set fee or piece rate for every truck of melon they filled.

Miguelito gestures at the open melon fields stretching toward the aqueduct, an area measuring roughly 150 acres. "Before, we would pick this whole area with four crews. In two hours." He draws a circle in the air that settles over the field on which we and seven other machine crews are harvesting, the glint of the far-off aqueduct, and the expanse of cloudless sky above. "People would die," he continues. "Every summer, three or four people would die in the melon," he repeats. "But no one cared then. No one paid attention. Because before, we workers had no say. But now there is a will and there is a way," he says (*porque antes, no ponían importancia. Porque no había voz ni mando. Pero ahora, hay voz y hay mando*).

Samuel nods his head. "Now, people are paying attention," he agrees.

The short man chimes in. Last year, he says, there were two deaths at Fresco—one in harvesting corn and the other melon.

I frown. I say I have heard that Fresco is one of the more responsible companies when it comes to worker safety. The short man dismisses this with a sardonic laugh. "Last year they were as bad as any other. Last year they brought one shade structure for a whole field of ten machines [crews]. And the water was warm and nasty. But this year, yes—every crew has its shade, they bring ice water, we have breaks. This year we work eight, nine, ten hours. Last year, we worked twelve or thirteen hours each day. It was obligatory."

"Because if you miss a day, the fruit rots," says another.

Lunch over, we walk to climb back onto the machine before it sets off into the field. As we trudge up the melon rows, the heat envelops us like a humid blanket. I think about the metaphor of *jugo* that men use to describe the "freshest" bodies—the ones, like those of Vicente and Jairo, who are deemed best fitted to work on the trailer in the open sun as stackers and shovers. It strikes me that there is an inverse relationship between a farmworker's *jugo* and a melon's. A farmworker's juice is depleted so that a melon's is preserved.

Conducting participant-observation in the fields shows that farmworkers' work behaviors cannot be separated from the immediate work and broader policy contexts that shape them. In introducing an intermediate layer of supervisors who must maximize field hands' labor to make a

profit, IRCA intensified the productivity pressures field hands face. Because men constitute the majority of fieldworkers, they establish a norm of labor capacity to which all workers aspire. Meanwhile, coworkers and supervisors enforce this standard to expedite production; they portray underperforming men as effeminate and deride women as weak. As men comply with the code of silence and work through high heat, they maintain their masculinity while facilitating the transfer of value to their employers.

Yet the efficacy of supervisors' gendered barbs, and men's desires to mask their vulnerability, cannot be understood by examining migrants' immediate work contexts alone. As we shall see in the next chapter, labor and immigration policies shape migrants' degree of economic security and therefore their need for work. Meanwhile, migrant men's proletarianization in the United States has helped forge the ideal of masculinity enacted on labor crews. Migrant men's work behaviors must be examined within the broader historical and political contexts that shape them.

CHAPTER 2

Entering Farm Work

Migration and Men's Work Identities

Manuel, who came to Mendota from Mexico in 1988 at the age of sixteen, remembers his first days of farm work very clearly. He came to the United States as an undocumented migrant with his father, Don Santiago, who himself had migrated to California's Central Valley each spring to provide for his family since 1970.[1] Manuel had worked on his father's small plot of land in La Capellanía, Zacatecas, since he was nine, tilling the fields with what he describes as "a plow made of sticks." Despite his farmworking background, he was unprepared for the fast pace of work and the rigid supervision he endured in the Central Valley. "With someone yelling at you and telling you that you have to go faster, that you can never stop for one minute, that was something I had never experienced before," he remembers. "When we were working really fast, some men even urinated in the fields so they would not have to stop to go to the bathroom."

As a new arrival, Manuel lacked the contacts to land one of the coveted jobs on a small family farm, where the pace is calmer. As an undocumented migrant, he was ineligible for work in packing and processing sheds, where work is better paid, year round, and additionally carries benefits. Instead he found work on *cuadrillas,* or labor crews, supervised by *mayordomos* and contractors. He harvested melon in the summer and fall and pruned almond trees and picked broccoli in the winter; in the spring, he spent his days weeding. Manuel remembers that his body gradually adjusted to the stooping required, the pace of the team,

and his field boss's demands. "When you pick and weed, you're hunched over all day. You only stand up at breaks. And you just have to keep going; no one wants to fall behind and draw the attention of the *mayordomo,*" he says.

This chapter examines Mexican and Salvadoran men's experiences of farm work, in both their countries of origin and the United States, as a means of explaining the disproportionate rates of occupational injuries and deaths among them. The peasant backgrounds of such men have made hard work a sign of masculine competence and the basis of self-worth. Emigration becomes a means of maintaining their dignity and their roles as providers when struggling family farms no longer provide a living. Yet the hierarchical organization of the labor crews where men like Manuel find jobs transforms their male identities. It places emphasis on their speed and strength even as it threatens their autonomy. The organization of contemporary industrial agriculture generates a habitus that discourages men from taking breaks when they are ill or injured, even as their exclusion from social assistance makes work the only means of economic security available to them.

MIGRATION CIRCUITS: LINKING RURAL MEXICO AND EL SALVADOR TO THE CENTRAL VALLEY

Scholars have long observed that whereas political-economic forces propel migration, social networks enable it. Prospective migrants turn to friends and family for information and assistance with their journeys, creating unique patterns of migration between particular sending and receiving communities.[2] In Mendota, migrants hail primarily from central Zacatecas and western Michoacán, two Mexican states that have long sent migrants to the United States, and Cabañas, a rural province in eastern El Salvador. Within these regions, Mendota has close links with three small "sister towns" in particular: Las Ánimas, Zacatecas; El Platanal, Michoacán (a town whose name means "the banana plantation"); and Sensuntepeque, Cabañas. For migrants from these towns, Mendota is but an extension of their communities. "When someone from El Platanal comes to Mendota, they know exactly on whose couch they will sleep while they try to find work, they may even know the foreman at some job," says Ricardo, whose father, Don Octavio, is one of the first *bananánecos* (as people from El Platanal are affectionately called) to settle in Mendota. Meanwhile, Salvadoran migrants have recreated some of the geography of Sensuntepeque in this small agricultural town: a corner

store named Sensunte marks the Salvadoran ghetto of Mendota, and a restaurant named Cabañas proudly serves traditional fare from both Mexico (*menudo*) and El Salvador (*pupusas*).

Mexican and Salvadorans have different histories of migration to the Valley, each shaped by U.S. trade and foreign policy. Because of a strong demand for their labor, men have migrated from central Mexico to California to work in agriculture since the late nineteenth century. This pattern was intensified by the bracero program, which imported 4.6 million men to work in the southwestern United States as agricultural laborers and on the railroads between 1942 and 1964, and which thus linked migration networks in the classic sending areas in Mexico even more tightly to the Central Valley.[3] In stadiums in Mexico, authorities selected men with a peasant background and callused hands; meanwhile, in reception centers in the United States, officials deloused and vaccinated potential applicants, sprayed them with DDT, and screened them for parasites and physical ailments.[4] This process changed the way Mexican men understood themselves, introducing them to the racialized objectification they would face in California's fields.[5] It also made tiny farming towns like Mendota household names in rural Mexican communities thousands of miles away.

The passage of the North American Free Trade Agreement (NAFTA) in 1994 spurred greater emigration from Mexico by exacerbating an inhospitable environment for farming. In the name of free trade, NAFTA required that Mexico remove taxes on U.S. imports, even as heavy U.S. government subsidies for agriculture make it difficult for Mexican producers to compete with U.S.-grown crops. NAFTA allowed the United States to flood Mexico with cheap corn, putting many rural farmers out of business.[6] As a result, many people from Las Ánimas say they are now more likely to run into an old neighbor on the streets of Mendota than in their hometown, and it is a truism that there are more *bananecos* in Mendota than in El Platanal itself. "Almost everyone lives here now," says Don Octavio.

Whereas Mexican migrants have a long tradition of migration to the Central Valley, Salvadorans began arriving in the area only in the late 1970s.[7] The first Salvadorans came to Mendota as economic migrants. Many first arrived in Los Angeles—a historic hub of Salvadoran settlement—but relocated to Fresno County in search of a calmer, more agricultural lifestyle. These arrivals blazed the trail for an unprecedented wave of refugee settlement after 1980, when a military coup sparked El Salvador's civil war. Rural eastern El Salvador, including the sending

provinces of Cabañas and Cuscatlán, became a stronghold for the coalition of left-wing guerrilla forces that formed the Farabundo Martí National Liberation Front (FMLN) and thus bore the brunt of the upheaval. Viewing the conflict as an extension of its Cold War priorities, the United States exacerbated the region's political instability by providing the right-wing government with financial support and military training. As ordinary civilians in these provinces faced the risk of being treated as collaborators targeted for "neutralization" by U.S.-backed government forces, United States involvement further fueled the outmigration.[8]

Since the signing of an official peace agreement in 1992 by the FMLN, the Salvadoran armed forces, and a civilian government, a crime wave has continued to convulse El Salvador in a manner reminiscent of the civil war itself.[9] The mass deportation of low-level offenders from the United States has transnationalized organized crime while importing new gang rivalries.[10] The United States' "War on Drugs"—which funded operations against the drug trade in Colombia and Mexico—had the ironic effect of diverting drug traffickers to Central America, further disrupting the region. To combat this, the United States has entered into regional "security agreements" with countries in the Northern Triangle of Central America (El Salvador, Honduras, and Guatemala). The U.S-funded expansion of police and military forces only fuels the existing tumult.[11] These three countries now lead the world in homicide rates: once-clear lines of wartime brutality have been replaced by the unpredictable violence of organized crime, gangs, and paramilitarism.[12] Thus recent U.S. trade and foreign policy have further destabilized agricultural livelihoods and intensified emigration.

MEXICAN PATRIARCHS' CIRCULAR MIGRATION TO THE VALLEY

The bracero program enshrined migration to the United States as an accepted strategy of achieving upward socioeconomic mobility in rural Mexico. Circular migration to work in agriculture in the U.S. became the means by which Mexican men earned money to purchase new land or maintain the farms they inherited when they no longer afforded a living. Emigration was a strategy to promote intergenerational socioeconomic mobility as well, as men hoped to pass their farms on to their children. After the bracero program ended in 1964, a second generation of Mexican men migrated to the United States undocumented in order to maintain their responsibilities as providers.

Don Octavio is one of these men, known as "El General" for his legendary work ethic. After his mother died when he was a child, his father remarried and had more children. Don Octavio's father had purchased a family farm of five acres with his own earnings from farm work in the Central Valley, but soon it could not sustain the growing family. To support his younger siblings, Don Octavio left school and went to work in a cow barn at the age of six. "They didn't pay him very much since he was just a kid [*chiquillo*], but they did give him milk for his siblings," says Don Octavio's wife, Doña Berta, with a wry smile. Because of his father's meager land and his own lack of education, Don Octavio had no option but to seek a living in the North when he came of age. So in 1974, at the age of seventeen, Don Octavio set out for California's fields as his father had done.

Don Octavio's goal was to save enough money to become a prosperous landowner and cattle rancher in El Platanal, realizing his father's dream of supporting his family with the produce he harvested. He had witnessed a handful of successful return migrants purchase large estates in the region; they even paid local peasants $15 a day to till them. Yet his earnings from farm work allowed him to buy only three *terrenos* (plots of land) and no animals, which were insufficient to sustain his family. Only in 1995, after twenty years of farm work in the United States, did Don Octavio finally succeed in building a new house for his wife and children—one with tile rather than dirt floors and a cement rather than a corrugated tin roof.

In her study of Latino migrants in Long Island, the anthropologist Sarah Mahler observes that migrants' "workaholism" is the result of their need to "generate more wealth than required for their own sustenance." Her migrant interviewees often failed to generate a surplus because they had not anticipated having to pay living expenses such as rent and electricity bills while simultaneously sending remittances to family "back home."[13] She writes: "[They] learn that their income must . . . cover expenses that they did not incur in their homelands and often did not anticipate incurring." A range of illegal "occupational taxes" that labor supervisors levy on their workers create additional obstacles to farmworkers' accumulating a nest egg. As Doña Berta puts it: "It's hard to save money when *mayordomos* charge you for everything—for *raites* [rides to work], your tools, and even sodas!"

Even though Don Octavio was unable to fulfill his dream of returning to Mexico as a self-sustaining farmer, he is known as a migrant success

story in El Platanal. According to Ricardo, his son, it was the house Don Octavio built—evidence of his self-discipline—that earned him his formidable nickname. Even so, the earnings that most men of his generation derived from farm work were too modest to allow them to retire as independent farmers in Mexico. Indeed, the few men who were able to purchase viable estates often did so via fortuitous bonanzas such as settlements for work injuries rather than through their earnings.

Don Miguel, now sixty-two, is an example. When I first meet him, he is sitting with his legs stretched out on his daughter-in-law's couch, slathering his knees with Vaseline to soothe their aches and pains. He arrived in the Valley just three months ago, and he has been working up to twelve hours a day, digging up broken irrigation pipes on a ranch. "It's just dig, dig, dig in the fields," he says (*es pura pala en el campo*). This is not the retirement Don Miguel envisioned for himself. Indeed, before a drought struck his region of Zacatecas in the mid-1990s, Don Miguel had accumulated the kind of nest egg Don Octavio only dreamed about.

Don Miguel first came to the Valley in 1973. He had worked in landscaping and agriculture for just over a decade when an accident profoundly changed his plans. A car slammed into the back of his landscaping truck, splitting open his head and sidelining him from work. Yet the accident yielded an unexpected windfall—a settlement of nearly $30,000. It was this payout, rather than his earnings, that transformed Don Miguel into a prosperous landholder. He returned to Las Huertas and invested the money in his house and his farm. He bought more land, cattle, chickens, and pigs, and a truck to haul water and transport his corn for sale. He thought he had left California's fields for good.

Gerardo, Don Miguel's son—who, as a child, had to travel more than an hour by donkey to the river to fetch water each day—remembers this as a period of prosperity for his family. "It was a relief—it seemed that finally, we were about to climb out of poverty," he says. Yet a few years later, the family's fortunes changed again. A series of droughts struck Las Huertas, and the natural springs that fed the property dried up. Don Miguel could no longer water his cattle or irrigate his fields. The land that represented fifteen years of hard work and suffering in the United States had become worthless. "All that's left is *pedregales* [hard rock]," Don Miguel says bitterly.

So Don Miguel sold his land and livestock and moved into the nearby city of Nochistlán. He was not alone. "There were twenty-two of us [in Las Huertas], but now there are only three," Don Miguel says. Some

left for Nochistlán, others for the United States. The drought had put a sudden end to Don Miguel's dreams of being an autonomous farmer, and the whole town of Las Huertas left with him.

Now Don Miguel is on a migration treadmill. His wife and two unmarried daughters in Nochistlán depend upon his earnings. His house in Nochistlán—which has electricity and phone service—requires money to maintain, yet he has no work. So in 1989, he set off for the United States once again. "It's a lot of sacrifice, but there's no other way," he says.

A few years ago, when Don Miguel was in the United States—staying with Gerardo and Gerardo's wife, Blanca—he swore he would leave for Nochistlán and never return. "But he's said that before," Blanca tells me. Blanca and Gerardo tried to convince him to stay; they knew that his departure would merely mean another border crossing they would have to finance. They pleaded in vain. To no one's surprise, Don Miguel returned two years later, with fresh debts to the *coyote* (professional human smuggler) for crossing the border. "The problem," Blanca says sympathetically, "is that he gets frustrated. You get fed up being here without papers, working hard in the jobs you have to work in, and feeling the insults of daily life. So he gets really irritated. So he keeps leaving and then coming back, leaving and then coming back. Because the problem is that there's no money to make in Mexico either."

Don Miguel's language of sacrifice and Blanca's description of his irritation illustrate the double bind that migration creates for Mexican rural men. Emigration allows men to retain a precarious hold on their roles as breadwinners, but only by exposing them to the indignities of the low-wage economy. As Deborah Boehm puts it in her study of the effect of migration on gendered subjectivities, "Men may have their masculinity stripped from them once they are in the U.S., as they leave behind their role as farmers to work in low-wage jobs."[14] As migrant men remain providers only at the cost of proletarianization, they experience what I call *embattled masculinities*.

In sum, emigration has failed to provide these men the nest egg in Mexico that they had hoped to accumulate. While meager wages in California prevented them from becoming prosperous landholders in their hometowns, arid and inhospitable land consumed the investments they did make. Emigration offered short-term cash but provided no permanent solution. Despite their sacrifices to achieve intergenerational mobility, few Mexican patriarchs have been able to pass on a legacy of independent farming to their children.

A YOUNGER GENERATION OF MEN: SETTLING IN THE UNITED STATES

Many of the sons of Mexican patriarchs like Don Octavio and Don Miguel followed in their fathers' footsteps, migrating in their teens and twenties. Yet this generation, now in their thirties and forties, found that two changes in immigration policy profoundly altered their residency patterns and their attachment to family farms. Beginning in the mid-1980s, the tightening of the border made return visits to Mexico increasingly difficult. Then the passage of IRCA in 1986 legalized 1.3 million undocumented farmworkers who could supply evidence of their work history.[15] These changes in immigration policy quietly transformed fathers' plans to establish independent landholdings in Mexico and pass them to their sons.

When Don Miguel left for California in the late 1970s, for example, he left his nine-year-old son, Gerardo, in charge of the family farm in Las Huertas. Gerardo wanted to join his elder brother in the United States, but his father would not let him. "He had too much land, and he needed someone to till the fields," Gerardo shrugs. As the eldest son left in Las Huertas, Gerardo was expected to fill his father's shoes. So Gerardo left school to help his family; he tilled the land, hauled water by donkey, and gathered firewood. It was only in 1988, when Don Miguel returned from the United States with his settlement, that Gerardo—then seventeen—was released from his adult responsibilities and was able to set off for the United States.

Gerardo says that he initially shared his father's migration goal. "My thoughts . . . were to buy land and a house in Mexico, to form a family and a household," he says. Yet the tightening of the U.S.-Mexico border, along with a budding romance, changed his plans. The cost of hiring a *coyote* to recross the border had spiked. And in 1995, on a return trip to Las Huertas, Gerardo met his wife, Blanca. Aware that immigration enforcement made maintaining a binational family a risky prospect, Gerardo persuaded Blanca to take the risk of crossing—hidden in the trunk of a *coyote*'s car—to the United States.

Although intensified border enforcement made life more difficult for undocumented couples like Gerardo and Blanca, the passage of IRCA in 1986—the nation's last major legalization program—also made resettlement easier for those who were able to attain legal status. IRCA's Special Agricultural Worker (SAW) program offered legal permanent residency to applicants who could prove that they had performed at

least ninety days of farm work during 1985 and 1986.[16] Under immigration law, legal permanent residents are eligible to seek immigrant visas for their spouses and children.[17] In allowing migrant farmworkers to obtain legal status, then, IRCA also made it possible for them to legally reunite their binational families. IRCA thus dramatically transformed farmworkers' migration and settlement patterns.[18]

Gaining legal status through the SAW program changed the lives of Don Octavio and his family. Because Doña Berta refused to cross the border without papers, she and Don Octavio used to see each other only during the three months he spent in Mexico each winter. In 1994, as a legal permanent resident, Don Octavio filed applications for permanent residency for Doña Berta and his eight children. In 2000, after more than twenty-three years of long-distance marriage, the visas were finally granted, and Doña Berta crossed the border with her children to settle in the United States.

Don Octavio's family's relocation to the United States has fundamentally changed his plans. Because a local farmer tills his land in El Platanal while he lives in California, he is able to collect farming subsidies from the Mexican government. Yet he and Doña Berta now speak of their land in Mexico as existing "in case of illness" (*en caso de enfermedad*)—as an asset to sell or a refuge to which they can retreat should hardship impede their work in the United States. In sum, IRCA redirected migrant men's attention to building a life in the United States and encouraged them to abandon their dreams of tilling family farms in Mexico. Rather than being a means of earning an independent livelihood, Don Octavio's hard-earned land now serves as mere insurance.

SALVADORAN MIGRANTS: ESCAPING THE CIVIL WAR

Whereas Mexican migrants have been migrating to the Central Valley to work for more than a century, Salvadoran migrants' journeys to Mendota date from the country's recent civil war (1979–1992). As scholars of migration argue, it is often fruitless to attempt to distinguish between political refugees and economic migrants.[19] Civil wars routinely dash hopes and thwart economic prospects. The stories of Salvadoran migrants reveal that the civil war not only directly put their lives at risk but also made earning a living impossible.

Born in 1969, Teo grew up in Sensuntepeque, Cabañas, as one of twelve children. Because his family owned no land, they worked as day laborers on the estates of large landowners, paying the owners a fixed

portion of their harvest and consuming the rest. When Teo was nine, the civil war transformed the rhythm of daily life. The teachers at his school refused to teach because their commute from the city had become unsafe, and the schools closed down. So Teo went to work. His mother and sisters prepared lunch, and Teo's task was to ferry it—barefoot, because his parents could not afford to buy him shoes—up the mountainside [*sierra*] to the estate where his father was harvesting. "And then I stayed there and worked—harvesting so that we could eat," he says.

Teo helped his father harvest beans, corn, and squash for nine years. When he turned eighteen, he was conscripted into the military. He saw bodies decapitated by the roadside and strung from electricity poles. Teo wished he could have emigrated to avoid military service, but he lacked the money to pay for an undocumented journey. "Those who had money fled. Those who didn't have the money to flee had to stay," he says. Teo served his compulsory two years. Then, in 1992—one year after Teo exited the army—the civil war ended.

Even after the peace treaty brought an official end to the war, its ravages lingered. The war had robbed Teo of his prospects; he had but four years of schooling to his name. Able to find only occasional farm work in Sensuntepeque, Teo decided to emigrate to start a family. He spent three years saving up the $875 he needed to pay a *coyote* to help him cross into the United States undocumented. In 1994, he left.

Although Teo cited work as his reason for emigration, his decision to migrate had its roots in the civil war, which limited his schooling and consequently decreased his access to jobs. Thus the civil war left a legacy of economic stunting, fueling emigration by interfering with men's ability to fulfill their responsibilities as providers.

Like his Mexican migrant peers, Teo intended to return to his hometown as an autonomous landholder, but he could not earn enough to do so. In addition, his tenuous legal status constrained his mobility. After some years in the United States, Teo received temporary protected status (TPS). Although this status grants him authorization to work, he cannot legally return to the United States if he leaves.[20] So Teo has resigned himself to supporting his family from afar.

Even today, the United States' regional policy of "securitization" continues to fuel political and economic tumult and has prompted a new generation of Salvadorans to flee.[21] Nine of Teo's twelve siblings have followed him to the United States. His youngest sister arrived in 2013 at the age of seventeen, escaping recruitment by members of a gang. Another sister, who had worked as an accountant for the Agricultural

Bank of El Salvador, fled because demands for a monthly "rent"—extorted under threat of death—left her penniless. Thus the liminal legality of Salvadorans prevents their circular migration, and the region's political and economic turmoil has killed migrants' dreams of return.[22]

ENTERING THE FIELDS

If their lack of productive land at home drove Mexican and Salvadoran migrants to the United States, barriers intrinsic to their migration histories consigned them to low-wage work once they arrived. For many, like Don Miguel, the lack of legal status foreclosed opportunities in the formal economy, where employers check work-authorization documents more stringently. But even those with legal status, like Don Octavio and Teo, found that their childhood environments of peasant scarcity and political instability impeded their economic mobility in the United States. Whether deprived of an education by war, as Teo was, or through economic hardship, like Gerardo, even migrants with legal status have found that a lack of literacy and of English skills have prevented them from entering sectors outside the low-wage economy.

Why did Mexican and Salvadoran men enter farm work as opposed to service work or factory work? In explaining their decisions, many say they find dignity in tilling the land and independence in working outdoors, relatively free from supervision, as they had in their homelands. They speak of farm work as a habitual preference or taste.[23] They say they shudder at the thought of being confined in a factory—or worse, doing the "women's work" of washing dishes in a restaurant.[24] As Gerardo, who works on a ranch, puts it: "I would be bored [in a factory or a restaurant]. I like being able to see nature, to walk around, do all different jobs." Thus men portray farm work as a means of maintaining their masculine dignity in the low-wage economy. Yet only a fortunate few are able to find work on small ranches that satisfies their desire for autonomy.

The Hierarchy of Farm Work

Migrants describe a hierarchy of farm work in the Central Valley. Jobs vary not only by the pace of work but also by security, pay and benefits, and the extent of labor controls and supervision. Landing better-paying, more secure jobs, such as those in packing and processing houses, requires legal status. And landing the jobs that allow the most autonomy, such as those on small ranches, requires connections.

FIGURE 7. A farmworker takes a brief rest on top of boxes of melons on a summer day.

Small family farms or ranches offer the most desirable employment for undocumented migrants. Workers on these farms typically do not receive benefits, raises, or overtime pay and only sometimes earn a wage higher than the state minimum. Yet because workers must carry out all the activities necessary to maintain the farm, the work offers the satisfaction of autonomy and diversified tasks. Because of the varied tasks, ranchers value workers' knowledge and skills over their speed and strength. As Gerardo says of the job he eventually found on a small ranch: "On labor crews, it's just racing up and down the field [*carreras*] all day. Here, I learned how to water cotton, how to water alfalfa, how to drive tractors and Caterpillars."

Packing and processing sheds offer the most lucrative employment in the Valley; sheds pay their workers a higher hourly wage and offer time-and-a-half overtime pay, raises, benefits, and the security of semipermanent employment. The work is repetitive and rigidly supervised, but workers are sheltered from the elements with ready access to bathrooms. However, these employers require valid work-authorization documents.[25]

The majority of jobs in the Valley are on labor crews.[26] In 2009, half the workers on California's crop farms were hired by labor contractors; they are particularly common in the Valley because of its large-scale farming enterprises and labor-intensive crops.[27] Labor crews, as described in chapter 1, are characterized by a hierarchical chain of command that makes the labor process quite unlike that in packing houses or small family farms. Unlike those on small family farms, labor-crew supervisors value workers' sheer labor power. Because growers typically hire contractors to accomplish a specific task—such as weeding or picking a field—the work is repetitive and specialized. And unlike workers in processing sheds, field hands work outdoors, exposed to the elements.

Because subcontractors turn a blind eye to questionable work-authorization documents, labor crews tend to be dominated by the most vulnerable workers—those who lack valid documents, underage workers, and migrants facing deportation orders. Aware that crews are an option of last resort, labor supervisors feel relatively insulated from the legal repercussions of engaging in labor abuses. The sociologist Elizabeth Fussell describes this phenomenon as the "deportation threat dynamic."[28] In her study of wage theft in New Orleans after Hurricane Katrina, Fussell suggests that it is the presumption of a group's illegality, rather than any single worker's known legal status, that encourages employers to disregard state and federal labor laws. Contractors know that some of their employees lack the valid papers to land a job in a packing shed; they know that others have records of immigration violations that prevent them from working under their legal names. Employers can rest confident that workers' fears of contacting the local authorities to contest abuses—a practice that could result in their deportation or arrest—ensure their quiescence.

For example, when Jessie, the Anglo-American wife of a *mayordomo*, began working in an onion processing plant after more than a decade of work on labor crews, she was surprised at the difference. The plant awarded "safety bucks" for each month a processing team avoided injury. Even if this strategy served as a backhanded means of discouraging workers from reporting their injuries (and thereby receiving workers'

FIGURE 8. A labor crew harvests corn.

compensation), it was a far cry from the blatant attempts at intimidation she had witnessed in the fields. "Who's gonna give you safety bucks in the fields?" she says. "[Working here] is not like in the field. Here, as long as you're doing the best you can, nobody tells you nothin'," she says.[29]

Thus because labor crews are dominated by those workers whom supervisors deem most exploitable, contractors feel relatively insulated from state and federal labor laws. The vulnerable status of workers on labor crews, combined with the financial incentives introduced by subcontracting, makes labor abuses common. In short, labor supervisors prey on the very vulnerabilities that channel migrants into labor crews in the first place—their lack of legal status, fear of law enforcement, and lack of social connections—to make a profit.

First Days: Reshaping Work Habitus

Many migrant men enter farm work in search of the autonomy and dignity they associate with the small family farms on which they grew up. However, the majority join labor crews, where they have to accustom

themselves to working as field hands under rigid controls and supervision. Every day they confront the contradiction between their pride in their breadwinning capacity and the humiliation they endure as field hands. Migrants' memories of their first days in California's fields provide a window onto such embattled masculinities and the reshaping of what I call work habitus.

Coined by Pierre Bourdieu, the term *habitus* refers to a set of mental attitudes and ways of holding our bodies that—because they are learned tacitly and internalized—are "placed beyond the grasp of consciousness."[30] It includes not only the tastes and dispositions but also a bodily style—what Bourdieu calls a "body hexis"— appropriate to our position in society. Bourdieu argues that our very social identities are formed by learning the postures and gestures specific to our classed and gendered positions. Although early childhood socialization forms our most enduring tastes and bodily deportments, our experiences in other environments—which Bourdieu calls "fields"—may either reinforce or transform our unconscious behaviors and attitudes. Migrant men's peasant backgrounds in both Mexico and El Salvador create a classed and gendered habitus in which hard manual labor is the basis of male identity. Many men respond to the degradation they endure on labor crews by asserting new pride in their labor capacity, even as the labor hierarchy instills in them a body hexis befitting their racialized identity and precarious occupational position.

Gerardo, for example, remembers that when he first arrived in California, he first sought work in landscaping, a job he describes as "lighter" than farm work. When his father, Don Miguel, returned to the Valley to harvest tomatoes on a crew, Gerardo decided he would join him. He was shocked. "Everyone was there on their knees in the dirt, scrabbling for tomatoes and throwing them onto the band. It was just gross [*cochino*]! And the *mayordomo* was standing over them, yelling insults at them; he wouldn't let them rest one second," Gerardo remembers. "And I said, 'This isn't for me!'" For Gerardo, the servile posture and dirt of tomato harvesting threw into relief the relative dignity of landscaping, work in which he could remain relatively clean, stand upright, and avoid surveillance and verbal abuse.

When Blanca joined Gerardo in California in 1995 and they had a daughter, he realized that a landscaper's earnings could not sustain them. It was Blanca who suggested that they move to Mendota, where she had an aunt, so that the pair could perform farm work. "In the city, they give you forty hours [of work], no more. You can't work the weekends. But

here you can work until 7 P.M., six days a week. Here you can work every day if you want to," he says. Thus Gerardo's need to support his young family led him back to labor crews, where he endured three more months of humiliation before eventually landing a job on a ranch.

Working on crews subtly changed Gerardo's attitudes toward work and his own body. Cognizant that his job security depended on maintaining a fast clip, he came to valorize his productivity. When he ran into old neighbors at the store, he would boast about how many trailers of melon he and his team had filled. He competed with his fellow pickers to see who could pile more melons onto the machine for women to pack. Yet when he returned home each night, Blanca remembers, he complained bitterly about his *mayordomo*'s insults and ploys. Even as he chafed against his demeaning work conditions, then, Gerardo found empowerment in displaying his labor capacity. Gerardo's story helps explain the power of the gendered slights inflicted by labor supervisors and coworkers. Demeaned by their status as racialized and proletarianized workers, migrant men see their breadwinning role as one of the few sources of pride they have left.

Like Gerardo, Blanca found the pace of labor crews harried and undignified. Blanca avoided working in the fields during her first fifteen years in California, but when her unmarried sister Lupita arrived in 2008 and invited her to sort tomatoes, she decided to give it a try. Blanca soon learned that the pace of production dictated that Lupita and her coworkers avoid visiting the bathroom during their eight-hour day. The tomato-sorting machine travels up and down the tomato furrows as men pick the fruit with knives; women ride on the machine and discard the bad produce. To visit the portable toilets placed on either edge of the field, they must honk a horn to signal the machine to stop, and the production process must halt to allow sorters to descend from the machine. When Blanca told her sister that she needed to stop, Lupita was alarmed. "Don't get off! Because when you get off to go to the bathroom, they'll laugh at you behind your back and say, 'There goes the itty-bitty bed-wetter [*meona*],'" Lupita told her. Lupita had learned to accommodate her *mayordoma*'s demands for unbroken productivity and avoid taunts by holding in her urine. However, Blanca refused to do so: she did honk for the machine to stop. Yet she did not return to tomato sorting.

As migrants enter labor crews, then, the farmwork hierarchy subtly reshapes their bodily dispositions and work attitudes. The hunched and stooped posture demanded by jobs such as tomato harvesting, picking and weeding reinforces workers' subordination, while the rigid supervision

they endure casts them as automatons, depersonalized units of labor.[31] Supervisors' valorization of men's speed and strength, combined with men's degraded status as field hands, heightens the emphasis men place on their labor capacity. They learn that they must disregard their physical needs to keep their jobs and to maintain the pace of production demanded of them.

The Legacy of the Bracero Program

A century of Mexican men's migration to the United States as contract workers leaves "historical sediments" that shape farmworkers' expectations even before they enter California's fields.[32] Six of my ten core Mexican interviewees remembered relatives—fathers, grandfathers, or uncles—who had served as braceros. These six had heard stories of working in California from their male relatives, and these tales shaped their expectations and understandings of industrial farm work.

Yadira, whose grandfather had purchased a *parcela,* or small plot of land, in Colima with money he earned as a bracero, says her grandfather never spoke of the program. "But I happened to overhear my mother talking about it once—something about him being ripped off or not getting paid," she says. Her mother's whispers of exploitation contrasted with the visible success of her grandfather's work—his land. Elisabeta, who eventually followed her father to the Valley from Jalisco, witnessed a similar contradiction. Her father and his three brothers, who had come as braceros, parlayed their hard-earned income into political and symbolic capital on their return. They rose to become prominent officials in Mexico's ruling party, the Partido Revolucionario Institucional (PRI); one brother even became mayor of San Nicolás. They helped build a hospital, church, new schools and installed electricity and a water pump. Thus the three were poster children for the national development and individual economic advancement that the Mexican state promised the program would provide its people.[33]

Yet Elisabeta's father also regaled her with stories of the humiliations he endured as a bracero. He told her that he had been "sprayed down with very cold water" when he crossed the border and had been forced to pass naked in front of a line of strangers. "They said that Mexicans carried diseases," she remembers him saying. He told her that he worked on a family farm and was unable to leave it. He said that his employers cheated him of wages by saying they had sent them to Mexico. And he told her his employers asked him to dress up in fine clothes to be photographed in

order to make the "Mexican government" think that braceros lived lives of great wealth. Two of her uncles died of rare skin diseases when she was a child, and the third developed what she described as lung cancer. "The doctors said the pesticides ate his lung," she says.

Elisabeta's father's stories colored her expectations of farm work before she even migrated.[34] They resonate with greater force now that she is tilling the same fields. She says she "was not surprised" to find that employers often "rushed" their workers, nor that they sometimes stiffed them of pay. Family members' tales of wage theft and of being treated as contagious vermin thus leave memory traces of racialized injustice that shape the work habitus of successive generations of migrants.

EXCEPTIONAL WORKERS: STATE AND FEDERAL POLICIES

Just as the history of Mexican and Salvadoran migration to the United States shapes farmworkers' work behaviors, so does the policy environment they find when they arrive. Labor and immigration policies are instrumental in determining their degree of economic security and their need for work. In exempting agricultural employers from the same regulations that protect workers in other industries, U.S. agricultural policy has in effect required that farmworkers be "exceptional workers."[35] If migrant farmworkers learn to subordinate their physical needs to their labor supervisors' demands, U.S. labor and immigration policies play a key role in teaching them this lesson.

Growers have used the unique vicissitudes of agriculture to argue for their exemption from the federal protections governing work in other industries. Premising their argument for agricultural exceptionalism on the conditions that distinguish agriculture from other forms of industrial production—the perishability of crops, the unpredictability of the weather and the labor supply, and the importance of agriculture in providing the nation's food—growers persuaded Congress to exclude the industry from the labor protections established in the New Deal. These included a standard minimum wage, restrictions on child labor, unemployment insurance, mandatory time-and-a-half overtime pay, the right to unionize, and retirement benefits. Thus the New Deal produced the anomaly that farmworkers—those in greatest need of legal protection—were excluded from the labor laws instrumental in building middle-class security.[36] States and the federal government have since undone some—though not all—of these original exemptions, granting farmworkers a

standard minimum wage, the right to unionize, and access to retirement benefits. However, the New Deal institutionalized farmworkers' status as second-class workers. The historic exclusion of farmworkers from the promises of liberalism makes them exceptional workers in the sense that they must expend exceptional effort to maintain their jobs.

The continuing exclusion of farmworkers from the requirement of time-and-a-half pay for overtime has a significant detrimental effect on their well-being and income. Mandatory overtime pay deters employers from requiring employees to work excessive hours. Moreover, because field hands often work long hours for a short period, time-and-a-half pay for overtime could dramatically mitigate their poverty. California is one of only seven states—including Colorado, Hawaii, Maine, Maryland, Minnesota, and Oregon—that mandate overtime pay for agricultural work.[37] Nevertheless, regulations regarding overtime pay maintain a double standard. In California, for example, overtime pay is required only for agricultural work in excess of ten hours a day or sixty hours a week.[38] In contrast, workers in packing and processing sheds, which are subject to the same overtime requirements as employers outside agriculture, receive time-and-a-half pay for work in excess of eight hours a day or forty hours a week.

The uneven inclusion of farmworkers in unemployment insurance is another key gap in agricultural labor protections. As low-income workers, many farmworkers depend heavily on federal and state benefits to supplement their income. A majority of farmworkers in California—61 percent—are employed seasonally.[39] Unemployment rates in major agricultural counties routinely exceed 17 percent during the winter.[40] Thus unemployment insurance provides a key supplement to meager earnings. In fact, according to the National Agricultural Workers' Survey, farmworkers use unemployment benefits more than any other form of public assistance.[41]

The New Deal established unemployment insurance as a federal benefit in 1935 to serve as a bulwark against economic recession. Yet, bowing to growers' concerns and the public's fears of a food crisis, it excluded farmworkers from eligibility.[42] Only in 1978 did Congress amend the Social Security Act to require that large agricultural employers include their workers in unemployment insurance programs.[43] Even so, undocumented workers remain universally excluded from unemployment coverage because they are legally ineligible for employment itself. Undocumented migrants' exclusion from unemployment insurance increases the stakes involved in pleasing their supervisors.[44]

Border Enforcement since 9/11: Creating an Indebted Workforce

If farmworkers' exclusion from these forms of social and employer assistance creates their economic insecurity, border enforcement intensifies it. In 1993, El Paso Border Patrol chief Silvestre Reyes piloted an experimental approach of deploying surveillance equipment, fencing, and 450 agents on the twenty-mile stretch of border around El Paso. Initially dubbed Operation Blockade, the show of visible force was a public relations success. Captivated by the image of an orderly border, the Immigration and Naturalization Service (INS) made Reyes's approach the centerpiece of border control. Under the policy of "prevention through deterrence," the Border Patrol (BP) concentrated its manpower and equipment on major ports of entry, including El Paso, San Diego, Tucson, and the Rio Grande Valley.[45] Between 1993 and 2000, the BP more than doubled in size, and the total INS budget nearly tripled.[46] Yet while the approach created the illusion of border control—and eventually won Reyes a seat in the House of Representatives—it merely altered the locations where migrants crossed. Rather than halt undocumented migration, it diverted migrants' journeys to the desert, where they risked dehydration and death.[47]

The events of September 11, 2001 radically transformed the border and the agency in charge of patrolling it. Amid fears about the nation's southern border being penetrated by terrorists, federal investment in the border as both a physical and symbolic entity escalated. In 1993, BP agents numbered 3,965; in 2009 there were 20,119. In 2004, the total budget for immigration enforcement was $9.5 billion; by 2010, it had increased to $17.2 billion.[48] Today, the border is not only fortified with steel fencing and motion sensors, as it had been before 9/11, but it is also patrolled by drones and light aircraft.[49]

It is well known that heightened border enforcement has increased not only the physical danger of an undocumented crossing but also the cost: the fees that *coyotes* charge for such crossings has tripled or quadrupled since 1993.[50] Less widely known is the fact that it has also affected migrants' labor conditions. Intensified border enforcement jeopardizes migrants' safety at work by saddling them and their families with unprecedented debts. U.S. relatives who serve as unofficial sponsors for undocumented migrants' journeys may borrow from moneylenders (*prestamistas*), often at a 20 percent interest rate. Whether paying off the fees for their own passage or saving money to pay for a

loved one's crossing, migrants must redouble their work to pay off sizable migration loans.

Yadira and her husband, René, for example, migrated from Colima in stages. René had been a construction worker in Colima, and the couple had long struggled to pay their bills; when his friend emigrated, René decided to follow suit. In 2000, the couple borrowed $1,500 from Yadira's brother in Los Angeles to pay a *coyote* to smuggle René through the desert. Although Yadira initially refused to join him in the United States, her mother persuaded her that it was the best option to keep the family together. René sometimes worked two jobs in California as he struggled to save the funds for Yadira's passage. Early the following year, Yadira crossed as well.

Yadira left her children with their grandmother in Colima, promising that she would send for them as soon as she could. Shortly after her arrival, however, the events of 9/11 increased the price and the risks of an undocumented border crossing. Instead of allowing their children to make the perilous desert crossing, Yadira and René worked for three years to be able to afford the safer option: paying a *coyote* to transport their children through the heavily patrolled ports of entry with false documents, at a cost of $10,500.

Yadira's memories of her first days of work in California highlight the way such hefty migration debts jeopardize undocumented migrants' work conditions. The very day after her arrival, Yadira's landlord, also a *mayordoma,* deposited her in the middle of the fields so that she could find employment. After some time, a contractor passed by and picked her up; he drove her to some tomato fields where workers were weeding. Yet Yadira had not been officially hired. She had not received the worker-safety training mandated by the state. She hadn't known to bring a water bottle to tie to her belt with twine to stay hydrated. Her husband had told her to wear a shirt with long sleeves to protect herself from the sun, but no one had told her to wear a hat. It was July, and Yadira had already waited in the sun for hours. A woman on her crew eventually took pity on her and lent her a bandanna so that Yadira could cover her forehead.

As a child, Yadira had occasionally helped her grandfather sow his small plot of land in Colima, which he had bought with his earnings as a bracero, but she found the pace of weeding on this labor crew a rude contrast. She had not anticipated that she would be walking several miles in the open sun without being able to take breaks. Yadira says, "When I saw the weeding, I thought to myself, 'My God, I don't think I'll make it.

FIGURE 9. A weeder wearing a hat, bandanna, and hooded sweatshirt to protect herself from the sun stops to rehydrate one July morning.

How can I walk so much? So I reminded myself of my children. I said, 'No, I have to work. I have to work because that's what I came to do!'"

Early in the day, Yadira had confided to a young coworker weeding the row next to her—whose age she put at seventeen or eighteen—that she was working to pay for her children's passage. As the day grew hotter, she told him she was uncertain she could continue. The young man listened sympathetically and gave her the encouragement she needed. "No *señora,* you have to go on. If you rest, they'll fire you. They'll say you can't do the work," he told her. "That young boy was very sweet," she says now. "He'd work extra fast to go on ahead, and then double back to finish my row too." The solidarity of Yadira's coworker kept her from drawing the attention of the *mayordomo* and helped her keep her job. Yet by the time she arrived home, she was trembling and had a fever.

Labor scholars have long noted the *superexploitation* of Latino migrants—their willingness to work harder and for less pay than other low-wage workers.[51] Yadira's story shows that heightened border enforcement facilitates workers' superexploitation by making their hard-earned

income from low-wage jobs vital to family reunification. Moreover, her story illustrates the invisible pressures that recent migrants like Jairo carry with them into the fields (see chapter 1). Unable to rely on unemployment income should she lose her job, Yadira had no safety net. As heightened border enforcement intersects with migrants' exclusion from employer protections, then, it only encourages migrants to work through illness.

AN INDUSTRY BUILT ON FOREIGN-BORN MIGRANTS

The exceptional vulnerabilities of foreign-born Latinos help explain their predominance in California's fields. Because of the prevalence of perishable-crop agriculture in California—a variant of farm work that is particularly labor-intensive—employers require a large and continuous supply of "willing" and tractable workers. As a result, established social networks continue to funnel recent arrivals directly into California's fields. Nationwide, 83 percent of farmworkers are Hispanic, and 78 percent are foreign born.[52] In California, the figures are 99 percent and 95 percent respectively. Ninety-one percent of the state's farmworkers were born in Mexico and 4 percent in Central America. Currently, more than half the state's farm labor force is estimated to be undocumented—a figure that has grown steadily since just after the last legalization program in 1986, when only 9 percent were undocumented.[53]

The stories of farmworkers born and raised in the United States throw into relief their different work attitudes. The advantages of U.S. citizenship, command of English, literacy, and therefore ability to find other jobs make their experiences in the fields quite different from those of their foreign-born peers. Even as supervisors behave as though their workers are legally vulnerable and therefore won't protest abuses, these individuals put the lie to this assumption. Such individuals' resistance to their supervisors' disciplinary tactics is instructive.

Raquel's son-in-law, Lalo, for example, is a relative outsider to the labor hierarchy in farmwork. Born in El Salvador, he moved to the United States when he was twelve and became a legal permanent resident. He previously worked in a factory making prefabricated houses in Sacramento—in a company which, according to Raquel, paid "for everything—overtime, insurance, everything, but sometimes you have to fight to get it." He had met Raquel's Salvadoran daughter, who came to the United States when she was seven, while she was working in customer service in Sacramento. The couple returned to the Valley to live with Raquel's parents, where, for the first time in his life, Lalo went to work in the fields.

Lalo recounts that while he was working in a cotton gin, some fluff from the cotton fell into his eye. He informed his supervisor that he wished to file an injury claim so that the company's workers' compensation insurance would pay for his treatment. His boss dismissed Lalo's report, implying that Lalo was attempting to finagle employer coverage for an injury he had sustained at home.[54] "You didn't get hurt here; who knows what you were doing [when you hurt your eye]!" Lalo's employer had said. Lalo was shocked. He replied that he would visit the doctor himself and inform him that he had been injured at work; he promptly followed up by threatening to sue the company for refusing to cover his care. Lalo says that his supervisor seemed surprised that his tactic of intimidation had failed; he sent Lalo to the doctor.

Lalo and his wife laugh and shake their heads at the supervisor's bald attempt to suppress Lalo's claim. "We're from Sacramento, so we know that if you get injured on the job, you're supposed to get care!" Lalo's wife exclaims. "People here just don't know that. Or if they *do* know, they're afraid to speak up." As this comment implies, the vulnerability of most migrants on labor crews resigns them to enduring this kind of abuse. In contrast, Lalo's history of work outside agriculture had accustomed him to particular labor protections. His outsider status explains his willingness to speak up, while his access to other jobs lessened the risks posed by losing his employment.

Similarly, Melissa's expectations as a U.S.-born worker—combined with her U.S. citizenship—made her comfortable contesting employer abuse. A forty-year-old, second-generation immigrant Latina, Melissa is the wife of Mike, the owner of the corner store in Mendota. Melissa managed the family's store in Mike's absence and supplemented the job with farm work. As a citizen, she enjoyed the relative privilege of working in the packing and processing plants. She also occasionally worked on labor crews in the fields, where she frequently found herself the only U.S.-born worker, apart from teenagers.

While working in the fields, Melissa witnessed a strategy *mayordomos* sometimes use to augment their earnings—that of adding phantom workers to the roster of employees. *Mayordomos* prepare a list of the crew's employees for the contractor, who pays them biweekly. Claiming nonexistent workers allows *mayordomos* to pad their income by appropriating the extra checks. The success of this ruse depends on the existing workers' superexploitation: because the contractor expects the output of a larger team, the *mayordomo* must drive his crew harder to make up for the missing employees.

Elisabeta first explained this strategy to me. Because she could read and write, she said, her *mayordomos* often asked her to sit in the van and help register workers on the first day of work. "And I'd take out the list of people who were there. And there were always, always, two extra people. And I'd say, 'Who are these extra people?'" Once a manager from the company came to the field and checked on the list. "He said, "Write out a list of all the female packers so I can check them and make sure the work is going well.'" So Elisabeta counted the packers and checked them against her *mayordomo*'s list, which bore the names of two additional workers. When she asked her *mayordomo* how to account for the discrepancy, he simply pointed to his roster. "And he'd say, 'Just put down their names and their numbers.' Because that supervisor didn't have a list, *verdad* [right]? And the *mayordomo* would say, 'Just put down their names.' And he'd make the machine go extra fast to pick as though there were two extra people working on it. And he must have thought I was a fool!"

While Elisabeta had grown accustomed to having to cover for her *mayordomo* in order to keep her job, Melissa protested the accelerated pace of work that this ploy required. Once, her *mayordomo* had begun pressuring workers to fill a trailer with melons before they left the field. "Hurry! I have to fill up this trailer by three o'clock!" he had yelled. Aware that the crew was working with four fewer members than the customary number, Melissa and her coworkers did not share the *mayordomo*'s sense of urgency. "*You* have to fill up this truck by three o'clock. *I* am a citizen, and I know my rights. I've sued a company before. I can sue you too!" Melissa retorted. Melissa urged her coworkers to protest too, but "they just stayed quiet," she says. Unwilling to put up with such exploitation, Melissa quit.

Thus even as supervisors behave as though their crew members' legal compromise will prevent them from contesting work abuses, the actions of Lalo and Melissa put the lie to this assumption. Lalo's prior employment in a factory, and Melissa's as a small business owner, have accustomed them to very different treatment at work. Moreover, because of their English skills and U.S. citizenship, they are unwilling to put up with the labor abuses that foreign-born workers must endure to keep their jobs. For the same reasons, however, they are less likely to remain in an industry that profits from the vulnerability of foreign-born migrants.

National studies consistently show that Latinos, and foreign-born Latinos in particular, account for a disproportionate number of work-related

injuries and deaths in the United States. This pattern cannot be explained by their concentration in the most dangerous occupations; foreign-born Latinos are overrepresented among the occupational injuries and mortalities within a single industry as well. Even as deaths at work have declined nationwide over the past fifteen years, the rate of such fatalities among Latinos has doubled—and that increase has been almost entirely accounted for by fatalities among foreign-born workers.[55]

These alarming statistics must be examined in the context of the U.S. labor and immigration policies that force Latino migrants to be exceptional workers. Growing up in peasant environments, migrant men learn to labor hard: they learn as young boys that their capability as breadwinners is integral to their masculine self-worth. They enter farm work because they view it as more dignified than the other low-wage options open to them. Yet the hierarchy of supervision on the labor crews in the Central Valley, combined with the vulnerability of the workforce, allows supervisors to reinforce productivity demands with abusive behavior. Meanwhile, the scarcity of jobs open to migrants, combined with their migration debts and limited labor protections, teaches men to work through illness. Indeed, as the next chapter shows, recent changes in immigration enforcement further deepen migrant workers' vulnerability at work.

CHAPTER 3

Ghost Workers

The Labor Consequences of Identity Loan

Elisabeta, an undocumented migrant farmworker from Jalisco, Mexico, learned the perils of being a ghost worker the hard way. Two years after arriving in the United States, she was topping onion plants. "There's a flower that grows above the onion, and it has spines. And one of those spines cut my eye, and it began to bleed," she remembers. Elisabeta's field supervisor told her he'd take her to the doctor; he even brought her the worker's compensation claim form for her to fill out. Yet as she stared at the form, Elisabeta faced a dilemma. "What name should I put down?" She was working with a set of loaned identity documents: as workers in the Central Valley put it, she was *trabajando fantasma* (working as a ghost). Her neighbor, María, had suggested that Elisabeta use María's Social Security card and green card in order to obtain work.

Elisabeta remembers that her supervisor was very stern in his response. "*Señora,* what have you done? If you were working in your own name, you could get help. I'd tell you to take out [workers' compensation]. But you can't get help if you're working under someone else's name," he said. Chastened and scared, Elisabeta simply went home. She stayed there for a month, treating her injured eye with a salve of boiled herbs.

As a result of this experience, Elisabeta now says that she "knows" that injured farmworkers cannot receive workers' compensation—a mandatory employer benefit in California—while working another person's papers. "Because how could you? What you're doing is fraud, no?

It's very serious. No, that's why they say in the fields, 'If it's fraudulent, the case is already over before it began.'"

This chapter examines the role of working other people's papers—or what I call *identity loan*—in shaping migrants' workplace conditions and behaviors. Identity loan occurs when a legally authorized worker—a legal permanent resident or citizen—loans his or her Social Security number (SSN) and photo identification to another person so that the recipient can present the required documents to an employer.[1] In contrast to the much-publicized phenomenon of identity theft, identity loan is a consensual and mutually beneficial exchange. The recipient gains the papers needed to find work, along with a bonus of $100 for every $1,000 earned.[2] Yet identity donors reap disproportionate financial benefit. Unemployment payments, on which farmworkers with legal status depend during the off-season, are based on a person's highest quarterly earnings during a continuous twelve-month period. Thus while María paid Elisabeta a modest tip, Elisabeta's labor contributed to María's official earning history and fattened her unemployment payments at the end of the season.[3]

Identity loan is a key income-generating strategy among migrant farmworkers, helping compensate for their status as "exceptional workers." It enables farmworkers with legal status—more established coworkers, relatives, even employers—to make a profit from the needs of their more vulnerable peers. Recently, however, changes in immigration enforcement have made the legal consequences of working with borrowed papers more serious. As Elisabeta's story illustrates, these changes have discouraged migrants from asserting their needs and claiming their workplace rights. Because migrant farmworkers fear the discovery of their engagement in identity loan, they are often unwilling to report illnesses or injuries to supervisors or even take breaks.

THE LEGAL PRODUCTION OF IDENTITY LOAN

Scholars of immigration law denaturalize migrant "illegality" by directing our attention to how it is legally produced.[4] Indeed, federal and state policies—specifically, IRCA and the exclusion of undocumented migrants from unemployment insurance—enable and encourage identity loan. The passage of IRCA in 1986 criminalized the employment of undocumented workers, making it illegal for employers to knowingly hire such workers. With the aim of reducing employment as an incentive for migration, IRCA requires employers to personally inspect each employee's documents proving their identity (usually a *mica*, or green

card) and their eligibility for work (a *seguro*, or Social Security card).[5] Employers must record this information on a federal I-9 form and keep a copy for three years. Although IRCA imposes sanctions on employers who violate its provisions, it contains a loophole that protects employers from such penalties: it does not require them to verify the authenticity of employees' documents. As a result, employers are considered to be complying with the law as long as the documents they accept "appear on their face to be genuine."[6] Thus while IRCA has done little to curb the employment of undocumented workers, it has created a thriving black market for fraudulent work-authorization documents.[7]

In migrant farmworker communities in the Central Valley, "papers" have become perhaps the most significant nonmonetary form of capital. IRCA has converted them into exchangeable commodities; migrants commonly speak of legal status as though it is inherent in *papeles* (papers) or *documentos* (documents) themselves. In legal theory, an individual's legal status is determinant: it confers rights, and legal documents merely serve as proof of that individual's eligibility to be accorded such rights. Yet because, in practice, documents are necessary to obtain legal employment and access state benefits, migrants' popular understandings of law assume that "status inheres in papers, not persons."[8] As a result, those privileged migrants *con papeles* (with papers) or *documentos* (documents) have found a brisk business in renting out and exchanging their papers with *los sinpapeles* (those without papers). In short, IRCA's requirement that employers inspect work authorization documents to verify a potential employee's eligibility for work has transformed legality into a fungible commodity—an object that can be circulated, exchanged, and rented.

Most media reports of the illicit market in papers focus on the underground vendors—operating in flea markets, corner stores, and out of their homes—who furnish migrants with fake documents for a fee. Yet because fake identity documents typically cost at least $150, migrant farmworkers say it is preferable to procure documents outside the market economy. In fact, interviewees say, identity loan is the most common means by which migrant farmworkers obtain the documents they need to work in the Central Valley.

The impoverishment of migrant farmworking communities—as well as the stark division among migrant farmworkers by legal status—encourages the treatment of papers as valuable resources. Nearly a quarter of all farmworker families nationwide lived in poverty between 2007 and 2009; the average total family income was less than $19,999

a year.[9] Unemployment benefits are a vital supplement to farmworkers' meager seasonal earnings. Indeed, the majority of farmworkers—61 percent in California—are employed seasonally, and according to the National Agricultural Workers' Survey, farmworkers use unemployment benefits more than any other form of public assistance. Yet only farmworkers with legal status are eligible for unemployment benefits in California, and it is estimated that 57 percent of the state's farmworkers lack legal status.[10] As a means of maximizing unemployment benefits, then, identity loan emerges as an important economic strategy. Circulating papers garners additional income for those with legal status while allowing those without it to secure work and obtain a financial bonus.[11]

THE MORAL ECONOMY OF EXCHANGE: "PAPERS" AS FAMILY ASSETS

Migrants describe a continuum of practices of identity loan; they say the risk of engaging in such loans varies according to the social distance between donor and recipient. The safest form of document exchange is between close family members. A citizen cousin may temporarily loan her undocumented cousin her identity documents, or an uncle who has returned to El Salvador or Mexico may give a nephew his Social Security card and green card to use on a permanent basis. Loans between kin, which rarely involve financial transactions and pose the least legal risk to the borrower, bind kin together and deepen ties of reciprocal obligation.

Loans between kin are enmeshed in what scholars call a "moral economy of exchange"—one in which individual monetary gain is not the primary objective. Scholars use the term *moral economy* to refer to the nonmarket norms and rationalities that govern exchanges in marginalized communities.[12] In communities with formidable barriers to socioeconomic mobility, maximizing individual profit may not in fact be the most rational goal. Instead, in communities alienated from the formal economy, engaging in reciprocal exchanges to build and strengthen social relationships may become an important end in and of itself.[13] Because documents constitute a scarce form of capital among migrant farmworkers, document exchange is a rational strategy to maximize the value of this precious family asset.

Manuel, for example, found that his uncle's valid documents opened the door to a more lucrative job in the formal economy. An undocumented migrant from Zacatecas, Manuel had first settled in the San

Francisco Bay Area and sought work in construction. Because the construction industry in San Francisco is unionized, Manuel had discovered that his potential employers would check his I-9 form with E-Verify, a federal database that matches Social Security numbers and names. Manuel's uncle had received a Social Security card in the early 1970s when he had first migrated to California. Because he had returned to Mexico and had no plans to return, Manuel's uncle agreed to let Manuel work his card.

When next applying for work, Manuel presented the Social Security card to the employer along with a fake green card in his uncle's name, which he had purchased from a local vendor. The employer was able to verify that the SSN was on file with the Social Security Administration (SSA) and that it matched the uncle's name. This strategy allowed Manuel the relative luxury of landing a unionized job normally closed to the undocumented, one that offered more comfortable working conditions and employer-provided benefits. Moreover, whereas Manuel had earned about $25,000 a year in agriculture, he was able to earn $60,000 to $80,000 a year in construction.

Manuel believes that borrowing his uncle's card is ethically superior to inventing an SSN and engaging in what he describes as a form of "identity roulette." He observes that his cousin—who purchased a fake Social Security card with a random number—has received notifications from the SSA informing him of a "duplicate user," meaning that the number on his fake card belonged to someone else. Manuel says he wished to avoid this "mess." "So some poor guy is walking around not knowing that a guy in the Central Valley is working his number. . . . At least I'm not using a number that might belong to someone I don't know," he says. Manuel views the circulation of documents among kin as a legitimate use of family property and takes comfort in the reciprocal nature of his exchange with his uncle. He explains, "This card belonged to my family; it's a family thing. My uncle can't do anything with it [his card] in Mexico. This way, if my uncle ever comes back here, he can get his benefits."

In a similar vein, Doña Rosa lent her daughter her work authorization documents with the understanding that valid Social Security cards should not be left "blank" (unused). Doña Rosa entered the United States legally three years ago, at the age of sixty-five. Her husband, Don Santiago, had been migrating seasonally to the Central Valley since the 1960s; Doña Rosa had stayed behind in Zacatecas until she could count on the security of a visa to join him. It was only in 2010—after more

than half a century of a long-distance marriage—that Doña Rosa became a legal permanent resident. She gained legal residency through her eldest daughter, who herself had the good fortune to become a legal permanent resident through marriage.

Having only recently immigrated to the United States, Doña Rosa had never set foot in the fields herself. However, her second-eldest daughter, Lupita, was struggling with the challenge of making a living as an undocumented farmworker. She picked melons and pruned grapes in the summer heat; she had worked alongside a young woman who died after being stung by an insect and a forty-year-old man who had expired on a 104-degree day. A single woman in her late thirties, Lupita felt her marriage prospects were dim; she saw no future ahead of her other than laboring in the hot fields. She was Doña Rosa and Don Santiago's only unmarried daughter, and they were given to fretting aloud about her future. "The field is no place for a woman," was Don Santiago's refrain, a preface to stories of his daughter's latest insults and injuries.

Having recently received her green card, Doña Rosa struck on what she thought was a brilliant plan to save her undocumented daughter from a future in the fields, an arrangement she thought would benefit them both. She would lend her SSN to Lupita, thus providing her daughter with the means to find less demanding work outside the fields; at the same time, her daughter's earnings would grant Doña Rosa—who had never worked in the United States— a way to amass a retirement fund.

When Doña Rosa announced her plan to her husband, Don Santiago tried to dissuade her. Having been privy to such schemes over his twenty years of working in the fields, Don Santiago was well aware that document exchange was not legal. Nevertheless, Doña Rosa promptly dispatched a hopeful Lupita to the tomato-packing shed—where packers have the luxury of working indoors and receiving both overtime and health insurance—to inquire whether she could use her mother's SSN to obtain more suitable employment there. According to Lupita, the secretary in the hiring office was adamant in her refusal but unperturbed. Slowly and carefully, she had explained to Lupita that not only was it not possible for her to use her mother's card to obtain employment but also that using another person's identity to secure employment constituted a form of identity fraud. According to Don Santiago, Lupita returned home chastened and scared—"with wide eyes," Don Santiago recounts, laughing in chagrin. "Ayy, that woman is so stubborn," he says of his wife, slapping his hand to his forehead. "And she had been so sure that it would not be a problem."

Doña Rosa's attempt to loan Lupita her documents was driven by the principle that valid Social Security cards—acquired only through great effort—should not be left unused. "Because her Social Security number is so blank [*tan blanquito*], she [Doña Rosa] thought that Lupita could work it," Don Santiago said. As he explained, Doña Rosa had felt that her idea would be acceptable. "She had just gotten her green card through her daughter, so why not give it to her other daughter to work?" Thus Doña Rosa's case shows that an immigration system in which adjustment of legal status is accomplished through family members fosters a perception of papers as a transferable family resource. Document loans among kin must be understood in the context of an immigration system in which legal status—most often obtained through family members—appears to be a transitive property.[14]

As Manuel and Doña Rosa's cases show, those who circulated documents among family members discussed the practice as means of maximizing the value of precious family assets. In farmworking families, papers serve as a form of symbolic capital that may be directly exchanged for social capital, jobs, and financial capital itself.[15] A set of unspoken moral principles appears to structure such exchanges: that valid papers must not be left "idle" and valid Social Security records must not be left "blank." Among migrant farmworking families, then, the pooling of scarce resources is a collective response to marginalization and impoverishment.

FATTENING THEIR UNEMPLOYMENT CHECKS: LOANS BY ACQUAINTANCES

Not all migrant farmworkers keep document exchange in the family. Identity loans sometimes bind together more distant acquaintances: neighbors, coworkers, and distant kin. Among parties separated by greater social distance, the primary objective is frequently maximizing individual profit. Thus these loans stand outside the moral economy of kin-based exchange. The donor seeks to harness the recipient's labor with the aim of receiving augmented benefits; to do so, he or she must typically entice the recipient by paying a fee. According to migrants, potential donors typically initiate the exchange. A lender may broach the topic by asking an acquaintance, "Are you going to work your own name? Or can you work my Social Security card?"[16]

According to migrants, workers with legal status may generate additional income through identity loan in two ways. They may loan undocumented workers their papers while resting at home, thereby maximiz-

ing their unemployment benefits and padding their pension accounts. Thus they may supplement their meager wages by taking advantage of undocumented workers' exclusion from unemployment benefits. Alternatively, they may collect unemployment earnings with their own documents while working under another person's identity, thereby supplementing their unemployment payments with earned income.

"Farm Work Finishes off the Body"

Although migrants with legal status disproportionately profit from identity loan, they engage in such practices out of need. Identity loan helps compensate for farmworkers' status as exceptional workers. Because of farm work's exclusion from state and federal protections that have created a middle-class standard of living, the annual incomes of farmworkers are the lowest of any wage-earning and salaried workers.[17] For farmworkers with the benefit of legal permanent residency and even citizenship, then, identity loan provides an opportunity to augment their earnings from a dangerous, difficult, and poorly compensated occupation.

To understand the pressures that make identity loan attractive—even necessary—for migrant farmworkers, let us take the case of Raquel and her husband. Raquel and Alberto are both in their early fifties. They left El Salvador in 1991 and received political asylum in the United States (see appendix C); they adjusted their status to become legal permanent residents a few years later. They have two adult daughters and another who is twelve.

After more than twenty years of picking and weeding, Raquel and her husband have come to the realization that their bodies carry no lifetime warranty. "Farm work finishes off the body," Raquel says (*se acaban los cuerpos en los fieles*). It is well known, she tells me, that a farmworker's body "finishes" well before the official retirement age. Alberto nods. "Bodies do meet their ends more quickly in the fields," he says. Over a lifetime, Alberto says, each kind of work takes its own particular toll. Bending to pick and pack melon strains the lower back. Squatting to weed tomatoes with a knife damages the knees. And packing asparagus into bunches produces *sobrehuesos,* spiny growths on the knuckles that are the hallmark of arthritis. At the end of a career in the fields, Alberto says, an astute observer can read a worker's history from his body, whether from the hunch of his back or the stiff limp of his gait.

Alberto works year-round; he prunes almond trees in the winter, weeds cotton and tomato in the spring, and picks melon in the summer

and fall. Raquel used to weed cotton and tomato alongside her husband during the spring, but is now limited to packing melon during the summer. Because of Raquel's age and increasing infirmity, few labor supervisors call her to work on their crews.

Farm work has left Raquel and Alberto with a host of ailments. For the past eleven years, Alberto has experienced recurring abdominal pain, that farm work often aggravates. In 2007, it struck him at the height of the melon season. He had been packing boxes of melons and throwing them onto the trailer. During his first hour of stacking boxes, which typically weigh twenty-five to forty pounds, he felt a stabbing pain in his abdomen that had made him double over; he returned home to recover. Fearful of being replaced if he missed another day, he returned to work the next day. He lasted only three hours before the pain knifed through his belly again. So Alberto drove himself home and made himself a tea from the grasses that grow outside his house. He rested for two hours. And then, gritting his teeth in quiet determination, he drove himself back to work.

Raquel has her own medical complaints. When I first talked to her about her health in 2008, she had complained of a pain in her back that eventually migrated to her hip. She had first experienced it while packing melon. "I think it's because of the weight—lifting box after box for so many hours," she says. X-rays revealed nothing. Raquel's doctor sent her home with a prescription for Vicodin; he told her that the pain was probably early arthritis and "would always be with her." For the doctor, the diagnosis was likely a routine event. Yet for Raquel—not yet fifty and facing ten years without retirement income—his answer provided little solace. Instead, Raquel took advantage of a trip to El Salvador to see her mother to visit a masseuse; the woman's patient kneading granted her a few weeks' reprieve from the pain.

Two years later, during a visit with the couple in the winter of 2010, I found that Raquel was now suffering pain in her right arm as well. Thrusting her finger into her elbow to describe her agony, she explained, "Pain strikes me right in the joints." It had begun when she was packing melons the previous summer and had continued through her spring job of weeding. Unsuccessful once again in finding relief at the clinic, she instead sought help in the Valley's underground medicine cabinet: the flea market. The vendor she consulted there recommended a bottle of arthritis pills called Rumoquin, a steroid and anti-inflammatory sold in Mexico. She took the pills every day, she said; they help "a little." Yet the pain now traveled from her elbow to her wrist, she added, grimacing as she traced its path with her finger.

The next winter, when I return to visit Raquel, she tells me she has been struck by knee pain so severe that it became difficult for her to stand. An MRI revealed that the cartilage in her left knee had worn down so much the bones in her knee were grating against each other. The doctor who treated her told her that he did not know how she had borne the pain for so long. Injuries as severe as Raquel's, he informed her, are typically caused by a serious fall. Yet Raquel was skeptical of the doctor's etiological claim: the last time she had fallen on her knee was twelve years ago. The doctor added that the damage might be the legacy of a lifetime of daily wear and tear, a cause he pronounced as "possible" but "difficult to prove." Obviously, Raquel tells me with a wry smile, the doctor had never worked in the *azadón* (weeding), which requires constant squatting and standing to uproot weeds along the rows of crops. Raquel remembers that a day of such work last summer had left her knee swollen like an overripe cantaloupe.

In the winter of 2012, Raquel had surgery to help repair the damaged cartilage. Her doctor certified her for two months of temporary disability so that she could recover. Although the surgery offered a solution for Raquel's damaged cartilage, it left a larger existential question unresolved. How could Raquel support herself after the disability benefits ended? Even if she were recertified for state disability benefits, they would last only twelve months. After that, her future would remain in doubt.

In short, Raquel's "used-up" knee has left her in a social assistance limbo. When I visited her in the summer of 2012, she had temporarily given up the knife and the hoe. Still hopeful that she might eventually return to the fields, she spent her days icing and rehabilitating her knee. Yet for now, she says, she is more comfortable supervising her grandchildren from the safety of her couch.

Identity Loan as a Safety Net

Raquel's involuntary retirement has left her and Alberto in a financial hole. Without her earnings, the couple now earns less than $8,000 in wages a year. Alberto receives $408 a week in unemployment payments for three months each year, and they also receive $300 a month in food stamps year-round. Their annual income, for a family of three, amounts to roughly $17,000 a year—well below the official poverty line.

As their annual incomes continue to decline because of their depleted bodies, Raquel and Alberto have adopted other strategies to meet their financial needs. They live across the street from a church that dispenses

food to the needy; Raquel stands in line to receive bags of rice and beans each month. The couple's adult daughters, whose husbands work in the fields, also help support them. But since their daughters' own annual wages amount to less than $15,000 each, and each has dependents, they cannot serve as the couple's sole support in their old age.

With their bodies used up and public assistance out of reach, Raquel and Alberto have decided to redeem the value of their last remaining asset. Raquel may be unable to work, but she still has a valid Social Security number. Since she cannot work, she will put it to good use by asking an undocumented relative to work it.

For his part, Alberto has already resorted to identity loan to compensate for his wife's lost income. He is working an acquaintance's SSN while also collecting unemployment. He uses his friend's number to earn wages while weeding onions; his friend pays him an additional $100 for each $1,000 he earns. At the same time, Alberto uses his own Social Security card to collect an additional $408 in unemployment benefits each week.

As Raquel and Alberto grow older, this deft use of document exchange will allow them to survive. Now that working in the fields has sapped their bodies of strength, their valid papers are one of their few remaining productive assets. For aging and elderly farmworkers, identity loan serves as a safety net in a social assistance system that fails to meet their needs.

"LOANS" BY EMPLOYERS: MAKING MONEY OFF THE MARGINS

Migrants' neighbors and coworkers are not the only ones who use document exchange in order to turn a profit. Labor supervisors—*mayordomos* in particular—are often tightly integrated into migrant communities. They are often bound to workers by ties of kinship and acquaintanceship. Many labor supervisors take advantage of their knowledge of migrants' personal circumstances to make deals that reduce their labor costs and yield additional income.

All the contractors and *mayordomos* I interviewed once worked in the fields themselves. Many, in fact, were former undocumented migrants who were able to adjust their legal status through IRCA's Special Agricultural Worker (SAW) program. Indeed, IRCA facilitated their ascent through the farm labor hierarchy in two different ways. First, the SAW program granted formerly undocumented farmworkers legal status, providing them an unprecedented opportunity to apply for state and federal contracting licenses. Second, as growers attempted to shield themselves from the fines associated with employing undocumented

workers, IRCA's documentation requirement placed labor intermediaries in high demand.[18]

Don Tomás, for example, worked as a field hand for twenty years and then as a *mayordomo* for an additional twelve years before retiring. Don Tomás migrated from El Salvador without documents in 1980 and first found work weeding cotton and picking melon for several large companies. "I know the pressure of work in *cuadrillas* [teams]—having to race up and down the field," he says. Through a friend, he eventually landed a job on a local ranch. During the spring and summer, he worked in the fields with the rest of the field hands. Then, over the winter, he was one of a select group of twenty men whom the ranch owner kept on to do the annual maintenance.

It was while he was working for this ranch that Don Tomás's fortunes changed. The passage of IRCA in 1986 allowed 1.3 million agricultural workers to obtain legal status through the SAW program.[19] "That's how I got my papers," Don Tomás says. Having proved himself a solid worker with "drive" and "skill," Don Tomás says, he soon drew the attention of the ranch's supervisors. Shortly after he adjusted his legal status, a friend of his—also a *mayordomo*—asked Don Tomás if he would like to try supervising a team himself. Thus a combination of consistency and sheer luck had transformed Don Tomás from field hand into field supervisor. His hard work had proved his ability to supervise a team, and his newly gained legal status allowed him to apply for and obtain a formal *mayordomo* license.

Having once been undocumented migrants themselves, many labor supervisors are deeply familiar with migrants' social and legal circumstances. As labor brokers who control the allocation of jobs, *mayordomos* occupy a position of advantage in migrant communities. Identity loan provides field bosses an additional source of gain. Exploiting their employees' vulnerability and their need for work, *mayordomos* often make an offer of employment contingent on a prospective employee's acceptance of a document loan. Field hands say that *mayordomos* themselves directly benefit from such loans; in exchange for an employee's use of a relative or friend's work authorization documents, the donor gives the supervisor a financial bonus.

In focus groups, migrant farmworkers reported that this strategy was common. As one focus group participant said: "A lot of field bosses . . . give their workers the names and SSNs of their family members. . . . And the poor guy without papers works the other person's Social Security card [*seguro*] and contributes to his account—unless he wants to go home." Another replied: "Or there are people who give their Social Security cards to the field bosses and say, 'You know what? Have them work my SSN, and I'll give you so much money.' . . . So the field boss puts

another [name] down for a worker who doesn't have a SSN, who doesn't have papers, and the field boss makes money!" Indeed, two migrant farmworkers in this group discovered that they had both fallen victim to the same labor supervisor's request that they work under another identity. "I asked [the *mayordomo*] for the [W-4] form and [he said] 'No, no! Why should we fill out the form? I already put this other name right here,'" one participant said. "The same thing happened to me [with that supervisor]!" another added. Thus labor supervisors have found a lucrative niche in exploiting undocumented migrants' need for identity documents.

Identity loan can be understood only in the context of the poverty and marginality of identity recipients that makes them agree to such loans. As one migrant put it, "Many people take advantage of the need one has [*necesidad*]." Indeed, document exchange benefits the donors more than the recipients. While it offers more established migrants and employers a means to "make money off the margins," it exposes identity recipients to the risk of arrest for Social Security fraud or identity theft.[20] As a result, interviewees say that common targets of loans are the individuals most in need of the legal disguise that document exchange provides: undocumented migrants, underage workers, and those facing deportation orders.[21] In short, labor supervisors are in a unique position to prey on the vulnerabilities produced by immigration enforcement and inadequately enforced labor laws.

DISGUISING UNLAWFUL EMPLOYEES AND LABOR PRACTICES

While document loans benefit labor supervisors as individuals, they also redound to their profit as employers. Because document exchange removes workers' identities from the official wage and employment records, labor supervisors often use the practice not only to augment their personal income but also to hide unlawful employees and labor practices from the authorities. Indeed, workers use the phrase *trabajando fantasma* (working as a ghost) to describe this process of legal disappearance.

Migrants say that labor supervisors are eager to transform particular categories of unlawful employees into ghost workers: undocumented migrants, minors, and those working overtime. For example, the employment of minors, like the employment of undocumented workers, often places agricultural employers at risk of being fined. In California, the state prohibits children under eighteen from working in agriculture for more than forty-eight hours a week, or eight hours a day.[22] Yet during the summer harvest season, when most minors seek work,

workers may labor for seventy to eighty hours a week. Labor supervisors often use minors' legal ineligibility for employment during the harvest season as an excuse to require that they work as ghosts. Thus labor supervisors engage in coercive loans as a means of what I call *identity masking*—that is, of disguising minors' employment from the federal and state governments (see also chapter 5).

Identity masking not only obscures employers' hire of unlawful employees; it also masks their engagement in unlawful labor practices. In the following exchange, five focus-group participants explain how document exchange allows the pervasive violation of overtime laws among agricultural employers:

> *Participant* #5: I say that also what's bad is that they only let me work Monday to Saturday. And sometimes you need to work Sunday, but on Sunday they make you work another . . .
>
> *Participant* #2: Another name.
>
> *Participant* #5: The Social Security number of another person.
>
> *Participant* #2: Exactly.
>
> *Participant* #3: To pay less.
>
> *Participant* #5: To not have to pay us "overtime." And if not, they look at you as if to say, "I'm going to lay Fulana [So-and-So] off, she won't work until Monday." . . . They make you lose a day [of work]. They lay you off on Sunday, or you work under another name.
>
> *SH*: So you have to choose to work with another name or not to work at all?
>
> *Participant* #2: That's right! Or you don't work on Sunday! [*¡O descansas!*]

Like restaurant owners in Chicago who use a "two-check" system,[23] agricultural employers use a "two-identity" system to avoid paying workers overtime wages. Indeed, migrants say that employers' pervasive use of document exchange to underpay workers for a seven-day work week has earned Sunday the moniker "the day of the ghost" in the Central Valley. As one migrant put it, "Sunday should be a holy day [*un día santo*], but instead it's the day of the ghost [*el día del fantasma*]." In short, the presence of ghost workers on a labor team reveals as much as it hides; it is a telltale sign of violations of immigration and labor laws.

WHEN GHOST WORKERS ARE INJURED: INVALIDATING WORKERS' COMPENSATION CLAIMS

Extending coercive loans to their employees allows employers to pad their own wallets while reducing their company's labor costs. Indeed, identity

loan helps employers cope with their competitive labor environments in several different ways. Identity masking not only helps them evade state and federal fines but also allows them to suppress ghost workers' compensation insurance (WCI) claims.

As Elisabeta discovered in the opening passage of the chapter, supervisors often inform migrants that working under other identities makes them ineligible for WCI when injured. Employers are required to offer WCI to workers to provide them with medical attention for job-related injuries and illnesses as well as compensation for their lost wages. Farmworkers have historically been excluded from labor protections such as workers' compensation. Undocumented workers are also excluded from workers' compensation benefits in many states. California, however, is one of thirteen states that require agricultural employers to offer the same coverage to employees as employers do in other industries.[24] Moreover, the state's undocumented migrants are legally entitled to the same benefits as workers with legal status. Yet identity loan accomplishes the exclusion that California's laws do not.

Being an identity recipient does not legally invalidate a worker's right to the benefit. However, my interviews with workers' compensation attorneys helped explain why identity loan poses difficulties for injured or ill workers. When migrants work under loaned identity documents, they disappear from the official roster of the company's insured employees.

According to the attorneys, document exchange prevents workers' use of the employer insurance by creating what they called "proof problems" for identity recipients. If an injured identity recipient were to file a WCI claim using his or her real name, the WCI carrier would have no record of the injured worker on the official list of the company's employees. One focus group participant explains why ghost workers have little legal recourse when injured: "Because who got injured? The ghost. . . . Do you think the guy who *didn't* work will sue? 'You weren't working! [the supervisor will say]. I saw someone else!' What's the poor guy [who got injured] going to do?" In short, identity loan precipitates a conflict between an injured worker's true identity and his or her assumed identity. Identity masking propels injured workers into what Susan Coutin calls "the space of nonexistence"—a space in which workers' social and physical presence clashes with their legal absence.[25]

Theoretically, the attorneys said, labor supervisors could intervene to assist ghost workers to reverse the process of disappearance that

identity loan creates. They could record the legal names of such workers on the list of that day's employees as though they were new hires. Alternatively, an injured identity recipient could call the insurance carrier and file a report under his own legal name. If the WCI carrier called the employer to investigate the claim for the unknown employee, the labor supervisor could disclose the identity switch to the WCI carrier to ensure that the worker was recognized as a company employee. Yet in practice, migrants said, labor supervisors rarely assisted their workers in this manner. Instead, they strategically manipulated their injured workers' fears in order to ensure that they did indeed disappear.

Labor Supervisors' Perspectives

Interviews with labor supervisors reveal why they turn to identity loan to suppress WCI claims. As intermediaries between growers and workers, labor supervisors face heavy financial, regulatory, and job-related stress. Growers pay contractors a commission that covers the contractor's overhead, expenses such as workers' compensation premiums, and employees' wages. Because growers shop for contractors based on reputation and cost, contractors strive to maintain low commission rates. High workers' compensation premiums—which rise with the number of paid claims—drive up a contractor's commission. To keep their premiums low and remain competitive, then, some labor intermediaries leverage the possibility of implicating workers in identity theft to discourage them from filing for WCI.

Most *mayordomos* and contractors denied engaging in such practices. However, one retired *mayordomo* for a small contractor, Don Tomás—with whom I had established a rapport by attempting to help him navigate the federal disability insurance system—was more candid. Don Tomás says that the contractor for whom he had worked for over fifteen years had explicitly informed supervisors during their training of an unofficial company policy of not paying claims for ghost workers. During the hiring process, he says, *mayordomos* and the secretary selectively informed workers whose photos did not match their faces that they ran "the risk of not being compensated" for their injuries. "They told us, 'Even if they're working with fake documents, they can get care, but they have to be using their own name,'" he says. "It's a very shrewd way [*manera muy caneja*] of reducing the company's costs."

GOVERNING MIGRANT WORKERS THROUGH CRIME

If identity loan provides employers a convenient pretext to suppress workers' compensation claims, federal immigration policy stokes the fears that make this ploy successful. Migrants' fears of being implicated in identity theft are the result of the increasing criminalization of undocumented migration over the past two decades. The anthropologists Julie Dowling and Jonathan Xavier Inda call this trend "governing immigration through crime," a process that makes "crime and punishment the institutional context in which efforts to guide the conduct of immigrants take place." The authors argue that the events of September 11, 2001, produced a "migration-crime-security complex" that polices immigrants as prototypical "criminal anti-citizens" who threaten the security of the homeland.[26] The perceived menace posed by such "internal foreigners" has led to a shift in the emphasis of immigration enforcement from policing the nation's borders to more vigilantly scrutinizing its interior.[27] As the border has migrated inward, the spaces of everyday life—including workplaces, homes, and neighborhoods—have been subjected to policing on an unprecedented scale. Immigration and Customs Enforcement's (ICE's) heightened worksite enforcement initiatives and its partnerships with local law enforcement officials are but two examples of the ratcheting up of internal surveillance.

At the federal level, for example, ICE officials used to summarily deport undocumented migrants apprehended during worksite raids. However, it is now common for federal prosecutors to charge migrants with document-related offenses as well as deport them. For example, during the 2008 raid of a kosher meatpacking plant in Postville, Iowa, ICE officers arrested and detained 389 undocumented migrants for aggravated identity theft, meaning that they had knowingly and intentionally used the identity of a third party without that party's consent. Federal prosecutors eventually offered most workers a plea agreement in exchange for admission to the lesser charge of Social Security fraud—that is, of using fraudulent Social Security cards.[28] After their deportation, evidence emerged that several plant supervisors and human services employees had furnished employees with the fraudulent documents that led to their convictions. In short, it may have been the plant managers themselves who committed identity theft as a form of identity masking—that is, precisely in an attempt to *avoid* a federal audit.[29]

Meanwhile, at the local level, law enforcement officials are entering into unprecedented partnerships with federal immigration authorities.

Under the federal 287(g) program, county and state law-enforcement officers may be deputized to arrest undocumented migrants on their own authority and collaborate with ICE to ensure their deportation as "criminal aliens."[30] In addition, Secure Communities, a federal program first launched in 2008, required that police provide the Department of Homeland Security (DHS) with the fingerprints of all arrestees in order to screen them against databases of known immigration offenders and hold them for removal. Its 2014 replacement, the Priority Enforcement Program (PEP), continues to require law enforcement officials to "cooperate" with DHS and to make undocumented migrants priority targets.[31] As undocumented migrants are increasingly governed through the criminal justice system, then, federal policies may increase migrants' vulnerability at work.

Labor scholars have long debated whether federal immigration policy plays a direct or indirect role in migrant workers' "superexploitation."[32] Nicholas De Genova argues that undocumented migrants' "deportability"—that is, the ever-present threat of deportation—allows employers to ensure that migrants serve as a profitable labor force. Anthropological scholarship has amply documented the ways that employers strategically manipulate the possibility of migrants' deportation to reduce their labor costs and maximize productivity.[33] For example, anthropologists have shown that "no-match" letters, sent by the Social Security Administration (SSA) to inform employers of a discrepancy between an employee's stated name and the name associated with that SSN, often indirectly provide employers with leverage over undocumented employees, enabling them to fire such workers under the pretext of obeying immigration laws. Angela Stuesse shows that Tyson Foods, a poultry processing giant in Mississippi, used no-match letters as a justification to fire only those migrant workers involved in a union.[34] Similarly, Ruth Gomberg-Muñoz and Laura Nussbaum-Barbarena found that a Chicago meatpacking plant used the letters to legitimize its firing of migrant employees in order to reduce labor costs by liquidating the plant and relocating it to Iowa.[35] Yet despite our understanding of how employers use federal workplace enforcement activities to their advantage, little scholarship has yet explored how the governing of immigration through the criminal justice system also facilitates the transfer of value from migrants to employers.[36]

The increasing criminalization of undocumented migrants' everyday conduct allows employers to wield greater power over migrants than merely leveraging the threat of their potential deportation. As states,

counties, and municipalities have increasingly criminalized migrants' everyday activities—such as driving, working, and standing on street corners—local law enforcement officers become de facto enforcers of federal immigration laws.[37] Both ICE's prosecution of migrants for document-related charges and local law enforcement officers' roles as surrogate immigration agents have made criminal rather than civil arrest a standard pathway to deportation. Thus what I call *denounceability*—that is, migrants' vulnerability to criminal arrest and imprisonment—only compounds their fears of deportation and ensures their quiescence.[38]

Producing Workers' Denounceability

Fear of being implicated in identity theft was pervasive among the workers I interviewed. They were unanimous in affirming that being an identity recipient renders a worker ineligible for WCI. "That's what they say. They say you don't have rights to receive any [death or injury] benefits if you work under another name," says Don Santiago, a seasoned worker of sixty-five. "Because they could say it was identity theft [*un robo de identidad*]," another elaborates. Workers say they learned of ghost workers' ineligibility from a variety of sources. Some *mayordomos* warned their crews of this on the first day of work; others, like Elisabeta's supervisor, informed workers of this policy only once they were injured. Workers repeated the supervisors' statement among themselves until it became accepted as truth.

For example, Elisabeta remembers that when she was packing cantaloupe for a large company from the border, the *mayordoma* called a special meeting to urge her employees to work under their rightful names. "I remember because she told us, 'Sure, working other people's papers may help earn you a little more money. But you run a huge risk because this job is very dangerous. If you work under another name, how will the company compensate you [if you are injured or killed]?'" Elisabeta says. The supervisor, Elisabeta recalls, seemed "truly worried." This earnest warning—in combination with her own experience while topping onions—left a lasting impression. "Since that time, I have only worked my own papers. Because what would happen to my children [if I were injured or killed]?" she says. "I need to leave them with some support" (*necesito dejarles algún respaldo*).

Sulema reported that she first heard this warning from her coworkers. "At work, people always ask: 'Are you going to work *derecho*—are you going to work your own name? I'd suggest that you do. Because if

you don't work your own name, they won't help you if anything bad happens to you at work.'" She calls this advice "popular wisdom." A new arrival, Sulema says that she had no idea that assistance was even available for injured workers until she heard her coworkers' warning. Ironically, Sulema says, she first learned about workers' compensation by hearing that identity loan invalidated a worker's entitlement to it. Laughing, she adds that the same workers who warn of the pitfalls of working as a ghost are of course eager to loan their documents if they find a willing taker.

MAKING GHOST WORKERS DISAPPEAR

Previous studies have suggested that the primary obstacle to farmworkers' receiving workers' compensation is that they are unaware of their eligibility.[39] In contrast, most of the workers I interviewed were aware that legal status is not a barrier: they had undocumented friends, acquaintances, and family members who had received the compensation. Yet their experience had also taught them that involvement in identity loan effectively invalidated a worker's eligibility. Workers reported that some *mayordomos* attempted to use their knowledge of employees' engagement in identity loan to discourage them from filing an injury report. When workers did file reports, they said, some contractors and growers threatened to expose their position of legal compromise to avoid paying injured workers remuneration for lost wages or bereaved family members death benefits. This suggests that even as undocumented workers have become more aware that lack of legal status is not a barrier to the submission of claims, employers have transformed identity loan into a powerful new tool for suppressing workers' access to benefits to which they are legally entitled.

Several workers reported that their supervisors had screened them for their engagement in identity loan before providing them with care. Yadira, an undocumented worker from Colima, successfully cleared this initial hurdle. Having tumbled from a tomato planting machine and lost consciousness, she awoke to her supervisor's question: "Are you working your own name?" When she said yes, he asked her, "Do you want to file a report?" Only when she responded affirmatively did he take her to the office to file an injury report.

Raquel, a legal permanent resident, had a similar story. Raquel once sliced open her thumb with a small knife used to weed tomato plants. Workers call the knife *la trucha*, or the "sly one," because it is stealthy

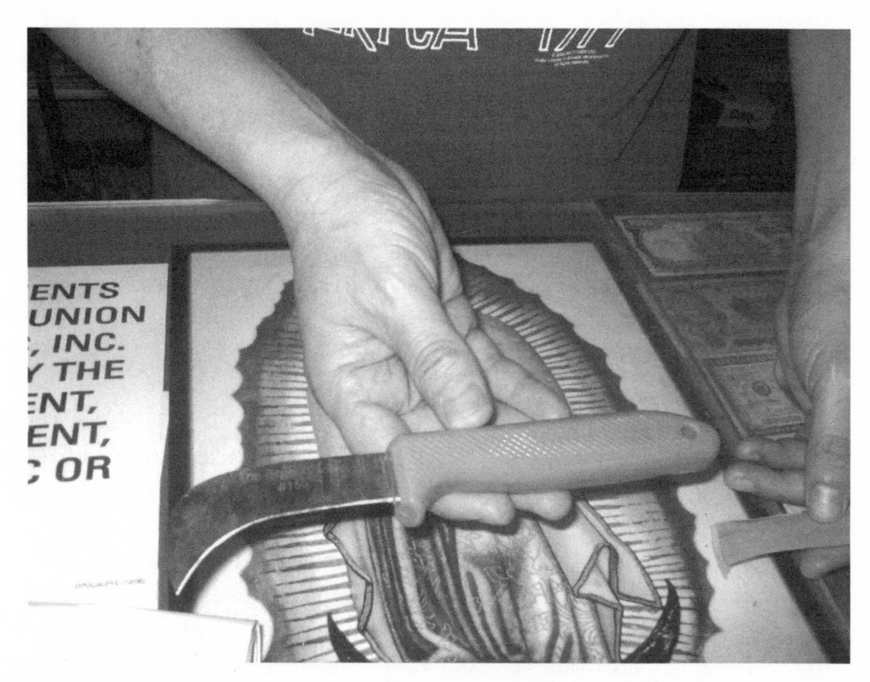

FIGURE 10. Supervisors require that workers use a short knife, called *la trucha,* to weed tomato plants, although its use is banned by Cal-OSHA for health and safety reasons.

in slicing not only tomato stems but also workers' hands. Raquel called her supervisor, who examined the wound with concern. It was a deep cut: it would require stitches and two full days of recuperation before she could comfortably use it again. Yet before taking her to the office to fill out a report, her supervisor asked: ("*¿Andas trabajando derecho?*" (Are you working straight?)[40] The question, Raquel says, was intended to screen out those workers committing identity loan; it was designed to discourage her from reporting the accident and filing a claim for care.[41]

As it happened, Raquel was working her own papers and told her supervisor so. She strongly suspects that the supervisor had asked her this question because he wished to avoid filing a report of the accident. As she discovered when he did take her to the doctor, it is illegal for *mayordomos* to require that workers weed using knives, which are among a variety of "short-handled tools" banned by the state of California in 1978. To Raquel's delight, the doctor stitched up her hand while roundly chastising her boss. Raquel's injury had drawn attention to this violation of health and safety standards: for her boss, it would have been most

convenient for Raquel and her injury to disappear. Indeed, the question he asked was designed to exploit Raquel's potential situation of legal compromise in order to obscure his own.

While Raquel's use of her own documents enabled her to access care, other migrants were not so lucky. Migrants reported that ghost workers using the documents provided by supervisors found themselves particularly disadvantaged in this regard. Employer-initiated loans are a false gift: workers refuse them at the risk of unemployment. Having direct knowledge—and even proof—of workers' involvement in identity loans, some supervisors have used this knowledge to withhold treatment or remuneration for injured workers.

One such case arose during a UFW meeting I attended. "Can't you do something about the woman who lost her eye?" a woman asked the organizers at the end of the meeting. After the meeting, she told me that her neighbor, Paula, had presented her fake Social Security card and green card to the *mayordomo* to be hired to pick grapes in a vineyard. The *mayordomo* had scoffed at the quality of her documents. "I can't hire you with these," he had told her. "That's okay, I'll give you a better set." The *mayordomo* had provided her with one set of documents that she worked for a week; the next week, he provided her with a different set. He paid wages but withheld her check stubs. Paula had no idea whose documents she was working; she assumed they must belong to relatives of her supervisor.

One day Paula was pruning grapes shortly after the field had been sprayed, and her eyes began to itch. She drove herself to the hospital after work because one eye had begun to burn. After two days of hospitalization, she eventually lost the eye. She left the hospital with a bill of over $20,000, yet she never dared to file a claim. Not only did her supervisor have direct proof of her engagement in identity loan, but Paula lacked the check stubs to prove that she had even worked for him. Although her neighbor had urged her to speak to the UFW or seek help elsewhere, and although I myself called her, Paula refused to speak with anyone else.

As Paula's case illustrates, employers' provision of identity documents places workers in a double bind. Supervisors use such loans as a means to harness the benefits associated with workers' labor for their own—and their family's—material gain. At the same time, such document loans jeopardize workers' access to compensation when injured. While loans by friends and acquaintances place identity recipients at risk of discovery by an employer, employer-initiated loans grant employers direct proof of workers' legal compromise.

Perpetual Illegality

An examination of changes in immigration law over the past two decades helps illuminate why identity loan has become such an effective tool of coercion. The Illegal Immigration Reform and Immigrant Responsibility Act (IIRIRA), passed in 1996 to help identify and remove "criminal aliens" from the nation, increased the penalties for document-related crimes. Prior to IIRIRA, migrants with legal status could be deported only for serious criminal offenses such as murder and felonies involving drugs and firearms. IIRIRA expanded the list of "aggravated felonies" for which legal residents are deportable to encompass nonviolent offenses such as petty theft, driving under the influence (in some states), and document fraud.[42] It also created additional penalties for undocumented migrants convicted of document fraud. It prevented undocumented migrants with criminal records from requesting judicial review of their removal proceedings and permanently barred those convicted of an aggravated felony from gaining legal residency.[43] Thus the convergence of immigration and criminal law creates a double penalty for migrants convicted of charges such as identity theft: the consequences of migrant denounceability far exceed those of migrant deportability alone. Conviction on such charges renders a migrant not merely subject to deportation but also permanently exiled from the United States.[44]

The sociologists Cecilia Menjívar and Leisy Abrego use the term *legal violence* to describe the way that the convergence of immigration and criminal law systematically impedes migrants' long-term incorporation. They use the term to highlight the invisible violence perpetrated by the law, which is often viewed as neutral and objective and yet has "cumulatively injurious effects" on migrants' family lives, education, and employment.[45] Legal violence refers to both the body of laws that allow such damage and the suffering they engender. Employers' manipulation of migrants' denounceability to reduce labor costs is an example of the intensified workplace abuses that legal violence abets.

As new federal and state laws increasingly cast undocumented migrants as criminals who undermine the security of the homeland, immigration enforcement has shifted from controlling the nation's borders to policing its interior. The criminalization of migrants' conduct over the past two decades has rendered them more vulnerable to manipulation and coercion by employers, and the penalty migrants face for

denunciation for offenses such as identity loan far exceeds that of deportation alone. As legal permanent residents work as ghosts to supplement their unemployment payments or work overtime, they too become vulnerable to denunciation. Thus legal violence jeopardizes the work conditions of all noncitizens.

Identity loan must be understood in the context of migrant farmworkers' poverty and marginality. It is the financial and legal vulnerability of migrants that makes them agree to work borrowed documents—a practice that places them at legal and physical risk. Yet even as migrant farmworkers' impoverishment makes engaging in identity loan attractive, immigration reforms have intensified its consequences. Although labor and immigration policies have long forced migrant farmworkers to work exceptionally hard, these punitive new changes only deepen their vulnerability at work. The risk of criminal prosecution for working with loaned documents degrades the working conditions of the entire migrant labor force.

CHAPTER 4

Presión Alta

The Physiological Toll of Farm Work

Less than two years apart, Sulema and Yadira, both under the age of forty, were hospitalized with *presión alta,* or hypertension. They joined Elisabeta, another undocumented woman and core research participant, who had been diagnosed with hypertension at the age of twenty-four. Sulema was diagnosed during a visit to the emergency room (ER) after her eye filled with blood during a family fight. Yadira found herself short of breath after the school nurse summoned her to her son's school to discuss his high blood pressure. After a friend checked her vitals with a monitor at home, Yadira had her reading confirmed by paramedics, who urged her to visit the ER. Yadira received antihypertensive medications intravenously before she was discharged.

When Sulema and Yadira talk about these episodes, both chalk their condition up to what they call *coraje.* In the anthropological literature, *coraje* is typically described as a culturally specific form of rage or deep-seated, embodied anger. As Ruth Behar notes, *coraje* denotes the kind of "rageful grief" that the anthropologist Renato Rosaldo experienced after losing his wife, Shelley, or that the Ilongot claim causes them to headhunt—an anger that demands death to soothe its pain.[1] In Rosaldo's account, this grief stems from rage at a misfortune one is powerless to correct.[2] Elsewhere, *coraje* is associated with sexual or physical victimization and abuse.[3] For Sulema and Yadira, *coraje* stemmed not from an insult dealt by a specific perpetrator or the hand of fate, but rather from the daily affronts they attributed to their undocumented status.

Studies suggest that migrant farmworkers suffer from hypertension at significantly higher rates than the general population.[4] Among my fifteen core research participants and their spouses, nine had been diagnosed and were taking medication at the time of their last interview. The average age of diagnosis was thirty-nine for men and forty-one for women. The true prevalence of hypertension among this group was likely higher, as it is a "silent epidemic," a condition that often exhibits no obvious symptoms and may be officially diagnosed only through a clinical exam. However, migrant farmworkers have only sporadic access to the subsidized health care that can detect and treat chronic disease; two of the seven men in my sample had not visited a doctor in the past five years.

In this chapter, I examine the forms of everyday violence—themselves the effects of legal violence—that cause self-reported *coraje* among migrant farmworkers and may lead to hypertension.[5] Scholars have argued that anthropologists are particularly well positioned to contribute to the analysis of health inequalities by "radically contextualizing" the high burden of chronic disease among marginalized groups.[6] Contextualizing the higher rates of hypertension among farmworkers in California's Central Valley suggests that work stress and immigration stress contribute to their disproportionate burden of chronic disease. This chapter uses migrants' narratives to suggest that these master stressors (an adaptation of Victor Turner's concept of the *master symbol*) trigger other anxieties and are interwoven with other related vulnerabilities.[7]

BEING AN UNDOCUMENTED FARMWORKER: CHRONIC STRESSORS

A growing body of anthropological research attempts to identify the discrete social stressors experienced by particular marginalized groups that ultimately lead to chronic diseases like hypertension.[8] The anthropologist Emily Mendenhall, for example, conducted life history interviews with 121 first- and second-generation Mexican women in Chicago who were diagnosed with type 2 diabetes. Mendenhall shows how the structural and legal violence in such women's lives—such as poverty and undocumented status—in turn precipitated multiple forms of "everyday violence," such as discrimination and sexual abuse. As the anthropologists Nancy Scheper-Hughes and Philippe Bourgois argue, violence begets violence.[9] Thus the macrosocial misfortunes such women suffered reverberated at the microsocial level as well. By analyzing their narratives, Mendenhall identifies nine common

stressors—including immigration stress, work stress, familial anxieties, and financial troubles—that are intrinsic to these women's experiences as migrants in the United States. These stressors—themselves the effect of political economic inequality—precipitously worsen Mexican women's health, culminating in both physical and mental distress.

Mendenhall persuasively argues that ethnographic narratives enhance our understanding of how such stressors affect migrants' bodies and psyches.[10] She emphasizes that traditional biomedical approaches often overlook the social and psychological causes of chronic disease, thereby missing important opportunities for intervention.[11] By allowing interviewees to discuss their lives and illness experiences in their own terms, ethnographic accounts not only radically contextualize the disproportionate burden of chronic disease so commonly observed among Mexican migrants but also illuminate the synergistic relationship between social, psychological, and physical distress.

Applying Mendenhall's insights to the cases of Sulema and Yadira suggests that we must listen to their stories to understand the role of stressors unique to their status in precipitating their onset of acute hypertension. Their narratives highlight the way that the legal violence of being an undocumented farmworker in turn triggers familial strife, financial misfortune, and interpersonal betrayal. The fact that work stress and immigration stress—both effects of legal violence—snowballed in significance over time and came to color all other domains of migrants' lives leads me to classify them as master stressors for undocumented migrant farmworkers in the Valley.

SULEMA: WORK STRESS AND PERCEIVED INJUSTICE

Undocumented migrants in the United States are concentrated in low-paid positions with little job security, high exploitation, and few benefits. Migrant farmworkers experience particularly high degrees of work stress. As temporary and seasonal workers, farmworkers have no job security and face high unemployment rates. Farm work is one of the three most dangerous occupations in the United States, and yet farmworkers are excluded from many state and federal labor protections.[12] In short, work stress is likely to be particularly pronounced among farmworkers; moreover, it is likely to take very particular forms.

Work injury—and attempts to obtain treatment through the workers' compensation system—is a common form of work stress among farmworkers. Forty-one percent of farmworkers surveyed in California in

1999 reported pain lasting more than a week that they attributed to a work injury. After skin disorders, musculoskeletal pain—particularly back pain—was the most common work-related health complaint. Nearly 20 percent of those surveyed reported having had a work-related injury that was remunerated through the workers' compensation system, but the number who filed claims is likely much higher.[13] Out of my core group of fifteen farmworkers, everyone who had done farm work for two years or more had experienced a work-related illness or injury.

Although complaints of delayed medical treatment, dismissive doctors, suppressed claims, and low settlement payouts were common among all farmworkers, undocumented migrants perceived that it was their legal status—a factor they could not control—that lay at the root of their negative experiences with the workers' compensation system. Below, I draw on Sulema's case to illustrate the continuing effects of such perceived unfair treatment, magnifying financial and familial stressors and ultimately causing internalized rage and stroke. I explore how Sulema's work injury unfolded between 2011 and 2014, when an acute hypertensive episode landed her in the ER. In the interest of brevity, I present a summaries of what transpired on each date rather than direct extracts from my field notes.[14]

June 2011

I first hear about Sulema's accident from Yadira, her *comadre* and sister-in-law. We are discussing how being a *sinpapel* (undocumented worker) affects one's treatment at work and why so few farmworkers bother to report injuries. She is trying to convince me that "it's not worth it" to report work accidents because companies deny payments, the doctors are in the pockets of the companies, and the payout is so small. Then Yadira brings up Sulema's story to drive her point home. "Like Sulema," she says. She tells me that Sulema fell while planting tomatoes for Álvarez Contracting this spring, and "they're not paying her any attention" (*no le hacen caso*). "They used her up," she says, slapping her hands together. I am startled. When I first met Sulema last year, she had been excited at the novelty of working in the fields and had just weathered her first summer packing melons.

Yadira tells me that Sulema cannot work any longer, but the company only sends her $280 every two weeks—less than half what she had earned before the accident—and the payment lasts only as long as the tomato-planting season. I ask whether the company is covering Sulema's

medical rehabilitation, as the law requires. Yadira tells me that that is another source of contention: the doctor tells Sulema that his exams reveal that nothing is wrong, even though Sulema's back is "completely twisted." "It's because the *mayordomo* and the doctor know she doesn't have papers," Yadira says. "It's because she's a *sinpapel.* If you're legal here, you can fight back."

When I arrive at Sulema's house, she escorts me to the kitchen table, where we used to chat and trade gossip. She walks carefully. When she pulls out the chair to sit down, the muscles around her mouth twitch. She recounts the accident, her narrative distilled to its essence from multiple tellings. "It happened," she begins, "while I was unpacking trays of tomato plants from the planting machine." It was 7:30 in the morning on April 4. She slipped, throwing down the empty trays in a vain attempt to break her fall. She landed on her left side, with her back twisted. "And that moment, I felt my back snap [*me tronó la espalda*]—such a horrible pain that I could barely get up."

Sulema kept working, afraid that she might lose her job if she stopped. After half an hour, she was in excruciating pain and reported the fall to her supervisor. Even as she waited for the contractor to take her to the doctor, she kept planting in order to hedge her bets. "Because what if I recovered?" Because he was busy with other teams of workers and other jobs, it took four hours for the contractor to arrive. "After some time, I couldn't even move to get off the machine. I was like this," she says, holding her body rigid.

The contractor took her to a doctor in Fresno, Dr. Jimenez, with whom Álvarez Contracting's insurance carrier, Apex, contracts to screen and handle its workers' compensation cases. He is one of the practitioners whom farmworkers like Yadira dismiss as "company doctors," saying they are more loyal to their clients—insurance companies—than to their farmworker patients. The doctor listened to Sulema's report of her injury and did a physical exam. To Sulema's surprise, he then pronounced her ready to return to work. He handed her a form with instructions to return to "modified work" and to visit the clinic for a follow-up appointment in three weeks. The form reads: "Return to work on 4/4/2011 with the following restrictions: No lifting over 20 lbs. No pushing and or pulling over 20 lbs of force." At the bottom of the report, under the heading "Remarks," it adds in small print: "No repetitive twisting."

When I translate Dr. Jimenez's report for Sulema, she is surprised. She says that despite this injunction against twisting, her contractor had asked her to return to planting tomatoes the following day. She had

complied because this job gave her six full months of employment each year; she could ill afford to lose it. We are left wondering whether the contractor read Dr. Jimenez's instructions and sent Sulema to plant tomatoes all the same, or whether Dr. Jimenez recorded this restriction on her activities yet never informed her supervisor.

Over the following two weeks, Sulema tried twice to return to work. Each time, twisting her spine to move the tomato seedlings from the tray to the planting wheel made her torso seize up. Each time, the supervisor took her to Dr. Jimenez, and each time, he insisted that she could return to work. Inexplicably, the injunctions against lateral rotation had dropped out of the "physician activity status reports" that Dr. Jimenez signed on Sulema's successive visits.

After her third appointment with Dr. Jimenez, Sulema called the contractor in a last-ditch effort to persuade him she was unable to work. "And he told me that I would have to work in the office the following week so that the insurance would not have to cover it," she says. Yet when Monday rolled around, she says, he never called.

May and June were a blur of treatments: X-rays and a bone density scan to see whether her pain was due to a spinal fracture, and finally—three months after her injury—an MRI. Because Dr. Jimenez had initially decreed the MRI unnecessary, it took a full month for the insurance provider to approve it. Without further explanation, Dr. Jimenez had informed her that all results were normal. "What I don't understand is how they were all normal if I can't stand the pain," she says.

Mistrustful of Dr. Jimenez's pronouncement, Sulema tried to switch doctors. Each employer contracts with a limited number of doctors to treat its workers' compensation cases, so the insurance provider merely sent her a list of the other doctors at that clinic. When Sulema called the local community clinics, she learned that care provided there would be "out of network" and therefore not covered by insurance. Sulema felt trapped. As she put it, she could not escape "*ese doctor tan corajudo*" (that nasty doctor) and his colleagues. Indeed, Sulema's frustration at her doctor's and supervisor's perceived indifference to her injury continued to mount over the following months, gathering intensity from financial and familial stressors and culminating in a stroke.

A Cardiovascular Paradox?

It is difficult to get an accurate estimate of rates of hypertension among migrant farmworkers like Sulema. Early epidemiological studies

suggested that Latino migrants—and the Mexican-origin population in particular—enjoyed lower rates of hypertension as well as lower mortality from cardiovascular disease than non-Latino whites, even after differences in the ages of the sample populations were taken into account.[15] Other early studies demonstrated a similar health advantage among Latino migrants with respect to several other health indicators, such as birth outcomes, mental health, and substance use; this pattern of better health became known as the *Latino paradox*. This research captured epidemiologists' attention because it appeared to contradict a main tenet of public health research, the social gradient in health: the finding that groups with higher socioeconomic status (SES) typically enjoy better health indicators than those with lower SES.[16] Attempts to explain this presumed epidemiological mystery often centered on the healthful characteristics of migrants' presumed traditional lifeways and the harmful effects of acculturating to modern American norms and behaviors.

Recent research has reevaluated the evidence for a Latino paradox with respect to both cardiovascular health and other health indicators. It suggests that simple artifacts of measurement may have led to the significant underdiagnosis of chronic disease in this population. First, the initial studies used different reference groups: some compared Latino migrants to the white, non-Latino population, while others compared recent Latino arrivals to second- and third-generation Latinos. Second, a "selection bias" has likely contributed to a perception of Latino migrants as particularly healthy; that is, the challenges of migration themselves select against unhealthy individuals, and the difficulty of living in the United States without health insurance swiftly repatriates less healthy migrants to their homelands.[17] Third, it is difficult to assess the true prevalence of cardiovascular disease in a population that has had limited access to the formal health care system both in the country of origin and in the United States. In short, basing determinations of hypertension on self-reporting alone rather than on clinical exams likely underestimates hypertension rates among Latino migrants.[18]

The few clinical studies on hypertension among migrant farmworkers paint a sobering portrait, suggesting that this population may be at particularly at high risk for cardiovascular disease. For example, the California Agricultural Workers Health Survey (CAWHS)—the most recent epidemiological study of California's farmworkers, and the only one to use clinical exams—found that young farmworkers, male and female, suffered from hypertension at more than twice the rate of the general population. About half of the workers examined in the CAWHS were

found to have one or more of the main risk factors for heart disease: high blood pressure, obesity, and high cholesterol. The authors note that farmworkers' risks for heart disease are "startlingly high for a group that is mostly comprised of young men who would normally be in the peak of physical condition."[19] Indeed, a review of death certificates in twenty-four states for the period 1984–93 found that farmworkers had significantly elevated mortality rates from a variety of conditions, including hypertension, heart disease, and stroke.[20] Sulema's case helps illustrate the everyday stressors that worm their way into farmworkers' physiologies, helping to account for their poor cardiovascular health.

June 2012

When I visit Sulema this June, she shows me the glossy brochures for a spine clinic she would like to visit in Los Angeles. Then she reaches into her purse to produce a bottle of supplements she recently purchased to relieve back pain. Apex may now cut off her medical care, she explains, and she is looking for hope.

Sulema says the problem began last fall, when she changed doctors the only way possible: she hired a lawyer. At her lawyer's request, Apex placed Sulema under the care of Dr. Sunjit Kapoor of the health maintenance organization Kaiser Permanente, who prescribed her naproxen (a painkiller and anti-inflammatory) and sent her to physical therapy. After six months, he told her there was nothing more he could do for her. He told her that she could never again do manual labor or lift more than thirty pounds. On her last visit, on March 15, 2012, he did a final physical exam and found "diffuse tenderness at the mid-line thoracic spine and left para-thoracic muscles," along the ribs, and at the lower lumbar spine. He wrote that "in my opinion, she does need future medical care and it should include physician visits including pain management."

A few weeks after her last appointment with Dr. Kapoor, Sulema received a letter from Apex. It read: "After careful consideration of all available information, we have concluded that we cannot pay you Temporary Disability benefits. Your claim is denied because you were found to have reached maximum medical improvement by Dr. Sunjit S Kapoor on 3/15/12." Dr. Kapoor's conclusion that Sulema had recovered from the accident as fully as she would ever be able to let Apex off the hook. Apex would cease paying Sulema the salary-remuneration portion of her workers' compensation benefits.

Then, in early June, the axe fell. Apex notified Sulema that it would end its payments not only for her disability benefit but also for her medical care, even though Dr. Kapoor's report stated that she required further medical care and pain management. Apex called a settlement conference and offered her $13,000. Sulema declined. Three weeks later, Apex tried again, upping the ante to $20,000; Sulema refused again. She says she told her lawyer to inform Apex that what she really wants is to be able to recuperate fully—and to have the option of medical care as long as she needs it. "Twenty thousand dollars—what's that going to do for me?"

The hardest part of the injury, Sulema tells me, has been its effect on her family. While she understood that the injury would diminish her capacities as a worker, she was not prepared for its interference with her domestic life. "I'm just not the same person I was before," she says. "I'm a person who's very devoted to being a good housewife. I try to prepare the meals every day. But there are days that I don't feel well and others that I wake up zonked [*durmida*] from taking painkillers at night."

Her youngest son—two and a half when she was first injured—used to run to have her pick him up. After the injury, whenever he barreled toward her, she had to tell him, "*Mijo,* I'm afraid I can't." Now the toddler has absorbed this lesson. "Remember, Mami, you can't pick me up," he admonishes her with a finger wag when she reaches down to hug him.

The rest of her family has had difficulty adjusting to the way the injury has affected her physically and emotionally. Her eldest daughter—who is training to become a nurse assistant—disappears early each morning to do her homework and does not return until late. Her two younger daughters slink by her when they see her slumped on the sofa holding her hand to her back. "It's sad for me [*es triste para mi*]. My family just doesn't understand what I'm going through," she says.

The chronic pain has left her feeling hopeless (*desesperada*) and makes easily angered. These changes have worsened her relationship with her husband, Mario. She says he becomes frustrated that dinner is not always ready after he returns from work and is increasingly unsympathetic with her testiness. "He just doesn't understand that I need to place my health first," she says.

Mario urged her to accept the settlement, but Sulema remains steeled against it. "Yes, of course I'd like to have the money," she tells me. "But what I really want is for them to take care of me so I can get better. I have three young children. I don't speak English, and out here there is nothing but farm work—work I can't do. And now my husband and I may separate—how will I support myself?"

August 2012

When I return to visit Sulema two months later, I find that her living room contains a makeshift gym. Between the sofa and the TV now stand an overstuffed recliner and a rower. Sulema found them at a yard sale and purchased them for twenty dollars. "I use them every day to stretch out my back," she tells me.

Mario and Sulema sit at the dining room table stiffly, not looking at each other as they discuss the aftermath of her injury. "It has affected us a lot; it has affected me too," Mario begins. Mario is a farm equipment mechanic and until recently worked for AgPro, an equipment supplier. Being a mechanic is a desirable job because few have the training: it pays above minimum wage and yields secure employment. Even in the winter, when finding farm work is difficult, Mario could always count on working for AgPro.

Yet in April this year, just after AgPro's contract to provide Álvarez with machinery had begun, Mario was fired. Mario suspects that Álvarez informed AgPro that his wife had retained a lawyer last fall. Mario called three *mayordomos* he knew who work for other companies, but none returned his calls. He inquired about work in person through an additional two *mayordomos* for a local grower, and both demurred. Mario says he finds this tepid response strange, because mechanics are usually in great demand.

Thanks to his wife's "complaint," as he puts it, Mario is now working as a field hand. He spends his weekdays weeding tomatoes in the sun, grateful for eight-hour days. "At first I couldn't even grab the plant," he says, setting his swollen hands on the table as proof. He earns a field hand's minimum-wage salary, $320 a week; he had earned twice that amount as a mechanic.

The couple expects to earn about $12,000 this year to support their family of seven—about half their income before Sulema's injury. They now receive food stamps ($290 a month) and welfare for their U.S. citizen children ($500 a month). To help with their finances, this summer, for the first time, they sent Vicente, their eighteen-year-old son, to work in the fields alongside his father.

Mario tells me that Sulema's accident has affected them in ways large and small. Because of her pain, she cannot do much around the house. Sulema agrees. "I try to cook or clean when the kids want something, and I just need to sit down because it's hurting so much," she says. Mario nods. At the same time, he tells me, she's more irritable (*enojona*) and has less patience with the kids.

In addition, Mario tells me, their former coworkers no longer greet them when they run into them in the supermarkets or corner stores. Sulema—and by association, Mario—has become persona non grata. "Why?" I ask. Sulema ponders the question, a smile slowly spreading across her face. "I think because they know that if their supervisors saw them talking with me, they would be fired," she says.

Thus Sulema's work injury has affected all aspects of her life. Her response to her discriminatory treatment cost her husband his job, and the couple their friends. Moreover, this master stressor precipitated a chain of further stressors: illness, family strife, financial insecurity, job loss, and social isolation. According to Sulema, it was the snowballing of these stressors that ultimately triggered the stroke that landed her in the Coalinga ER.

Migration as a Risk Factor in Cardiovascular Health

In their survey on the health of California farmworkers in 1999, researchers noted a disturbing finding. Not only were migrant farmworkers more likely to suffer from heart disease than the general population, but their cardiovascular health appeared to decline in proportion to the length of time they had spent in the United States. Through clinical exams, the CAWHS found that 32 percent of men with legal status had hypertension, in comparison to 20 percent of undocumented men. This contrast was also observed among female farmworkers. Other risk factors for cardiovascular disease—including obesity and high cholesterol—were also significantly higher among male and female migrants with legal immigrant status.[21]

Why would migrant farmworkers with legal status face a significantly higher burden of chronic disease? The authors of the study initially presumed that the differences were due to the difference in the average age of the two groups, but the age difference was only two years. Instead, the researchers concluded that the variable responsible for the difference between the cardiovascular risk of the two groups was their length of residence in the United States: the undocumented group had been in the United States for an average of 7.4 years, compared to 19 years for the documented workers.[22]

In 2000, when this study was first published, the authors declared the harmful effect of duration of time in the United States "surprising."[23] Since then, however, other studies have corroborated the finding that being a migrant in the United States is itself detrimental to cardiovascular

health. One study, for example, found that a much higher percentage of Mexican-origin women and men living in the United States had hypertension than their counterparts in Mexico. Furthermore, among Mexican women who had migrated to the United States and eventually returned to Mexico, rates of hypertension were "strikingly similar" to those of their Mexican American peers in the United States. This finding persisted even after adjusting for rates of obesity and smoking, suggesting that the negative health behaviors often associated with adapting to life in the United States were not to blame. Instead, the authors speculate, "stress associated with the [migrant] experience may exhibit itself in poor mental health and physiological damage to the body over the years," potentially leading to chronic illnesses such as high blood pressure.[24]

The Internalization of Everyday Violence

If being a migrant leads to deteriorating cardiovascular health, through what physiological pathways does chronic stress enter the body? A provocative new field of research investigates how chronic stressors such as social stigma and discrimination may contribute to the development of hypertension and heart disease. For example, demonstrating that differences in rates of hypertension between racial/ethnic groups persist even after socioeconomic and behavioral factors (such as smoking and obesity) are taken into account, some studies suggest that the chronic anticipation of racism or perseveration over past discrimination contributes to the hardening of arterial walls and the narrowing of arterial passages.[25] This research suggests that socially mediated and recurrent stress may be as damaging to cardiovascular health as a high-cholesterol diet or smoking.[26] For example, a study in Chicago that performed both clinical measures of hypertension and assessed subjects' racism-related "vigilance" found that reports of anticipatory stress increased the odds of hypertension among African Americans and, to a lesser degree, Latinos.[27]

This research suggests that racial minorities—and African Americans in particular—suffer from higher rates of hypertension than the dominant white population because of their constant exposure to what Scheper-Hughes and Bourgois call the "everyday violence" of discrimination. These anthropologists describe a "violence continuum" ranging from overtly brutal physical acts to the invisible forms of violence that pervade everyday social interactions. They write: "Violence can never be understood solely in terms of its physicality—force, assault, or the

infliction of pain—alone. Violence also includes assaults on the personhood, dignity, sense of worth or value of the victim."[28] Everyday violence is so normalized as to become routine: expected and dismissed by those who perpetrate it, those who condone it, and even its victims. In physiological terms, it is precisely because discrimination is so pervasive—and yet uncontrollable—that it is so corrosive. The mind and body must brace for it each day.

Researchers have introduced the concept of *allostatic load* to describe the physiological pathways through which such chronic social stress is embodied. It refers to the cumulative wear and tear that the constant release of stress hormones such as adrenaline and cortisol exerts on both the body and the brain.[29] It is well known that humans' physiological response to sudden threats is evolutionarily adaptive: a "fight or flight" response enabled by the sudden release of stress hormones allows us to avoid acute, short-term dangers. However, recent research suggests that for racial minorities facing the possibility of chronic racism, this stress response becomes pathological.[30] Everyday discrimination sends minorities' bodies into a state of hyperarousal, and the continual release of adrenaline and cortisol weakens organ systems and erodes cardiovascular health. As the heart pumps rapidly to bring fuel to the muscles, arteries harden and cardiac valves tire. The everyday violence of racism enters the body in the form of atherosclerotic plaque and hypertension.

July 2013

In the winter of 2012, Sulema's prospects looked brighter. Mario had found a job as a mechanic on a farm an hour's drive away—far enough that none of the supervisors had heard of Sulema's lawsuit. And there was progress in the case. In early 2013, she went to court to discuss a settlement, and the company increased its offer. Sulema declined, still insisting that she wanted the possibility of continued medical care. The judge decreed that an independent evaluator agreed upon by both parties should have the final word; she has an appointment this August.

When I visit in July, I find that Sulema's cache of papers—once limited to a tidy stack of Dr. Jimenez's reports—has now filled three manila folders, and she considers its unwanted bulk glumly. "None of this would have happened if that Dr. Jimenez had actually listened to me," she says. "None of this would have happened if he hadn't kept sending me back to work."

I ask Sulema whether—like Yadira—she thinks that being a *sinpapel* affected her treatment at all. "Yes, it did. Because I reported the injury at noon, and the contractor came to get me at four. Now, if I had my papers in order, he would have come sooner," she says. "And that *doctor corajudo,* all he'd say was, 'You can keep working.' From the moment that he looked at me, that doctor really did not want to help. Now if I had my papers in order, they would have taken me seriously. Because it took two people to get me down out of the car when we got to the clinic," she says.

But how would the doctor, let alone her supervisor, even know that she was undocumented, I ask? She laughs sardonically, and her husband, entering the kitchen in his pajamas after his evening shower, laughs as well. "They *know,*" she says. "The company has copies of my card on file. Because when they hire you, they take copies of your *mica* [green card] to the office. Plus they've probably checked my number or something, I don't know."

Examining Sulema's story through her own eyes illustrates the social significance she attributes to her unattended work injury and consequent physical debilitation. She believes that it was her status as an undocumented worker that condemned her to this struggle for her pain to be heard and her injury legitimized. She was sure that workers who "had their papers in order" would have instead been taken to the hospital and had their complaints taken seriously. In Sulema's view, the dismissive treatment she received was due to her immigration status.

The Everyday Violence of Being a Legal Minority

While recent studies of chronic stress and cardiovascular disease have focused specifically on racial minorities, the findings are suggestive for other minority groups that also face chronic, pervasive stress.[31] Many researchers observe that being a legal minority—that is, an undocumented migrant or a migrant with tenuous legal status—may provoke unprecedented anticipatory stress and chronic worry in the current antimigrant climate.[32] Cecilia Menjívar and Leisy Abrego's analysis of legal violence focuses on how it exerts material effects on migrants' schooling, family life, and employment.[33] Complementing their analysis, this chapter explores the subjective and physiological effects of such legal violence.

Rogelio Sáenz and colleagues point out that a climate of increasing hostility toward migrants in the United States affects their psychological (and presumably physiological) health. They show that the passage of

Arizona's "Show Me Your Papers" law in 2010 caused distress and anxiety even among migrants in neighboring states.[34] They compare the microaggressions with which undocumented migrants contend to the "racial battle fatigue" that racial and ethnic minorities experience.[35] Similarly, in her study of eighteen return migrants at a public psychiatric hospital in Oaxaca, Whitney Duncan found that all but two attributed their mental illness to the migration experience—in particular its "solitude, discrimination, [and] unremitting anxiety and stress." Most of her sample had never experienced mental health problems prior to leaving for the United States.[36] In the current antimigrant climate, legal minority status may also lead to perpetual vigilance. Like being "Black," being "illegal" or tenuously legal may result in hyperarousal—the chronic perception of the body's being under attack.

March 2014

When I return to visit Sulema this March, the tension over her case has come to a head. First, the worsening drought in California has cost Mario his new job. Her husband's unemployment aggravated tensions between the couple over their dwindling finances and Sulema's potential payout. "We'd fight in the morning when there was no milk, and then we'd fight again at night when we opened bills we couldn't pay," she says. Sulema began taking a popular over-the-counter Mexican medication, Neurobion, to try to calm her nerves. Exiled from the bedroom, she often sought a night's rest on the recliner she had bought to soothe her muscles. She says she was full of *coraje*. "Anger at my husband for not understanding, anger at the doctors for not listening to me, and anger at myself for not being able to provide for my children," she says.[37]

During one such argument, she developed a throbbing headache. Shortly afterward, her left eye began filling with blood. Her husband drove her to the ER in Coalinga, where the doctors took cranial X-rays and examined the eye to discern the cause of the hemorrhage. Her systolic blood pressure was 280. The doctors said she had suffered a stroke provoked by acute hypertension. Fortunately, the blood vessel that ruptured was in her eye rather than her brain. They kept her in the hospital all night, administering intravenous medication to reduce her blood pressure, and discharged her in the morning with strict injunctions to "relax and reduce [her] stress levels."

Sulema had initially thought of her disability settlement as a bitter concession to her family. But with her husband's unemployment and

their marital strife, it now appeared a lifeline. She accepted the company's payout offer of $20,000 in November; after paying the lawyer's fees, she was left with $14,000. "It'll be three years that I've been fighting them. And I'm no different. With the need we have, there's nothing I can do but close the case," she says.

Following Sulema's attempts to seek rehabilitation through the workers' compensation system reveals the multiple forms of everyday violence that undocumented farmworkers face. As a temporary and seasonal worker, Sulema had reason to fear that reporting her injury to her supervisor would cost her her job. Her delay in reporting it, however, jeopardized her health. Meanwhile, not only did Sulema face perceived indifference to her injury from her doctor and supervisor, but retaining a lawyer indirectly cost her husband his job. This, in turn, increased the pressure on Sulema to close her case. Thus Sulema's work injury triggered a chain of further stressors.

Sulema's story yields clues as to why Mexican migrants may experience deteriorating cardiovascular health in the United States. Research has suggested that recent African migrants are protected from the harmful effects of racism; it is the next generation that exhibits elevated rates of high blood pressure and premature births similar to those of African Americans.[38] In short, classification as a minority by others does not automatically erode cardiovascular health; rather, it is an individual's awareness of her devalued status in society that most affects her physiology. Sulema's story shows the dawning of a consciousness of what it means to be a legal minority—the anticipatory stress of further discrimination and potential deportation—and the simmering resentment about her perceived powerlessness. As Sulema tells it, her *coraje* at her sociopolitical status ultimately expressed itself in the form of a hypertensive stroke.

IMMIGRATION STRESS: THE CASE OF YADIRA

While Sulema's narrative shows the damaging effects of work stress, migrants' hypertension narratives also illustrate the role of immigration stress. In the Central Valley, a legacy of racial segregation and a history of ICE raids make the threat of deportation a constant, menacing backdrop. The transfer of immigration functions to the police has introduced the threat of denounceability into migrant neighborhoods, transforming the common avenues by which deportation occurs. As we saw in chapter 3, the prosecution of migrants for document-related fraud

and programs such as Secure Communities and its replacement, the Priority Enforcement Program, have made criminal, rather than civil, arrest a common pathway to deportation. Migrants in the Central Valley thus face anxiety stemming not only from their deportability, but also from their denounceability for everyday activities.

In February 2007, Mendota made national news when ICE officials apprehended roughly two hundred undocumented migrants in this town of ten thousand under Operation Return to Sender.[39] Ostensibly targeting "fugitive aliens"—that is, convicted felons and gang members—this program sent ICE officers to the addresses of specific targets with arrest warrants; once inside, they swept up all the undocumented migrants who happened to be on the premises in what they dubbed "collateral arrests." Because of the high proportion of residents in Mendota who are undocumented, Operation Return to Sender gave ICE a pretext for deportations on a massive scale. In Mendota, the ICE vans—white and unmarked—were indistinguishable from the vans of the *raiteros*, the taxi drivers of the fields. Knocking on doors at 5 A.M.—the hour when farmworkers await a knock from their *raiteros*—ICE agents succeeded in swelling the ranks of their targets with dozens of ordinary workers and parents. Some growers complained that the raids brought agricultural production to a halt, as farmworkers stayed home, afraid to open their doors when the *raitero* knocked or risk an ICE stop on the way to work. The Mendota City Council passed a resolution condemning the "emotional turmoil and financial hardship" the raids created, and the Republican mayor of Fresno, Alan Autry, denounced ICE's tactics as "mind-boggling in [their] callousness."[40]

ICE has since ceased large-scale operations in the Valley, and raids on farms themselves are virtually nonexistent. Yet everyday racialized policing presents a continuing threat to undocumented migrants. The convergence between immigration and criminal law enforcement has introduced the threat of deportation even further into migrant neighborhoods, and the possibility of denunciation for minor infractions makes migrants wary of interactions with authorities. Yadira's story illustrates the pervasive effects of the coupling of immigration and criminal law enforcement.

April 2005

When I first meet Yadira in 2005, she is living with her husband and four children in a one-bedroom wooden shack the size of a horse trailer

on Lolita Street. Located on the poor east side of town, Lolita Street is lined with rickety apartments stuffed to the seams with recently arrived migrant men; they pile their mattresses into garages rented from family members or are immediately dubbed brothers through sharing the confines of a single bedroom. When Yadira opens the door, I squeeze into a narrow kitchen with a fridge but no stove—almost holding my breath to fit—and then take one more step through a low doorway into the family room. Her boys, Ramón and José Luis, nine and six years old, sit in front of a black-and-white TV, its rabbit-ear antenna cocked, while her three-year-old daughter, Elmira, nibbles at uncooked ramen noodles in a Styrofoam cup.

Five years ago, Yadira was working toward a nursing degree in Colima, Mexico—she had only one semester left before graduating—when her husband decided that he and Yadira should leave for the United States. Her husband, René, who is toiling under the hood of a rusted 1970s pickup truck outside, had been a bricklayer. When they departed, they had to leave her three eldest children with her mother. She and her husband worked year-round in the fields for three years to pay off the *coyote* debts she had assumed to bring them to the United States. Although winter work is scarce, and the *mayordomos* prefer not to hire women, Yadira's husband was able to persuade his boss to make an exception and hire her so that they could reunite their family.

When I knock on Yadira's door in 2008, three years after our initial meeting, a mustached man in a white tank top—a man I don't know—opens the door. I had all but given up Yadira for deported when I caught sight of her on the other side of town, stepping out of a gleaming white pickup truck on her way back from church. She is transformed, her hair pulled back, wearing a diaphanous dress. She beams as she tells me that she now lives in the federally subsidized farmworker housing units on Tuft Street. She is legally ineligible for such housing because of her undocumented status, but a retired farmworker with legal status is subletting it to her *debajo del agua* (under the table). On the outside, the units look like a cluster of colorless stucco units with low ceilings, but inside, they are spacious, clean, and solidly built.

July 2010

When I return to visit Yadira this summer, I find her wooden front door reinforced by a new security door made of wrought iron. I bang on the security door to no avail. I am about to leave when the interior door

slides open just wide enough to reveal a tuft of hair and a child's slender arm. "*¿Quién?*" (who?) a voice booms.

Yadira arrives to usher me in, guardedly. After we sit down, she tells me how a knock on the door this past May transformed everything on Tuft Street.

Early on a spring morning, René had just left to drive the youngest kids to elementary school. Minutes later, there was a pounding at the door. She thought René had forgotten something, but she opened the door to find what seemed to be three police officers in plain clothes with her three youngest children, who were crying. She caught sight of another officer at the edge of the carport, standing over her husband, who was kneeling, handcuffed (*esposado*). "Your husband has been arrested," the officer at the door told her. She remembers thinking he spoke Spanish well. "What are the charges?" She asked. "He's been deported before," the man replied. Her stomach knotted as it began to dawn on her that perhaps this was not a police arrest. She told the man that she would take the kids inside "so they wouldn't have to see their father like this," then closed and locked the door. She grabbed her children and hauled them to their rooms. Then she crept back to watch the scene from the kitchen window.

While three of the officers wore plain clothes, one was wearing a black vest (*chaleco*) with yellow stripes. "I'd seen that vest when they show the raids [*redadas*] on the news," she tells me. The ICE officers were still waiting in her driveway—for what, she tells me, she didn't want to know—but at least she still had the safety of the wall between them. They stared at each other silently through the open window. Then the officers asked, "Do you have any identification or any money you want to give him? Do you want to come out to hug him to say goodbye?" She did not dare reply. She simply shook her head and displayed her empty hands to indicate she had nothing to give, and watched as they hauled him into the van. How, she has asked herself each night since, how had she not seen that van, the white van waiting at the curb? It could have been anyone's van. White with tinted windows, it could have belonged to the *raiteros* who drive farmworkers to work, except that—as she remembers now—it lacked the state-mandated lettering to identify it as such.

At least her three eldest, all born in Mexico, had already set out for middle school that morning, she thought. At least she hadn't stepped outside. "Because then what would have happened to my kids, my youngest kids?" she asks.

Hence the new door. Her children know, she says, that ICE officers cannot enter unless they let them in.

Now, sitting at her dining room table with me, she says she often wonders how ICE found René in their carport that spring morning. He had been deported in 2009; back then, the officers happened to catch him outside a grocery store in town.[41] It had taken him four months, and cost the couple all of her winter earnings, to return. Since he returned, he had taken the precaution of never working under his own name; he had always borrowed other people's papers to protect himself from being caught. She will probably never know how ICE obtained a warrant for his arrest or how the federal government even knew that he had reentered the country.

On the advice of her brother, who reassured her that "if they were looking for you, they would have grabbed you by now," Yadira tells me that she finally left the house for the first time last month. She says she has three relatives who are U.S. citizens; she thinks her aunt and uncle would be the best guardians and that it would be best for the children if they were not split up. On her to-do list now is the task of writing out detailed instructions—which she will have officially witnessed by a notary—explaining who she wishes to take custody of her children should she be taken too.

June 2011

When René finally was able to call a month after his apprehension, he told Yadira that ICE had transferred him to a maximum-security prison in Georgia. He spent six months there in a cell without a window. "Like he was a criminal," she says. He witnessed fights and saw people knife each other. She sent him money so he could call to talk with her and with the children. To pass the time, he worked in the kitchen, where he was paid fifteen cents an hour. And he drew. In his cell, he made drawings of animals and cartoon characters for her and the children.

René was finally deported last November. He is now living with his mother and working in construction in Colima. He and Yadira talk every week and sometimes Skype. He tells her he doesn't want to return because he is afraid that he will be imprisoned again, this time for five or ten years. This leaves Yadira "with her back against the wall" (*entre la espada y el pared*), as Sulema later confides in me. Yadira herself is more "reserved," as Sulema puts it. Yadira says she has had to accept his decision. IIRIRA makes repeat unlawful entry an offense that may lead to imprisonment for up to two years. "I don't want to demand that he come back because I don't want him to wind up in jail again," she explains.

Now Yadira lies awake nights debating whether she should return to Mexico to reunite the family. The arguments for and against play like a constant loop in her head. She wants her children to be with their father, but it doesn't seem fair to her to deprive her youngest children—all U.S. citizens—of the privileges of growing up in the United States, the country of their birth. "I want to go back to Mexico, but life is hard there. My children would all have to work in the fields, just like here. They would have no opportunity. It just doesn't seem fair to the ones who were born here," she says.

In the months after René's apprehension, the tenor of the family's lives changed. All of a sudden, Yadira says, it was as though they were back in Mexico. They ate beans and rice for dinner because she could no longer afford to buy meat. When her children wanted to go to the market to get a soda, she had to tell them they could no longer afford to. And, she says, her kids once again ran around in "dirty and tattered shoes"—a symbolic marker of poverty in Mexico that she had been proud to escape. This sudden poverty felt all the more acute because of her family's recent relative financial security.

Before René was deported, the couple had earned about $15,000 a year. They planted and sorted tomatoes together in the spring and summer, and he worked pruning and sweeping almonds in the winter. After he was gone, Yadira had to rely on her son Ramón, now fourteen, to earn a living. She dispatched him to work in the fields for the first time last summer. He worked planting tomatoes and picking melons, and then sweeping almonds in the fall, just like his father. Yet because state law prohibits minors from working overtime, Ramón had to use the identity his *mayordomo* gave him in order to be able to work. This frightens Yadira, as she fears he would be ineligible for care through workers' compensation if he were injured.

The three youngest remain traumatized by René's deportation. "They saw their dad with his hands tied behind his back," she says. "They were too young to know that he did not do anything wrong." Meanwhile, the three eldest "*tienen coraje,*" she says: they have become angry at the world. Recently, Ramón returned home from picking melon, disgruntled. He had spent the afternoon trudging in the fields while his brothers and sisters were home watching TV; he had cut his thumb while trying to sever a melon from its stem with his pocketknife, and his coworkers had laughed at him. "All the other boys' fathers taught them how to work. Why can't mine?" He had said. As Yadira tells me the story, her

lip begins to wobble, and although her expression is barely altered, I see that she is crying.

After I leave Yadira's house, I visit Sulema, and we discuss Yadira's situation with concern. "She doesn't know how to reach them," she says, shaking her head. "They're rebelling against her and against their teachers; they talk back and have to stay after school." I ask whether the school district can offer them counseling, or whether there is any county assistance for families separated by deportations. Sulema sighs in exasperation and opens her hands, as though she thought the same thing but has had to let it go. "She won't talk to the teachers. She won't talk to a social worker. She won't talk to anyone because she's afraid they'll take them away," she says.

TRANSFORMING POLICE INTO BORDER CONTROL AGENTS

Yadira's story illustrates the heightened stress created by programs such as Secure Communities, which requires that the police turn over the fingerprints of arrestees to ICE. Although ICE has currently ceased large-scale immigration raids like Operation Return to Sender in the Central Valley, the transfer of immigration functions to the police, in conjunction with the new immigration-related consequences of criminal offenses, has transformed police and other authorities into internal agents of border control.[42]

Secure Communities was launched in 2008 with the stated purpose of identifying and removing "serious felons." Yet, because arrestees' fingerprints are checked against federal immigration databases before their trial, migrants may be detained for deportation without ever being convicted of a criminal offense.[43] Indeed, according to DHS, the vast majority of undocumented migrants deported during the first year of the program were arrested for minor offenses; only 10 percent were violent felons.[44] Thus Secure Communities has had the effect of turning police officers in some precincts into antimigrant vigilantes, encouraging them to take immigration control into their own hands.[45]

Programs such as Secure Communities encourage racial profiling, placing Latinos—both undocumented and legal residents—at risk during even casual encounters with the police. A report by the Warren Institute at UC Berkeley found that Latinos were overrepresented among those arrested through Secure Communities; they constitute 77 percent of the undocumented population in the United States but accounted for 93 percent of

deportations.[46] Because of the antimigrant sentiment of many Anglo-Americans in the Central Valley, Secure Communities became a pretext for vigilante policing in the area.[47] Of all California counties, Fresno County had the second highest percentage of noncriminal deportations through Secure Communities in 2010—after Madera County, its neighbor to the north.[48] Because the United States passed legislation in both 1988 and 1996 to make noncitizens deportable for a greater number of minor offenses, differential policing poses a threat even to migrants with legal status.[49] Secure Communities thus established the groundwork for migrant denounceability: that is, migrants' arrest for "crimes"—often ordinary activities—that itself inevitably triggers deportation.

The unfolding of Yadira's narrative illustrates the emotional toll of deportation on migrant families, as well as the threat that migrant denounceability constitutes for single undocumented mothers in the Central Valley. Yadira found herself in a double bind. Her husband's deportation led to disruptive behavior by her elder sons, but her fear that state intervention would lead to the separation of her family dissuaded her from contacting social workers or teachers for help.

August 2012

When Ramón opens the security door to the house on Tuft Street this hot August, the lights are off, and the TV is quiet. Without the family's main breadwinner, Yadira is saving money on electricity and air conditioning. Her daughter colors a book on the couch in the living room as a large fan blows the hot air around.

We sit in the dim dining room as Yadira elaborates on the financial and emotional hardships she has faced in the wake of René's deportation. These hardships are exacerbated by her mounting fears that because she is a single mother without legal status, the state might take away her children at the slightest provocation. She tells me that she is at a loss as to how to support her family while she is the sole caretaker for her children. Even though she deems José Luis, now twelve, mature enough to take care of his younger siblings while she and Ramón are at work, she worries about leaving him in sole charge of the younger children. "You hear 'Don't leave them alone,' all the time," she says. "What would happen if I left them with him, and someone were to knock and think they were all alone? What if they called social services, or worse, the police?" If Yadira were to be charged with child neglect, she says, the state might take her children. Equally awful, she might be deported.

To avoid this scenario, she pays $20 a day for a babysitter to take care of the three youngest children while she works. This is on top of the $8 she pays each day to the *raitero* to drive her to and from the fields. Being appointed a *raitero* is a favor bestowed on friends of the *mayordomo;* therefore, driving herself to work to save the fare would cost her her job. With these deductions, her take-home pay for an eight-hour day is $35. Rent is $465 a month. If it weren't for her son's earnings—$6,000 last summer—and federal assistance, she could not make it. "I work all week to just pay the bills. I don't know how anyone saves with this kind of a schedule," she says.

Her husband's deportation has also intensified her dependence on the state. Reluctantly, she applied for welfare last winter for her U.S.-born children and now receives $490 a month. She also receives $503 a month in food stamps. The irony of this situation is not lost on her. "It would have been better for everyone if he hadn't been deported," she says. She says she had never even known such assistance was available before this time of need.

Here again, the mixed legal status of her family members counts against her: as noncitizens, she and her eldest three children do not qualify for federal help. Had all her children been born in the United States, she would receive twice as much government assistance. Instead, they make do on resources intended for a family of three. "I just can't make the money last," she says (*no alcanza para todos*).

And then there is the problem of her eldest sons. She says that for them—and for José Luis in particular—she can do nothing right. He takes out his anger on her and his younger sister. He's mad at Yadira for not being able to buy the family what they need. Then he's mad at her for working. "He says I should stay home with them; he doesn't understand why I have to work. But how can they survive? I tell him I'm not going to do bad things. I'm not going to get involved in crime. No, I have to work," she says.

Ramón is now sixteen. He used to be named student of the month, but in the past year, he has earned four Fs and will have to attend an after-school program to graduate. She has thought of applying for temporary legal status for him through the Deferred Action program—as he is the only member of the family who can qualify—but she cannot pay the fees.[50]

José Luis, the second eldest, is in seventh grade. He had been a straight-A student, but in the first year after René's apprehension, he, like Ramón, received several Fs. Now his grades have improved slightly; he is mostly

getting Bs, she says. He will be going to summer school this year in order to continue on to junior high. She sighs. "They just don't know how to express how they feel," she says (*no saben sacar lo que sienten*).

Yadira's story shows how the legal violence of René's deportation created interpersonal strife in her family, and how her immigration stress has intensified over time. René's apprehension led to Yadira's own deportation-related vigilance. She braced herself for the possibility of her own arrest; she placed a security door on her house and refused to step outside. It has also led to chronic worry—or perseverative stress—as she has blamed herself for not noticing the parked van on the day of his arrest, agonized over whether to relocate her children to Mexico, and constantly worried about how to make ends meet.

Yadira's husband's deportation unleashed a series of additional stressors. Meanwhile, her potential denounceability—that is, her fear of the consequences of seeking help from the authorities for her troubled sons—only compounded her anxiety. A narrative account of how immigration stress unfolds in Yadira's life allows us to trace the dense connections that developed between these related stressors and reveals new anxieties created by the coupling of immigration and criminal law enforcement.

June 2013

When I arrive at Yadira's house this July, I learn that a visit to the ER earlier this summer had cost her her usual job planting tomato for Álvarez Contracting.

"I don't know why my blood pressure went up so high," she begins. The school district had called and said there was a problem with José Luis, now fourteen. She had arrived at the principal's office with dread, fearing that he had gotten into a fight. Instead she learned something completely unexpected: he had been taken to the school nurse during PE class because he was feeling *agitado* (worked up). A checkup revealed that he had high blood pressure. José Luis later reassured her that it was likely simply a temporary state provoked by exercise, but his teacher and the school nurse were more concerned. "They said he was too young to have high blood pressure," she says, as though about to cry. They had given him strict instructions not to drink sodas and to "remain calm," and Yadira will need to take him in for a follow-up appointment.

Yadira left the school relieved that José Luis hadn't been expelled. Thinking about the toll of her son's pent-up anger as she walked back

home, however, she began to tremble under the weight of her family's predicament. She tried to keep walking, but she felt out of breath. "It felt like something was squeezing my chest," she says. She stopped and called a friend to pick her up; the friend transported her to the house of a woman they knew who owned a blood pressure monitor. Because her blood pressure was 220/150—dangerously high—they called emergency services. When the paramedics arrived, they confirmed the reading. They offered to take Yadira to the ER, but she refused, to avoid being charged for the ambulance ride. Instead, Yadira's friend rushed her to the ER in Fresno. "I was worried I might be having a heart attack," she says.

That was how she lost her spring job planting tomatoes—and likely her summer job planting melons for the same *mayordoma,* she says. She called her *mayordoma* from her friend's car to let her know she would be missing work, but the woman told her she could not keep Yadira's job open while she recovered.

As she sat in the hospital with the tentacles of the EKG taped to her chest and an intravenous drip in her arm, Yadira thought of her children. "All I could think was that if anything happened to me, what would happen to my children? They only have me," she says. She worried that this new development—itself caused by the knotting of multiple stressors unleashed by her husband's deportation—might provoke the very outcome she feared most.

The hospital discharged her with three weeks' worth of blood pressure medication and the simple injunction to avoid stress. They told her to follow up with a doctor when the medication ran out, but her lack of regular insurance has prevented her from doing so. She says she will seek follow-up care at the health fair in the park, where the local clinic performs blood pressure checks for free. And perhaps, she tells me, she will follow her friend's example and buy a blood pressure monitor for herself and her son.

Coraje, *Hypertension, and Sociopolitical Status*

Yadira's and Sulema's narratives suggest that the higher burden of cardiovascular risk among migrant farmworkers stems, at least in part, from the chronic stressors associated with their sociopolitical status. The stress of life as undocumented farmworkers takes a toll on their emotional health as well: both Yadira and Sulema describe episodes of *coraje,* or rage, that preceded and accompanied their episodes of acute

hypertension. Other migrant farmworkers I interviewed who suffered from hypertension offered related explanatory models of the disease, attributing it to extreme emotions. Elisabeta, for example, attributes her hypertension to suffering *una gran tristeza* (a great sadness) when her mother died in Mexico and her undocumented status made it impossible for her to return to pay her respects; she subsequently felt *coraje* at herself for ever having left. Don Santiago and his wife say that hypertension struck them after they suffered *un gran apuro* (a great hardship) when their eldest son was killed in a car crash in the United States. Raquel attributes her high blood pressure to her *coraje* at her husband's drinking and carousing.

In the anthropological literature, *coraje* typically denotes powerlessness within a social system: it is an internalized rage at the moral insults associated with subordinate status. It is often experienced as the result of interpersonal victimization, such as wife beating, rape, and child abuse: it is most commonly reported by women.[51] Some assert that *coraje* is the most commonly reported cause of illness in Mexico, a "folk illness" that is believed to precipitate physical distress.[52] Indeed, Emily Mendenhall has found that Mexican women often link this culturally specific form of distress to the etiology of diabetes.[53]

Yadira's and Sulema's accounts raise interesting questions about the relationship between *coraje* and hypertension, suggesting that for these farmworking women, it may be the embodied sensation that ultimately takes a toll on cardiovascular health.[54] *Coraje* may be the socioemotional correlate of undocumented farmworkers' sociopolitical status, the felt experience of their perceived vulnerability. Yadira's narrative further suggests that *coraje* is intersubjective and thus contagious: it is not unique to the undocumented members of a family but is experienced also by others affected by their legal status.[55] *Coraje* is the embodied register through which Yadira feels her son's powerlessness.

The sociologists Cecilia Menjívar and Leisy Abrego call attention to the fact that legal violence is structural in form: it is enshrined in law and leads to the systematic disadvantaging of noncitizens, much as the institutionalization of racial discrimination exacerbates the systematic harm to racial minorities (see chapter 3). Yet the stories of Yadira and Sulema show that legal violence also has subjective and physiological effects. As migrants learn what it means to be an undocumented migrant in the United States, the everyday experience of legal violence is embodied in the form of hypertension.

If the experience of being undocumented varies according to time and place, recent changes in immigration law have intensified the emotional distress associated with the status. Yet legal residents are not immune to such chronic stressors. As IIRIRA has made legal residents deportable for a greater number of minor offenses, the shifting of immigration functions to local authorities has heightened the anxiety of all noncitizens.[56]

An analysis of migrants' narratives helps identify the master stressors that contribute to their anxiety and their high burden of chronic disease. A longitudinal analysis allows us to see how such stressors grow in intensity, how they gain meaning from their connection to other stressors, and how they permeate the most intimate details of migrants' lives. Looking at daily events through the eyes of migrants allows us to see how they interpreted them through a lens colored by such master stressors: seemingly mundane occurrences, such as interactions with teachers, triggered broader fears. Examining the processes through which social inequality is embodied reveals a set of stressors shaped by historically and locally contingent contexts and policies. A radical contextualization of migrant farmworkers' high rates of hypertension reveals the physiological effects of legal minority status.[57]

CHAPTER 5

Álvaro's Casket

Heat Illness and Chronic Disease at Work

One afternoon in July 2012, I travel to a town south of Fresno to speak with a small contractor, Humberto, about heat deaths. So far this year, there has been one death in California's fields that has been conclusively ruled as due to heat; several others are being investigated. I ask Humberto what he thinks are the causes. He tells me that he routinely conducts the state-mandated trainings for his crews of workers to help prevent heat illness, but that there are always factors beyond his control. "I go and talk to my crews and tell them what to watch out for, 'Here's what you gotta follow.' And I tell people, 'Be careful! It's a hot day.' Then people go out and get a six-pack before they go home, and then they come to work the next day already dehydrated. Or they'll drink those energy drinks. Monster and Red Bull. Yeah, that can cause heat stroke real quick," he says.

Then he brings up the case of a worker who had died in the fields that summer, and whose death the county coroner had ruled as due to hypertension, exacerbated by heat. "So it's the same thing with the heat illness prevention standard," he continues. "I don't screen you before you work! You might have high blood pressure, you might have heart disease, I don't know. But then we have a 109-degree day, and you're out there sweating, and you're out there losing fluids. And if you have high blood pressure, well, then, we both got a problem."

Humberto's statement suggests that heat illness, hypertension, and cardiovascular disease constitute a *syndemic* among migrant farmworkers—a cluster of conditions that interact biologically and socially. "Burning

up" is not a uniform process, and heat mortality may encompass many different physiological conditions. If the heart is already strained by clogged arteries or by hypertension, its working overtime to attempt to cool the body may trigger cardiac arrest. Hypertension causes excessive water loss when sweating, increasing the risk of dehydration and heat stroke.[1] Undiagnosed or unmanaged diabetes expedites this chain reaction; it is a known risk factor for heart disease and accelerates its course.[2]

Yet Humberto's statement naturalizes the phenomenon of heat death, deflecting attention away from the role played by farmworkers' work circumstances. It portrays heat mortality as simply an unfortunate consequence of working outdoors with undiagnosed chronic disease. Here I show that a host of public policies and private interests, including state and federal policies and agribusiness's desires for profits—are implicated in the unhappy outcomes that Humberto describes. I show that migrant men's longstanding exclusion from subsidized health insurance has alienated them from health care, posing an obstacle to treatment even once they are included. At the same time, subcontracting and migrants' exclusion from overtime laws allow their undiagnosed chronic disease to interact with heat illness. Attention to the synergistic relationship between hypertension and heat illness raises provocative questions about how to accurately count heat deaths and sheds new light on farm work's death toll.

SYNDEMIC INTERACTIONS

The anthropologist Merrill Singer coined the term *syndemic* to describe the unique biological interactions between diseases like hypertension and heat illness, which exacerbate the negative health effects of one or both conditions.[3] Diabetic heart disease, for example, is more severe and leads to earlier death than heart disease by itself. Thus disease interaction may influence the expression, severity, and course of each single affliction. Syndemics are combinations of particular diseases that interact in recognizable and unique patterns, creating a qualitatively different phenomenon from any of the single contributing conditions.

Yet the distinctive biological synergy of particular epidemics is not enough to explain why syndemics appear with regularity among vulnerable populations. Just as the diseases constituting a syndemic are not self-contained, isolated entities, neither are the bodies of the individuals they afflict. As Singer and Clair write: "Diseases do not exist in a social vacuum . . . thus their transmission and impact is never merely a biological

process."[4] As in the case of infectious disease, a disease agent is a necessary but not sufficient cause of a syndemic. Rather, adverse social circumstances—including stress, malnutrition, and poverty—weaken a group's natural defenses and expose it to a set of intertwined and mutually aggravating ailments. In short, the patterned clustering of particular diseases among different marginalized populations is encouraged and sustained by their sociopolitical circumstances. Thus the concept of syndemics is part of a social scientific movement to *resocialize* epidemiology, a science that has long neglected consideration of disease cofactors that resist quantification.[5]

Singer first struck on the concept of synergistic epidemics when studying what he called the SAVA epidemic—the combination of substance abuse, violence, and AIDS—among Puerto Ricans in inner-city Hartford, Connecticut.[6] At the time, the dominant public health approach to combating AIDS in this population used the same measures as those employed among the middle-class gay male population, primarily safe-sex programs. Singer realized, however, that the SAVA epidemic was a different phenomenon that required a different approach. Just as the treatment of SAVA needed to address the broader context that encouraged its spread, examining this inner-city epidemic as though separate from the other conditions and diseases that accompanied it was a "distortion."[7]

Singer argued that AIDS clustered with social conditions like substance abuse and violence and biological conditions like tuberculosis and hepatitis B because they were "not wholly separable." The common denominator was the encompassing social context: Puerto Ricans' poverty, low levels of education, and high rates of unemployment fueled the AIDS epidemic by prompting youth participation in the drug trade, violence, and gang activity. Singer identified additional "behavioral and biological" connections that encouraged and sustained disease interaction.[8] For example, it is well-accepted that HIV/AIDS can be transmitted through intravenous drug users' sharing of contaminated needles. Yet at the biological level, Singer speculated that the stress of being a victim of violence may enhance HIV transmission. He also hypothesized another behavioral component to disease transmission: an AIDS diagnosis may lead to greater drug use. Singer's framework thus underscores the way that marginalized status amplifies the harmful effects of any single affliction.

The concept of syndemics helps explain why vulnerable populations bear a disproportionate burden of disease. It suggests that rather than zeroing in on each disease alone, anthropologists and public health researchers should take a holistic approach that situates intertwined

conditions in the social and political contexts that encourage and sustain them. Indeed, if farmworkers' hypertension is socially and politically produced, their lack of access to health care aggravates it by preventing its prompt detection. Meanwhile, an interlocking set of labor laws and food safety policies increases farmworkers' susceptibility to heat illness, only fueling the syndemic interactions Humberto describes.

HEALTH CARE ACCESS: COLLATERAL DIAGNOSES

Migrants, and migrant farmworkers in particular, suffer from higher rates of chronic disease than the general population. California's farmworkers have twice the risk of hypertension of the general population, and farmworking men in particular have higher-than-average risk factors for cardiovascular disease.[9] In addition, Latinos have a higher risk of developing type 2 diabetes than non-Latino whites, and those of Mexican origin bear the highest risk of diabetes of all Latino subgroups.[10]

Despite their higher rates of chronic disease, migrant farmworkers experience significant barriers to accessing the formal health care system. Excluded from Medicaid and many county insurance programs because of their legal status, undocumented migrants are also ineligible for subsidized health insurance through the exchanges established under the Affordable Care Act.[11] In California, undocumented migrants are eligible for the state's Emergency Medicaid program, Emergency Medi-Cal, if they meet federal income guidelines, but Emergency Medi-Cal covers only the limited treatment required to resolve acute emergencies.[12] Moreover, until recently, single "sojourners"—that is, migrants (typically male) who maintain families in their sending countries and whose legal status has allowed them to migrate to the United States seasonally for work—have been excluded from subsidized health care as well. Only in 2014 did California make childless men and women with legal resident status eligible for Medi-Cal if they meet federal income guidelines.

Limited forms of subsidized care are available to undocumented migrants beyond the scope of emergency treatment. The extent of such services varies by gender. Uninsured migrant women are often eligible for state-subsidized prenatal care and reproductive care. Uninsured migrant men occasionally receive medical screenings that are mandated by their employers. Instead of preventive and diagnostic care, then, uninsured migrant men and women often receive what I call *collateral diagnoses* of serious conditions: that is, diagnoses that are the unintentional and chance by-product of care delivered for other purposes.

Migrant Women: Receiving Government-Subsidized Care

When they become pregnant, uninsured migrant women become eligible for Restricted Medi-Cal, a program that covers prenatal care, deliveries, and post-partum care for sixty days. The program entitles such women to diagnostic services and care more extensive than those provided through Emergency Medi-Cal. Their brief window of Restricted Medi-Cal eligibility thus affords women an important opportunity to receive preventive screenings and to learn of disabling conditions. Because their eligibility for such services ends two months after they deliver their babies, however, they rarely receive treatment for their chronic conditions.

Elisabeta, for example, first learned she had gestational diabetes while pregnant with her son, Carlos, when she was twenty-one. Gestational diabetes, a common side-effect of pregnancy that disappears after the baby's delivery, leaves a woman at higher risk of developing type 2 diabetes. Her doctor prescribed Elisabeta pills and told her to watch her diet, and—as he had hoped—her blood sugar levels returned to normal after her delivery. When her access to Restricted Medi-Cal ended two months after her delivery, however, Elisabeta could not afford to further monitor her condition. It was only during a second pregnancy nine years later, when she was again eligible for the insurance, that Elisabeta discovered that her diabetes had returned. Her blood sugar levels had risen so high that her doctor sent her to Fresno to take weekly "classes about blood sugar," as Elisabeta puts it. "That's how I learned how to control my blood sugar," she says. Yet Restricted Medi-Cal covered the treatment of Elisabeta's diabetes only because it posed a risk to her pregnancy: the care that Elisabeta received was aimed primarily at ensuring the health of her unborn citizen child.

Similarly, Yadira found out that she had anemia when she was pregnant with her youngest daughter. She had been working ten- to twelve-hour days in one of the toughest winter jobs—clearing weeds from around almond and pistachio trees—and was continually exhausted. "I just wanted to sleep all the time," she remembers. It was only when she became pregnant and qualified for Restricted Medi-Cal that she was able to visit the doctor: Yadira was then told that her hemoglobin level was 7.3, well below the lower limit of the range for "normal," 12. After her diagnosis, Yadira took iron pills three times a day for three months. Since her eligibility for Restricted Medi-Cal ended, however, she has been unable to return for a check-up. "Sometimes, you just can't make

it—with my six kids, the rent, food, and shoes, sometimes you just can't go to the doctor [*a veces no alcanza para ir al doctor*]," she says.

Migrant women who receive medical care for conditions like these are the collateral—that is, indirect and unintentional—beneficiaries of the subsidized care that the state provides their citizen children. Yet both cases show the serious limitations of a system that offers migrants only collateral care. While it allows migrant women an invaluable period of subsidized screenings, its benefits are fleeting.[13]

Migrant Men: Receiving Employer-Subsidized Care

Whereas migrant women often discover hidden ailments only during subsidized prenatal or post-partum check-ups, migrant men—especially undocumented men and single sojourners with legal status—have no such benefit. Instead, they often learn of chronic ailments only when seeking the medical certifications occasionally required by employers. Because these screenings are not common, collateral diagnoses occur more frequently among migrant women.

Don Tomás, for example, found out that he had advanced diabetes when he applied for a commercial driver's license. He had just been promoted to *mayordomo* and wished to be able to drive his crew to the fields. The California Department of Motor Vehicles (DMV) requires that applicants for a commercial license undergo a vision test and provide certification of a medical exam. So Don Tomás, at the age of forty-one, visited a doctor for the first time since he had arrived in the United States some twenty years earlier. He got his license, but he also came away with an unexpected death sentence. The urine test the doctor had ordered came back with a blood sugar level of 300, indicating advanced diabetes. The doctor informed him that he had but a few years left to live—that is, unless he changed his diet dramatically.

Similarly, Don Raúl, a single male sojourner with temporary protected status (TPS; see chapter 2), first learned of his high blood pressure in 2000 at the age of forty-four, when he underwent medical tests required by his employer. He was working in a beef and pork processing plant in Iowa and had applied for a position with greater authority, for which he was first required to pass tests of his vision, strength, bone density, and blood pressure. "The idea is that if you faint, and the conveyor belt carries you away, they can't have that happening," he says. Now that he knows of his condition, Don Raúl tries to make an appointment for a monthly checkup at the local community health center—paying a $100

fee for each visit—so that the doctor can adjust his medications. "Blood pressure is a very delicate thing because it affects the heart—so they won't give you a prescription for more than a month," he says.

Employer-provided diagnostic care is a form of collateral care aimed primarily at reducing employers' liability for work accidents. Like migrant women's reproductive health care, these screenings are no substitute for comprehensive health care coverage. As Don Raúl's case shows, although they may provide migrant men with valuable information about their health, they do not provide access to treatment. In addition, as Don Tomás' case shows, collateral care is by no means preventative. Because it is irregular and episodic, collateral care often delays the diagnosis of migrants' chronic ailments and prevents them from better managing their conditions at an earlier stage.

Migrants' limited inclusion in the health care system sends divergent messages to migrant men and women that shape an enduring health-care seeking habitus. Undocumented women learn that they can expect only fleeting bursts of collateral care, and that they merit these medical services only by virtue of carrying and birthing the state's new citizens. Meanwhile, migrant men are led to regard government health care programs as intended for women alone.

The limited and sporadic collateral care migrant men receive creates and reinforces habitual patterns of prioritizing their work over their health—patterns long forged by labor, immigration, and health care policies. We have seen in chapter 2 that U.S. immigration and labor policies restrict the forms of government and employer assistance available to migrants, making them particularly reliant on their jobs. The limited diagnostic screenings provided by employers only reinforce this lesson for migrant men, who learn that they are eligible for diagnostic screenings only because of the value their employers attach to their labor capacity. A system of collateral care further teaches migrant men that their health is important to employers only if it affects their immediate ability to work, and that they must subordinate their physical well-being to their productivity.

Migrant Women: Opportunistic Care

In the United States, a patchwork of programs offered by nonprofit organizations and government agencies partly mitigates the widespread lack of health insurance: the American way of funding health care reflects contradictory principles of "exclusion and generosity."[14] Like others

who are uninsured, migrant women devise creative strategies to cope with the health care mélange they encounter in the United States. One of these is resourcefully using the services offered at little or no cost by government and informal agents, a strategy I refer to as *opportunistic care.*

Migrant women become adept at locating sources of opportunistic care. They attend health fairs hosted by the migrant clinic and send their uninsured children to the screenings offered by the county mobile van or to the school nurse. When formal care is unavailable, they rely on the medical equipment of friends and family. It is through these ancillary channels that migrant women often learn of hidden ailments.

Elisabeta, for example, found out she had high blood pressure at the annual health fair hosted by the migrant clinic in the city park. She was twenty-four at the time and had been doing farm work in the Valley for eight years. After the clinic worker strapped the blood-pressure cuff around her arm, he informed her that her systolic pressure was more than 200. "And I asked him, '*Oye* [listen], is that high?'" Elisabeta remembers. "And he said, 'Very high, ma'am.' And then he offered to call me an ambulance." Because she did not have the benefit of a full clinical consultation and explanation of her condition, Elisabeta remained skeptical. "And I thought, what is this illness? I don't believe I have anything," she says. Indeed, it was not until Elisabeta's doctor certified her for pregnancy-related medical disability eleven years later that he explained what hypertension is and Elisabeta realized its severity.

Similarly, Yadira, whose hypertension remained silent until a hemorrhagic stroke landed her in the ER, says that she plans to use a visit to the annual health fair as her annual checkup. Now that her second-eldest son, José Luis, has also shown signs of hypertension, Yadira is anxious to find preventive screenings for him as well. Because he is undocumented, this is not easy. Yadira knows that the county mobile van offers physical exams and hearing, dental, and vision screenings to migrant students, as well as referrals for immunizations.[15] But the van only visits Mendota once a year and serves migrant students only for three years after their arrival in the school district. It is no surprise, then, that José Luis's hypertension remained undetected until his shortness of breath landed him in the school nurse's office.

Uninsured migrant women also self-diagnose by borrowing the medical equipment of friends and family. Indeed, their social networks become an even more vital source of health care in the United States than in their homelands because of their exclusion from formal care.[16] Whether they use friends' and family's peak-flow monitors to measure

shortness of breath, finger sticks to measure blood glucose, or blood pressure cuffs, women use such home tests to avoid paying for the cost of a doctor's visit.

Migrant Men: Fortuitous Diagnoses

Migrant men are less likely to draw on the limited forms of charity and informal care used by women. Because labor and immigration policies have long forced migrant men to privilege their work over their health, they have learned to view their health as secondary to their productivity. Moreover, because of their historical exclusion from Medicaid and other forms of state-subsidized care, the government has taught migrant men to regard health care as a women's domain. The effect of these lessons is perverse. Although migrant farmworking men suffer higher rates of hypertension and cardiovascular disease than their female counterparts, their lack of access to care allows such conditions to remain silent.[17]

Elisabeta's husband, Teo, for example, was diagnosed with asthma only after severe pneumonia landed him in the hospital for a week. As a single, childless migrant farmworker, Teo had never had health insurance and had long avoided the doctor. While he was picking lettuce in Salinas, however, he had become sick with a fever, chest congestion, and a cough. Teo continued working, even though he had to sleep sitting up in order to breathe. Finally, one evening, Teo's landlady, hearing his hacking cough, insisted on taking him to the ER. There, the doctors diagnosed him with pneumonia complicated by asthma. The doctors told him that his lungs were severely inflamed and kept him in the hospital with an oxygen mask for a week; he was discharged with inhalers.

Thus state and federal policies that have historically excluded migrant men—combined with labor policies that make work men's only form of economic security—have left an enduring legacy. Although single migrant men with legal status are now eligible for Medi-Cal, they continue to operate with a health care habitus forged by longstanding policies of exclusion. Reliant on fortuitous screenings rather than routine preventive care, many men are confronted with illnesses detected only once they are beyond the point of intervention.

Sulema's husband, Mario, lost his mother to diabetes when she was in her fifties; his father now suffers from it as well. His younger brother was hospitalized for a week when his heart stopped; he was released with a defibrillator vest to keep his heart beating. Yet Mario refuses to visit the

doctor for even a routine checkup. Sulema herself learned she had high blood cholesterol after she paid out of pocket for a checkup following her hospitalization for high blood pressure. Yet when I ask Sulema whether Mario also suffers from any chronic diseases, she shrugs. "Who knows? That man is terrified of visiting the doctor," she says. Witnessing his family's decline has left Mario with a profound skepticism about the value of medical care. Mario visited a doctor in the United States only once, eight years ago, when a bout of acute pain—ultimately diagnosed as gallstones—left him bedridden.

As Mario's case shows, delayed diagnoses create a vicious cycle, begetting further mistrust of the medical system. As migrants see their friends and family diagnosed with conditions at stages well past the point of effective intervention, many understandably regard seeking formal medical care as an as unprofitable gamble. Thus migrants' health-care-seeking behaviors must be understood in the context of their historic exclusion from subsidized care and a system of collateral care that causes diagnoses to occur only by chance. This contributes to the situation Humberto describes, as migrants enter the fields unaware that their chronic conditions predispose them to heat stroke.

WORK AND HEALTH: PHYSIOLOGICAL INTERACTIONS

To understand the second half of the deadly chain reaction that Humberto outlines, we must consider the effect of farm work on the body. Farm work typically entails strong pressure to meet quotas imposed by supervisors, vigorous physical exertion, potential exposure to pesticides, and exposure to sun and heat. Stress, exertion, and heat are often contraindicated for those with uncontrolled hypertension, cardiovascular disease, and diabetes. In addition, pesticide exposure has been linked to a higher incidence of diabetes, which in turn aggravates cardiovascular disease.[18] Although the long-term effects of pesticide exposure remain shrouded by what the anthropologist Dvera Saxton calls "toxic ignorance," it is well known that overexposure to particular pesticides may cause excessive sweating and thereby worsen heat stress.[19] Thus if a system of collateral care prevents the prompt diagnosis of farmworkers' chronic disease, farm work initiates a series of physiological interactions that themselves exacerbate it.

As Humberto states, working in the heat with hypertension and cardiovascular disease is a dangerous combination. Blood pressure levels rise with the stress of maintaining equilibrium, as the body struggles to

keep cool. High blood pressure, in turn, causes excess sweating and dehydration; it can also trigger a heart attack.[20]

What Killed Timoteo Cruz?

The concept of syndemics powerfully challenges biomedicine's partitioning of diseases into discrete, bounded categories. Because diseases interact at the physiological and even cellular level, they may be said to become a whole greater than the sum of its parts. In the case of heat-related syndemics, then, attempting to isolate a single cause of mortality can be a tricky, even futile, enterprise. If a worker who suffers from high blood pressure dies of a heart attack on a hot day, who is to say whether the primary cause of death is hypertension, heart disease, or heat exhaustion?

The lawsuit the UFW filed against Cal-OSHA in 2012 (see chapter 1) ends with an appendix listing the cases of fourteen farmworkers whose deaths in the fields the plaintiffs claim Cal-OSHA should recognize as heat-related. Of these deaths, one is listed as having an undetermined cause, and one does not appear on the Cal-OSHA list. According to the county coroners who performed the autopsies, the other twelve deaths were exclusively due to three chronic illnesses from which farmworkers disproportionately suffer: hypertension, cardiovascular disease, and diabetes. One death was ruled as primarily due to "complications related to diabetes mellitus," three were attributed to hypertension, and eight were attributed to cardiac arrest, including "congestive heart failure . . . with secondary hypertensive cardiovascular disease" and "arteriosclerotic CVD."[21]

Number 14 on the list is a thirty-five-year-old named Timoteo Castro Cruz, who died on September 23, 2011, while working for George Masih Pagany Labor Contractors in Yuba City. The case concludes with the medical opinion of a Dr. Prudhomme, who adamantly rules out heat as the cause of Timoteo's death. Yet even his vehemence points up the difficulty of distinguishing the roles played by cardiovascular disease and by heat in Timoteo's demise. Dr. Prudhomme overrules the opinion of the forensic pathologist and coroner, writing: "I would NOT classify this as a heat fatality even though I agree with the pathologist that performing work (even light work) in the heat DID contribute to his death." Under "Cause of Death," Dr. Prudhomme writes: "Congestive heart failure exacerbated by the physical exertion during hot humid weather."[22]

FIGURE 11. A memorial to a fallen farmworker adjacent to a table-grape orchard on the road from Firebaugh to Fresno.

As the CDC warns, autopsies can rarely identify the role of heat in precipitating a death like Timoteo's. Because heat exacerbates other chronic diseases, and heat death may be preceded by a variety of symptoms, heat deaths are often underreported.[23] Moreover, as the Fresno deputy coroner, Kelly Matlock, states, autopsies are often performed the day after a body arrives at the morgue, by which time the clinical signs of heat illness—such as an elevated core body temperature and elevated liver and muscle enzymes—are no longer evident. As a result, the National Association of Medical Examiners has suggested that coroners should rely primarily on circumstantial evidence—such as a history of exposure to high temperatures—in diagnosing heat death.[24] Yet

as Dr. Prudhomme's assessment shows, doctors' medical training often leads them to privilege the visible organic pathology evident during an exam—such as Timoteo's heart disease—over the less perceptible social causes of ill health and death. [25]

Every summer, there are dozens of Timoteos—young, reasonably healthy farmworkers who die in the fields—whose deaths are ruled by county coroners as being primarily due to cardiovascular disease or hypertension, with heat stress playing a lesser or no role. Unless heat is recorded as a cause of death on their death certificates, these deaths will disappear from official statistics, such as the tally that state officials keep of farmworkers who have died since the implementation of the heat-illness standard. As state officials privilege the information yielded by autopsies over farmworkers' actual work circumstances, the social and political pathologies that lead to farmworkers' deaths fade from view. Resocializing deaths like Timoteo's yields a very different picture. It suggests that not only work but also the sociopolitical organization of farm work itself may have played a role in Timoteo's heart failure.

PUBLIC POLICY INTERACTIONS

Just as it is facile to view hypertension as a condition isolated from migrants' tenuous legal status and marginality, it is short-sighted to view farmworkers' heat illness as an inevitable effect of work. Work does not occur in a social and political vacuum; nor is it separable from the social relations that structure it. Rather, federal and state policies—combined with the farm labor hierarchy—profoundly shape the labor process and structure farmworkers' need for excessive and continuous work.

Overtime and Overwork

Overtime laws were created to discourage excessive work and protect workers' job security. Yet farmworkers' status as "exceptional workers"—specifically, their exclusion from federal overtime laws—leads to work weeks that far exceed the forty-hour standard that prevails in other industries. The California legislature has decreed that farmworkers be paid overtime once they work in excess of sixty hours a week, or ten hours a day. But because *mayordomos* transform their employees into ghost workers to disguise their violation of overtime laws, farmworkers exceed even this limit. During the harvest season, employers may demand that field hands work seventy- to eighty-hour weeks to

clear the fields of quickly ripening melons. The legislative double standard in overtime, together with *mayordomos'* violation of the laws that exist, contributes to heat illness by leading to excessive work.

I learn this one July afternoon during a historic heat wave, when I visit Elisabeta. It is 109 degrees when I arrive, and I find Elisabeta anxiously thumbing through the Spanish-language yellow pages. Her air conditioning is broken, and her landlord—a notorious slumlord—refuses to repair it. For Elisabeta, the timing could not be worse. Her son, Oscar, starts work picking melon tomorrow. "I think to myself, 'If something happens to my son, what will I do?' He'll be out there in the heat, and if we don't have AC at home, his body will never have a chance to cool down," she says.

Oscar, seventeen years old, has been working in the fields as a ghost for three years now. Elisabeta is particularly concerned about his health at present because his current employer requires that field hands work seven-day weeks, and often up to eleven hours a day, for the duration of the harvest. Elisabeta remembers her own experience of working in the high heat for weeks on end. She says that even once her body was able to cool down at night, she found herself sweating constantly—"*sudi y sudi y sudi y sudi.*" And her eyes became quite bloodshot (*la vista se pone roja, roja*)—the result, she thinks, of a spike in her blood pressure. Now that her broken air conditioning will not allow Oscar's body to recover after work, Elisabeta fears that he will suffer in the same way.

Contract Work and Skipping Breaks

Another example of the health hazards created by the sociopolitical conditions of farm work is the peer pressure engendered by contract work. Labor supervisors agree to pay their workers on contract when they wish to create an incentive for workers to clear the fields quickly and are less concerned about the quality of their work. In contract work, an individual's pay depends directly on the performance of the team: a crew of workers is paid a fixed amount for each flatbed trailer they stack full of boxes or each box of melons they fill.

Working by contract is often more lucrative than being paid by the hour, and crews made up of healthy young men approach the melon harvest as they would a prime-time sports event. Crews compete to see who can fill more trailers in a day, trading jabs as they work and bragging about their prowess. They elect to work the melon harvest in smaller crews—of seventeen instead of the traditional twenty-one—to

take home more money. Crew members working by contract exert considerable pressure on their peers. They may demand that the *mayordomo* weed out underperforming members, holding teammates to a high rate of production.

Contract work entails the expectation that workers will skip state-mandated breaks so that they can return home early. When Elisabeta harvests watermelon for a large contractor, the crews put in seven-hour days, and the machine never stops. "All day it goes up the rows. It never stops for more than a minute," she says. As a result, Elisabeta and her coworkers don't even bring lunches, although they sometimes eat a watermelon straight from the field. The *mayordoma* works alongside five of her family members, and the in-group forms an aggressive posse. They snap at workers to work harder and insult them when they appear to be slowing. "They push us harder," she says (*andan empuchando a nosotros*). Few workers dare to ask for a break. Once, when the tractor driver got out of his seat to go the bathroom, the *mayordoma* complained: "And why does he choose to go now? Doesn't he see that we have a field of melons to pick?"

Elisabeta says that trying to manage her diabetes while working for this crew only aggravated her condition. She was twenty-eight at the time, but pregnancy had caused her blood sugar to skyrocket. Her doctor prescribed twice-daily injections of insulin. She carried her syringes of insulin to work in a cooler packed with ice and deposited them in the *raitero*'s van at the edge of the field while she worked. To maintain her image as a capable team member, she never told her supervisor or coworkers what the cooler contained. "I put a soda in there to disguise [the syringes]," she says. Yet because her supervisor and crew routinely went without breaks, Elisabeta was never able to inject her medication. "The cooler just sat there all season," she says.

Soon Elisabeta's blood sugar was at 400, and her pregnancy was at risk. When Elisabeta told her doctor that she was furtively trying to steal a moment to inject her insulin in the open field, he certified her for temporary disability and sent her to a diabetes specialist in Fresno. Her extremely high blood sugar levels, combined with uncontrolled blood pressure, caused her doctors to opt to deliver her baby, Andrea, two months early. Thus the pressure of working on contract is particularly harmful for workers with chronic disease. To meet their teams' demands for productivity, migrants conceal chronic illness and work through breaks.

Food Safety Policies: Sustaining the Syndemic

If the anemic enforcement of California's heat illness standard has failed to prevent heat-related syndemics, the industry's heightened scrutiny of "worker hygiene" actively encourages them. As we saw in chapter 1, he cantaloupe industry has adopted new regulations that prohibit the state's melon harvesters and packers from bringing their own water supplies into the fields. These are merely the most recent iteration of a series of food safety standards intended to burnish the industry's public image.

After a series of widespread outbreaks of food-borne illness in the 1980s and 1990s, retailers began searching for a branding mechanism to assure consumers of the safety of fresh produce. In order to protect their markets, major retailers—such as Kroeger's, Subway, Walmart, and Costco—required that suppliers of fresh fruits and vegetables undergo third-party food-safety audits based on U.S. and global guidelines.[26] Yet this system has not succeeded in eliminating food-borne illness.[27] A 2006 multistate *E. coli* outbreak linked to contaminated spinach, followed by national outbreaks of salmonella and listeriosis linked to contaminated cantaloupe, again tarnished the industry's image and threatened its profits.

To restore consumer confidence, the produce industry giants formed their own trade associations. In 1998, California cantaloupe producers formed the California Cantaloupe Advisory Board (CCAB); in 2007, spinach and lettuce growers followed suit with the California Leafy Green Marketing Agreement (LGMA).[28] In an attempt to maintain the industry's reputation and hold their peers accountable, these associations of growers most affected by foodborne illness devised their own food-safety certifications. Together with food-safety experts, and with the approval of state and federal governments, they created detailed audit checklists specifying how each crop should be picked, packed, and transported: the LGMA in 2007 and the CCAB in 2012.

All major cantaloupe growers and distributors in California are bound by the CCAB guidelines, which specify in detail how workers should behave while harvesting. Since 2012, when the guidelines went into force, all these producers have begun prohibiting workers from taking personal water supplies onto the farm machinery in order to maintain their CCAB certification. As we saw in chapter 1, workers routinely go without water rather than request that the production process stop to let them drink from the company-provided water supply. Thus in its

zeal to maintain consumer confidence, the food industry has sanctioned a different kind of harm: it safeguards its own legitimacy at the price of risking workers' health.

FOOD SAFETY REGULATIONS AT WORK

The farmwork hierarchy, together with immigration and labor policies, has long taught migrant men to remain quiet (*callados*) even when they are on the brink of burning up. No farmworker wants to be dismissed with the barb "*ese flojón no quiere trabajar*" (that lazy ass just doesn't want to work) or derided by colleagues for having "limp hands." Workers know that being perceived as weak may cost them their jobs. Each summer, there are many *callados* who successfully make it through the day. And each summer, there are some who do not.

Elisabeta's husband, Teo, worked alongside one such *callado*. He and Álvaro had worked together picking watermelons—the supersized "jambo" melons—in El Centro, California, for fifteen years. Both men were from Mendota but traveled south to El Centro each summer because the pay was better; they worked on contract and were paid by the box.

Elisabeta, in contrast, preferred to spend her summer harvesting watermelons in Mendota, earning less money per box. She said she preferred to accept the lower pay rather than risk discovery of her undocumented status while passing through an internal immigration checkpoint. "And with the raids they have there? *Ni modo* [no way]," she said.

During the first week of July in 2013, I visited Elisabeta while Teo was in El Centro. Teo had called the day before and reported that Álvaro, a coworker of his, had died. Álvaro was a *paisano,* a Salvadoran like Teo, and he was forty-two. When I visit, Elisabeta is worried; Teo has three more days of work left. Fresno County is in the midst of a heat wave, yet it is still cooler in the Central Valley than in the southern California desert. I find Elisabeta sitting at her kitchen table, her face flushed with heat because of her broken air conditioner, her eyes anxious as she recounts her conversation with Teo. "He said he could hardly see straight. I told him he should come home."

When he finally does return, Teo tells me that jambo watermelons are cut and picked assembly-line style. One man severs the thick stem of the melon with a pocketknife and then tosses it to the next in line, who relays it to the next. Expert jambo pickers are like professional jugglers, conveying melon up the line in one fluid motion. They bounce the melons on

their way, never letting the fruit settle in their hands, for hours at a time. Álvaro had worked on his team as a cutter, the first man in the line.

The crew had been working six- to seven-hour days without breaks, entering the field at 5:30 A.M. and stopping at noon. In the heat of the Imperial Valley, skipping breaks is not a matter of convenience but a way for the crews to avoid the worst of the heat. The faster the crew works, the more likely they are to be able to finish before the afternoon heat sets in.

Álvaro had been in a good mood because he had just returned from El Salvador. He had initially had TPS, just like Teo. He had married a U.S. citizen two years earlier and had finally been able to adjust his immigration status earlier that year so that he could legally return after leaving the country. For the first time since he had arrived in the United States fifteen years ago, he had been able to visit his aging mother.

Álvaro spent three months in El Salvador with his mother and returned to pick melon in the Imperial Valley that July. He returned on Monday and worked fine on Tuesday, Teo says, with a shake of his head. He died on Wednesday.

Teo says that when the crew gathered to talk about Álvaro's death the following morning—after the shock of the supervisor's announcement had somewhat abated—nothing had stood out as particularly unusual about that day in El Centro. It is true that it was 115 degrees, as it often is midsummer, and the National Weather Service had issued an excessive heat warning. It is true that the elderly, young children, and those with heart conditions were advised against staying outdoors too long, and that their crew had been working strenuously all morning. It is true that they hadn't taken breaks, and that Álvaro—as a cutter—worked the farthest from the sole water jug riding under the field-packing machine. It is true that the machine hadn't stopped in its journey up and down the furrows, and that Álvaro likely didn't drink all morning. But, he shrugs, these things are business as usual when picking watermelon on the U.S.-Mexico border in the summer.

Teo says that in retrospect, he could see scattered clues. In the morning, he found out later, Álvaro had confided to an older coworker—a friend of his—that his stomach hurt. Nausea is often a sign of heat illness, so the coworker—who had had the luxury of packing melons in the shade of the field-packing machine's canopy—voluntarily traded places with Álvaro to let him cool off. But Álvaro never complained to his supervisor or asked for a break. He continued to pack, finished his workday without comment, and went home.

At home that afternoon, Álvaro complained to his wife that his stomach still hurt. According to his supervisor, who had spoken with Álvaro's wife, Álvaro told her he didn't know why or what the problem was. He took an antacid pill, thinking it was indigestion. The couple crossed the border into Mexico for dinner—again, a first for him—where he ate a bowl of shrimp. He seemed to relax, she said. But when they returned home, the pain grew worse. Teo recounts what the supervisor told them the morning after Álvaro died: "He said it kept hurting, and the pain kept growing, and perhaps they delayed in calling an ambulance, because when it arrived he could no longer breathe."

On the Saturday evening after Álvaro's death, I join Elisabeta, Teo, and their two children, Carlos and Andrea, in attending his funeral at the Catholic church in Mendota. The service has already started; the ceiling fans buzz as the priest delivers his sermon. As we walk down the side aisle to find a seat, we see a gray casket flanked by two large wreaths—serving as halos to statues of Jesus and the Virgin Mary—and, on the mantle above it, an ample bouquet of red and white roses. We find a seat in a pew in front. After we are settled, I turn around to see that there are nearly a hundred people in the church. The men's faces are flushed; they look as if they have just come in from the fields. Yet, in deference to the occasion, they wear button-down shirts instead of T-shirts, and their jeans are freshly starched. They lay their baseball caps in their laps.[29]

Álvaro's family sits in the three front left pews. The men are in dark jeans, button-down shirts, leather boots with polished tips, and black sombreros, with red ribbons pinned to their lapels. The women wear dresses and heels. Their hair is straightened, coiffed, and kept in place with decorative combs.

In the front pew sit three broad-shouldered Salvadoran men with sunburned faces and black moustaches. I later learn these are Álvaro's brothers. To their right, a woman is slouched in her pew, her long black hair hanging loose and disheveled. She is wearing a black T-shirt and jeans; her face is swollen, and she wears no makeup. The audience is still except for an elderly woman in the pew behind her, who is massaging and stroking the woman's back. Throughout the sermon, she stares straight ahead, her gaze fixed on no point in particular. The priest is saying that Jesus taught his followers not to believe in revenge, nor to fight evil with evil. She continues to stare. When the sermon reaches a crescendo and the priest tells the crowd that Jesus died but was reborn (*resuscitado*), she begins to cry, hard, as though a knife that had been

buried deep in her has finally been pulled out and she can at last feel its sting. Throughout the whole service, the elderly woman sitting behind her continues touching her, stroking her shoulders, and teasing her hair.

At the end of the service, when the priest opens the top half of the casket for the viewing of the body, this woman is the first to approach. She brings a framed studio portrait of herself and Álvaro and sets it inside the lid of the casket. She stands there, with her hand half covering her open mouth, for several seconds. Then she moves to the side as the center aisle of the church fills with men queuing up to pay their respects. They shift uncomfortably in their boots, holding their caps in their hands.

Teo gets up to pay his respects while Elisabeta and I stay with the children. They are seated on either side of Elisabeta, and she pulls them close for a hug. Andrea, just four, is wearing a starched black and white checked dress and pigtails; she is busy toying with her rhinestone-studded butterfly hairpin. "See, it's a butterfly! It will sail through the sky," she tells me. Carlos, eleven years old, is crying. He is not moving, but there are tears welling in his eyes. When we exit the church, Carlos pulls his baseball cap down over his eyes to prevent others from seeing.

When Teo returns, we exit to the church courtyard, where refreshments have been provided — coolers of sodas and Gatorade. We stay to visit just briefly. Elisabeta's face is flushed, and she is fanning it as though she were still packing watermelon in the fields. "Let's go," Teo urges. Elisabeta is ready. She tells me she is feeling *coraje*. "Whenever I go to one of these, whenever there's a worker killed in the fields, I just feel like I can't breathe. I feel like that hot air is suffocating me," she says.

We walk back through the cooling city streets as the evening darkens, Andrea blithely sailing her butterfly hairpin through the air. Carlos walks quietly, listening intently as Teo tries to make sense of the week's events. "It's horrible to see your brother [*paisano*] in a casket. You just feel awful [*se siente perro*]! Working at his side one day and seeing him in his casket the next."

"When death comes, it comes suddenly," Elisabeta says.

Teo shakes his head. "On Tuesday, I asked him, I said, 'Are you going to return with us to Mendota to keep working?' And he said: '*Si Dios quiere*' [God willing]. *Si Dios quiere,*" he repeats.

"Well, God didn't will it then, right?" Elisabeta responds.

I ask Teo why he thinks it happened. "He told a coworker that he suffers from high blood pressure," Teo tells me. Álvaro's gaining legal status had been a watershed in many ways: not only had it allowed him to return

to El Salvador, but it also had made him eligible for Medi-Cal. Álvaro had visited a doctor, who had prescribed pills to combat his hypertension.

That day in El Centro, however, Álvaro had just returned to farm work after a three-month break. He had worked alongside Teo picking lettuce near Fresno earlier that year, Teo says, but maybe his body had not yet acclimatized to the heat. Maybe the heat had caused his blood pressure to spike. He had barely begun picking jambos when the temperature in El Centro hit 115 degrees.

I ask why Álvaro had been unable to drink water. I had seen workers tie water bottles to their belts with twine when weeding. Why hadn't Álvaro taken this precautionary measure? "Because they're the precious ones," Teo says with a wry smile—referring to the watermelon. That year, he says, supervisors had made their workers surrender their bottles. While California's watermelon growers aren't subject to the same food safety regulations as its cantaloupe growers, this particular company was trying to pass more stringent audits in order to sell its produce to larger retailers.

We walk in silence for a few minutes. Then Teo turns to Elisabeta to comment that Fito and Kevin—two of Álvaro's brothers seated in the front row—had paid $7,000 to hold the funeral and to return Álvaro's body to El Salvador in the hold of a plane. Those were Álvaro's wishes, Teo says: to be buried alongside his parents "in his land" (*en su tierra*).

I ask why the company isn't treating Álvaro's death as work related, which would mean that some of these expenses would be covered by workers' compensation insurance. "The supervisor said it wasn't the company's fault because he died at home," Teo says. He adds that "good companies" sometimes reimburse families for the expense of flying a deceased worker home to be buried, particularly if the worker had a long and consistent record. He says that so far there has been no word.

As the sun sets, the shadows of bushes in the yards and of the cars parked on the streets grow longer and stranger. Elisabeta and Teo trade stories of that summer's close calls. Elisabeta tells me that when she went to pack watermelon this past week, she got so hot that by the time she took her break inside the *mayordomo*'s van, her arms were already beginning to cramp up. "Cramps. That's the first step of *insolación,*" she says.

Teo replies that while he was picking in the Imperial Valley, his legs began to cramp so hard that he had to grab the side of the field-packing machine to stretch them out as he walked. "They say that when your muscles begin to cramp, you have to hold them tight, tight, until they stop," he tells me. "And if you're not careful, your whole body can seize up."

Elisabeta will not be outdone. That Monday, when it was 111 in Mendota, she tells us, a young man working on another crew in her same company died. She hadn't been at work that day; she had gone to the clinic to refill her blood pressure medication. She hadn't known the dead worker by name, but she had heard from a coworker how it had happened. "They say he was sweating and sweating and sweating, and then it just stopped. His mouth got dry, and he couldn't talk. That's what they say happened before he fell."

Every farmworker can tell stories of close calls, of appointments with their maker narrowly averted. The constraining web of public policies and private interests could have ensnared any farmworker in its net. Mere happenstance could have placed Elisabeta or Teo in that casket. "That's why Carlos was crying," Elisabeta tells me later. "He said it could have been his *papá* in there."

The stories of Álvaro and Timoteo reveal the hidden hand of work in the deaths of farmworkers who reportedly die of natural causes, as well as the ambiguity in the way that heat death itself is defined and counted.[30] Because Timoteo had heart disease, his death was not ruled as due to heat. Because Álvaro never mentioned his stomach pain to his supervisor, his death at home was not recognized as work related. The part played by their work is blanched from history, preserving the mystery of why the average life span of a farmworker is only forty-nine years.[31]

Deaths accounted for in this way relieve growers and companies of the financial burden of compensating farmworker families for their loss. Workers' compensation insurance policies not only cover the care of workers sickened on the job but also cover funeral expenses and the care of dependents when workers die on the job. The way that death is reckoned and the silence imposed by the farmwork hierarchy conspire to make these deaths go unreimbursed. As in Álvaro's case, dependents go unsupported, and families are left to pick up the funeral expenses for their deceased.

The ways county coroners determine cause of death and state epidemiologists compile their official reports make deaths like these disappear from the death toll of farm work. Yet attending to the cases that state epidemiologists ignore—listening to the ethnographic "noise" eliminated from epidemiological data sets—reveals the complex interaction of public policies and social processes that culminate in heat death each summer. Analyzing cases like Álvaro's and Timoteo's—cases that trouble the boundaries of official categories—allows a different narrative about heat death to snap into focus. Our peculiar accounting of workplace

fatalities helps conceal a public and occupational health travesty that would not be tolerated in middle-class workplaces.

Differential Enforcement and the Politics of Visibility

Scholars suggest that corporations often produce some kind of harm in the pursuit of profit: the tobacco and firearms industries are particularly visible examples of "harm industries" but by no means the only ones.[32] Because public health crises— such as outbreaks of food-borne illness, mass shootings, and scientific studies revealing smoking's link to cancer—threaten to delegitimize such industries and erode their profits, they can serve as critical tipping points that reveal corporate strategies to "shape the social management of harm."[33] They also reveal what kinds of harm the public will tolerate. Álvaro's death shows that the produce industry's attempts to maintain consumer confidence have replaced one kind of corporate harm with another: containing the threat of food-borne illness has come at the expense of workers' health.

The public's relative tolerance of different types of harms is evident from a comparison of the produce industry's enforcement of food safety regulations and the state's enforcement of its heat illness standard. Growers are much more likely to face a food safety audit—whether by the state or an industry association—than a visit by Cal-OSHA to enforce the heat-illness standard. Steve, the food-safety supervisor I spoke with (see chapter 1), told me that Fresco's cantaloupe harvesters had undergone four food-safety inspections in 2012 and eight in 2013 but none by Cal-OSHA. During those two years, Cal-OSHA had visited the company only once, to inspect its bell-pepper harvesters. Indeed, in 2012, the agency audited only four thousand of California's thirty-five thousand farms.[34]

The prioritization of consumer confidence over farmworker health is part of a politics of visibility that keeps farmworkers' concerns relatively hidden, while contaminated food makes headlines.[35] A history of agricultural exceptionalism has long legitimized farmworkers' exclusion from the labor and health protections extended to members of other occupational classes. Invoking the myth of beleaguered family farmers hampered by excessive regulation, the agribusiness industry has been able to disguise the fact that the majority of farm employees in fact work for large agricultural growers and corporations.[36] By so doing, they have succeeded in quashing legislation that would bring agricultural working conditions out of the early industrial era while placing protections for farmers on the agendas of state and federal policy makers. In short, the

"plight" of farmers has been placed in the spotlight, while farmworkers have labored in its shadow.[37]

The gap in stringency and frequency between audits ensuring consumer safety and farmworker health is part of this politics of visibility. Consumers' deaths due to outbreaks of listeriosis and *E. coli* on contaminated melon, lettuce, and spinach consistently make national news while the deaths of those who harvest these crops often go unremarked and uncounted. The privileging of consumers' over workers' safety helps explain the gaps in the state's heat-illness standard as well as its erratic enforcement. Only when workers' plight is made as visible as that of farmers' and consumers' will it be possible to enact meaningful legislation to address the synergistic interaction of chronic disease and heat illness in California's fields.

Tacking back and forth between social and political structures and the behaviors they produce, this chapter has explored the multiple contexts encouraging farmworkers' undiagnosed chronic ailments. Attention to how the immediate work context and broader public policies interact to encourage disease clustering helps flesh out the existing statistics, explaining why foreign-born farmworkers like Álvaro bear the highest risk of heat death.[38] Merrill Singer notes that the synergistic interaction of multiple afflictions has an additively negative effect on the health of vulnerable populations. In a similar way, the knot of public policies and private interests implicated in heat death constrains farmworkers' health in an exponential manner. Álvaro's story illustrates the cumulative embodied effects of farmworkers' exclusion from public insurance, their precarious work status, and the imposition of new food-safety standards.

Detailing the precise behavioral and structural factors that exacerbate syndemics can help identify potential points of intervention.[39] As Bobby Milstein of the Syndemics Prevention Network puts it, "To prevent a syndemic, one must not only prevent or control each disease but also the forces that tie those diseases together."[40] Thus while California's heat-illness prevention standard narrowly targets heat illness alone, uncoupling the discrete conditions that lead to deaths in the fields requires untying the dense knot of public policies and private interests that produce them. Any effort to reduce heat death will fail without efforts to expand migrant farmworkers' access to preventive health care, to reduce the physiological stress of legal minority status, to diminish the pressures of the farmwork hierarchy, and to alter the produce industry's food-safety certification system—measures I return to in the book's conclusion.

CHAPTER 6

Desabilitado

Kidney Disease and the Disability-Assistance Hole

When Don Ramón, fifty-two years old, reflects on the past, he thinks that maybe the reason he is now *desabilitado* (disabled) dates all the way back to the mid-1980s—the heyday of melon harvesting in the Valley—when he used to pick melon by contract. We are sitting in the living room of his subsidized apartment on an overcast fall day, a few hours before Don Ramón will go to dialysis and the day before the cataract surgery that he hopes will restore his sight—and he is ruminating on what landed him in this predicament. "Back when we used to pick melon with a sack, we used to rush up and down the field all day long," he remembers. Before field packing was invented and before farmwork was better regulated, he says, he would work without breaks, ferrying up to forty melons in a sack slung over his shoulders from the fields to the truck. His team of thirteen would fill up to eleven trucks a day. "We were working on contract, so we could earn good money," he remembers. "And we wouldn't even stop to drink."

Don Ramón recalls that he often experienced pain in the right side of his lower back during the harvest season—which, at the time, he chalked up to the result of hours of stooping. Yet he also found himself sweating excessively, even after the harvest ended. When he returned to his hometown of El Platanal, Mexico, to see his family, this struck his wife as odd. "At night, when he slept, he'd be drenched in sweat. And I'd ask him, 'Why do you sweat so much?'" his wife recalls. "And I'd tell her, 'It's because of the work I do,'" Don Ramón says with pride. Then

he stops, his expression darkening. "But now, I wonder if it was more than that."

The warning signs of kidney decline are typically mild. Don Ramón's excessive sweating may have been a symptom of chronic kidney disease (CKD), and the pain in his lower back is consistent with rhabdomyolysis, a syndrome triggered by heatstroke or excessive exertion that can also lead to kidney damage. However, because kidney disease typically remains silent until it is very advanced, none of the farmworkers I interviewed were diagnosed until they had end-stage renal disease (ESRD).

A growing body of literature links kidney damage to the harsh working conditions faced by farmworkers in Central America.[1] Yet because of policies that keep farmworkers' health concerns relatively obscure, research has only now begun to explore the relationship between work circumstances and kidney decline among farmworkers in the United States. Rather than examining the immediate effect of work on health, this chapter explores farm work's cumulative physiological toll. It suggests that farmworkers' repeated exposure to heat stress may yield long-term kidney damage and examines why a potential epidemic of kidney disease among U.S. farmworkers may remain undetected.

Social Security Disability Insurance (SSDI) is a staple in the patchwork of government assistance programs that sustain farmworking families. Yet while SSDI provides those with ESRD with income and medical assistance, its failure to intervene at earlier stages only contributes to kidney failure among farmworkers. If the anemic enforcement of labor regulations contributes to long-term kidney decline among U.S. farmworkers, the U.S. disability insurance system only hastens its course. In addition, federal disability programs teach migrant men a perverse lesson. Men who have long prized their self-sufficiency learn that their receipt of the insurance comes at the price of complete dependence.

AN AGRICULTURAL EPIDEMIC

Recent research on kidney disease among agricultural workers in Central America casts Don Ramón's kidney failure in a new light. For the past two decades, Central American public health officials and researchers have documented a "Mesoamerican epidemic" of chronic kidney disease of unknown origin—dubbed CKDu—widely affecting farmworkers across El Salvador, Nicaragua, and Costa Rica.[2] CKDu differs significantly from the form of CKD documented in developed nations, which is caused primarily by diabetes and hypertension and typically

afflicts an older, unhealthier population. CKDu, in contrast, usually strikes young, predominantly healthy men without the usual risk factors for the disease: often called an "agricultural nephropathy," it occurs disproportionately among farmworkers.[3]

Margaret Lock has shown that human biology is not an invariant universal: rather, the expression and experience of disease may vary according to environment, culture, and other contextual factors.[4] Indeed, those afflicted with CKDu appear to have a different illness trajectory than those suffering the kidney disease known to U.S. nephrologists. Whereas the form of CKD known in the United States is characterized by damage to the filter (glomerulus) of the kidney, biopsies of kidneys diseased by CKDu instead show damage originating in the tubules of the kidney—a pattern consistent with chronic dehydration.[5] Moreover, because of the lack of access to preventative health care, dialysis, and transplants in developing countries, CKDu is rarely treatable. It appears to be deadlier than its better-known variant in the Global North, progressing more rapidly to kidney failure.[6]

CKDu is concentrated among Central American sugarcane cutters. Studies commissioned by sugar mill owners initially blamed the epidemic on workers themselves. They pointed to workers' "overuse" of nonsteroidal anti-inflammatories and their consumption of a homemade moonshine called *lija*.[7] Yet a growing body of research points to the very explanations offered by Don Ramón, documenting the damage to the kidneys caused by the conditions of agricultural work. Mounting evidence from epidemiological studies suggests that dehydration, heat stress, and kidney damage constitute a syndemic—one that especially strikes otherwise-healthy farmworking men.

A population-based study in El Salvador was among the first to definitively identify heat stress and dehydration as risk factors for CKDu. Researchers measured the blood-serum creatinine levels—a biological marker of kidney damage—of more than six hundred men and women living in five different Salvadoran communities. They ensured that the communities varied by altitude—as a proxy for the extent of heat exposure—and by dominant occupation. They found that a history of work on sugarcane and cotton plantations at low altitudes was associated with more signs of kidney damage than less strenuous work on coffee plantations and in subsistence crops, in which workers had greater control over their work conditions, or work in sugarcane plantations at a high altitude, where workers were exposed to less heat

stress. The longer the duration of work on lowland sugarcane and cotton plantations, the more severe the damage: 44 percent of the men and 40 percent of the women who had worked for more than ten years in coastal cotton or sugarcane plantations had elevated markers of kidney damage.[8] Thus the researchers concluded that the conditions faced by workers in lowland sugar mills and on cotton plantations—involving strenuous physical activity in high heat—may cause kidney decline.

A 2015 study directly measured the effect of strenuous physical activity on workers' kidneys. Researchers collected blood and urine samples from 189 full-time sugarcane cutters before and after their work shifts over the course of eight different days and correlated the results with the ambient temperature. They found that workers experienced a 2 percent increase in serum creatinine for each degree increase in temperature. Moreover, they found elevated serum creatinine levels in 20 percent of the male sugarcane cutters even before their work shift, indicating preexisting kidney damage. This particular group of men experienced a greater increase in serum creatinine levels after their workday than the others, suggesting greater kidney damage over time. Fourteen percent of the men surveyed met the criteria for CKD.[9] Thus the Salvadoran study challenges the tenet among nephrologists that dehydration-induced damage to the kidney is reversible. Instead, the fact that workers' serum creatinine levels increased over the course of a workday suggests that the researchers were observing ESRD in the making.[10]

THE DIAGNOSIS: WORK AND KIDNEY DISEASE

The Central American data would not surprise Don Ramón, nor many other farmworkers in the Central Valley. Many farmworkers in the Valley know neighbors, family members, or coworkers who have kidney failure and are on dialysis, the mechanical process of blood filtration that substitutes for diseased kidneys. Even young, otherwise healthy men require this procedure. Indeed, dialysis is a household word among farmworkers in the Valley. Coining a Spanglish verb from a medical term, farmworkers say that such workers are *dialysisando*.

In the Central Valley, it is a truism that kidneys "dry up" (*se secan*), "go bad" (*se echan a perder*), or "finish" (*se acaban*) because of the physical stress of farmwork. This is why Blanca told me, on that summer day in 2008, that farmworkers "leave their kidneys in the fields." Interviews with U.S. farmworkers about how they first learned of their

chronic kidney disease bear out the findings in Central America. They suggest that working the summer harvest aggravated—if not single-handedly caused—workers' kidney decline.

Silvestre, now thirty-two, first noticed that something was amiss while he was working as a stacker (*cargador*) during the corn harvest. He was then twenty-seven years old and had done farmwork in the Valley since he was sixteen. In September 2010, Silvestre began experiencing extreme nausea and headaches; he also routinely began vomiting shortly after entering the corn fields at 4 A.M. His doctor later told him this was a sign of early-morning hypertension. When Silvestre finally took a day off work to visit the doctor, his systolic blood pressure was 280. The doctor suggested that Silvestre return and undergo a panel of tests to try to discern the cause. Undocumented and unable to pay for the tests, Silvestre worked for an additional month and a half, retching each morning. Only when his landlady encouraged him to return to Mexico "to get cured" did a nephrologist there diagnose him with kidney failure—"just by looking at the color of my eyes," he says.

Martín first began feeling tired in September 2014, during the melon harvest. He was thirty at the time. After a few days of working as a stacker, he switched to driving the tractor because he wanted a break. Because of cantaloupe companies' stringent rules against workers bringing their own drinking water, Martín could drink only during the two breaks provided—at 9 A.M. and noon. Driving the open tractor, Martín was exposed directly to the sun and began to feel "exhausted." By the end of the melon season, Martín noticed that he was barely urinating—a symptom that he chalked up to a routine urine infection.

In March 2015, Martín was working staking grape vines for a particularly strict *mayordomo*. They put in nine-hour days, and the *mayordomo* rebuked them if they paused to drink. The temperature sometimes rose to 90 degrees by noon, and the heat index was even higher due to the humidity among the vines. Martín began to feel that he might vomit. "And when I bent down to pick up the vine [to stake it], my vision sometimes would go black," he says.

After a few days, Martín noticed that his lower abdomen was distended, and he developed a sharp pain below his ribs. Martín asked the *mayordomo* if he could have a day off so he could visit the hospital. When he entered the ER in Fresno on March 2, 2015, blood tests revealed that his kidneys were working at 15 percent of their normal capacity. The doctors inserted a catheter in his chest to perform his first session of dialysis.

Studies of CKDu in Central America suggest that the timing of these men's diagnoses is not coincidental. Because the melon and corn harvests occur at the height of summer, and only the packers—usually women—have the benefit of shade, men face particular risk of heat stress. The three young men I interviewed had all worked as stackers, piling pallets of melons into columns more than eight feet high. Because of the pace of work and new food-safety regulations, they were able to rehydrate only infrequently. Whether or not their working conditions were the sole cause of their illness, it is clear that heat exposure and intensive exertion aggravated a disease that had long remained silent.

The Geography of Complacence

In seeking to identify the cause of the epidemic of CKDu in Central America, international NGOs have pointed to lax regulation that allows overwork, farmworkers' lack of access to shade and water, and the use of child labor.[11] Despite international concern for the poor labor conditions on the far side of the sugar commodity chain, however, researchers have only recently begun to investigate whether the disease is common among U.S. farmworkers.[12]

The late attention to this issue in the United States is the result of what I call a *geography of complacence*—a comforting sense that the problems of overwork, lack of breaks, and scarce opportunities for rehydration among farmworkers are confined to the Global South. The anthropologist and physician Paul Farmer introduced the term *geography of blame* to describe the way that emerging public health problems in the Global North, such HIV/AIDS and multi-drug-resistant tuberculosis, are often blamed on the unhealthy practices of populations in the Global South, thereby diverting attention from the structural circumstances that contribute to disease.[13] Like the geography of blame, the geography of complacence is content to relegate the harsh labor practices that create premature kidney failure to other times and other places. This complacence leads policy makers and the public to overlook the tightly interlocked bundle of policies that have maintained U.S. farmworkers' status as exceptional workers—workers with a higher ceiling for overtime, wages that make child labor incumbent, and a history of lax regulation that permits labor abuses to flourish. As we shall see, migrants' inadequate health care access may allow a U.S. variant of the Central American epidemic to go undetected.

DELAYED DIAGNOSIS: THE PRICE OF EXCLUSION FROM MEDI-CAL

Prior to the episodes of acute illness that precipitated their diagnoses, only one of the men I interviewed with ESRD had ever visited a doctor in the United States. As Martín puts it, "Because as an undocumented migrant, how? How are you going to pay for it?" Because kidney disease often remains asymptomatic until it is very advanced, none of the farmworkers with kidney disease whom I interviewed were diagnosed until they had ESRD. Thus while the summer harvest set the stage for the emergence of men's latent kidney disease, their inadequate access to care had long incubated it.

Don Ramón's story illustrates the way U.S. policies discourage migrant male breadwinners from seeking health care. Even though single men with legal status became eligible for Medi-Cal in January 2014, the legacy of their exclusion from Medi-Cal lingers. Because these single male sojourners have spent most of their years in the United States ineligible for Medi-Cal—first as undocumented migrants and then as childless men with legal status—federal policies have long taught them to cope without health insurance.

Like many other men of his generation, Don Ramón first came to the United States as an undocumented migrant in order to support his family in El Platanal. He subsequently obtained legal status through IRCA's Special Agricultural Worker program. Because his wife, Doña Luisa, refused to face the risks of crossing the border *mojada* (unlawfully), Don Ramón applied for visas for her and their three children in 1994. It was not until 2000 that the visas were granted and she and her children could be reunited with Don Ramón. Even though Don Ramón himself became "legal" in 1986, then, he was ineligible for Medicaid for the intervening fourteen years because U.S. policy viewed him as a childless male. As a result, the only time he visited a doctor in the United States was at the behest of an employer in a laundromat, who ordered physicals for all employees to improve the efficiency of his workforce.

Even when they qualified for Medi-Cal, Don Ramón and his wife—then in their early forties—had other reasons to manage without it. Receiving Medicaid benefits has historically been cause for labeling migrants as "public charges" likely to become dependent on the state, justifying their deportation or barring their legal reentry to the United States. Because the federal government did not clarify until 1999 that receipt of Medicaid would not be cause for a public-charge determination,

many migrants—like Don Ramón and Doña Luisa—scrupulously avoided the insurance.[14] "We always paid for our children's care out of pocket," Doña Luisa explains. Indeed, in keeping with the messages communicated to them by federal health care and immigration policies, Don Ramón and Doña Luisa continue to take pride in their ability to cope without assistance. "We've always been relatively healthy," she says. So when Don Ramón was first diagnosed with ESRD, "We didn't know anything about Medi-Cal or how the system works."

As a result of these circumstances, Don Ramón did not learn of his advanced diabetes until he was fifty years old, when it was already destroying his kidneys and affecting his vision. He first noticed that he felt unwell while picking chile in the summer of 2012. "I had a lot of nausea. And I wondered, what could this be? Why do I feel like this?" He remembers. He thought it could be the sun; after all, it was 108 degrees that day. Yet he continued to feel poorly while working indoors in a fish cannery in Alaska later that summer. He began losing his sight and noticed that his feet were swelling, then his hands, and then his whole body. The nausea continued. "I had to take two or three antacids a day to hold out," he remembers. He was also having difficulty urinating. Essentially, he says, water was accumulating in his body. "They said that if I had gotten help then, to release some of the water, I could have prevented the damage. But now the damage is permanent," he says.

Doña Berta, who first introduced me to Don Ramón—her neighbor in their hometown of El Platanal—tried to prepare me in advance for his state. "They are giving him dialysis" (*lo están dialysisando*), she told me, "and now he cannot see. I didn't know until I ran into him last year, and he did not recognize me; he could not see my face." Later, when I tell her that Don Ramón has a cataract surgery scheduled and that Doña Luisa has great hopes that his sight will return, Doña Berta looks at me skeptically. "Faith is a very great thing," she responds, her mouth pursed.

Don Ramón is not alone. Other men of his generation—Don Octavio, Don Tomás, and Don Wilfredo, a *bananeneco* like Don Ramón—all followed the same pattern of family step-migration. Of the four, only Don Octavio has used Medi-Cal after becoming eligible. Thus the advanced kidney disease and premature disability of men like Don Ramón are the legacy of their exclusion from subsidized care. Migrant men's long history in the United States as single sojourning men, combined with Medicaid policies that have historically emphasized the health of women and children, discourage them from seeking health care and contribute to their delayed diagnoses.

EXCEPTIONAL DIAGNOSES: EXPLAINING ESRD AMONG YOUNG MEN

The cases of the older men in my sample fit the dominant biomedical narrative of kidney failure in the United States. Don Ramon's condition can easily be chalked up to late-diagnosed diabetes and Don Wilfredo's to hypertension. However, the younger men with kidney disease whom I interviewed—Martín, Silvestre, and Eufemio—did not fit this mold. None of them had diabetes or a family history of kidney disease or hypertension. Indeed, because of their youth and their lack of obvious risk factors, these young men's doctors initially provided them with unusual etiological explanations, attributing their disease to pesticides, sepsis, and congenital conditions.

Silvestre, whose ESRD was diagnosed in Mexico when he was only twenty-seven, never spoke to a U.S. doctor about his condition. The nephrologist he visited in Mexico was at a loss to explain the presence of ESRD in a man so young. After taking a medical history, he told Silvestre that his exceptionally high blood pressure might have been caused by pesticides, and that this in turn might have caused his kidneys to fail. "He asked me if I had worked in the U.S., and when I said yes, he said, 'Ahh. They use a lot of heavy pesticides there,'" Silvestre says. Eufemio, who visited a doctor in the United States when he was twenty-three, also had his disease attributed to an unusual cause: sepsis resulting from an infection of his leg. When blood tests failed to confirm that initial diagnosis, however, the doctors fell back on a different explanation. "Now they say it is likely due to hypertension," he shrugs.

When Martín first came to the nephrologist with advanced kidney failure, he was told that he had—according to the nephrologist's notes from his first visit—"bilateral small kidneys." Martín understood this to be a congenital condition. "They said that that when I was a kid, they were big enough to function adequately, but not for an adult," he says. When I ask the nephrologist whether Martín's small kidneys were in fact congenital, however, he says that at this late stage, it is difficult to know what destroyed them. Whereas having one small kidney may be a birth defect, bilateral small kidneys are more frequently a consequence rather than a cause of kidney disease. Because Martín's kidneys were already irreparably damaged by the time his nephrologist saw him, a biopsy would have been useless. Thus the source of Martín's disease remains a mystery. Indeed, in his progress notes, Martín's nephrologist resolves the uncertainty by attributing Martín's small kidneys to "hypertension

and likely underlying GN" (glomerulonephritis, a disease affecting the glomeruli).

However, high blood pressure typically damages the kidney only if it is uncontrolled for a prolonged period. Martín was diagnosed at the age of thirty, Silvestre at twenty-seven, and Eufemio at twenty-three. Moreover, although hypertension is a common cause of kidney failure, it is also a consequence of the condition. Because the kidney releases a hormone, renin, that regulates blood pressure, and kidney failure itself leads to fluid retention that increases blood pressure, kidney failure is always accompanied by hypertension. Thus Martín, Silvestre, and Eufemio have unorthodox cases of kidney disease. At a loss to explain the kidney failure of such exceptionally young men, nephrologists' attributing it to hypertension may represent an attempt to fit these men's cases into the accepted paradigm of kidney failure in the United States. Because of their lack of prior medical history, it is impossible to know whether their hypertension triggered their kidney failure or followed it.

Thus migrant men's exclusion from health care not only causes preventable morbidity and mortality but also masks the very etiology of their conditions. Their late medical attention makes the cause of their conditions a black box. The inadequate medical attention farmworkers receive may be allowing an American counterpart to the Mesoamerican epidemic to go undetected.

FACILITATING THE SYNDEMIC: THE FEDERAL DISABILITY-ASSISTANCE HOLE

The public and private policies that dictate the circumstances of farmworkers' labor—their exposure to high heat for extended periods of time, their inability to take breaks, and their difficulty rehydrating sufficiently—may permanently damage the kidneys. Chronic heat stress and recurrent dehydration appear to both trigger kidney disease and hasten the organs' decline. Thus heat stress, intensive physical exertion, dehydration, and kidney disease constitute a syndemic—a cluster of physiological states produced and sustained by the conditions of farmwork.

An undiagnosed epidemic of kidney disease may play an unrecognized role in the physiological interactions that place men like Álvaro in their caskets. Chronic kidney disease is a significant risk factor for cardiovascular disease and is known to accelerate its course. Diseased kidneys fail to regulate blood pressure, increasing the risk of hypertensive heart disease. Cholesterol levels increase as the kidneys fail to filter the blood

efficiently.[15] Because hypertension—also a consequence of kidney disease—may weaken and narrow blood vessels, the buildup of cholesterol-related plaque in these vessels poses additional risk. In short, the type of dehydration-induced kidney damage experienced by Central American farmworkers may contribute to deaths from heart attack and stroke among migrant farmworkers in the United States—whether inside the fields or at home.

As Merrill Singer reminds us, syndemics do not occur in a social vacuum. Just as it is facile to view kidney disease as isolated from the work circumstances that may provoke it, it is myopic to view farmworkers' need to work as isolated from public policy. In excluding them from many forms of social assistance, immigration and labor policies make farmwork one of migrant workers' few sources of reliable income. The federal disability assistance system reinforces farmworkers' lack of economic security by failing to provide them with an alternative to work when their bodies begin to decline.

A patchwork of state and federal disability programs are responsible for covering disabled farmworkers when their bodies "finish." State and federal disability assistance vary in the duration of their coverage as well as their eligibility criteria. California State Disability Insurance (SDI), a state program funded by mandatory wage deductions, covers a worker for a maximum of a year. To qualify, a worker must supply a doctor's certification that he has been unable to perform his previous job for at least eight days.[16] Workers often refer to SDI as "temporary disability." Meanwhile, the federal Social Security Administration (SSA) manages two programs to assist workers with legal status who are permanently disabled: Social Security Disability Insurance (SSDI) and Supplemental Security Income (SSI), a stipend for low-income elderly, blind, and disabled individuals.[17] These complementary federal programs provide disabled workers with vital income support and access to health insurance; SSDI entitles recipients to Medicare, and SSI makes them eligible for Medicaid.

ESRD is a federally recognized disability. Thus a diagnosis of kidney failure automatically qualifies individuals with legal status for both SSDI and for Medicare. Yet farmworkers with chronic diseases that may eventually lead to ESRD—such as hypertension and diabetes—face formidable obstacles to receiving the insurance. Even though these diseases are the primary known causes of ESRD in the United States, the federal disability system extends farmworkers a helping hand only once their kidney disease has reached its end stage. Thus farmworkers with acute chronic illnesses fall through the holes of the social assistance

safety net. If work contributes to farmworkers' kidney disease, then, the disability assistance system only accelerates its course.

Desabilitado: *Retirement*

Federal disability insurance provides vital support for elderly and disabled farmworkers who can no longer work. Indeed, it is so important a staple among farmworking families that workers have created a word in Spanglish, *desabilitarse,* to refer to the receipt of such insurance. I learn this when, to my surprise, my long-term interviewee, Elisabeta, innocently inquires as to whether my seventy-five-year-old father, an attorney in Oakland, is still working by asking, "And has he been officially disabled yet?" (*¿Y ha sido desabilitado ya?*) The formal Spanish translation of "to become disabled" is *descapacitarse,* but I learn that *desabilitarse* implies something quite different. Being *desabilitado* refers not only to the bodily state of being physically incapable of work but also to its bureaucratic validation. Being *desabilitado,* then, is both a feared end and a considerable accomplishment. It means receiving the income support and medical assistance entailed by the official certification of one's condition by the federal government—often a lengthy and cumbersome process.

Medical anthropologists have long shown that the cultural significance of medicine in industrialized nations has led us to understand and characterize the natural stages of the life course in medicalized ways, permeating our everyday language with terms borrowed from biomedicine.[18] The term *desabilitado* illustrates that everyday life in the Central Valley is not only medicalized but also bureaucratized. Because farmworkers are excluded from many state and federal labor protections, the government must step in to help their families survive. Just as food stamps and Medicaid provide vital support to low-income families, federal disability insurance is a staple aid for farmworker families at the end of a breadwinner's productive career.

A farmworker's life course does not follow the uniform trajectory of aging assumed by the standard retirement age established by federal authorities. The average life expectancy of a farmworker in the United States is forty-nine years, and progressive disability often sets in much earlier.[19] Indeed, farmworkers say that the receipt of federal disability assistance, rather than federal retirement payments, more frequently marks the end of a career in the fields. They often use the term *desabilitarse* (to be deemed disabled) to refer to the end of work instead of the more common *jubilarse* (to retire) or *pensionarse* (to receive a pension).

Even so, physical disability often long precedes the federal government's official certification of the condition. To qualify for permanent disability, a worker must show the federal government that not only is he unable to perform his previous job but also that he is unable to "adjust to other work due to [his] medical condition."[20] In short, the federal government requires evidence of "total disability."[21] This high burden of proof creates a hole in the social safety net. According to Lucinda, an eligibility worker in the Mendota branch of a state agency, "The problem is that gray area, where someone may need disability for more than a year but can't yet prove they're permanently disabled."

Trying to Escape the Hole: Don Ramón and Don Tomás

The contrasting cases of Don Ramón and Don Tomás illustrate the consequences of this gap in disability assistance. When Don Ramón returned to Mendota after experiencing fluid retention in Alaska, he visited the clinic with his wife to seek care. They talked to the social worker at the clinic but learned that their income exceeded the program's limit. Shortly afterward, Don Ramón's father died in El Platanal, so he and his wife flew back to Michoacán and took the opportunity to visit specialists. It was there that Don Ramón learned that he had diabetes and high blood pressure. "And the doctor told me, 'I'm not going to lie to you and take your money. Care costs too much here. You should go back to the US and see if you qualify for a program.'" When Don Ramón returned to Mendota, he immediately went to the emergency room in Fresno, where the clinicians did blood and urine tests to confirm the Mexican doctor's diagnoses. They also diagnosed him with kidney failure and immediately began dialysis.

As a federally recognized disability, an ESRD diagnosis opened doors to insurance for Don Ramón where diabetes had not. Within a week of his hospitalization, a social worker began helping him apply for permanent disability (SSDI), which would automatically entitle him to Medicare. It also granted him income support so that he did not have to work while he received dialysis. In short, after years of being ineligible for Medi-Cal, Don Ramón's diagnosis of ESRD had finally earned him the care he needed. Ironically, his failing kidneys qualified him for the health insurance that, had it been provided at an earlier stage, could have helped avert his disabling condition.

Despite Don Ramón's delayed diagnosis, he counts himself relatively fortunate. Farmworkers with chronic diseases that lead to ESRD, such

as diabetes, often find that the federal government's failure to intervene has unexpected consequences. Below, I draw on my field notes to provide a chronological account of the struggles of Don Tomás, a *mayordomo* to whom Elisabeta and Teo introduced me, to receive the income support and medical assistance his disease required.

March 12, 2008

When I first met Don Tomás, he and his wife, Doña Linda, were living in a well-tended house with rose bushes in front—a house that they owned. At the time, Don Tomás was forty-nine and had worked as a *mayordomo* for eight years, supervising weeding and melon harvesting for two different companies. Because of his house and his car, and his income of roughly $35,000 a year, Don Tomás and his wife never qualified for Medi-Cal. This became a particular problem for Don Tomás in 2000, when he discovered that he had advanced diabetes.

Don Tomás has worked in the fields for a total of twenty-nine years—ever since he arrived in 1980 as a twenty-year-old boy (*mozo*) fleeing the Salvadoran civil war. He supported his parents from afar during the war while starting a family in the United States with Doña Linda, a widow whom he met during a return trip to El Salvador. Despite his relative success, Don Tomás now feels that the disease is catching up with him. "There are days when I feel okay, but there are more days now that I don't," he tells me.

Because Don Tomás does not have health insurance, he found out he had diabetes only by chance, while applying for a commercial driver's license. His doctor informed him that he had just two more years left to live unless he changed his habits dramatically (see chapter 5). That was eight years ago. Don Tomás credits his relative longevity to the changes he made in his lifestyle. He avoided beer; he avoided bars. Sodas were often the coldest beverage available in the fields, but he shunned them, too. He admits that he often ate fried foods and beans for his work lunches. "Vegetables and boiled fish just don't sustain you in the fields," he says. Otherwise, he says, he followed the doctor's prescribed diet to the letter.

Lacking Medi-Cal coverage, Don Tomás had to continue to work to pay for his diabetes medications and hospital appointments. Working, in turn, jeopardized his health. Weeding made his feet swell; he was losing sensation in his toes. The pressure of the job sometimes caused his blood sugar levels to spiral out of control. If his crew made an error and left weeds in the field and the grower called to complain, or if he had to

admonish a lagging crew member, his blood sugar would spike. "As a *mayordomo,* you're struggling with people all day long. It's difficult to control your sugar when you're under constant stress at work," he says.

The heat of the summer seemed to aggravate Don Tomás's symptoms and make him fatigued. Working in the direct sun to harvest melons that his pickers had missed, he felt exhausted. After particularly hot days, he returned home weak. Don Tomás was well aware that working aggravated his diabetes, but he did not know that it might have played a role in his development of kidney failure as well.

Don Tomás soon found himself on a treadmill. At first he only had to pay for his pills and injections, but soon he also had to work to pay for his hospitalizations. Meanwhile, his continuing to work led to yet more medical expenses. In 2005, he was hospitalized for three days when he forgot to take his pills and fainted at work. The cost was $12,000, and it took him a year to pay it. The following year, he again fainted at work and was hospitalized for three days. This time, the cost was $18,000.[22]

Shortly after he was discharged from the hospital the first time, Don Tomás visited a local doctor in the hopes of being able to retire permanently. Too young to draw a federal pension, he hoped the doctor could certify him for disability payments. Because temporary disability (SDI) would offer Don Tomás only a year's reprieve from work, the doctor told him he should apply for permanent disability; he helped Don Tomás file his application for both SSDI and SSI. He told him that the state Disability Determination Services (DDS) office, which manages federal disability insurance benefits for the federal government, would look for five different criteria in making its decision, including evidence that he was no longer able to do his previous job and that he was also unable to do any other work in the national economy.[23] After several months, Don Tomás received a letter that he had been rejected. Although the DDS agreed that he could no longer perform farmwork, it considered him "trainable" for other occupations.

As Lucinda, an eligibility worker in a local state agency, clarified, the DDS determines eligibility for its permanent disability programs based on criteria established by the federal government: age, education, work history, and the nature of the applicant's impairment. Don Tomás spoke only Spanish, had a fourth-grade education, had never done any type of work other than farmwork, and was forty-five years old at the time of his application. Yet the DDS agents maintained that he should be able to find another type of work in "his region" or "other regions of the

country."[24] Don Tomás's eligibility worker told him to apply again the following year. Indeed, as Lucinda later told me, the federal government deems few workers under fifty eligible for permanent disability, regardless of their skills or the severity of their impairment.

Thus the federal government's one-size-fits-all criteria for disability pose a particular conundrum for farmworkers like Don Tomás. Farmworkers' limited language abilities, low education levels, and segregation in areas dependent on agriculture limit their options of obtaining other work. The government assumes that farmworkers can find less physically taxing jobs outside farmwork, even though they are eligible for few other occupations in the agricultural areas where they live. Indeed, even if they could relocate, the very vulnerabilities that first channeled them into farmwork often make it difficult to find work in other industries.

June 28, 2012

Without social assistance, Don Tomás had no other option but to continue to work. He felt his legs grow progressively weaker, as though they were "limp rags" (*trapos flojos*). Because of his fluid retention, he had to buy shoes one size bigger. Around midday, he found that his vision "got blurry," and an optometrist told him that blood was collecting behind his left eye. He eventually decided he was no longer competent to drive. Yet Don Tomás would receive the disability insurance he required only when his kidneys were truly worn out; only a diagnosis of kidney failure would earn him his long-needed assistance.

When Don Tomás opens the door this morning four years after our initial meeting, there is a hospital admission band dangling from his wrist, along with an orange band with the word "Spanish" scrawled on it in ink. His other wrist bears a band with the label "Future dialysis access blood draw."

Don Tomás tells me he now has kidney failure. On February 4, he had noticed a pustule on his left testicle and went to the hospital to have it checked. As he was waiting in his hospital gown to meet the doctor, his nervousness made his blood sugar spike. By the time the doctor arrived, he found Don Tomás unconscious on the floor. Don Tomás flitted in and out of consciousness for eight days. After a series of tests, the doctors found that his kidneys were failing. He was finally discharged—with instructions to begin dialysis—twenty-seven days later.

While he was hospitalized, his doctor certified Don Tomás for what he calls *la incapacidad,* or temporary disability (SDI). The program will

last a year, and provides him with a checks of $844 a month. Yet his goal of receiving what he calls *desabilidad por vida,* or lifelong (permanent) disability, remains elusive. At the local office of the state Employment Development Department (EDD), his social worker told him that the federal government often takes a few months to make this determination. "And here I was, thinking that it would be quick," he says.

As Don Tomás's case shows, the federal government's imposition of universal criteria for disability neglects the lived realities of occupations such as farm work, in which injury and chronic illness often set in by middle age. The government's disproportionate weighting of applicants' age in determining eligibility automatically disqualifies many middle-aged farmworkers with severe chronic disease. The price of such delayed assistance is seen in aggravated chronic illness and a diminished quality of life.

July 5, 2013

The embodied effects of a faulty disability insurance system become apparent when I visit Don Tomás this evening. I find Doña Linda watering the garden outside. As she walks me to the front door of their house, a gaggle of grandchildren emerge and run into the yard. The house is dark, and I see Don Tomás sitting on the couch, seemingly staring into space. Doña Linda tells him I am here. Don Tomás's eyes are covered with a pink film. He moves his head searchingly as he tries to locate the source of my voice. He is wearing a white T-shirt and jeans that betray spindly legs. He says, "I'm doing really badly. I lost my sight. I'm still on dialysis, and now they say the diabetes is going to my heart."

Don Tomás's sight had been blurry for some time. Then one day last winter, his left eye began throbbing, and a white splinter appeared in his line of vision. He visited the doctor and was sent to the ER. The doctors there informed him that he had cataracts and would need surgery to try to save his left eye. They said that if his right eye was not affected by glaucoma, the surgery should save it. Yet Don Tomás awoke to darkness. "I came in partially sighted, and I left the hospital blind. The diabetes and high blood pressure have eaten my sight."

Don Tomás says that the severity of his diabetes derailed him. "It happened to me like a car doing sixty that suddenly loses a wheel" (*me pasó a mi como un coche que va a 60 millas por hora y pierde una llanta).* He is often dizzy and tired. His feet go numb, and his blood pressure is worsening. He tells me that he feels as though something heavy is sitting on his chest; it often feels compressed (*oprimido*), and he

cannot breathe. The doctors have prescribed him fast-acting blood pressure medications; he places lozenges under his tongue and uses an oral spray for immediate relief.

Yet his worsening health has yielded a perverse benefit. After he went blind, he was finally granted both types of federal disability assistance; he now receives $870 a month. In addition, SSDI pays his wife $900 a month to care for him. His two confirmed disabilities have finally earned Don Tomás both a long-delayed "retirement" and health care coverage. SSI automatically makes him eligible for Medi-Cal, and SSDI for Medicare. Because Medicare imposes a waiting period on covering Don Tomás' dialysis, Medi-Cal will cover it in the interim.

These benefits, however, come with strings attached. While he was receiving dialysis, a social worker explained the bargain he had unwittingly struck: the state would take his house and other assets if he did not give them away. Medi-Cal requires that recipients report their income and assets each month to ensure that their income does not exceed the limit of 138 percent of the federal poverty level. To ensure that Medi-Cal would continue to cover Don Tomás's dialysis, the couple had been forced to shed their possessions. They divested themselves of their savings and made Don Tomás's house over to his son-in-law. Don Tomás also forfeited his life insurance policy, worth $35,000. "At least they let me keep the interest," he says. Ultimately, Doña Linda says, the couple were so successful at shedding their assets that the state no longer requires them to report their income and assets each month. "Because we no longer have any," she says, lifting empty hands.

To Don Tomás, the lesson of this exchange was perverse. Although he had spent the first thirty-four years of his life in the United States attempting to acquire the trappings of material security, he now had to assiduously divest himself of them. Don Tomás's spent body had finally entitled him to a payout from the government, but it had come at the price of complete dependence. He had to relinquish the symbols of success in which he had taken such pride in order to treat an illness that had deteriorated only because of his initial lack of public assistance.

For chronically ill farmworkers who are too young to qualify for retirement benefits, then, disability assistance inverts the lessons instilled in them by their jobs. Whereas their worth once derived from their bodily vigor, they now find that their bodies have once again accrued value only because they are "finished" (*acabados*). Only when Don Tomás experienced kidney failure and went blind could he finally receive federal assistance—the very support that could have averted his premature

disability. Federal disability programs provide a faulty safety net for ailing farmworkers, who learn that the only remaining value their bodies offer them derives from their complete debilitation.

TREATMENT OPTIONS: TRANSPLANTS, MEDICAL RETURNS, AND THE DIALYSIS LIMBO

Don Tomás's case highlights the paradoxes that federal disability criteria create for ailing farmworkers with legal status. Because they are ineligible for income support until they are certified as permanently disabled, they must continue to work. As they struggle to disguise their progressive disabilities from their supervisors in order to keep their jobs, their working in turn hastens the decline of their health.

Chronically ill farmworkers without legal status face a similar predicament. Ineligible for federal disability insurance, they must survive without the income support that their disability requires. Yet once undocumented farmworkers receive an ESRD diagnosis, they face a new set of challenges.

Men with Legal Status: Waiting for a Transplant

Dialysis only slows the internal damage caused by the accumulation of waste products in the blood. After they have begun dialysis, patients between the ages of forty and forty-four can expect to survive for an average of eight years.[25] Moreover, dialysis treatments, which typically involve visiting a clinic for three four-hour sessions each week, make it difficult to maintain normal activities. Organ transplant offers patients a better qualify of life as well as lower mortality rates and fewer complications.[26]

The migrant men with ESRD I interviewed all wished to be registered on the United Nations Organ Sharing (UNOS) waiting list to receive a kidney transplant. However, the team of financial counselors, doctors, nurses, social workers, and nutritionists at the University of California at San Francisco (UCSF)—the closest transplant center to the Central Valley—takes a number of factors into account before adding a candidate to the waiting list. Potential transplant recipients must be sufficiently healthy to survive the transplant. This factor disqualified Don Ramón, whose diabetes was still uncontrolled. If they meet this criterion, they must pass a second test. They must also provide evidence of insurance that will cover both their surgery and their post-transplant care—a hurdle that fells all undocumented farmworkers.

Don Wilfredo is the only man in my sample who passed both tests. He has been receiving dialysis three times a week at a public hospital in

Fresno for the past four years. His blood pressure has now stabilized, and he has no other chronic medical conditions. In addition, because he is a legal resident, his ESRD makes him eligible for Medicare, which the UCSF Transplant Center deems to be sufficient insurance. So Don Wilfredo is now a candidate for a transplant. This prospect gives him hope: he sees it as a means of reclaiming a "normal" life. He takes particular pleasure in the fact that his doctor has told him that if he does well after the surgery, he will certify him as able to return to work in three years. Don Wilfredo cannot wait. "I want to get a transplant so I can keep being productive for this country [*produciéndole al país*]," he says.

Men without Legal Status: Medical Returns

While legal permanent residents like Don Wilfredo may be eligible for Medicare and therefore for kidney transplants, undocumented migrant men face scarce options. Aware that they can expect limited assistance from the government, undocumented migrants often depart for their homelands permanently once they become cognizant of the severity of their conditions. They make "medical returns," seeking the care the U.S. government will not provide in their sending communities instead.[27]

Silvestre is one such case. After his U.S. doctor told him he would need to perform further diagnostic tests to discern the cause of his high blood pressure—tests that Silvestre could not afford—he returned to El Platanal, Michoacán, to stay with his wife and three children. He paid out of pocket to visit several private doctors and was eventually diagnosed with ESRD by a nephrologist in the nearby city of Zamora. Knowing that he is ineligible for any long-term care in California, Silvestre has decided to take his chances in Mexico. By selling the home he had long worked to purchase for his family in El Platanal and depleting his savings, Silvestre paid out of pocket for his dialysis in Mexico—at roughly $4,200 a month—for six months. "And all that without being able to work and without being able to earn money," he says. Thus even as undocumented men's work aggravates—if not causes—their kidney failure, their conditions in turn consume the fruits of their labor.

When these men return to their homelands, the burden of their care to their families, sending communities, and governments. When Silvestre sold his house, he moved in with his uncle. He eventually found health insurance through his sister, who added him to the plan offered by her employer, at an additional cost of $400 per year. Moreover, Silvestre's friends and family in Mendota band together to hold bake sales to help him out. "We get a bunch of women from El Platanal together,

and we make cookies and *posole* to sell to raise money for him," says Doña Berta, Silvestre's relative. As the Marxist sociologist Michael Burawoy famously observed, then, the exclusion of migrant men from federal assistance serves to divert the costs of their health care and "retirement" to sending states.[28]

Perpetual Dialysis

While Mexico's universal insurance plan for the poor, Seguro Popular, did not cover organ transplant when Silvestre began dialysis, his sister's insurance does. His transplant is scheduled for December, and his sister has agreed to be his kidney donor.

Yet as Silvestre is aware, his eligibility for a transplant makes his case something of an anomaly. An older man with kidney failure in his hometown has no hope of a transplant because of the lack of a donor. In El Salvador and Nicaragua—countries ravaged by the epidemic of CKDu—resources for dialysis and transplantation are so scarce that many patients with kidney disease die in the hospital of uremia, the buildup of urea and other toxins in their blood—a condition usually averted by dialysis in the United States.[29] However, even in the United States, the scarce resources available for undocumented men afford them limited options. Ineligible for federally funded transplants, young undocumented men with kidney disease are trapped in a state of perpetual dialysis.

The federal statute governing Emergency Medicaid, the federal-state partnership that covers the emergency medical care of low-income residents, defines "emergency conditions" broadly.[30] In effect, states determine which conditions count as "emergencies" under their Medicaid plans. Most states cover dialysis for undocumented migrants only on an emergency, short-term basis.[31] California is one of only five states that use Emergency Medicaid funds to cover "maintenance dialysis" services for undocumented patients. Yet the federal statute that creates Emergency Medicaid specifically prohibits the insurance from covering organ transplants for undocumented migrants.[32] Thus even though undocumented migrants tend to be younger and healthier, and therefore better transplant candidates, than most dialysis patients, federal policy precludes this option.[33] Instead, federal statute, combined with transplant centers' policy of demanding "sufficient insurance," consigns undocumented migrants to a dialysis limbo. They receive dialysis in outpatient clinics as they wait for a resolution to this endgame—either in the form of an opportunity to adjust their immigration status or in the form of death.

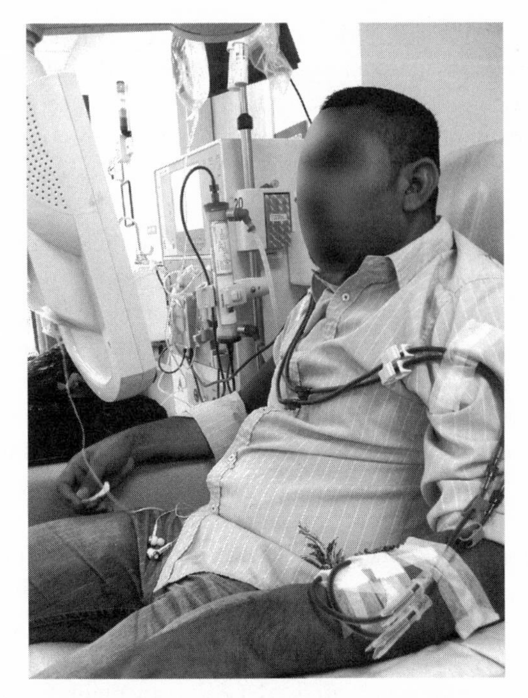

FIGURE 12. A young undocumented farmworker receives dialysis. (His face is intentionally blurred).

Martín is one such case. A thirty-one-year-old Honduran, he lives in a one-room apartment that he shares with a Salvadoran roommate, a man he met at work. Martín, who sleeps in the bottom bunk of their bunk bed, has taped an image of the Virgin of Guadalupe to watch over his bed. He is affable and sociable and often entertains Honduran friends who come to visit. "It's good because it helps me get my mind off of it [my condition]," he says.

Because of his kidney failure, Martín cannot work; instead, his daily life is dictated by the rhythms of mechanical filtration. He visits a dialysis center in the nearby city of Madera three times a week. Yet the "machine," Martín tells me, extends its reach beyond the confines of the dialysis center. After the procedure, he is dizzy and exhausted and immediately goes to sleep. On the other days, Martín tries to conserve his strength. He kills time by visiting with his younger brother, who also lives in Mendota and on whom Martín now relies to pay his rent and food. He also whiles away the days by attending church, cooking and cleaning, and teaching himself to play the guitar.

Unlike many patients with kidney failure, Martín does not have the complications of hypertension or uncontrolled diabetes. Yet because Martín's undocumented status precludes his being placed on the waiting list for a transplant, his future remains unclear. The one thing that is certain, Martín says, is that he must visit the dialysis center three times a week for the foreseeable future.

At the hospital where he was initially treated, the social worker asked Martín if he would prefer a transplant to long-term dialysis. Unaware of the predicament created by his legal status, Martín said yes. Yet when we visit his nephrologist in Fresno for his bimonthly appointment, the doctor has already received a denial letter from the transplant center, which is sitting in his inbox alongside two new referral requests from a social worker at the clinic. Because the nephrologist's office continuously processes transplant referrals in vain, he is frustrated. "Can you please tell him that he is not a candidate for transplant until he gets a better insurance?" the doctor asks me. He then turns to Martín. "You're an ideal candidate for a transplant—you're young, you're healthy, you don't have diabetes," he says. "The only thing is a little high blood pressure, but just a little. But until your insurance changes, we can't do anything."

As the finance manager of the UCSF Transplant Center explains, patients with Emergency Medi-Cal insurance find themselves in a double bind. Because eligibility for Medi-Cal is based on income, raising philanthropic funds to cover the surgery would disqualify a patient from the insurance. "If you qualify for Medi-Cal, you can't receive the donations that would pay for the transplant," she says. In addition, Emergency Medi-Cal does not cover the post-transplant medications, which cost between $3,000 and $5,000 a month for as long as the patient lives. In fact, she says, "Patients with emergency-only Medi-Cal are not eligible to come into our transplant center. We're not an emergency room; their insurance won't pay for the visit." In short, competing state and federal definitions of emergency care have perverse consequences for undocumented migrants with ESRD. The state of California allows undocumented migrants to receive maintenance dialysis treatment, but the federal bar to their eligibility for organ transplants leaves otherwise healthy young men indefinitely on dialysis.

The Waiting Game

Martín's cellphone's screen saver displays a photo of his wife holding his five-year-old son in his hometown in Honduras. He says that he

would like nothing more than to see his son again. Yet because treatment options for kidney disease are scarce in Honduras, he bides him time in the United States. Unable to support his family, he feels the frustration of being a failed breadwinner with each week that passes. His only hope, he says, is that a legalization program in the United States will eventually make him eligible for an insurance plan that will cover organ transplant. In the meantime, however, Martín must wait.

Martín takes great precautions to avoid worsening his condition. To prevent his dialysis port from becoming infected, he keeps his apartment clean. To avoid overburdening his kidneys, he does not drink alcohol or eat foods high in potassium and sodium. He does not venture outside during the afternoon heat. Because water intake taxes the kidneys, Martín endures perpetual thirst. "I just wet my lips and that's it," he says. By training his focus on the immediate present—which he can control—Martín avoids the anxiety of a future that remains opaque.

Medical anthropologists have described the state of uncertainty induced in patients by chronic, unpredictable illnesses. In analyzing the illness narratives of patients with epilepsy in Turkey, for example, Byron Good and Mary-Jo DelVecchio Good argue that patients are like readers who find themselves "in the midst of stories" with uncertain endings. Such patients, they say, live "in the subjunctive mode": they anxiously and expectantly revise the potential endings of their stories based on the unfolding of events in the present. They write of such patients' illness narratives: "Endings were often hypothetical; outcomes which were feared were juxtaposed against those desperately hoped for."[34] Undocumented migrants with kidney failure are similarly trapped in a limbo not of their own making. But for these young, otherwise healthy migrants, it is federal and transplant center policy—not their diagnoses—that dictates the plot of their illness narratives and blurs their stories' endings.

The anthropologist Margaret Lock has proposed the concept of "local biologies" to draw attention to the way that the expression and experience of human disease may vary according to environment, culture, and other contextual factors.[35] Studies of sugarcane cutters in Brazil and Central America suggest that kidney decline serves as a barometer of the intensity and inhumanity of their working conditions—conditions that may be shared by some farmworkers in the United States. Yet as the cases of Don Ramón and Don Tomás show, farmworkers' premature disability is not caused by their work conditions alone. Migrant men's historic exclusion from Medicaid allows their disease to progress undiagnosed,

while federal disability insurance intervenes too late. Even though ESRD is a known disability, the federal government withholds the income assistance and treatment that could prevent migrant men's early disease from reaching its end stage.

Disability insurance creates a series of paradoxes for migrant farmworking men, contradicting the lessons that U.S. labor and health care policies have long taught them. Whereas these men's meager access to social assistance has made bodily vigor their primary source of economic security, the disability system grants them support only at the moment of their bodies' utter physical debilitation. In addition, while their historic exclusion from Medicaid has long led men like Don Ramón and Don Tomás to pride themselves on their self-reliance, the federal disability system penalizes them for their hard-won economic success. As their bodies wear out in middle age, migrant men learn that the assistance for which they are eligible comes at the cost of their much-prized independence.

Undocumented migrant men encounter a different set of policy ironies. Even as farmwork demands that such men "leave their kidneys in the fields," competing definitions of emergency care condemn them to life attached to a dializer. While our food-production system drains such men's bodies of their *jugo* (life essence), our health care system offers them limited support. The lack of adequate transplantation options for young, undocumented migrant men illustrates their treatment as a disposable resource.[36]

Conclusion

Strategies for Change

At the start of my research in the Central Valley in 2005, I rarely heard of any state or federal agencies visiting the fields to monitor workers' health and safety. "The Valley is a different world," one workers' compensation attorney from the central coast told me. Agricultural supervisors noted that workers in the Salinas Valley "knew their rights," implying that those in the Central Valley did not. One said that workers from the cooler coasts objected to work in the Valley as being "too hot," "too dirty," and "too hard." One supervisor for a large contracting company told me, "I brought a crew out from Salinas to work in the garlic earlier in the spring. And some of them just said, 'Uh-uh. This isn't for me!'" Undocumented migrants tended to gravitate to the interior of California, he said, because the relative lack of federal and state enforcement there allowed them to "fly under the radar." Yet by 2011, even the Valley had changed. The reduction of immigration from Mexico after the recession had raised growers' fears about labor shortages. Flyers advertising jobs suddenly appeared on the doors of pool halls, corner stores, and *pupuserías* (Central American eateries). And the UFW began organizing tomato pickers in western Fresno County—the union's first successful organizing drive near Mendota in decades.

Under the leadership of Jerry Brown, the Democrat who succeeded the Republican Arnold Schwarzenegger as governor of California, the state began more aggressively defending labor rights. In February 2015, the Cal-OSHA Standards Board—with five of seven members appointed

by Brown—adopted many of the heat illness regulations that the ACLU and UFW had advocated in their lawsuit (see chapter 1). Under the revised standard, employers are required to bring shade structures sufficient to accommodate all workers at any one time, provide water that is not only "potable" but "fresh" and "pure," and provide a ten-minute cool-down period every two hours once the heat rises above 95 degrees. Then, on June 10, 2015, Cal-OSHA announced its settlement with the UFW, acceding to more of the union's demands. The settlement makes Cal-OSHA more accountable for its role as a work safety watchdog: it will conduct internal audits of its enforcement activities (and allow the UFW to review them), it will allow the UFW to help report and refer violators of the heat-illness standards, and it will dedicate all inspectors to monitoring outdoor workplaces during periods of high heat.[1]

As Don Tomás recounted in June 2012, shortly after he had stopped working because of his advanced diabetes, the enforcement climate was beginning to worry some of his *mayordomo* and contractor friends. His own contractor was fined by Cal-OSHA in 2011 for not bringing sufficient water to the fields. Another contractor was fined by Cal-OSHA for bringing what Don Tomás described as "yellow water" and having filthy bathrooms. "They told him that if he gets one more violation, he will lose his license," Don Tomás reported with a raised eyebrow. As he sat on his couch with the cane he used to navigate the house, staring into space because he could not see my face, he said he viewed the changes as "a good thing for the people." He recalled, "When I first came to this country [in 1980], the bathrooms were awful, and the water was *fea* [unpotable and] from the tap. And the *mayordomos* were strict. It was just *corri, corri, corri* [run, run, run] up and down the field. Slowly, things are getting better and better."

POLICY CHANGE: ENDING THE SYNDEMIC

As labor conditions in the fields are buffeted by intensified regulation, a decline in Mexican immigration, and the possibility of employers' resistance to state interference, what do the changes portend for farmworkers' health? Farmworkers' labor conditions and health must be understood within the context of the nexus of immigration and labor policies that has long abetted their exploitation. As Merrill Singer notes, to combat a syndemic we must address not only its constituent elements but also the sociopolitical conditions that bring them together.[2] It is worth reprising the major findings of this book to help illuminate the

policy changes that are necessary if we are to ensure the safety of those who harvest our food.

Farmworkers as a group experience death from heatstroke at higher rates than members of other outdoor occupations—such as construction workers—because their limited inclusion in the labor protections afforded workers in other industries requires that they be "exceptional workers." By excluding farmworkers from paid time-and-a-half overtime, agricultural exceptionalism makes work one of the few forms of economic security available to farmworkers, even as immigration policy makes undocumented workers ineligible for unemployment insurance. Yet if federal labor and immigration policies ensure that farmworkers are particularly "willing to work," the harsh conditions on labor crews only intensify this disposition.[3] IRCA, which created a subcontracting boom in agriculture, introduced an intermediate layer of labor supervisors, many of them former migrants. It created a financial incentive for these supervisors to intensify field hands' workloads and to use their knowledge of the vulnerable status of their workforce to maximize profit. By heightening the productivity pressures on field hands, subcontracting makes workers particularly vulnerable to heat illness. Migrants on labor crews learn that they must privilege their supervisors' immediate demands over their physical needs in order to keep their jobs.

Meanwhile, the convergence of immigration and criminal law abets new forms of legal violence that further erode migrants' workplace rights.[4] Farmworkers' uneven inclusion in employer protections—and their exclusion from many forms of social assistance—compels many to turn to illicit income-generating strategies such as identity loan. As identity recipients face the possibility of being implicated in identity theft, with the attendant risks of prison, deportation, and extended bars on their legal return, the trend toward governing immigration through crime worsens the working conditions of all noncitizens. Thus any meaningful efforts to address heat illness among migrant farmworkers must take into account the recent policy changes that have entrenched migrants' vulnerability, as well as the historical weight of migrant workers' subordination.

Finally, the labor and immigration policies that place farmworkers at risk in the fields also saddle them with long-term ailments. The convergence of immigration and criminal law has intensified the anxiety of being a legal minority, which in turn is embodied in the form of hypertension and stroke. These chronic diseases interact with the sociopolitical organization of farm work—which leads to migrants' overwork and

limited ability to rehydrate—to place them at risk of heatstroke and cardiac arrest. Moreover, recurrent heatstroke may culminate in kidney failure. Migrant workers' longstanding exclusion from Medicaid, in combination with Social Security disability programs that intervene too late, further aggravate the clustering of such ailments.

Various forms of symbolic violence naturalize the causes of heat deaths. As we have seen, policymakers and the press portray heat death as a matter largely of rising temperatures. The state's heat illness campaign emphasizes workers' responsibility to rest and rehydrate, diverting attention from the fact that the pressure of the farm labor hierarchy makes such choices impossible. Moreover, the attribution of deaths like Álvaro's to heart failure—and therefore to migrants' "faulty" lifestyle choices—makes the harmful effects of the sociopolitical organization of work disappear. This book provides a corrective to such explanations by analyzing the social and political pathologies that place men like Álvaro in their caskets.

Analyzing migrants' health at work in the context of the public policies that affect it—overtime policies, unemployment policies, immigration policies, Medicaid, and disability assistance—provides a holistic perspective. Together, these policies exert a compounded and deleterious effect on migrants' health. Moreover, examining these policies in combination shows how they shape migrants' health care and work habitus in converging and diverging ways. Public policies may have mutually reinforcing effects, as in the case of labor and health care policies that encourage men to place their work above their health. Or they may send contradictory messages that cause demoralization, as in the case of labor and immigration policies that lead men to prize self-sufficiency even as disability policies that intervene late in their lives demand the sacrifice of their hard-earned independence. The fate of men like Don Tomás, blind and disabled at forty-nine, testifies to our obligation to undo the thickly knitted web of policies that together result in such needless suffering.

Ending Agricultural Exceptionalism

What can anthropologists and the public do to improve farmworkers' health and to protect them from heat stress, overwork, and dehydration? And in what strategies of "pragmatic solidarity" can we engage in the continuing struggle over farmworkers' labor conditions?[5] Policy change on multiple fronts is necessary. At a minimum, we must end the exclusion of agricultural workers from standard labor protections. Exceptions

to policies regarding overtime pay, child labor, and workers' compensation for farmworkers have historically been justified as necessary for securing the nation's food supply and subsidizing the cost of food for the middle class.[6] Yet the embodied effects of farmworkers' exceptional status are exceptionally inhumane. After nearly a century, the injustice of farmworkers' exclusion from the provisions of the New Deal must be fully rectified.

Over the past fifty years, farmworker advocates have proposed various initiatives to chip away at agricultural exceptionalism at the state level. In New York State in the fall of 2014, for example, State Senator Diane J. Savino sponsored the Farmworker Fair Labor Practices Act, a bill that would have required time-and-a-half overtime pay after sixty hours of work in a week and guaranteed farmworkers a day off. However, the New York Farm Bureau, which represents fifteen thousand farmers in the state, successfully blocked the bill by mobilizing the image of the beleaguered family farmer, claiming it would be the "death knell of family farms." (As Senator Savino aptly rebutted, "Most family farms would not be affected, because family farms don't actually employ farmworkers.")[7] This was the fifth year that senators had brought the bill to the floor. Yet farmworker advocates remain optimistic. With the backing of the Hispanic Federation and the Brooklyn Food Coalition, they have mounted greater pressure for its passage through rallies and marches.[8]

While the farm lobby has continued to quash efforts to repeal the double standard in overtime pay in New York, an appeals court in New Mexico recently overturned the state law excluding farmworkers from workers' compensation insurance. In 2009, the New Mexico Center on Law and Poverty filed suit on behalf of three injured dairy workers, arguing that their exclusion from workers' compensation insurance violated the state constitution's equal protection clause. In 2011, the District Court ruled in favor of the injured workers, but the state's Workers' Compensation Administration appealed the decision. In June 2015, the state's Court of Appeals upheld the District Court's ruling, stating that its review of workers' compensation statutes back to 1929 "has not revealed an articulable purpose for the exclusion."[9] The ruling makes New Mexico one of only thirteen states to mandate the inclusion of farmworkers in workers' compensation insurance to the same extent as workers in other industries.[10] To change farmworkers' status as a pocket of exceptional ill health, the paradox that the most vulnerable workers receive the most paltry labor protections must be ended.

Immigration Reform, Labor Reform

Combined with legislation institutionalizing farmworkers' second-class status, punitive immigration reforms since the mid-1990s have made migrants more vulnerable at work. Granting undocumented migrants legal status is an obvious first step to ending the climate of fear in migrant workplaces. It would allow migrants' entry into other occupations—with better pay and better labor standards—in which legal status is required. Moreover, legalization—even through a temporary work permit, such as that granted to qualifying migrants by the Obama Administration's executive order in November 2014—would offer migrants benefits beyond an exit from farm work. In making undocumented migrants legally eligible for work, legalization programs would override their exclusion from unemployment insurance programs nationwide. By making formerly undocumented migrants eligible for unemployment benefits, even a temporary work permit would go some way to reducing the poverty that makes migrant farmworkers' engagement in illicit income-generating strategies incumbent.

However, given the scale of the harsh immigration reforms the nation has seen over the past two decades, legalization programs are only a first step. In an environment in which law enforcement officers serve as vigilante immigration agents,[11] and in which the security promised by the status of legal permanent residency is undermined by the practice of deportation for petty offenses, even migrants with legal status remain *callados* in the face of workplace hazards and injustices. To remedy these forms of institutionalized discrimination requires the active promotion of migrant workers' rights. The Protect Our Workers from Exploitation and Retaliation Act (POWER Act)—identified by the National Immigration Law Center as an essential component of any immigration reform—is intended to ensure that threats of deportation or arrest do not deter migrants from reporting workplace violations.[12] The POWER Act would grant those who have filed a workplace claim a stay of removal and employment authorization until the claim is resolved. It would protect workers against whom employers have retaliated for their claims by making them eligible for a U visa—that is, by granting them temporary legal status—as long as they cooperate with local authorities in investigating the alleged abuse. Legislation such as the POWER Act could help remove the sway that labor supervisors hold over migrants engaged in identity loan, ensuring that injured migrants receive the workers' compensation they are due.

State legislation can also mitigate the labor abuses associated with subcontracting. In 2014, for example, California Governor Jerry Brown signed into law Assembly Bill 1897, which holds companies with more than twenty-five employees jointly liable—alongside labor contractors—for wage violations as well as for failures to provide workers' compensation insurance. AB 1897 explicitly prevents subcontracting from serving as a firewall for employers. By making growers jointly accountable for the labor violations of their labor contractors, the new law creates incentives for growers to scrutinize farmworkers' labor conditions, safety, and pay more closely. It will limit growers' ability to shift the responsibility for complying with the state's heat illness standard to these labor intermediaries. California's new law serves as a model for other states, offering the potential to reduce the damage caused by the farm labor hierarchy and mitigate the labor abuses and health risks that workers face on labor crews.[13]

Health Reform

Health reform is a vital complement to these changes in immigration and labor policy. The federal government's recent extension of Medicaid benefits to low-income, childless adults through the Affordable Care Act (ACA) was an important first step in remedying the historical exclusion of migrant men from Medicaid. Yet because the ACA's Medicaid expansion has come at the expense of funding for California's county indigent-care programs, it has, paradoxically, only further reduced health-care options for undocumented migrants.[14]

While federal law explicitly bars undocumented migrants from receiving federally subsidized health care, states and localities can step in to offer their own programs. Some localities and states have devised plans to provide free or discounted primary care to all residents, regardless of legal status. In 2006, for example, Massachusetts created the Health Safety Net, a health insurance program that provides primary health care to all low-income state residents, regardless of citizenship status. The following year, San Francisco enacted a program to provide subsidized primary health care to all uninsured city residents whose incomes fall below 500 percent of the federal poverty level. Funded through city and federal monies as well as a health care tax on businesses, Healthy San Francisco provides basic primary care to an excluded group, reinforcing safety net providers' perspectives that undocumented migrants are "deserving" of health care and sending a message of inclusion to the migrants themselves.[15]

Healthy San Francisco accepts alternative forms of evidence of local residency (such as a landlord's affidavit) and of low income (such as an employer's signed letter). Nevertheless, because the program's eligibility requirements are modeled on Emergency Medicaid's, structural barriers continue to prevent some undocumented migrants from qualifying. Not only does Healthy San Francisco require proof of city residency and income, but it also requires proof of denial from Medi-Cal.[16] To effectively include the undocumented, programs like this would need to create novel ways of proving eligibility that do not replicate the bureaucratic disentitlement effected by federal and state Medicaid policies.

Moreover, while Healthy San Francisco and Massachusetts' Health Safety Net provide basic, much-needed primary care, they do little to reverse undocumented migrants' historic exclusion from federal disability insurance and their ineligibility for organ transplantation. Given that migrants' farm work exacerbates their chronic disease—and may in fact cause the very kidney failure for which transplantation is denied—the public has a moral obligation to help tend to their ailments.

Worker Safety Is Food Safety

The final major policy change necessary to improve migrant workers' health is the inclusion of worker-safety provisions in food-safety branding mechanisms. Responding to the public's fears about contaminated produce, retailers increasingly demand that their suppliers undergo "market-access" food-safety audits—conducted by USDA-trained inspectors or by third-party auditors. Certifications of food safety have become a stamp of approval that the large national and international chains require. Preparing for such audits, supervisors are imposing increasingly strict controls on the measures workers use to combat dehydration and mitigate chronic illness.

As outbreaks of food-borne illness continue despite third-party auditing, consumer concerns over the safety of fresh fruits and vegetables are bound to persist. The public concern with the safety of fresh produce clearly must be counterbalanced by concern for the lives of those who produce it.

The food-safety certification boom provides a model for worker-safety advocates. The FDA's lack of staff to inspect the nation's farms and food facilities has allowed the third-party inspection industry to mushroom. Its growth demonstrates that consumer pressure—refracted through the large retailers—can do what inadequately funded and staffed government agencies cannot. By harnessing the power of consumer demand, new

FIGURE 13. A team I packed melons with waits during a break.

"fair labor" certifications, based on guidelines issued by worker advocacy organizations, can help offset proliferating food-safety certifications.

One such model is the Equitable Food Initiative, cofounded by Oxfam, which issues a certification based not only on companies' meeting particular food-safety and pesticide-management standards but also on their providing "improved working conditions" for farmworkers.[17] Particularly innovative is the fact that the EFI incorporates farmworkers as stakeholders in the certification process, with the philosophy that food safety *is* worker safety. The EFI model anticipates that one of the best ways to guarantee food safety is to ensure that farmworkers buy into the process. Farmworkers help design, implement, and enforce the EFI standards on each farm. Along with managers, they serve on a leadership team that ensures the farm's continuous adherence to the standards. This arrangement also addresses a common criticism of the current third-party audit system, which is that an audit measures compliance only at one point in time.

If the produce industry balks at having to undergo additional certifications such as the EFI, an alternative solution would be to permanently incorporate protections for worker health and safety into national food-safety guidelines. The produce industry, the FDA, and the USDA closely collaborate in drafting the guidelines used for food safety audits. Including

worker advocacy groups in this process would help reduce the need for additional certifications. Granting worker advocacy groups a place at the drafting table along with industry and government groups would help modify restrictive guidelines that compromise workers' health.

Special Legislative Protections for Stackers

While the proposals above focus on broad policy change, applied anthropology can identify micro-level interventions necessary in the fields as well. Close attention to the labor process in melon and corn harvesting, along with grounded analysis of the multiple policy environments influencing it, can help guide future policies to lessen morbidity and mortality.

We have seen that a gender- and age-specific division of labor places the youngest migrant men in precisely the most vulnerable positions on labor crews in melon harvesting—as stackers. Because of the intensive physical demands and conditions of the job, stackers face the highest risk of recurrent dehydration and heat stress. They work in direct sunlight, which is reflected and magnified by the trailer's metal floor. They also work farthest from the water that is usually stored under the field-packing device and face pressure not to slow the pace of production by taking breaks to rehydrate. Thus stackers face the highest risk of heatstroke and an increased risk of kidney disease over the long term. Indeed, stackers were overrepresented among the young men with kidney failure whom I interviewed.

Stackers' work conditions make it impossible for them to drink eight ounces of water every fifteen minutes, as Cal-OSHA recommends.[18] Stackers, then, require particular legislative protections. Employers could be required to cycle their employees through the stacker position and the less taxing positions of picking and packing. Moreover, given the obstacles to their staying hydrated, it is unconscionable that stackers are not allowed to carry their own water supplies. As a short-term measure to counteract draconian food-safety regulations, lawmakers should require that growers provide their farmworkers with hydration packs (such as the CamelBak) or plastic water jugs that can be attached to their belts.

Farmworkers' poor health indicators are reinforced by their "hiddenness" as a population and a lack of understanding of the complex ways in which a farm working occupation and precarious legal status combine to cause illness.[19] Careful ethnographic research can document the concrete pathways through which inequalities are embodied and

bring to light this population's extreme health risks. This is a research agenda to which anthropology, sociology, and the health sciences can all contribute—and one that is vital to avert the preventable suffering of farmworkers like Don Ramón and Don Tomás.

Remembering Don Tomás

Don Tomás did not live to see Cal-OSHA's new requirement that workers receive breaks every two hours in high heat conditions or its historic settlement with the UFW. When I called Doña Linda shortly after my last visit with them in September 2014, I learned that he had died of a heart attack in the bathroom early one October morning. He was fifty-six years old. Elisabeta and Teo, who attended his funeral, told me that even Doña Linda's granddaughter, whom Don Tomás had adopted as his own along with Doña Linda's other children (because, as Teo had put it with a shake of his head, the poor man "was shooting blanks" [*no pudo pegar hijos*]), had flown in from Sensuntepeque to pay her respects to the man who had for so long supported her from afar.

Yet across town, in the housing units for farmworkers on Social Security disability, Don Wilfredo, another former *mayordomo* who is now battling kidney failure at the age of fifty-two, offered his perspective on the policy changes. Don Wilfredo has worked in the fields since 1985. In 2011, while working as a *mayordomo,* he began experiencing extreme fatigue while picking stray melons under the September sun. "I was drinking too much water," he remembers. "And when I got home, I was so weak I could barely walk a block." After visiting a doctor at the local clinic and learning that he would need an additional battery of tests, Don Wilfredo, who—as a single legal permanent resident, was ineligible for Medi-Cal—threw up his hands. Like Don Ramón and Silvestre, Don Wilfredo returned to Mexico for further care. He and his wife settled in Guadalajara, and he sold his truck and assets to pay for three months of visits to specialists, who were unable to reduce his blood pressure with sublingual medications. After being diagnosed with kidney failure, he decided to return to Mendota. When he appeared at the local clinic with a systolic blood pressure reading of more than 300, his primary physician "got scared," he says. She immediately referred him to the emergency room of the nearest hospital. "And that very day in the hospital, they inserted a catheter in me and began dialysis," he says.

Like Don Ramón, Don Wilfredo thinks that his kidney damage likely began in the 1980s, when he and other men harvested melon by the

sackful. Because of the lack of state surveillance and a surplus of labor, *mayordomos* had free rein. Before the introduction of field-packing machines that consolidated picking and packing and sped up the production process, employers routinely paid teams of men by contract as an incentive for speed. "We'd spend all day running—running to toss melons into our sack, running up the plank that led to the truck, and then running back down. You didn't stop for a minute—unless you wanted to look for work elsewhere," he chuckles darkly. Men routinely worked outside without shade; they sometimes worked without water. Once, Don Wilfredo remembers, the heat led a worker to drink straight from the irrigation hose—likely ferrying agrochemical pollutants along with the life-saving water—in an adjacent orchard.

The harried work conditions Don Wilfredo experienced then contrast starkly with the privileges he assumed decades later when he became a *mayordomo,* supervising the crew while riding atop the field-harvesting machine, under the shade provided by its canopy. "Back in the eighties, that's when the damage was done. It's not like work today—with their shade structures and water jugs," Don Wilfredo says. "But once it's done, the problem is that it is too late—now the damage is irreparable [*ya es irremediable*]," he says.

Today, the prospect of heightened enforcement is slowly encouraging greater adherence to the heat illness prevention standard. But the cases of Don Wilfredo and Don Tomás stand as a reminder of the costs of a geography of complacence and the need for continued vigilance. We do not yet know what invisible damage may be occurring in the bodies of young migrants, to be detected only when it is beyond repair.

Although men of Don Wilfredo's generation may consider the working conditions of today's farmworkers a far cry from the past, there is still much work to be done. Farmworkers in forty-eight states do not have the benefit of regulations protecting them against heat stress—which is likely to become more common with the effects of global climate change. Moreover, occupational safety is only one strand in the web of immigration, labor, health care, and food safety policies that constrains farmworkers' health. As the cases of younger men with kidney failure suggest, these policies encourage disease states that not only interact syndemically but also reinforce each other in multiply damaging ways. Until the legacy of such policies is rectified, farmworkers will continue to be exceptional workers whose exceptional vulnerability is manifest in health outcomes anomalous in a modern industrial nation.

APPENDIX A

On Engaged Anthropology and Ethnographic Writing

Although I first came to Mendota with the objective of studying children's oral health, I soon found that my interlocutors had other ideas for me. The men and women I met were often puzzled over my intense interest in their children's mouths. They had many other agendas—related both to research and to the simple practicalities of daily living—that they would have preferred I pursue. In this predominantly monolingual, Spanish-speaking migrant community, my legal status, English skills, and familiarity with U.S. bureaucracies were unusual assets, and my interviewees quickly put them to use. After interviews, undocumented parents—who could not legally drive—asked me to transport them and their children to their medical and dental appointments. Some asked me to help them arrange appointments with dental specialists; others enlisted my help in approaching school officials and social service providers. Soon I was immersed in a second career as a kind of researcher-cum-social worker: translating letters from U.S. Citizenship and Immigration Services, corresponding with the Social Security Administration, and communicating with workers' compensation attorneys.

Three years later, I had moved from the study of children's oral health to that of migrants' workplace vulnerabilities and illnesses. With some prodding from my long-term interviewees, I had exchanged interviews in living rooms for trips to the open fields and traded observing dentists' treatment practices for observing different types of farm work. As I grew more deeply embedded in the fabric of my interviewees' lives, they suggested that I assume yet new roles. At a focus group on the health risks of farm work in March 2015, for example, workers explained how labor supervisors prevented them from taking bathroom breaks so as to not slow the pace of production. One man who suffered from diabetes told me that such policies placed workers like him at particular risk of dehydration. A woman ventured that she had had a urinary tract infection because she could not take a break. Elisabeta, whom I had interviewed about her son's cavities some ten years

before, turned to me with a glimmer in her eye. Perhaps, she suggested, I would organize a meeting with the companies the workers had named—armed with my notepad and the latent threat of a press release—to suggest that they kindly grant their workers their legally mandated bathroom breaks?

Ethnography draws anthropologists into the lives of the populations we study. Those who work with vulnerable populations over a long period find that we cease to be what Michael Agar calls "professional strangers" who are but casual interlopers in the lives of our subjects and incur deepening obligations.[1] Witnessing the daily struggles of a population that faces stresses not only as migrants but also as one of the most disadvantaged occupational groups in the United States compels a form of moral engagement that stems from empathic listening.[2] Just like the everyday acts of support in which I first engaged, a turn toward advocacy is a logical extension of the norm of reciprocity that underlies anthropologists' intense engagement with our subjects.[3]

ON ENGAGED, PUBLIC, AND ADVOCACY ANTHROPOLOGY

An *advocacy anthropology* is part of a broader movement toward *engaged anthropology*—that is, toward making the discipline of cultural anthropology more relevant by engaging more deeply with problems of real-world significance and the communities with whom anthropologists work. This shift has included making space for our interlocutors in choosing the topics of our research, as I suggest above. It also entails involving research participants in determining how our research is formulated and carried out, as well as increasing attention to how our results are disseminated and what kinds of "publics" we wish to reach. As Rob Borofsky asks in his manifesto on the topic: "What would happen if anthropologists were judged not in terms of how many books they added to the academic pile, but in terms of the pragmatic effectiveness of their analyses—to what degree they influenced public debates, addressed and clarified serious social problems that interested the broader public?"[4]

Borofsky advocates for a particular variant of engaged anthropology—which he dubs a "public anthropology"—that fashions anthropologists as public intellectuals in the style of Margaret Mead. In his vision of public anthropology, anthropologists serve as cultural critics who illuminate important social issues in a new light for an informed reading public.

This momentum toward public anthropology builds on decades of work among applied anthropologists.[5] Yet some argue that the publics imagined by public anthropology are quite distinct from those targeted by applied anthropology. Some applied anthropologists, for example, suggest that the move toward public anthropology privileges the act of writing over community actions and that public anthropology's emphasis on finely crafted and accessible ethnographies comes at the expense of formulating concrete policy solutions to improve the lives of those with whom anthropologists work.[6] Should anthropologists wishing to "influence public debates" tailor their books to the lay reading public or to policy makers? How can engaged anthropologists best make an impact: by changing the public's perceptions of particular social problems or by engaging with policy makers and influencing policy?

Some argue that the twin aims of cultural critique and of advocating for the well-being of vulnerable populations are not mutually exclusive. They argue for a "big tent" approach, emphasizing the shared goals of various brands of anthropology: public, applied, activist, and advocacy.[7] For example, some use their books to situate a social problem such as homelessness and drug use in a new light, using the critical insights offered by anthropological theory to propose policy solutions.[8] Others tailor their publications for distinct audiences. They may don a "public intellectual" hat to write books and opinion pieces geared toward academics and the lay public while also drafting white papers for policy audiences, sitting on advisory boards, and serving as expert witnesses.[9]

This book is purposely written for an undergraduate and lay reading public with the aim of opening a window onto migrant farmworkers' lives, but it ultimately aims to catalyze changes in public policy. I hope that broadening awareness of migrants' suffering will increase momentum for social change, as the popular success of recent ethnographies by authors like Seth Holmes suggests it can, and mobilize the public in favor of legislation that can ameliorate farmworkers' suffering. At various points in this book, however, I exchange the hat of public intellectual for that of engaged advocate. I suggest that intensive and sustained engagements with vulnerable groups entails a moral obligation for anthropologists that extends beyond representation. In the spirit of what Nancy Scheper-Hughes calls an "ethically grounded anthropology," I also discuss my engagements with farmworkers that venture beyond academic research and into the spheres of advocacy and activism.[10]

ON ETHNOGRAPHIC WRITING

The move toward writing for the public has encouraged greater attention to ethnographic form and voice, giving rise to what appears to be a second "experimental moment" in ethnographic writing.[11] In their efforts to craft books that are more accessible and compelling while remaining transparent about the research process, ethnographers seem to be increasingly borrowing techniques from creative nonfiction. As a result, recent public ethnographies exhibit attention to voice, character, and even plot—devices unimaginable in the dry monographs produced by the omniscient "ethnographic authorities" of old.

One such device involves the ethnographer's inserting herself and her own research experiences into the text. This strategy helps decenter the authority of the ethnographer and purposely reveal the partiality and subjective investments of her analysis.[12] Yet centering ethnographies around the personal experience of the ethnographer appears to serve an additional purpose in ethnographies about vulnerable populations whose lives may be hard to imagine. By providing the reader with more comfortable shoes to inhabit as they navigate foreign landscapes, making the ethnographer into the book's protagonist may also help diminish a reader's discomfort in engaging with apparently "alien" and unfamiliar ways of living. It draws in the reader by granting her a kind of personal avatar to inhabit in an alien world. As attested by the success of some recent ethnographies, this tactic appears to be effective for many readers. Yet because it invites the reader to identify with the ethnographer (often white and middle class) rather than with the "exotic"

subjects, I worry that this slippage of identification may diminish the radical potential of anthropology to humanize and demystify the "Other."

In this ethnography, I include a selection of my own thoughts and experiences, but I attempt to place the experiences and narratives of farmworkers front and center. A primary aim of this book is unabashedly humanistic: to render the texture of farmworkers' everyday lives so that their worlds appear less foreign to readers. To accomplish this, I employ another representational strategy that public ethnographers have increasingly borrowed from nonfiction accounts: following the lives of subjects over time.[13] This narrative device shifts the focus from the ethnographer as protagonist to his or her subjects, in an effort to foster greater identification with them than is achieved in the more traditional distanced and impersonal accounts produced by the classic participant-observers. This approach allows readers to come to acquaint themselves with farmworkers as individuals and to see how their lives unfold. I hope to highlight the diversity in migrant farmworkers' experiences as readers inhabit the shoes of farmworkers of different genders and at varying stages in the life course.

A common criticism of many ethnographic classics is that they establish the authority of the ethnographer on the backs of a variety of unacknowledged "key informants": that is, that they represent the statements and opinions of informants as the seamless analysis of an omniscient participant-observer. Part of the movement to decenter ethnographic authority has included the unmasking of the politics of ethnographic production and the revelation that behind every great classic ethnographer stands at least one great key informant—or native fieldworker.[14] I place farmworkers' own accounts and experiences at the center of this ethnography to accord credit to their own informed analyses and grant recognition of their pointed critiques.[15]

This book is based on sustained and intensive research with farmworkers at the bottom of the farm labor hierarchy. While this positioning granted me a privileged window onto migrants' vulnerabilities, it also revealed the illicit strategies farmworkers must use to circumvent immigration policies, find work, and make a viable living. Intensive engagement with vulnerable populations thus requires greater attention to strategies of representation and dissemination. It demands care in deciding which parts of the story to divulge to which audiences and how to package potentially controversial material. It also requires care to ensure that research participants are appropriately represented as complex, sympathetic characters rather than as one-dimensional victims of suffering.

Finally, intensive engagement with vulnerable populations requires action.[16] As part of an engaged anthropology that actively seeks the "promotion of social justice,"[17] this book attempts not only to diagnose the causes of migrant farmworkers' suffering but also to propose remedies and community-based interventions. Thus it serves as a form of "critically applied public anthropology;"[18] while my approach is theoretically informed, my research is intended to illuminate concrete changes that could help ameliorate farmworkers' suffering. Below, I discuss an intervention that put my research findings to practical use by attempting to help mitigate the kind of legal violence that prevents migrant farmworkers from making workers' compensation insurance (WCI) claims.

THE WORKERS' COMPENSATION INSURANCE INTERVENTION

The convergence of immigration and criminal law has led federal and local law enforcement officers to increasingly prosecute migrants' work-related conduct, such as working with another person's documents. Although undocumented workers are increasingly aware that their lack of legal status does not exclude them from WCI, labor supervisors wield the threat of their prosecution for identity theft to discourage them from filing insurance claims for workplace injuries and remuneration for lost work.

In February 2015, I organized an informational meeting for farmworkers in Mendota to help dispel the myth that injured workers are ineligible for WCI if they are working another person's papers. I collaborated with workers' compensation attorneys who serve a farmworking clientele and the Migrant and Seasonal Farmworker Division of the state's Employment Development Department to create a guide for workers concerned about the implications of the practice.

In the days before the meeting, I distributed flyers in the restaurants and *lavanderías* (laundromats) downtown, discussing the issue with dozens of workers. Some had workers' compensation cases that had dragged on without resolution; others had friends who had been denied benefits due to identity loan. They accepted the flyers and eagerly asked for the contact information of the attorneys. Yet on the day of the meeting, fewer than two dozen attended. As Mike, the former mayor later explained, labor supervisors are sometimes stationed outside UFW meetings to take note of the "*leyistas*"—those law-abiding "rabble-rousers"—who entered. In this small town dependent on farmwork, workers' fears of employer retaliation depressed attendance.

The low turn-out for this meeting highlighted the intense structural vulnerability produced by the labor hierarchy, by workers' need for work—itself structured by immigration and labor policies—and by *mayordomos*' intimate knowledge of workers' lives. It showed the relative futility of individual-level interventions in the face of powerful social structures that dampened the movement towards change. Yet if the meeting failed to remove the hold labor supervisors exert over workers, it at least communicated resolve and served to empower those present. It allowed attendees to ask questions of attorneys, and served as a space for workers to air other concerns.

After the meeting, Elisabeta, a long-time interviewee, paused to reflect. Having long fielded questions from me, Elisabeta was pleased to finally have had the opportunity to question the "experts" on the panel. Moreover, having often produced account after account of labor abuses at my request, it was comforting for Elisabeta to see action being taken. "Because tonight you did something for us," she said.

Concrete interventions to disseminate research results help shift the balance of power in ethnographic research, allowing research participants a greater role in shaping the dialogue. They create a place for research participants at the table, allowing them to inform researchers what information is valuable to them and how they can best be of assistance. During the meeting itself, research participants identified additional ways that we could intervene: by encouraging labor

supervisors to allow the farm machinery to stop so that workers can drink and use the bathrooms, by asking employers to install seatbelts on the onion and tomato planting machines to prevent falls, and by drawing attention to the fact that new food-safety regulations for melon harvesting make rehydration difficult for workers.

Advocacy is a logical extension of the interpersonal engagements created through long-term research. It is no longer sufficient for an anthropologist to publish a monograph and move on. Public anthropologists who conduct in-depth research with vulnerable populations have an obligation to reciprocate with advocacy. The benefits of longitudinal research stem not only from the breadth of knowledge that researchers obtain about the lived experience of vulnerable populations but also from the deep interpersonal commitments created by our sustained engagement with individuals. As ethnographers are "'called' into the stories and lives of others,"[19] the process of engaged listening to members of vulnerable groups requires a long-term commitment to their well-being.

APPENDIX B

Methods

To write this book, I followed the lives, work circumstances, and health status of eight farmworking women and seven farmworking men over nearly a decade. (The husband of one woman was deported early in my research.) At the start of my project, eight of my participants had legal permanent residency, seven were undocumented, and one had a temporary work visa (temporary protected status, or TPS). The median age of the women was thirty-five, and the median age of the men was thirty-nine. Altogether, they had been in the United States for a median of fifteen years: eleven for women and eighteen for men. Although their work patterns changed over time, at the start of my research, all but two participants were employed in farm work for at least four months each year: eleven in temporary and seasonal work in the fields (on labor crews and ranches), and two indoors in year-round, more permanent jobs in a tomato processing plant.

I also conducted repeat interviews with seven of these participants' family members—fathers and mothers, brothers, sisters, in-laws, and children. These interviews helped provide additional perspectives on the issues raised by core research participants, such as a father's memory of the circumstances on family farms in Mexico that caused his son to migrate (chapter 1), and identity loan and work injuries (chapter 3).

My race, gender, and nationality both abetted and foreclosed access to aspects of my research participants' lives. As a Spanish-speaking *gabacha* (white North American) who sought out interactions with the local migrant population, I did not fit into the racial and ethnic hierarchies of this highly segregated region. Because of the pervasive hostility toward migrants in the area, both Anglo-Americans and middle-class Mexican Americans strove to distance themselves from the region's recent arrivals. The Mexican Americans who worked in Mendota's vast social service bureaucracy, themselves often the children of

migrant farmworkers, sometimes expressed astonishment that I was living in town. They made it clear that they had long ago left Mendota—which they pejoratively referred to as a "migrant labor camp"—to settle in the more comfortable suburbs closer to Fresno. Anglo-Americans who passed through town and casually asked me where to eat were often puzzled by my efforts to give the Spanish pronunciations of Mexican restaurants their due. "You *Spanish?*" one man asked quizzically, wrinkling his nose, using the local euphemism for *Mexican* so as to not provoke offense. Meanwhile, the local Spanish-speaking residents had me pegged because of the nasal inflection of my Spanish. "Are you *American?*" one bread vendor asked with surprise. In a region in which *American* and *migrant* are diametrically opposed terms, his question reveals the conflation of nationality, nativity, and race.

As a *gabacha,* I was immediately marked as an outsider by many migrants; yet this status implied that I had access to valuable knowledge unavailable to most migrants. The *gabachos* who entered the community to interact with migrants were usually brokers of social services of some kind: school officials, social service workers, dental outreach coordinators. Thus being a *gabacha* sometimes made it more difficult to gain participants' trust. In other cases, it facilitated access—and also conferred responsibility. Migrants often assumed that I must have greater familiarity with the health care and social service bureaucracies and enlisted my help. As I was called into migrants' lives in deeper and more intimate ways, I had to weigh how to represent the sensitive data to which I was privy—data that might be misinterpreted by the less sympathetic and yet was valuable in illustrating the structural violence that affects migrants' lives.

Just as my race and nationality were a mixed blessing, so was being a woman. My interactions with migrant women about their children's health provided a foundation of trust and interdependence. However, as an unmarried woman, and a *gabacha* at that—and therefore viewed as not bound by the same gendered norms of propriety as my female interlocutors—I had more circumscribed relationships with migrant farmworking men. Because it would have been inappropriate to interview women's husbands outside my relationship as their wives' confidante and friend, I often interviewed women and their husbands together. I compensated for the limitations on my access to migrant men by interviewing women's brothers and fathers, with whom my relationship was less constrained.

I also conducted interviews with middle-aged male sojourners in the town's corner store and pool hall, where unaccompanied men—many of whom had left their families in their homelands—relaxed and socialized after work. Their unaccompanied status diminished the social proscriptions against my interacting with them, and the intervention of Mike—the owner of these twin institutions—lessened the potential scandal associated with my own presence in these traditionally male spaces. (I did, however, shock one long-term female research participant one afternoon when she found me chatting with men in the corner store, where she had gone to pay her bills.) Finally, conducting participant-observation in and of farm work allowed me to interact with migrant men without the mediation of their wives. These encounters deepened my understanding of the unique vulnerabilities men experience at work and as a result of physical disabilities.

Conducting research with vulnerable populations such as migrant farmworkers is inherently challenging.[1] Migrants' long workdays and workweeks—eight- to ten-hour workdays, often seven days a week, combined with commutes of one to two hours—makes their free time a rare commodity. The winter fallow season, when work is scarce, is often the most opportune time to conduct research, but by the same token, it is an inappropriate time to conduct in-depth interviews about work. Finally, the very hiddenness of agricultural work—the fact that it often occurs out of plain sight, in segregated and remote rural areas, on an unpredictable schedule, and in changing locations—makes accessing migrants' workplaces difficult.[2] These impediments to research partially explain why farmworkers remain a hidden population whose health problems remain poorly understood by researchers and poorly addressed by public health programs.[3]

If merely catching up with migrant farmworkers to learn about their lives is a formidable task, following them over time presents additional challenges. Migrants are by definition mobile, crossing international borders and state lines. The social chaos of poverty further complicates long-term research among vulnerable populations like farmworkers: relocations, evictions, deportations, and terminated cell-phone numbers all make it difficult to stay in touch. Finally, institutional review boards (IRBs)—committees that exist at research institutions to protect the subjects of research studies from physical or psychological harm—often impose safeguards more appropriate for biomedical research protocols than for intensive ethnography built on long-term relationships of rapport and trust. While IRBs were established to protect vulnerable populations from being conscripted into research studies without a full understanding of the risks involved, their regulations threaten to transform ethnographers' interaction with their subjects into one-time transactional encounters.[4] In the interest of protecting research subjects' confidentiality, for example, such boards often prohibit researchers from maintaining the contact information of their subjects after their study's expiration date.[5]

As the anthropologist Nancy Scheper-Hughes has put it, the unique engagement of the ethnographer with her subjects enables her to serve as a kind of "clerk of the records . . . a minor historian of ordinary lives of people often presumed to have no history."[6] She writes: "The clerk, or the 'keeper,' of the records is the one who listens, observes, records, and tries to interpret human lives, as does the traditional country doctor." This book chronicles many significant events in my lives of my research participants: chronic illnesses, work injuries, retirements, and deaths. Ethnographers of the poor acknowledge that explorations of the lives of marginalized groups have the potential to degenerate into a kind of pornography of poverty, sacrificing a sympathetic portrayal of such groups for the sheer voyeurism of providing a window onto difficult, and exotic, lives.[7] This book aims to avoid this trap. It strives to balance its examination of the gritty realities farmworkers face with a sympathetic account of their humanity—their hopes and disappointments, joys and fears.

APPENDIX C

Core Research Participants

This appendix provides a sketch of the families of the core interviewees whom I have followed since 2005, including details of their migration and work histories, health problems, income, and access to benefits. Their stories are up to date as of 2015, and names of family members mentioned in the text are italicized on first mention.

Blanca (forty-two) met her husband, *Gerardo* (forty-three), in 1995 when he returned to Zacatecas for the winter holidays. Gerardo had migrated to the United States undocumented in 1989 when he was seventeen, after his father, *Don Miguel* (now sixty-six), returned from the United States with a settlement from a work injury. Blanca joined Gerardo, undocumented, one year later. Gerardo works on a ranch year-round, doing a variety of tasks, which he enjoys. Blanca usually earns $45 a day by providing informal daycare for three children while their parents work in the fields. In 2005, they earned about $25,000 a year for a family of five.

Blanca suffers from migraines; Gerardo had a bout of high blood pressure but says it is now controlled. Because both Blanca and Gerardo are undocumented, neither qualifies for unemployment insurance or regular Medi-Cal; their three U.S.-born children receive regular Medi-Cal. Don Miguel suffers from high blood pressure, diabetes, and swollen, arthritic knees, which he slathers with Vaseline each night. He stopped working in 2011 after an accident while he was harvesting pomegranates for a large company. A trailer slammed into the back of the van in which he and his coworkers were riding, knocking out Don Miguel's teeth and causing whiplash. Don Miguel received $800 in state disability insurance every month while he waited for a settlement. In 2013, the company finally paid him a cash settlement of $10,000—which Blanca calls "a pittance" (*un dinerito*). "He hasn't even been able to pay his debts," Blanca says. "And he can't find work here; they don't give work to senior citizens." Don Miguel

returned to Mexico "for good" in 2013 with no earnings to show for his efforts. "Sometimes we send him and his wife money, but we also need it," Blanca says.

Elisabeta, now thirty-five, crossed the border without authorization at the age of fourteen to support her widowed mother in Jalisco, Mexico. She toiled in the same fields that her father, a bracero, had worked before her. Elisabeta met her husband, *Teo* (now forty-six), a Salvadoran with temporary protected status, when she was harvesting lettuce in Huron at the age of twenty-two. "She wouldn't let me out of her sight," Teo jokes (*me echó la ley encima.*) Teo himself had come to the United States without papers in 1994 to escape the lack of economic opportunities in El Salvador. Both Elisabeta and Teo work in the fields for a variety of large companies and contractors. Elisabeta usually works five to six months a year; she picks lettuce in the spring and weeds tomato fields and harvests watermelons in the summer. Teo works year-round picking and pruning almonds, picking lettuce, weeding tomato fields, and harvesting melons in southern California. Elisabeta suffers from diabetes (diagnosed when she was twenty-three), hypertension (diagnosed when she was twenty-four), and also from anxiety and depression (which she alternately describes as either *una gran tristeza*—a "great sadness"—or *nervios,* "nerves"), which she attributes to her inability to return to Mexico to pay her respects to her mother when she died. Teo's most pressing complaint is his chronic asthma; he has also had an inflamed liver. In 2015, the couple earned $17,000 for a family of five; Teo additionally receives about $3,000 a year in unemployment benefits. The couple receives sporadic health care through Emergency Medi-Cal while their children, all U.S.-born, are insured through regular Medi-Cal. Their children include *Oscar* (eighteen), *Carlos* (thirteen), *Andrea* (now five), and Lisette, who was born in January 2015.

Leticia (thirty-eight) and *Claudio* (forty-two) are both legal permanent residents. Claudio's parents owned a trucking company in a more prosperous community near El Platanal; they migrated to Mendota undocumented in 1984, after their business went bankrupt. The timing of their arrival was fortuitous: Claudio's whole family received legal permanent residency through IRCA two years later. Claudio met Leticia on a return visit to the area in 1996, and the couple married. They work primarily in processing plants, sorting asparagus February through April and sorting tomatoes for a tomato processing company May through November; he also works in a cotton gin from October through December. The work is semipermanent, indoors, and carries benefits; they earn overtime pay for work in excess of an eight-hour-day and receive raises each year. In 2015, the couple earned about $25,000 a year for a family of five.

Claudio suffers from varicose veins, which his doctor attributes to his standing at work all day long, and from hypertension. When he walks, his legs throb and ache. Leticia suffers from what she calls *nervios,* or anxiety and depression. Claudio and Leticia own a three-bedroom home on the west side of Mendota, a prosperous area called Bunny Hill. They are the only couple I interviewed who owns their own home.

Don Octavio (now fifty-eight) claims to be the first migrant from El Platanal to have settled permanently in Mendota. In 1974, at the age of seventeen, he

migrated undocumented to work on a ranch alongside his uncles, for the same *mayordomo* as his own father, who had been a bracero. Don Octavio caught a glimpse of *Doña Berta* (now fifty-seven) on a float during a return trip to El Platanal; the couple married three days later. Don Octavio adjusted his legal status through IRCA and was able to bring his family to the United States with visas in 2000. He works on a ranch year-round and enjoys the outdoor work. Doña Berta remembers starting work in 2000, two days after she arrived, at the age of forty-two. When she returned home from her first day of work weeding melon, she simply lay down on the carpet. "I couldn't even get up," she remembers. She did not last the season.

Doña Berta suffers from hypertension and *nervios,* or anxiety/depression, and she says that Don Octavio "almost never goes to the doctor." Their son, *Ricardo* (now twenty-seven), began working in the fields when he was fifteen, alongside his older brother. Because they are legal permanent residents, the couple is eligible for regular Medi-Cal, unemployment, and food stamps. Don Octavio earned about $19,000 to support a family of five in 2005.

Raquel (fifty-four) and her husband, *Alberto* (fifty-five), are Salvadoran legal permanent residents who arrived in the United States from the eastern province of Cuscatlán at the height of El Salvador's civil war. As asylum seekers, they gained legal permanent residence through a law passed in 1997 to remedy the bias against granting asylum to Central American migrants fleeing U.S.-backed regimes during the Cold War. The couple began working in the fields in 1991. Raquel suffers from hypertension, anxiety and depression (*nervios*), and severe arthritis. Alberto suffers from recurrent abdominal pain and missing fillings. He now works seven months a year on labor crews weeding cotton and tomato fields, picking melons, and pruning grapevines and almond trees. Raquel used to work on labor crews packing melon, weeding tomato, cotton, and onion fields, and sorting tomatoes. After her mid-forties, it became increasingly difficult for her to find work, and she stopped working entirely in 2010 due to severe arthritic pain. Raquel finally began receiving Social Security disability (SSDI) in 2013 at the age of fifty-three, two years after Medi-Cal funded an operation to "clean the cartilage" in her knee that did little to resolve the problem. SSDI also entitled her to Medicare, which paid for reconstructive surgery on her other knee (which Medi-Cal would not have covered). She is now waiting for a third knee surgery to correct the original botched operation. The couple has two adult daughters born in El Salvador, who went to school and worked in Sacramento before returning to Mendota; a grandson; and a twelve-year-old daughter born in the United States. Their son-in-law, *Lalo,* a legal permanent resident, works in a cotton gin in Mendota. As legal permanent residents, the couple receives Medi-Cal and are eligible for unemployment benefits. In 2010, they earned $11,000 a year for a family of three.

Don Santiago (now seventy), Blanca's father, initially came to Mendota as an undocumented worker in 1970 from La Capellanía, Zacatecas, supporting his family by migrating each year to work in the fields. He had intended to retire in Mexico in the early 2000s and never risk an undocumented crossing again. However, a family tragedy ironically provided him with the opportunity to reunite

with his children in the United States. In March 2006, a car crash left his undocumented son, Silvestre, brain-dead, and the hospital contacted Don Santiago and his wife, *Doña Rosa* (now sixty-five), in Zacatecas to inquire whether they would consent to have Silvestre's organs donated. They did. The hospital was able to arrange for visitors' visas for the couple and their daughter *Lupita* to pay their respects to Silvestre before he was buried. Because Don Santiago's four other children (including Blanca and Manuel) lived in the United States, the three decided to overstay their visas.

Both Don Santiago and Doña Rosa were diagnosed with hypertension and diabetes in the fall of 2006 (she at fifty-seven, he at sixty-two), which they attribute to the *gran apuro* (the great shock) of Silvestre's death. Don Santiago also suffers from high cholesterol and painful varicose veins, which he calls *bolas de sangre* (balls of blood). The couple's younger son, *Manuel* (now thirty-five), migrated to the United States undocumented in 1996 at the age of sixteen. He tore his shoulder while moving heavy irrigation pipes on a large commercial farm in 2012 and received workers' compensation. When the doctor decreed that he could return to light duty in August 2014, the farm sent him to weed melon, and he tore his shoulder once again. At thirty-five, he worries that he may not work again.

Don Santiago obtained a Social Security card from the Social Security Administration in 1973, but he missed the opportunity for legalization offered by the Immigration Reform and Control Act (IRCA) in 1986 because he had returned to Zacatecas the previous year, when his mother became gravely ill. Don Santiago continued to work in the fields in the Central Valley, hoping that another amnesty would eventually allow him to access the forty years of retirement earnings he had sunk into his "real" Social Security card. Although no such opportunity arose, he and Doña Rosa succeeded in becoming legal permanent residents in 2012 through a daughter who married a U.S. citizen. Don Santiago and Doña Rosa now live with their unmarried daughter, Lupita.

Don Santiago used to work on labor crews weeding tomato fields and picking cantaloupe. In 2008, he was hit on the head with a discarded melon and stopped work entirely. He received about $3,300 in state disability insurance in total and then a settlement of $20,000; after paying the lawyer's fees, he was left with $8,000. His settlement spent, he now earns about $280 a month by recycling. Don Santiago and Doña Rosa each receive $190 a month through Social Security. The Personal Responsibility and Work Opportunities Act of 1996 imposed a five-year bar on access to Supplemental Security Income, additional payments to which their low incomes would otherwise have entitled them. Both gained access to regular Medi-Cal in 2012 when they became legal permanent residents. Lupita, who is undocumented, works on labor crews "in whatever [she] can" to help support her parents and a newborn; she earns about $8,000 a year and is ineligible for unemployment benefits. She works six to seven months a year weeding tomato fields, picking cantaloupe and watermelon, sorting tomato, pruning grape vines and almond trees, and sorting asparagus.

Sulema (forty-one) is Yadira's *comadre,* her sister-in-law. She is married to Yadira's cousin, *Mario* (forty-two). Sulema is an undocumented farmworker originally from Puebla, Mexico. She and Mario met while working in a factory

in Los Angeles more than twenty years ago; Mario eventually worked as a mechanic and owned his own repair shop. They moved to Mendota in late 2007, when Mario lost his shop during the recession. In Mendota, Mario worked year-round maintaining the equipment for a medium-sized contractor; he earned more than minimum wage and had a secure job in the winter. Sulema worked for the contractor for about four months a year planting tomatoes. When Sulema was injured in a fall at work in 2011 and eventually sued, Mario lost his job. Sulema's eldest son, *Vicente,* began working in the fields at eighteen to help support the family.

Sulema suffers from high cholesterol and musculoskeletal issues caused by her fall, and she suffered en episode of acute hypertension in 2013 that led to a cranial hemorrhage. Her husband worries about his hereditary predisposition toward cardiovascular disease and diabetes but has not received preventive screenings. In 2015, Sulema and Mario were finally able to gain legal permanent residency through their eldest daughter, who turned twenty-one in 2014. This entitles them both to legal status and the perks it entails—legal employment, unemployment benefits, and routine health checkups covered by regular Medi-Cal.

Don Tomás (who died in 2014 at the age of fifty-six) arrived in the Central Valley from El Salvador in 1980. He met *Doña Linda* (now fifty-eight), a widow, during a return visit to his hometown of Sensuntepeque; after they married, he adopted her five children as his own. Don Tomás was able to adjust his legal status in 1986 through IRCA and then petitioned for the legal permanent residency of his new family; he brought Doña Linda and her children to the United States with legal visas. Don Tomás worked in the fields for twenty years before he came to supervise a team himself.

When work slowed down, in 2000, he found a job as a *mayordomo* for a large contractor. It was then that Don Tomás learned he had advanced diabetes. Ineligible for Medicaid because of his assets and income, Don Tomás continued to work. He applied to the Social Security Administration for permanent disability at the age of forty-five but was deemed capable of working in another occupation. He stopped working in 2011 after a twenty-eight-day hospital stay and qualified for Social Security disability only in 2013, after losing his sight and beginning dialysis. He also suffered from hypertension and high cholesterol; his wife suffers from diabetes and high blood pressure. Before he stopped work, Don Tomás had earned about $35,000 a year for a family of two; he was additionally eligible for unemployment. In 2014, Don Tomás received $870 in Social Security disability every month, and Doña Linda received $900 from the state as his caretaker—"to wash me, to feed me, to wash my clothes."

Yadira (thirty-eight) migrated from Colima, Mexico, undocumented, to join her husband, *René,* in 2001. After unsuccessfully trying to support his family as a construction worker, René had migrated to the United States undocumented the previous year. After paying a *coyote* to bring their three children across the border, the couple had another three children in the United States. After René was deported in 2010, Yadira remained in the United States with the children,

the eldest of whom, *Ramón* (eighteen), began working in the fields at fourteen to help support the family.

Yadira typically works on labor crews planting tomatoes in the spring and picking melons in the summer and fall, although she lost her job planting tomatoes when she missed work because of her acute hypertension. Prior to René's deportation, the couple earned $15,000 a year for a family of six. In 2012, she earned $3,000, and Ramón earned $6,000 in the fields; she also received $490 a month in welfare and $503 a month in food stamps. Yadira suffers from untreated hypertension and bouts of anemia. Her three U.S.-born children are covered by regular Medi-Cal, while she and her eldest three children—all undocumented—are only able to access Emergency Medi-Cal. Yadira's mother, who migrated undocumented in 2008 to join her, was able to take care of Yadira's children after René's deportation. However, she died in 2011 at the age of fifty-six due to cirrhosis of the liver, complicated by a blow to her arm after a fall from a tomato-planting machine for which she received no treatment or compensation.

Notes

INTRODUCTION

1. I use the term *undocumented* to refer to migrants without legal status because this is the English translation of *sinpapeles,* the term my interviewees used. As Heyman and colleagues (2009) note, however, many members of the group I refer to as undocumented did in fact have various forms of documentation, as some workers entered the United States legally and overstayed their visas. I follow De Genova (2002) in using the term *migrant* as opposed to *immigrant* because the former captures the "intrinsic incompletion and consequent irresolution" of migration rather than a unidirectional and purposeful movement. Moreover, the term *immigrant* itself describes new arrivals from the perspective of the nation-state, often connoting a linear process of assimilation.

2. Arax 2005.

3. Ibid.

4. Ibid; Barbasssa 2005.

5. Branco 2006; Martin 2005.

6. Bethel and Harger 2014; CDC 2008; Jackson and Rosenberg 2010; Rao 2007.

7. Martin 2005.

8. Barbassa 2005; Calvan 2005.

9. Klinenberg 2002.

10. Jackson and Rosenberg 2010.

11. Burke 2008.

12. Jackson and Rosenberg 2010; NWFM 2016b.

13. CDC 2008. The country of origin of was recorded only for crop workers who died between 2003 and 2006.

14. Bethel and Harger 2014.

15. Adams 2013; Das 1995; Klinenberg 2002.

16. Klinenberg 2002.
17. Lam et al. 2013.
18. Bethel and Harger 2014; Jackson and Rosenberg 2010; Lam et al. 2013.
19. Lam et al. 2013; Stoecklin-Marois et al. 2013.
20. Bethel and Harger 2014; Lam et al. 2013.
21. Some research does propose helpful workplace protections to reduce farmworkers' risk of heat illness, such as access to regular breaks, shade, and medical attention (Fleischer et al. 2013), and altering work hours and activities (Mirabelli et al. 2010). Yet even when studies of occupational health emphasize the role of the work environment as opposed to farmworkers' own behaviors, they fail to examine the impact of public policies in structuring farmworkers' immediate work environments, let alone the historical structures shaping farmworkers' own behaviors.
22. Holmes 2013a: 158.
23. Farmer 1999.
24. Slack and Whiteford 2011.
25. Quesada, Hart and Bourgois: 2011: 341.
26. Ibid.: 342.
27. NFWM 2016a.
28. Bourdieu 1977: 66.
29. See Gravlee 2009; Horton and Barker 2010.
30. Lamphere 2004: 432.
31. U.S. Census 2010.
32. Whittaker 2012.
33. U.S. Census 2010.
34. Bourgois 2003.
35. Bourgois and Schonberg 2009; Horton and Barker 2010. See also Saxton 2015 on the importance of attending to the "chronicity" of illness.
36. Bourgois and Schonberg 2009: 14; Holmes 2013b: 38.
37. Kleinman 1998: 417–18; Oliver 2004, cited in Zavella 2011: 18.
38. I use pseudonyms throughout this book to protect the anonymity and confidentiality of my interviewees.
39. Local companies have also begun topping the stalks of corn before workers enter in order to reduce humidity and to reduce workers' exposure to pesticides and pollen. As one supervisor for the company puts it: "If it's not cut and you walk into that field ten feet, you just want to shower. It's all just over you. We cut it so people aren't getting all those particles and all that pollen in their face. Because inside that field, the corn grows really thick. Inside that field, the humidity is at like 90 percent." In discussing the death of the young man in the corn in 2008, this supervisor says: "We had three weeks of temperatures of about 107 to 115. It was ridiculous." Yet, as Klinenberg argues (2002), emphasizing the role of natural factors in the production of heat deaths serves to short-circuit inquiry into the social production of such deaths.
40. I took field notes in the language spoken by my interviewees. Where possible, I digitally recorded interviews. All quotes are my English translations of the Spanish; I have attempted to capture the nuance, dialect, and inflection of interviewees' statements in my translations. Yet translations of speech are rarely

adequate to convey the nuances of body language, emotion, and tone. Not only does a speaker's choice of words carry connotations of meaning and social position that are difficult to capture in English, but word order itself can heighten the emphasis placed on particular parts of speech. Throughout the manuscript, I include the original quotations in Spanish where the poetry or import of a statement is lost in translation.

CHAPTER 1. BURNING UP

1. DIR n.d.a.

2. The heat-illness standard also requires that employers develop a plan for emergencies and offer heat-stress training to both supervisors and workers in their native language.

3. Burke 2008.

4. On June 10, 2015, Cal-OSHA announced its settlement with the UFW and its pledge to increase its enforcement activities. I discuss the settlement in the book's conclusion.

5. Le 2013.

6. Philip Martin, a scholar of agricultural economics, has documented the concentration of California's farmworkers in fruit, vegetable, and horticultural production on a relatively small number of farms: he notes that the largest 10 percent of the state's farm employers accounted for over 90 percent of the state's farm-labor expenditures in 2010 (Martin 2011: 5).

7. I made repeat visits to observe and participate in various kinds of farmwork in 2011, 2012 and 2013. In most cases, I was able to stay only a few minutes before contractors intervened. This is, in fact, how I was able to interview several midlevel supervisors (in charge of quality control and food safety) and one contractor. However, on a few occasions, the contractors were slow to arrive, and the *mayordomos* kindly invited me up onto the field-packing machine. I attribute this acceptance to fact that as my fieldwork wore on, and Cal-OSHA inspections began to increase, supervisors became inured to the prospect of outsiders observing their work. Moreover, as the description provided here suggests, working alongside field hands made it more likely that labor supervisors would tolerate my presence the following day. My novelty as a *gabacha* also likely abetted my access. "It's a rare thing. . . . It's not often that people come to visit us in the fields," said the wife of one *mayordomo* who packed alongside me in 2012.

8. Grossi 2013.

9. Cal-OSHA 2013.

10. Bourdieu 1977: 66.

11. Massey, Durand, and Malone 2002: 119–21; see also Martin 1994.

12. Commercial growers and companies hire contractors to complete a specified task, such as picking several fields of melons or weeding fields of tomatoes. Because contractors may command a labor force of several hundred to several thousand employees, and one labor contractor often works for several growers at once, contractors in turn delegate workers' direct supervision to *mayordomos,* who supervise labor crews of twelve to forty people. The *mayordomo* is

responsible for recruiting the crew members, supervising their work, and ensuring their health and safety in the fields. The term *mayordomo* is historically derived from the Spanish term used to refer to the principal post in the civil-religious hierarchy in Latin America that organizes community festivals; therefore, it denotes a position of great authority and responsibility (Brandes 1988).

13. Aguirre International 2005: 20.

14. Bourdieu 2001: 30.

15. Ibid.: 49, 52.

16. According to the CDC, there are multiple stages of heat illness, beginning with *heat stress:* warning symptoms such as the swelling of hands and feet, muscle spasms, and dizziness. The next stage, *heat exhaustion,* is marked by excessive sweating, weakness, nausea, and sometimes fainting. In *heatstroke,* the body heats up faster than its cooling mechanisms can handle: simply ceasing activity may not allow the body's internal temperature to return to normal. Heatstroke is distinguished by red, hot, dry skin—as blood vessels dilate in the body's attempt to increase heat loss—neurological impairment, a, strong, rapid pulse, and a core body temperature above 103°F. It may also lead to seizures or coma (CDC 2008; Rao 2007).

17. Companies' recent concerns about food safety inspections have led them to exchange their old wooden trailers for metal trailers, which increase stackers' heat exposure. A food safety supervisor for Fresco explained, "Once you do field-packing as we do, you have to clean and sanitize those particular implements, and wood is porous."

18. DIR n.d.a.

19. The CCAB guidelines are based on the Food and Drug Administration's own guidelines to reduce the contamination of fresh produce, which it released in 1998 after a series of outbreaks of food-borne illness (see FDA 1998). Many food safety audits performed by industry and by third-party auditors are based on this original guide. Any cantaloupe producer or distributor in California that sells more than five thousand cartons of cantaloupe a year is bound by the CCAB guidelines. "If you're producing cantaloupe in California, you're going to be audited," says an official in the CCAB.

20. Contrary to this supervisor's statement, the CCAB guidelines do not state that the use of gloves is mandatory during harvesting. Although some pickers wear gloves to protect their fingers from the cantaloupe's rough skin, most do not. Packers must often attach stickers to the melons, and wearing gloves would greatly hinder this process.

21. See CCAB 2014, a checklist of the items that food safety inspectors from the California Department of Food and Agriculture, trained by the U.S Department of Agriculture (USDA), must examine when auditing melon harvesting companies.

22. Wozniacka 2012.

23. Ibid.

24. Morehouse 2013.

25. DIR n.d.a.

26. Wozniacka 2012.

27. Ibid.

28. Bourdieu 2001.

29. The CCAB checklist for cantaloupe field-harvesting and packing, approved by the U.S. Food and Drug Administration (FDA), includes ninety-seven items. Under the rubric of worker hygiene, item 26 prohibits workers from taking "personal items" into the harvest area. Item 27 states: "Smoking, eating and drinking (except water) shall be confined to designated areas" (CCAB 2014). However, as a member of the CCAB clarified, that restriction is intended to specifically exclude any water not provided by the company. Fresco's food safety director defends the policy by saying: "Imagine if everyone brought a little plastic bottle that looks like water and it was full of vodka. We don't have personnel to check every water bottle."

CHAPTER 2. ENTERING FARM WORK

1. In keeping with the usage of my interviewees, I use the honorifics *Don* and *Doña* to refer to migrants who command respect due to their age, occupational position, or status in the community.

2. Massey, Durand, and Malone 2002: 19–20; Menjívar 2000.

3. Cohen 2011; Massey et al: 42; Ngai 2004: 138. The United States first established the bracero program through a bilateral agreement with Mexico on September 27, 1942. Under this initial wartime agreement (which was extended until 1947), the United States imported 215,000 Mexican nationals to work in agriculture and 75,000 to maintain the tracks for more than twenty railroads. The U.S. Congress extended the program several times. In 1951, Congress passed Public Law 78, which continued to govern the program until its end in 1964, along with a diplomatic agreement negotiated in Mexico, known as the Migrant Labor Agreement (see Ngai 2004: 138–40). At the height of the program, the United States imported between 400,000 and 450,000 braceros a year (Massey, Durand, and Malone 2002: 37).

4. Cohen 2011: 89–117.

5. Ibid.

6. Otero 2011; Smith-Nonini 2011; Stephen 2007.

7. Although only recently arrived in Mendota, Salvadoran migrants have had a presence in San Francisco for over a hundred years. Cecilia Menjívar (2000) shows that because San Francisco was a central processing center for coffee from Central America, the commercialization of coffee in Central America led El Salvador's coffee elites to settle in the city in the early 1900s.

8. Coutin 2007: 78.

9. Moodie 2010.

10. Coutin 2007; Castañeda, Heidbrink, and Yarris 2014; Zilberg 2011.

11. Vogt 2013: 9.

12. Coutin 2007: 160–65.

13. Mahler 1995: 92, 93.

14. Boehm 2012: 73, 71–80.

15. Massey, Durand, and Malone 2002: 91.

16. Martin 1994; Massey, Durand, and Malone 2002: 91. Not all migrants qualified for SAW, however. Injured men like Don Miguel were ineligible

because they could not supply the requisite evidence of work, and, later arrivals like Gerardo missed the cutoff date.

17. The Immigration and Nationality Act of 1965 made family reunification a core principle of U.S. immigration policy. As a result, U.S. citizens and legal permanent residents may petition for permanent resident visas (green cards) for their immediate family. However, U.S. immigration policy allots each country a uniform number of visas each year. This policy penalizes Mexicans, whose long-standing cultural, social, and historical ties to the United States create a particularly high demand for visas (see De Genova 2002, 2005; Gomberg-Muñoz 2016). As a result, Mexican applicants must wait much longer for visas than applicants of many other nationalities.

18. Massey, Durand, and Malone 2002: 91.

19. Mahler 1995: 43.

20. Salvadorans' ambiguous legal status is directly related to the United States' support of the military during the country's civil war and its historic refusal to grant Salvadoran refugees political asylum. After a decade of public activism on behalf of Nicaraguans, Salvadorans, and Guatemalans, the U.S. Congress compromised by creating temporary protected status (TPS) for migrants deemed unable to safely return to their countries of origin because of war, natural disasters, or other "extraordinary and temporary conditions" (see Merry and Coutin 2014: 9). It permits them to work in the United States for a maximum of eighteen months. However, migrants must be continuously physically present in the United States to retain this status. The temporary nature of the program is underscored by the fact that its extension is routinely announced just a month or two prior to its expiration (Menjívar and Abrego 2012: 1393). Thus TPS is one of a proliferating number of temporary and provisional immigration statuses (see Menjívar and Kanstroom 2014), a form of "liminal legality" that leaves bearers with "long-term uncertainty" (Menjívar 2006: 1001). Currently, the TPS program is in effect through September 9, 2016 (see USCIS n.d.).

21. Vogt 2013.

22. Menjívar 2006.

23. Most migrant farmworkers in California come from agricultural backgrounds. The National Agricultural Workers' Survey found that 64 percent of the state's farmworkers had performed agricultural work prior to arriving in the United States (Aguirre International 2005: 8).

24. Boehm 2012: 77.

25. Packing and processing sheds generally offer workers better labor conditions and pay than labor contractors, although their payment structures, benefits, and labor controls vary widely. In general, the documented status of most workers at such plants, which enables them to find work elsewhere, requires that supervisors avoid engaging in obvious labor abuses.

26. Throughout the book, I use the term *labor crew* to refer to crews of workers hired by labor contractors. It does not necessarily mean, however, that the workers are working by a piece rate or "on contract."

27. Martin 2011, 2014: 5. Because of their ability to provide companies with a large workforce on demand, contractors tend to predominate in the

cultivation of labor-intensive crops such as fruits, nuts, and vegetables. Thus they are particularly common in the San Joaquin Valley (Aguirre International 2005: 6–7).

28. Fussell 2011.

29. In contrast to coercively suppressing the workers' compensation claims of undocumented workers through the explicit threat of retaliation, deportation, or arrest (see chapter 3), the practice of offering workers "safety bucks" encourages less vulnerable workers to silence themselves. Moreover, because workers in packing and processing sheds usually work in a fixed position on a moving conveyor belt or assembly line, they often find it difficult to leave that spot to drink water or visit the bathroom.

30. Bourdieu 1977: 94.

31. In his compelling ethnography of berry pickers in Washington State, Seth Holmes shows that body posture during work reflects one's position in the social hierarchy (2013b: 174–76). Jobs performed while sitting behind a desk are symbolically linked to the mind and therefore more prestigious. Those performed while standing or walking are associated with the body, and yet such workers still command respect—as evidenced by common terms such as *upstanding citizen* and *upright character*. However, jobs that involve squatting or kneeling in the dirt are at the bottom of the labor hierarchy, and the individuals who perform them are viewed as less than human.

32. Bourdieu 1977, 2000; Bourgois and Schonberg 2009: 18.

33. Cohen 2011.

34. Most couples I interviewed engaged in what scholars call *step migration;* that is, husbands took the risky step of migrating first, and their wives and children joined them later. As Pierrette Hondagneu-Sotelo (1994) argues, men typically pioneer decisions to migrate, although women play critical roles in the process, for example by contesting such decisions and deciding the timing of their own journeys. Women usually migrate with their husbands or fathers (see Boehm 2012: 83), although a handful of women in my sample, like Elisabeta, migrated alone, and the number of Mexican and Central American women who migrate alone to support families from afar is growing (Hondagneu-Sotelo and Ávila 1997; O'Leary 2009).

35. The term *exceptional workers* captures the double-edged nature of the work ethic required of farmworkers on labor crews. Farmworkers' exceptional work effort is compelled by the U.S. labor and immigration policies that exclude them from labor protections and render them vulnerable. Ruth Gomberg-Muñoz (2010, 2011) draws attention to the similar double meaning of Mexican workers' reputed "willingness to work."

36. Friedland and Thomas 1974: 60; López 2007; Schell 2002.

37. Berger 2014.

38. LCC n.d.

39. Aguirre International 2005: viii.

40. Martin 2012.

41. Aguirre International 2005: 28.

42. See López 2007: 99.

43. Schell 2002: 150.

44. The scarcity of work further exacerbates workers' dependence on their labor supervisors. *Mayordomos* often maintain a list of "regulars" on their labor crews, and a worker's performance each season determines future opportunities. Workers who miss a day of work jeopardize both their current jobs and their future employment opportunities.

45. Andreas 1998.

46. Cornelius 2001: 661.

47. Ibid.

48. Marquandt et al. 2013: 66.

49. Andreas 1998; Massey 2006.

50. Cornelius and Salehyan 2007: 143.

51. Heyman 2001; see also Chavez 1992: 139–151; Gomberg-Muñoz 2010, 2011; Quesada, Hart, and Bourgois 2011: 394.

52. U.S. DOL 2010.

53. Aguirre International 2005: 15.

54. Although injured workers may qualify for State Disability Insurance (SDI), SDI payments are typically less generous than workers' compensation. Therefore labor supervisors believe that workers have an incentive to claim injuries sustained at work as work injuries instead.

55. U.S. DOL 2014a.

CHAPTER 3. GHOST WORKERS

1. Under identity loan, an identity recipient typically receives wages in the form of a check made out to the donor: in this case, Elisabeta received a check in María's name. This arrangement is facilitated by lax check-cashing practices. While banks require official identification and a signature in order to cash checks, many corner stores and check-cashing outlets in the Central Valley do not.

2. Migrants say that until the late 1990s, it was customary for identity recipients to pay document donors $100 for each $1,000 they earned from working on the donors' papers. However, this "rental" of papers has become less common since 1996, when the Internal Revenue Service began issuing Individual Taxpayer Identification Numbers (ITINs) to undocumented workers. Because legal status is a requirement for receiving a Social Security number, undocumented workers had previously been unable to file taxes. However, once ITINs allowed the undocumented to build a record of their presence that could count toward eventual legalization and perhaps even to receive tax refunds, undocumented workers found it more desirable to use fake Social Security and green cards with their own names when obtaining work. To attract identity recipients, document donors must now entice borrowers by offering them a bonus.

3. In some cases, identity recipients work "idle" documents—that is, documents lent by donors who are disabled, pregnant, or no longer able to work. In other cases, donors and recipients may share the same set of identity documents to earn money at the same time.

4. De Genova 2002, 2005, 2007, 2009.

5. Massey et al. 2002: 119.

6. Calavita 1990: 1063.

7. Mahler 1995: 167–71; Martin 1994; Massey et al. 2002: 119.

8. Coutin 2000: 55.

9. NCFH 2012.

10. Aguirre International 2005: viii, 28, 15.

11. Identity loan is likely particularly common in agriculture. In her ethnography of undocumented migrants in Long Island, Sarah Mahler points to the practice of using friends' or relatives' documents when the I-9 form must be filled out; she states that this was successful in the case of cousins "who look somewhat alike" (1995: 170). While Mahler's particular case centered on a woman seeking work in a factory—in an industry where employers may in fact check documents' authenticity—few labor contractors in agriculture rigorously scrutinize work authorization documents because the seasonality and rapid turnover of the workforce make audits and raids uncommon. Indeed, according to the California Agricultural Worker Health Survey (CAWHS), 62 percent and 52 percent of undocumented female and male farmworkers, respectively—and 29 percent of men and 20 percent of women with legal status—said they had used another person's Social Security card for the purposes of employment (Villarejo et al. 2010: 393).

12. Bourgois 1998; Bourgois and Schonberg 2009. See also Lomnitz and Hammel 1977 and Stack 1983 for a discussion of the importance of social networks in the economic survival of marginalized groups. Scholars of immigration have long noted the fact that migrant social networks play a key role in migrant adaptation, but they caution that such networks may be strained by hostile policies in the receiving context. See Menjívar (1997, 2000).

13. Newell 2006; Stack 1983.

14. On family reunification as a principle of the U.S. immigration system, see Boehm 2012: 53–70.

15. Bourdieu 1977.

16. Mahler (1995) observes that predatory economic practices such as the ones discussed in this chapter may result from migrants' exclusion from the formal economy. Preying on the vulnerability of recently arrived and/or undocumented migrants is one of the few forms of entrepreneurial activity available to more established migrants.

17. NFWM 2016a.

18. See Martin 1994.

19. Massey et al. 2002: 91.

20. Mahler 1995: 138.

21. See also Horton 2015, n.d.b.

22. Agricultural employers are excluded from the federal labor laws that govern underage workers in other industries. California is one of only four states that have raised the legal minimum age of employment in agriculture during school sessions to eighteen. See CA DLSE 2013: 64–5.

23. Gomberg-Muñoz 2010, 2011.

24. Farmworker Justice 2009.

25. Coutin 2000.

26. Dowling and Inda 2013: 2, 7.

27. Ibid.: 3. See also Kanstroom 2007.

28. Camayd-Freixas 2009; Dowling and Inda 2013: 1.

29. See Horton n.d.b. In 2008 alone, ICE arrested more than 960 migrants on charges of aggravated identity theft and Social Security fraud (Dowling and Inda 2013: 17).

30. Gilbert 2013; Stuesse and Coleman 2014.

31. In November 2014, an executive order by President Barack Obama replaced Secure Communities (S-Comm) with the Priority Enforcement Program (PEP). When an individual is arrested, both S-COMM and PEP require local and state law enforcement officials to share fingerprints with DHS. Under S-COMM, if fingerprints matched a record in the DHS databases, ICE could request that the law enforcement agency detain the individual for retrieval by ICE. PEP replaces immigration detainers with "requests for notification"—that is, requests that the local agency notify ICE of the individual's release date. However, PEP continues to target undocumented migrants who have not been convicted of a crime as "priorities" for removal. Moreover, according to the memo regarding the new program, under "special circumstances"—which remain undefined—ICE may issue an immigration detainer as well (NILC 2015). On S-Comm, see Kohli, Markowitz, and Chavez 2011.

32. See, for example, Gomberg-Muñoz and Nussbaum-Barberena 2011; Heyman 1998.

33. De Genova 2002, 2007, 2009.

34. Stuesse 2010.

35. Gomberg-Muñoz and Nussbaum-Barberena 2011: 369.

36. On immigration laws as transferring value, see Heyman 2001.

37. See De Genova 2009: 456.

38. Attention to migrant denounceability is not new: Josiah Heyman notes that migrants' necessary immersion in "conspiracies to avoid the law" may lead to the transfer of value to employers and the state (1998: 157). He suggests that the criminalization of undocumented migration as well as of migrants' everyday activities often implicates them in forms of legal compromise that render them liable to exploitation by others. However, two new developments in immigration enforcement and immigration law make this issue particularly deserving of analysis at present. First, in 1996, IIRIRA significantly strengthened the immigration-related consequences of being convicted of practices such as identity theft, imposing extended bars on such migrants' legal re-entry. Then, more recently, ICE has begun charging migrants with criminal violations for document-related charges as a strategy to deter undocumented immigration to the United States (Dowling and Inda 2013: 16–17). Under IIRIRA, then, migrants convicted of such charges face the possibility of permanent exile.

39. Villarejo et al. 2010: 393.

40. *Derecho*—which means both "straight" and "legal"—is often colloquially used to modify "papers," as in the phrase *papeles derechos*. The expression *papeles chuecos* refers to papers that have something wrong with them—that is, papers that are fraudulent or forged (Coutin 2000: 58). Both authorized and undocumented migrants may work *chueco:* that is, they may work under the valid SSN and legal name of another person.

41. Although Raquel did manage to obtain care, her inconvenient injury would cost her compensatory pay. The contractor refused to report the injury to his insurance carrier, as the use of knives violated the conditions of his insurance policy. Ultimately, the contractor paid Raquel under the table to avoid involving the insurance company.

42. Stumpf 2006.

43. Sarabia 2012.

44. Ibid.

45. Menjívar and Abrego 2012: 1380.

CHAPTER 4. *PRESIÓN ALTA*

1. Behar 1993: 163.

2. Rosaldo 1993.

3. Mendenhall et al. 2012.

4. Villarejo et al. 2000: 19.

5. On "everyday violence," see Scheper-Hughes and Bourgois 2004.

6. Chapman and Berggren 2005.

7. Turner 1967.

8. Gravlee 2009.; Singer and Clair 2003; Singer 2009; Mendenhall 2012.

9. Scheper-Hughes and Bourgois 2004.

10. Mendenhall 2012.

11. Ibid.: 24.

12. NFWM 2016b.

13. Villarejo et al. 2000: 27–28.

14. The narrative structure of this chapter, describing events in these women's lives in the present tense rather than retrospectively, attempts to capture the anxiety of living life "in the subjunctive mode"(Good and DelVecchio Good 1994)—that is, with uncertain and constantly shifting outcomes. Those grappling with adverse circumstances are "are in the midst of the stories they tell" and do not know the ending (1994: 838). A retrospective telling risks obliterating the issues most at stake for each woman in the moment.

15. Liao et al. 1997; Pappas, Gergen, and Carroll 1990; Pérez-Stable, Juarbe, and Moreno-John 2001; Ramírez 1996; Sorlie et al. 1993.

16. Acevedo-García and Bates 2008.

17. Ibid.: 107; Lerman-Garber, Villa, and Caballero 2004.

18. Barcellos, Goldman, and Smith 2012.

19. Villarejo et al. 2000: 19, 7.

20. Villarejo 2003: 180.

21. This chapter examines the way that legal minority status causes a range of master stressors for migrant farmworkers, with immigration stress and work stress being principal among them. However, I do not intend to suggest that these master stressors can be easily separated, as either one may precipitate the other.

22. Lighthall 2001: 224.

23. Villarejo et al. 2000: 7.

24. Salinas, Eschbach, and Markides 2008: 297.

25. Brosschot, Gerin, and Thayer 2006; Clark, Benkert, and Flack 2006; Redmond, Baer, and Hicks 2011.

26. Brosschot, Gerin, and Thayer 2006.

27. Hicken et al. 2014.

28. Scheper-Hughes and Bourgois 2004: 1.

29. McEwen 2000; McEwen and Wingfield 2003; Seeman et al. 2010.

30. Duru et al. 2012.

31. See Castañeda 2010: 19; Castañeda et al. 2015: 383.

32. Castañeda 2009: 1553, McGuire and Georges 2003.

33. Menjívar and Abrego 2012.

34. Sáenz, Menjívar, and García. 2013: 166.

35. Heide Castañeda notes similar findings among migrants in Germany, where clinicians used the term *illegal syndrome* to describe the constellation of stress-related health conditions—including depression and anxiety—that they often found among the undocumented migrants they treated, regardless of their national origin (2009: 1558).

36. Duncan 2015: 28.

37. Although Sulema's and Yadira's narratives are redacted, I present the women's descriptions of their internal emotional states verbatim. I retain the Spanish terms they used, as English translations rarely capture the nuances of culturally specific forms of distress such as *coraje, tristeza, susto* (roughly translated as "fright"), and *nervios* (roughly translated as "nerves").

38. David and Collins 1997; Hyman et al. 2000.

39. Colon 2007; McKinley 2007.

40. Chawkins 2007; McKinley 2007.

41. As a former deportee, René was likely apprehended through the National Fugitive Operations Program (NFOP), an ICE program that is intended to focus on migrants with criminal convictions but also targets individuals with deportation orders who have no prior criminal convictions (see Menjívar and Abrego 2012: 1390). The publicity granted NFOP operations—and their targeting of individuals as "fugitives" from the law—further conflates undocumented migrants and "criminals" in the minds of the public.

42. See Stuesse and Coleman 2014.

43. See Kohli, Markowitz, and Chavez 2011.

44. New York Times Editorial Board 2014.

45. Because of concern that Secure Communities (S-Comm) jeopardized relations between the police and migrant communities and led to the deportation of law-abiding residents, the California legislature significantly modified the program by passing the Trust Act in 2013. Under this legislation, only arrestees convicted of serious crimes—such as rape or murder—are subject to immigration holds by police. Those arrested for less serious offenses are not detained for deportation by ICE. The law went into effect on January 1, 2014. Inspired in part by the Trust Act, in November 2014 President Obama created the Priority Enforcement Program (PEP) to replace S-Comm and reduce the risk of deporting "families" rather than "felons" (Linthicum 2014). However, critics of PEP point out that undocumented migrants remain a priority for removal under the program and that ICE has retained its prerogative to issue detainers under "special circumstances," which are not defined (see NILC 2015).

46. Kohli, Markowitz, and Chavez 2011.

47. See Holmes 2013: 158–72.

48. See Phelan 2011.

49. See Chacón 2013; Kanstroom 2007; Stumpf 2006; Golash-Boza 2014; Menjívar and Abrego 2012.

50. On June 15, 2012, President Obama created the Deferred Action for Childhood Arrivals program for undocumented youths who came to the United States before the age of sixteen. The status grants youths a temporary stay of deportation and allows them to apply for authorization to work. To be eligible, however, youths must be at least fifteen when they apply, a rule that disqualifies Ramón's younger undocumented siblings.

51. Finkler 1991, 1997; Mendenhall et al. 2010, 2012; Mercado-Martínez and Ramos-Herrera 2002.

52. Finkler 1994.

53. Mendenhall et al. 2010, 2012.

54. In a similar fashion, researchers have recently suggested that depression be viewed not only as a consequence of diabetes but also a potential cause (see Mendenhall 2012: 21).

55. Thus the burden of *coraje* may be borne by family members in migrants' sending communities as well.

56. Golash-Boza 2014; Kanstroom 2007; Menjívar and Abrego 2012.

57. Chapman and Berggren 2005.

CHAPTER 5. ÁLVARO'S CASKET

1. On the cardiovascular implications of heat strain, see Jackson and Rosenberg 2010.

2. NHLBI 2011.

3. Singer 1996, 2009.

4. Singer and Clair 2003: 428.

5. Farmer 1999; Gravlee 2009; Krieger 2005, 2008.

6. Singer 1996.

7. Singer 2009: xiv.

8. Singer and Clair 2003: 431.

9. Villarejo et al. 2000: 19–21.

10. Mendenhall 2012. The 1999 California Agricultural Worker Health Survey (CAWHS) is perhaps the only study to attempt a clinical assessment of the serum glucose measures of farmworkers, although it did not conduct a fasting serum glucose measure. While the recommended range is 65–115 milligrams per deciliter (mg/dl) for fasting subjects, the CAWHS found that 4.3 percent of men had serum glucose levels above 200 mg/dl, and nearly all of these had levels above 260 mg/dl. The report concludes that further research is needed to "clarify the extent of this condition among agricultural workers" (Villarejo et al. 2000: 24).

11. Even as the Affordable Care Act has allowed more migrants with legal status to receive subsidized care, it has had the ironic effect of increasing barriers to care for undocumented migrants in California by leading to diminished funding for county indigent programs. By state law, county health care programs

have historically served as health care providers of last resort for the uninsured, many of them undocumented. Fresno County's Medically Indigent Services Program (MISP) makes low-income uninsured adults eligible for up to three months of reduced-cost specialty treatment at a variety of community health centers. Yet the state used the reduction of the number of the state's uninsured that resulted from ACA as a justification to divert $900 million in funding from county indigent programs to finance the Medi-Cal expansion. To cope with the reduction in state funds, the Fresno County Board of Supervisors voted to exclude the undocumented from the program in January 2014 (Plevin 2014). Because undocumented migrants now constitute over half of the state's uninsured population (Karlamangla 2015), the reduction in funding for county programs disproportionately penalizes those without legal status.

12. In 1986, Congress amended the Emergency Medical Treatment and Labor Act (EMTALA) to specifically exclude undocumented migrants from full Medicaid benefits while providing for the treatment of their "emergency medical condition[s]" (Rodriguez 2015: 62). This federal exclusion created the state programs we know as Emergency Medicaid, which cover undocumented migrants' emergency care. The state of California created two such programs: Emergency Medi-Cal, which covers emergency treatment for low-income migrant men and women, and Restricted Medi-Cal, which covers low-income migrant women's prenatal care, labor and delivery services, and up to sixty days of post-partum care. U.S.-born children of undocumented parents who meet eligibility requirements qualify for full Medicaid coverage.

13. In addition to the temporary care they receive through Restricted Medi-Cal, undocumented migrant women occasionally receive limited screenings through the Family Planning, Access, Care and Treatment Program, or Family PACT. Delivered through the California Department of Health Care Services, Family PACT provides free family planning services and contraception to low-income men and women who do not qualify for Medi-Cal (CA DHCS n.d.). The program provides migrant women not only with free contraception but also with Pap smears; in rare cases, kindly doctors extend its reach to provide them with additional diagnostic care. For many undocumented migrant women, Family PACT is the closest they come to receiving a regular checkup. Yet, like Restricted Medi-Cal, Family PACT is a form of collateral care. Once migrants lose their reproductive capacity—whether through age or through medical procedures—they become ineligible for the program's services. Moreover, Family PACT's focus on reproductive health circumscribes its reach among men, who typically view it as for "women's issues" alone.

14. Castañeda 2010: 13; Hoffman 2006: 237–38.

15. The federal Migrant Education program, established through Title I of the Elementary and Secondary Education Act of 1965, funds the mobile van that visits Mendota once a year, along with an annual school clinic that offers preventive screenings to the district's migrant students.

16. Menjívar 2002.

17. Villarejo et al. 2000: 19–21.

18. The syndemic interaction between pesticide exposure and diabetes deserves further study. Cox et al. (2007), for example, found that blood serum

concentrations of certain pesticides were associated with a higher prevalence of self-reported diabetes among Mexican Americans.

19. Even as a burgeoning literature links pesticide exposure to both metabolic and endocrine disorders, the state, agribusiness companies, and insurance companies continue to normalize pesticide exposure. In fact, some agribusiness companies portray the use of pesticides as essential not only to company survival but also to farmworkers' economic well-being (Saxton 2015: 176). On the connection between pesticides and heat stress, see Rao 2007: 8.

20. According to an analysis performed by the CDC of death certificates in which heat was a contributing rather than an underlying factor, cardiovascular disease was recorded as the underlying cause of death in more than half of these cases (CDC 2006).

21. Bautista v. Cal-OSHA n.d.: 43–46.

22. Ibid.: 46.

23. CDC 2006. As the CDC observes, unless a clinician is immediately present and able to observe and record the clinical signs of heat illness, heat death may often go undetected.

24. Donoghue et al. 1997.

25. Good 1994; Luhrmann 2000.

26. In 1998, the U S. Food and Drug Administration (FDA) issued a set of general recommendations for the produce industry to minimize "microbial hazards" in the production of fresh fruits and vegetables; these guidelines served as a benchmark for the checklists created by U.S.-based third-party auditors. In 2000, major food retailers formed a nonprofit foundation called the Global Food Safety Initiative (GFSI), which issued its own food-safety standards based on guidelines established by European trade associations. Thus, while U.S. chains and restaurants such as Subway and Wegman's may require that their produce suppliers undergo audits based on the FDA regulations, global retailers such as Walmart and Kroeger's demand that they be certified through a GFSI-recognized scheme. The net result is what industry experts call *audit fatigue:* large growers may find themselves facing as many different food-safety audits as they have buyers.

27. There is no mandatory government audit system for the produce industry. FDA inspections and fines are triggered only by outbreaks, such as the 2011 listeriosis outbreak linked to Jensen Farms in Colorado that led to at least thirty deaths. The FDA has only 1,100 inspectors to monitor 167,000 domestic farms or food facilities in the United States (Bronstein and Griffin 2012).

28. See CCAB 2014; LGMA 2013.

29. In order to protect the privacy of Álvaro's family, I have changed the distinguishing characteristics of the individuals described at the funeral as well as the location where he worked.

30. CDC 2006.

31. Bugarin and Lopez 1998.

32. Benson 2011, 2014; Benson and Kirsch 2010.

33. Benson and Kirsch 2010: 460.

34. The lax monitoring of farmworkers' safety by the state is due to insufficient personnel: a federal oversight report on Cal-OSHA found that it had staffing

adequate to conduct an audit of each of California's workplaces once every 170 years (OSHA 2014).

35. On the "hiddenness" of farmwork, see Holmes 2013: 51.

36. Martin 1994.

37. On the "plight" of farmers, see Benson 2011.

38. CDC 2008.

39. González-Guarda, Florom-Smith, and Thomas 2011.

40. Milstein 2001: 2, cited in Singer and Clair 2003: 425.

CHAPTER 6. *DESABILITADO*

To write this chapter, I supplemented my long-term ethnography with Don Tomás, whom I met in 2008 and who was diagnosed with kidney failure in 2012, with interviews and ethnography with five additional migrant men with kidney failure. I also conducted interviews with two nephrologists, the Finance Manager at UCSF's Transplant Center, and two scientists in the Division of Renal Diseases and Hypertension at the University of Colorado, Denver, about the epidemic of chronic kidney disease of unknown origin in Central America and its potential existence in California's Central Valley.

1. Almaguer et al. 2014; Lebov et al. 2015; Ordunez et al. 2014; Peraza et al. 2012; Trabanino et al. 2015; Weaver, Fadrowski, and Jaar 2015.

2. Ibid.

3. The epidemic is widespread. In El Salvador, kidney failure was the leading cause of hospital deaths among men and the fifth among women in 2011 (Orantes et al. 2011). Researchers suggest that up to 13 percent of the population in Nicaragua may suffer from the disease, with documented prevalence rates of greater than 8 percent in some mining and agricultural communities (Almaguer et al. 2014).

4. Lock 1993.

5. Wijkstrom et al. 2013.

6. Ordunez et al. 2014.

7. Brooks 2009; see also Lakhani 2015 for a critical analysis of the World Bank's use of the Brooks study—funded in part by Ingenio San Antonio (ISA), the largest sugar mill in Nicaragua—to defend its multimillion-dollar loans to the sugarcane industry, including ISA.

8. Peraza et al. 2012.

9. Trabanino et al. 2015.

10. While mounting data suggest that physiological changes initiated by intensive agricultural work are implicated in kidney damage, these findings do not rule out pesticide exposure as a contributing factor. Indeed, the Salvadoran study of the effects of work on kidney function also found that 74 percent of the workers with elevated serum creatinine levels reported the use of carbamate pesticides, as opposed to 29 percent of those without (Trabanino et al. 2015). As one review of the literature states, the kidney may be "hit doubly hard" by pesticide exposure, as such toxins accumulate in the kidneys before they are excreted. Dehydration and profuse sweating in hot environments may further concentrate the levels of toxins in the kidneys (Almaguer et al. 2014).

11. See Fairfood International n.d.

12. As in the Central American epidemic—which may have been going on for decades—the lack of adequate health care access and surveillance systems may be preventing the identification of CKDu among farmworkers in the United States. A poster presented at the Second International Workshop on Mesoamerican Nephropathy in Costa Rica in 2015 suggests that CKDu may be occurring among California farmworkers. It found an 11 percent prevalence of acute kidney injury, which may develop into CKDu, and suggests that dehydrated workers bear twice the risk of developing it (Moyce et al. 2015).

13. Farmer 2001, 2006.

14. Horton 2014; Park et al. 2000: 9.

15. For reasons not yet understood, chronic kidney failure appears to reduce the activity of the clearing enzymes of the liver, increasing the blood levels of unhealthy cholesterols—triglycerides and LDL—while reducing HDL, the healthy cholesterol (Foley and Parfrey 1998; National Kidney Foundation n.d.)

16. Because SDI is funded through wage deductions, undocumented migrants are eligible for this benefit if they can show proof of earning at least $300 in the twelve-month period prior to filing a claim.

17. SSDI is funded in part through Federal Insurance Contributions Act (FICA) deductions from workers' paychecks, whereas SSI is funded through general tax revenues. Undocumented migrants contribute to the SSDI fund through wage deductions and to SSI by paying taxes. However, the Social Security Protection Act of 2004 made undocumented workers ineligible for both disability programs (Nuschler and Siskin 2005: CRS-4). Moreover, because SSI is a means-tested public benefit, access to SSI for noncitizens is restricted. The 1996 Personal Responsibility and Work Opportunity Reconciliation Act rendered legal permanent residents ineligible for such means-tested benefits for the first five years of their residence in the United States and barred migrants with only a temporary work authorization (TPS status) from collecting the benefit (Wasem 2014: 1).

18. See Conrad 2007; Lock 1993; Scheper-Hughes 1992.

19. Bugarin and Lopez 1998.

20. SSA n.d.b.

21. SSA n.d.c.

22. The company's workers' compensation insurance carrier was able to disclaim responsibility for Don Tomás's hospital stay because his diabetes was a "preexisting condition." Ironically, Don Tomás says it would have benefited him if his diabetes had not been diagnosed until he fainted at work.

23. SSA n.d.b.

24. SSA n.d.c.

25. Collins et al. 2010.

26. Linden, Cano, and Coritsidis 2012.

27. Many studies document the phenomenon of migrants' returning to their homelands for care following acute illnesses, mental health crises, and accidents. See Bergmark, Barr, and García 2008; Duncan 2015.

28. Burawoy 1976.

29. Wijkstrom et al. 2013.

30. In 1986, Congress amended the Emergency Medical Treatment and Labor Act (EMTALA) to specifically exclude undocumented migrants from full-scope Medicaid benefits while providing for the treatment of such migrants' "emergency medical condition[s]." It also specifically barred undocumented migrants from receiving "care and services" "related to an organ transplant procedure." Yet the Act defines an "emergency medical condition" quite broadly—as "a medical condition (including emergency labor and delivery) manifesting itself by acute symptoms of sufficient severity (including severe pain) such that the absence of immediate medical attention could reasonably be expected to result in placing the patient' s health in serious jeopardy, serious impairment to bodily functions, or serious dysfunction of any bodily organ or part." Moreover, it limits the covered services to those required "after the sudden onset" of such an emergency (Rodriguez 2015: 62).

31. Linden, Cano, and Coritsidis 2012. For excellent analyses of the treatment of undocumented patients on dialysis in states in which Emergency Medicaid covers only emergency dialysis, see Kline 2015; Melo and Fleuriet 2016.

32. According to the finance manager of the UCSF Transplant Center, undocumented migrants are eligible to be placed on the UNOS organ-transplant list if they have insurance that will cover their post-transplant care. This could be private insurance or the Major Risk Medical Insurance Plan, a state plan that individuals may purchase that has a $750,000 lifetime maximum payout. "So that's a limit that's good enough for a transplant, and it covers them for some of the post[-transplant care]," she says. However, the cost of the insurance is a barrier; she says that the monthly premium for a middle-aged patient without children is about $500.

33. Linden, Cano, and Coritsidis 2012.

34. Good and DelVecchio Good 1994: 837.

35. Lock 1993.

36. See Smith-Nonini 2011.

CONCLUSION

1. Mohan 2015.

2. Singer 2009.

3. See Gomberg-Muñoz 2010, 2011.

4. Menjívar and Abrego 2012.

5. Farmer 2001; Holmes 2013: 190–91.

6. López 2007: 99–100; Martin 1994.

7. Berger 2014.

8. Fuller 2015.

9. Sorrentino 2015.

10. Farmworker Justice 2009.

11. Kohli, Markowitz, and Chavez 2011.

12. See NILC 2013.

13. AB 1897 also addresses the difficulty that labor contractors are often transient and difficult to hold accountable: they may declare bankruptcy and

reincorporate under a new name, escaping past judgments for lost wages or labor violations (Horn 2014). Thus the new law allows workers additional legal recourse if they are stiffed pay or suffer heatstroke.

14. Karlamangla 2015.

15. See Marrow 2012.

16. Ibid.

17. Oxfam 2014.

18. DIR n.d.b. To comply with this recommendation for hydration, stackers require protections that exceed the current Cal-OSHA requirement of a ten-minute break every two hours when the temperature exceeds 95 degrees. If stackers were to rehydrate only every two hours, they would need to drink two quarts of water during each break. Not only is this impractical, but rapid, excessive water consumption can lead to water intoxication, which itself may be deadly.

19. See Holmes 2013; Rothenberg 1998.

APPENDIX A

1. Agar 2008.

2. Kleinman 1998: 417.

3. See Kirsch 2002; Low and Merry 2010.

4. Borofsky 2007.

5. See Rylko-Bauer, Singer, and Van Willigen 2006; Singer 2000.

6. Ibid.

7. See Lamphere 2004; Low and Merry 2010.

8. Bourgois and Schonberg 2009.

9. See, for example, Johnston and Barker 2008.

10. Hale 2006; Scheper-Hughes 1995; Speed 2006.

11. See Marcus and Fischer 1986.

12. See Clifford 1983.

13. See Biehl 2005; Bourgois and Schonberg 2009; Gomberg-Muñoz 2011.

14. Sanjek 2014.

15. I am indebted to Bill Alexander for his analysis of the implications of this book's privileging of farmworkers' critiques of policy.

16. Bourgois and Schonberg 2009; Hale 2006; Speed 2006.

17. Low and Merry 2010.

18. Bourgois and Schonberg 2009.

19. Kleinman 1998: 418.

APPENDIX B

1. See Singer 1999.

2. Holmes 2013b; Rothenberg 1998.

3. Singer 1999.

4. For a discussion of the research abuses of the past, see Singer 1999.

5. In order to abide by IRB regulations, I deliberately wrote a section into my consent form requesting permission to retain interviewees' contact information

after the conclusion of my study. I also obtained a Certificate of Confidentiality from the National Institutes of Health—an important measure to protect my participants' anonymity and confidentiality, as my research uncovered sensitive information.

6. Scheper-Hughes 1992: 29.

7. For a discussion of this dilemma, see Bourgois and Schonberg 2009: 15.

References

Acevedo-García, Dolores, and Lisa M. Bates. 2008. "Latino Health Paradoxes: Empirical Evidence, Explanations, Future Research, and Implications." In *Latinas/os in the United States: Changing the Face of America,* ed. Havidan Rodríguez, Rogelio Sáenz, and Cecilia Menívar, 101–13. New York: Springer.

Adams, Vincanne. 2013. *Markets of Sorrow, Labors of Faith: New Orleans in the Wake of Katrina.* Durham, NC: Duke University Press.

Agar, Michael H. 2008. *The Professional Stranger: An Informal Introduction to Ethnography.* Bingley, UK: Emerald Group Publishing.

Aguirre International. 2005. *The California Farm Labor Force: Overview and Trends from the National Agricultural Workers Study.* Burlingame, CA: Aguirre International.

Almaguer, Miguel, Raúl Herrera, and Carlos M. Orantes. 2014. "Chronic Kidney Disease of Unknown Etiology in Agricultural Communities." *MEDICC Review* 16 (2):9–15.

American Civil Liberties Union of California and American Friends Service Committee. 2014. "CHP Vehicle Impoundments Disproportionately Impacted Latinos." August 14.www.aclunc.org/news/chp-vehicle-impoundments-disproportionately-impacted-latinos.

Andreas, Peter. 1998. "The U.S. Immigration Control Offensive: Constructing an Image of Order on the Southwest Border." In *Crossings: Mexican Immigration in Interdisciplinary Perspectives,* ed. M. Marcelo Suárez-Orozco, 342–61. Cambridge, MA: David Rockefeller Center for Latin American Studies, Harvard University.

Arax, Mark. 2005. "Deaths Rally Farm Laborers." *Los Angeles Times,* July 28. http://articles.latimes.com/2005/jul/28/local/me-heat28.

Associated Press. 2013. "Calif. Officials Probe Worker Deaths." *San Jose Mercury News*. July 5. www.mercurynews.com/ci_23605063/calif-officials-probe-worker-deaths, accessed October 12, 2014.

Barbassa, Julian. 2005. "New Rules Make Toil under the Sun Safer." *San Diego Tribune*, August 17. http://www.sandiegouniontribune.com/uniontrib/20050817/news_1n17heat.html.

Barcellos, Silvia Helena, Dana P. Goldman, and James P. Smith. 2012. "Undiagnosed Disease, Especially Diabetes, Casts Doubt on Some of Reported Health Advantage' of Recent Mexican Immigrants." *Health Affairs* 31 (12): 2727–37.

Bautista v. Cal-OSHA. n.d. Complaint for Declaratory and Injunctive Relief and Writ of Mandate. Los Angeles: Superior Court of the State of California, City and County of Los Angeles. www.publiccounsel.org/tools/assets/files/Bautista-v-Cal-OSHA-Complaint-10–18–2012-with-exhibits.pdf, accessed August 12, 2014.

Behar, Ruth. 1993. *Translated Woman: Crossing the Border with Esperanza's Story*. Boston: Beacon Press.

Belluck, Pam. 2008. "Settlement Will Allow Thousands of Mexican Laborers in U.S. to Collect Back Pay." *New York Times*. October 15. www.nytimes.com/2008/10/16/us/16settle.html?fta=y&_r=1&, accessed October 12, 2015.

Benson, Peter. 2011. *Tobacco Capitalism: Growers, Migrant Workers, and the Changing Face of a Global Industry*. Princeton, NJ: Princeton University Press.

———. 2014. "Corporate Paternalism and the Problem of Harmful Products." *PoLAR* 37 (2): 218–30.

Benson, Peter, and Stuart Kirsch. 2010. "Capitalism and the Politics of Resignation." *Current Anthropology* 51 (4): 459–86.

Berger, Joseph. 2014. "Long Day in the Fields, without Earning Overtime." *New York Times*. August 7, 2014. www.nytimes.com/2014/08/08/nyregion/in-harvest-season-endless-hours-with-no-overtime-for-new-york-farmworkers.html, accessed February 6, 2015.

Bergmark, R., D. Barr, and R. García. "Mexican Immigrants in the U.S. Living Far from the Border May Return to Mexico for Health Services." Journal of Immigrant and Minority Health 12 (4): 610–14.

Bethel, Jeffrey W., and Renee Harger. 2014. "Heat-Related Illness among Oregon Farmworkers." *Journal of Environmental Research in Public Health* 11 (9): 9273–85.

Biehl, João. 2005. *Vita: Life in a Zone of Social Abandonment*. Berkeley: University of California Press.

Boehm, Deborah A. 2012. *Intimate Migrations: Gender, Family, and Illegality among Transnational Mexicans*. New York: New York University Press.

Borofsky, Robert. 2007. "Defining Public Anthropology: A Personal Perspective." Center for Public Anthrolopology blog, www.publicanthropology.org/public-anthropology/, accessed June 2, 2015.

Bourdieu, Pierre. 1977. *Outline of a Theory of Practice*. Translated by Richard Nice. Cambridge: Cambridge University Press.

———. 1984. *Distinction: A Social Critique of the Judgment of Taste*. Translated by Richard Nice. Cambridge, MA: Harvard University Press.

———. 2000. *Pascalian Meditations*. Translated by Richard Nice. Stanford, CA: Stanford University Press.

———. 2001. *Masculine Domination*. Translated by Richard Nice. Stanford, CA: Stanford University Press.

Bourgois, Philippe. 1998. "The Moral Economies of Homeless Heroin Addicts: Confronting Ethnography, HIV Risk, and Everyday Violence in San Francisco Shooting Camps." *Substance Use and Misuse* 33 (11): 2323–51.

———. 2003. *In Search of Respect: Selling Crack in El Barrio*. 2nd ed. Cambridge: Cambridge University Press.

Bourgois, Philippe, and Jeffrey Schonberg. 2009. *Righteous Dopefiend*. Berkeley: University of California Press.

Branco, Shellie. 2006. "Settlement Made in Death." *Bakersfield Californian*, October 7, www.bakersfield.com/news/2006/10/07/settlement-made-in-death.

Brandes, Stanley. 1988. *Power and Persuasion: Fiestas and Social Control in Mexico*. Philadelphia: University of Pennsylvania Press.

Bronstein, Scott, and Drew Griffin. 2012. "Third-Deadliest U.S. Food Outbreak was Preventable, Experts Say." *CNN News*. May 3, 2012. www.cnn.com/2012/05/03/health/listeria-outbreak-investigation, accessed July 12, 2015.

Brooks, Daniel. 2009. *Final Scoping Study Report: Epidemiology of Chronic Kidney Disease in Nicaragua*. Boston University School of Public Health. www.cao-ombudsman.org/cases/document-links/documents/03H_BU_FINAL_report_scopestudyCRI_18.Dec.2009.pdf, accessed September 1, 2015.

Brosschot, Jos F., William Gerin, and Julian F. Thayer. 2006. "The Perseverative Cognition Hypothesis: A Review of Worry, Prolonged Stress-related Physiological Activation, and Health." *Journal of Psychosomatic Research* 60 (2): 113–24.

Bugarin, Alicia, and Elias Lopez 1998. "Farmworkers in California." California Research Bureau, www.library.ca.gov/crb/CRBReports.html, accessed January 5, 2012.

Burawoy, Michael. 1976. "The Functions and Reproduction of Migrant Labor: Comparative Material from Southern Africa and the United States." *American Journal of Sociology* 81 (5): 1050–87.

Burke, Garance. 2008. "More Farm Deaths in Heat despite Calif. Crackdown." *USA Today*, August 20. http://usatoday30.usatoday.com/news/nation/2008-08-20-3205167992_x.htm, accessed September 25, 2014.

CA DHCS (California Department of Health Care Services) n.d. *Welcome to Family PACT*, www.familypact.org/, accessed September 10, 2014.

Calavita, Kitty. 1990. "Employer Sanctions Violations: Toward a Dialectical Model of White-Collar Crime." *Law and Society Review* 24 (4): 1041–69.

———. 1994. "United States Immigration and Policy Responses: The Limits of Legislation." In *Controlling Immigration*, ed. Wayne Cornelius, Philip Martin, and James Hollifield, 55–82. Stanford, CA: Stanford University Press.

California Department of Food and Agriculture. 2015. *California Department of Food and Agriculture: 96 Years Protecting and Promoting Agriculture in the Golden State*. Sacramento, CA: California Department of Food and Agriculture. www.cdfa.ca.gov/CDFA-History.html, accessed July 12, 2015.

Cal-OSHA (California Occupational Safety and Health Program). 2013. "High Heat Advisory: Cal/OSHA Cautions Employers of Increased Risks as Heat Wave Continues in Central Valley." News Release No: 13–35. www.dir.ca.gov/DIRNews/2013/IR2013-35.pdf, accessed July 3, 2013.

———. 2014a. *Heat Illness Prevention Training*. www.dir.ca.gov/DOSH/HeatIllnessInfo.html, accessed March 2014.

———. 2014b. *Pocket Guide: Protect Yourself from Heat Illness*. www.dir.ca.gov/dosh/dosh_publications/HeatIllnessEmployeeEngSpan.pdf.

———. 2014c. *State OSHA Annual Report (SOAR), Federal FY 2013*, www.dir.ca.gov/dosh/reports/State-OSHA-Annual-Report-%28SOAR%29-FY-2013.pdf.

Cal-OSHA Reporter. 2015. "Flash Report! Heat Illness Changes Approved—It's Training Time." *Cal-OSHA Reporter*. February 20. www.cal- osha.com/Heat-Illness-Changes-Approved-Its-Training-Time.aspx, accessed February 21, 2015.

Calvan, Bobby Caina. 2005. "Heat Takes Its Toll in Fields, and California Seeks Relief." *Boston Globe*, August 7, www.boston.com/news/nation/articles/2005/08/07/heat_takes_its_toll_in_fields_and_california_seeks_relief/.

Camayd-Freixas, Eric. 2009. "Interpreting after the Largest ICE Raid in U.S. History: A Personal Account." *Latino Studies* 7 (1): 123–39.

Cartwright, Elizabeth. 2011. "Immigrant Dreams: Legal Pathologies and Structural Vulnerabilities along the Immigration Continuum." *Medical Anthropology: Cross-Cultural Studies of Health and Illness* 30 (5): 475–95.

Castañeda, Heide. 2007. "Paternity for Sale: Anxieties over Demographic "Theft" and Undocumented Migrant Reproduction in Germany." *Medical Anthropology Quarterly* 22 (4): 340–59.

———. 2009. "Illegality as Risk Factor: A Survey of Unauthorized Migrant Patients in a Berlin Clinic." *Social Science and Medicine* 68: 1552–60.

———. 2010. "Im/migration and Health: Conceptual, Methodological, and Theoretical Propositions for Applied Anthropology." Special issue, "Anthropological Perspectives on Migration and Health," *Annals of Anthropological Practice* 34 (1): 6–27.

Castañeda, Heide, Laura Heidbrink, and Kristin Yarris. 2014. "From Alienation to Protection: Central American Child Migration." *Access Denied*, September 4, 2014. https://accessdeniedblog.wordpress.com/2014/09/04/from-alienation-to-protection-central-american-child-migration-heide-castaneda-lauren-heidbrink-and-kristin-yarris, accessed November 16, 2014.

Castañeda, Heide, Seth M. Holmes, Daniel S. Madrigal, Maria-Elena Trinidad Young, Naomi Beyeler, and James Quesada. 2015. "Immigration as a Social Determinant of Health." *Annual Review of Public Health* 36: 375–92.

CCAB (California Cantaloupe Advisory Board). 2014. *Food Safety Audit: California Cantaloupe Advisory Board Audit Verification Checklist-Field & Harvesting*. April 17. www.californiacantaloupes.com/sites/default/files/Audit%20Checklist—%20Field%20and%20Harvest.pdf, accessed March 3, 2015.

CDC (Centers for Disease Control and Prevention). 2006. "Heat-Related Deaths: United States, 1999–2003." *Morbidity and Mortality Weekly Report* 55 (29): 796–98.

———. 2008. "Heat-Related Deaths among Crop Workers: United States, 1992–2006." *Morbidity and Mortality Weekly Report* 57 (24): 649–53.

Chacón, Jennifer M. 2013. "The Security Myth: Punishing Immigrants in the Name of National Security." In *Governing Immigration through Crime: A Reader,* ed. Julie A. Dowling and Jonathan Xavier Inda, 77–94. Stanford, CA: Stanford University Press.

Chapman, Rachel, and J.R. Berggren. 2005. "Radical Contextualization: Contributions to an Anthropology of Racial/Ethnic Health Disparities." *Health* 9 (2): 145–67.

Chavez, Leo. 1992. *Shadowed Lives: Undocumented Immigrants in American Society*. New York: Harcourt Brace.

Chawkins, Steve. 2007. "A Big Voice in a Heated Debate." *Los Angeles Times*. June 24. http://articles.latimes.com/2007/jun/24/local/me-autry24/2.

Clark, Rodney, Ramona A. Benkert, and John M. Flack. 2006. "Large Arterial Elasticity Varies as a Function of Gender and Racism-Related Vigilance in Black Youth." *Journal of Adolescent Health* 39 (4): 562–69.

Clifford, James. 1983. "On Ethnographic Authority." *Representations* 2: 118–46.

Cohen, Deborah. 2011. *Braceros: Migrant Citizens and Transnational Subjects in the Postwar United States and Mexico*. Chapel Hill: University of North Carolina Press.

Collins A.J., R.N. Foley, C. Herzog, B.M. Chavers, D. Gilbertson, A. Ishani, B.L. Kasiske, et al. 2010. "US Renal Data System 2009 Annual Data Report." *American Journal of Kidney Disease* 55 (1 Suppl 1): S1.

Colon, Vanessa. 2007. "Roundup of Illegals Shakes Mendota: Federal Action Splits Families, Empties Streets; City to Consider Resolution Opposing the Raids." *Fresno Bee*. February 27, 2007. www.capsweb.org/roundup-illegals-shakes-mendota, accessed June 2, 2015.

Conrad, Peter. 2007. *The Medicalization of Society: On the Transformation of Human Conditions into Treatable Disorders*. Baltimore: Johns Hopkins University Press.

———. 2001. "Death at the Border: Efficacy and Unintended Consequences of US Immigration Control Policy." *Population and Development Review* 27 (4): 661–85.

Cornelius, Wayne, and Idean Salehyan. 2007. "Does Border Enforcement Deter Unauthorized Immigration? The Case of Mexican Migration to the United States of America." *Regulation and Governance* 1: 139–53.

Coutin, Susan Bibler. 2000. *Legalizing Moves: Salvadoran Immigrants' Struggle for US Residency*. Ann Arbor: University of Michigan Press.

———. 2007. *Nations of Emigrants: Shifting Boundaries of Citizenship in El Salvador and the United States*. Ithaca, NY: Cornell University Press.

Cox, John. 2012. "Lawsuit Accuses California of Overlooking Heat Illness Threats to Farmworkers." *Bakersfield Californian*. October 18. www.bakersfieldcalifornian.com/business/x1250042700/Lawsuit-accuses-Cal-OSHA-of-overlooking-heat-illness-threats-to-farmworkers, accessed July 23, 2014.

———. 2013. "UFW Calls for "Aggressive" Heat Illness Enforcement." *Bakersfield Californian*. July 8. www.bakersfieldcalifornian.com/local/x1538233434

/UFW-calls-for-aggressive-heat-illness-enforcement-after-farmworker-dies, accessed July 22, 2014.

Cox, Shanna, Amanda Sue Niskar, K.M. Venkat Narayan, and Michele Marcus. 2007. "Prevalence of Self-Reported Diabetes and Exposure to Organochlorine Pesticides among Mexican Americans: Hispanic Health and Nutrition Examination Survey, 1982–1984." *Environmental Health Perspectives* 115 (2): 1747–52.

Das, Veena. 1997. *Critical Events: An Anthropological Perspective on Contemporary India.* Delhi: Oxford University Press.

David, Richard J., and James W. Collins, Jr. 1997. "Differing Birth Weight among Infants of U.S.-Born Blacks, African-Born Blacks, and U.S.-Born Whites." *New England Journal of Medicine* 337: 1209–14.

De Genova, Nicholas. 2002. "Migrant 'Illegality' and Deportability in Everyday Life." *Annual Reviews of Anthropology* 31: 419–47.

———. 2005. *Working the Boundaries: Race, Space, and "Illegality" in Mexican Chicago.* Durham, NC: Duke University Press.

———. 2007. "The Production of Culprits: From Deportability to Detainability in the Aftermath of 'Homeland Security.'" *Citizenship Studies* 11 (5): 421–48.

———. 2009. "Conflicts of Mobility, and the Mobility of Conflict: Rightlessness, Presence, Subjectivity, Freedom." *Subjectivity* 29: 445–66.

DIR (Department of Industrial Relations). n.d.a. *Heat Illness Prevention Standard.* California Code of Regulations, Title 8, Section 3395. www.dir.ca.gov /Title8/3395.html, accessed July 22, 2014.

———. n.d.b. *Pocket Guide: Protect Yourself from Heat Illness.* www.dir .ca.gov/dosh/dosh_publications/HeatIllnessEmployeeEngSpan.pdf, accessed August 29, 2015.

Donoghue, E.R., M.A. Graham, J.M. Jentzen, B.D. Lifschultz, J.L. Luke, and H.G. Mirchandani. 1997. "Criteria for the Diagnosis of Heat-related Deaths: National Association of Medical Examiners; Position Paper." *American Journal of Forensic Medical Pathology* 18: 11–14.

Dowling, Julie A., and Jonathan Xavier Inda. 2013. *Governing Immigration through Crime: A Reader.* Stanford, CA: Stanford University Press.

Duncan, Whitney L. 2015. "Transnational Disorders: Return Migrants at Oaxaca's Psychiatric Hospital." *Medical Anthropology Quarterly* 29 (1): 24–41.

Duru, O. Kenrik, Nina T. Harawa, Dulcie Kermah, and Keith C. Norris. 2012. "Allostatic Load Burden and Racial Disparities in Mortality." *Journal of the National Medical Association* 104 (1–2): 89–95.

Everett, Charles J., Ivar L. Frithsen, Vanessa A. Diaz, Richelle J. Koopman, Wiliam M. Simpson Jr., and Arch G. Mainous III. 2007. "Association of a Polychlorinated Dibenzo-p-dioxin, a Polychlorinated Biphenyl, and DDT with Diabetes." *Environmental Research* 103 (3): 413–18.

Fairfood International. n.d. *Sugarcane Workers and Chronic Kidney Disease.* www.fairfood.org/sugarcane-workers-and-chronic-kidney-disease/, accessed November 1, 2015.

Farmer, Paul. 1999. *Infections and Inequalities: The Modern Plagues.* Berkeley: University of California Press.

———. 2006. *AIDS and Accusation: Haiti and the Geography of Blame*. Berkeley: University of California Press.

Farmworker Justice. 2009. *State Workers' Compensation Coverage for Agricultural Workers*. http://farmworkerjustice.org/sites/default/files/documents/6.3.a.1State_Workers_Comp_Information_for_Health_Centers_11-09.pdf, accessed November 12, 2014.

FDA (U.S. Food and Drug Administration). 1998. *Guidance for Industry: Guide to Minimize Microbial Food Safety Hazards for Fresh Fruits and Vegetables*. Center for Food Safety and Applied Nutrition, U.S. Department of Health and Human Services. www.fda.gov/downloads/Food/GuidanceRegulation/UCM169112.pdf, accessed July 12, 2015.

Finkler, Kaja. 1991. *Physicians at Work, Patients in Pain: Biomedical Practice and Patient Response in Mexico*. Boulder, CO: Westview Press.

———. 1994. *Women in Pain: Gender and Morbidity in Mexico*. Philadelphia: University of Pennsylvania Press.

———. 1997. "Gender, Domestic Violence, and Sickness in Mexico." *Social Science and Medicine* 45 (8): 1147–60.

Foley, R.N. and P.S. Parfrey. 1998. "Cardiovascular Disease and Mortality in ESRD." *Journal of Nephrology* 11 (5): 239–45.

Fleischer, Nancy L., Hope M. Tiesman, Jeri Sumitani, Terry Mize, Kumar Kartik Amarnath, A. Rana Bayakly, and Matthew W. Murphy. 2013. "Public Health Impact of Heat-Related Illness among Migrant Farmworkers." *American Journal of Preventive Medicine* 44 (3): 199–206.

Friedland, William H., and Robert J. Thomas. 1974. "Paradoxes of Agricultural Unionism in California." *Society* 11 (4): 52–60.

Fuller, Nicole. 2015. "Farmworkers Rally on Long Island for Overtime Pay." *Newsday*. March 29. www.newsday.com/business/farmworkers-rally-in-long-island-for-overtime-pay-1.10152719, accessed August 1, 2015.

Fussell, Elizabeth. 2011. "The Deportation Threat Dynamic and Victimization of Latino Migrants: Wage Theft and Street Robbery." *Sociological Quarterly* 52 (4): 593–615.

Gazette Staff. 2014. "Former Agriprocessors Manager to Serve 10 Months in Prison." *Iowa Gazette Online*. March 31, 2014, www.thegazette.com/2010/05/26/former-agriprocessors-manager-to-serve-10-months-in-prison.

Gilbert, Liette. 2013. "Immigration as Local Politics: Re-bordering Immigration through Deterrence and Incapacitation." In *Governing Immigration through Crime*, ed. Julie A. Dowling and Jonathan Xavier Inda, 181–94. Stanford, CA: Stanford University Press.

Golash-Boza, Tanya. 2014. "From Legal to 'Illegal': The Deportation of Legal Permanent Residents from the United States." In *Constructing Immigrant "Illegality": Critiques, Experiences, and Responses*, ed. Cecilia Menjívar and Daniel Kanstroom, 203–24. New York: Cambridge University Press.

Gomberg-Muñoz, Ruth. 2010. "Willing to Work: Agency and Vulnerability in an Undocumented Immigrant Network." *American Anthropologist* 112 (2): 295–307.

———. 2011. *Labor and Legality: An Ethnography of a Mexican Immigrant Network*. Oxford: Oxford University Press.

———. 2012. "Inequality in a 'Postracial' Era: Race, Immigration, and Criminalization of Low-Wage Labor." *DuBois Review* 9 (2): 339–53.

———. 2016. *Becoming Legal: Mixed-Status Couples and U.S. Immigration Processing*. Oxford: Oxford University Press.

Gomberg-Muñoz, Ruth, and Laura Nussbaum-Barberena. 2011. "Is Immigration Policy Labor Policy? Immigration Enforcement, Undocumented Labor, and the State." *Human Organization* 70 (4): 366–75.

González-Guarda, R., A. Florom-Smith, and T. Thomas. 2011. "A Syndemic Model of Substance Abuse, Intimate Partner Violence, HIV Infection, and Mental Health among Hispanics." *Public Health Nursing* 28 (4): 366–78.

Good, Byron J. 1994. *Medicine, Rationality and Experience: An Anthropological Perspective*. Cambridge: Cambridge University Press.

Good, Byron J., and Mary-Jo DelVecchio Good. 1994. "In the Subjunctive Mode: Epilepsy Narratives in Turkey." *Social Science and Medicine* 38 (6): 835–42.

Gravlee, Clarence C. 2009. "How Race Becomes Biology: Embodiment of Social Inequality." *American Journal of Physical Anthropology* 139 (1): 47–57.

Griffith, David, Ed Kissam, Jeromino Camposeco, Anna García, Max Pfeffer, David Runsten, and Manuel Valdes Pizzini. 1995. *Working Poor: Farmworkers in the United States*. Philadelphia, PA: Temple University Press.

Grossi, Mark. 2013. "Valley Swelters in Historic Heat Wave." *Fresno Bee*. June 30. http://muckrack.com/link/s8ml/valley-swelters-in-potentially-historic-heat-wave, accessed July 22, 2014.

Hale, Charles. 2006. "Activist Research vs. Cultural Critique: Indigenous Land Rights and the Contradictions of Politically Engaged Anthropology." *Cultural Anthropology* 21: 96–120.

Hansen, Helena, Seth Holmes, and Danielle Lindemann. 2013. "Ethnography of Health for Social Change: Impact on Public Perception and Policy." *Social Science and Medicine* 99: 116–18.

Heyman, Josiah. 1998. "State Effects on Labor Exploitation: The INS and Undocumented Immigrants at the Mexico-United States Border." *Critique of Anthropology* 18 (2): 157–80.

———. 2001. Class and Classification at the United States-Mexico Border. *Human Organization* 60 (2): 128–40.

Heyman, Josiah McC., Guillermina Gina Nunez, and Victor Talavera. 2009. "Health Care Access and Barriers for Unauthorized Immigrants in El Paso County, Texas." *Family and Community Health* 32 (1): 4–21.

Hicken, Margaret T., Hedwig Lee, Jeffrey Morenoff, James S. House, and David R. Williams. 2014. "Racial/Ethnic Disparities in Hypertension Prevalence: Reconsidering the Role of Chronic Stress." *American Journal of Public Health* 104 (1): 117–23.

Hoffman, Beatrix. 2005. "Sympathy and Exclusion: Access to Health Care for Undocumented Immigrants in the United States." In *A Death Retold: Jesica Santillan, the Bungled Transplant, and Paradoxes of Medical Citizenship*, eds. Keith Wailoo, Julie Livingston and Peter Guarnaccia, viii-378. Chapel Hill, NC: University of North Carolina Press.

Holmes, Seth. 2013a. ""Is it Worth Risking Your Life?": Ethnography, Risk and Death on the U.S.–Mexico Border." *Social Science Medicine* 99: 153–161.

———. 2013b. *Fresh Fruit, Broken Bodies: Migrant Farmworkers in the United States.* Berkeley: University of California Press.

Holtcamp, Wendee. 2012. "Obesogens: An Environmental Link to Obesity." *Environmental Health Perspectives* 120 (2): a62–a68.

Hondagneu-Sotelo, Pierette. 1994. *Gendered Transitions: Mexican Experiences of Immigration.* Berkeley: University of California Press.

Hondagneu-Sotelo, Pierette, and Ernestine Avila. 1997. "'I'm Here, but I'm There': The Meanings of Latina Transnational Motherhood." *Gender and Society* 11 (5): 548–71.

Horn, Megan. 2014. "Positive Developments for California Farmworkers and Other News." *Harvesting Justice: A Blog by Farmworker Justice.* October 3, 2014. www.farmworkerjustice.org/fj-blog/positive-developments-california-farmworkers-and-other-news, accessed February 22, 2015.

Horton, Sarah. 2014. "Debating 'Medical Citizenship': Policies Shaping Immigrants' Learned Avoidance of the US Health Care System." In *Hidden Lives and Human Rights in the United States: Understanding the Controversies and Tragedies in Undocumented Immigration,* ed. Lois A. Lorentzen, 3: 297–320. Santa Barbara, CA: ABC-CLIO.

———. 2015. "Identity Loan: The Moral Economy of Migrant Document Exchange in California's Central Valley." *American Ethnologist* 42 (1): 55–67.

———. n.d.a. "From 'Deportability' to 'Denounce-ability': New Forms of Labor Subordination in an Era of Governing Immigration through Crime." *Political and Legal Anthropology Review.*

———. n.d.b. "Ghost Workers: The Implications of Governing Immigration through Crime for Migrant Workplaces." *Anthropology of Work Review.*

Horton, Sarah, and Judith C. Barker. 2009. "'Stains' on Their Self-Discipline: Public Health, Hygiene, and the Disciplining of Undocumented Immigrant Parents in the Nation's Internal Borderlands." *American Ethnologist* 36 (4): 784–98.

———. 2010. "Stigmatized Biologies: Examining the Cumulative Effects of Oral Health Disparities for Mexican American Children." *Medical Anthropology Quarterly* 24 (2): 199–219.

Hyman, David J., K. Ogbonnaya, V.N. Pavlik, Walker S. Poston, and K. Ho. 2000. "Lower Hypertension Prevalence in First-Generation African Immigrants Compared to U.S.-Born African Americans." *Ethnicity and Disease* 10 (3): 343–49.

Industrial Welfare Commission. n.d. *Order No. 13–2001 Regulating Wages, Hours, and Working Conditions in the Industries Preparing Agricultural Products for Market, on the Farm.* California Department of Industrial Relations, https://www.dir.ca.gov/IWC/IWCArticle13.pdf, accessed March 12, 2015.

Jackson, L.L., and H.R. Rosenberg. 2010. "Preventing Heat-Related Illness among Agricultural Workers." *Journal of Agromedicine* 15 (3): 200–215.

Jayasumana, Channa, Sarath Gunatilake, and Sisira Siribadda Johnston. 2015. "Simultaneous Exposure to Multiple Heavymetals and Glyphosate may Contribute to Sri Lankan Agricultural Nephropathy." *BMC Nephrology* 16 (103): 1–8.

Johnston, Barbara Rose. 2010. "Social Responsibility and the Anthropological Citizen." "*Current Anthropology* 51 (S2):S235–S247.

Johnston, Barbara Rose, and Holly M. Barker. 2008. *The Consequential Damages of Nuclear War: The Rongelap Report.* Walnut Creek, CA: Left Coast Press.

Kanstroom, Daniel. 2007. *Deportation Nation: Outsiders in American History.* Cambridge, MA: Harvard University Press.

Karlamangla, Soumya. 2015. "For Those in California Illegally, Health Services Vary Greatly by County." *Los Angeles Times.* June 11. www.latimes.com/local/countygovernment/la-me-remaining-uninsured-20150611-story.html.

Kirsch, Stuart. 2002. "Anthropology and Advocacy: A Case Study of the Campaign Against the Ok Tedi Mine." *Critique of Anthropology* 22: 175–200.

Kleinman, Arthur. 1998. "Experience and Its Moral Codes: Culture, Human Conditions, and Disorder." Tanner Lectures on Human Values, Stanford, CA. April.

Kline, Nolan. 2015. "Pathogenic Policy: Health-Related Consequences of Immigrant Policing in Atlanta, Georgia." PhD diss., University of Florida.

Klinenberg, Eric. 2002. *Heat Wave: A Social Autopsy of Disaster in Chicago.* Chicago, IL: University of Chicago Press.

Kohli, Aarti, Peter L. Markowitz, and Lisa Chavez. 2011. *Secure Communities by the Numbers: An Analysis of Demographics and Due Process.* University of California Berkeley Law School, Chief Justice Earl Warren Institute on Law and Social Policy. www.law.berkeley.edu/files/Secure_Communities_by_the_Numbers.pdf, accessed February 12, 2015.

Krieger, Nancy. 2001. "Theories for Social Epidemiology in the 21st Century: An Ecosocial Perspective." *International Journal of Epidemiology* 30: 668–77.

———. 2005. "Embodiment: A Conceptual Glossary for Epidemiology." *Journal of Epidemiology and Community Health* 59: 350–355.

———. 2008. "Proximal, Distal, and the Politics of Causation: What's Level Got to Do with It?" *American Journal of Public Health* 98 (2): 221–30.

La Cooperative Campesina de California (LCC). n.d. *Overtime Pay for California's Farmworkers.* www.lacooperativa.org/overtime-pay-californias-farmworkers/, accessed February 6, 2015.

Lakhani, Nina. 2015. "Nicaraguans Demand Action over Illness Killing Thousands of Sugar Cane Workers." *Guardian.* February 16, 2015. www.theguardian.com/world/2015/feb/16/-sp-nicaragua-kidney-disease-killing-sugar-cane-workers, accessed September 1, 2015.

Lam, Michelle, Jennifer Krenz, Pablo Palmández, Maria Negrete, Martha Perla, Helen Murphy-Robinson, and June T. Spector. 2013. "Identification of Barriers to the Prevention and Treatment of Heat-Related Illnesses in Latino Farmworkers Using Activity-Oriented, Participatory Rural Appraisal Focus Group Methods." *BMC Public Health* 13: 1004.

Lamphere, Louise. 2004. "The Convergence of Applied, Practicing and Public Anthropology in the 21st Century." *Human Organization* 63 (4): 431–43.

Le, Ellen. 2013. "Central Valley Farmworkers Still Vulnerable to Heat-Related Illnesses, Study Finds." *Sacramento Bee*. July 7. www.sacbee.com/2013/07/07/5549706/central-valley-farmworkers-still.html, accessed July 22, 2014.

Lebov, Jill F., Eliette Valladares, Rodolfo Peña, Edgar M. Peña, Scott L. Sanoff, Efren Castellón Cisneros, Romulo E. Colindres, Douglas R. Morgan, and Susan L. Hogan. 2015. "A Population-Based Study of Prevalence and Risk Factors of Chronic Kidney Disease in León, Nicaragua." *Canadian Journal of Kidney Health and Disease* 2: 6.

Lerman-Garber, I., A.R. Villa, and E. Caballero. 2004. "Diabetes and Cardiovascular Disease: Is There a True Hispanic Paradox?" *Revista de investigación clínica* 56 (3): 282–96.

LGMA (Leafy Green Marketing Agreement). 2013. *Commodity Specific Food Safety Guidelines for the Production and Harvest of Lettuce and Leafy Greens*. www.lgma.ca.gov/wp-content/uploads/2014/09/California-LGMA-metrics-08–26–13-Final.pdf, accessed March 3, 2015.

Liao, Youlian, Richard S. Cooper, Guichan Cao, Jay S. Kaufman, Andrew E. Long, and Daniel L. McGee. 1997. "Mortality from Coronary Heart Disease and Cardiovascular Disease among Adult U.S. Hispanics: Findings from the National Health Interview Survey (1986–1994)." *Journal of the American College of Cardiology* 30 (5): 1200–1205.

Lighthall, David. 2001. "The Poor Health of Farm Workers." *Western Journal of Medicine* 175 (4): 223–24.

Linden, Ellena A., Jeannette Cano, and George N. Coritsidis. 2012. "Kidney Transplantation in Undocumented Immigrants With ESRD: A Policy Whose Time Has Come?" *American Journal of Kidney Disease* 60 (3): 354–59.

Linthicum, Kate. 2014. "Obama Ends Secure Communities Program as Part of Immigration Action." *Los Angeles Times*. November 21. www.latimes.com/local/california/la-me-1121-immigration-justice-20141121-story.html.

Lock, Margaret. 1993. *Encounters with Aging*. Berkeley: University of California Press.

Lomnitz, Larissa Adler, and E.A. Hammel. 1977. *Networks and Marginality: Life in a Mexican Shantytown*. New York: Academic Press.

López, Ann Aurelia. 2007. *The Farmworkers' Journey*. Berkeley: University of California Press.

Low, Setha M., and Sally Engle Merry. 2015. "Engaged Anthropology: Diversity and Dilemmas: An Introduction to Supplement 2." *Current Anthropology* 51 (S2): S203–S226.

Luhrmann, Tanya Marie. 2000. *Of Two Minds: the Growing Disorder in American Psychiatry*. New York: Vintage Books.

Lydgate, Joanna. 2010. *Assembly-Line Justice: A Review of Operation Streamline*. University of California, Berkeley, Law School, Chief Justice Earl Warren Institute on Race, Ethnicity and Diversity.

Mahler, Sarah. 1995. *American Dreaming: Immigrant Life on the Margins*. Princeton, NJ: Princeton University Press.

———. 1996. *Salvadorans in Suburbia: Symbiosis and Conflict.* New York: Pearson.

Marcus, George E., and Michael M.J. Fischer. 1986. *Anthropology as Cultural Critique.* Chicago: University of Chicago Press.

Marquandt, Marie, Timothy J. Steigenga, Philip J. Williams, and Manuel A. Vásquez. 2013. *Living "Illegal" The Human Face of Unauthorized Immigration.* New York NY: The New Press.

Marrow, Helen. 2012. "Deserving to a Point: Unauthorized Immigrants in San Francisco's Universal Access Healthcare Model." *Social Science and Medicine* 74 (6): 846–54.

Martin, Mark. 2005. "State Seeks to Halt Farmworker Deaths." *SFGate.* August 3. www.sfgate.com/bayarea/article/SACRAMENTO-State-seeks-to-halt-farmworker-2650740.php, accessed January 15, 2016.

Martin, Philip L. 1994. "Good Intentions Gone Awry: IRCA and US Agriculture." *Annals of the Academy of Social Science* 534: 44–57.

———. 2011. *California Hired Farm Labor 1960–2010: Change and Continuity.* UC Davis Agricultural and Resource Economics. https://migrationfiles.ucdavis.edu/uploads/cf/files/2011-may/martin-california-hired-farm-labor.pdf, accessed July 21, 2015.

Martin, Philip, and J. Edward Taylor. 2013. *Ripe with Change: Evolving Farm Labor Markets in the United States, Mexico and Central America.* Washington, DC: Migration Policy Institute.

Massey, Douglas. 2006. "Borderline Madness." *Chronicle of Higher Education* 52 (43): 11–12. June 30.

Massey, Douglas, S. Jorge Durand, and Nolan J. Malone. 2002. *Beyond Smoke and Mirrors: Mexican Immigration in an Era of Economic Integration.* New York: Russell Sage Foundation.

McEwen, Bruce S. 2000. "Allostasis and Allostatic Load: Implications for Neuropsychopharmacology." *Neuropsychopharmacology* 22: 108–24.

McEwen, Bruce, and John Wingfield. 2003. "The Concept of Allostasis in Biology and Biomedicine." *Hormones and Behavior* 43 (1): 2–15.

McGuire, Sharon, and J. Georges. 2003. "Undocumentedness and Liminality as Health Variables." *Advances in Nursing Science* 26 (3): 185–95.

McKinley, Jesse. 2007. "San Francisco Bay Area Reacts Angrily to Series of Immigration Raids." *New York Times.* April 28. www.nytimes.com/2007/04/28/washington/28immig.html, accessed November 12, 2014.

McWilliams, Carey. 2000 [1939]. *Factories in the Field: The Story of Migratory Farm Labor in California.* Berkeley: University of California Press.

Melo, Milena, and K. Jill Fleuriet. 2016. "Who Has the Right to Health Care and Why? Immigration, Health Care Policy, and Incorporation." In *Mexican Migration to the United States: Perspectives from Both Sides of the Border,* ed. H. Romo and O. Mogollon-Lopez, 159–183. Austin: University of Texas Press.

Mendenhall, Emily. 2012. *Syndemic Suffering: Social Distress, Depression, and Diabetes among Mexican Immigrant Women.* Walnut Creek, CA: Left Coast Press.

Mendenhall, Emily, Alicia Fernandez, Nancy Adler, and Elizabeth A. Jacobs. 2012. "*Susto, Coraje,* and Abuse: Depression and Beliefs about Diabetes." Culture, Medicine, and Psychiatry 36 (3): 480–492.

Mendenhall, Emily, R.A. Selgiman, A. Fernandez, and E.A. Jacobs. 2010. "Speaking through Diabetes: Rethinking the Significance of Lay Discourse on Diabetes." *Medical Anthropology Quarterly* 24 (2): 220–39.

Menjívar, Cecilia. 1997. "Immigrant Kinship Networks and the Impact of the Receiving Context: Salvadorans in San Francisco in the Early 1990s." *Social Problems* 44 (1): 104–23.

———. 2000. *Fragmented Ties: Salvadoran Immigrant Networks in America.* Berkeley: University of California Press.

———. 2002. "The Ties that Heal: Guatemalan Immigrant Women's Networks and Medical Treatment." *International Migration Review* 36 (2): 437–66.

———. 2006. "Liminal Legality: Salvadoran and Guatemalan Immigrants' Lives in the United States." *American Journal of Sociology* 111 (4): 999–1037.

Menjívar, Cecilia, and Leisy T. Abrego. 2012. "Legal Violence: Immigration Law and the Lives of Central American Immigrants." *American Journal of Sociology* 117 (5): 1380–1421.

Menjívar, Cecilia, and Daniel Kanstroom, eds. 2014. *Constructing Immigrant "Illegality": Critiques, Experiences, and Responses.* New York: Cambridge University Press.

Mercado-Martínez, Francisco J., and Igor M. Ramos-Herrera. 2002. "Diabetes: The Layperson's Theories of Causality." *Qualitative Health Research* 12 (6): 792–806.

Merry, Sally Engle, and Susan Bibler Coutin. 2014. "Technologies of Truth in the Anthropology of Conflict: AES/APLA Presidential Address, 2013." *American Ethnologist* 41 (1): 1–16.

Millman, Joel. 2011. "Captive Labor on the Farm." *Wall Street Journal.* October 18, 2011. www.wsj.com/articles/SB10001424052970204774604576630972860034248, accessed February 6, 2015.

Milstein, Bobby. 2001. *Introduction to the Syndemics Prevention Network.* Atlanta: Centers for Disease Control and Prevention, www.cdc.gov/syndemics, accessed November 10, 2010.

Mirabelli, M.C. S.A. Quandt, R. Crain, J.G. Grzywacz, E.N. Robinson, Q.M. Vallejos, and T.A. Arcury. 2010. "Symptoms of Heat Illness among Latino Farm Workers in North Carolina." *American Journal of Preventive Medicine* 39 (5): 468–71.

Mohan, Geoffrey. 2015. "Cal-OSHA Settles Farmworker Suits over Heat-Related Deaths." *Los Angeles Times.* June 11. www.latimes.com/business/la-fi-cal-osha-farm-workers-20150612-story.html, accessed August 1, 2015.

Moodie, Ellen. 2010. *El Salvador in the Aftermath of Peace: Crime, Uncertainty and the Transition to Democracy.* Philadelphia: University of Pennsylvania Press.

Moore, Joe. 2014. "Fresno County to Fund Health Care For Undocumented, Partially." Valley Public Radio, NPR for Central California, November 5,

http://kvpr.org/post/fresno-county-fund-health-care-undocumented-partially, accessed July 28, 2015.

Morehouse, Lisa. 2013. "Heat Wave Worrisome for Worker Health." *California Report,* July 19–21, www.californiareport.org/archive/R201307191630/b, accessed July 23, 2014.

Moyce, Sally, Joseph J. Tancredi., D. Mitchell, T. Armitage, and Marc Schenker. 2015. "Heat Exposure, Volume Depletion, and Acute Kidney Injury in California's Agricultural Workers." Poster presented at the Second International Workshop on Mesoamerican Nephropathy, Universidad Nacional de Costa Rica, November 18–25, 2015.

NCFH (National Center for Farmworker Health, Inc.). 2012. *National Center for Farmworker Health Fact Sheets: Demographics.* www.ncfh.org/docs/fs-Migrant%20Demographics.pdf, accessed September 30, 2014.

Newell, Sasha. 2006. "Estranged Belongings: A Moral Economy of Theft in Abidjan, Côte d'Ivoire." *Anthropological Theory* 6 (2): 179–204.

New York Times Editorial Board. 2014. "The 'Secure Communities' Illusion." *New York Times.* September 5. www.nytimes.com/2014/09/06/opinion/the-secure-communities-illusion.html, accessed November 12, 2014.

NFWM (National Farm Worker Ministry). 2016a. "Low Wages." http://nfwm.org/education-center/farm-worker-issues/low-wages/, accessed March 1, 2016.

——— 2016b. *"Health and Safety."* http://nfwm.org/education-center/farm-worker-issues/health-safety/, accessed March 1, 2016.

Ngai, Mae. 2004. *Impossible Subjects: Illegal Aliens and the Making of Modern America.* Princeton, NJ: Princeton University Press.

NHLBI (National Heart, Lung and Blood Institute). 2011. *What Is Diabetic Heart Disease?* National Institutes of Health, www.nhlbi.nih.gov/health/health-topics/topics/dhd, updated September 20, 2011.

NILC (National Immigration Law Center). 2013. *The POWER Act: An Essential Component of Immigration Reform.* www.nilc.org/powerir.html, accessed February 22, 2015.

———. 2015. *Priority Enforcement Program: Why "PEP" Doesn't Replace S-COMM's Failings.* www.nilc.org/issues/immigration-enforcement/pepnotafix/, accessed March 15, 2016.

NKF (National Kidney Foundation). n.d. *About Chronic Kidney Disease.* www.kidney.org/kidneydisease/aboutckd, accessed September 8, 2015.

Nuschler, Dawn, and Alison Siskin. 2005. *Social Security Benefits for Noncitizens: Current Policy and Legislation.* Congressional Research Service Report No. RL32004.

O'Leary, Anna Ochoa. 2009. "*Mujeres en el Cruce:* Remapping Border Security through Migrant Mobility." *Journal of the Southwest* 51 (4): 523–42.

O'Leary, Lizzie, and Aaron Cooper. 2012. "Rules 'Hold-Up' Puzzles Food Industry and Food-Safety Advocates." *CNN News.* May 3, 2012. www.cnn.com/2012/05/03/us/food-safety-rules-delay/index.html, accessed July 12, 2015.

Oliver, Kelly. 2004. "Witnessing and Testimony." *Parallax* 10 (1): 79–88.

Orantes, C.M., R. Herrera, M. Almaguer, E.G. Brizuela, C.E. Hernández, H. Bayarre, J.C. Amaya, et al. 2011. "Chronic Kidney Disease and Associated

Risk Factors in the Bajo Lempa Region of El Salvador: Nefrolempa Study 2009." *MEDICC Review* 13 (4): 14–22.

Ordunez, Pedro, Ramón Martinez, Ludovic Reveiz, Evelina Chapman, Carla Saenz, Agnes Soares da Silva, and Francisco Becerra. 2014. "Chronic Kidney Disease Epidemic in Central America: Urgent Public Health Action Is Needed amid Causal Uncertainty." *PLoS Neglected Tropical Diseases* 8 (8): 1–3.

OSHA (Occupational Safety and Health Administration). 2014. *FY 2013 Comprehensive Federal Annual Monitoring and Evaluation (FAME) Report.* San Francisco, CA: US Department of Labor Occupational Safety and Health Administration (OSHA). www.osha.gov/dcsp/osp/efame/2013/ca_report.pdf, accessed October 2, 2014.

Otero, Gerardo. 2011. "Neoliberal Globalization, NAFTA, and Migration: Mexico's Loss of Food and Labor Sovereignty." *Journal of Poverty* 15 (4): 384–402.

Oxfam America. 2014. *Equitable Food Initiative, March 30, 2014*, http://policy-practice.oxfamamerica.org/work/in-action/equitable-food-initiative/, accessed March 2, 2015.

Pappas, G., P.J. Gergen, and M. Carroll. 1990. "Hypertension Prevalence and the Status of Awareness, Treatment, and Control in the Hispanic Health and Nutrition Examination Survey (HHANES), 1982–84." *American Journal of Public Health* 80 (12): 1431–36.

Park, Lisa Sun-Hee, Rhonda Sarnoff, Catherine Bender, and Carol Korenbrot. 2000. "Impact of Recent Welfare and Immigration Reforms on Receipt of Medicaid for Prenatal Care by Immigrants in California." *Journal of Immigrant Health* 2 (1): 5–22.

Paula Santos, Ubiratan, Dirce Maria T. Zanetta, Mário Terra-Filho, and Emmanuel A. Burdmann. 2015. "Burnt Sugarcane Harvesting is Associated with Acute Renal Dysfunction." *Kidney International* 87 (4): 792–9.

Peraza, Sandra, Catharina Wesseling, Aurora Aragon, Ricardo Leiva, Ramón Antonio García-Trabanino, Cecilia Torres, Kristina Jakobsson, Carl Gustaf Elinder, and Christer Hogstedt. 2012. "Decreased Kidney Function among Agricultural Workers in El Salvador." *American Journal of Kidney Disease* 59 (4): 531–40.

Pérez-Stable, E., T. Juarbe, and G. Moreno-John. 2001. "Cardiovascular Disease." In *Health Issues in the Latino Community,* ed. M. Aguirre-Molina, C.W. Molina, and R.E. Zambrana, 245–76. San Francisco, CA: Jossey-Bass.

Phelan, Sarah. 2011. "SF in Top 38 Counties Nationwide that Deport 'Noncriminal Aliens.'" *San Francisco Bay Guardian.* March 31. www.sfbg.com/politics/2011/03/31/sf-top-38-counties-nationwide-deport-non-criminal-aliens, accessed November 12, 2014.

Plevin, Rebecca. 2014. "Fresno County Plan to End Care for Undocumented Meets Resistance." *Valley Edition,* Valley Public Radio, NPR for Central California. January 14. http://kvpr.org/post/fresno-county-plan-end-care-undocumented-meets-resistance, accessed July 28, 2015.

Quesada, James, Laurie K. Hart, and Philippe Bourgois. 2011. "Structural Vulnerability and Health: Latino Migrant Laborers in the U.S." *Medical Anthropology* 30 (4): 339–62.

Ramírez, A.G. 1996. "Hypertension in Hispanic Americans: Overview of the Population." *Public Health Reports* 3 (Suppl.2): 25–26.

Rao, Pamela. 2007. *Heat-Related Illnesses: An Occupational Health Concern for Farmworkers.* Washington, DC: Farmworker Justice. https://farmworkerjustice.org/sites/default/files/documents/Heat20Related20Illnesses.pdf, accessed May 12, 2014.

Redmond, Nicole, Heather J. Baer, and LeRoi S. Hicks. 2011. "Health Behaviors and Racial Disparity in Blood Pressure Control in the National Health and Nutrition Examination Survey." *Hypertension* 57 (3): 383–89.

Rodriguez, R.A. 2015. "Dialysis for Undocumented Immigrants in the United States." *Advanced Chronic Kidney Disease* 22 (1): 60–65.

Rosaldo, Renato. 1993 [1989]. *Culture and Truth: The Remaking of Social Analysis.* Boston: Beacon Press.

Rothenberg, Daniel. 1998. *With These Hands: The Hidden World of Migrant Farmworkers Today.* Berkeley: University of California Press.

Rylko-Bauer, Barbara, Merrill Singer, and John Van Willigen. 2006. "Reclaiming Applied Anthropology: Its Past, Present, and Future." *American Anthropologist* 108 (1): 178–90.

Sáenz, Rogelio, Cecila Menjívar, and San Juanita Edilia García. 2013. "Arizona's SB 1070: Setting Conditions for Violations of Human Rights here and Beyond. In *Governing Immigration through Crime: A Reader,* ed. Julie A. Dowling and Jonathan Xavier Inda, 165–80. Stanford, CA: Stanford University Press.

Salinas, Jennifer J., Karl A. Eschbach, and Kyriakos S. Markides. 2008. "The Prevalence of Hypertension in Older Mexicans and Mexican Americans." *Ethnicity and Disease* 18 (3): 294–98.

Sanjek, Roger. 2014. "Anthropology's Hidden Colonialism: Assistants and Their Ethnographers." Chapter 5 in *Ethnography in Today's World: Color Full before Color Blind,* 72–81. Philadelphia: University of Pennsylvania Press.

Sanoff, Scott L., Luis Callejas, Carlos D. Alonso, Yichun Hu, Romulo E. Colindres, Hyunsook Chin, Douglas R. Morgan, and Susan L. Hogan. 2010. "Positive Association of Renal Insufficiency with Agriculture Employment and Unregulated Alcohol Consumption in Nicaragua." *Renal Failure* 32 (7): 766–77.

Sarabia, Heidy. 2012. "Perpetual Illegality: Results of Border Enforcement and Policies for Mexican Undocumented Migrants in the United States." *Analyses of Social Issues and Public Policy* 12 (1): 49–67.

Saxton, Dvera I. 2015. "Strawberry Fields as Extreme Environments: The Ecobiopolitics of Farmworker Health." *Medical Anthropology* 34 (2): 166–83.

Schell, Greg. 2002. "Farmworker Exceptionalism under the Law: How the Legal System Contributes to Farmworker Poverty and Powerlessness." In *The Human Cost of Food: Farmworkers' Lives, Labor, and Advocacy,* ed. Charles D. Thompson Jr. and Melissa F. Wiggins, 139–66. Austin: University of Texas Press.

Schenker, Marc B. 2010. "A Global Perspective of Migration and Occupational Health." *American Journal of Industrial Medicine* 53 (4): 329–37.

Scheper-Hughes, Nancy. 1992. *Death without Weeping: The Violence of Everyday Life in Brazil.* Berkeley: University of California Press.

———. 1995. "The Primacy of the Ethical: Propositions for a Militant Anthropology." *Current Anthropology* 36: 409–20.

Scheper-Hughes, Nancy, and Philippe Bourgois. 2004. "Introduction: Making Sense of Violence." In *Violence in War and Peace: An Anthology,* ed. Nancy Scheper-Hughes and Philippe Bourgois, 1–31. New York: Blackwell.

Seeman, Teresa, Elissa Epel, Tara Gurenewald, Arun Karlamangla, and Bruce S. McEwen. 2010. "Socio-economic Differentials in Peripheral Biology: Cumulative Allostatic Load." *Annals of the New York Academy of Sciences* 1186: 223–39.

Singer, Merrill. 1996. "A Dose of Drugs, a Touch of Violence, a Case of AIDS: Conceptualizing the SAVA Syndemic." *Free Inquiry in Creative Sociology* 24 (2): 99–110.

———. 1999. "Studying Hidden Populations." In *Mapping Social Networks, Spatial Data, and Hidden Populations,* ed. J. J. Schensul, M. LeCompte, R. T. Trotter II, E. K. Cromely, and M. Singer, 125–192. Lanham, MD: AltaMira Press.

———. 2000. "Why I Am Not a Public Anthropologist." *Anthropology News* 41 (6): 6–7.

———. 2009. *Introduction to Syndemics: A Critical Systems Approach to Public and Community Health.* San Francisco, CA: John Wiley & Sons.

Singer, Merrill, and Scott Clair. 2003. "Syndemics and Public Health: Reconceptualizing Disease in Biosocial Context." *Medical Anthropology Quarterly* 17 (4): 423–41.

Slack, Jeremy, and Scott Whiteford. 2011. "Violence and Migration on the Arizona Sonora Border." *Human Organization* 70(1): 11–21.

Smith-Nonini, Sandi. 2011. "The Illegal and the Dead: Are Mexicans Renewable Energy?" *Medical Anthropology* 30 (5): 454–74.

Sorlie, P.D., E. Backlund, N.J. Johnson, and E. Rogot. 1993. "Mortality by Hispanic Status in the United States." *Journal of the American Medical Association* 270 (20): 2464–68.

Sorrentino, Joseph. 2015. "N.M. Field and Dairy Laborers Win Right to Workers' Comp—Court Calls Exemption 'Absurd.'" *In These Times,* July 20, http://inthesetimes.com/working/entry/18214/n.m._field_and_dairy_laborers_win_the_right_to_workers_compexemption_was_ab, accessed August 1, 2015.

Speed, Shannon. 2006. "At the Crossroads of Human Rights and Anthropology: Toward a Critically Engaged Activist Research." *American Anthropologist* 108: 66–76.

SSA (Social Security Administration). n.d.a. *DI 45001.001: End-Stage Renal Disease (ESRD) Entitlement Provisions.* https://secure.ssa.gov/poms.nsf/lnx/0445001001, accessed September 8, 2015.

———. n.d.b. *Disability Planner: What We Mean by "Disability."* www.ssa.gov/dibplan/dqualify4.htm, accessed October 23, 2014.

———. n.d.c. *Disability Benefits.* www.ssa.gov/pubs/EN-05-10029.pdf, accessed October 23, 2014.

———. n.d.d. *Code of Federal Regulations: 401.4566. Work Which Exists in the National Economy*. www.ssa.gov/OP_Home/cfr20/404/404–1566.htm, accessed October 23, 2014.

Stack, Carol. 1983. *All Our Kin: Strategies for Survival in a Black Community*. New York: Basic Books.

Stephen, Lynn. 2007. *Transborder Lives: Indigenous Oaxacans in Mexico, California, and Oregon*. Durham, NC: Duke University Press.

Stoecklin-Marois, M., Burt T. Hennessy, D. Mitchell, and M. Schenker. 2013. "Heat-Related Illness Knowledge and Practices among California Hired Farm Workers in the MICASA Study." *Industrial Health* 51 (1): 47–55.

Stuesse, Angela C. 2010. "What's 'Justice and Dignity' Got to Do with It? Migrant Vulnerability, Corporate Complicity, and the State." *Human Organization* 69 (1): 19–30.

Stuesse, Angela, and Mathew Coleman. 2014. "Automobility, Immobility, Altermobility: Surviving and Resisting the Intensification of Immigrant Policing." *City and Society* 26 (1): 105–26.

Stumpf, Juliet. 2006. "The Crimmigration Crisis: Immigrants, Crime, and Sovereign Power." *American University Law Review* 56: 367–419.

Trabanino, Ramón García, Raúl Aguilar, Carlos Reyes Silva, Manuel Ortiz Mercado, and Ricardo Leiva Merino. 2002. "End-Stage Renal Disease among Patients in a Referral Hospital in El Salvador." *Revista Panamericana de Salud Pública* 12 (3): 202–6.

Trabanino, Ramón García, Emmanuel Jarquín, Catharina Wesseling, Richard J. Johnson, Marvin González-Quiroz, Ilana Weiss, Jason Glaser, et al. 2015. "Heat Stress, Dehydration, and Kidney Function in Sugarcane Cutters in El Salvador: A Cross-Shift Study of Workers at Risk of Mesoamerican Nephropathy." *Environmental Research*. 142: 746–55.

Turner, Victor. 1967. *The Forest of Symbols: Aspects of Ndembu Ritual*. Ithaca, NY: Cornell University Press.

U.S. Census Bureau. 2010. "State and County Quick Facts: Mendota (City), California." http://quickfacts.census.gov/qfd/states/06/0646828.html, accessed October 31, 2014.

USCIS (U.S. Customs and Immigration Service). 2016. *Temporary Protected Status*. www.uscis.gov/humanitarian/temporary-protected-status-deferred-enforced-departure/temporary-protected-status#Countries Currently Designated for TPS, updated February 19, 2016.

U.S. DOL (Department of Labor (). 2010. *The National Agricultural Workers Survey*. Employment and Training Administration (ETA). www.doleta.gov/agworker/report9/chapter1.cfm#summary, updated January 11, 2010. Accessed March 15, 2015.

———. 2006. *Census of Fatal Occupational Injuries*. Washington, DC: Bureau of Labor Statistics.

———. 2014. *National Census of Fatal Occupational Injuries in 2013 (Preliminary Results)*. USDL-14–1674.Washington, DC: Bureau of Labor Statistics. www.bls.gov/news.release/pdf/cfoi.pdf, accessed September 11, 2014.

Villarejo, Don. 2003. "The Health of Hired US Farm Workers." *Annual Review of Public Health* 24: 175–93.

Villarejo, Don, David Lighthall, Daniel Williams, Ann Souter, Richard Mines, Bonnie Bade, Steve Samuels, and Stephen A. McCurdy. 2000. *Suffering in Silence: A Report on the Health of California's Agricultural Workers.* Davis, CA: California Institute for Rural Studies.

———. 2001. "Access to Health Care for California's Hired Farmworkers: A Baseline Report." Working paper, California Program on Access to Care, California Policy Research Center, University of California.

Villarejo, Don, Stephen A. McCurdy, Bonnie Bade, Steve Samuels, David Lighthall, and Daniel Williams III. 2010. "The Health of California's Immigrant Hired Farmworkers." *American Journal of Industrial Medicine* 53: 387–97.

Vogt, Wendy. 2013. "Crossing Mexico: Structural Violence and the Commodification of Undocumented Central American Migrants." *American Ethnologist* 40 (4): 764–80.

Waddington, Lynda. 2009. "US Supreme Court Slaps Postville Prosecutions." *Des Moines Register.* May 4.

Wasem, Ruth Ellen. 2014. *Noncitizen Eligibility for Federal Public Assistance: Policy Overview and Trends.* Congressional Research Service Report no. RL 33809. September 24.

Weaver, Virginia M., Jeffrey J. Fadrowski, and Bernard G. Jaar. 2015. "Global Dimensions of Chronic Kidney Disease of Unknown Etiology (CKDu): A Modern Era Environmental and/or Occupational Nephropathy?" *BMC Nephrology* 16 (145): 1–8.

Whittaker, Max. 2012. "The Detroit of California: A Slideshow." *New York Times.* September 17. www.nytimes.com/slideshow/2012/09/17/us/20120917-MENDOTA.html, accessed March 12, 2013.

Wijkstrom, Julia, Ricardo Leiva, Carl-Gustaf Elinder, Silvia Leiva, Zulma Trujillo, Luis Trujillo, Magnus Söderberg, Kjell Hultenby, and Annika Wernerson. 2013. "Clinical and Pathological Characterization of Mesoamerican Nephropathy: A New Kidney Disease in Central America." *American Journal of Kidney Disease* 62 (5): 908–18.

Wozniacka, Gosia. 2012. "Farmworkers Sue California over Heat Regulation Violations." *Huffington Post.* October 18. www.huffingtonpost.com/2012/10/18/farm-workers-sue-california_n_1982706.html, accessed July 23, 2014.

Zavella, Patricia. 2011. *I'm Neither Here nor There: Mexicans' Quotidian Struggles with Migration and Poverty.* Durham, NC: Duke University Press.

Zilberg, Elana. 2011. *Space of Detention: The Making of a Transnational Gang Crisis between Los Angeles and El Salvador.* Durham, NC: Duke University Press.

Index

Abrego, Leisy, 94, 109, 122
acculturation, effect on migrant health, 101–3
ACLU (American Civil Liberties Union), 18, 36, 174
Affordable Care Act: effect on county indigent care programs in California, 179, 213n11; exclusion of undocumented from, 127; inclusion of single childless men, 132, 179; Medicaid expansion, 132, 179
advocacy anthropology, 11, 186–87, 188, 189–90
Agar, Michael, 186
agriculture, U.S.: child labor laws and, 84–85; dependence on foreign-born workers, 68; exceptionalism in, 146–47, 176–77; exclusion from standard labor laws, 63–64, 153, 176–77; hierarchy of jobs in, 56–59; organization of, 19, 23–24; overtime laws and, 84–85, 136–37; uniqueness in California, 20, 58, 68, 203n6; uniqueness in Central Valley, 58
agricultural exceptionalism: food safety and, 146–47; need to end, 175–77; New Deal and, 63–64
allostatic load, 108
anemia, 128–29
anthropology: advocacy and engaged anthropology, 186–87, 188, 189–90; anthropologist as "clerk of the records," 193; applied anthropology, 182, 186; "critically applied anthropology," 188; "ethically-grounded anthropology," 187; need for research on health effects of farmwork, 182–83; public anthropology, 186–87; vulnerable populations and, 186. *See also* ethnography; fieldwork; participant observation

back pain, 79, 80, 99, 100–101, 103–6, 148
bananaecos (residents of El Platanal), 47–48, 155
bathroom breaks: labor crews and, 46, 61, 138; pace of production and, 37, 46, 185–86, 190; packinghouses and, 207n29
bell peppers, 1, 33, 35, 146
biomedicine: 159, 134–36
Boehm, Deborah, 52
border enforcement, 53, 65–68, 88, 94, 117
border patrol, 65
Borofsky, Bob, 186
Bourdieu, Pierre, 6, 22, 28–29, 36–37, 43, 60
Bourgois, Philippe, 97, 107
bracero program, 48, 49, 62–63, 196, 197, 205n3
breaks: Cal-OSHA rules on, 2, 18, 22, 36, 38, 183, 219n18; code of silence and, 23–24; contract work and, 3, 137–38,

breaks *(continued)*
148; geography of complacence and, 153; heat deaths and, 3–4, 12; heat illness and, 41, 42, 66–67; kidney damage and, 157; labor policies and, 5–6; masculinity and, 28–29; need for normalization of, 37; rehydration and, 152, 182; skipping of, 3–4, 30–31, 42, 47, 87, 137–38, 148, 141
Brown, Jerry (governor of California), 173, 179
Burawoy, Michael, 168

Cabañas (province in El Salvador), 47, 48, 49, 54
California: health and safety laws in, 92; health care access in, 127–29, 168, 179–80, 213n11, 214n12; health issues of farmworkers in, 97, 98–99, 102–3, 106–7, 127, 213n10; heat deaths in, 1, 2, 5, 17, 124; heat illness legislation, 2, 17–18, 173–74; immigration legislation in, 212n45; labor laws in, 64, 72, 84–85, 86, 136–37, 209n22; location of study, 6–7; migration to, 47–48, 62–63; an "Other" California, 8–9; statistics on farmworkers in, 28, 64, 68, 75, 206n23; subcontracting boom in, 23–24; uniqueness of agriculture in, 20, 58, 68, 203n6. *See also* Advisory Board; California Cantaloupe ; Cal-OSHA; Central Valley
California Agricultural Workers' Health Survey, 102–3, 106–7, 213n10
California Assembly Bill 805, 2, 17–18. *See also* heat-illness prevention standard
California Assembly Bill 1897, 179, 218n13
California Cantaloupe Advisory Board (CCAB), certifications, 34, 139–40; emergence of, 139–40; food safety checklists, 34, 37, 204n19, 205n29
California Department of Food and Agriculture, 204n21
Cal-OSHA: ban of short-handled tools, 92, 92*fig.;* billboards, 17, 18*fig.*, 19, 19*fig.*, 20, 23, 37, 41; enforcement activities of, 33, 174; heat wave warnings, 20; inadequate enforcement, 146–47; inadequate staffing, 35–37, 215n34; lawsuit against, 18, 36, 134, 174; settlement with UFW, 174; Standards Board, 173. *See also* heat-illness prevention standard
cantaloupe harvesting: author's work in, 11, 20; description of, 21; division of labor in, 25–28; food safety inspections of, 146; food safety rules in, 34, 139–40, 152; heatstroke in, 2, 8, 44; in Mendota, 8; stacking in, 29–31, 153, 182; timing of harvest, 42
cardiovascular disease. *See* heart disease
Centers for Disease Control and Prevention (CDC), 3, 136–37, 204n16, 215n23
Central America: conditions of farmwork in, 153; kidney disease among farmworkers in, 149–51; migration from, 48–49; 54–56
Central Valley (California): heat deaths in, 1, 2, 5, 17, 124; hierarchy of farm work in, 56–59; immigration raids and, 111–12; labor enforcement and, 173–74; location of study, 6, 8–9; migration to, 15, 47–48, 62–63; as "Other" California, 8–9; predominance of labor crews in, 58; Secure Communities and, 117–18
child labor, 63, 84–85, 116, 137, 153, 177, 209n22
cholesterol, high blood levels of: kidney disease and, 157–58, 217n15; migrants and, 103, 136, 198, 199
chronic disease. *See* diabetes; heart disease; hypertension
CKD (chronic kidney disease): blood cholesterol levels and, 217n15; causes of, 156–57; delayed diagnosis of, 149, 154–55; diabetes and, 149; farmwork's role in, 148–49, 151–53; heatstroke and, 149; hypertension and, 149, 156–57; lax regulation of farmwork and, 153; syndemic interactions and, 157–59
CKDnT. *See* CKDu
CKDu (chronic kidney disease of unknown origin): difference from CKD, 149–51; delayed attention to in Central America, 217n12; farmwork's role in, 150–51; lax labor regulations and, 153; prevalence in Central America, 216n3; possible existence in United States, 148–49, 171, 217n12
code of silence, 23–24, 33, 35–37, 41, 45, 140
collateral care: employer-subsidized care as, 129–30; Family PACT as, 214n13; health care seeking behaviors and, 130, 133; Restricted Medi-Cal as, 127–29

coraje (rage), 110, 116, 143; anthropological literature on, 96, 122; hypertension and, 111, 121–22; legal violence and, 97, 121–22; stroke and, 111
Certificate of Confidentiality, 219n5
corn harvesting, 59*fig8;* author's participant observation of, 10–11; description of, 12, 41–42; heatstroke in, 8, 12, 14, 44; naturalization of deaths in, 13, 202n39; stackers' risks in, 153; timing of harvest, 12, 42
corporate harm, 146–47. *See also* harm industries
county coroners, 18, 124, 134–35, 136, 145–46
coyote (human smuggler), 52, 53, 55, 65, 66, 113, 199
crew bosses. *See mayordomos*
criminalization, of undocumented migration, 88–90, 94–95, 210n38, 212n41; denounceability and, 111–12, 120; detention and, 115; IIRIRA and, 94, 115, 210n38; remedy for, 178; Secure Communities and, 117–18
critically applied public anthropology, 188
Cuscatlán (province in El Salvador), 49, 197

Deferred Action for Childhood Arrivals (DACA) program, 119, 213n50
dehydration: border crossing and, 65; food safety rules and, 180; hypertension and, 125, 134; kidney disease and, 150, 151, 157; lack of breaks and, 185; pesticide exposure and, 216n10; stackers and, 196; work deaths due to, 14, 159
denounceability: effect on migrant neighborhoods, 111–12; Josiah Heyman on, 210n38; legal production of, 88–90; Secure Communities and, 117–88; workers' compensation and, 91–93; workplace conditions and, 90–91
Department of Homeland Security (DHS), 89, 117, 210n31
deportability, 15, 89, 90, 94–95, 111–12
deportation: denounce-ability and, 94–95; "deportation threat dynamic," 57–58; document-related offenses and, 88; effects on family, 118–20; ghost workers and, 84; immigration enforcement and, 15, 88–89, 94, 117–18, 121–23; legal residents and, 15, 123, 178; Postville workers and, 88; public charge and, 154; René and, 114–17, 199–200; transnational gangs and, 49; vigilance, 120
desabilitado (disabled), 148, 160
diabetes, 195, 196, 198, 199; contract work and, 137–38; delayed diagnosis of, 129, 154–55; disability insurance and, 158–66; emotional distress and, 97–98, 122; farmworkers' rates of, 213n10; food safety policies and, 185; gestational, 128; heat illness and, 125, 133, 134; kidney disease and, 149, 156; Mexican migrants' higher risk of, 97–98, 127; organ transplant and, 166, 170; pesticide exposure and, 133
dialysis: in Central America, 150, 168; compared to organ transplant, 166–67; emergency dialysis, 218n31; Medi-Cal coverage of, 163–65; in Mexico, 167–68; normalization of in Central Valley, 151–3; perpetual dialysis, 168–70
disability: author's fieldwork on, 9, 10, 87; federal policies, 7, 149, 158, 162–63; housing for disabled workers, 183; kidney failure and, 158–66; perverse lessons of, 149, 165–66, 172, 176; pregnancy-related, 131, 138; premature disability, 79–82, 160, 155; "retirement" and, 6, 159; state policies, 158, 162; undocumented migrants' exclusion from, 180; workers' compensation payments and, 103–4, 110. *See also desabilitado;* SDI; SSDI; SSI
document exchange. *See* identity loan
documents: *chuecos* or *derechos*, 210n40; employers' scrutiny of, 23, 56, 58–59, 73–74, 209n11; "idle," 78, 208n3; prosecution for document fraud, 189, 210n38
Dowling, Julie, 88
drought, 51–52, 110
Duncan, Whitney, 110

E. coli, 34, 139, 147
El Platanal (town in Michoacán), 47, 48, 50, 51, 54, 148, 154, 155, 160, 167, 196, 197
El Salvador, 10, 60, 68, 75, 79, 80, 83, 141, 144, 149, 150, 168, 196, 199; civil war in, 48–49, 54–56, 161, 197, 206n20; migration from, 47–49, 54–56
embattled masculinities, 52, 60
Emergency Medi-Cal, 196, 200; compared to Restricted Medi-Cal, 128–29; creation by state of California, 214n12; organ transplant and, 168–70;

Emergency Medi-Cal *(continued)*
undocumented migrants' eligibility for, 127. *See also* Emergency Medicaid
Emergency Medical Treatment and Labor Act (EMTALA): 214n12, 218n30. *See also* Emergency Medi-Cal
Emergency Medicaid, 168, 180, 214n12. *See also* Emergency Medi-Cal
Employment Development Department (EDD), 164, 189
engaged anthropology, 186–87
English language, and economic opportunities, 56, 68, 70, 104
Equitable Food Initiative (EFI), 181
epidemiology, 7–8, 126
ESRD (End-Stage Renal Disease), 149, 151, 154, 155; delayed diagnosis of, 154–55; insurance coverage of, 158–66; young men and, 156–57
ethically-grounded anthropology, 187
ethnography: author's methods in, 8–11, 191–93; epidemiology and, 7–8; ethnographic authority and, 188; moral engagement and, 186; positionality and, 191–92; protections of vulnerable populations, 193, 219n5; as "transgressive," 11; writing and, 187–88. *See also* anthropology; fieldwork; participant observation
experimental moment, in ethnography, 188
exceptional workers: 63–64, 71, 73, 79, 136, 175, 184, 207n35
experience-near, 7
everyday violence, 97, 107–8; as effect of legal violence, 109–10

family farms: diversified tasks on, 56–57; pace of work on, 24, 46, 58; mythology of , 146–7; 176–77
farm labor hierarchy, 19, 44–45; code of silence in, 28, 35, 140, 145; desirability of jobs in, 56–59; habitus and, 59–62; heat illness and, 28, 37, 43, 147, 176; hierarchy of supervision in, 23–24, 71; joint liability and, 179; outsiders to, 68–70; overwork in, 135–37; skipping breaks in, 137–38
Farmer, Paul, 4–5, 153
Farmworker Fair Labor Practices Act (2014), 177
Family PACT (Family Planning, Access, Care and Treatment Program), 214n13
family reunification, 54, 78, 206n17
Farabundo Martí National Liberation Front (FMLN), 49
field hands: hierarchical supervision of, 23–24, 59–62; job security of, 24; masculinity and, 28–29; overwork and, 135–37; productivity demands on, 15, 23–24, 44–45, 175; skipping breaks and, 137–38; subcontracting and, 15, 23–24, 44–45, 175; vulnerability of, 56–59
field notes: 20, 99, 161, 202-n40
fieldwork: 188; 193, 203n7, 219n5. *See also* anthropology; ethnography; participant observation
Food and Drug Administration (FDA): approval of CCAB guidelines, 205n29; audit system, 180, 215n27; food safety guidelines, 181, 204n19, 215n26; lack of inspectors, 215n27. *See also* food safety
food-borne illness, outbreaks of: 139–40, 146–47, 180, 204n19
food safety, 7, 10, 42, 127; audits, 139, 144, 147, 180–82, 204n19, 215n27; as counterproductive, 37; Global Food Safety Initiative, 215n26; guidelines, 33–34, 139–40; incorporating worker safety into, 180–82; workers' rehydration and, 30–31, 35–37, 140–45, 146–47, 153
fortuitous diagnoses, 132–33
Fresco, 20, 31, 33–34, 40, 41, 44, 146, 204n17, 205n29
Fresno County: county coroner in, 135; heat deaths in, 2; heat wave in, 19–20, 140; Salvadoran settlement in, 48–49; Secure Communities in, 118; UFW organizing in, 173
Fussell, Elizabeth, 58

gabachos (white North Americans): outsiders in migrant communities, 192; racial hierarchy in Valley and, 191–92; role in migrant communities, 9; visitors from state, 21
gender: author's research and, 192; division of labor in melon harvesting, 26–29; health care seeking and, 128–33, 154–55; health insurance and, 127
geography of blame, 153
geography of complacence, 153, 184
Good, Byron, 171
Good, Mary-Jo, 171
Gomberg-Muñoz, Ruth, 89, 206n17, 207n35

grape harvesting, 2, 24, 77, 93, 135*fig11*, 152, 197–98

habitus (Bourdieuian concept), 6, 22, 47, 60; bracero program and, 62–63; definition of, 6, 60; health care habitus, 6; health care system and, 130–32; labor crews and, 59–62; policies' conflicting effects on, 176; work habitus, 6
harm industries, 146–47
health care access: in Central America, 150; kidney failure and, 158–66; Medi-Cal and, 127–33, 154–55; need to expand, 147, 179–80; organ transplants and, 166–71; silent epidemics and, 97, 102, 149, 153, 157
health care seeking: collateral diagnoses and, 127–30; 214n13; fortuitous diagnoses and, 132–33; gender and, 127–33, 154–55; in Mexico, 167–68; opportunistic care and, 130–32
health fairs, 121, 131
Healthy San Francisco, 179–80
heart disease: diabetes and, 125; farmworkers' rate of deaths from, 103; farmworkers' risk factors for, 101–3, 132; heat and, 124–25, 133–36, 145; kidney disease and, 157–58; lack of health care access and, 127; legal violence and, 107–8, 109–10; migration as risk factor for, 106–7; as pre-existing condition, 124, 176; symbolic violence and, 176. *See also* hypertension
heat illness, 20–23, 24–25, 38–41; border enforcement and, 65–68; breaks and, 41, 42, 66–67, 137–38; code of silence and, 23–25, 33, 35, 41; colloquial terms for, 31; deaths from, 1–3, 5, 17–18, 124; diabetes and, 125, 133, 134; document exchange and, 73; exclusion from labor laws and, 63–64; experience-near account of, 7–8, 11–14, 42–43; farm labor hierarchy and, 28, 37, 43, 147, 176; farmworkers' susceptibility to, 2, 3; food safety rules and, 34, 37–38, 42, 127, 139–40, 146–47; gender and, 25–29, 44–45; heart disease and, 124–25, 133–36, 145; hypertension and, 124–25, 133–36, 144–46; kidney disease and, 149–51, 157–59; social and political production of, 3, 5–6, 7, 15–16, 147, 175–76; misplaced autonomy and, 3–5; naturalization of, 3, 13, 28–29, 43, 124–25, 134–36, 124, 176, 202n39; occupational health sciences' approach to, 4, 202n21; stages of, 204n16; state billboards and, 19–20; subcontracting and, 23–24, 44–45, 125, 175; stackers' vulnerability to, 29–31, 153, 182. *See also* heat-illness prevention standard
heat-illness prevention standard: acclimatization and, 33; changes to due to UFW lawsuit, 173–4; creation of, 17–18, 203n2; enforcement of, 33, 174; inadequate enforcement of, 35–37, 38–39, 146–47; reduction of shift length and, 33; supervision and, 33; violations of, 33, 36, 174
hiddenness of farmwork, 146, 182, 193
hidden populations, research with, 193, 219n5
Holmes, Seth, 4–5, 187, 207n31
housing, 113, 183
hypertension: acute episodes of, 96, 106, 110–11, 131, 120–21; delayed diagnosis of, 127–33; emotions and, 121–22; farmworkers' rates of, 97, 101–3, 106–7, 132; heat exposure and, 124–25, 133–36, 144–46; kidney disease and, 149–50, 156–58, 170; legal violence and, 97–98, 107–8, 109–10, 136, 175; migration as risk factor for, 106–7; stroke and, 106, 110–11, 175

ICE (U.S. Immigration and Customs Enforcement), 88–90, 111–12, 114–15, 117–18
identity loan: acquaintances and, 78–81; arrangement of, 73, 208nn1,3; definition of, 73; employers and, 82–83; "exceptional workers" and, 73; family members and, 75–78; labor abuses and, 84–85; legal production of, 73–75; particularly common in agriculture, 209n11; potential prosecution of, 88–90, 94; as safety net, 81–82; workers' compensation and, 85–96. *See also* identity masking
identity masking: definition of, 85; minors and, 84, 116, 137; overtime and, 85; workers' compensation and, 85–93; undocumented migrants and, 84
identity theft, 73, 84, 87, 88–90, 94, 175, 189, 210n29, 210n38
Illegal Immigration Reform and Immigrant Responsibility Act (IIRIRA), 94, 115, 123, 210n38

immigration. *See* migration
Immigration and Nationality Act (1965), 206n17
immigration control policies. *See* border enforcement; interior immigration enforcement; Illegal Immigration Reform and Immigrant Responsibility Act; Immigration Reform and Control Act
Immigration Reform and Control Act (IRCA): employer sanctions, 23–24; 44–45, 73–74; labor crews and, 23–24, 175; labor supervisors and, 82–83, 175; legalization and, 53–54, 154, 196, 197, 198, 199
immigration status. *See* legal status
Inda, Jonathan Xavier, 88
industrial agriculture: habitus and, 59–62; hierarchy of supervision and, 23–24, 71; joint liability and, 179; labor hierarchy in, 23–24; organization of, 19, 47, 56–59; overwork and, 135–37; skipping breaks and, 137–38
Institutional Review Board (IRB), 193, 219n5
intergenerational mobility, 49, 52

job security: impressing *mayordomo* and, 14, 23–24, 59–62; labor crews and, 23–24, 28–29, 59–62; overtime and, 136; undocumented migrants and, 98; unemployment insurance and, 64, 68

kidney disease. *See* CKD; CKDu
Klinenberg, Eric, 3, 7
knee injuries, 79, 81, 195, 197

"*La trucha*" (the "sly" knife), 92, 92*fig*
labor abuses: foreign-born workers and, 70; health and safety rules and, 92–93; joint liability and, 179; lax regulation and, 153; overtime and, 84–85; packinghouses and, 206n25; subcontracting and, 15, 58–59, 179; workers' compensation and, 85–93; workers' superexploitation and, 69–70; U.S. workers and, 68–70; verbal abuse, 60–61; workers' vulnerability and, 58–59
labor contractors: familiarity with field hands' circumstances, 82–83; fines and, 174; interviews with, 10, 124, 203n7; IRCA and, 23–24; job stresses of, 87; joint liability and, 179; labor abuses and, 1, 15, 58–59; 85–93, 179, 220n27; pace of production and, 23–24, 38; predominance in California agriculture, 20, 58; work injuries and, 100–101, 109
labor crews: author's work on, 20; definition of, 206n26; degradation workers face on, 59–62, 71, 175; gendered division of labor on, 25–28; hierarchical supervision of, 23–24, 47, 59–60, 71; least desirable employment in Valley, 56–59; pace of production on, 23–24, 38, 43, 57, 59–60, 175; peer pressure on, 28–30, 45; predominance in California, 57; skipping breaks on, 137–38, 175; vulnerable workers on, 58–59; workers' quiescence on, 70
labor hierarchy. *See* farm labor hierarchy
labor laws: child labor, 63–64, 84–85, 137, 209n22; New York Farmworkers' Fair Labor Practices Act, 177; overtime, 63–64, 85, 153, 175, 176; unemployment insurance, 64, 68
labor supervisors. *See mayordomos,* labor contractors
ladder of farmwork, 23–24
Lamphere, Louise, 8
Las Ánimas (town in Zacatecas), 47, 48
Latino paradox, 101–3
Latino migrants: chronic disease and, 127; concentration in California agriculture, 68; difficulty generating a surplus, 50; disproportionate rate of work injuries and deaths, 70–71; higher risk of heat death, 3, 7, 15; migration debts, 65–68, 113; migration histories, 47–56; presumed health, 101–2; racial profiling of, 117–18; racism-related "vigilance" and, 107; reasons entered farmwork, 56; reasons entered labor crews, 57–60
Leafy Green Marketing Agreement (LGMA), 139
legal status: *coraje* and, 121–22; disability insurance and, 159, 217n16; 217n17; documents and, 74; family reunification and, 54, 78, 199; farmworker housing and, 113; health insurance and, 127–30, 143, 154–55, 179–80, 213n11; hypertension and, 106–7; identity loan and, 73, 74–75; IIRIRA and, 94; IRCA and, 53–54, 82–83, 197–99; labor crews and, 58–59; low-wage work and, 56; minority stress and, 109–10; mixed-status families and, 119; organ transplant and, 168, 170, 218n30, 218n32; reform

and, 178; sample and, 191; Secure Communities and, 118; temporary legal status, 55, 119, 178, 206n20; workers' compensation and, 86, 91, 99, 189; unemployment benefits and, 75. *See also* undocumented workers; visas
legal violence, 94–95, 97–98, 109–10, 120, 122–23, 175, 188
listeriosis, 39, 139, 215n27
liminal legality, 56, 206n20
literacy, and economic opportunities, 56, 68
local biologies, 150, 171
Lock, Margaret, 150, 171

Mahler, Sarah, 50, 209n16
marginalized populations, research with, 193, 219n5
Massachusetts' Health Safety Net, 179–80
master stressors, 97–98, 123, 211n21
mayordomos (crew bosses): document loans and, 83–84, 87, 90–91, 93, 116; health and safety violations of, 92–93; heat illness and, 12, 13, 22, 25, 34–35, 38, 40, 42; integration into migrant communities of, 82–83; interviews with, 10, 32–33; job responsibilities of, 23–24, 162, 203n1; job security and, 14, 23–24, 67, 189, 208n41; labor violations of, 85–87, 136–37; meaning of term, 203n1; occupational taxes and, 50; pace of production and, 47, 69, 138, 152; superexploitation and, 69; verbal abuse by, 60–61; work conditions of, 184
Mead, Margaret, 186
Medically Indigent Services Program (MISP), 213–4n11
Medi-Cal: asset reporting and, 165; delayed diagnosis and, 154–55; dialysis and, 168–70; Emergency Medi-Cal, 127, 170; Healthy San Francisco and, 180; kidney failure and, 158–66; migrant men's exclusion from, 129–30, 154–55; organ transplant and, 168–70; public charge provisions and, 154; Restricted Medi-Cal, 128–29
Medicare, 158, 160, 165, 167, 197
Mendota, town of, 6, 8–9, 47–48, 54, 112, 131, 173, 185, 189, 191–92
Mendenhall, Emily, 97–98, 122
Menjívar, Cecilia, 94, 109, 122, 205n7, 206n20, 209n12
mental health: Latino paradox and, 101–2; legal violence and, 109–10, 121–22; medical returns and, 217n27; migration and, 106–7. *See also coraje; nervios*
Mesoamerican epidemic, 149. *See also* CKDu
Mexican migrants: bracero program and, 48, 62–63, 205n3; diabetes rate among, 127; hypertension rate among, 101–2, 111; immigration policy and, 206n17; migration histories of, 15, 47–54; percentage of California's farmworkers, 68; racism in Valley against, 191–92. *See also* Latino migrants
Michoacán (Mexican state), 1, 47, 160, 167
middle class, New Deal and, 63, 79; farmworkers' subsidy of, 177
Migrant Education Program (1965), 214n15
migration: bracero program and, 48, 62–63; effects on health, 101–3, 106–7, 109–10; externalized costs of, 168; economic versus political migration, 54; El Salvador's civil war and, 54–55; gang violence and, 55–56; inequality and, 56; medical migration, 167–68; motivations for, 47–56; social networks' role in, 47–48; women and, 207n34
moral economy, 75–78
mothers, single undocumented, 118
musculoskeletal injuries, 99, 109. *See also* back pain

National Agricultural Workers' Survey, 64, 75
National Fugitive Operations Program (NFOP), 211n41
National Immigration Law Center (NILC), 178
naturalization, of heat death: by county coroners, 134–36; by field hands, 28–29, 43; by labor supervisors, 124–25, 202n39; by media, 2–3, 176; by policymakers, 2–3, 176. *See also* symbolic violence
nervios (anxiety/depression), 196, 197
New Deal, 63–64, 177
NIH (National Institutes of Health) Certificate of Confidentiality, 219n5
Nochistlán (city in Zacatecas), 51, 52
North American Free Trade Agreement (NAFTA), 48
Northern Triangle (El Salvador, Guatemala, Honduras), 49
Nussbaum-Barberena, Laura, 88

Obama Administration, 178, 210n31, 212n45, 213n50

occupational health studies: 4–5, 202n21
Operation Blockade (1993), 65
Operation Return to Sender (2007), 112, 117
opportunistic care, 130–32
organ transplant, 166–70, 180, 218n30
overtime laws: excessive work and, 136; farmworkers' exclusion from, 63–64, 153, 175, 176; New York Farmworkers' Fair Labor Practices Act (2014), 177; packinghouses and, 64; violations of, 84–85, 136–37
Oxfam, 181

packing and processing sheds: desirability of employment in, 56, 58, 69, 206n25; employer verification of work authorization documents in, 23–24, 46, 58; overtime benefits in, 64, 77, 196; workers' compensation in, 207n29; health hazards of, 79, 207n29
participant observation: 19, 21, 44, 188. *See also* anthropology; ethnography; fieldwork
perpetual illegality, 94
Personal Responsibility and Work Opportunity Reconciliation Act (PRWORA), 217n17
Pesticides: carbamate pesticides, 216n10; diabetes and, 214n18; heat stress and, 133; kidney disease and, 156, 216n10
Postville (Iowa), workplace raid in, 88
poverty: health and, 126–27; identity loan and, 73, 81–82, 84, 95, 178; legalization and, 178; Medi-Cal eligibility and, 127, 165; Mendota and, 8–9; New Deal and, 63–64; rates among farmworkers, 74–75; as reason for migration, 47–56; research with marginalized populations and, 193; as result of migration, 56; symbolic marker of, 116
POWER (Protect Our Workers from Exploitation and Retaliation) Act, 178
pragmatic solidarity, 176
Priority Enforcement Program (PEP), 89, 201n31, 210n31, 211n45
production, pace of: bathroom breaks and, 37, 61–62, 185; contract work and, 137–38, 184; farm labor hierarchy and, 23–24; masculinity and, 25–30, 45; rehydration and, 22, 37, 139–40, 182
public anthropology, 186–87
public charge determination, 154
public health research, 4–5, 101–3, 125–27, 193

Quesada, James, 5

racial/ethnic hierarchy in Central Valley, 191–192
racialization, 48, 60, 61, 63, 112
racism, 107–8, 191–92
raiteros, 112, 114, 119, 138
remittances, 50
Restricted Medi-Cal, 128–29, 214n12
Retirement, 6, 79–82, 159–60, 162, 165–66, 168, 198
Rosaldo, Renato, 96
Reyes, Silvestre, 65

Saénz, Rogelio, 109
Salmonella, 30, 34, 139
Salvadoran migrants: civil war and, 48–49, 54–56, 161, 197, 206n20; labor crews and, 56–59; low-wage work and, 56; masculinity and, 59–62; migration histories of, 15, 48–49, 54–56; political asylum and, 79, 197; temporary protected status and, 55, 56, 129, 191, 206n20
SAW (Special Agricultural Worker) program (1986), 53–54, 55, 82–83, 154, 205–6n16
Saxton, Dvera, 133
Scheper-Hughes, Nancy, 97, 107, 187, 193
seasonal labor, 64, 74–75, 98, 127
Secure Communities, 89, 112: critiques of, 117–18, 201n31, 211n45; replacement with Priority Enforcement Program, 210n31; replacement with Trust Act in California, 211n45; requests for notification, 201n31
segregation, in Central Valley, 8–9, 111–12, 163, 191–92
Seguro Popular, 168
Sensuntepeque (town in Cabañas, El Salvador), 47–48, 54, 55, 183, 199
shade, 1, 2, 17–18, 36, 44, 153, 174, 184, 202n21
short-handled tools, 92, 92*fig*
small family farms. *See* family farms
Singer, Merrill, 125–26, 147, 158, 174
social gradient in health, 102
social epidemiology from the ground up, 8
social networks, 47, 48, 68, 131, 209n12
Social Security. *See* retirement
Social Security Administration (SSA), 89, 158
Social Security Disability Insurance (SSDI). 149, 158; difficulty qualifying for,

160–66, 197; perverse lessons of, 172, 149, 176; as "retirement," 6, 159–60; undocumented migrants' ineligibility for, 217n17. *See also* disability
Social Security fraud, 84, 88, 210
stackers: description of work, 12, 25–27, 27*fig6;* rehydration needs of, 219n18
special legislative protections for, 182, 219n18; special workplace vulnerabilities of, 29–30, 33, 35, 40, 44, 152–53
State Disability Insurance (SDI), 158, 162–63, 195–96, 198, 208n54, 217n16. *See also* disability
step migration, 154–55, 207n34
stress, chronic. *See* allostatic load
structural violence, 4–5, 192
structural vulnerability, 5–6, 13, 41, 189
Stuesse, Angela, 88
subcontracting: heat illness and, 125, 175; IRCA and, 23–24; job security and, 24; joint liability and, 179; labor abuses and, 56–59, 136–37; 85–96, 179; labor supervisors and, 82–83; pace of production and, 7, 15, 23–24, 44–45, 175. *See also* labor contractors; *mayordomos*
subjunctive mode, 171, 211n14
sugarcane industry, in Central America, 150–51, 153, 171, 216n7
superexploitation, 67–68, 69–70, 89–90
Supplemental Security Income (SSI), 158, 162, 165, 217n17. *See also* disability
symbolic violence, 28–29, 43, 176. *See also* naturalization
syndemics: definition of, 125–27; disability insurance and, 157–58; food safety and, 139–40; health care access and, 127–30; heat illness and, 124, 125–27, 134–36, 147; policy changes necessary to end, 174–76; work and heat illness, 136–38; kidney disease and heat illness, 150–51

temporary protected status (TPS), 55, 129, 191, 206n20
tomato harvesting, 2, 10, 27–28, 29, 40, 60, 61, 66, 77, 79–80, 91, 92, 92*fig10,* 99–101, 105, 116, 120, 121, 173, 190
Trust Act (213), 211n45
Turner, Victor, 97
287(g) program, 89

UFW (United Farmworkers of America), 1, 2, 10, 18, 36, 93, 134, 173–74, 183, 189
undocumented migrants: border crossings of, 65; in California agriculture, 68; chronic stressors of, 97–98; constrained work opportunities, 15, 23–24, 46, 56–59, 76; *coraje* and, 96, 121–22; criminalization of, 88–90, 94–95, 111–12, 117–18; deportation of, 111–12, 117–18; driver's licenses and, 39; everyday violence and, 109–10; exclusion from federal disability insurance, 217; exclusion from unemployment benefits, 64, 73, 75; health care access of, 127–29, 166–70, 179–80, 217n17; hypertension and, 96–97, 106–7, 121–22; identity loan and, 73–75, 84; inclusion in state disability insurance, 217; labor conditions of, 5–6, 13; legal violence and, 97–98, 109–10, 122–23; legalization of, 53–54, 82–83, 178; medical returns and, 167–68; mental health and, 121–22; migration debts and, 39, 65–68; terminology for, 201n1; workers' compensation and, 86, 91–93, 98–99
unemployment insurance: determination of amount, 73; farmworkers' exclusion from during New Deal, 63–64; identity loan and, 73–74, 78–82, 95; importance to farmworkers of, 64, 75, 196, 197, 199; job security and, 64, 68; legalization and, 178, 199; undocumented workers' exclusion from, 64, 73, 75, 175, 195, 197
United Nations Organ Sharing (UNOS) waiting list, 166, 218n32
urinary tract infections, 185
"used up" workers, 14, 81, 82
U.S. Border Patrol (USBP). *See* border patrol
U.S. Department of Agriculture (USDA), 10, 180, 181, 204n21

violence. *See* everyday violence; legal violence; structural violence; symbolic violence
violence continuum, 107–8
visas, 54, 76, 154, 178, 191, 197, 198, 199, 201n1, 206n17
vulnerable populations, research with, 193, 219n5

"willingness to work," 67, 207n35
workers' compensation insurance, 39–40, 69, 99–101, 103–6, 108–9, 110–11;

workers' compensation insurance *(continued)* agricultural exceptionalism and, 176–77; deaths at home and, 144–145; denounceability and, 88–90, 94; document exchange and, 72–73, 85–87, 90–93, 116; intervention, 188–90; joint liability and, 179; in New Mexico, 177; POWER Act and, 178; undocumented migrants eligibility for in California and, 86; work stress and, 98–99
"worker hygiene," 205n29
World Bank, 216

Zacatecas (Mexican state), 46, 47, 51, 75, 76, 195, 197, 198
Zamora (city in Michoacán), 167